IRISH HOTELS FEDERATION

13 Northbrook Road, Dublin 6, Ireland
Telephone 01-497 6459   Fax: 01-497 4613

Web Site: http://www.beourguest.ie

Be Our Guest

2000

Featuring over 1,000 Hotels & Guesthouses
as well as details on
·   Golfing
Angling
Conference Facilities
and
Touring Maps

Printed & Published by The Wood Printcraft Group, Greencastle Parade, Clonshaugh, Dublin 17. Tel: 847 0011. Fax: 847 5570. Design & Origination by Printcraft Imaging, Unit 95 Newtown Industrial Estate, Clonshaugh, Dublin 17.

Telephone and fax numbers will change in some areas during 2000, please consult directory enquiries in case of difficulty.

CONTENTS

FACILITIES

🛏	Total number of rooms	🔍	Games room
🛁	Number of rooms with bath/shower and toilet	🎾	Squash court
☎	Direct dial facilities	∪	Horse riding/pony trekking on site or nearby
🖵	TV in all bedrooms	▶9	9-hole golf course on site
↕	Elevator/Lift	▶18	18-hole golf course on site
T	Can be booked through travel agent / tourist office and commission paid	↲	Angling on site or nearby
/🛝	Childrens playground	♫	Evening Entertainment
🪀	Childrens playroom	P	Car parking
C	Price reduction for children	🐾	Facilities for pets
🐤	Babysitter service	S	Price reduction for senior citizens excl. July/August and subject to availability
CM	Childrens meals	♀	Wine Licence only
CS	Creche	🍾	Dispense Bar Service Only
�֍	Garden for visitors use	🍺	Licensed to sell all alcoholic drink
🏊	Indoor swimming pool	àlc	À la carte meals provided
🏊	Outdoor swimming pool	☕	Tea/coffee making facilities in bedroom
🧖	Sauna	♿	Facilities and services are accessible to disabled persons
🏛	Gym only	👤	Suitable for disabled persons, with the assistance of one helper
🏠	Leisure Complex (including sauna / swimming pool / gym)	Inet	Modem access in room
		FAX	Fax machine in room
🎾	Tennis court - hard / grass	☺	Special Offer

 Denotes that premises are members of the *Irish Hotels Federation* as at 18 September 1999.

 Denotes that premises are members of the *Northern Ireland Hotels Federation* as at 18 September 1999.

ACTIVITY SECTIONS

Green symbols Illustrated below denote that the hotel or guesthouse is included in a particular activity section. Further details of the facilities available and the arrangements made on behalf of guests for participation in these activities are shown on pages 400 to 455.

 Golf   Angling   🏛 Conference

MARKETING GROUPS

Many of the hotels and guesthouses in the guide are members of Marketing Groups. Those properties which are members of the Marketing Groups will have the name of the group displayed within their entry. Some of these groups operate a central reservation system and can make reservations for you. Marketing Groups are featured on page 398.

SELECTING YOUR HOTEL AND GUESTHOUSE

REGIONS

Begin by selecting the region(s) you wish to visit. This guide divides into eight separate Regions – West, North West, North, East Coast, Midlands / Lakelands, South East, South West, Shannon – and they are represented in that order.

COUNTIES

Within each region, counties are presented alphabetically.

LOCATIONS – CITIES, TOWNS, VILLAGES

Within counties, locations are also presented alphabetically, see Index Pages 4 & 6.

PREMISES

Hotels and guesthouses are also presented in alphabetical order, see Index Pages 481 to 496.

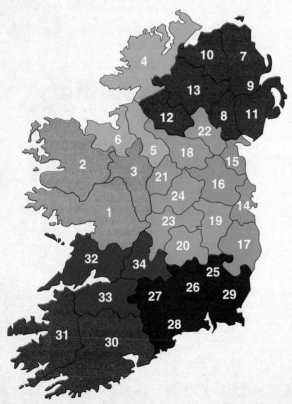

	COUNTIES	REGION	PAGES
1	GALWAY	West	Page 24 to 60
2	MAYO	West	Page 60 to 72
3	ROSCOMMON	West	Page 72 to 74
4	DONEGAL	North West	Page 76 to 89
5	LEITRIM	North West	Page 89 to 90
6	SLIGO	North West	Page 90 to 95
7	ANTRIM	North	Page 97 to 102
8	ARMAGH	North	Page 102 to 102
9	BELFAST CITY	North	Page 103 to 107
10	DERRY	North	Page 107 to 110
11	DOWN	North	Page 110 to 114
12	FERMANAGH	North	Page 114 to 116
13	TYRONE	North	Page 116 to 116
14	DUBLIN	East Coast	Page 118 to 185
15	LOUTH	East Coast	Page 185 to 189
16	MEATH	East Coast	Page 189 to 193
17	WICKLOW	East Coast	Page 194 to 205
18	CAVAN	Midlands & Lakelands	Page 207 to 209
19	KILDARE	Midlands & Lakelands	Page 210 to 215
20	LAOIS	Midlands & Lakelands	Page 215 to 217
21	LONGFORD	Midlands & Lakelands	Page 218 to 218
22	MONAGHAN	Midlands & Lakelands	Page 218 to 220
23	OFFALY	Midlands & Lakelands	Page 220 to 223
24	WESTMEATH	Midlands & Lakelands	Page 224 to 227
25	CARLOW	South East	Page 229 to 231
26	KILKENNY	South East	Page 231 to 238
27	TIPPERARY SOUTH	South East	Page 238 to 244
28	WATERFORD	South East	Page 245 to 257
29	WEXFORD	South East	Page 258 to 270
30	CORK	South West	Page 272 to 315
31	KERRY	South West	Page 315 to 360
32	CLARE	Shannon	Page 362 to 385
33	LIMERICK	Shannon	Page 385 to 394
34	TIPPERARY NORTH	Shannon	Page 394 to 397

INDEX TO LOCATIONS

GUINNESS

AVOCA
HANDWEAVERS

Welcome to the colourful world of Avoca, where our six magical shops are crammed
with beautiful things, most of which are made exclusively by Avoca. Savour our restaurants
where our delicious lunches are legendary. Visit any one of our shops and be
sure of a warm welcome and an experience with a difference.

Kilmacanogue	Avoca Village	Powerscourt House Shop	Molls Gap	Bunratty	Letterfrack
Bray, Co. Wicklow	Avoca Co. Wicklow	Enniskerry Co. Wicklow	Killarney, Co. Kerry	Co. Clare	Co. Galway

Tel: 01 286 7466
Fax: 01 286 2367

Open 7 Days

GUINNESS

live
life
to
the
power
of

William Power
President, Irish Hotels Federation

Hotels and Guesthouses in Ireland are very special. The majority are family owned with the proprietor and members of the family there to welcome guests and to extend to them renowned Irish hospitality. Even when they are owned by a company, or are part of a group, they still retain the character and ambience of a family premises - a place where you will be truly welcome.

The Irish hotel is unique, in that more often than not, it acts as a social centre for the community. Hotels offer a lot more than just a bed and a meal - they are fully fledged social, leisure, business and community centres with every imaginable facility and amenity, providing food, accommodation, sports, leisure facilities, entertainment and other attractions.

If you are moving around the country, you'll find that "Be Our Guest" is an invaluable help in choosing your next location.

Ireland's hoteliers and guesthouse owners want to welcome you and want to play their part in ensuring that your stay in Ireland is a happy one. We hope that you will stay with us and that you will use this guide to select the hotel or guesthouse of your choice, so that we can personally invite you to -

Be Our Guest

Ní haon ní coitianta é an Óstlann nó an Teach Lóistín in Éirinn. Is í seilbh teaghlaigh iad a bhformhór acu agus bíonn an t-úinéir agus baill den teaghlach romhat chun fáilte Uí Cheallaigh a chur romhat. Fiú nuair is le comhlacht iad, nó is cuid de ghrúpa iad, baineann meon agus atmaisféar áitreabh teaghlaigh leo – áiteanna ina gcuirfí fíorchaoin fáilte romhat.

Rud ar leith is ea an óstlann in Éirinn agus is dócha ná a mhalairt go bhfeidhmíonn sí mar lárionad sóisialta don phobal. Cuireann an óstlann i bhfad níos mó ná leaba agus béile ar fáil - is lárionad sóisialta,a siamsaíochta, gnó agus pobail ar fheabhas í chomh maith agus gach aon áis faoin spéir aici, a chuireann bia, lóistín, imeachtaí spóirt, áiseanna siamsíochta agus só agus tarraingtí nach iad ar fáil.

Agus tú ag taisteal timpeall na tíre gheobhaidh tú amach go mbeidh "Bí i d'Aoi Againn" an-áisiúil agus an chéad suíomh eile á roghnú agat.

Is mian le hóstlannaithe agus le lucht tithe lóistín na hÉireann fáilte a chur romhat agus a bheith in ann a dheimhniú go mbainfidh tú sult as do sheal in Éirinn. Tá súil againn go bhfanfaidh tú linn agus go mbainfidh tú leas as an treoir seo

chun do rogha óstlann nó teach lóistin
a aimsiú, i dtreo is go mbeimid in ann
a rá leat of pearsanta -

Be Our Guest

Les hôtels et les pensions en Irlande
sont d'un caractère particulier.

Ils sont très souvent gérés par le pro-
priétaire et des membres de sa famille,
présents pour accueillir les visiteurs et
leur faire découvrir la célèbre hospital-
ité irlandaise.
Même s'ils appartiennent à une entre-
prise ou font partie d'un
groupe de sociétés, ils possèdent tou-
jours ce caractère et cette
ambiance des lieux familiaux - un
endroit où vous serez sincèrement
bien accueillis.

L'hôtel irlandais est unique en ce
qu'il joue très souvent le rôle de
centre social pour la communauté.
Les hôtels offrent beaucoup plus
qu'un lit et un repas - ce sont, pour
la communauté, de véritables centres
sociaux, de loisirs et d'affaires,
équipés de toutes les infrastructures
et installations imaginables.
Ils vous proposent le gîte et le
couvert, mais aussi activités sportives
et de loisir, divertissements et autres
attractions.

Si vous voyagez dans le pays, vous
trouverez que le guide "Be Our Guest"
est d'une aide précieuse pour vous
aider à choisir votre prochaine destination.

Les hôteliers et les propriétaires de
pensions irlandais veulent vous accueillir et être là pour vous assurer un
séjour agréable en Irlande. Nous
espérons que vous resterez avec nous
et que vous utiliserez ce guide pour
sélectionner l'hôtel ou la pension de
votre choix, afin que nous ayons le
plaisir de vous compter parmi nos visiteurs.

Be Our Guest

Die Hotels und Pensionen in Irland sind
von ganz besonderer Art.

Zum größten Teil handelt es sich
dabei um private Familienbetriebe,
in denen der Besitzer und die
Familienmitglieder ihre Gäste mit
der vielgerühmten irischen
Gastfreundschaft willkommen heißen.
Aber auch wenn sich diese Häuser in
Unternehmensbesitz befinden oder
einer Kette angehören, strahlen sie
dennoch den Charakter und die
Atmosphäre von Familienbetrieben
aus - ein Ort, an dem Sie immer herz-
lich willkommen sind.

Hotels in Irland sind einzig in ihrer
Art und dienen oftmals als
Mittelpunkt geselliger Treffen.
Hotels haben viel mehr zu bieten als
nur ein Bett und eine Mahlzeit - sie
sind Gesellschafts-, Freizeit-,
Geschäfts- und öffentlicher
Treffpunkt mit allen nur erdenklichen
Einrichtungen und Annehmlichkeiten,
angefangen bei Essen, Unterkunft,
Sport und Freizeitmöglichkeiten bis
zur Unterhaltung und anderen
Anziehungspunkten.

Auf Ihren Reisen im Land werden Sie
feststellen, daß Ihnen der "Be Our
Guest"-Führer eine wertvolle Hilfe bei
der Suche nach der nächstgelegenen
Unterkunft leistet.

Irlands Hotel- und Pensionsbesitzer
heißen Sie gerne willkommen und
möchten ihren Anteil dazu
beitragen, daß Ihnen Ihr
Aufenthalt in Irland in angenehmer
Erinnerung bleibt. Wir hoffen, daß Sie
uns besuchen werden und diesen
Führer bei der Auswahl Ihres Hotels
oder Ihrer Pension zu Rate ziehen, so
daß wir Sie persönlich willkommen
heißen können.

Be Our Guest

+800 36 98 74 12

res ireland

www.ireland.travel.ie

Be Our Guest

2000
HOTEL AND GUESTHOUSE
RESERVATIONS
FREEPHONE

To book any of the premises in this Guide ring toll free on

+800 36 98 74 12 *

Be Our Guest

* + denotes international access code in country where call is made
e.g. from UK   access code 00
        USA   access code 011

Powered by:  **res**ireland

IRISH TOURIST BOARD OFFICES
www.ireland.travel.ie

IRELAND
Dublin
Bord Fáilte - Irish Tourist Board,
Baggot Street Bridge, Dublin 2.
Tel: 1850 23 0330
Fax: 01 - 602 4100
For general postal enquiries:
Bord Fáilte - Irish Tourist Board,
P.O. Box 273, Dublin 8.

NORTHERN IRELAND
Belfast
Bord Fáilte - Irish Tourist Board,
53 Castle Street, Belfast BT1 1GH.
Tel: 028 - 9032 7888
Fax: 028 - 9024 0201

Derry
Bord Fáilte - Irish Tourist Board,
44 Foyle Street, Derry BT48 6AT.
Tel: 028 - 7136 9501
Fax: 028 - 7136 9501

EUROPE
Great Britain
Bord Fáilte - Irish Tourist Board,
150 New Bond Street,
London W1Y OAQ.
Tel: 020 - 7493 3201
Fax: 020 - 7493 9065

All Ireland Information,
Britain Visitor Centre, 1 Regent Street,
London SW1Y 4XT.

France
Office National du Tourisme Irlandais,
33, rue de Miromesnil, 75008 Paris.
Tel: 01 - 53 43 12 12
Fax: 01 - 47 42 01 64

Italy
Ente Nazionale del Turismo Irlandese,
Via S. Maria Segreta, 6, 20123 Milano.
Tel: 02 - 869 05 41
Fax: 02 - 869 03 96

Germany
Irische Fremdenverkehrszentrale,
Untermainanlage 7,
D60329 Frankfurt/Main.
Tel: 069 - 92 31 85 50
Fax: 069 - 92 31 85 88

Netherlands
Iers Nationaal Bureau voor Toerisme,
Spuistraat 104, 1012VA Amsterdam.
Tel: 020 - 622 31 01
Fax: 020 - 620 80 89

Belgium
Irish Tourist Board,
Avenue de Beaulieulaan 25/12,
1160 Brussels.
Tel: 02 - 673 99 40
Fax: 02 - 672 10 66

Spain
Oficina de Turismo de Irlanda,
Paseo de la Castellana 46, 3 Planta,
28046 Madrid.
Tel: 91 - 577 17 87
Fax: 91 - 577 69 34

Sweden
Irlandska Turistbyran,
Sibyllegatan 49,
PO Box 5292, 10246 Stockholm
Tel: 08 - 662 85 10
Fax: 08 - 661 75 95

Denmark
Det Irske Turistkontor, Klostergaarden,
Amagertorv 29B, 3,
DK 1160 Kobenhavn K.
Tel: 33 - 15 80 45
Fax: 33 - 93 63 90

Finland
Irlannin Matkailutoimisto,
Embassy of Ireland,
Erottajankatu 7A,
PL33 00130 Helsinki.
Tel: 9 - 608 966
Fax: 9 - 646 022

USA & CANADA
New York
Irish Tourist Board,
345 Park Avenue,
New York NY 10154.
Tel: 1800 22 36 470
Fax: 212 - 371 9052

JAPAN
Tokyo
Irish Tourist Board,
Ireland House 4th floor,
2-10-7 Kojimachi,
Chiyoda-ku, Tokyo 102 - 0083
Tel: 03 - 5275 1611
Fax: 03 - 5275 1623

SOUTH AFRICA
Braamfontein
c/o Development Promotions
Everite House, 7th floor,
20, De Korte Street,
Braamfontein 2001
Tel: 011 - 339 4865
Fax: 011 - 339 2474

AUSTRALIA
Sydney
Irish Tourist Board,
5th Level, 36 Carrington Street,
Sydney, NSW 2000.
Tel: 02 - 9299 6177
Fax: 02 - 9299 6323

NORTHERN IRELAND TOURIST BOARD

Belfast
Northern Ireland Tourist Board,
59 North Street,
Belfast BT1 1NB.
Tel: 028 - 9023 1221
Fax: 028 - 9024 0960

Dublin
Northern Ireland Tourist Board,
16 Nassau Street,
Dublin 2.
Tel: 01 - 679 1977
Fax: 01 - 679 1863

Glasgow
Northern Ireland Tourist Board,
98 West George Street,
7th Floor, Glasgow G2 1PJ.
Tel: 0141 - 572 4030
Fax: 0141 - 572 4033

London
Northern Ireland Tourist Board,
24 Haymarket,
London SW1Y 4DG.
Tel: 020 - 7766 9920
Fax: 020 - 7766 9929

France
Northern Ireland Tourist Board,
Centre PO 166,
23 rue Lecourbe,
75015 Paris
Tel: 1 - 49 39 05 77

Germany
Northern Ireland Tourist Board,
Westendstr. 16-22
D-60325, Frankfurt
Tel: 0049 69 - 234504
Fax: 0049 69 - 233480

United States
Northern Ireland Tourist Board,
551 Fifth Avenue, Suite 701,
New York, NY 10176.
Tel: 212 - 922 0101
Fax: 212 - 922 0099

Canada
Northern Ireland Tourist Board,
2 Bloor Street West, Suite 1501,
Toronto, ON M4W 3E2.
Tel: 416 - 925 6368
Fax: 416 - 925 6033

LOCAL TOURIST INFORMATION OFFICES

The offices below operate throughout the year; approximately one hundred others are open during the summer months.

Aran Islands
Kilronan
Tel: 099 - 61263

Armagh
40 English Street
Tel: 028 - 3752 1800

Belfast
59 North Street
Tel: 028 - 9024 6609
Fax: 028 - 9031 2424

Blarney
Tel: 021 - 381624

Bru na Boinne
Bru na Boinne Visitor Centre
Donore, Co. Meath
Tel: 041 - 988 0305

Carlow
Town Centre
Tel: 0503 - 31554

Carrick-On-Shannon
The Quays
Tel: 078 - 20170

Cavan
1 Farnham Street
Tel: 049 - 4331942

Clonmel
Town Centre
Tel: 052 - 22960

Cork City
Tourist House,
Grand Parade
Tel: 021 - 273251
Fax: 021 - 273504

Derry
44 Foyle Street
Tel: 028 - 7126 7284

Dublin
Dublin Tourism Centre,
Suffolk Street, Dublin 2
Ferry Terminal,
Dun Laoghaire Harbour
Arrivals Hall, Dublin Airport
Baggot St. Bridge, Dublin 2
The Square Town Centre,
Tallaght
E-mail:
information@dublintourism.ie
reservations@dublintourism.ie
Internet: www.visitdublin.com

For reservations in Dublin
contact Ireland Reservations
Freephone
Tel: +800 668 668 66

Dundalk
Jocelyn Street
Tel: 042 - 933 5484
Fax: 042 - 933 8070

Dungarvan
Town Centre
Tel: 058 - 41741

Ennis
Arthur's Row
Tel: 065 - 682 8366

Enniskillen
Wellington Road
Tel: 028 - 6632 3110

Galway
Victoria Place,
Eyre Square
Tel: 091 - 563081
Fax: 091 - 565201

Giant's Causeway
Bushmills
Tel: 028 - 2073 1855

Gorey
Town Centre
Tel: 055 - 21248

Kilkenny
Rose Inn Street
Tel: 056 - 51500
Fax: 056 - 63955

Killarney
Beech Road
Tel: 064 - 31633
Fax: 064 - 34506

Killymaddy
Dungannon (off A4)
Tel: 028 - 8776 7259

Letterkenny
Derry Road
Tel: 074 - 21160
Fax: 074 - 25180

Limerick City
Arthur's Quay
Tel: 061 - 317522
Fax: 061 - 317939

Monaghan
Market House
Tel: 047 - 81122

Mullingar
Market House
Tel: 044 - 48650
Fax: 044 - 40413

Newcastle
(Co. Down)
10-14 Central Promenade
Tel: 028 - 4372 2222

Omagh
1 Market Street
Tel: 028 - 8224 7831

Rosslare
Tel: 053 - 33622 /33232
Fax: 053 - 33421

Shannon Airport
Tel: 061 - 471664

Skibbereen
North Street
Tel: 028 - 21766
Fax: 028 - 21353

Sligo
Temple Street
Tel: 071 - 61201
Fax: 071 - 60360

Tralee
Ashe Hall
Tel: 066 - 7121288

Tullamore
Tullamore Dew
Heritage Centre
Bury Quay
Tel: 0506 - 52617

Waterford
The Granary
Tel: 051 - 875788
Fax: 051 - 877388

Westport
James Street
Tel: 098 - 25711
Fax: 098 - 26709

Wexford
Crescent Quay
Tel: 053 - 23111
Fax: 053 - 41743

Wicklow
Fitzwilliam Square
Tel: 0404 - 69117
Fax: 0404 - 69118

QUALITY EMPLOYER PROGRAMME SYMBOL AN ASSURANCE TO GUESTS OF THE HIGHEST STANDARDS OF EMPLOYMENT

Readers will notice our Quality Employer Programme (QEP) logo in the right hand corner of a large number of hotel and guesthouse entries throughout this guide. It is an assurance to you as a guest, that the property you choose offers excellence in all standards of employment and treatment of staff. This ultimately benefits all guests, as the staff in these premises enjoy high job satisfaction, which in turn leads to an enhanced quality of service for you to experience.

The QEP is a defined code of practice with standards set in all areas of employment including; training, personnel relations, rostering and the arrangement of work hours. It also makes recommendations on meals, uniforms and pensions. Once a property has fulfiled all elements of the programme it faces an annual review to ensure that standards are achieved and maintained. The QEP development by the Irish Hotel Federation, is in effect a guarantee to you, that the accredited properties have reached an important standard in relation to all their employment practices in these areas. It also means that staff are trained to carry out their job to set criteria and receive ongoing training to update their skills. All in all, this means a better service for guests.

The QEP status enjoyed by the properties in this guide also means that they attract the highest calibre of staff. Highly skilled staff in the hospitality sector, want to work in best hotels and guesthouses so they can experience the best conditions of employment and career progression.

So you when you choose a QEP hotel or guesthouse, you can be assured you will experience Irish hospitality and friendliness at its best.

INTRODUCTION

It is essential that when booking your accommodation you request the "Be Our Guest 2000" Rate

Our Guide features a broad selection of Irish Hotels, including stately Country Houses, luxurious Castles, old-world Inns and homely Guesthouses. The majority of these hotels and guesthouses are members of the Irish Hotels Federation or the Northern Ireland Hotels Federation and we hope that the illustrations and descriptions of these premises and the amenities they offer will help you to choose the most suitable premises for your holiday.

All of the hotels and guesthouses registered at the time of going to print (19th Oct 1999) and the facilities and services they provide have been inspected by Bord Failte / Irish Tourist Board or by the Northern Ireland Tourist Board, in accordance with the Statutory Registration Regulations which they administer. *(See also Activity Sections pgs 400-455)*

RATES

The only rates featured in this publication relate to Per Person Sharing or a Room Rate.

Per Person Sharing: relates to the cost of Bed & Full Breakfast per person per night, on the basis of two persons occupying a double/twin bedded room, most having private bath/shower.

Room Rate: relates to the cost of a room per night. There may be a restriction on the number of persons allowed to share the room. It is advisable to check this when making your reservation.

The rates range from minimum to maximum and are those generally in operation throughout the year, but may not apply during special occasions such as Public Holiday Weekends, Christmas and New Year, International Events, Major Festivals and Sporting Fixtures, or on such other occasions as individual premises may decide.

These are guideline rates, please ensure that you contact the premises to verify the rates applicable to your reservation.

Rates are inclusive of Value Added Taxes at current (1999) rates and Services Charges (if any).

Supplements may be payable for suites or superior / de luxe rooms. Also, where single or double/ twin bedded rooms are occupied by one person, a supplement may be payable. Correspondingly, if more than two persons share a family room, special reduced rates may be arranged.

In the case of hotels and guesthouses in the Republic of Ireland, rates are quoted in IR£, whereas in Northern Ireland they are quoted in STG£.

Rates are also quoted in Euros except in the case of Northern Ireland. 1 € = IR£ 0.787564

STANDARD SPECIAL OFFERS (Per Person Sharing) ☺

Many of the hotels / guesthouses in the Guide feature special offers :

- **Weekend Specials** include 2 nights' accommodation, 2 Breakfasts and 1 Dinner.
- **Midweek Specials** include 3 nights' accommodation and 3 breakfasts.
- **Weekly Partial Board** includes 7 nights' accommodation, 7 breakfasts and 7 dinners.

Alternative Special Offers may be featured

HOTEL CLASSIFICATION

FIVE STAR   ★★★★★

These include Ireland's most luxurious hotels, all of which are of high international standard. They range from elegant, stately castles to prestigious country clubs and top class city hotels catering for both the business and tourist visitor. All guest accommodation is luxurious and spacious suites are also available.

These fine hotels boast of some of the country's best restaurants and offer table d'hôte and / or à la carte lunch and dinner menus. Exceptional service and a personalised welcome are the norm in these hotels.

FOUR STAR   ★★★★

These include contemporary hotels of excellent quality and charming period houses renovated to very high standards complete with all modern comforts. All guest accommodation is luxurious with suites and half suites available in most

follow in a giant's footsteps.
start with his breakfast.

Next time you fancy a holiday break, try Northern Ireland for size. The massive, mysterious Giant's Causeway (built by giant Finn MacCool, some say, to reach his lady love in Scotland) will take your breath away. And just wait till you see the size of the breakfasts we serve here. One on its own is enough to keep you going for a whole holiday!

We're big on welcomes, too. Nobody's a stranger for long in Northern Ireland - because making new friends is one of our favourite hobbies. Just you try *not* joining in with the music, the singing and the chat when you spend an evening in one of our pubs!

It's ever so easy to get here - and there's so much to see and do you'll never, ever find yourself at a loose end.

Enjoy a wander along one of our beautiful, uncrowded beaches. Take a picnic to your very own secret, hideaway glen (there are nine in County Antrim alone!) or head for our magnificent rolling hills and blow a few cobwebs away.

Come and live it up in our superb restaurants, famous theatres and night clubs. Stroll our first class shopping avenues. Feed your mind in our heritage parks, galleries and museums. Come pony trekking, mountain biking or hang gliding. Or relax on a boating holiday, an angling break or a golfing package.

If you want much, much more from your next holiday or short break ring the CallSave number below.

It's easy to find out more. Callsave

1850 230 230

(Mon - Fri, 9.15am - 5.30pm. Sat, 10am - 5pm.)

Ireland
(www.ni-tourism.com)

Northern Ireland Tourist Board
16 Nassau Street, Dublin 2.

Ireland. It's a different holiday altogether.

cases. Restaurant facilities provide excellent cuisine and service for the discerning diner. Table d'hôte and / or à la carte lunch and dinner menus are available.

THREE STAR ★★★

These range from small, family operated premises to larger, modern hotels. Guest rooms are well decorated with the emphasis on comfort and all have a private bathroom with a bath and / or shower. Some hotels may also have colour TV, direct dial phones, hairdryers, tea / coffee facilities and room service. Many hotels also have lesiure facilities, car parking, safety deposit boxes.

Restaurants offer high standards of cuisine in relaxed and hospitable surroundings. Table d'hôte and / or à la carte dinner menus are available.

GUESTHOUSE CLASSIFICATION

FOUR STAR ★★★★

This is the top classification for guesthouses in Ireland. Guest accommodation includes half suites and all guest rooms have private bathroom with bath and / or shower, direct dial telephone, colour TV and radio. Room service offers full breakfast. Many premises provide dinner, with table d'hôte and / or à la carte menus. Guesthouse facilities include car parking, safety deposit boxes, fax.

THREE STAR ★★★

All guest rooms have private bathroom with bath and / or shower and direct dial telephone. Guesthouse facilities include a TV lounge, travellers cheques are exchanged and major credit cards are accepted. Restaurant facilities are available in some guesthouses.

TWO STAR ★★

Half or more of the guest rooms have private bathroom with bath and / or shower. Guesthouse facilities include a reading / writing room or lounge area for residents' use. Restaurant facilities are available in some guesthouses.

ONE STAR ★

These premises meet all the mandatory requirements for guesthouses and offer simple accommodation, facilities and services to a satisfactory standard. Restaurant facilities are available in some guesthouses.

TWO STAR ★★

These are more likely to be family operated premises, selected for their charm and their comfortable facilities.

All guest rooms have a telephone and most have a private bathroom with a bath and / or shower. Full dining facilities are available, representing excellent value and good wholesome food.

ONE STAR ★

Here you can enjoy the comforts of a pleasantly simple hotel where a warm welcome prevails. These premises offer all the mandatory services and facilities to a satisfactory standard, necessary for a most enjoyable and relaxed visit. Some guest rooms have a private bathroom with a bath or a shower.

OPENING DATES

Some of the premises featured in the guide were not open at the guide print date (19 October 1999). The planned date of opening as supplied by these premises is displayed.

Hotels and Guesthouses may have the symbols, U, N, R, P, CR for the following reasons:

U Under the terms of the classification scheme a premises may opt to remain unclassified and will be shown U in this guide. Of course these premises meet all the mandatory requirements for hotel/guesthouse registration.

N These are premises that have recently registered with Bord Fáilte / Northern Irish Tourist Board but, at the time of going to print, have not been long enough in operation for their standards to be fully assessed.

R These premises were undergoing major refurbishment at the time of printing this guide. Their classification will be assessed when the work is completed.

P Applied to Bord Fáilte/Northern Ireland Tourist Board for registration at time of going to print.

CR Classification Rescinded - At the time of going to print (19 October 1999) the classification of these properties had been rescinded and the registration was under review by Bord Fáilte.

Kerry County Museum

Kerry County Museum at the Ashe Memorial Hall is the ideal starting point for tours of County Kerry .It consists of 3 superb attractions which tell the story of Kerry and Ireland over 8,000 years:

Kerry in Colour - a panoramic multi-image audio-visual tour of County Kerry featuring scenery, historic sites, people and traditions.

Kerry County Museum - a museum with a difference. Interactive media and reconstructions stand side-by-side with priceless treasures dating from the Stone and Bronze Age to the Present Day. The Museum also hosts major international temporary exhibitions.

Geraldine Tralee - This is well worth a detour on its own! Imagine being transported 600 years back in time to the Middle Ages and experiencing a day in the life of an Irish medieval town. Visitors are seated in time cars and brought on a fascinating journey through the reconstructed streets, houses, Abbey and Castle of Geraldine Tralee complete with sounds and smells. Commentaries in 7 languages.

Opening Hours: 10.00 - 18.00 hrs (17.00 Nov 1st - Dec 31st)
March 17 - December 31. Closed Dec. 24-26, Jan. 1 - March 16.

GROUP BOOKINGS - Kerry County Museum,
Ashe Memorial Hall, Denny Street, Tralee, Co. Kerry, Ireland.
Telephone: **066 7127777** Facsimile: **066 7127444**

The JEANIE JOHNSTON

TRALEE · NEW YORK · BOSTON · QUEBEC

The *Jeanie Johnston (1847-58)* was the most famous of the Kerry 19th century emigrant vessels. During the Great Famine Jeanie made 16 successful voyages to North America without losing a passenger. Now a life-size sailing replica of the 150ft Long Tall Ship is being built at a visitor friendly shipyard at Blennerville on the main Tralee-Dingle Road. Young people from Ireland, North and South, come together with trained craftsmen from Ireland and Overseas to rebuild the tripple masted barque which carried a full complement of 200 passengers and a crew of 17. When completed in the Year 2000, *Jeanie* will make her Millennium Voyage to the United States and Canada. The Jeanie Johnston Shipyard is open to visitors right through the various phases of construction Visitors are introduced to traditional shipbuilding, the design of the sailing ships and life aboard the emigrant vessels in the Visitor Centre. Then they are guided through the workshops and shipyard site to view the shipwrights, metal workers, riggers, sailmakers and apprentices at work. Each visit to the yard is a new experience as no day is exactly the same.

GROUP BOOKINGS
The Jeanie Johnston Visitor Shipyard, Blennerville,
Tralee, County Kerry.
Telephone:066-7121064. Facsimile:066-7181888

RESERVATIONS

Courtesy Onward Reservations

If you are moving around the country, the premises in which you are staying will be delighted to help you select and make your next accommodation reservation from the Be Our Guest Guide.

The following are other ways in which a booking can be made :

1. Advance enquiries and reservations may be made directly to the premises by phone, fax, e-mail or letter and details of the reservation should be confirmed by both parties. A deposit should be forwarded if requested.

2. Some of the hotels and guesthouses in the Guide participate in a Central Reservations system and the contact number of their agency in various countries, **may be included** in their entry. Some Marketing Groups are featured in the Guide pages 398 to 399 and will make reservations for you on request.

3. Travel Agent - your travel agent will normally make a booking on your behalf without extra charge where the premises pays travel agents' commission (this is indicated by the symbol T in the Guide). In other cases, agents will usually charge a small fee to cover the cost of telephone calls and administration.

4. Some Irish Tourist Board offices listed in this guide (see pages 12 & 13) operate an enquiry and booking service and will make an accommodation reservation on your behalf.

5. "resireland" - Ireland's tourism information and reservations system. This system enables visitors to make reservations with ease. To book any premises in the guide ring toll free on **+ 800 36 98 74 12.**

COMPLAINTS

Should there be cause for complaint, the matter should be brought to the notice of the Management of the premises in the first instance. **Failing satisfaction, the matter should be referred to the Tourist Information Office concerned (see list on pages 12 & 13).** In the case of Northern Ireland premises, complaints should be addressed to the Customer Relations Section, **Northern Ireland Tourist Board,** 59 North Street, Belfast BT1 1NB.

ERRORS AND OMISSIONS

The information contained in the accommodation section has been supplied by individual premises. While reasonable care has been taken in compiling the information supplied and ensuring its accuracy and compliance with consumer protection laws, the Irish Hotels Federation cannot accept any responsibility for any errors, omissions or misinformation regarding accommodation, facilities, prices, services, classification or any other information whatsover in the Guide and shall have no liability whatsoever and howsoever arising to any person for any loss, whether direct, indirect, economic or consequential, or damages, actions, proceedings, costs, claims, expenses or demands arising therefrom.

The listing of any premises in this guide is not and should not be taken as a recommendation from the IHF or a representation that the premises will be suitable for your purposes.

THINK ABOUT INSURANCE

We strongly advise you to take out an insurance policy against accidents, cancellations, delays, loss of property and medical expenses. Such travel and holiday insurance policies are available quite cheaply and are worth every penny for peace of mind alone.

CANCELLATIONS

Should it be necessary to amend or cancel your reservation advise the premises immediately as there may be a cancellation penalty.

Ireland's Millennium Festivals

ST. PATRICK'S FESTIVAL, DUBLIN
16th - 19th March 2000

GALWAY ARTS FESTIVAL
19th - 30th July 2000

KILKENNY ARTS FESTIVAL
11th - 20th August 2000

ROSE OF TRALEE FESTIVAL
19th - 23rd August 2000

FLEADH CHEOIL NA hÉIREANN
21st - 27th August 2000

WEXFORD FESTIVAL OPERA
19th October - 5th November 2000

GUINNESS CORK JAZZ FESTIVAL
27th - 30th October 2000

BELFAST FESTIVAL AT QUEEN'S
27th October - 12th November 2000

www.millennium-ireland.com email: **info@millennium-ireland.com**
Millennium Festivals phone cards available at selected outlets.

SAMPLE ENTRY

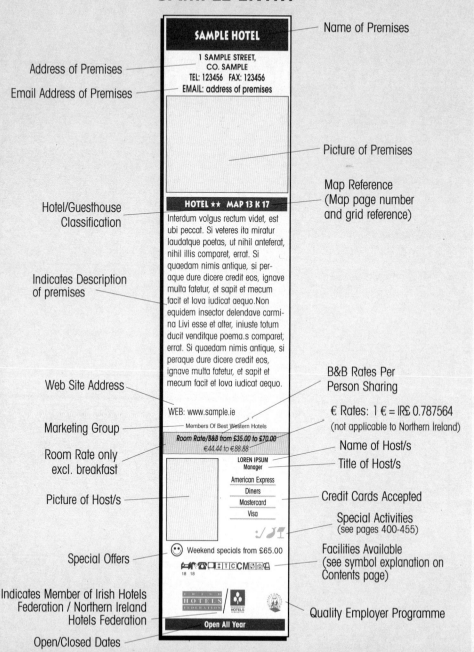

Name of Premises

SAMPLE HOTEL

1 SAMPLE STREET,
CO. SAMPLE
TEL: 123456 FAX: 123456
EMAIL: address of premises

Address of Premises

Email Address of Premises

Picture of Premises

HOTEL ★★ MAP 13 K 17

Hotel/Guesthouse Classification

Map Reference (Map page number and grid reference)

Interdum volgus rectum videt, est ubi peccat. Si veteres ita miratur laudatque poetas, ut nihil anteferat, nihil illis comparet, errat. Si quaedam nimis antique, si peraque dure dicere credit eos, ignave multa fatetur, et sapit et mecum facit et Iova iudicat aequo. Non equidem insector delendave carmina Livi esse et alter, iniuste totum ducit venditque poema.s comparet; errat. Si quaedam nimis antique, si peraque dure dicere credit eos, ignave multa fatetur, et sapit et mecum facit et Iova iudicat aequo.

Indicates Description of premises

B&B Rates Per Person Sharing

WEB: www.sample.ie

Web Site Address

€ Rates: 1 € = IR£ 0.787564 (not applicable to Northern Ireland)

Members Of Best Western Hotels

Marketing Group

Room Rate/B&B from £35.00 to £70.00
€44.44 to €88.88

Room Rate only excl. breakfast

Name of Host/s

LOREN IPSUM
Manager

Title of Host/s

American Express
Diners
Mastercard
Visa

Picture of Host/s

Credit Cards Accepted

Special Activities (see pages 400-455)

☺ Weekend specials from £65.00

Special Offers

18 18

Facilities Available (see symbol explanation on Contents page)

Indicates Member of Irish Hotels Federation / Northern Ireland Hotels Federation

IRISH HOTELS FEDERATION

Quality Employer Programme

Open All Year

Open/Closed Dates

Galway, Mayo and Roscommon are noted for their traditional Irish music and song, and there's a wide range of activities and amenities, with secluded sandy beaches and beautiful scenery. Among the many famous Festivals which are held throughout the year are the Galway Arts Festival, Galway and Clarinbridge Oyster Festivals, Ballinasloe Horse Show, Ballina Salmon Festival, Westport Street Festival and the O'Carolan Harp Festival in Keadue, Co. Roscommon, Clifden Arts Week (Co. Galway) Castlebar 4 day Walks Festival (Co. Mayo).

MAJOR ATTRACTIONS

Galway City has a host of attractions on offer, including Galway Irish Crystal Heritage Centre, Lynch's Castle, the Spanish Arch, Nora Barnacle House and the Talbhdhearc – Ireland's only Irish-speaking theatre. In Co. Galway you have Thoor Ballylee, the home of the poet W.B. Yeats, and Coole Park Visitor Centre, former home of Lady Gregory, both located just north of Gort. The Battle of Aughrim Interpretative Centre near Ballinasloe gives a fascinating account of one of the most decisive battles in European history. Other major attractions include Aughnanure Castle in Oughterard, Dan O'Hara's Pre-Famine Farm near Clifden, Leenane Cultural Centre, Kylemore Abbey in Letterfrack, Connemara, Glengowla Mines near Oughterard and Ionad Arann, Aran's Heritage Centre on Inishmore.

Amongst the attractions worth a visit in Co. Mayo are the Ceide Fields in Ballycastle, Foxford Woollen Mills, Knock Shrine and Folk Museum, Ballintubber Abbey and the Westport Heritage Centre. Westport Heritage Centre Ballintubber Abbey.

While Roscommon can boast the County Heritage and Genealogical centre in Strokestown, Strokestown Park House, Garden and Famine Museum, Clonalis House in Castlerea, Douglas Hyde Interpretative Centre in Porthard, King House and Boyle Abbey in Boyle and the magnificent Lough Key Forest Park.

For information and accommodation bookings in Counties Galway, Mayo and Roscommon contact:

Ireland West Tourism,
Aras Fáilte, Eyre Square, Galway.
Tel: (091) 563081. Fax: (091) 565201
Self Catering Tel: (091) 567673

Tourist Information Office,
James Street, Westport, Co. Mayo.
Tel: (098) 25711. Fax: (098) 26709.

Tourist Information Office,
Boyle, Co. Roscommon.
Tel: (079) 62145.

GUINNESS

Galway Arts Festival, Co. Galway.
July

Guinness Galway Races, Co. Galway.
July / August

Galway International Oyster Festival, Co. Galway.
September

Guinness Ballinasloe International October Fair & Festival, Co. Galway.
October

Event details correct at time of going to press

ABBEY HOUSE

113 UPPER NEWCASTLE,
GALWAY
TEL: 091-524394 FAX: 091-528217
EMAIL: johndarby@eircom.net

GUESTHOUSE ★★ MAP 6 F 10

Family run guest house located on
the N59 leading to Connemara.
Convenient to city centre. Rooms are
en suite with cable TV, and DD
phones. Private car parking. Close to
golf, fishing, tennis, swimming pool,
horse riding, seaside and city centre.
Excellent location for touring
Connemara, Aran Islands and the
Burren. A warm welcome awaits you
from the Darby family.

WEB: homepage.eircom.net/~johndarby/

B&B from £18.00 to £28.00
€22.86 to €35.55

JOHN DARBY

Mastercard

Visa

Midweek specials from £54.00

12 11

IRISH HOTELS FEDERATION

Open All Year

ABBINGTON GUEST HOUSE

12 BISHOP O'DONNELL'S ROAD,
TAYLORS HILL, GALWAY
TEL: 091-525530 / 525531
EMAIL: abbingtonguesthouse@eircom.net

GUESTHOUSE N MAP 6 F 10

New luxurious, purpose-built
guesthouse within walking distance
of Salthill promenade and 5 mins
drive from city centre. All rooms
interior design with power shower,
bath, DD phone, cable TV, hairdryer,
iron press and complimentary
tea/coffee facilities. Private car
parking. Convenient to Leisureland,
tennis, wind surfing, fishing and
horseriding. Ground floor rooms
available.

WEB: www.galway.net/pages/abbington

B&B from £17.00 to £35.00
€21.59 to €44.44

COLETTE NUGENT
Proprietor

American Express

Mastercard

Visa

8 8

Closed 24 - 25 December

ACORN GUESTHOUSE

19 DUBLIN ROAD,
GALWAY
TEL: 091-770990 FAX: 091-770173
EMAIL: acorn1@eircom.net

GUESTHOUSE ★★★ MAP 6 F 10

Acorn Guesthouse is a family run
registered guesthouse. Within
walking distance from Galway city.
An ideal base for holiday makers
and business people. Bedrooms
contain en suite bathrooms,
orthopaedic beds, DD phones,
hairdryers, remote control multi-
channel TV, complimentary tea and
coffee. Private car park. Acorn
Guesthouse is adjacent to Ryan's
Hotel and Corrib Great Southern.

WEB: www.acorn-guesthouse.com

Room Rate from £20.00 to £40.00
€25.39 to €50.79

GARRY & CAROL MCKEON
Owners

Mastercard

Visa

7 5

IRISH HOTELS FEDERATION

Closed 23 - 27 December

B&B rates are per person sharing per night incl. Breakfast

ADARE GUEST HOUSE

9 FR. GRIFFIN PLACE,
GALWAY
TEL: 091-582638   FAX: 091-583963
EMAIL: adare@iol.ie

GUESTHOUSE ★★★   MAP 6 F 10

Adare guesthouse is a family managed guesthouse, within 5 mins from city centre (train/bus). Refurbished with old time pine furniture & floors, you can enjoy your multi choice breakfast in our dining room overlooking our beautiful patio area. All bedrooms have en suite, DD phones, cable TV & hairdryers. Tea/coffee & ironing facilities are available. 2 new suites built to a high standard with baths, DD fax phone, trouser press/iron, tea/coffee/cable TV/Radio. Safe facilities available.

B&B from £20.00 to £30.00
€25.39 to €38.09

GRAINNE & PADRAIC CONROY
Proprietors

American Express
Mastercard
Visa

14 14

Closed 24 - 27 December

ANNO SANTO HOTEL

THREADNEEDLE ROAD, SALTHILL,
GALWAY
TEL: 091-523011   FAX: 091-522110
EMAIL: annosant@iol.ie

HOTEL ★★   MAP 6 F 10

Small family run hotel located in quiet residential area. Galway's major tennis/badminton and squash club lies opposite the hotel. The golf club is also close by (1km), while Galway city and beaches are within easy reach. We are also on a main bus route. All rooms are en suite, TV, tea/coffee and direct dial telephone. Your hosts, the Vaughan family, provide high class service in comfortable bedrooms at budget prices.

B&B from £25.00 to £42.00
€31.74 to €53.33

GERARD & JOANNA VAUGHAN
Proprietors

American Express
Diners
Mastercard
Visa

14 14

Closed 20 December - 20 January

ARDAWN HOUSE

31 COLLEGE ROAD,
GALWAY
TEL: 091-568833   FAX: 091-563454
EMAIL: ardawn@iol.ie

GUESTHOUSE ★★★★   MAP 6 F 10

Ardawn House is a luxurious haven for the discerning visitor to Galway. Located within five minutes walking of city centre, train & bus. Antiques, fresh flowers, silver and china help to make our multi choice home cooked breakfast famous. All bedrooms have en suite, D.D. phones, cable TV & hairdryers. Tea/coffee & ironing facilities are also available. Highly recommended in Guide du Routard, AA and many other guide books.

B&B from £25.00 to £40.00
€31.74 to €50.79

MIKE & BREDA GUILFOYLE
Proprietors

American Express
Mastercard
Visa

8 8

Closed 22 - 26 December

Room rates are per room per night

ARDILAUN HOUSE HOTEL, CONFERENCE CENTRE & LEISURE CLUB

TAYLOR'S HILL,
GALWAY
TEL: 091-521433 FAX: 091-521546
EMAIL: ardilaun@iol.ie

HOTEL ★★★★ MAP 6 F 10

The Ardilaun is a privately owned 89 bedroomed 4**** hotel, in 5 acres of beautiful grounds. All rooms en suite with *DD phone *TV *Trouser press *Tea and coffee making facilities *Hairdryer *Award winning restaurant *New state of the art leisure club *Deck level pool *Hydro-spa *Jacuzzi *Sauna *Steamroom *Aerobics *Hi-tech gym *Sun-room therapy suites *Billiard room *Golf *Tennis *Beach & city within 5 mins. drive. Conference centre -25-500 persons. Bookable world-wide Utell Intl.

WEB: www.ardilaunhousehotel.ie

Members Of Signature Hotels

B&B from £49.00 to £80.00
€62.22 to €101.58

T.A. MACCARTHY O'HEA
General Manager

American Express
Diners
Mastercard
Visa

☺ Weekend specials from £135.00

🏨🖐📞🛎📺Ⓒ🅿CM❄️🐾⛵🏦♨
⛵🅿❓🅂🄰alc 🖥 Inet

89 89

IRISH HOTELS FEDERATION

Closed 22 - 28 December

ASHFORD MANOR

NO 7 COLLEGE ROAD,
GALWAY
TEL: 091-563941 FAX: 091-563941
EMAIL: ashfordmanor@esatclear.ie

GUESTHOUSE N MAP 6 F 10

Centrally located in the heart of Galway's city centre, Ashford Manor offers a unique combination of stylish en suite accommodation in a prestigious location at affordable prices. All rooms include multi-channel TV, radio, DD phone, professional hairdryer and tea/coffee facilities. Ideal base for touring Connemara, the Burren and the Aran Islands. AA selected ◆◆◆◆ and as featured in Bon Voyage. Credit cards accepted.

B&B from £20.00 to £35.00
€25.39 to €44.44

CORINNE MANNION
Proprietor

American Express
Mastercard
Visa

🏨🖐📞🛎📺Ⓒ🅿CM⛵🅿🖥

5 5

Closed 24 - 25 December

ATLANTA HOTEL

DOMINICK STREET,
GALWAY
TEL: 091-562241 FAX: 091-563895

HOTEL ★ MAP 6 F 10

Atlanta Hotel is a family run hotel with a homely atmosphere, where a friendly welcome awaits you. Located in the city centre with guests car park. Convenient to theatre, cinema, golf links, tennis club, swimming and horse riding. 5 minutes walk to beach. Gulliver Reservations. Fully licensed.

B&B from £25.00 to £40.00
€31.74 to €50.79

JOSEPH OWENS
General Manager

American Express
Diners
Mastercard
Visa

🏨🖐📞🅿Ⓒ❄️⛵🅿🔒alc 🖥

16 16

IRISH HOTELS FEDERATION

Open All Year

B&B rates are per person sharing per night incl. Breakfast

ATLANTIC VIEW HOUSE

4 OCEAN WAVE,
GALWAY CITY
TEL: 091-582109 FAX: 091-528566
EMAIL: jennifertreacy@ireland.com

GUESTHOUSE ★★★ MAP 6 F 10

Atlantic View House is a luxurious haven overlooking Galway Bay with a large sun balcony. Some of our rooms have stunning views of the sea, with balconies. The house overlooks the beach with spectacular views of the Aran Islands and the Burren mountains. We are only a short walk from the medieval city of Galway and the seaside resort of Salthill. Our rooms are luxuriously decorated with DD phone, satellite TV, trouser press, hair dryer, hospitality tray and clock-radio.

B&B from £17.00 to £50.00
€21.59 to €63.49

BREDA & JENNIFER TREACY
Proprietors

Mastercard
Visa

5 5

Closed 23 - 28 December

BRENNANS YARD HOTEL

LOWER MERCHANTS ROAD,
GALWAY
TEL: 091-568166 FAX: 091-568262

HOTEL ★★ MAP 6 F 10

A refurbished city centre hotel, Brennans Yard is a charming, intimate hotel with excellent standards of accommodation, food and service. Our en suite bedrooms have been individually designed and are furnished with antique pine furniture. In our restaurant, you can dine in discreet elegance, choose from a wide range of dishes prepared from the freshest ingredients. The Spanish Bar offers an intimate, warm and lively atmosphere, or join us in the new Terry's Restaurant. Bookable worldwide through UTELL International.

B&B from £35.00 to £50.00
€44.44 to €63.49

CONNIE FENNELL
General Manager

American Express
Diners
Mastercard
Visa

45 45

Closed 24 - 29 December

CONNEMARA COAST HOTEL

FURBO,
GALWAY
TEL: 091-592108 FAX: 091-592065
EMAIL: sinnott@iol.ie

HOTEL ★★★★ MAP 6 F 10

A spectacular setting, with grounds that sweep down to the shores of Galway Bay and panoramic views of the coastline, make this the ideal base from which to explore Connemara and enjoy the bustling city of Galway, just ten minutes drive away. Luxurious public areas, well appointed bedrooms, two restaurants, a state of the art conference suite, free car-parking, an award winning bar and leisure centre provide the unique setting to relax and enjoy Galway at its best.

WEB: www.sinnotthotels.com

B&B from £62.50 to £90.00
€79.36 to €114.28

PAUL O'MEARA
General Manager

American Express
Diners
Mastercard
Visa

Weekend/midweek specials available

112 112

Open All Year

Room rates are per room per night

CORRIB GREAT SOUTHERN HOTEL

RENMORE,
GALWAY
TEL: 091-755281 FAX: 091-751390
EMAIL: res@corrib.gsh.ie

HOTEL ★★★★ MAP 6 F 10

This 4**** hotel overlooks Galway Bay. It has 180 rooms, all en suite with radio, TV, DD phone, hairdryer, tea/coffee making facilities and trouser press. Leisure facilities include indoor heated swimming pool, steam room, jacuzzi, gym. Evening entertainment and childrens play centre during summer months. Currach Restaurant and O'Malley's bar. Convention centre accommodates up to 800 delegates. Bookable through central reservations 01-214 4800 or UTELL International.

WEB: www.gsh.ie

B&B from £50.00 to £91.00
€63.49 to €115.55

MICHEAL CUNNINGHAM
General Manager

American Express
Diners
Mastercard
Visa

☺ Weekend specials from £96.00

🏢🅿️🚗📺🛁T🅰️♿C♨CMCS❄
📶🏠⬛U🏊P🅿️S🏮alc🔥

180 180

Closed 24 - 26 December

CORRIB HAVEN

107 UPPER NEWCASTLE,
GALWAY CITY
TEL: 091-524171 FAX: 091-524171
EMAIL: corribhaven@eircom.net

GUESTHOUSE ★★★ MAP 6 F 10

Corrib Haven's motto is Quality Hospitality for discerning people. AA selected ◆◆◆◆. Its new, purpose built, located in Galway city on the N59 leading to Connemara. All rooms en suite, power showers, posture sprung beds, cable TV, video, DD phones. Tea/coffee facility, breakfast menu, private parking. Convenient to city centre, good restaurants, nightly entertainment. Ideal for touring Connemara, Aran Islands. Smooth professionalism with personal warmth to our visitors. Non-smoking.

B&B from £18.00 to £30.00
€22.86 to €38.09

FRANK KELLY
Owner

Mastercard
Visa

☺ Midweek specials from £54.00

🏢🅿️🚗📺TPS

9 9

Closed 24 - 27 December

EGLINTON HOTEL

THE PROMENADE, SALTHILL,
GALWAY
TEL: 091-526400 FAX: 091-526495

HOTEL U MAP 6 F 10

Located right in the centre of Salthill. 48 brand new top quality bedrooms, sleeping up to 4 people. Entertainment on premises most nights; 100 metres from Leisureland swimming and entertainment complex. Galway golf course nearby. Free private car park. Groups and parties welcome any time. (Special rates available). Enjoy comfortable accommodation at keen rates in a lovely seafront location.

B&B from £25.00 to £47.50
€31.74 to €60.31

PATRICK MCGOVERN
Manager

American Express
Diners
Mastercard
Visa

🏢🅿️🚗📺🛁TCU🏊♫P🅿️alc

48 48

Closed 24 - 27 December

B&B rates are per person sharing per night incl. Breakfast

EYRE SQUARE HOTEL

FORSTER STREET, OFF EYRE SQUARE,
GALWAY
TEL: 091-569633 FAX: 091-569641

HOTEL ★★★ MAP 6 F 10

Opened in February 1996, the Eyre Square Hotel is situated right in the heart of Galway, adjacent to both bus & rail stations. The Eyre Square Hotel caters for both the tourist and the business person offering a very high standard of accommodation. Rooms en suite with DD phone, multichannel TV and tea/coffee making facilities. Enjoy excellent cuisine in our restaurant or visit the lively Red Square pub. A warm and friendly welcome awaits you at Eyre Square Hotel.

B&B from £35.00 to £80.00
€44.44 to €101.58

JOHN HUGHES
General Manager

American Express
Diners
Mastercard
Visa

☺ Weekend specials from £85.00

45   45

IRISH
HOTELS
FEDERATION

Closed 25 - 26 December

FLANNERYS HOTEL

DUBLIN ROAD,
GALWAY
TEL: 091-755111 FAX: 091-753078

HOTEL ★★★ MAP 6 F 10

Family owned and operated 98 bedroomed hotel situated 2km from Galway city centre on the main approach road, extensive car parking. An ideal base for touring the west of Ireland. The hotel features a table d'hôte/à la carte restaurant, bars. All rooms en suite with TV, tea making facilities, hair dryer. You are assured of a warm welcome. A member of Best Western Hotels.

Members Of Best Western Hotels

B&B from £30.00 to £60.00
€38.09 to €76.18

MARY FLANNERY
Proprietor

American Express
Diners
Mastercard
Visa

98   98

IRISH
HOTELS
FEDERATION

Closed 20 - 30 December

GALWAY BAY GOLF AND COUNTRY CLUB HOTEL

ORANMORE,
GALWAY
TEL: 091-790500 FAX: 091-790510
EMAIL: gbaygolf@iol.ie

HOTEL U MAP 6 G 10

This hotel is the ideal venue for leisure breaks and for corporate events. Within its private grounds, on the shore of Galway Bay we offer the challenge of a European PGA championship golf course and the tranquillity of forest walks. Our restaurant has been awarded two AA Rosettes for its cuisine and the conference and banqueting facilities cater for up to 200 people. The vibrant city of Galway is within 10 minutes drive from the hotel.

WEB: www.galwaybay.com

B&B from £45.00 to £95.00
€57.14 to €120.63

MR J CASSIDY
Managing Director F.I.C.H.I.

American Express
Diners
Mastercard
Visa

90   90

IRISH
HOTELS
FEDERATION

Closed 24 - 27 December

Room rates are per room per night

GALWAY BAY HOTEL, CONFERENCE & LEISURE CENTRE

THE PROMENADE, SALTHILL, GALWAY
TEL: 091-520520 FAX: 091-520530
EMAIL: info@galwaybayhotel.net

HOTEL N MAP 6 F 10

The Galway Bay Hotel which opened in May 1998 is situated on the Promenade with spectacular views of Galway Bay. All rooms are tastefully appointed with all the modern facilities the discerning traveller has come to expect. The hotel combines excellent facilities with superb customer care all enhanced by a view of the bay unrivalled in the area.

WEB: www.galwaybayhotel.net

B&B from £72.50 to £80.00
€92.06 to €101.58

TERRY BRENNAN
Managing Director

American Express
Diners
Mastercard
Visa

Weekend specials from £89.00

150 150

Open All Year

GALWAY GREAT SOUTHERN HOTEL

EYRE SQUARE, GALWAY
TEL: 091-564041 FAX: 091-566704
EMAIL: res@galway.gsh.ie

HOTEL ★★★★ MAP 6 F 10

A blend of 19th century elegance and modern amenities, Galway Great Southern (built in 1845) overlooks Eyre Square in Galway city. All bedrooms are en suite with TV, direct dial phone, radio, hairdryer, trouser press and tea/coffee making facilities. Enjoy dining in the Oyster Room restaurant - the atmosphere of the cocktail bar or O'Flahertys pub. Facilities include indoor heated pool, sauna, steamroom. Bookable worldwide through UTELL International/Central Res. 01-214 4800.

WEB: www.gsh.ie

B&B from £62.00 to £99.00
€78.72 to €125.70

ROBERT BYRNE
General Manager

American Express
Diners
Mastercard
Visa

Weekend specials from £107.00

115 115

Closed 24 - 26 December

GALWAY RYAN HOTEL & LEISURE CENTRE

DUBLIN ROAD, GALWAY CITY EAST, GALWAY
TEL: 091-753181 FAX: 091-753187
EMAIL: ryan@indigo.ie

HOTEL ★★★ MAP 6 F 10

This hotel offers the ultimate in relaxation and leisure facilities. 96 en suite rooms, the air-conditioned Oranmore Room, 2 air-conditioned meeting rooms, Toddy's bar and a relaxing lobby lounge. A magnificent leisure centre with a 2,500 sq ft. pool incorporating 60ft. swimming lanes, lounger, geyser and toddlers pools, steam room, jacuzzi, sauna, multi purpose sports hall, aerobics studio, a state of the art gym and floodlit tennis courts. Parking. AA, RAC & Egon Ronay recommended.

WEB: www.ryan-hotels.com

B&B from £45.00 to £90.00
€57.14 to €114.28

PAUL COLLERAN
General Manager

American Express
Diners
Mastercard
Visa

Weekend specials from £89.00

96 96

Open All Year

B&B rates are per person sharing per night incl. Breakfast

GLENLO ABBEY HOTEL

BUSHYPARK,
GALWAY
TEL: 091-526666 FAX: 091-527800
EMAIL: glenlo@iol.ie

HOTEL ★★★★★ MAP 6 F 10

Glenlo Abbey Hotel-an 18th century country residence, is located on a 138 acre lake side golf estate just 4km from Galway city. Now a Bord Failte rated 5***** hotel, Glenlo Abbey is a haven for all discerning travellers. All 46 rooms have marbled bathrooms, personal safe, DD phones, trouser press, cable TV, radio and 24 hour room service. The Pullman restaurant, two unique orient express carriages, offers a totally new dining experience. Other activities include fishing, etc.

WEB: www.glenlo.com

Members Of Small Luxury Hotels

B&B from £140.00 to £195.00
€177.76 to €247.60

PEGGY & JOHN BOURKE
Proprietors

American Express
Diners
Mastercard
Visa

46 46

P ♿ a/c inet

IRISH HOTELS FEDERATION

Open All Year

GUIDER'S OSTERLEY LODGE

142 LOWER SALTHILL,
GALWAY
TEL: 091-523794 FAX: 091-523565
EMAIL: osterleylodge@eircom.net

GUESTHOUSE ★★ MAP 6 F 10

Osterley Lodge is family owned with private car park, 200 metres from promenade and famous Galway Bay. It is close to theatres, cinemas, ten-pin bowling, restaurants, tennis, golf, horse riding. City centre bus stop at door. Ideal base for motorists to explore breathtaking beauty of Connemara, Aran Islands, Cliffs of Moher, the Burren. Rooms are en suite with multi-channel TV, tea/coffee facilities, direct dial telephones. Ground floor rooms available.

B&B from £20.00 to £25.00
€25.39 to €31.74

PAT & BARBARA GUIDER
Proprietors

Mastercard
Visa

12 12

IRISH HOTELS FEDERATION

Closed 23 - 28 December

HOLIDAY HOTEL

181 UPPER SALTHILL, SALTHILL,
GALWAY
TEL: 091-523934 FAX: 091-527083

HOTEL CR MAP 6 F 10

Holiday Hotel is closely set near beaches, amusements, a new state of the art aquarium, and nightly entertainment. A Bord Failte approved hotel, with all rooms en suite, DD phone, multi-channel TV, hairdryer and trouser-press. Ideally located for golfing, fishing, family holidays and relaxing breaks. The Holiday Hotel offers a recently renovated bar, where you can be guaranteed a relaxing time following a tough day at the office.

B&B from £25.00 to £35.00
€31.74 to €44.44

BARRY WARD
Proprietor

American Express
Mastercard
Visa

10 10

IRISH HOTELS FEDERATION

Closed September - June

Room rates are per room per night

HOTEL SACRE COEUR

LENABOY GARDENS, SALTHILL,
GALWAY
TEL: 091-523355 FAX: 091-523553

HOTEL ★★ MAP 6 F 10

Hotel Sacre Coeur is a family owned and managed hotel where a Cead Mile Failte awaits you. All of our 40 rooms are en suite, direct dial telephone, with colour TV and tea/coffee making facilities. Within five minutes walk of the hotel we have Salthill's magnificent promenade, tennis club and a wonderful 18 hole golf course. Renowned for its friendly service and excellent food you will enjoy your stay at the Sacre Coeur.

B&B from £27.00 to £32.00
€34.28 to €40.63

SEAN OG DUNLEAVY
Manager

Mastercard
Visa

✓

☺ Midweek specials from £90.00

40 40

IRISH HOTELS FEDERATION

Closed 22 - 30 December

HOTEL SALTHILL

SALTHILL, GALWAY,
CO. GALWAY
TEL: 091-522711 FAX: 091-521855
EMAIL: infosh@indigo.ie

HOTEL ★★★ MAP 6 F 10

Family run 3*** hotel, 50 metres from Salthill's sandy beach. Piano bar music most nights, every night from June to Sept (Thu-Sun rest of year). All rooms en suite, DD telephone, tea making facilities, hair dryer. Excellent cuisine and service. 100m from Leisureland and indoor swimming pool. Overlooking Galway Bay with large car park. Ideal location for family holidays and over 55's in off season. Less than 2 miles from the mediaeval city of Galway. Many sporting activities nearby.

WEB: www.indigo.ie/infosh

B&B from £35.00 to £90.00
€44.44 to €114.28

MICHAEL & BRIAN MURRAY
Proprietors

American Express
Diners
Mastercard
Visa

75 75

IRISH HOTELS FEDERATION

Closed 22 - 30 December

HOTEL SPANISH ARCH

QUAY STREET,
GALWAY
TEL: 091-569600 FAX: 091-569191
EMAIL: emcdgall@iol.ie

HOTEL ★★★ MAP 6 F 10

Situated in the heart of Galway this is a 20 roomed boutique style hotel. Rooms of unsurpassed elegance created and individually designed by Easter McDonagh. Our unique Victorian bar which has original wooden panelled walls from the home of Lilly Langtree, confidante to King Edward VII. A 16th Century stone wall was uncovered and can be found in the back bar where locals and visitors mingle - where late nightly music can be enjoyed and various functions/weddings. Bistro. Carpark.

WEB: www.irishholidays.com/sp-index.shtml/

B&B from £45.00 to £95.00
€57.14 to €120.63

EASTER MCDONAGH GALLAGHER
Managing Director

American Express
Diners
Mastercard
Visa

20 20

inet FAX

IRISH HOTELS FEDERATION

Open All Year

B&B rates are per person sharing per night incl. Breakfast

IMPERIAL HOTEL

EYRE SQUARE,
GALWAY
TEL: 091-563033   FAX: 091-568410
EMAIL: imperialhtl@hotmail.com

HOTEL ★★★   MAP 6 F 10

A bustling hotel in the centre of Galway City with modern comfortable 3 star bedrooms. Located in the main shopping area surrounded by a large choice of restaurants, pubs and quality shops. Five minutes walk from the new Galway Theatre, main bus and rail terminals. Beside main taxi rank with multi storey parking nearby. Full service hotel; friendly and informative staff. No service charge. R.A.C. 3 star.

B&B from £35.00 to £57.50
€44.44 to €73.01

KEVIN FLANNERY
General Manager

American Express
Diners
Mastercard
Visa

85 85

Closed 24 - 25 December

INISHMORE GUESTHOUSE

109 FR. GRIFFIN ROAD,
LOWER SALTHILL, GALWAY
TEL: 091-582639   FAX: 091-589311
EMAIL: inishmorehouse@eircom.net

GUESTHOUSE ★★★   MAP 6 F 10

A charming family residence with secure carpark within 5 mins walk of city and beach. All rooms contain DD phone, multi-channel TV and hairdryers. Tea/coffee and ironing facilities available. German spoken. An ideal base for touring the Aran Islands, Burren and Connemara. Golf holidays, sea angling trips and coarse or game fishing arranged. Recommended by many leading travel guides.

B&B from £20.00 to £30.00
€25.39 to €38.09

MARIE & PETER
Proprietors

Mastercard
Visa

☺ Midweek specials from £60.00

8 5

Closed 23 - 28 December

JAMESONS HOTEL

SALTHILL,
GALWAY
TEL: 091-528666   FAX: 091-528626
EMAIL: jamesons@iol.ie

HOTEL ★★★   MAP 6 F 10

Jamesons Hotel is located in the heart of Salthill, overlooking Galway Bay. All rooms are en suite with special jacuzzi suites available. We offer excellent cuisine in the pleasant surroundings of our restaurant. Live entertainment 7 nights a week in summer and at weekends over the winter period. Conference suites facilitating up to 60 people. Private car parking. Special weekend rates available.

B&B from £34.00 to £80.00
€43.17 to €101.58

JOSEPH BOYLE
Proprietor

American Express
Diners
Mastercard
Visa

☺ Weekend specials from £97.95

20 20

Open All Year

Room rates are per room per night

JURYS GALWAY INN

QUAY STREET,
GALWAY
TEL: 091-566444 FAX: 091-568415
EMAIL: info@jurys.com

HOTEL ★★★ MAP 6 F 10

Modern attractive rooms capable of
accommodating up to 3 adults or 2
adults and 2 children. All rooms are
en suite with multi-channel TV, radio,
DD phone and tea/coffee making
facilities. Located in the heart of
Galway city the Inn has an informal
restaurant and a lively pub, a
business centre, conference rooms
and an adjoining public multi-storey
car park (fee payable). Jurys Doyle
Hotel Group central reservations Tel.
01-607 0000 Fax. 01-631 6999.

WEB: www.jurys.com

Room Rate from £47.00 to £69.00
€59.68 to €87.61

KAREN CREMINS
General Manager

American Express
Diners
Mastercard
Visa

128 128

Closed 24 - 26 December

KNOCKREA GUEST HOUSE

55 LOWER SALTHILL,
GALWAY
TEL: 091-520145 FAX: 091-529985
EMAIL: knockrea@eircom.net

GUESTHOUSE ★★★ MAP 6 F 10

A 3*** family run guesthouse
established 1950. Refurbished to a
high standard with pine floors
throughout. Car park at rear. 1km
from city centre on bus route. 300
metres from Salthills promenade.
Restaurants, theatres, golf, tennis,
horseriding close by. Perfect base for
touring Connemara, Burren and Aran
Islands. Within walking distance of
Spanish Arch and Quay Street. Irish
pub music entertainment available
locally. All rooms en suite, TV, and
DD phone. Frommers guide
recommended.

WEB: www.galway.net/pages/knockrea/

B&B from £18.00 to £27.00
€22.86 to €34.28

EILEEN STORAN
Proprietor

Mastercard
Visa

9 9

Closed 23 - 26 December

LOCHLURGAIN HOTEL

22 MONKSFIELD, UPPER SALTHILL,
GALWAY
TEL: 091-529595 FAX: 091-522399
EMAIL: loclurgn@eircom.net

HOTEL U MAP 6 F 10

Welcome to Lochlurgain. Completely
refurbished elegant Town House
Hotel, AA***. Beside church off Main
St, 5 mins beach and leisure centre.
City centre 5 minutes. Fresh home
cooked food served. Seafood also
featured. Enjoy comfort, peace,
tranquility and relaxation.
Lochlurgain is 62ml/100km north of
Shannon Airport. One hour from the
Burren and Connemara. On parle
français. Bed, breakfast and dinner
breaks, please ask for details.
Peadar and Joan Cunningham
welcome you.

WEB: www.failte.com/salthill/loch.htm

B&B from £27.50 to £50.00
€34.92 to €63.49

PEADAR & JOAN CUNNINGHAM
Proprietors

Mastercard
Visa

3 B&B and 3 Dinners from
£130.00

10 10

Closed 31 October - 10 March

B&B rates are per person sharing per night incl. Breakfast

MARIAN LODGE GUESTHOUSE

KNOCKNACARRA ROAD,
SALTHILL UPPER, GALWAY
TEL: 091-521678 FAX: 091-528103
EMAIL: celine@iol.ie

GUESTHOUSE ★★★ MAP 6 F 10

Family-run, adjacent to Promenade and beach in Salthill Upper. Private parking. On bus route/city centre/Aran Islands/Connemara. Home baking lounge with rustic fireplace displaying pots and pans of old. Bedrooms en suite, cable TV, DD phone, clock radios, orthopaedic beds, hairdryers, tea/coffee facilities. Ironing facilities & trouserpress available. Convenient to Leisureland, tennis, wind surfing, fishing, horseriding. Beside golf course, driving range, restaurant, pubs, shops.

WEB: www.marian-lodge.com

B&B from £19.00 to £25.00
€24.13 to €31.74

CELINE MOLLOY

Mastercard
Visa

☺ Midweek specials from £57.00

Closed 23 - 28 December

MENLO PARK HOTEL

TERRYLAND, HEADFORD ROAD,
GALWAY
TEL: 091-761122 FAX: 091-761222
EMAIL: menlopkh@iol.ie

HOTEL ★★★ MAP 6 F 10

Situated near Galway's city centre the Menlo Park offers the best of modern facilities with old fashioned hospitality. All rooms have TV/teletext, welcome tray, power showers, rich colour schemes. Executive rooms also feature king beds, sofas, trouser press/iron, fax machines, extra workspace and modem points. Contemporary chic but casual restaurant; MP's Bar. Easy access to main roads. Free car parking. Meeting and conference facilities.

WEB: www.menloparkhotel.com

B&B from £37.50 to £80.00
€47.62 to €101.58

DAVID KEANE
Manager

American Express
Diners
Mastercard
Visa

Closed 24 - 26 December

OCEAN CREST HOUSE

OCEAN WAVE, SEAPOINT
PROMENADE, SALTHILL, GALWAY
TEL: 091-589028 FAX: 091-529399
EMAIL: oceanbb@iol.ie

GUESTHOUSE ★★★ MAP 6 F 10

We chose this site and built this guesthouse to provide what our guests love, a taste of subtropical elegance, overlooking Galway Bay and beaches with panoramic views of the Burren mountains. We are walking distance from the bustling medieval city of Galway and across the road we have the Promenade. Our bedrooms are beautifully appointed with multi channel TV, en suite facilities, phone, trouser press, hair dryers, hospitality tray and armchairs.

B&B from £18.00 to £25.00
€22.86 to €31.74

JILLIAN RUANE
Manager

American Express
Mastercard
Visa

Closed 24 - 28 December

Room rates are per room per night

ORANMORE LODGE HOTEL, CONFERENCE & LEISURE CENTRE

ORANMORE,
GALWAY
TEL: 091-794400 FAX: 091-790227
EMAIL: orlodge@eircom.net

HOTEL ★★★ MAP 6 G 10

This manor house hotel 8k from Galway city in the picturesque village of Oranmore, overlooking Galway Bay and on the edge of oyster country. 3k from Galway airport. Equestrian, golfing and walking pursuits all within 3k of the hotel. Full leisure facilities with a 17m swimming pool and 21st century TechnoGym. Your host and his efficient staff radiate a welcome and warmth reminiscent of the old country houses of Ireland.

Members Of Logis of Ireland

B&B from £35.00 to £90.00
€44.44 to €114.28

BRIAN J. O'HIGGINS
Proprietor

American Express
Diners
Mastercard
Visa

😊 Weekend specials from £89.00

56 56

Closed 24 - 27 December

OYSTER MANOR HOTEL

CLARENBRIDGE,
CO. GALWAY
TEL: 091-796777 FAX: 091-796770

HOTEL ★★★ MAP 6 F 10

Located in the famous oyster village of Clarenbridge the Oyster Manor Hotel was opened in May 1996. The building dates back some 150 years and has been tastefully redecorated in mature grounds. The hotel is family run which adds to its relaxing and friendly atmosphere. The hotel boasts a wide reputation for excellent cuisine in the Pearl restaurant. Music and craic every weekend in the Leanach bar.

B&B from £35.00 to £70.00
€44.44 to €88.88

NED & JULIANNE FORDE
Proprietors

American Express
Diners
Mastercard
Visa

26 26

Closed 24 - 26 December

PARK HOUSE HOTEL & EYRE HOUSE RESTAURANTS

FORSTER STREET, EYRE SQUARE,
GALWAY
TEL: 091-564924 FAX: 091-569219
EMAIL: parkhousehotel@eircom.net

HOTEL ★★★★ MAP 6 F 10

An oasis of luxury and hospitality in the heart of Galway city centre. We are Bord Failte 4****, AA 4 star and RAC 4 star. All 57 rooms are en suite with bath and shower, DD phone, ISDN line, multi channel TV, tea/coffee making facilities, trouser press, awards of excellence winning restaurant over many years. Les Routiers Restaurant of the Year Ireland 1998-1999. Our high standards are your guarantee. Private residents car park on hotel grounds.

B&B from £40.00 to £75.00
€50.79 to €95.23

EAMON DOYLE & KITTY CARR
Proprietors

American Express
Diners
Mastercard
Visa

57 57

Closed 24 - 29 December

B&B rates are per person sharing per night incl. Breakfast

QUALITY HOTEL AND LEISURE CENTRE GALWAY

ORANMORE,
GALWAY
TEL: 091-792244 FAX: 091-792246
EMAIL: qualityhotelgalway@eircom.net

HOTEL ★★★ MAP 6 G 10

This luxury hotel is ideally located on the N6 approach to Galway, adjacent to the picturesque village of Oranmore & just 5 mins drive from Galway city. Facilities incl spacious rooms, Furey's Well traditional pub with regular entertainment & all day menu, Furey's Relish restaurant, residents lounge & a superb leisure centre with a 20m pool, jacuzzi, hi-tech gym, steamroom, sauna, therapy & solarium. Rooms to accommodate up to 2 adults & 2 children. Golf, karting, horseriding nearby.

WEB: www.qualityhotelgalway.com

Members Of Choice Hotels Ireland

Room Rate from £39.00 to £105.00
€49.52 to €133.32

DERMOT COMERFORD
General Manager

American Express
Diners
Mastercard
Visa

☺ Weekend specials from £65.00

93 93

Open All Year

ROCKBARTON PARK HOTEL

ROCKBARTON PARK, SALTHILL,
GALWAY
TEL: 091-522286 FAX: 091-527692

HOTEL ★★ MAP 6 F 10

Owned and managed by the Tyson family, fully licensed, in a quiet residential cul de sac. 200 metres from seafront and Leisureland Centre. Golf, tennis, badminton and squash just 5 minutes walk. Tyson's Restaurant offers a homely comfortable atmosphere noted for fresh local fish and prime steaks, prepared and cooked delightfully by chef/proprietor Terry. Bar food also available. Friendly service.

B&B from £25.00 to £35.00
€31.74 to €44.44

PATRICIA AND TERRY TYSON
Proprietors

American Express
Diners
Mastercard
Visa

10 10

Closed 24 - 31 December

ROCKLAND HOTEL

SALTHILL,
GALWAY
TEL: 091-522111 FAX: 091-526577

HOTEL U MAP 6 F 10

Overlooking the scenic splendour of Galway Bay, the Rockland Hotel is ideally situated to capture all the charm of the rugged beauty of Connemara. All bedrooms are en suite with TV, DD phone, tea/coffee making facilities and many with panoramic views of Galway Bay. Enjoy our good food, comfortable bar, nightly entertainment during high season and of course our friendly staff.

B&B from £20.00 to £45.00
€25.39 to €57.14

BRIAN MURPHY
Manager

Mastercard
Visa

☺ Weekend specials from £69.00

14 14

Closed 22 - 29 December

Room rates are per room per night

SALT LAKE GUESTHOUSE

4 LOUGH ATALIA ROAD,
GALWAY
TEL: 091-564572   FAX: 091-567037
EMAIL: oceanbb@iol.ie

GUESTHOUSE N   MAP 6 F 10

Salt Lake House is a beautifully purpose-built guesthouse with exquisite views of Lough Atalia (inlet of Galway Bay). We offer luxurious accommodation within easy reach of Galway city centre, only minutes from bus/train station. Each room is beautifully appointed with en suite facilities, multi-channel TV (12 channels), armchairs and table, hospitality tray, iron and board and hairdryer.

B&B from £18.00 to £25.00
€22.86 to €31.74

JILLIAN RUANE
Manager

American Express
Mastercard
Visa

8 8

Closed 24 - 30 December

SKEFFINGTON ARMS HOTEL

EYRE SQUARE,
GALWAY
TEL: 091-563173   FAX: 091-561679

HOTEL ★★★   MAP 6 F 10

The Skeffington Arms Hotel has been caring for guests for over a 100 years. Overlooking Eyre Square, within walking distance of rail and bus terminal, it enjoys an enviable position in the heart of Galway. This privately owned hotel is justifiably proud of its new bars and à la carte menu which is very popular with both locals and guests alike. The bedrooms, which are newly refurbished have multi-channel TV, DD phone and bath/shower en suite.

B&B from £35.00 to £80.00
€44.44 to €101.58

SELENE JONES
Reservations Manager

American Express
Mastercard
Visa

23 23

IRISH
HOTELS
FEDERATION

Closed 25 - 26 December

B&B rates are per person sharing per night incl. Breakfast

SPINNAKER HOUSE HOTEL

KNOCKNACARRA, SALTHILL,
GALWAY
TEL: 091-525425 FAX: 091-526650

HOTEL ★★ MAP 6 F 10

The newly refurbished Spinnaker Hotel is a family run hotel overlooking Galway golf course and has spectacular views of Galway Bay and the Burren. All 20 rooms, most with private balconies, are newly built with en suite facilities, telephone, TV and tea/coffee maker. Within 2k of the hotel we have beaches, fishing, horse riding, golf and tennis clubs, Leisureland complex and the ferry port to the Aran Islands.

> **B&B from £27.50 to £45.00**
> €34.92 to €57.14

SEAN DIVINEY

American Express
Mastercard
Visa

☺ Weekend specials from £70.00

Closed 25 - 26 December

VICTORIA HOTEL

VICTORIA PLACE, OFF EYRE
SQUARE, GALWAY
TEL: 091-567433 FAX: 091-565880
EMAIL: bookings@victoriahotel.ie

HOTEL ★★★ MAP 6 F 10

The Victoria Hotel is centrally located just 100 yards off Eyre Square, within walking distance of all shops, theatres, pubs and cinemas. Each of the 57 spacious en suite rooms are beautifully appointed with DD phone, trouserpress and hairdryer. A hotel restaurant serving à la carte dinner along with a lively bar serving lunches will all add up to make your stay at the Victoria as enjoyable as possible. The Victoria is your enclave in the city, dedicated to pleasing you.

> **B&B from £37.50 to £70.00**
> €47.62 to €88.88

LINDA GORDON-MARVILLE
Manager

American Express
Diners
Mastercard
Visa

☺ Weekend specials from £79.00

Closed 24 - 26 December

WATERFRONT HOTEL

SALTHILL,
GALWAY
TEL: 091-588100 FAX: 091-588107

HOTEL P MAP 6 F 10

Located on Salthill's promenade, all of our 66 luxurious rooms have a panoramic view of beautiful Galway bay. DD phone, cable TV, tea/coffee making facilities, trouser press, hairdryer and clock radio in all rooms. There is also a choice of kitchenette or lounge. Secure parking and only 5 minutes from city centre. Incorporating Kitty O'Shea's bar and restaurant which provides regular live entertainment. Reservations Freephone 1800 588 488.

> **Room Rate from £45.00 to £70.00**
> €57.14 to €88.88

KEN BERGIN
General Manager

American Express
Mastercard
Visa

☺ Weekend specials from £70.00

Closed 24 - 26 December

Room rates are per room per night

WEST WINDS

5 OCEAN WAVE, SALTHILL,
GALWAY
TEL: 091-520223 FAX: 091-520223
EMAIL: westwinds@eircom.ie

GUESTHOUSE N   MAP 6 F 10

Westwinds is a charming family-managed guesthouse overlooking Galway Bay, 10 minutes walk from Galway city, an ideal base for all travellers wishing to explore the Burren, Connemara and the Aran Islands. We are situated at the city-end of Salthill's Promenade, restaurants, nightly entertainment and all other amenities 5-10 minutes walk. All rooms have en suite bathrooms with power shower, hairdryer, cable TV, tea/coffee making facility. Our hospitality awaits!

WEB: homepage.eircom.ie/~westwinds

B&B from £18.00 to £30.00
€22.86 to €38.09

RITA & PATRICK JOYCE
Proprietors

Mastercard
Visa

😊 Midweek specials from £57.00

10 10

Closed 12 December - 01 April

WESTWOOD HOUSE HOTEL

DANGAN, UPPER NEWCASTLE,
GALWAY
TEL: 091-521442 FAX: 091-521400
EMAIL: westwoodhotel@eircom.net

HOTEL N   MAP 6 F 10

The Westwood House Hotel, commands a prime location on the edge of Galway city and at the gateway to Connemara. Tastefully designed to international standards and air conditioned throughout the Westwood boasts 58 superbly appointed bedrooms which include 6 junior suites, 8 executive rooms, 44 deluxe bedrooms, the award winning Meridian Restaurant, a themed bar along with Conference/Banqueting facilities with ample car parking.

WEB: westwoodhousehotel.com

Members Of Signature Hotels

B&B from £44.50 to £89.50
€56.50 to €113.64

RACHAEL COYLE
General Manager

American Express
Diners
Mastercard
Visa

58 58

Inet FAX

IRISH
HOTELS
FEDERATION

Closed 24 - 26 December

WHITE HOUSE

2 OCEAN WAVE,
GALWAY CITY
TEL: 091-529399 FAX: 091-529399
EMAIL: oceanbb@iol.ie

GUESTHOUSE ★★★   MAP 6 F 10

New and beautiful purpose-built guest house in Galway's finest location, overlooking Galway Bay and the Burren mountains, minutes walk to Galway's medieval city and Salthill's new hotel, the Galway Bay. Large bedrooms with armchairs and tables, iron and board, multi-channel TV, hospitality tray and hairdryer.

B&B from £18.00 to £25.00
€22.86 to €31.74

MARY MORAN/TOM MCEVADDY
Owners

American Express
Mastercard
Visa

6 6

Open All Year

B&B rates are per person sharing per night incl. Breakfast

ARD EINNE GUESTHOUSE

INISMOR, ARAN ISLANDS,
CO. GALWAY
TEL: 099-61126 FAX: 099-61388
EMAIL: ardeinne@eircom.net

GUESTHOUSE ★★ MAP 5 D 10

A few days on historical Inismor (Aran Islands) is an essential part of an Irish holiday. Enjoy the stress-free experience in the relaxed atmosphere of spectacularly situated and high quality Ard Einne, with sweeping panoramic views of Galway/Clare coastlines, mountains and Galway Bay. Earth has not anything to show more fair. Walks, tours, cycle trips organised. Artists, writers, groups, clubs, societies offered very attractive rates. Convenient to air-sea services, beach and pub.

B&B from £17.00 to £20.00
€21.59 to €25.39

KEVIN AND ENDA GILL
Proprietors

Mastercard

Visa

☺ Weekend specials from £40.00

🖐🔥☎☀🚶🎵🅿️🆂☂
15 9

IRISH HOTELS FEDERATION

Closed 10 November - 10 February

KILMURVEY HOUSE

KILRONAN, ARAN ISLANDS,
CO. GALWAY
TEL: 099-61218 FAX: 099-61397
EMAIL: kilmurveyhouse@eircom.net

GUESTHOUSE ★★★ MAP 5 D 10

Kilmurvey House is a 150 year-old country house situated at the foot of Dun Aonghus, beside Dun Aongusa visitor centre. 3 minutes walk from a blue flag beach in one of the more peaceful locations on the island. We are the ideal setting for cyclists, walkers, botanists and those that just want to relax. Special group rates available.

B&B from £20.00 to £25.00
€25.39 to €31.74

BRIDGET HERNON/TERESA JOYCE
Proprietors

Mastercard

Visa

🖐🔥☎🆃🅲☀🆄🅿️
12 12

IRISH HOTELS FEDERATION

Closed 31 October - 01 April

PIER HOUSE GUESTHOUSE

LOWER KILRONAN, ARAN ISLANDS,
CO. GALWAY
TEL: 099-61417 FAX: 099-61122
EMAIL: pierh@iol.ie

GUESTHOUSE ★★★ MAP 5 D 10

Pier House is perfectly located less than 100m from Kilronan Harbour and village, within walking distance of sandy beaches, pubs, restaurants and historical remains. This modern house is finished to a very high standard, has a private gym for guest use and many other extra facilities. Its bedrooms are well appointed and have perfect sea and landscape views. If it is comfort and old fashioned warmth and hospitality you expect, then Pier House is the perfect location to enjoy it.

B&B from £20.00 to £25.00
€25.39 to €31.74

MAURA & PADRAIG JOYCE
Proprietors

Mastercard

Visa

🖐🔥☎🆃🅲☀🎵🅿️🆂☂
12 12

IRISH HOTELS FEDERATION

Closed 01 November - 01 March

Room rates are per room per night

TIGH FITZ

KILLEANY, KILRONAN,
ARAN ISLANDS, CO. GALWAY
TEL: 099-61213 FAX: 099-61386

GUESTHOUSE ★★ MAP 5 D 10

Tigh Fitz, a family run Guest house, bar, lounge, is in Killeany, Inishmore. Offering a luxurious accommodation in this unspoilt area of the Aran Isles. Tigh Fitz is unique in its situation, in its spaciousness and proximity to beaches and areas of archaeological and historical remains. In this area are the tall cliffs of Aran and the magnificent pre-historic forts. Tigh Fitz is 1.6km from the Island capital Kilronan and close to the Aer Arann Airstrip.

B&B from £18.00 to £25.00
€22.86 to €31.74

PENNY MAHON
Proprietor/Owner

Mastercard
Visa

13 9

Closed 01 November - 01 March

NEWPARK HOTEL

CROSS STREET, ATHENRY,
CO. GALWAY
TEL: 091-844035 FAX: 091-844921

HOTEL ★ MAP 6 G 10

The Newpark Hotel under the management of Alacoque Feeney and family since Feb '99. The hotel is situated in a quiet part of this medieval heritage town surrounded by the famed 'Fields of Athenry' and only 15 mins drive from Galway city. Our rooms are tastefully decorated and furnished to enhance your stay. Our dining room menu offers the guest an excellent choice of Irish and international cuisine in warm relaxed surroundings. Unwind and enjoy a drink in our warm comfy bar. Music each weekend.

Room Rate from £25.00 to £35.00
€31.74 to €44.44

ALACOQUE FEENEY
Proprietor

Mastercard
Visa

18 7

☺ Weekend specials from £80.00

Closed 23 - 31 December

HAYDEN'S GATEWAY BUSINESS AND LEISURE HOTEL

DUNLO STREET, BALLINASLOE,
CO. GALWAY
TEL: 065-682 3000 FAX: 065-682 3759
EMAIL: cro@lynchotels.com

HOTEL ★★★ MAP 6 I 11

Ideal location off main Dublin-Galway road, famous for hospitality and award winning coffee dock/carvery and à la carte restaurant. 48 recently refurbished en-suite rooms including Executive rooms with spa bath. 40 mins from Galway, 15 mins from Athlone. Award winning traditional Irish pub, Planet nite club with free admission for residents. Conference facilities for up to 300. Car parking 100. 6 championship golf courses nearby.

WEB: www.lynchotels.com

Members Of Lynch Hotels

B&B from £33.00 to £45.00
€41.90 to €57.14

MICHAEL B LYNCH Group MD
JOE MELODY Gen Mgr

American Express
Diners
Mastercard
Visa

48 48

☺ From £39.00 Dinner, B&B per person sharing

Open All Year

B&B rates are per person sharing per night incl. Breakfast

BALLYNAHINCH CASTLE HOTEL

BALLYNAHINCH, RECESS, CONNEMARA, CO. GALWAY
TEL: 095-31006 FAX: 095-31085
EMAIL: bhinch@iol.ie

HOTEL ★★★★ MAP 5 D 11

Once home to the O'Flaherty Chieftains, pirate queen Grace O'Malley, Humanity Dick Martin and Maharajah Ranjitsinji, Ballynahinch is now a 4★★★★ hotel. With casual country elegance overlooking the river and ringed by mountains, Ballynahinch offers an unpretentious service and is an ideal centre from which to tour the west. Log fires and a friendly fisherman's pub complement a restaurant offering the best in fresh game, fish and produce. Ballynahinch, the Jewel in Connemara's Crown.

WEB: www.commerce.ie/ballynahinch/

Members Of Manor House Hotels

B&B from £57.00 to £167.00
€72.38 to €212.05

PATRICK O'FLAHERTY
General Manager

American Express
Diners
Mastercard
Visa

☺ Weekend specials from £119.00

40 40

Closed Christmas Week & February

SILVERSEAS

CAPPAGH ROAD, BARNA, CO. GALWAY
TEL: 091-590575 FAX: 091-590575
EMAIL: silverseas@eircom.net

GUESTHOUSE ★★★ MAP 5 F 10

Newly built ultra modern luxury residence, 1.6km from Salthill overlooking Galway bay, unsurpassed view and landscaped gardens. AA selected ♦♦♦. Family run Guesthouse with high standard of accommodation, all bedrooms en suite with power showers, TV, radio clock, hairdryer, Trouser press, guest sitting room with tea/coffee making facilities, large private car park. Riding stables, golf, surfing, beach nearby, cycling, nature walks and historical tours, Aran Island trips arranged.

B&B from £18.00 to £27.00
€22.86 to €34.28

GEULAH MCGRATH
Proprietor

Mastercard
Visa

8 8

Open All Year

CARNA BAY HOTEL

CARNA, CONNEMARA, CO. GALWAY
TEL: 095-32255 FAX: 095-32530
EMAIL: carnabay@iol.ie

HOTEL ★★★ MAP 9 D 11

Are you looking for somewhere special? Allow us to plan your carefree days in the most magical scenery in Ireland. Connemara, unique landscape, flora and fauna, unspoilt beaches, mountain ranges. Beautiful Western Way walking routes. Cycling, bicycles provided free. Our kitchen offers the finest fresh Irish produce. 26 well appointed rooms, most with sea or mountain views. Locally: St. McDara's Island, Connemara National Park, Kylemore Abbey, Aran and Inisbofin ferry 40 mins drive.

WEB: www.iol.ie/~carnabay

Members Of Village Inn Hotels

Room Rate from £30.00 to £50.00
€38.09 to €63.49

PARAIC & MARY CLOHERTY
Proprietors

American Express
Mastercard
Visa

26 26

Open All Year

Room rates are per room per night

HOTEL CARRAROE BEST WESTERN

CARRAROE,
CO. GALWAY
TEL: 091-595116 FAX: 091-595187

HOTEL ★★ MAP 5 D 10

The Best Western Hotel Carraroe is a 25 bedroomed en suite family run hotel situated in the heart of the Connemara Gaeltacht. Facilities include outdoor swimming pool, tennis court, play area and games room. The village of Carraroe itself is renowned for its traditional values and music. Daily boat trips to the Aran Islands are from nearby Rossaveal Harbour. Our local friendly staff will provide information on where to fish, play golf, horse ride or tour beautiful Connemara.

Members Of Best Western Hotels

B&B from £30.00 to £45.00
€38.09 to €57.14

BRID NI CHEALLAIGH
Manager

American Express
Mastercard
Visa

Weekend specials from £75.00

25 25

Closed 01 October - 02 May

CASHEL HOUSE HOTEL

CASHEL,
CO. GALWAY
TEL: 095-31001 FAX: 095-31077
EMAIL: info@cashel-house-hotel.com

HOTEL ★★★★ MAP 5 D 11

Elegance in a wilderness on the shores of the Atlantic. It is set amidst the most beautiful garden in Ireland. Enjoy long walks, bicycle or horseback rides, and fishing. Later, relax in front of a peat fire in this elegant residence appointed with antique furniture and period paintings. Most guestrooms look onto the gardens and some onto the sea. Dine on bounty from the sea and garden - enjoy vintage wine. Also member of Ireland's Blue Book.

WEB: http://www.cashel-house-hotel.com

Members Of Relais & Châteaux

B&B from £60.75 to £90.00
€77.14 to €114.28

MCEVILLY FAMILY
Proprietors

American Express
Diners
Mastercard
Visa

Weekend specials from £135.00

32 32

Closed 10 January - 10 February

GLYNSK HOUSE HOTEL

CASHEL BAY, CONNEMARA,
CO. GALWAY
TEL: 095-32279 FAX: 095-32342
EMAIL: glynsk@iol.ie

HOTEL ★★ MAP 5 D 11

Overlooking Cashel bay and Twelve Bens mountains, this small family-run hotel is the ideal location for touring Connemara. Enjoy the best of local seafood and Connemara lamb in our restaurant, à la carte and bar menu also available. Local attractions: Connemara National Park, Kylemore Abbey, safe white sandy beaches, Aran and Inisbofin ferry 40 mins drive. Golf and pitch & putt also a short drive away. Bicycles free. Western Way walking route close by.

Room Rate from £25.00 to £35.00
€31.74 to €44.44

PARAIC & MARY CLOHERTY
Proprietors

American Express
Mastercard
Visa

Midweek specials from £70.00

12 12

Closed 30 September - 01 May

B&B rates are per person sharing per night incl. Breakfast

ZETLAND COUNTRY HOUSE HOTEL

**CASHEL BAY, CONNEMARA,
CO. GALWAY
TEL: 095-31111 FAX: 095-31117
EMAIL: zetland@iol.ie**

HOTEL ★★★★ MAP 5 D 11

Overlooking Cashel Bay this 19th century manor house is renowned for its peace and commanding views. The bedrooms and superb seafood restaurant overlook the gardens and Cashel Bay. Facilities include tennis court and billard room and there are many activities, hill walking and golf in the surrounding area. Good Hotel Guide recommended '98, AA Courtesy of Care Award '98 and Gilbeys Gold Medal Winner '97. 4**** Manor House Hotel, GDS Acess Code, US 1-800-44-UTELL

WEB: www.connemara.net/zetland/

Members Of Manor House Hotels

B&B from £57.50 to £70.00
€73.01 to €88.88

JOHN & MONA PRENDERGAST
Proprietors

American Express
Diners
Mastercard
Visa

Closed 01 November - 10 April

ACTONS GUESTHOUSE

**LEEGAUN, CLADDAGHDUFF,
CO. GALWAY
TEL: 095-44339 FAX: 095-44309
EMAIL: actonsbandb@eircom.net**

GUESTHOUSE ★★★★ MAP 9 C 12

Our 4**** guest house is situated 7k from Clifden. We have direct access to our own sandy beach with uninterrupted views of the sea and islands. We are an ideal location for touring Connemara, the Aran Islands, Kylemore Abbey and a host of other interesting scenic locations. All bedrooms en suite with TV, telephone, tea/coffee making facilities. Warmly recommended by the Lonely Planet. AA Premier Selected ◆◆◆◆◆.

B&B from £25.00 to £30.00
€31.74 to €38.09

MARTIN & RITA ACTON
Proprietors

American Express
Diners
Mastercard
Visa

Closed 01 October - 01 April

ABBEYGLEN CASTLE HOTEL

**SKY ROAD, CLIFDEN,
CO. GALWAY
TEL: 095-21201 FAX: 095-21797
EMAIL: info@abbeyglen.ie**

HOTEL ★★★★ MAP 9 C 12

Abbeyglen Castle Hotel was built in 1832 in the heart of Connemara by John D'Arcy of Clifden Castle. Abbeyglen is romantically set in beautiful gardens with waterfalls and streams, has a panoramic view of Clifden and the bay with a backdrop of the Twelve Bens. Abbeyglen provides a long list of indoor and outdoor facilities, cuisine of international fame, unique qualities of peace, serenity and ambience. Complimentary afternoon tea a speciality. AA 1 rosette for good food and service.

WEB: www.abbeyglen.ie

Members Of Manor House Hotels

B&B from £55.00 to £67.50
€69.84 to €85.71

BRIAN/PAUL HUGHES
Manager/Proprietor

American Express
Diners
Mastercard
Visa

Week partial board from
£394.00

Closed 10 January - 01 February

ALCOCK AND BROWN HOTEL

CLIFDEN, CONNEMARA,
CO. GALWAY
TEL: 095-21206 FAX: 095-21842
EMAIL: alcock-brown@connemara.net

HOTEL ★★★ MAP 9 C 12

Alcock and Brown Best Western Hotel is family owned and operated. Situated in the centre of Clifden Village. The Hotel has 19 en suite bedrooms. Splendid restaurant with AA rosette rating. Ideal base for touring Connemara. Pursuits to be enjoyed are pony trekking, golfing on Connemara Championships Links Course, sea angling, guided heritage walks and mountain climbing. Numerous sandy beaches nearby. Member of Best Western Hotels Central Reservations 01-6766776.

Members Of Best Western Hotels

B&B from £31.00 to £39.00
€39.36 to €49.52

DEIRDRE KEOGH
Manager

American Express
Diners
Mastercard
Visa

Weekend specials from £80.00

19 19

Closed 22 - 26 December

ARDAGH HOTEL & RESTAURANT

BALLYCONNEELY ROAD, CLIFDEN,
CO. GALWAY
TEL: 095-21384 FAX: 095-21314
EMAIL: ardaghhotel@eircom.net

HOTEL ★★★ MAP 9 C 12

A quiet family-run 3*** hotel, 2km from Clifden on Ardbear Bay, AA and RAC recommended. Bedrooms individually decorated with television, telephone and tea/coffee facilities. Award-winning restaurant specialises in lobsters, salmon, oysters and Connemara lamb with homegrown vegetables and a wide selection of wines. Local amenities: golf, fishing and beaches. Reservations by post, phone, fax. Superior suites with bay view available.

WEB: www.commerce.ie/ardaghhotel

Members Of Coast and Country Hotels

B&B from £47.50 to £55.00
€60.31 to €69.84

STEPHANE & MONIQUE BAUVET
Proprietor/Manager/Chef

American Express
Diners
Mastercard
Visa

3 Dinner B&B from £175

17 17

Closed 01 November - 31 March

BEN VIEW HOUSE

BRIDGE STREET, CLIFDEN,
CONNEMARA, CO. GALWAY
TEL: 095-21256 FAX: 095-21226

GUESTHOUSE ★★ MAP 9 C 12

Charming mid 19th century town house of immense character. Owned and managed by our family since 1926. We have been extending traditional family hospitality to our guests since then. Recommended by Frommer and Le Petit Fute Guides. Enjoy all the modern comforts and special ambience of this elegant guesthouse, surrounded by antiques and old world atmosphere. Wishing all our guests a pleasant and safe journey.

B&B from £18.50 to £23.50
€23.49 to €29.84

EILEEN MORRIS
Proprietor

American Express
Mastercard
Visa

Midweek specials from £55.50

10 10

Closed 24 - 26 December

B&B rates are per person sharing per night incl. Breakfast

BUTTERMILK LODGE

WESTPORT ROAD, CLIFDEN,
CO. GALWAY
TEL: 095-21951   FAX: 095-21953
EMAIL: buttermilk@anu.ie

GUESTHOUSE ★★★   MAP 9 C 12

A warm friendly home from home,
400m from Clifden town centre
(5mins walk). Our spacious en suite
rooms have satellite TV, DD phone,
radio/alarm clock and hairdryer.
Your warm welcome includes
tea/coffee and home baking by the
turf fire where there is always a
cuppa available. Our breakfast
options, tasteful decor and many
extra touches bring our guests back.
Internet access for guests. ITB 3***,
AA Selected ♦♦♦♦ and RAC Highly
Acclaimed.

WEB: www.connemara.com/buttermilk-lodge

B&B from £20.00 to £25.00
€25.39 to €31.74

PATRICK & CATHRIONA O'TOOLE
Proprietors/Hosts

Mastercard
Visa

Closed 10 January - 01 February

DUN RI GUESTHOUSE

HULK STREET, CLIFDEN,
CO. GALWAY
TEL: 095-21625   FAX: 095-21635
EMAIL: dunri@anu.ie

GUESTHOUSE ★★★   MAP 9 C 12

Centrally located in picturesque
Clifden. Dun Ri is newly built and
specially designed to offer a high
standard of accommodation. The
spacious and luxurious bedrooms
are all en suite. Facilities include TV,
phone, hairdryer and tea/coffee.
Private parking is available. Ideal
base to enjoy all Connemara has to
offer - golf, fishing, walking, sandy
beaches, cycling, horse riding,
excellent restaurants and pubs.

WEB: www.connemara.net/dun-ri

B&B from £18.00 to £25.00
€22.86 to €31.74

MICHAEL KING
Proprietor

Mastercard
Visa

Midweek specials from £54.00

Closed 03 November - 01 March

ERRISEASK HOUSE HOTEL & RESTAURANT

BALLYCONNEELY, CLIFDEN,
CO. GALWAY
TEL: 095-23553   FAX: 095-23639
EMAIL: erriseask@connemara-ireland.com

HOTEL ★★★   MAP 9 C 11

Set amidst breathtaking scenery right
on the shore of Mannin Bay - with
our beach just a short walk away
over own fields. Starting from here,
you can explore the coastline and
walk along the numerous sandy
beaches for hours. Enjoy the
excellent cuisine in our own
restaurant overlooking Erriseask
peninsula and bay, (table d'hôte, à
la carte, menu dégustation). Local
amenities include Connemara golf
course, pony trekking, sea and lake
fishing.

WEB: erriseask.connemara-ireland.com

B&B from £40.00 to £48.00
€50.79 to €60.95

CHRISTIAN & STEFAN MATZ
Proprietors

American Express
Diners
Mastercard
Visa

Week partial board from
£333.00

Closed 25 September - 01 May

Room rates are per room per night

FOYLES HOTEL

CLIFDEN, CONNEMARA,
CO. GALWAY
TEL: 095-21801 FAX: 095-21458
EMAIL: foyles@anu.ie

HOTEL U   MAP 9 C 12

Foyles Hotel, formerly Clifden Bay
Hotel, is situated on the square in
Clifden. Connemara's longest
established hotel, it has been owned
and managed by the Foyle family
since 1917. Facilities include, DD
phone, tea/coffee tray, multi-channel
colour TV and hair dryers in all
bedrooms. There is a pleasant patio
garden to the rear of the hotel. Golf,
horse riding, deep sea fishing and
tennis are all available locally. Logis
of Ireland, Central Reservations tel.
01-6689743.

WEB: www.connemara.net/foyles-hotel

B&B from £33.00 to £50.00
€41.90 to €63.49

EDDIE FOYLE
Proprietor

American Express
Diners
Mastercard
Visa

☺ Weekend specials from £80.00

28 28

Closed 01 November - 01 May

JOYCES WATERLOO HOUSE

GALWAY ROAD, CLIFDEN,
CONNEMARA, CO. GALWAY
TEL: 095-21688 FAX: 095-22044
EMAIL: waterloo@anu.ie

GUESTHOUSE ★★★   MAP 9 C 12

Relax with a genuine Irish coffee
after you've settled into your
spacious 4-poster en suite room
with all mod cons to hand. All south
facing rooms are furnished with
sofas in own balcony to enjoy
glorious countryside views. A
refreshingly relaxed home tempered
with our vast knowledge of local
activities. Lone travellers catered for
with our 2 single standard rooms. A
superb breakfast menu and our
evening meals are a must!! Secure
private parking. AA ◆◆◆◆.

WEB: www.connemara.net/waterloo-house

B&B from £20.00 to £30.00
€25.39 to €38.09

PATRICIA & P.K. JOYCE
Hosts

Mastercard
Visa

☺ Midweek specials from £54.00

8 6

Open All Year

MALDUA GUEST HOUSE

GALWAY ROAD, CLIFDEN,
CO. GALWAY
TEL: 095-21171 FAX: 095-21739
EMAIL: maldua@iol.ie

GUESTHOUSE ★★★★   MAP 9 C 12

4**** guest house, 1.25km from
Clifden (N59) capital of Connemara.
This comfortable family run guest
house has a warm atmosphere and
pleasant surroundings. All non
smoking bedrooms are individually
decorated, spacious and offer a high
level of luxury and comfort. All en
suite bath/shower, DD phone,
hairdryer, trouser press,
radio/satellite TV, tea/coffee tray.
Private car parking and landscaped
gardens. AA ◆◆◆◆, RAC Highly
Acclaimed. A warm welcome awaits
you. Member of Les Routiers.

WEB: www.galway-guide.com/pages/maldua/

Members Of Premier Guesthouses

B&B from £23.00 to £33.00
€29.20 to €41.90

PETER & AIDEEN BYRNE
Proprietors

American Express
Mastercard
Visa

14 14

Closed 01 November - 01 March

B&B rates are per person sharing per night incl. Breakfast

O'GRADY'S SUNNYBANK GUESTHOUSE

CHURCH HILL, CLIFDEN,
CO. GALWAY
TEL: 095-21437 FAX: 095-21976
EMAIL: sunnybank@anu.ie

GUESTHOUSE ★★★★ MAP 9 C 12

A tastefully furnished period residence of 4**** rating ideally situated one hundred metres from town. The guesthouse is surrounded by landscaped gardens which contain many interesting features. It is owned and run by the O'Grady family who have long experience in the restaurant and hospitality industry and are recipients of many awards of excellence. AA ◆◆◆◆ and Highly Acclaimed RAC. Galtee Breakfast Award. Amenities include swimming pool, sauna, tennis court.

Members Of Premier Guesthouses

B&B from £20.00 to £30.00
€25.39 to €38.09

THE O'GRADY FAMILY
Proprietors

Mastercard

Visa

Closed 06 November - 01 March

ROCK GLEN COUNTRY HOUSE HOTEL

CLIFDEN, CONNEMARA,
CO. GALWAY
TEL: 095-21035 FAX: 095-21737
EMAIL: rockglen@iol.ie

HOTEL ★★★★ MAP 9 C 12

A delightful country house hotel run by the Roche family. The restaurant is well known for its excellent cuisine (2AA Rosettes). Lovely rooms, have the full range of facilities for your comfort. All weather tennis court, croquet, putting green and snooker room. A short drive is Connemara's 18-hole golflinks, horse riding, trekking and fishing arranged nearby. Guided walks to historical sites. Clifden has many art galleries and shops where you can buy local handcrafts, tweeds, linens. Visit Kylemore Abbey, Victorian Gardens and National Park.

WEB: www.connemara.net/rockglen-hotel

Members Of Manor House Hotels

B&B from £55.00 to £67.50
€69.84 to €85.71

JOHN & EVANGELINE ROCHE
Proprietors

American Express

Diners

Mastercard

Visa

Closed 20 December - 12 February

SMUGGLERS LODGE HOTEL

BRIDGE STREET, CLIFDEN,
CO. GALWAY
TEL: 095-21187 FAX: 095-21701
EMAIL: smuggler@oceanfree.net

HOTEL ★★ MAP 9 C 12

Smugglers Lodge is a friendly family run hotel. Originally built in 1809. It maintains the charm of a country inn yet providing the convienences of a modern hotel. Centrally located in the town of Clifden and overlooking the Twelve Bens mountain range, the hotel is an ideal base for golfing, touring, angling, hill walking, cycling, mountain climbing. Our restaurant provides excellent seafood and local dishes. In the hotel bar, you are likely to find live music or impromtu sessions.

B&B from £25.00 to £40.00
€31.74 to €50.79

SHARON & MICHAEL PRENDERGAST
Proprietors

American Express

Mastercard

Visa

☺ Midweek specials from £65.00

Closed from 10 October - 01 April

Room rates are per room per night

STATION HOUSE HOTEL

CLIFDEN, CONNEMARA,
CO. GALWAY
TEL: 095-21699 FAX: 095-21667
EMAIL: station@eircom.net

HOTEL U MAP 9 C 12

Modern hotel adjacent to the old station house which has been restored as a pub and restaurant. Rooms are spacious, warm and designed for the modern traveller. Leisure centre with indoor pool and conference facilities for 250. A heritage site complete with museum, old railway buildings, a village of crafts, antique and designer shops and 11 holiday homes complete what is the most exciting resort complex in Ireland. A warm, friendly and relaxed atmosphere awaits you at the Station House.

Members Of Signature Hotels

B&B from £35.00 to £70.00
€44.44 to €88.88

CIAN LANDERS
General Manager

American Express
Diners
Mastercard
Visa

78 78

Open All Year

PASS INN HOTEL

KYLEMORE, CONNEMARA,
CO. GALWAY
TEL: 095-41141 FAX: 095-41377
EMAIL: passinn@indigo.ie

HOTEL ★★ MAP 9 D 12

Family owned and managed where you are assured a warm welcome, comfortable & restful holiday. Beautifully situated on a 4 acre site overlooking mountains and Kylemore Lake. Ideal base for leisure activities including fishing, diving, pony trekking and hiking. In both restaurant & lounge bar each window affords a view of magnificent scenery, serves vegetarian menu & local caught fish a speciality, also when available organic produce. Restaurant (and 1st Floor Bedrooms) Non-Smoking.

WEB: http://passinn.irishbiz.com

B&B from £25.00 to £40.00
€31.74 to €50.79

ROSE RIMA
Owner

American Express
Diners
Mastercard
Visa

3 day specials from £119.00
and £139.00

10 10

Open All Year

ST. CLERANS

CRAUGHWELL,
CO. GALWAY
TEL: 091-846555 FAX: 091-846600
EMAIL: stclerans@iol.ie

GUESTHOUSE ★★★★ MAP 6 G 10

The Georgian style house is situated 35k east of Galway city. It was considered by the late owner, film director John Huston, to be 'one of the most beautiful houses in Ireland'. American entertainer and present owner, Merv Griffin, has carefully restored St. Clerans to its original splendour and decorated the house with art treasures from around the world. St. Clerans provides a calm and serene location for true relaxation.

WEB: www.merv.com/stclerans

B&B from £85.00 to £130.00
€107.93 to €165.07

ELIZABETH O'MAHONY
Director

American Express
Mastercard
Visa

Inet

12 12

Open All Year

B&B rates are per person sharing per night incl. Breakfast

LADY GREGORY HOTEL

ENNIS ROAD, GORT,
CO. GALWAY
TEL: 091-632333 FAX: 091-632332
EMAIL: ladygregoryhotel@eircom.net

HOTEL ★★★ MAP 6 G 9

Situated in the west of Ireland near Coole Park, home of Lady Gregory in the town of Gort, with its many historic and local attractions. A warm friendly welcome awaits you as you enter the architectural splendour of the Lady Gregory Hotel. 48 beautifully appointed rooms, Copper Beech Restaurant, lively Jack B Yeats bar and magnificent Gregory Suite. Relax in our Kiltatan Reading Room. Discounted green fees available from reception for Gort course located less than 1 hour from Shannon Airport.

WEB: www.ladygregoryhotel.com

B&B from £38.00 to £50.00
€48.25 to €63.49

LEONARD MURPHY
General Manager

American Express
Diners
Mastercard
Visa

☺ Weekend specials from £89.00

48 48

P inet FAX

Closed 24 - 27 December

SULLIVAN'S ROYAL HOTEL

THE SQUARE, GORT,
CO. GALWAY
TEL: 091-631257 FAX: 091-631916

HOTEL ★★ MAP 6 G 9

Sullivans Hotel is family run and managed, fully licensed and open all year round. Situated on main west of Ireland road, in close proximity to Coole Park, home of Lady Gregory, Thoore Ballylee, Kilmacduagh and the Burren. TV and telephone in all bedrooms, en suite rooms, meals served all day - bar food, à la carte dinner at reasonable rates. Available locally: golf, pony trekking, fishing.

B&B from £22.50 to £22.50
€28.57 to €28.57

JOHNNY & ANNIE SULLIVAN
Proprietors

American Express
Diners
Mastercard
Visa

10 10

IRISH
HOTELS
FEDERATION

Open All Year

DAY'S HOTEL

INISHBOFIN ISLAND,
CO. GALWAY
TEL: 095-45809 FAX: 095-45803

HOTEL ★★ MAP 9 C 12

Inishbofin, 6 miles from the mainland of Connemara, is one of the most westerly in Ireland. Day's Hotel, formerly the landlord's residence, commands exquisite views over the harbour. This long-established family-run hotel has well-appointed rooms and most are south facing. The family specialise in offering a warm welcome, friendly efficient service and excellent food, particularly seafood. In the evening social life in the hotel or the adjoining pub tends to be lively and musical.

B&B from £30.00 to £35.00
€38.09 to €44.44

BRENDAN & BRIDIE DAY
Proprietors

American Express
Mastercard
Visa

14 8

IRISH
HOTELS
FEDERATION

Closed 31 September - 01 April

Room rates are per room per night

DOONMORE HOTEL

INISHBOFIN ISLAND,
CO. GALWAY
TEL: 095-45804   FAX: 095-45804

HOTEL ★★   MAP 9 C 12

Uniquely situated on a beautiful and historic island, commanding magnificent views of the surrounding sea and islands. Inishbofin, a haven for artists, fishermen, bird watchers, nature lovers or those who just wish to escape from the hectic pace of the nineties. Fine sandy beaches. Sea trips and boat angling can be arranged. Facilities for divers. Excellent shore fishing. Doonmore Hotel is owned and managed by the Murray family, unpretentious but friendly and comfortable

B&B from £26.00 to £29.00
€33.01 to €36.82

AILEEN MURRAY
Manager

American Express
Mastercard
Visa

Closed 10 October - 14 April

MERRIMAN INN & RESTAURANT

MAIN STREET, KINVARA,
CO. GALWAY
TEL: 091-638222   FAX: 091-637686

HOTEL ★★★   MAP 6 G 10

Merriman Inn opened in April 1997, and is located in the picturesque fishing village of Kinvara on the shores of Galway Bay. The Hotel has the largest thatched roof in the country and boasts 32 beautifully decorated bedrooms. Located 20 mins from Galway and a short distance from the Burren, it is an ideal touring base. Excellent restaurant and M'Asal Beag Dubh Bar, provide for a friendly, comfortable and value for money Hotel.

B&B from £30.00 to £40.00
€38.09 to €50.79

NIAMH O'DONNELL
Manager

American Express
Diners
Mastercard
Visa

IRISH
HOTELS
FEDERATION

Closed 01 January - 17 March

LEENANE HOTEL

LEENANE, CONNEMARA,
CO. GALWAY
TEL: 095-42249   FAX: 095-42376

HOTEL P   MAP 9 D 12

On the shores of spectacular Killary Harbour at the start of the Western Way lies one of Europe's oldest coaching inns playing host to kings and mortals for centuries. All lovers of fine fresh food will find much to appreciate in the restaurant. Enjoy golden tranquil beaches, mountain climbing, adventure centres, scuba diving and pony trekking all within ten minutes drive.

B&B from £20.00 to £50.00
€25.39 to €63.49

BRIAN & CONOR FOYLE
Proprietors

Mastercard
Visa

☺ Weekend specials from £69.00

Closed 01 November - 31 March

B&B rates are per person sharing per night incl. Breakfast

PORTFINN LODGE

LEENANE,
CO. GALWAY
TEL: 095-42265 FAX: 095-42315
EMAIL: rorydaly@anu.ie

GUESTHOUSE ★★ MAP 9 D 12

Portfinn Lodge is a family run guest house offering 8 comfortable rooms en suite including double and triple bedrooms, a guest lounge and a restaurant which has an international reputation for its fresh seafood. Rory and Brid Daly will be delighted to make you feel welcome and at home. An ideal centre from which beaches, walking, angling, clay shooting, watersports etc. are easily reachable. When in Connemara, then stay at Portfinn.

WEB: www.anu.ie/portfinn

B&B from £20.00 to £27.00
€25.39 to €34.28

BRID & RORY DALY
Owners

Mastercard
Visa

8 8

IRISH
HOTELS
FEDERATION

Closed 01 November - 31 March

ROSLEAGUE MANOR HOTEL

LETTERFRACK, CONNEMARA,
CO. GALWAY
TEL: 095-41101 FAX: 095-41168

HOTEL ★★★★ MAP 9 C 12

Rosleague is a Regency manor now run as a first class country house hotel by Anne Foyle and Patrick Foyle. It lies 7 miles north west of Clifden on the coast overlooking a sheltered bay and surrounded by the Connemara mountains and beside the National Park. It is renowned for its superb cuisine personally supervised by the owners with all the amenities expected by todays discerning guest. Also a member of Ireland's Blue Book.

Members Of I.C.H.R.A. (Blue Book)

B&B from £50.00 to £75.00
€63.49 to €95.23

ANNE FOYLE
Manager/Owner

American Express
Mastercard
Visa

16 16

Closed 01 November - 01 April

MEADOW COURT HOTEL

CLOSTOKEN, LOUGHREA,
CO. GALWAY
TEL: 091-841051 FAX: 091-842406
EMAIL: meadowcourthotel@eircom.net

HOTEL P MAP 6 H 10

Newly extended and refurbished the Meadow Court Hotel's en suite rooms have full facilities, multi channel TV and garment press. Superb dining is on offer in our award-winning restaurant renowned for its outstanding cuisine. Enjoy after dinner drinks in our Derby Bar. Situated on the main Galway Dublin road 2mls from Loughrea, 18mls from Galway, convenient to all local 18-hole golf courses, angling, horseriding, water sports. Banqueting & conference facilities. Carpark.

B&B from £30.00 to £50.00
€38.09 to €63.49

TOM & DAVID CORBETT
Directors

20 20

Closed 25 December

Room rates are per room per night

O'DEAS HOTEL

BRIDE STREET, LOUGHREA,
CO. GALWAY
TEL: 091-841611   FAX: 091-842635

HOTEL ★★★   MAP 6 H 10

O'Deas Hotel is a family hotel, a Georgian town house hotel, of character with open fires and within walking distance of Loughrea's game fishing lake. It is an ideal touring base situated on the N6 (exactly halfway between Clonmacnoise, 35 miles to the east and the Cliffs of Moher, 35 miles to the west). The start of the Burren country is just 12 miles away. Galway city 20 miles.

WEB: www.commerce.ie/odeashotel

Members Of Logis of Ireland

B&B from £35.00 to £40.00
€44.44 to €50.79

MARY O'NEILL
Proprietor/Manager

American Express
Mastercard
Visa

25 25

alc

IRISH HOTELS FEDERATION

Open All Year

MORAN'S CLOONNABINNIA HOUSE HOTEL

MOYCULLEN, CONNEMARA,
CO. GALWAY
TEL: 091-555555   FAX: 091-555640
EMAIL: cbinnia@iol.ie

HOTEL ★★★   MAP 6 F 11

A hidden jewel, 16k from Galway city just off route N59. Overlooking Ross lake and the rolling hills of Connemara. Quality food and magnificent views. It's the warmth and genuine hospitality of the Moran family that make a visit to this delightful hotel a memorable experience. Angling centre on hotel grounds, own boats and gillies. 60,000 acres of internationally renowned lake and river systems. Atlantic ocean 20 minutes. 5 golf courses and many walking routes nearby.

B&B from £40.00 to £47.00
€50.79 to €59.68

PETER & BERNADETTE MORAN
Proprietors

Mastercard
Visa

20 20

IRISH HOTELS FEDERATION

Open All Year

MOORINGS RESTAURANT & GUEST HOUSE

MAIN STREET, ORANMORE VILLAGE,
CO. GALWAY
TEL: 091-790462   FAX: 091-790462

GUESTHOUSE ★★★   MAP 6 G 10

Located in the famous village of Oranmore, just 5 mins from Galway city on the main Dublin-Galway road and the main Limerick-Galway road, close to Galway airport and just 1hr from Shannon. Golf, sailing, windsurfing close by. The Moorings houses a delightful nautical fully licensed restaurant and guest accommodation. All rooms en suite, DD phone and tea/coffee facilities. Guests' patio, garden and private car park. Your hosts Michael and Anne Lynch welcome you!

B&B from £22.50 to £25.00
€28.57 to €31.74

MICHAEL LYNCH

American Express
Diners
Mastercard
Visa

6 6

Open All Year

B&B rates are per person sharing per night incl. Breakfast

BOAT INN

THE SQUARE, OUGHTERARD,
CO. GALWAY
TEL: 091-552196   FAX: 091-552694
EMAIL: boatinn@indigo.ie

GUESTHOUSE ★★★   MAP 5 E 11

3★★★ guesthouse in the heart of
Oughterard, just 30 minutes from
Galway. 5 minutes to Lough Corrib
and 18 hole golf course. Ideal base
to explore Connemara. The Boat Bar
and Restaurant offer an imaginative
choice of food, drinks and wine.
Enjoy the continental feel of our
terrace. Live music in the bar. All
bedrooms are en suite with TV,
radio/phone and tea/coffee making
facilities.

B&B from £23.00 to £27.00
€29.20 to €34.28

MICHAEL & NOREEN O'CALLAGHAN
Proprietors

American Express
Diners
Mastercard
Visa

☺ Weekend specials from £60.00

10 10

Closed 25 - 26 December

CONNEMARA GATEWAY HOTEL

OUGHTERARD,
CO. GALWAY
TEL: 091-552328   FAX: 091-552332
EMAIL: sinnott@iol.ie

HOTEL ★★★   MAP 5 E 11

An award winning hotel full of
character and style, just 16 miles
from Galway city at the gateway to
Connemara. Set in attractive
grounds, the emphasis is on warmth
and hospitality. Turf fires, pine
panelled lobby and bedrooms all en
suite with tea/coffee making
facilities, add to the overall comfort.
The bar, restaurant and indoor
heated swimming pool are equally
attractive and nearby, there is golf
and fishing in abundance.

WEB: www.iol.ie/bizpark/s/sinnott

B&B from £35.00 to £65.00
€44.44 to €82.53

TONY BELLEW
Manager

American Express
Diners
Mastercard
Visa

☺ Weekend specials from £85.00

62 62

Closed 01 December - 14 February

CORRIB HOUSE HOTEL

BRIDGE STREET, OUGHTERARD,
CO. GALWAY
TEL: 091-552329   FAX: 091-552522

HOTEL ★★   MAP 5 E 11

Character at the gateway to
Connemara the Corrib House Hotel
is 20 miles from Galway city and 1
mile from Connemara. 27
comfortable en suite rooms, turf fires
and our renowned Owenriff
restaurant with superb food and
wine list. 4 championship golf
courses within 30 miles, the world
famous fishing on Lough Corrib (1
mile) and magnificent walking and
hiking - a few of the past-times
available while staying with us.

Members Of MinOtel Ireland Hotel Group

B&B from £30.00 to £45.00
€38.09 to €57.14

FRANCIS & HELEN CASEY
Proprietors

American Express
Diners
Mastercard
Visa

☺ Weekend specials from £69.00

27 27

Closed 23 - 28 December

Room rates are per room per night

CORRIB WAVE GUEST HOUSE

PORTACARRON, OUGHTERARD,
CONNEMARA, CO. GALWAY
TEL: 091-552147 FAX: 091-552736

GUESTHOUSE ★★★ MAP 5 E 11

Panoramic lakeside guest house - the home of Michael & Maria Healy. As our guests, you are assured of a warm welcome to a family home with every comfort and Irish hospitality, superb home cooking, excellent wines, beautiful en suite bedrooms (all with double and single beds), TVs, hairdryers. Spectacular views, turf fire, peace & tranquillity. Angling specialists, boats, engines. Boatmen for hire. Wild brown trout, salmon, pike, lakeside walks. 18 hole golf 1k. Colour brochure on request.

B&B from £22.50 to £25.00
€28.57 to €31.74

MICHAEL & MARIA HEALY
Proprietors

Mastercard
Visa

:/♪

☺ 3 day special 3 B&B + 3 dinners
£99.00 - £110.00
🛏🏃☎️TC❄️♒🎵📺
10 10

IRISH
HOTELS
FEDERATION

Closed 01 November - 15 March

CURRAREVAGH HOUSE

OUGHTERARD, CONNEMARA,
CO. GALWAY
TEL: 091-552312 FAX: 091-552731

GUESTHOUSE ★★★★ MAP 5 E 11

A charming country mansion, built in 1842, situated beside Lough Corrib in 60 hectares of private woodland. The relaxing atmosphere and classically simple menus receive much international praise. Own fishing, boats, tennis court, with golf and riding locally. Recommendations: Egon Ronay, Guide Michelin, Fodor, Karen Brown's Irish Country Inns, Good Food Guide, Good Hotel Guide and many other international hotel and food guides. "To absorb the atmosphere you really should stay 3 nights".

Members Of Ireland's Blue Book

B&B from £49.00 to £66.00
€62.22 to €83.80

HARRY & JUNE HODGSON
Proprietors

🛏🏃❄️♒🚶📺📶
15 15

IRISH
HOTELS
FEDERATION

Closed 21 October - 31 March

LAKE HOTEL

OUGHTERARD,
CO. GALWAY
TEL: 091-552275 FAX: 091-552794

HOTEL ★★ MAP 5 E 11

Longest established hotel in Oughterard. Home cooking, family run. Seafood a speciality. Completely refurbished 1996. D.D. phone and TV in all rooms. Turf fire in cosy lounge. Excellent fishing nearby in Lough Corrib for Trout, Salmon and Pike. Boats and boatmen arranged. 18 hole Golf course and 18 hole Pitch and Putt within 3km. Pony trekking and walks.

B&B from £25.00 to £40.00
€31.74 to €50.79

GERRY & MARY MCDONNELL
Proprietors

American Express
Diners
Mastercard
Visa

:/♪

🛏🏃🐕☎️TC♿CM♒🎵📶Ⓢ🍽alc
19 19

Open All Year

B&B rates are per person sharing per night incl. Breakfast

MOUNTAIN VIEW GUEST HOUSE

AUGHNANURE, OUGHTERARD,
CO. GALWAY
TEL: 091-550306 FAX: 091-550133

GUESTHOUSE ★★★ MAP 5 E 11

Situated just off the N59, 24km from Galway city and within 2.4km of Oughterard, with the Connemara mountains in the distance and Lough Corrib nearby. Leisure activities include; golf at the renowned Oughterard Golf Club, established walks along scenic routes, boating or fishing on Lough Corrib. Guests can relax in the lounge with open turf fire and sample some of the cuisine before retiring to en suite bedrooms with TV, DD phone, tea/coffee making facilities and hairdryer.

B&B from £18.00 to £23.00
€22.86 to €29.20

PATRICIA & RICHARD O'CONNOR
Proprietors

Mastercard
Visa

☺ Weekend specials from £50.00

10 10

Closed 24 - 26 December

RIVER RUN LODGE

GLANN ROAD, OUGHTERARD,
CO. GALWAY
TEL: 091-552697 FAX: 091-552669
EMAIL: rivrun@indigo.ie

GUESTHOUSE ★★★★ MAP 5 E 11

River Run Lodge sits on the Owenriff which flows into Lough Corrib. Just minutes walk from the heart of Oughterard you'll find landscaped gardens, patios and riverside walks. A lodge warmed by light wood and lit by natural hues. Comfortably traditional spacious bedrooms and cosy lounges. A riverside restaurant with menus to rival any city repertoire. Book your slice of peace and quiet in the ideal base for exploring Connemara.

B&B from £25.00 to £35.00
€31.74 to €44.44

ANNE & TOM LITTLE
Proprietors

American Express
Mastercard
Visa

☺ Midweek specials from £75.00

6 6

Open All Year

ROSS LAKE HOUSE HOTEL

ROSSCAHILL, OUGHTERARD,
CO. GALWAY
TEL: 091-550109 FAX: 091-550184
EMAIL: ireland@greenbook.ie

HOTEL ★★★ MAP 5 E 11

Ross Lake House is a wonderful Georgian house set in the magnificent wilderness of Connemara. This splendid house stands serenely in its estate of woods and gardens beckoning the worldweary with its own refreshing charm. A high-quality Irish menu is delightfully prepared and presented featuring a tempting variety of fresh produce from nearby Connemara hills, streams and lakes as well as fish straight from the Atlantic.
Green Book-
US Toll Free 01180016762555
Europe 0080016762555.

Members Of Green Book of Ireland
B&B from £45.00 to £68.00
€57.14 to €86.34

ELAINE & HENRY REID
Proprietors

American Express
Diners
Mastercard
Visa

☺ Special offers on request

13 13

Closed 31 October - 15 March

Room rates are per room per night

SHANNON OAKS HOTEL & COUNTRY CLUB

PORTUMNA,
CO. GALWAY
TEL: 0509-41777   FAX: 0509-41357
EMAIL: sales@shannonoaks.ie

HOTEL R   MAP 6 I 9

Shannon Oaks Hotel & Country Club lies adjacent to the 17th century Portumna Castle and estate, by the shores of Lough Derg. All our rooms have satellite television, D.D. phone and an en suite bathroom. A distinguished menu of classic and fusion Irish dishes are available each evening. Our leisure centre, with its indoor heated swimming pool, sauna, steam room and gymnasium provides the stress free atmosphere in which to relax and unwind.

WEB: www.shannonoaks.ie

Members Of Signature Hotels

B&B from £55.00 to £58.00
€69.84 to €73.64

DENIS DEERY
General Manager

American Express
Diners
Mastercard
Visa

63 63

Open All Year

LOUGH INAGH LODGE

RECESS, CONNEMARA,
CO. GALWAY
TEL: 095-34706   FAX: 095-34708
EMAIL: inagh@iol.ie

HOTEL ★★★   MAP 5 D 11

Lough Inagh Lodge was built in 1880. It offers all the comforts of an elegant modern hotel in an old world atmosphere, open log fires in the library and oak panelled bar symbolises the warmth of Inagh hospitality. The lodge is surrounded by famous beauty spots including the Twelve Bens mountain range and the Connemara National Park. Kylemore Abbey is also nearby.

WEB: www.commerce.ie/inagh/

Members Of Manor House Hotels

B&B from £55.00 to £79.20
€69.84 to €100.56

MAIRE O'CONNOR
Proprietor

American Express
Diners
Mastercard
Visa

☺ Weekend specials from £108.90

12 12

Closed 13 December - 12 March

RENVYLE HOUSE HOTEL

RENVYLE, CONNEMARA,
CO. GALWAY
TEL: 095-43511   FAX: 095-43515
EMAIL: renvyle@iol.ie

HOTEL ★★★   MAP 9 C 12

Historic coastal hotel set amid the magical beauty of sea, lake and mountains, the keynotes are warmth and comfort with award winning fine fare. Turf fires and cosy lounges make you relax and feel at home. Golf, tennis, horse riding, swimming pool, snooker, boating, fishing are the facilities to name but a few. Wonderful walking and cycling routes throughout an area that hosts a vast National Park.

WEB: www.renvyle.com

B&B from £25.00 to £75.00
€31.74 to €95.23

VINCENT FLANNERY
General Manager

American Express
Diners
Mastercard
Visa

65 65

Closed 02 January - 29 February

B&B rates are per person sharing per night incl. Breakfast

ELDONS HOTEL

ROUNDSTONE, CONNEMARA,
CO. GALWAY
TEL: 095-35933 FAX: 095-35722

HOTEL ★★ MAP 9 C 11

Situated in the village of Roundstone, has a view of the harbour and Twelve Ben's mountain range. We are a newly built, family run hotel, offering bedrooms all with private bathrooms, colour TV and D.D. phones. Locally; 18 hole golf course, sea angling and windsurfing school. Our Beola restaurant has been operating successfully for many years and is renowned for its fine food, with lobster being its speciality. Credit cards taken. New Annex consisting of 6 superior rooms with a lift.

B&B from £30.00 to £45.00
€38.09 to €57.14

ANN & NOLEEN CONNEELY
Owner/Chef

American Express
Diners
Mastercard
Visa

19 19

Closed 11 November - 17 March

ROUNDSTONE HOUSE HOTEL

ROUNDSTONE, CONNEMARA,
CO. GALWAY
TEL: 095-35864 FAX: 095-35944
EMAIL: diar@eircom.net

HOTEL ★★ MAP 9 C 11

Roundstone House Hotel is a family hotel situated in the picturesque village of Roundstone. Roundstone is a fascinating place for a holiday offering a wide range of interests for the holiday makers. Many outdoor activities are available locally including sea angling, watersports, hillwalking, pony trekking and a championship 18 hole golf course nearby. Come to beautiful Roundstone for a holiday to remember.

Members Of Village Inn Hotels

B&B from £29.00 to £36.50
€36.82 to €46.35

MAUREEN VAUGHAN
Proprietor

American Express
Mastercard
Visa

13 13

Closed 30 October - 15 March

BRIDGE HOUSE HOTEL

SPIDDAL, CONNEMARA,
CO. GALWAY
TEL: 091-553118 FAX: 091-553435

HOTEL ★★ MAP 5 E 10

Enjoy a friendly relaxed atmosphere at Bridge House, a small hotel set in the heart of Spiddal Village - the home of traditional Irish music. Ideally situated to tour the many beauty spots of Connemara. Minutes walk from the sea. Trips to the Aran Islands arranged. All rooms en suite, colour TV, direct dial telephone. Award winning restaurant - fresh seafood a speciality - privately owned - personal service. Discover the difference for yourself.

B&B from £30.00 to £55.00
€38.09 to €69.84

ESTHER FEENEY
Manager

American Express
Mastercard
Visa

Weekend specials from £75.00

10 10

Closed 20 December - 01 March

Room rates are per room per night

PARK LODGE HOTEL

PARK, SPIDDAL,
CO. GALWAY
TEL: 091-553159 FAX: 091-553494
EMAIL: parklodgehotel@eircom.net

HOTEL U   MAP 5 E 10

The Park Lodge Hotel is owned and run by the Foyle family. It is situated on the coast road from Galway to Connemara, 16k west of Galway City and just east of Spiddal village. Most of the 23 bedrooms have a view of Galway Bay. There are also seven detached cottages on the grounds, each self-catering and fully equipped for 5 persons. Cottages open all year.

WEB: www.failte-ireland.com/parklodgehotel

B&B from £27.00 to £40.00
€34.28 to €50.79

JANE MARIE FOYLE
Manager

Mastercard

Visa

23 23

Closed 01 October - 31 May

TIGH CHUALAIN

KILROE EAST, SPIDDAL,
CO. GALWAY
TEL: 091-553609 FAX: 091-553049

GUESTHOUSE ★★★   MAP 5 E 10

Tigh Chualain is a charming, family run 3*** guesthouse, 16km west of Galway city and 2km west of Spiddal village, en route to the Aran Islands' ferry. Overlooking Galway Bay, with a nearby Blue Flag beach it is in the heart of the Connemara Gaeltacht. An obvious starting point for exploring the rugged beauty of Connemara with its manifold attractions. All bedrooms are en suite with direct dial telephone and colour TV.

B&B from £18.00 to £20.00
€22.86 to €25.39

THE FOLAN FAMILY
Proprietors

☺ Midweek specials from £50.00

9 9

Closed 31 October - 01 April

ACHILL CLIFF HOUSE & RESTAURANT

KEEL, ACHILL ISLAND,
CO. MAYO
TEL: 098-43400 FAX: 098-43007
EMAIL: achwch@anu.ie

GUESTHOUSE ★★★★   MAP 9 C 14

A superbly appointed 4**** guesthouse & restaurant with panoramic cliff/sea views. RAC Highly Acclaimed. The beautiful spacious non-smoking rooms have DD phone, TV, hairdryer, power showers, baths, orthopaedic beds for a good nights sleep. Full NRB approved room. AA ♦♦♦♦. The excellent cuisine at the fully licenced restaurant includes lamb, succulent steak, wild salmon, oyster and lobster. In the evening you can relax in the sauna. Experience the peaceful unhurried atmosphere.

Members Of Premier Guesthouses

B&B from £25.00 to £45.00
€31.74 to €57.14

J.J. MCNAMARA
Proprietor

American Express

Mastercard

Visa

☺ Midweek specials from £72.00

11 11

Open All Year

B&B rates are per person sharing per night incl. Breakfast

GRAYS GUEST HOUSE

DUGORT, ACHILL ISLAND,
CO. MAYO
TEL: 098-43244

GUESTHOUSE ★★★   MAP 9 C 14

Vi McDowell welcomes you to Grays where you are assured of a restful holiday, with good food, comfort and personal attention. Turf fires and electric blankets. Late dinner is served at 7pm. There are three lounges, coloured TV, Table Tennis room and Croquet lawn and swings in an enclosed garden.

B&B from £25.00 to £35.00
€31.74 to €44.44

VI MCDOWELL
Owner/Manager

Closed 24 - 26 December

MCDOWELL'S HOTEL

SLIEVEMORE ROAD, DUGORT,
ACHILL, CO. MAYO
TEL: 098-43148   FAX: 0902-94801

HOTEL ★★   MAP 9 C 14

McDowell's Hotel is nestled at the base of Slievemore mountain in a rugged Atlantic setting. Cuisine is the best of homecooked local fresh produce and local seafood. Children's menu available. En suite accommodation has TV, DD phone. Some rooms have breathtaking views of cliffs, lake and ocean. Adventure and leisure activity facilities. Richard and Tina O'Hara offer personal service and welcome all who visit the hotel.

B&B from £30.00 to £30.00
€38.09 to €38.09

RICHARD & TINA O'HARA
Proprietors

Mastercard

Visa

Closed 01 November - 31 March

SLIEVEMORE HOTEL

DUGORT, ACHILL,
CO. MAYO
TEL: 098-43224   FAX: 098-43236

HOTEL ★   MAP 9 C 14

This historic building dates back to the 1830s and became Achill's first hotel in 1840. Standing on the slopes of Slievemore mountain (Achill's highest point 2,204ft) it affords the energetic a start for walks and climbs with stunning beauty and views. Within a few minutes walk you have one of Dugort's two blue flag beaches with views of north Mayo across Blacksod Bay. Beside this beach is a small harbour and nearby the famous seal caves.

B&B from £20.00 to £25.00
€25.39 to €31.74

TIM & AIDEEN STEVENSON
Owners

Mastercard

Visa

Open All Year

Room rates are per room per night

BARTRA HOUSE HOTEL

PEARSE STREET, BALLINA,
CO. MAYO
TEL: 096-22200 FAX: 096-22111

HOTEL ★★ MAP 10 F 15

Bartra House Hotel, situated in Ballina, is a family business run by brothers Paul and Noel Regan. Located near the famous River Moy and with two golf courses within easy reach, it is the ideal base for such holidays. The hotel boasts 24 bedrooms all en suite, with colour television and telephone. Our restaurant is famous for its superb food and service and our function room can cater for up to 300 people.

B&B from £32.00 to £38.00
€40.63 to €48.25

PAUL AND NOEL REGAN
Directors

American Express
Diners
Mastercard
Visa

Weekend specials from £80.00

20 20

Closed 25 December

BELLEEK CASTLE

BALLINA,
CO. MAYO
TEL: 096-22400 FAX: 096-71750

HOTEL U MAP 10 F 15

Historic, romantic, set in 1000 acres of woodland on banks of river Moy - Wine/dine till midnight - Gourmet organic food enthusiasts welcomed - 'Perchance to Dream' in a four poster. For your added pleasure: tour of 16c castle armoury, giant fossil exhibits, Spanish Armada Bar, dramatic artifacts and timbers salvaged from Galleons wrecked off Irish west coast 1588. Sporting: international surfing, golf, fishing, tennis, riding, ten stables in castle.

B&B from £38.50 to £71.50
€48.88 to €90.79

MARSHALL & JACQUELINE DORAN

American Express
Mastercard
Visa

10 10

Open All Year

DOWNHILL HOTEL

BALLINA,
CO. MAYO
TEL: 096-21033 FAX: 096-21338
EMAIL: thedownhillhotel@eircom.net

HOTEL ★★★ MAP 10 F 15

A 3*** family run hotel beside Europe's best salmon fishing river, the Moy, 1k outside Ballina, adjacent lake, course & deep sea fishing. Golfers paradise, 6x18-hole courses nearby. Set in tranquil gardens, personal and friendly service, excellent cuisine and superb facilities. Eagles health and leisure club, heated pool, children's pool, sauna, jacuzzi, sunbed and all weather playdeck floodlit tennis courts. 'Cats' conference centre. Frogs Piano Bar with international entertainment June-Sept. Rest of year weekends (entertainment).

Members Of Signature Hotels Collection

B&B from £48.00 to £58.00
€60.95 to €73.64

MICHAEL MCKEIGUE
General Manager

American Express
Diners
Mastercard
Visa

Weekend specials from £120.00

50 50

Closed 22 - 27 December

B&B rates are per person sharing per night incl. Breakfast

DOWNHILL INN

SLIGO ROAD, BALLINA,
CO. MAYO
TEL: 096-73444 FAX: 096-73411
EMAIL: thedownhillinn@eircom.net

HOTEL ★★★ MAP 10 F 15

A family-run Inn, located 1 mile outside Ballina town on the main Sligo road. Contemporary in its design with 45 well-appointed triple rooms. All rooms are en suite with multi-channel TV, hairdryer and DD phone. The region offers superb fishing on the river Moy, Lough Conn and Killala bay. An excellent selection of golf courses: Enniscrone, Ballina, Carne, to mention but a few. Enjoy a drink at the bar or a meal in our Terrace restaurant. Rest assured!

WEB: www.downhillinn.ie

Members Of Logis of Ireland

Room Rate from £39.00 to £55.00
€49.52 to €69.84

NICOLA MOYLETT/JOHN RAFTERY
Proprietors

American Express
Mastercard
Visa

:/

☺ Weekend specials from £65.00

45 45

IRISH HOTELS FEDERATION

Closed 24 - 30 December

MOUNT FALCON CASTLE

BALLINA,
CO. MAYO
TEL: 096-70811 FAX: 096-71517
EMAIL: mfsalmon@iol.ie

GUESTHOUSE U MAP 10 F 15

Mount Falcon - a pleasantly different holiday whether you wish to relax in the quiet comfort of a log fire, catch your first salmon, or explore one of the beautiful deserted beaches a few miles away. Mount Falcon offers preserved salmon fishing on the river Moy and free trout fishing on lakes and rivers, with excellent estuary and sea fishing nearby. Children welcome, member of Irish Country Houses and Restaurants Assoc. Award winning Breakfasts and Egon Ronay Host of the year 1997.

Members Of Ireland's Blue Book

B&B from £35.00 to £60.00
€44.44 to €76.18

THE ALDRIDGE FAMILY

American Express
Diners
Mastercard
Visa

:/

☺ Week partial board from £300.00

9 9

IRISH HOTELS FEDERATION

Closed 01 February - 31 March

ROCKS

FOXFORD ROAD, BALLINA,
CO. MAYO
TEL: 096-22140
EMAIL: therocks@eircom.net

GUESTHOUSE ★★ MAP 10 F 15

Built and designed by the present owners. This beautiful residence offers good hospitality and atmosphere. All rooms en suite with hairdryers, TV and internal phone system. Guest tea & coffee room and guest lounge. Large landscaped gardens - front & rear - childrens playground and barbeque. Ideal location for touring the scenic North West. All fishing arranged on river Moy - Lough Conn - estuary and sea with gillie and boats. Pony riding, golf, swimming and mountain climbing nearby.

B&B from £18.00 to £22.00
€22.86 to €27.93

MARGARET CUMISKEY

6 6

IRISH HOTELS FEDERATION

Open All Year

Room rates are per room per night

BREAFFY HOUSE HOTEL

CASTLEBAR,
CO. MAYO
TEL: 094-22033 FAX: 094-22276
EMAIL: breaffyhotel@anu.ie

HOTEL ★★★ MAP 9 E 14

Breaffy House Hotel is a 3*** manor style country house hotel, situated on 100 acres of grounds and gardens, just 4km from Castlebar. All 59 rooms are en suite, with DD phone, TV/radio, hairdryer, trouserpress and tea/coffee making facilities. Enjoy the relaxed and comfortable Mulberry Bar and lounge, with superb food in the Garden Restaurant. The hotel is the ideal base to explore the beauties of Co Mayo and 30 mins from Knock and Westport. Leasure Centre planned to open Summer 2000.

WEB: www.breaffyhouse.ie

Members Of Best Western Hotels

B&B from £40.00 to £65.00
€50.79 to €82.53

DAVID RYAN
General Manager

American Express
Diners
Mastercard
Visa

Weekend specials from £78.00

59 59

Closed 23 - 26 December

DALY'S HOTEL

THE MALL, CASTLEBAR,
CO. MAYO
TEL: 094-21961 FAX: 094-22783

HOTEL U MAP 9 E 14

The longest established hotel in Castlebar (1795) tastefully renovated and refurbished. Combines all of what is good from both old and new. Centre piece of the beautiful Mall - a mature, tree lined park in the heart of the town. Attractive bar, charming restaurant and spacious bedrooms ensure an enjoyable and pleasurable stay. Indoor pool and leisure complex closeby (.5km). Outdoor activities including angling can be arranged. Ideal base for touring the west, blue flag beaches nearby.

B&B from £28.00 to £32.00
€35.55 to €40.63

PATRICK MC HALE
Proprietor

American Express
Diners
Mastercard
Visa

23 23

Open All Year

HENEGHAN'S GUEST HOUSE

NEWTOWN STREET, CASTLEBAR,
CO. MAYO
TEL: 094-21883 FAX: 094-26476
EMAIL: heneghans@eircom.net

GUESTHOUSE ★★★ MAP 9 E 14

Charming town house, built by our grandparents in 1932, it has hosted generations of Irish and international guests. Restored and tastefully refurbished while retaining the old character, we offer warmth, comfort and great food in the centre of Castlebar. Relax in our courtyard garden and library or use as the ideal base for touring the west. Genealogical information supplied. Arrangements made for walking, golfing and fishing. Packed lunches available. Extensive breakfast menu.

WEB: http://castlebar.mayo-ireland.ie/heneghan.htm

B&B from £20.00 to £22.00
€25.39 to €27.93

BRIDGET & ROISIN HORKAN
Proprietors

Mastercard
Visa

7 nights - one night free

8 8

Closed 24 - 25 December

B&B rates are per person sharing per night incl. Breakfast

JENNINGS HOTEL & TRAVELLERS FRIEND

OLD WESTPORT ROAD, CASTLEBAR,
CO. MAYO
TEL: 094-23111 FAX: 094-21919
EMAIL: patj@anu.ie

HOTEL ★★★ MAP 9 E 14

Jennings Hotel & The Travellers Friend, Hotel & Theatre is a luxurious family 3*** facility. Contemporary style new rooms and suites with air-conditioning, data-ports, VCR, hairdryer, trouser press. Combine with a new 1920s style restaurant and new conference rooms to provide excellent facilities for meetings/banquets in this town centre hotel. Personalised service, excellent cuisine, theatre shows, afford total comfort without compromise. Dedicated Business Centre.

Members Of Green Book of Ireland

B&B from £35.00 to £55.00
€44.44 to €69.84

MARY AND PAT JENNINGS
Proprietors

American Express
Mastercard
Visa

Weekend specials from £89.00

27 27

alc

HOTELS
FEDERATION

Closed 24 - 25 December

KENNYS GUESTHOUSE

LUCAN STREET, CASTLEBAR,
CO. MAYO
TEL: 094-23091

GUESTHOUSE N MAP 9 E 14

Our family-managed guesthouse is tastefully decorated and furnished to a very high standard. All guests rooms are en suite with DD phone, TV and hairdryer. Relax in our residents' lounge with complimentary tea/coffee or avail of the numerous facilities nearby e.g. organised walks, fishing trips, bowling, swimming, golf, fine restaurants and entertainment. Ideal base to explore the unspoilt areas in the west. Private car parking. Reasonable prices for business or leisure.

B&B from £20.00 to £25.00
€25.39 to €31.74

RAYMOND & SUSANNA KENNY
Owners/Proprietors

Mastercard
Visa

8 8

HOTELS
FEDERATION

Open All Year

WELCOME INN HOTEL

NEW ANTRIM STREET, CASTLEBAR,
CO. MAYO
TEL: 094-22288 FAX: 094-21766
EMAIL: ifh@iol.ie

HOTEL ★★ MAP 9 E 14

The Welcome Inn Hotel is a professionally managed family hotel in the capital town of County Mayo. We provide first class service at reasonable rates. We have ultra modern facilities combined with a very friendly and welcoming attitude. Ours is an ideal base from which to tour and view some of the world's most breathtaking scenery. We look forward to welcoming you. A member of Irish Family Hotels Marketing Group Int. Tel 353 45867307.

Members Of Irish Family Hotels

B&B from £28.00 to £42.00
€35.55 to €53.33

ANN MCHUGH
General Manager

American Express
Mastercard
Visa

40 40

alc

HOTELS
FEDERATION

Closed 24 - 27 December

Room rates are per room per night

ASHFORD CASTLE

CONG,
CO. MAYO
TEL: 092-46003   FAX: 092-46260

HOTEL ★★★★★   MAP 9 E 12

5* Ashford Castle has long been considered one of Ireland's most outstanding properties - and has adapted the facilities to cater for the demands of today's discerning clientele. Now a total resort, guests can enjoy complimentary golf and the health club facilities which comprise of a fully equipped gymnasium, sauna, steamroom and whirlpool. Other sports to be enjoyed are horseback riding outdoor & indoor, cruising and fishing on Lough Corrib. Nightly entertainment is provided.

Members Of Relais & Châteaux

Room Rate from £140.00 to £342.00
€177.76 to €434.25

BILL BUCKLEY
Manager

American Express
Diners
Mastercard
Visa

83 83

Open All Year

LYDONS LODGE

CONG,
CO. MAYO
TEL: 092-46053   FAX: 092-46523
EMAIL: lydonslodge@eircom.net

HOTEL ★★   MAP 9 E 12

Lydons Lodge combines the most modern amenities with old world charm. Located in Cong, village of 'Quiet Man' film fame it offers salmon, pike and the famous Lough Corrib wild trout fishing. Choice of 3 local golf clubs, horse riding and tennis. Minutes walk from Ashford Castle and gardens. Hill walks and mountain climbing with spectacular lake views; an archaeological and geological paradise. Traditional music nightly. Bar food all day and also evening dinner.

B&B from £25.00 to £25.00
€31.74 to €31.74

FRANK LYDON
Owner

American Express
Diners
Mastercard
Visa

11 11

Closed 05 November - 01 February

RYAN'S HOTEL

CONG,
CO. MAYO
TEL: 092-46243   FAX: 092-46634

HOTEL ★★   MAP 9 E 12

The idyllic riverside setting of Ryan's Hotel is more than matched by the outstanding service and lovely surroundings inside. Just a few minutes walk from the infamous free fishing Brown Trout lake Lough Corrib, the hotel is ideally situated for touring the west coast including the breathtaking views of Connemara. Because of its unique beauty, Cong was chosen by John Ford for his film The Quiet Man.

Members Of MinOtel Ireland Hotel Group

B&B from £29.00 to £42.00
€36.82 to €53.33

MICHAEL & GERALDINE RYAN
Owners

Mastercard
Visa

12 12

Closed 04 January - 08 February

B&B rates are per person sharing per night incl. Breakfast

TEACH IORRAIS

**GEESALA, BALLINA,
CO. MAYO**
TEL: 097-86888 FAX: 097-86855
EMAIL: teachior@iol.ie

HOTEL N MAP 10 F 15

Teach Iorrais stands amidst the rugged landscape of the Mullet Peninsula, boasting breathtaking views of the Atlantic ocean and the Nephin mountain range. Situated in Mayo's Gealtacht region and within one hour of Ballina and Westport, it is also easily accessible from both Knock and Sligo airports. Teach Iorrais features 30 tastefully decorated en suite bedrooms and a master suite, each bedroom includes DD phone and multi channel television.

B&B from £28.00 to £48.00
€35.55 to €60.95

MARY GINTY
General Manager

American Express
Diners
Mastercard
Visa

☺ Weekend specials from £79.00

🛏🔌☎🅿🆃🅲🍴CM✵♿♪🅿🍴
31 31
🆂🅿 alc

IRISH HOTELS FEDERATION

Open All Year

CILL AODAIN HOTEL

**MAIN STREET, KILTIMAGH,
CO. MAYO**
TEL: 094-81761 FAX: 094-81838
EMAIL: cillaodain@eircom.net

HOTEL R MAP 10 F 14

This RAC 3*** hotel is set in the centre of historic Kiltimagh. Furnished with flair and imagination. Has pannelled lounges and open fires. The restaurant which has received many accolades is open for dinner each evening. The bedrooms, with all amenities, are individually furnished and decorated. Kiltimagh is one of Ireland's most famous small towns. 5km off Galway to Sligo road. Member of Village Inns of Ireland, Freephone 1 800 201 801.

Members Of Village Inn Hotels

B&B from £26.00 to £42.00
€33.01 to €53.33

TONY MCDERMOTT
Innkeeper

American Express
Diners
Mastercard
Visa

🛏🔌☎🅿🆃🅲🍴CM✵♿🅿🍴🆂
12 12
alc ◼

IRISH HOTELS FEDERATION

Closed 24 - 26 December

KNOCK INTERNATIONAL HOTEL

**MAIN STREET, KNOCK,
CO. MAYO**
TEL: 094-88466 FAX: 094-88428

HOTEL ★★ MAP 10 G 13

Knock International Hotel was opened in 1986 by Mary and Edward Curry, who have been catering for pilgrims for years at Fairfield Restaurant. Set in own gardens only minutes from Knock Shrine. Also only 10 minutes from Knock Airport. The Currys are joined in the operations by their family and the hotel is especially suited for weddings and functions. Credit cards, Access, Visa and American Express.

B&B from £25.00 to £30.00
€31.74 to €38.09

MR & MRS EDWARD CURRY
Owners

Mastercard
Visa

🛏🔌☎🅿🆃🅲🆃CM✵🅿🅲 alc
10 10

IRISH HOTELS FEDERATION

Closed 13 October - 29 March

Room rates are per room per night

HEALY'S HOTEL

PONTOON, FOXFORD,
CO. MAYO
TEL: 094-56443 FAX: 094-56572
EMAIL: healyspontoon@eircom.net

HOTEL ★★ MAP 9 F 14

The perfect hideaway, Healy's masters the art of relaxation in this beautiful part of Ireland. Scenically overlooking Lough Cullen, close to Lough Conn (renowned for it's fishing), we are only 15 minutes from the river Moy, probably the best salmon fishing river in Europe. The hotel is also central to Mayo's best golfing locations. With sumptuous cuisine and excellent wines, the friendly staff will make your stay a memorable one.

Members Of Logis of Ireland

B&B from £28.00 to £35.00
€35.55 to €44.44

JOHN DEVER
Proprietor

American Express
Diners
Mastercard
Visa

14 14 alc

IRISH HOTELS FEDERATION

Open All Year

PONTOON BRIDGE HOTEL

PONTOON, FOXFORD,
CO. MAYO
TEL: 094-56120 FAX: 094-56688
EMAIL: pontoon@mayo-ireland.ie

HOTEL ★★★ MAP 10 F 14

Family managed hotel on the shores of Lough Conn and Cullin in the centre of Mayo. Famous for trout and salmon fishing - river Moy, golf, horseriding, scenery, central for touring. Twin Lakes Restaurant. Live musical entertainment nightly during season. Tennis court, sandy beaches, conference facilities. Families welcome. School of flyfishing and school of bog crafts, landscape painting and cookery. Leisure Centre opening Summer 2000.

WEB: www.pontoon.mayo-ireland.ie

B&B from £55.00 to £65.00
€69.84 to €82.53

BREETA GEARY
General Manager

American Express
Mastercard
Visa

28 28

S alc

Closed 01 November - 01 April

ARDMORE COUNTRY HOUSE AND RESTAURANT

THE QUAY, WESTPORT,
CO. MAYO
TEL: 098-25994 FAX: 098-27795

HOTEL P MAP 9 E 13

Ardmore Country House has recently been renovated to 4 star sandards. It has 13 luxuriously appointed bedrooms tastefully adorned with exquisite fabrics and furniture. Pat and Noreen offer their guests the ultimate in comfort and relaxation. Renowned for it's excellent cuisine and fine wines Ardmore Country House is an experience not to be missed.

B&B from £40.00 to £80.00
€50.79 to €101.58

NOREEN & PAT HOBAN

American Express
Mastercard
Visa

13 13

IRISH HOTELS FEDERATION

Closed 20 - 30 December

B&B rates are per person sharing per night incl. Breakfast

ATLANTIC COAST HOTEL

THE QUAY, WESTPORT,
CO. MAYO
TEL: 098-29000 FAX: 098-29111
EMAIL: achotel@iol.ie

HOTEL P MAP 9 E 13

Stylish new hotel, in a tranquil quayside setting. The Harbourmaster Bar - an ideal rendezvous for a quiet drink or gathering of friends. The Blue Wave Restaurant - unique top floor location with stunning ocean views and exciting contemporary cuisine. The Atlantic Club - superb leisure facility featuring pool, gym, sauna, steamroom and relaxing treatments. Golf, angling, horseriding, walks and blue flag beaches nearby. Your perfect base in beautiful Westport, - A masterchef's company.

Members Of Business & Leisure Ltd.

B&B from £45.00 to £60.00
€57.14 to €76.18

BRIAN FAHY
General Manager

American Express
Mastercard
Visa

:/♪♫Ⓣ

😊 Weekend specials from £90.00

🛏🏠☎🖥🅃CM🕯🛎⊙♪♫
85 85
🅿🆂🅰alc💻 Inet

IRISH
HOTELS
FEDERATION

Closed 23 - 28 December

AUGUSTA LODGE

GOLF LINKS ROAD, WESTPORT,
CO. MAYO
TEL: 098-28900 FAX: 098-28995
EMAIL: augustalodge@anu.ie

GUESTHOUSE ★★★ MAP 9 E 13

Augusta Lodge is a purpose-built 3*** guesthouse situated just 5 minutes walk from the town centre of Westport. A warm and friendly welcome awaits you in this family run guesthouse and Liz and Dave will ensure that your stay is a memorable one. A golfer's haven with tee times and reduced green fees arranged at Westport and adjacent courses. US PGA spec putting green on site for guests use. Listed in all leading guides.

WEB: www.anu.ie/augustalodge/

B&B from £18.00 to £25.00
€22.86 to €31.74

LIZ O'REGAN

Mastercard
Visa

:/

😊 Midweek specials from £54.00

🛏🏠☎Ⓣ🅲🏡❄🔅⊙🆄🅿🆂📺
10 10

IRISH
HOTELS
FEDERATION

Closed 23 - 27 December

CASTLECOURT HOTEL CONFERENCE AND LEISURE CENTRE

CASTLEBAR STREET, WESTPORT,
CO. MAYO
TEL: 098-25444 FAX: 098-28622
EMAIL: castlecourt@anu.ie

HOTEL ★★★ MAP 9 E 13

The family run 3*** Castlecourt Hotel is set in the heart of the County Mayo resort of Westport, on the shores of the island strewn and golden stranded Clew Bay. The hotel boasts 140 bedrooms including suites, indoor swimming pool, sauna, steam bath and jacuzzi, gymnasium, creche and playroom, health suites for aromatherapy and massage and the Orchard restaurant offering sumptuous cuisine. A new conference facility for up to 1,000 people is also available.

WEB: www.castlecourthotel.ie

Members Of Holiday Ireland Hotels

B&B from £40.00 to £72.00
€50.79 to €91.42

JOSEPH & ANNE CORCORAN
Managers

American Express
Diners
Mastercard
Visa

:/Ⓣ

😊 Weekend specials from £79.00

🛏🏠☎🖥🅃🅲🔱CMCS❄🔆
140 140
📷🔍🆄♪♫🅿🆂🅰alc💻 Inet FAX

IRISH
HOTELS
FEDERATION

Closed 24 - 26 December

Room rates are per room per night

CENTRAL HOTEL

**THE OCTAGON, WESTPORT,
CO. MAYO**
TEL: 098-25027 FAX: 098-26316
EMAIL: centralhotel@anu.ie

HOTEL U   MAP 9 E 13

A warm, friendly newly renovated hotel, perfectly located in the heart of Westport's beautiful town. Easy distance to Westport championship golf course. Arrangements made for sea, river or lake fishing, horse riding, pony trekking, etc. Restaurant open all day, carvery lunch and à la carte menu. Swimming pool and beach located nearby. A newly renovated lively bar with open turf fires. Walking distance from Westport's famous restaurants and pubs.

B&B from £37.50 to £45.00
€47.62 to €57.14

CIARA TEMPLE
General Manager

American Express
Mastercard
Visa

😊 Weekend specials from £94.00

36 36

Closed 24 - 25 December

CLEW BAY HOTEL

**JAMES STREET, WESTPORT,
CO. MAYO**
TEL: 098-28088 FAX: 098-25783
EMAIL: clewbay@anu.ie

HOTEL U   MAP 9 E 13

Enjoy our warm friendly family run hotel situated in Westport town centre. Our newly renovated hotel has 28 en suite rooms finished to the highest standard of comfort. Guests can enjoy the Old World charm of the Tubber bar that features traditional music. The Riverside Restaurant overlooking the Carrowbeg river offers an imaginative menu, modestly priced with bar lunches served daily. Local attraction, angling, golf, pony trekking, scenic walks/drives, beaches or gold trekking!!!.

WEB: www.clewbay.anu.ie

Members Of Village Inn Hotels

B&B from £32.50 to £40.50
€41.27 to €51.42

DARREN MADDEN & MARIA RUDDY
Proprietors

Mastercard
Visa

😊 Weekend specials from £75.00

28 28

Closed 22 - 27 December

HOTEL WESTPORT

**THE DEMESNE, NEWPORT ROAD,
WESTPORT, CO. MAYO**
TEL: 098-25122 FAX: 098-26739
EMAIL: sales@hotelwestport.ie

HOTEL ★★★   MAP 9 E 13

This uniquely comfortable, friendly hotel is set in its own tranquil parklands, in the heart of Westport town, offering a unique experience in relaxation and leisure. Our state of the art conference centre and ultra modern swimming pool/leisure centre offer an excellent range of accommodation with delightful food, wine, entertainment for your business or leisure break. Local attractions: golf, scenic walks/drives, cycling, angling, pony trekking, beaches. Callsave: 1850 53 63 73

WEB: www.hotelwestport.ie

B&B from £60.00 to £70.00
€76.18 to €88.88

GERRY WALSHE
General Manager

American Express
Diners
Mastercard
Visa

😊 Weekend specials from £95.00

129 129

Open All Year

B&B rates are per person sharing per night incl. Breakfast

KNOCKRANNY HOUSE HOTEL

WESTPORT,
CO. MAYO
TEL: 098-28600 FAX: 098-28611
EMAIL: info@khh.ie

HOTEL ★★★★ MAP 9 E 13

A warm welcome awaits you at the unique Knockranny House Hotel, Mayo's first and only 4★★★★ hotel. This elegant, luxurious, stylish hotel has unrivalled panoramic views, discreet, secluded grounds, majestic guest areas, prize winning bar, award winning restaurant, excellent cuisine, fine wines and spacious, comfortable bedrooms and suites all combining to ensure you have a truly memorable enjoyable stay.

WEB: www.khh.ie

B&B from £65.00 to £75.00
€82.53 to €95.23

ADRIAN & GERALDINE NOONAN
Proprietors

American Express
Mastercard
Visa

😊 Weekend specials from £105.00

Closed 23 - 27 December

KNOCKRANNY LODGE

KNOCKRANNY, WESTPORT,
CO. MAYO
TEL: 098-28595 FAX: 098-28805
EMAIL: knockranny@anu.ie

GUESTHOUSE ★★★★ MAP 9 E 13

Knockranny Lodge is a beautifully appointed 4★★★★ guesthouse. It has the peace and tranquillity of the country and yet is only 5 mins walk to town. Relax and enjoy a cup of tea or coffee in our welcoming lounge. All of our en suite bedrooms have DD phone, multi-channel TV, trouserpress and hairdryer. Private tennis court and car park. We have full use of swimming pool and leisure complex in nearby sister hotel.

B&B from £25.00 to £45.00
€31.74 to €57.14

MARY MCDERMOTT

Closed 01 - 29 December

OLDE RAILWAY HOTEL

THE MALL, WESTPORT,
CO. MAYO
TEL: 098-25166 FAX: 098-25090
EMAIL: railway@anu.ie

HOTEL ★★★ MAP 9 E 13

Get away from it all and be pampered in this tastefully appointed 18th Century coaching inn. Standard and superior accommodation. Renowned for traditional country fare and fine wines. Genuine hospitality and warm welcome in relaxing intimate surroundings. Conservatory restaurant, residents lounge and library, turf fires, original antique furniture adorn. Patio and garden area. Organic vegetable garden for restaurant. Recommended in all leading guides, Egon Ronnay, AA Rosette winner.

WEB: www.anu.ie/railwayhotel

B&B from £30.00 to £60.00
€38.09 to €76.18

KARL ROSENKRANZ
Owner/Manager

American Express
Diners
Mastercard
Visa

😊 Weekend specials from £85.00

Open All Year

Room rates are per room per night

WESTPORT WOODS HOTEL & LEISURE CENTRE

QUAY ROAD, WESTPORT,
CO. MAYO
TEL: 098-25811 FAX: 098-26212
EMAIL: woodshotel@anu.ie

HOTEL ★★★ MAP 9 E 13

Friendly, cosy hotel with fabulous brand new leisure centre, set in mature wood-land, overlooking private lake. Enjoy unforgettable family holidays with our famous Kiddies Club or treat yourself to a terrific theme break, ranging from golf and murder mystery to bridge and bowls. Glorious golden getaways are a speciality in this welcoming establishment.
Situated on the road to the harbour, the hotel is ideally located for lots of fascinating day trips - Kylemore Abbey, Achill, Clare Island, Croagh Patrick to name but a few.

Member of the Brian McEniff Hotel Group

B&B from £40.00 to £65.00
€50.79 to €82.53

MICHAEL LENNON
General Manager

Mastercard
Visa

95 95

Open All Year

ABBEY HOTEL

GALWAY ROAD,
ROSCOMMON TOWN
TEL: 0903-26240 FAX: 0903-26021
EMAIL: cmv@indigo.ie

HOTEL ★★★ MAP 10 I 12

This eighteenth century manor has been carefully transformed into an exceedingly well appointed country house hotel beautifully set in four acres of private lawns, the Abbey offers excellent accommodation, the old wing rooms are a special feature, and a fine restaurant open to non residents. The hotel is three star rated by Bord Failte, AA and RAC. Recommended in most guide books. Roscommon town is on these holiday routes, Dublin/Westport, Shannon/Donegal and Belfast/Galway.

Members Of Coast and Country Hotels

B&B from £45.00 to £55.00
€57.14 to €69.84

TOMMY & ANYA GREALY
Manager/Manageress

American Express
Diners
Mastercard
Visa

25 25

Closed 24 - 26 December

GLEESONS GUESTHOUSE & RESTAURANT

MARKET SQUARE,
ROSCOMMON TOWN
TEL: 0903-26954 FAX: 0903-27425
EMAIL: gleerest@iol.ie

GUESTHOUSE ★★★ MAP 10 I 12

Magnificent Guesthouse/Restaurant in a tastefully restored listed 19th Century Town House with an attractive finish of cut limestone and blue bangor quarry slates. Located in the town centre next door to the Tourist Office/Museum. We offer superb accommodation with all 19 rooms appointed to a 4 star standard. Private car parking. Experience "The Manse" restaurant where all the old values of guest satisfaction comfort and value for money prevail. Fully licensed for beers/spirits/wine. Anglers/Golf facility centre on-site.

WEB: www.dragnet-system.ie/dira/gleerest

B&B from £22.50 to £30.00
€28.57 to €38.09

MARY & EAMONN GLEESON
Proprietors

American Express
Diners
Mastercard
Visa

😊 Weekend specials from £69.00

19 19

Open All Year

B&B rates are per person sharing per night incl. Breakfast

O'GARAS ROYAL HOTEL

CASTLE STREET,
ROSCOMMON TOWN
TEL: 0903-26317 FAX: 0903-26225

HOTEL ★★ MAP 10 I 12

O'Gara's Royal Hotel family run, situated on the Dublin to Castlebar/Westport route. 19 bedrooms en suite, radio, DD telephone, TV, video, hair dryer. Comfortable modern dining room with good food and friendly service. Coffee dock/carvery. Spacious lounge bar with pleasant surroundings. Entertainment 3 nights a week in Roscommon's premier night spot Rockfords. Private car park. A warm welcome awaits you. Available 3 new conference rooms fully equipped with the latest facilities.

B&B from £25.00 to £32.00
€31.74 to €40.63

AILEEN & LARRY O'GARA
Proprietors

American Express
Mastercard
Visa

☺ Weekend specials from £70.00

🛏♿☎⬜T C CM❄P🅿alc
19   19

IRISH HOTELS FEDERATION

Open All Year

REGANS

THE MARKET SQUARE,
ROSCOMMON TOWN
TEL: 0903-25339 FAX: 0903-27833

GUESTHOUSE ★★★ MAP 10 I 12

Regan's is a family run 3*** licenced guesthouse situated in Roscommon town centre. It provides a central base to explore the town and environs. Regans boasts a fine bar, restaurant and 12 en suite bedrooms, all with satellite TV and DD phone facilities. We have also added a new dimension by way of two bedroom self-catering apartments. Our restaurant offers good quality food at a reasonable price. also available is a fully equipped conference room. A warm welcome awaits you.

B&B from £20.00 to £25.00
€25.39 to €31.74

EAMON & DOMINIC REGAN
Managers

Mastercard
Visa

🛏♿☎⬜T C ▶CM↻JP S🅿
12   12

alc

Open All Year

FOREST PARK HOTEL

DUBLIN ROAD, BOYLE,
CO. ROSCOMMON
TEL: 079-62229 FAX: 079-63113

HOTEL ★★ MAP 10 I 14

Family run hotel, in own gardens on main Dublin road. 1km from town centre. All rooms en suite with T.V. & Welcome Tea Tray, most with a garden view. Full Restaurant & Bar facilities with Foodbar open daily. Ideal touring centre close to Lough Key Forest Park, Boyle Abbey, Arigna Drive & newly restored King House. Available locally are 9 Hole Golf, Fishing, Walking, Cycling & Animal Farm. Close to Knock & Sligo Airports. We wish you a pleasant visit.

B&B from £30.00 to £45.00
€38.09 to €57.14

MICHAEL GILMARTIN
Manager

American Express
Diners
Mastercard
Visa

☺ Midweek specials from £85.00

🛏♿☎⬜T C CM❄JP S🅿alc
12   12

IRISH HOTELS FEDERATION

Closed 24 - 26 December

Room rates are per room per night

ROYAL HOTEL

**BRIDGE STREET, BOYLE,
CO. ROSCOMMON
TEL: 079-62016   FAX: 079-62016**

HOTEL ★★   MAP 10 I 14

Royal Hotel is over 250 years old, owner managed. 16 rooms en suite, TV, direct dial phone, tea/coffee facility. An ideal venue for angling, shooting, botany, archaeology, or touring holiday. Coffee shop open daily serving snacks/carvery luncheon. The Riverside Restaurant is renowned. AA**. Private car park. Member of Minotels Marketing Group, Ballycanew, Co. Wexford. Tel.353-55-27291. Fax:353-55-27398

Members Of MinOtel Ireland Hotel Group

B&B from £45.00 to £45.00
€57.14 to €57.14

VINCENT REGAN
Manager

American Express
Diners
Mastercard
Visa

16 16

WHITE HOUSE HOTEL

**BALLINLOUGH, CASTLEREA,
CO. ROSCOMMON
TEL: 0907-40112 FAX: 0907-40112**

UNDER CONSTRUCTION OPENING MAR 2000

HOTEL P   MAP 10 H 13

The newly-constructed White House Hotel offers a wide range of luxurious facilities for both the tourist and the business traveller. It is situated in an ideal location to explore the many attractions of the area including Knock Shrine, Lake Flynn and many scenic walks and fishing. The hotel indorporates a unique mix of modern technology with traditional Irish hospitality.

B&B from £40.00 to £50.00
€50.79 to €63.49

MR & MRS G.GANNON
Proprietors

American Express
Diners
Mastercard
Visa

20 20

Inet FAX

SHANNON KEY WEST HOTEL

**THE RIVER EDGE, ROOSKEY,
CO. ROSCOMMON
TEL: 078-38800 FAX: 078-38811
EMAIL: shnkywst@iol.ie**

HOTEL ★★★   MAP 11 J 13

Situated on N4 Dublin Sligo route, 2k from Dromod train station, this beautiful 40 bedroom hotel with Greek, Georgian and modern architecture offers panoramic views of Shannon river from both bedrooms and roof gardens. All rooms are well appointed with DD phone - modem compatible. Rooskey Inn and Kilglass restaurants offer excellent choice of cuisine. Leisure club and tennis court. Enjoy scenic trips on Shannon Queen. While away your time in elegant and peaceful surroundings.

WEB: keywest.firebird.net

Members Of Best Western Hotels

B&B from £39.50 to £46.50
€50.15 to €59.04

DAVID O'CONNOR
General Manager

American Express
Diners
Mastercard
Visa

☺ Weekend specials from £65.00

40 40

B&B rates are per person sharing per night incl. Breakfast

NORTH WEST
Atlantic and Lakelands

Ireland's North West spans a huge variety of landscape, from the rolling drumlins and tranquil lakes of counties Cavan and Monaghan in the east, to the lovely valleys of Leitrim and Sligo and the dramatic wild landscape of Co. Donegal in the west. Three of the counties, Donegal, Leitrim and Sligo bathe their feet in the restless Atlantic and the Shannon Erne Waterway connects the other great water courses in the region, the Shannon and the Erne Rivers.

FESTIVALS AND EVENTS

The North West offers many unexplored peaceful beauty spots, but lively action too. Festivals and events abound, from the Letterkenny and Ballyshannon Folk Festivals, Sligo International Choral Festival, the Mary from Dungloe International Festival, to the Yeats International Summer School and the North Leitrim Walking Festival and the Monaghan Jazz Festival.

MAJOR ATTRACTIONS

Two major attractions are Bundoran's Waterworld and the Visitor Centre at Carrowmore near Sligo, the largest and most important megalithic site in Europe. Also not to

Lough Muckno Park, Co. Monaghan

be missed in Co. Donegal are the Lakeside Museum at Dunlewy, Glencolumbkille Folk Museum, Glenveagh National Park, Donegal Castle and the Vintage Car Museum in Buncrana. Parke's Castle on the shore of Lough Gill on the Sligo/Leitrim border is located in the heart of Yeats' country.

Visit Cavan Crystal, Parian China and Celtic Weave in Ballyshannon, Swan Island

Open Farm in Co. Leitrim, the Patrick Kavanagh Centre in Inniskeen and the award winning Monaghan County Museum, or follow the sculpture trail through Hazelwood, near Sligo Town.

Tra Na Rosann Bay, Co. Donegal

ENTERTAINMENT

In Sligo, experience the Yeats' Candle-Lit Supper - a 3 course evening meal with entertainment, dramatising the loves and frailties of the Nobel poet, William Butler Yeats. Alternatively, discover our culture in the lively traditional music sessions that are held in pubs throughout the region

For further information and assistance in planning your holiday and making accommodation reservations please contact:–

The North West Tourism Authority, Temple Street, Sligo.
Tel: 071 61201. Fax: 071 60360
OR
Tourist Information Office, Derry Road, Letterkenny, Co. Donegal.
Tel: 074 21160. Fax: 074 25180.

GUINNESS

Sligo Arts Festival, Co. Sligo.
June

Guinness Mary from Dungloe International Festival, Co. Donegal.
July / August

Yeats International Summer School, Co. Sligo.
August

Event details correct at time of going to press

ABBEY HOTEL

**THE DIAMOND,
DONEGAL**
TEL: 073-21014   FAX: 073-23660

HOTEL ★★★   MAP 13 I 18

A comfortable 3*** hotel. All bedrooms are en suite equipped with modern facilities, some rooms with delightful views of Donegal Bay. Situated in the centre of Donegal town it is an ideal base for touring the scenic county of Donegal. Available locally: sandy beaches, golf, fishing, boating, pitch & putt, all water sports, horse riding, hill walking. In our Abbey restaurant we serve a full à la carte menu, a dinner menu daily and lunches, hot meals/snacks in our Eas Dun Bar.

Members Of White Hotel Group

B&B from £45.00 to £55.00
€57.14 to €69.84

JIM WHITE
Proprietor

American Express
Diners
Mastercard
Visa

Weekend specials from £90.00

49 49

Closed 25 - 27 December

HARVEY'S POINT COUNTRY HOTEL

**LOUGH ESKE, DONEGAL TOWN,
CO. DONEGAL**
TEL: 073-22208   FAX: 073-22352
EMAIL: harveyspoint@eircom.net

HOTEL ★★★   MAP 13 I 18

Hidden in the hills of Donegal, you will discover the secret paradise of Harvey's Point Country Hotel situated on the shores of Lough Eske, 6km from Donegal town. Exquisite French and Swiss gourmet cuisine in our award winning restaurant. Luxurious accommodation to international standards. Fabulous facilities, privacy and peace. Open weekends only from 1st November to 31st March.

B&B from £49.00 to £55.00
€62.22 to €69.84

DEIRDRE MCGLONE & MARK GYSLING
Manager/Head Chef

American Express
Diners
Mastercard
Visa

20 20

Closed 01 November - 31 March

HYLAND CENTRAL HOTEL

**THE DIAMOND,
DONEGAL**
TEL: 073-21027   FAX: 073-22295

HOTEL ★★★   MAP 13 I 18

This family run hotel, modern in comfort but old world in decor and courtesy, is an ideal base for discovering Donegal's dramatic scenery. Situated in the middle of the enterprising town of Donegal, it combines, with its garden views of Donegal Bay, the convenience of a town centre location with the peace and quiet of the countryside. Leisure centre, fully equipped gym, indoor swimming pool, steam room, jacuzzi, solarium.

Members Of Best Western Hotels

B&B from £35.00 to £50.00
€44.44 to €63.49

LIAM HYLAND
Managing Director

American Express
Diners
Mastercard
Visa

90 90

Closed 24 - 28 December

B&B rates are per person sharing per night incl. Breakfast

ST ERNAN'S HOUSE HOTEL

DONEGAL TOWN,
CO. DONEGAL
TEL: 073-21065 FAX: 073-22098
EMAIL: info@sainternans.com

HOTEL ★★★★ MAP 13 I 18

St Ernan's House Hotel is situated on its own wooded island and joined to the mainland by a causeway. This graceful house offers a homely atmosphere where good food and tranquillity is a way of life. Golfing, swimming and angling are close by. The surrounding countryside offers beautiful scenic tours of mountains, sea and lakes. St Ernan's is the perfect respite from the hectic pace of life. Children under 6 not catered for. Member of Irish Country Houses and Restaurants Association.

WEB: www.sainternans.com

Members Of I.C.H.R.A.

B&B from £73.00 to £79.00
€92.69 to €100.31

BRIAN O'DOWD
Proprietor

Mastercard

Visa

12 12

Closed 29 October - 20 April

WOODHILL HOUSE

ARDARA,
CO. DONEGAL
TEL: 075-41112 FAX: 075-41516
EMAIL: yates@iol.ie

GUESTHOUSE ★★★ MAP 13 H 18

An historic country house, the site dates back to the 17th century. The house is set in its own grounds, overlooking the Donegal Highlands. There is a quality restaurant, with fully licensed bar and occasional music. The area, famous for its Donegal tweeds and woollen goods, also offers salmon and trout fishing, shooting, pony trekking, golf, boating, cycling, bathing beaches, many archaeological sites, Sheskinmore Wildlife Reserve and some of the most unspoiled scenery in Europe.

WEB: www.woodhillhouse.com

B&B from £30.00 to £40.00
€38.09 to €50.79

NANCY & JOHN YATES
Owners

American Express

Diners

Mastercard

Visa

9 9

Closed 24 - 27 December

Room rates are per room per night

JACKSON'S HOTEL

BALLYBOFEY,
CO. DONEGAL
TEL: 074-31021 FAX: 074-31096
EMAIL: bjackson@iol.ie

HOTEL ★★★ MAP 13 J 19

Jackson's award winning family run hotel is situated in its own gardens with all 88 bedrooms en-suite with mod cons. Relax at the log fire at reception or enjoy breathtaking views of the River Finn and Drumboe woods. Close to Glenveagh National Park and ideal for golf, fishing, hill walking and horse riding. Indulge in fine cuisine in the Bally Buffet Bistro or Garden Restaurant. Leisure club with swimming pool, jacuzzi, sauna, sun beds, massage and gym.

B&B from £40.50 to £47.50
€51.42 to €60.31

MARGARET & BARRY JACKSON
Proprietors

American Express
Diners
Mastercard
Visa

Weekend specials from £95.00

88 88

Open All Year

KEE'S HOTEL

STRANORLAR, BALLYBOFEY,
CO. DONEGAL
TEL: 074-31018 FAX: 074-31917

HOTEL ★★★ MAP 13 J 19

This charming historic family run hotel in its pleasant village situation overlooking the Blue Stack mountains has that special atmosphere, a combination of excellent facilities, caring staff and management, which draws guests back time and again. The elegant looking Glass restaurant awarded 2AA Rosettes of Excellence. The Old Gallery restaurant for more casual dining. Delightful en suite rooms with TV, tea/coffee facilities, hairdryer, trouser press. Comprehensive leisure club.

B&B from £40.00 to £48.00
€50.79 to €60.95

ARTHUR KEE
Proprietor

American Express
Diners
Mastercard
Visa

Weekend specials from £95.00

53 53

Open All Year

BALLYLIFFIN HOTEL

BALLYLIFFIN, INISHOWEN,
CO. DONEGAL
TEL: 077-76106 FAX: 077-76658

HOTEL ★★ MAP 14 K 21

Family-run hotel situated in the picturesque village of Ballyliffin. 5 minutes walk to the beach and 2 minutes drive to Ballyliffin golf club. Renowned for its excellent cuisine and warm hospitality. All 36 rooms en suite, with satellite TV, DD phone, hairdryer and tea/coffee making facilities, with access to all bedrooms by lift or stairs. Access for wheelchairs.

B&B from £27.50 to £30.00
€34.92 to €38.09

MR & MRS P. MCGONIGLE

Mastercard
Visa

Weekend specials from £65.00

36 36

Open All Year

B&B rates are per person sharing per night incl. Breakfast

DORRIANS IMPERIAL HOTEL

MAIN STREET, BALLYSHANNON,
CO. DONEGAL
TEL: 072-51147 FAX: 072-51001

HOTEL R MAP 13 I 17

Town centre family run hotel (built 1781). All rooms en suite with TV, phone and tea/coffee making facilities. Small leisure centre - gym, jacuzzi and steamroom. Private car park. Hotel recently renovated embracing old and new decor, elevator. Ideally suitable for touring North West Donegal, Fermanagh, Sligo and Derry. Ideally located for golfing, fishing and a base for discovering the North of Ireland, Sligo 45km, Belfast 202km, Dublin 216km.

Members Of Logis of Ireland

B&B from £38.50 to £45.00
€48.88 to €57.14

BEN & MARY DORRIAN
Proprietors

Mastercard

Visa

☺ Weekend specials from £85.00

47 47

Closed 23 - 31 December

AN CHUIRT GWEEDORE COURT HOTEL

MEENDERRYGAMPH, GWEEDORE P.O.,
LETTERKENNY, CO. DONEGAL
TEL: 075-32900 FAX: 075-32929
EMAIL: anchuirt@eircom.net

HOTEL N MAP 13 J 19

Situated in some of the most breathtaking scenery in Ireland, An Chuirt, the Gweedore Court Hotel, stands on the original hostelry built by Lord George Hill in the middle of the last century. The present owners have recreated the building to provide a happy blend of modern convenience and the dignified elegance of the past. Against a backdrop of Mount Errigal and just a few mins drive from the Donegal coast, An Chuirt is fronted by the River Clady, famous for its trout and salmon.

B&B from £35.00 to £50.00
€44.44 to €63.49

PATRICIA DOHERTY

Mastercard

Visa

☺ Weekend specials from £100.00

19 19

Open All Year

MUSAEM CHONTAE
Dhun na nGall
DONEGAL COUNTY MUSEUM

Donegal County Museum is based in a fine old stone building which was once part of the Letterkenny Workhouse. The Museum houses a fascinating range of artefacts from Pre-history to the Twentieth century and covering all aspects of life in Donegal.

The Museum caters for school groups and is fully accessible to the disabled.

Open

Monday-Friday
10.00-4.30

Saturday
1.00-4.30

Closed for Lunch
12.30-1.00

Admission Free

**The Curator, Donegal County Museum
High Road, Letterkenny
Tel. (074) 24613
Fax. (074) 26522**

Room rates are per room per night

BUNBEG HOUSE

THE HARBOUR, BUNBEG,
CO. DONEGAL
TEL: 075-31305 FAX: 075-31420

GUESTHOUSE ★★★ MAP 13 I 20

Beautifully situated overlooking Bunbeg Harbour on the Clady River. High class accommodation, all rooms en suite, TV's and tea making facilities. Restaurant open each evening with emphasis on home cooking. We use the fresh foods produced by sea and land nearby and have a well-pondered wine list and bar. An ideal base for discovering Donegal.

B&B from £20.00 to £25.00
€25.39 to €31.74

ANDREW AND JEAN CARR

American Express
Diners
Mastercard
Visa

14 14

Closed 01 November - 01 March

OSTAN GWEEDORE HOTEL & LEISURE COMPLEX

BUNBEG,
CO. DONEGAL
TEL: 075-31177 FAX: 075-31726

HOTEL ★★★ MAP 13 I 20

Luxury hotel, all major guides approved, with 36 bedrooms & 3 executive suites, leisure centre with 19m swimming pool, childrens' pool, sauna, steam room & jacuzzi. Our award winning restaurant, overlooking the Atlantic, specialises in salmon & lobster fresh from the ocean. The Library Bar is the ideal place to relax with a quiet drink and a good book. 9-hole golf course & fishing available locally.

WEB: www.celticinternet.com/ostangweedore/index.htm

B&B from £90.00 to £140.00
€114.28 to €177.76

CHARLES BOYLE
Managing Director

American Express
Mastercard
Visa

☺ Weekend specials from £100.00

39 39

IRISH HOTELS FEDERATION

Closed 01 December - 31 January

OSTAN RADHARC NA MARA

SEA VIEW HOTEL, BUNBEG,
CO. DONEGAL
TEL: 075-31159 FAX: 075-32238
EMAIL: boylec@iol.ie

HOTEL ★★ MAP 13 I 20

In an area where nature remains untouched, the air is rich and pure, ensuring a heavy appetite. In the Seaview Hotel, guests are treated to wonderful food. The à la carte menu always includes a seasonal selection of fresh, local seafood dishes, with salmon, trout, lobster and oysters a speciality.

B&B from £40.00 to £90.00
€50.79 to €114.28

JAMES BOYLE
General Manager

Mastercard
Visa

39 39

IRISH HOTELS FEDERATION

Open All Year

B&B rates are per person sharing per night incl. Breakfast

INISHOWEN GATEWAY HOTEL

RAILWAY ROAD, BUNCRANA,
INISHOWEN, CO. DONEGAL
TEL: 077-61144 FAX: 077-62278
EMAIL: inigatho@iol.ie

HOTEL ★★★ MAP 14 K 20

Luxurious hotel, 63 bedrooms, Peninsula Restaurant, exciting barfood menu, conference & banqueting, disabled facilities, Keycard security, free carparking, Gateway health and fitness club. 20m deck level swimming pool, sauna, steam room, jacuzzi, fitness suite and aerobics studio. Coastal location, white sandy beaches, coastal walks, fresh sea breeze, breathtaking views, free golf, inexpensive rates.

Members Of Irish Family Hotels

B&B from £34.50 to £52.00
€43.81 to €66.03

SEAN O'KANE
General Manager

American Express
Mastercard
Visa

Midweek specials from £89.00

63 63

Open All Year

LAKE OF SHADOWS HOTEL

GRIANAN PARK, BUNCRANA,
CO. DONEGAL
TEL: 077-61902 FAX: 077-62131

HOTEL ★★ MAP 14 K 20

Located close to the shorefront and town centre, this elegant Victorian building is the ideal base for a holiday on the scenic Inishowen peninsula. All bedrooms have bathroom en suite, satellite TV, video, direct dial phone, hairdryer and hospitality tray. White sandy beaches, championship golf links, game/sea angling, watersports, horseriding, coastal walks available locally. Weekly live entertainment, excellent hospitality and a genuine warm welcome awaits you here.

Members Of Logis of Ireland

B&B from £25.00 to £30.00
€31.74 to €38.09

PATRICK DOHERTY
Proprietor

American Express
Mastercard
Visa

Midweek specials from £69.00

23 23

Closed 24 - 26 December

ALLINGHAM ARMS HOTEL

MAIN STREET, BUNDORAN,
CO. DONEGAL
TEL: 072-41075 FAX: 072-41171
EMAIL: allingham@tyrconnell-group.iol.ie

HOTEL ★★★ MAP 13 I 17

The Allingham Arms Hotel has been significantly extended and completely refurbished. It is recognised as a leading hotel in the North West. Owned by Sean McEniff & family, traditional hospitality is ensured in a congenial atmosphere with every modern facility available. Attached to the hotel is our pitch and putt course which is extremely popular and is free to residents.

B&B from £30.00 to £45.00
€38.09 to €57.14

PETER MCINTYRE
Manager

American Express
Diners
Mastercard
Visa

88 88

Closed 22 - 27 December

Room rates are per room per night

GREAT NORTHERN HOTEL

BUNDORAN,
CO. DONEGAL
TEL: 072-41204 FAX: 072-41114

HOTEL U MAP 13 I 17

The Great Northern Hotel and Leisure Centre, Bundoran is situated in the middle of its own 18 hole championship golf course overlooking Donegal Bay. This hotel has all en suite bedrooms, a restaurant, grill room, lounge, ballroom and syndicate rooms. Leisure centre with swimming pool, gymnasium, private jacuzzi, sauna, steam room, plunge pool, beauty salon and hairdressing salon. We now offer a new state of the art conference centre.

B&B from £60.00 to £65.00
€76.18 to €82.53

PHILIP MCGLYNN
General Manager

American Express
Mastercard
Visa

☺ Weekend specials from £140.00

Open All Year

HOLYROOD HOTEL

MAIN STREET, BUNDORAN,
CO. DONEGAL
TEL: 072-41232 FAX: 072-41100
EMAIL: hrood@indigo.ie

HOTEL ★★★ MAP 13 I 17

The Holyrood Hotel, situated on the main street of Bundoran, just a few minutes walk from the beach. All bedrooms are luxuriously furnished with multi-channel TV, DD phone, bath/shower and hairdryer. Entertainment available at our Waterfront Bar. Leisure centre available at sister hotel nearby.

Members Of Holiday Ireland Hotels

B&B from £42.00 to £45.00
€53.33 to €57.14

SEANIE MCENIFF
Manager

Mastercard
Visa

☺ Weekend specials from £85.00

Open All Year

CAMPBELL'S PIER HOUSE

THE HARBOUR, BURTONPORT,
LETTERKENNY, CO. DONEGAL
TEL: 075-42017 FAX: 075-42017
EMAIL: campbellh@boinet.ie

GUESTHOUSE ★★ MAP 13 J 19

Campbell's Pier House is located overlooking the picturesque fishing harbour at Burtonport in the heart of the Rosses and gateway to the many local islands. The premises has been totally renovated and all rooms are en suite with TV, tea/coffee facilities, telephone, etc. The surrounding countryside offers beautiful tours of the mountains and local attractions including Glenveagh National Park, Dunlewey Heritage Centre, etc.

B&B from £20.00 to £25.00
€25.39 to €31.74

PATRICIA MCGETTIGAN
Manageress

Mastercard
Visa

☺ Weekend specials from £57.50

Closed 20 December - 02 January

B&B rates are per person sharing per night incl. Breakfast

MCGRORYS OF CULDAFF

CULDAFF, INISHOWEN,
CO. DONEGAL
TEL: 077-79104 FAX: 077-79235
EMAIL: mcgr@eircom.net

GUESTHOUSE ★★★ MAP 14 L 21

Recently refurbished family run guesthouse, bar and restaurant, incorporating Mac's Backroom Bar, famous live music venue. Specialising in music, all tastes are catered for, from traditional sessions to rock and jazz. The restaurant at McGrorys offers great food in a stylish setting and includes locally sourced seafood. Situated on the scenic Inishowen peninsula, McGrory's is an ideal base for golfing, angling and leisure breaks.

WEB: www.mcgrorys.ie

B&B from £30.00 to £40.00
€38.09 to €50.79

JOHN/NEIL MCGRORY/
ANNE DOHERTY

American Express
Mastercard
Visa

10   10

HOTELS

Closed 23 - 27 December

OSTAN NA TRA (BEACH HOTEL)

DOWNINGS, LETTERKENNY,
CO. DONEGAL
TEL: 074-55303 FAX: 074-55907

HOTEL ★ MAP 13 J 21

The Beach Hotel is family run, situated on the breath taking Atlantic Drive, having safe Downings blue flag beach at the back door. In the heart of Rosguill golf enthusiasts can avail of both Carrigart and Rosapenna 18 hole championship course. Ideally placed for angling, diving and walking, within easy driving distance of Glenveagh National Park, Glebe Gallery, Horn Head and Letterkenny. Sea trips to Tory Island, and diving for wrecks and shark fishing easily arranged.

B&B from £19.00 to £26.00
€24.13 to €33.01

CHARLIE & MAIREAD MCCLAFFERTY

20   14

Closed 31 October - 01 April

ROSAPENNA HOTEL

DOWNINGS,
CO. DONEGAL
TEL: 074-55301 FAX: 074-55128
EMAIL: rosapenna@eircom.net

HOTEL ★★★★ MAP 13 J 21

Rosapenna is a 4**** hotel situated in North West Donegal beside the fishing village of Downings. Set in 700 acres between Sheephaven and Mulroy Bays, the hotel has its own 18 hole course designed by old Tom Morris of St. Andrews in 1893. Spacious lounges and a magnificent dining room overlooking the bay contribute to a relaxing atmosphere. Fresh seafood, locally caught, served daily. Indoor pool scheduled for completion in 2000. Rosapenna, a place to remember and return to.

WEB: www.rosapenna.ie

B&B from £50.00 to £55.00
€63.49 to €69.84

HILARY & FRANK CASEY
Owners

American Express
Diners
Mastercard
Visa

3 Dinners, B&B and green fees
from £187.50

48   48

HOTELS

Closed 31 October - 17 March

Room rates are per room per night

ARNOLDS HOTEL

**DUNFANAGHY,
CO. DONEGAL
TEL: 074-36208 FAX: 074-36352
EMAIL: arnoldshotel@eircom.net**

HOTEL ★★★ MAP 13 J 21

Situated at the entrance to the village and overlooking Sheephaven Bay and Horn Head, the hotel has been in the Arnold family for three generations. Good food, the friendly relaxed atmosphere and our helpful staff are just some of the compliments we receive from our guests who return each year. We are an ideal base for touring North West Donegal, Glenveagh National Park and gardens. GDS Access Code UI Toll Free 1-800-44-UTELL.

Members Of Coast and Country Hotels

B&B from £40.00 to £50.00
€50.79 to €63.49

WILLIAM ARNOLD
Manager

American Express
Diners
Mastercard
Visa

☺ Weekend specials from £95.00

🖐📞☎🖥️TCM☀♒UJ♫PS
30 30
📠🅰️lc♿

I R I S H
HOTELS
FEDERATION

Closed 01 November - 16 March

CARRIG-RUA HOTEL

**DUNFANAGHY,
CO. DONEGAL
TEL: 074-36133 FAX: 074-36277
EMAIL: carrigruahotel@eircom.net**

HOTEL ★★★ MAP 13 J 21

A charming Coaching Inn offering high standards. All 22 bedrooms en suite, colour TV, telephones. Ideally situated for touring, beaches, golf, watersport, Glenveagh Castle and historic sites in close proximity. Meet old and new friends in the Highwayman Bar and enjoy a meal in the Copper Grill or Sheephaven Room main restaurant. The hotel is famous for its seafood, friendly staff. A warm welcome awaits you at the Carrig-Rua Hotel.

B&B from £35.00 to £45.00
€44.44 to €57.14

GERARDA ARNOLD
Manager

Mastercard
Visa

☺ Midweek specials from £105.00

🖐📞☎🖥️TCMUJ♫PS📠🅰️lc
22 22

I R I S H
HOTELS
FEDERATION

Open All Year

SHANDON HOTEL & LEISURE CENTRE

**MARBLE HILL STRAND,
PORT-NA-BLAGH, CO. DONEGAL
TEL: 074-36137 FAX: 074-36430
EMAIL: shandonhotel@eircom.net**

HOTEL ★★★ MAP 13 J 21

Nestled into the lee of a hill, in its own grounds that slope down to Marble Hill Strand. All rooms at the Shandon Hotel command panoramic views of Sheephaven Bay. 18 new superior bedrooms, new air conditioned dining room and a new purpose built childrens activity centre. Leisure centre includes a 17.5m swimming pool, childrens pool, whirlpool spa, sauna and steam room. Three 18 hole golf links nearby. Water sports on beach.

WEB: www.shandonhotel.com

B&B from £45.00 to £65.00
€57.14 to €82.53

CATHERINE & DERMOT MCGLADE
Proprietor/Manager

American Express
Mastercard
Visa

☺ 3 B&B and 3 Dinners from £189.00

🖐📞☎🖥️T♿🛗CM☀♒🖐
70 70
🏠♒UJ♫PS📠

I R I S H
HOTELS
FEDERATION

Closed 05 November - 16 March

B&B rates are per person sharing per night incl. Breakfast

ATLANTIC HOUSE

MAIN STREET, DUNGLOE,
CO. DONEGAL
TEL: 075-21061 FAX: 075-21061

GUESTHOUSE ★★ MAP 13 I 19

The Atlantic House is family run. It is within easy access of the airport, golf courses, pitch 'n putt course, shopping and lots of beaches to choose from. There is also lake fishing, sea angling and hill walking close by. We have one of the most beautiful coastlines in Ireland as well as some of the most beautiful scenery to offer the tourist who just wants a quiet, peaceful holiday.

B&B from £18.00 to £25.00
€22.86 to €31.74

JAMES & MARY CANNON
Owners

Mastercard

Visa

☺ Midweek specials from £50.00

13 13

Closed 20 - 27 December

OSTAN NA ROSANN

MILL ROAD, DUNGLOE,
CO. DONEGAL
TEL: 075-22444 FAX: 075-22400
EMAIL: ostannarosann@iol.ie

HOTEL ★★★ MAP 13 I 19

The hotel is situated in the rugged area of the Rosses amidst some of the finest scenery in Ireland and is an ideal location for golf, fishing, riding, walking and sailing. All 48 bedrooms are en suite and come fully equipped with TV, tea/coffee making facilities, hairdryer and DD phone. The hotel features a leisure centre with a splendid heated indoor swimming pool. The function room can cater for up to 330 people.

B&B from £30.00 to £50.00
€38.09 to €63.49

ALAN SWEENY
General Manager

American Express

Mastercard

Visa

48 48

Closed 06 January - 22 February

BAY VIEW HOTEL & LEISURE CENTRE

MAIN STREET, KILLYBEGS,
CO. DONEGAL
TEL: 073-31950 FAX: 073-31856
EMAIL: bvhotel@iol.ie

HOTEL ★★★ MAP 13 H 18

Donegal's newest hotel, overlooking the splendor of Donegal Bay. We offer 40 en suite bedrooms with satellite TV, hair dryer, trouser press, tea/coffee makers, D.D., wheelchair rooms, lift. Theme bar and carvery, seafood restaurant. Fully equipped leisure centre, indoor swimming pool. Deep sea angling, fresh water fishing, golf, hill walking. Guided tours of the Veronica, when in harbour, the queen of the Irish fishing fleet. An ideal touring base.

WEB: www.bayviewhotel.ie

Members Of Signature Hotels

B&B from £45.00 to £57.00
€57.14 to €72.38

NOEL O'MAHONY
Managing Director

American Express

Mastercard

Visa

☺ Weekend specials from £75.00

40 40

Closed 25 - 27 December

Room rates are per room per night

MOORLAND GUESTHOUSE

**LAGHEY, DONEGAL TOWN,
CO. DONEGAL
TEL: 073-34319 FAX: 073-34319**

GUESTHOUSE ★★★ MAP 13 I 18

Have a break from the hustle and bustle. A newly-built guesthouse with family character, situated in a wild, high moor/hill landscape. We offer good cuisine. Available on the premises:- cosmetic treatment, reflexology, massage, lymphatic drainage, chiropody and sauna. The ideal starting point for unlimited walks, angling, bicycle tours, riding and touring. Excellent golf links and sandy bathing beaches nearby. Very quiet and remote. German spoken.

B&B from £18.00 to £23.00
€22.86 to €29.20

ROSEMARIE & WALTER SCHAFFNER
Proprietors

Mastercard

Visa

88

IRISH HOTELS FEDERATION

Open All Year

CASTLE GROVE COUNTRY HOUSE HOTEL

**BALLYMALEEL, LETTERKENNY,
CO. DONEGAL
TEL: 074-51118 FAX: 074-51384**

HOTEL N MAP 13 J 19

Castle Grove is a 17th Century country house set on its own rolling estate overlooking Lough Swilly. Its bedrooms are spacious and with all modern facilities. Downstairs in both drawing room and library you find a perfect blend of old and new. The dining room offers excellent cuisine, much of its produce from the Walled Garden. To the discerning guest Castle Grove has to be visited to be appreciated. While here you can, shoot, fish, golf, or simply enjoy the locality.

B&B from £35.00 to £65.00
€44.44 to €82.53

MARY T SWEENEY
Owner

American Express

Diners

Mastercard

Visa

14 14

Closed 23 - 28 December

GALLAGHERS HOTEL

**100 MAIN STREET, LETTERKENNY,
CO. DONEGAL
TEL: 074-22066 FAX: 074-21016**

HOTEL ★★ MAP 13 J 19

Gallaghers Hotel situated in the centre of Letterkenny in the heart of Donegal. The hotel offers the ultimate in comfort and personal attention with its home-like atmosphere and friendly staff. Each bedroom complete with private bath/shower, colour satellite T.V. and direct dial telephone, personal hair dryers, tea/coffee making facilities. Enjoy delicious food served in our Restaurant and Bar daily. 18-hole golf course nearby and leisure complex - 5 mins walk, convenient to all shops, bars, nite clubs.

B&B from £25.00 to £30.00
€31.74 to €38.09

AIDAN COMISKEY
Manager

American Express

Diners

Mastercard

Visa

☺ Weekend specials from £75.00

27 27

IRISH HOTELS FEDERATION

Open All Year

B&B rates are per person sharing per night incl. Breakfast

MOUNT ERRIGAL HOTEL & LEISURE CENTRE

BALLYRAINE, LETTERKENNY,
CO. DONEGAL
TEL: 074-22700 FAX: 074-25085
EMAIL: info@mounterrigal.com

HOTEL ★★★ MAP 13 J 19

The hotel is situated approximately 1k from Letterkenny on main entry road from Galway, Dublin and Derry. The hotel has 82 bedrooms, all en suite with all facilities. The hotel has an indoor leisure centre which has a swimming pool, sauna, gym, steam room, jacuzzi, sun beds and massage available. Entertainment at weekends and nightly during the summer season.

WEB: www.mounterrigal.com

B&B from £38.00 to £54.00
€48.25 to €68.57

TERRY MCENIFF
General Manager

American Express

Diners

Mastercard

Visa

☺ Weekend specials from £94.00

82 82

Closed 23 - 27 December

MALIN HOTEL

MALIN, INISHOWEN,
CO. DONEGAL
TEL: 077-70645 FAX: 077-70770
EMAIL: malinhotel@eircom.net

HOTEL ★★ MAP 14 L 21

Situated on the scenic Inishowen peninsula the newly-refurbished old world style family-run hotel offers a large variety of good homecooked food and locally caught seafood in pleasant surroundings. Ideal area for walking, cycling, etc. Golf locally (10 mins drive). All rooms en suite, DD phone, colour TV, tea/coffee making facilities and hair dryer.

WEB: www.inishowen.com

B&B from £25.00 to £35.00
€31.74 to €44.44

MARTIN & BRIDIE MCLAUGHLIN
Proprietors

Mastercard

Visa

☺ Weekend specials from £60.00

10 10

Open All Year

LAKE HOUSE HOTEL

GLEBE, CLOONEY, NARIN,
PORTNOO, CO. DONEGAL
TEL: 075-45123 FAX: 075-45444
EMAIL: lakehouse@iol.ie

HOTEL R MAP 13 H 19

Recently renovated and refurbished the Lake House Hotel has a friendly and relaxing atmosphere. 10 mins drive from Ardara and centrally located for exploring Donegal, the hotel is ideally situated for discovering the safe beaches, lakes, walks, an 18-hole links golf course and the archaeological heritage of this beautiful and unspoilt area. The bar and restaurant specialise in dishes created using fresh seafood and local produce.

WEB: www.lakehousehotel.net

B&B from £25.00 to £30.00
€31.74 to €38.09

KAREN MCGILL
Proprietor

Mastercard

Visa

14 14

Open All Year

Room rates are per room per night

FORT ROYAL HOTEL

RATHMULLAN, LETTERKENNY,
CO. DONEGAL
TEL: 074-58100 FAX: 074-58103
EMAIL: fortroyal@eircom.net

HOTEL ★★★ MAP 14 K 20

One of the most beautifully situated hotels in Ireland with 7 hectares of lovely grounds and gardens beside Lough Swilly include a sandy beach, hard tennis court, par 3 golf course. Especially friendly welcome accounts for the large number of regular visitors from all parts of the world to this peaceful unspoilt part of Donegal. Recently awarded two rosettes for food by AA. Member of Manor House Hotels, Irish Tourist Board and AA ***. GDS Access Code: UI Toll Free 1-800-44-UTELL

Members Of Manor House Hotels

B&B from £35.00 to £60.00
€44.44 to €76.18

ANN & ROBIN FLETCHER
Owners

American Express
Diners
Mastercard
Visa

☺ Midweek specials from £120.00

15 15

Closed 01 November - 31 March

RATHMULLAN HOUSE

LOUGH SWILLY, RATHMULLAN,
CO. DONEGAL
TEL: 074-58188 FAX: 074-58200
EMAIL: rathhse@iol.ie

HOTEL ★★★★ MAP 14 K 20

A country house with a glorious seaside setting on Lough Swilly amid award winning gardens which stretch down to a sandy beach. Inside, elegant sitting-rooms are in period style. Bedrooms vary in size and cost, from simple family rooms to luxurious suites. Renowned for good food. Indoor heated pool, steamroom and tennis. 4 golf courses nearby. Special weekend and half board rates on request. Member of Blue Book. RAC*** (Comfort Award). Dublin - 3.5 hours, Belfast - 2 hours.

Members Of Ireland's Blue Book

B&B from £52.25 to £57.75
€66.34 to €73.33

ROBIN & BOB WHEELER
Hosts

American Express
Diners
Mastercard
Visa

☺ Weekend specials from £134.75

25 25

Closed 02 January - 12 February

REDCASTLE HOTEL

REDCASTLE, MOVILLE,
CO. DONEGAL
TEL: 077-82073 FAX: 077-82214

HOTEL ★★★ MAP 14 L 21

Redcastle Hotel is ideally situated along the banks of Lough Foyle in the beautiful Inishowen Peninsula. The hotel's challenging 9 hole golf course and indoor leisure centre provides the perfect form of relaxation. Cochranes Restaurant offers a wide choice of dishes with warm and friendly service guaranteed. The welcoming staff look forward to greeting old and new customers.

B&B from £35.00 to £55.00
€44.44 to €69.84

MARGARET PATTERSON
General Manager

American Express
Diners
Mastercard
Visa

☺ Weekend specials from £95.00

31 31

Open All Year

B&B rates are per person sharing per night incl. Breakfast

SAND HOUSE HOTEL

ROSSNOWLAGH,
CO. DONEGAL
TEL: 072-51777 FAX: 072-52100
EMAIL: info@sandhouse-hotel.ie

HOTEL ★★★★   MAP 13 I 17

A delightful seaside setting overlooking the Atlantic ocean on Donegal Bay. This small 4* luxury hotel, a transformed mid 19th century fishing lodge, is an oasis of comfort and relaxation on a 2ml golden sandy beach. It combines elegant accommodation, open log fires and an award winning restaurant. A splendid location to explore the spectacular Donegal landscapes. Nearby 3 Ch'ship golf links courses. Described as one of Ireland's west coast treasures. Dublin 3 $\frac{1}{2}$ hrs, Shannon 4hrs.

WEB: www.sandhouse-hotel.ie

Members Of Manor House Hotels

B&B from £50.00 to £67.50
€63.49 to €85.71

PAUL DIVER
Manager

American Express
Diners
Mastercard
Visa

☺ Weekend specials from £120.00

45 45

Closed 30 October - 01 April

RIVERSDALE FARM GUESTHOUSE

BALLINAMORE,
CO. LEITRIM
TEL: 078-44122 FAX: 078-44813

GUESTHOUSE ★★★   MAP 11 J 15

Riversdale is an impressive residence beautifully situated in parkland overlooking the Shannon-Erne waterway. Spacious rooms and lounges mean a comfortable and peaceful ambience. We have our own heated indoor pool, squash court, sauna, fitness suite and games room for when the weather is unkind - or hot! Local golf, horse riding, walking, riverbus, boat trips and scenic drives. Wide choice of interesting day trips. Brochure available - special family suites.

B&B from £26.00 to £30.00
€33.01 to €38.09

THE THOMAS FAMILY
Owners

Mastercard
Visa

☺ Midweek specials from £69.00

9 9

Closed 19 - 31 December

AISLEIGH GUEST HOUSE

DUBLIN ROAD, CARRICK-ON-SHANNON, CO. LEITRIM
TEL: 078-20313 FAX: 078-20313

GUESTHOUSE ★★★   MAP 10 I 14

A warm welcome awaits you at our family run guest house situated 1km from the centre of the picturesque town of Carrick on Shannon, Ireland's best kept secret. Facilities include en-suite bedrooms with TV, direct dial telephones (fax also available) games room, and sauna. Local genealogy a speciality. Nearby there is golfing, swimming, tennis, squash, cruising, fishing (tackle & bait supplies) horse riding, walking, cycling, etc.

B&B from £19.00 to £19.00
€24.13 to €24.13

SEAN & CHARLOTTE FEARON
Owners

American Express
Mastercard
Visa

10 10

Open All Year

Room rates are per room per night

BUSH HOTEL

CARRICK-ON-SHANNON,
CO. LEITRIM
TEL: 078-20014   FAX: 078-21180
EMAIL: bushhotel@eircom.net

HOTEL ★★★   MAP 10 I 14

An hotel of ambience, style and comfort, the Bush Hotel (one of Ireland's oldest) has recently undergone major refurbishment whilst retaining its olde world character and charm. Centrally located in the village, the hotel backs onto courtyard, gardens and N4 by-pass with private access and parking. 28 en suite bedrooms, theme bars, coffee shop, restaurant overlooking courtyard. Amenities: National parks, period houses, river Shannon.

WEB: www.homepage.eircom.net/~bushhotel

Members Of Logis of Ireland

B&B from £30.00 to £35.00
€38.09 to €44.44

JOSEPH DOLAN
Managing Director

American Express
Mastercard
Visa

Weekend specials from £79.00

28 28

Closed 24 - 26 December

GLEBE HOUSE

BALLINAMORE ROAD, MOHILL,
CO. LEITRIM
TEL: 078-31086   FAX: 078-31886
EMAIL: glebe@iol.ie

GUESTHOUSE ★★★   MAP 11 J 14

Dating back to 1823 this lovely Georgian former Rectory set in fifty acres of woods and farmland has been completely restored by the Maloney Family. Enjoy the tranquility of this peaceful part of Ireland. Plenty to see and do. Visit the stately homes and gardens, sample golf, horse riding, pony trekking, fishing and cruising. Or take to the country roads by bike or on foot. Assistance given with genealogy. 10% discount on bookings if more than one night. Special discount for seniors.

WEB: www.glebehouse.com

B&B from £24.00 to £30.00
€30.47 to €38.09

JOHN & MARION MALONEY
Proprietors

American Express
Mastercard
Visa

Weekend specials from £63.00

8 8

Open All Year

BALLINCAR HOUSE HOTEL

ROSSES POINT ROAD,
SLIGO,
TEL: 071-45361   FAX: 071-44198

HOTEL ★★★   MAP 10 H 16

Your secret hideaway in beautiful and peaceful surroundings within 4 minutes of Sligo town and Rosses Point seaside village. Dine at our Rose Garden Restaurant and enjoy the warm atmosphere, the superb cuisine, the rare wines from around the world and our professional service. Unlimited outdoor activities including golfing (Co. Sligo Golf Club, Strandhill...), walking, angling and blue flag beach.

WEB: www.infowing.ie/ballincarhousehotel

B&B from £37.00 to £47.00
€46.98 to €59.68

RESIDENT MANAGER

American Express
Diners
Mastercard
Visa

Weekend specials from £85.00

25 25

Closed 23 December - 07 January

B&B rates are per person sharing per night incl. Breakfast

CLARENCE HOTEL

WINE STREET,
SLIGO
TEL: 071-42211 FAX: 071-45823
EMAIL: clarencehotel@eircom.net

HOTEL ★★ MAP 10 H 16

Listed for its striking architectural design, the hotel is situated in the centre of Sligo. Its location makes it the perfect base to explore one of Ireland's most beautiful counties. You will find all of Sligo's business, shopping and historic centres just steps away with a modern new entertainment complex adjoining the hotel. Our restaurant, a gourmet delight, atmospheric throughout brings an exciting dimension to wining and dining in Sligo. All rooms en suite with all amenities.

B&B from £28.00 to £45.00
€35.55 to €57.14

CARMEL FOLEY
Managing Director

American Express
Mastercard
Visa

11 11

HOTELS
FEDERATION

Open All Year

HOTEL SILVER SWAN

HYDE BRIDGE,
SLIGO
TEL: 071-43231 FAX: 071-42232

HOTEL U MAP 10 H 16

Uniquely situated on the banks of the Garavogue river and close to shops, art gallery and theatre. All rooms recently refurbished and our de-luxe rooms have Aero-spa baths. Relax and watch the swans glide by as you dine in the Cygnet Restaurant renowned for excellent French cuisine with a special emphasis on fresh oysters, lobster and game in season. Traditional Irish music Wednesday nights. A member of Logis of Ireland.

Members Of Logis of Ireland
B&B from £28.00 to £40.00
€35.55 to €50.79

MICHAEL HIGGINS
Manager

American Express
Diners
Mastercard
Visa

:/ ♪

😊 Weekend specials from £75.00

29 29

HOTELS
FEDERATION

Closed 25 - 28 December

INNISFREE HOTEL

HIGH STREET,
SLIGO
TEL: 071-42014 FAX: 071-45745

HOTEL ★★ MAP 10 H 16

Located in the heart of Sligo town, this comfortable hotel has a special, friendly atmosphere. All rooms are en suite with TV, DD phone and tea making facilities. Excellent food served all day or visit the lively Ark Bar with its seafaring theme. Convenient to theatre and shops. Explore W.B. Yeats breathtaking countryside, the Lake Isle of Innisfree, Glencar, Lisadell, renowned for its golf courses and seaside resorts. Specialising in commercial traveller rates and golf holidays.

B&B from £25.00 to £35.00
€31.74 to €44.44

GERRY & CATHERINE GURN
Owners

Mastercard
Visa

:/ ♪ ♫

19 19

HOTELS
FEDERATION

Closed 24 - 26 December

Room rates are per room per night

LISADORN

DONEGAL ROAD,
SLIGO
TEL: 071-43417 FAX: 071-46418
EMAIL: cjo'connor@eircom.net

GUESTHOUSE ★★★ MAP 10 H 16

Sligo Town's 1st and only 3* guesthouse situated on the N15 within 5 minutes of town centre. Ideal base for North bound traffic. All rooms en suite, remote control colour TVs, direct dial telephones, fax, hairdryers and hospitality tray. Beside pitch & putt and 10 minutes to Rosses Point. Beside Sligo's Tennis & Squash Club. In the heart of Yeats' Country. It's the ultimate in luxury accommodation. A friendly welcome and service is guaranteed.

C32

B&B from £18.00 to £19.50
€22.86 to €24.76

CYRIL O'CONNOR
Proprietor

Mastercard
Visa

Midweek specials from £49.00

7 7

Open All Year

SLIGO PARK HOTEL

PEARSE ROAD,
SLIGO
TEL: 071-60291 FAX: 071-69556
EMAIL: sligopk@leehotels.ie

HOTEL ★★★ MAP 10 H 16

Situated one mile south of Sligo on the Dublin road, the Sligo Park Hotel is set on seven acres of gardens. A 3*** hotel with 110 bedrooms, the hotel has one of the finest leisure centres in the country. In the heart of the Yeats country, the Sligo Park is surrounded by some of the most scenic countryside in Ireland ranging from the majestic Benbulben to the gentle waters of Lough Gill. For that special break, the Sligo Park has all the facilities for your enjoyment.

WEB: www.iol.ie/lee

Members Of Lee Hotels

B&B from £40.00 to £56.00
€50.79 to €71.11

MICHELE HAUGH
General Manager

American Express
Diners
Mastercard
Visa

Weekend specials from £79.00

110 110

IRISH
HOTELS
FEDERATION

Open All Year

SLIGO'S SOUTHERN HOTEL & LEISURE CENTRE

STRANDHILL ROAD,
SLIGO
TEL: 071-62101 FAX: 071-60328

HOTEL ★★★ MAP 10 H 16

The Southern Hotel & Leisure Centre is situated in the heart of Sligo town, adjacent to the railway and bus stations. The Southern Hotel blends old world intimacy with every modern convenience. All 105 rooms are en suite, cable TV, telephone, hairdryers, tea/coffee making facilities. Indoor swimming pool, gym, jacuzzi, sauna and steam room. Indoor bowls and bridge tables available. Entertainment most nights in high season. Reservations 1 850 520052 or Free phone NI & UK 0 800 7839024.

Members Of Brian McEniff Hotels

B&B from £35.00 to £75.00
€44.44 to €95.23

KEVIN MCGLYNN
Manager

American Express
Diners
Mastercard
Visa

Weekend specials from £75.00

105 105

IRISH
HOTELS
FEDERATION

Closed 24 - 26 December

B&B rates are per person sharing per night incl. Breakfast

TOWER HOTEL

**QUAY STREET,
SLIGO
TEL: 071-44000   FAX: 071-46888
EMAIL: towersl@iol.ie**

HOTEL ★★★   MAP 10 H 16

A Tower Group Hotel - the Tower Hotel is Sligo's most central and convenient hotel. Situated on Quay Street beside City Hall, the Tower is an impressive red brick building with clock tower. With 58 bedrooms, it is small enough to offer a truly personal service. The bedrooms are all en suite with multi-channel TV, DD phone, tea/coffee facilities and trouser press. The Links Bar and Lady Eleanor Restaurant offer the perfect relaxation after a busy day touring or a rewarding day's golf.

WEB: www.towerhotelgroup.ie

Members Of Tower Hotel Group

B&B from £35.00 to £55.00
€44.44 to €69.84

JOE LEONARD
General Manager

American Express
Diners
Mastercard
Visa

☺ Weekend specials from £69.00

58 58

Closed 24 - 29 December

CROMLEACH LODGE

**CASTLEBALDWIN, VIA BOYLE,
CO.SLIGO
TEL: 071-65155   FAX: 071-65455
EMAIL: cromleac@iol.ie**

HOTEL ★★★★   MAP 10 H 16

Good Hotel Guide - Hotel of the Year 1999. Cromleach Lodge is set in the quiet hills above Lough Arrow - a spectular vista of unspoiled mountain, lake & woodlands. The superior minisuites are appointed to a very high standard & each enjoys the breathtaking panorama. The atmosphere is warm & relaxed with complimentary liquers, fruit, newspapers & the scent of fresh flowers everywhere. But Cromleach's pièce de résistance is its Restaurant, where the creations of Moira & her team are a gastronomic delight.

Members Of Blue Book Of Ireland

B&B from £69.00 to £99.00
€87.61 to €125.70

MOIRA & CHRISTY TIGHE
Proprietors

American Express
Diners
Mastercard
Visa

☺ Weekend specials from £165.00

10 10

alc ▮

Closed 01 November - 01February

MARKREE CASTLE

**COLLOONEY,
CO. SLIGO
TEL: 071-67800   FAX: 071-67840
EMAIL: markree@iol.ie**

HOTEL ★★★   MAP 10 H 15

Charles and Mary Cooper have restored Sligo's oldest inhabited house and made it a spectacular family hotel. Home of the Cooper family since 1640 and set in the middle of a large estate, Markree boasts spectacular plasterwork, a fine Irish oak staircase yet all the comforts of a 3* hotel. Good food, peace, quiet, lots of space and warm family welcome. Riding is also available on the estate.

WEB: www.markreecastle.ie

B&B from £53.50 to £65.50
€67.93 to €83.17

CHARLES & MARY COOPER
Owners

American Express
Diners
Mastercard
Visa

29 29

▮

Closed 24 - 27 December

Room rates are per room per night

CASTLE ARMS HOTEL

ENNISCRONE,
CO. SLIGO
TEL: 096-36156   FAX: 096-36156

HOTEL ★★   MAP 10 F 15

The Castle Arms Hotel is a 2** family run hotel and upholds the tradition of offering a warm and friendly welcome with excellent home cooking and 27 rooms. It is adjacent to a three mile long sandy beach, an 18 hole championship golf links, aqua leisure centre, seaweed and steam health baths, tennis courts and many other amenities. For other information contact a member of the Grimes family at 096 36156.

B&B from £27.50 to £27.50
€34.92 to €34.92

LIAM & SHANE GRIMES

Mastercard
Visa

☺ Weekend specials from £67.50

27 27

Open All Year

BEACH HOTEL AND LEISURE CLUB

THE HARBOUR, MULLAGHMORE,
CO. SLIGO
TEL: 071-66103   FAX: 071-66448
EMAIL: beachhot@iol.ie

HOTEL ★★   MAP 13 H 17

The Beach Hotel overlooks the harbour and Ben Bulben mountains in the charming and beautiful village of Mullaghmore. All rooms are en suite with DD phone, satellite TV and tea/coffee facilities. Enjoy our indoor swimming pool, jacuzzi, sauna, steam room and fitness suite. 5 golf courses, angling, horseriding, watersports, walking, boat trips and blue flag beach locally. Excellent cuisine. Free Kiddies Club, Murder Mystery & activity weekends. Fall under the spell...

B&B from £30.00 to £40.00
€38.09 to €50.79

COLM HERRON
Proprietor

American Express
Mastercard
Visa

☺ Weekend specials from £70.00

28 28

IRISH HOTELS FEDERATION

Open All Year

PIER HEAD HOUSE

MULLAGHMORE,
CO. SLIGO
TEL: 071-66171   FAX: 071-66473
EMAIL: pierhead@eircom.net

GUESTHOUSE ★★★   MAP 13 H 17

With it's unique setting in the picturesque seaside/fishing resort of Mullaghmore this family run premises offers superb sea & harbour views. All rooms en suite, cafe style bar, restaurant, function rooms and conference facilities. Regular entertainment by top Irish and international artistes. Next door is the renowned Olde Quay Bar & Seafood Restaurant with its attractive stone facade and old world nautical charm, making it a popular haunt for locals and tourists alike. Ideal for touring NW. Golf 8mls. Horse Riding, Fishing.

B&B from £27.50 to £40.00
€34.92 to €50.79

JOHN MCHUGH

American Express
Diners
Mastercard
Visa

16 16

IRISH HOTELS FEDERATION

Open All Year

B&B rates are per person sharing per night incl. Breakfast

YEATS COUNTRY HOTEL AND LEISURE CLUB

ROSSES POINT, SLIGO,
CO. SLIGO
TEL: 071-77211 FAX: 071-77203

HOTEL ★★★ MAP 10 H 16

A family run, 3*** hotel. All rooms en suite, cable TV, DD phone, tea/coffee facilities, hairdryer. 3k of sandy beaches and Sligo's 18 hole ch'ship golf courses at consession rates locally. Amenities include de-luxe leisure club with 18m swimming pool, sauna, jacuzzi, steam room and hi-tech gymnasium. Also available tennis, basketball, indoor bowling. Supervised creche and indoor play areas on bank holiday weekends/July/August. Local activities: golf, yachting, fishing, scenic drives.

Members Of Brian McEniff Hotels

B&B from £30.00 to £80.00
€38.09 to €101.58

RONAN & FIONA LONG
Managing Directors

American Express
Diners
Mastercard
Visa

😊 Weekend specials from £79.00

79 79

IRISH HOTELS FEDERATION

Closed 02 January - 02 February

OCEAN VIEW HOTEL

STRANDHILL,
CO. SLIGO
TEL: 071-68115 FAX: 071-68009
EMAIL: oceanviewhotel@eircom.net

HOTEL ★★★ MAP 10 H 16

Ocean View Hotel, nestling at the foot of Knocknarea mountain, overlooking the Atlantic, is a long established family hotel which offers a unique blend of all modern comforts with old-fashioned courtesy and charm. Its Rollers Restaurant is renowned for its home oak-smoked salmon and fresh local produce. Bar food also available. This picturesque area invites you to stroll its sandy beaches, pony trek, golf, explore the hidden glens, visit the oldest megalithic tombs in Europe.

Members Of Village Inn Hotels

B&B from £35.00 to £45.00
€44.44 to €57.14

SHAY BURKE/JEAN BURKE
Proprietors

American Express
Diners
Mastercard
Visa

10 10

alc

IRISH HOTELS FEDERATION

Closed 24 December - 01 March

CAWLEY'S

EMMET STREET, TUBBERCURRY,
CO. SLIGO
TEL: 071-85025 FAX: 071-85963

GUESTHOUSE ★★ MAP 10 G 15

Cawley's, a large 3 storey family run guesthouse. We offer high standards in accommodation with tastefully decorated rooms. Our home cooking and personal service makes this premises your home for the duration of your stay. Private parking, landscaped gardens, easily accessed by air, rail and bus. Local amenities include fishing, 9 hole golf, horse riding. Sea side resorts close by. Major credit cards accepted.

B&B from £22.50 to £30.00
€28.57 to €38.09

JEAN CAWLEY
Proprietor

Mastercard
Visa

10 10

alc

IRISH HOTELS FEDERATION

Closed 25 - 26 December

Room rates are per room per night

follow in a giant's footsteps.
start with his breakfast.

Next time you fancy a holiday break, try Northern Ireland for size. The massive, mysterious Giant's Causeway (built by giant Finn MacCool, some say, to reach his lady love in Scotland) will take your breath away. And just wait till you see the size of the breakfasts we serve here. One on its own is enough to keep you going for a whole holiday!

We're big on welcomes, too. Nobody's a stranger for long in Northern Ireland - because making new friends is one of our favourite hobbies. Just you try *not* joining in with the music, the singing and the chat when you spend an evening in one of our pubs!

It's ever so easy to get here - and there's so much to see and do you'll never, ever find yourself at a loose end.

Enjoy a wander along one of our beautiful, uncrowded beaches. Take a picnic to your very own secret, hideaway glen (there are nine in County Antrim alone!) or head for our magnificent rolling hills and blow a few cobwebs away.

Come and live it up in our superb restaurants, famous theatres and night clubs. Stroll our first class shopping avenues. Feed your mind in our heritage parks, galleries and museums. Come pony trekking, mountain biking or hang gliding. Or relax on a boating holiday, an angling break or a golfing package.

If you want much, much more from your next holiday or short break ring the CallSave number below.

It's easy to find out more. **CallSave**
1850 230 230
(Mon - Fri, 9.15am - 5.30pm. Sat, 10am - 5pm.)

Ireland

(www.ni-tourism.com)

Northern Ireland Tourist Board

16 Nassau Street, Dublin 2.

Ireland. It's a different holiday altogether.

ADAIR ARMS HOTEL

BALLYMONEY ROAD, BALLYMENA,
CO. ANTRIM BT43 5BS
TEL: 028-2565 3674 FAX: 028-2564 0436
EMAIL: reservations@adairarms.com

HOTEL ★★★ MAP 15 O 19

A warm welcome awaits you at the Adair Arms Hotel, which is owned and run by the McLarnon family. The hotel was built in 1846 by Sir Robert Adair, and designed by the famous architect Charles Lanyon. Situated in the heart of Ballymena, ideally located for touring the romantic Glens of Antrim, Slemish Mountain and north Antrim coast. The hotel has recently been refurbished and has the added attraction of a new 18 hole golf course within one mile, courtesy transport provided for guests.

WEB: www.adairarms.com

B&B from £32.50 to £42.50

G MCLARNON
Manager/Proprietor

American Express
Diners
Mastercard
Visa

Weekend specials from £75.00

40 40

Open All Year

TULLYGLASS HOUSE HOTEL

178 GALGORM ROAD,
BALLYMENA, CO. ANTRIM BT42 1HJ
TEL: 028-2565 2639 FAX: 028-2564 6938
EMAIL: guest@tullyglass.com

HOTEL ★★★ MAP 15 O 19

Situated in its own private grounds close to the north Antrim Coast and Glens of Antrim, Tullyglass House Hotel has something for everyone with 29 beautifully decorative en suite bedrooms, all with tea/coffee making facilities, trouser press, hairdryer, DD telephone, 3 bars, a superb restaurant and daily carvery. Regular entertainment and a choice of conference and wedding facilities. Activities close by include fishing, horseriding and golf.

WEB: www.tullyglass.com

B&B from £40.00 to £60.00

MR & MRS C MCCONVILLE

American Express
Mastercard
Visa

29 29

Closed 25 - 26 December

BEACH HOTEL

61 BEACH ROAD, PORTBALLINTRAE,
BUSHMILLS, CO. ANTRIM BT578RJ
TEL: 028-2073 1214 FAX: 028-2073 1664
EMAIL: info@beachhousehotel.com

HOTEL ★★★ MAP 14 N 21

Located one mile from the famous Old Bushmills Distillery in the picturesque village of Portballintrae, overlooking the Atlantic Ocean and within easy reach of the world famous Giant's Causeway, Carrick-a-Rede rope bridge, Dunluce Castle. Ideal base to relax or play golf at Royal Portrush, Portstewart, Castlerock, Ballycastle, Bushfoot, Gracehill and Galgorm Castle golf courses. Private car park.

WEB: www.beachhousehotel.com

Members Of Kennedy Hotel Group

B&B from £42.50 to £50.00

MARY O'NEILL
Marketing Manager

Diners
Mastercard
Visa

Weekend specials from £90.00

32 32

Open All Year

Room rates are per room per night

BUSHMILLS INN

9 DUNLUCE ROAD, BUSHMILLS,
CO. ANTRIM BT57 8QG
TEL: 028-2073 2339   FAX: 028-2073 2048
EMAIL: info@bushmills-inn.com

HOTEL ★★★   MAP 14 N 21

"It's one of those places where you hope it rains all day so you have an excuse to snuggle indoors".
At the home of the world's oldest distillery between the Giant's Causeway and Royal Portrush Golf Club this award winning hotel and restaurant, with its open peat fires, pitched pine and gas lights, has been outstandingly successful in re-creating its origins as an old coaching inn and mill house.

WEB: www.bushmills-inn.com/

Members Of Best Loved Hotels Of The World

B&B from £44.00 to £64.00

ALAN DUNLOP & STELLA MINOGUE
Managers

American Express
Mastercard
Visa

32 32

Inet

Open All Year

CAUSEWAY HOTEL

40 CAUSEWAY ROAD, BUSHMILLS,
CO. ANTRIM BT57 8SU
TEL: 028-2073 1226   FAX: 028-2073 2552

HOTEL ★★   MAP 14 N 21

Situated on the north Antrim coast at the entrance to the world famous Giant's Causeway and the new visitors' centre, this old family hotel established in 1836 has been tastefully renovated and restored to provide modern facilities while retaining its old grandeur and charm. The thirty centrally heated bedrooms have TV, telephone, tea/coffee making facilities and bathrooms en suite.

B&B from £32.50 to £35.00

STANLEY ARMSTRONG
Proprietor

Mastercard
Visa

☺   Special Offer 2 B&B and
2 Dinners from £95.00

28 28

Open All Year

LONDONDERRY ARMS HOTEL GLENS OF ANTRIM

20 HARBOUR ROAD, CARNLOUGH,
CO. ANTRIM BT44 0EU
TEL: 028-2888 5255   FAX: 028-2888 5263
EMAIL: lda@glensofantrim.com

HOTEL ★★★   MAP 15 P 20

This beautiful Georgian hotel was built in 1847. Once owned by Sir Winston Churchill, it is now owned and managed by Mr Frank O'Neill. With its open log fires, private lounges and award-winning restaurant this premier hotel in the Glens of Antrim is the perfect place to stay and discover the north eastern part of Ireland.

WEB: www.@glensofantrim.com

Members Of N.I. Best Kept Secrets

B&B from £40.00 to £45.00

FRANK O'NEILL
Proprietor

American Express
Diners
Mastercard
Visa

35 35

Open All Year

QUALITY HOTEL

75 BELFAST ROAD, CARRICKFERGUS,
CO. ANTRIM BT38 8PH
TEL: 028-9336 4556   FAX: 028-9335 1620
EMAIL: info@qualitycarrick.co.uk

HOTEL ★★★   MAP 15 P 18

3*** Mediterranean style hotel situated just 15 mins from Belfast city centre, enroute to the beautiful Antrim coast. With two bars and the Boardwalk Restaurant the hotel offers a variety of menus to suit all tastes. Each of the deluxe 68 en suite bedrooms offers a hospitality tray, trouser press, kingsize bed, hairdryer, DD phone and colour TV with satellite channels.

WEB: www.qualityinn.com

Members Of Choice Hotels International

B&B from £60.00 to £85.00

FRANK BARBER
General Manager

American Express
Diners
Mastercard
Visa

😊 Weekend specials from £70.00

68 68

Closed 24 - 26 December

ALEXANDRA

11 LANSDOWNE CRESCENT,
PORTRUSH, CO. ANTRIM
TEL: 028-7082 2284

GUESTHOUSE U   MAP 14 N 21

The Alexandra, a charming period townhouse, traditionally furnished but with modern day facilities offers the discerning visitor an ideal base to explore the surrounding countryside. Your choice of room will range from cosy and charming to spacious and gracious. Located in a tranquil crescent with uninterrupted sea views and ample car parking.

B&B from £20.00 to £30.00

MARY MCALISTER

Mastercard
Visa

:✓

10 5

Open All Year

CAUSEWAY COAST HOTEL & CONFERENCE CENTRE

36 BALLYREAGH ROAD, PORTRUSH,
CO. ANTRIM BT56 8LR
TEL: 028-7082 2435   FAX: 028-7082 4495
EMAIL: info@causewaycoast.com

HOTEL ★★★   MAP 14 N 21

Located one mile from Royal Portrush golf course on the coast road between Portrush and Portstewart, overlooking the Atlantic ocean and within easy reach of the Giant's Causeway, Carrick-a-Rede rope bridge, Dunluce Castle. Ideal base to relax and play golf at Royal Portrush, Portstewart, Castlerock, Ballycastle, Bushfoot, Gracehill and Galgorm Castle golf courses. Private car park.

WEB: www.causewaycoast.com

Members Of Kennedy Hotel Group

B&B from £42.50 to £50.00

MARY O'NEILL
Marketing Manager

American Express
Mastercard
Visa

✓🍴

😊 Weekend specials from £90.00

21 21

Open All Year

Room rates are per room per night

CLARMONT

10 LANSDOWNE CRESCENT,
PORTRUSH, CO. ANTRIM
TEL: 028-7082 2397   FAX: 028-7082 2397
EMAIL: clarmont@talk21.com

GUESTHOUSE ★   MAP 14 N 21

An established, family run, period town house, situated in beautiful award winning Lansdowne Cresent, enjoying panoramic views of Skerries Islands and picturesque Causeway coastline. Convenient to town centre, golf clubs, harbour, restaurants and entertainment. Weekend or midweek bookings welcome. All rooms en suite / TV. Ample car parking.

B&B from £22.50 to £27.50

JOHN & FRANCES DUGGAN
Owners

Mastercard

Visa

⚞🛏️🔌🅲🍴♨

10   10

🏨 HOTELS

Closed 20 - 30 December

MAGHERABUOY HOUSE HOTEL

41 MAGHERABOY ROAD,
PORTRUSH, CO. ANTRIM
TEL: 028-7082 3507   FAX: 028-7082 4687

HOTEL ★★★   MAP 14 N 21

The perfect base for the shopping/sporting enthusiast. Quietly located 1 mile from Portrush town and central to all the Causeway coast's beautiful attractions. Bistro serving good value meals daily. À la carte restaurant. Sunday carvery. The Magherabuoy is the ideal location for a relaxing break, a golfing weekend, a business meeting or your annual conference. E-mail: administration@magherabuoy. freeserve.co.uk

B&B from £40.00 to £50.00

T. CLARKE
General Manager

American Express

Diners

Mastercard

Visa

😊 Midweek specials from £70.00

⚞🛏️🐾🔌🅣🅲🅼☀🔌♨🎵🅿
38   38
🆂 a/c

🏨 HOTELS

Closed 24 - 26 December

ROYAL COURT HOTEL

233 BALLYBOGEY ROAD,
PORTRUSH, CO. ANTRIM BT56 8NF
TEL: 028-7082 2236   FAX: 028-7082 3176

HOTEL ★★★   MAP 14 N 21

The Royal Court occupies one of the best positions on Northern Ireland's world famous Causeway coast. The hotel offers unrivalled views over the harbour town of Portrush, its world famous Royal Portrush golf course and probably the best stretch of beach anywhere on the island. The hotel's 14 bedrooms and 4 suites are all en suite and have DD phone, tea/coffee making facilities, satellite TV and trouser press.

B&B from £37.50 to £45.00

JENNIFER O'KANE
General Manager

American Express

Mastercard

Visa

😊 Weekend specials from £80.00

⚞🛏️🐾🔌🅣🅲♥🅼☀🔌♨🎵🅿🆂
18   18
 a/c

🏨 HOTELS

Open All Year

B&B rates are per person sharing per night incl. Breakfast

BALLYMAC

**7A ROCK ROAD, STONEYFORD,
CO. ANTRIM BT28 3SU
TEL: 028-9264 8313 FAX: 028-9264 8312
EMAIL: info@ballymachotel.ie**

GUESTHOUSE ★★★ MAP 15 O 18

The Ballymac is a new accommodation and conference development comprising of 15 en suite rooms with excellent facilities including satellite TV, tea/coffee making facilities, DD phone and hairdryer. Our grill bar and à la carte restaurants feature outstanding cuisine from award winning chefs. The Ballymac also boasts well-equipped function suites suitable for weddings, parties, trade shows and conferences. Extensive private parking available in our grounds.

WEB: www.ballymachotel.ie

B&B from £27.50 to £39.50

CATHY MULDOON
General Manager

American Express
Mastercard
Visa

15 15

HOTELS
FOUNDATION

Closed 25 December

STAKIS PARK

**CASTLE UPTON ESTATE, TEMPLEPATRICK,
CO. ANTRIM BT39 0DD
TEL: 028-9443 5500   FAX: 028-9443 5511
EMAIL: res.manager@park.stakis.co.uk**

HOTEL ★★★★ MAP 15 O 18

Stakis Park, set in 220 acres of parkland, just 10 mins from Belfast International Airport is the perfect retreat for a short break. 130 en suite rooms offering views of the surrounding countryside. All rooms are equipped with satellite TV, phone, trouser press, hairdryer and hospitality tray. Dine in style in one of the hotel's restaurants or bars. Play a round of golf on the hotel's own 18 hole championship course or relax in the LivingWell Health Club.

WEB: www.stakis.co.uk

Room Rate from £60.00 to £150.00

MATTHEW MULLAN

American Express
Diners
Mastercard
Visa

130 130
18

Open All Year

TEMPLETON HOTEL

**882 ANTRIM ROAD, TEMPLEPATRICK,
BALLYCLARE, CO. ANTRIM
TEL: 028-9443 2984 FAX: 028-9443 3406**

HOTEL ★★★ MAP 15 O 18

This luxury hotel is in a prime location close to Belfast International Airport, Belfast city centre and Larne Harbour. Mixing the best of modern facilities with the appeal of yesterday, the hotel offers total quality for all tastes and needs. Upton Grill Room serving lunch and dinner daily, Templeton à la carte restaurant, spacious new lounge, 24 bedrooms including bridal suite and family rooms, Sam's Bar with pub grub and big screen.

B&B from £35.00 to £55.00

ALISON MCCOURT/CLAIRE KERR
Gen Manager/Mkt Manager

☺ Weekend specials from £91.50

24 24

HOTELS
FOUNDATION

Closed 25 - 26 December

O'NEILL ARMS HOTEL

MAIN STREET, TOOMEBRIDGE,
CO. ANTRIM BT41 3TQ
TEL: 028-7965 0202   FAX: 028-7965 0970

HOTEL ★   MAP 14 N 18

Experience hospitality at its best in the O'Neill Arms Hotel, located on the main Belfast to Derry road. Convenient to both the city and the international airport. The hotel comprises of 10 bedrooms, 3 function suites, an excellent lounge/restaurant and the new Arby's Nightclub offering weekend entertainment. Situated beside the famous eel fishery in Lough Neagh, the O'Neill Arms is a haven for anglers. Local amenities: fishing, golf and horse riding.

B&B from £20.00 to £25.00

KATHLEEN MCCONVILLE
Owner

Mastercard

Visa

10 5

Closed 25 December

ASHBURN HOTEL

81 WILLIAM STREET, LURGAN,
CO. ARMAGH BT66 6JB
TEL: 028-3832 5711   FAX: 028-3834 7194

HOTEL ★   MAP 15 O 17

Owned and managed by the McConaghy Family, the Ashburn Hotel is friendly and efficient. Conveniently situated with easy access to the motorway (M1), rail network and town centre. An ideal base for angling or golfing trips - 5 miles from the river Bann and 1 mile from local golf course. All bedrooms are en suite with colour TV, direct dial telephone and hospitality tray. Entertainment each weekend in our popular nightclub.

B&B from £28.00 to £28.00

JOHN F. MCCONAGHY

Mastercard

Visa

12 12

Closed 24 - 26 December

SILVERWOOD GOLF HOTEL AND COUNTRY CLUB

KILN ROAD, LURGAN, CRAIGAVON,
CO. ARMAGH
TEL: 028-3832 7722   FAX: 028-3832 5290

HOTEL ★   MAP 15 O 17

Silverwood Golf Hotel, situated in pleasant rural surroundings, is only 2 mins from the M1 motorway which links the hotel to Belfast and sea/airports within 20 minutes. The centre of business life at Craigavon is also close at hand. The hotel has a reputation for excellent food combined with friendly and efficient service in a relaxed and charming setting. Family owned. Golf course on doorstep; live entertainment at weekends; overlooks artificial ski slope (details available).

Members Of Best Western Hotels

B&B from £20.00 to £35.00

SEAN HUGHES
Proprietor

American Express

Diners

Mastercard

Visa

Weekend specials from £55.00

29 29

Open All Year

B&B rates are per person sharing per night incl. Breakfast

ALDERGROVE HOTEL

BELFAST INTERNATIONAL AIRPORT,
CRUMLIN, BELFAST
TEL: 028-9442 2033   FAX: 028-9442 3500

HOTEL ★★★   MAP 15 P 18

Situated 50m from entrance to Belfast International Airport and 17 miles from Belfast city centre. Fully air conditioned, this modern 3*** hotel has 108 rooms, fully equipped to the highest standard, including 3 award winning disabled rooms. Restaurant open 6 am - 10 pm daily. Fitness suite and sauna available free to all guests. Purpose built conference and banqueting facilities and free guest parking.

B&B from £32.50 to £37.50

HUGH SLEVIN / MARY LOUGHRAN
Managers

American Express

Diners

Mastercard

Visa

108 108

HOTELS

Open All Year

BALMORAL HOTEL

BLACKS ROAD, DUNMURRY,
BELFAST
TEL:028-9030 1234   FAX: 028-9060 1455

HOTEL ★★   MAP 15 P 18

A budget hotel five minutes from city centre in residential south Belfast at Dunmurry junction of the M1 motorway. Forty four comfortable en suite bedrooms with eight designed especially to cater for the needs of the disabled person. The hotel is also 30 minutes travelling time from either Belfast International Airport or Belfast Harbour Airport.

B&B from £35.00 to £35.00

FRANK WARD
Managing Director

American Express

Diners

Mastercard

Visa

44 44

HOTELS

Open All Year

CORR'S CORNER HOTEL

315 BALLYCLARE ROAD,
NEWTOWNABBEY, CO. ANTRIM BT36 4TQ
TEL: 028-9084 9221   FAX: 028-9083 2118

HOTEL ★★   MAP 15 P 18

Corr's Corner is a family-run business located 7 miles north of Belfast at the M2 and A8 junction, 14 miles from Larne Harbour and Belfast International Airport. The hotel has 30 en suite rooms with 2 rooms specifically designed for guests with disabilities. Meals are served all day in the Lady R Bar and the Corriander Room Restaurant. The Ballyhenry lounge is open every evening and the Cedar Room caters for meetings and private parties up to 60 persons.

Room Rate from £45.00 to £55.00

EUGENE & CATHERINE MCKEEVER

American Express

Diners

Mastercard

Visa

☺ Weekend specials from £65.00

30 30

HOTELS

Closed 25 - 26 December

Room rates are per room per night

DUKES HOTEL

65/67 UNIVERSITY STREET,
BELFAST BT7 1HL
TEL: 028-9023 6666   FAX: 028-9023 7177

HOTEL ★★★   MAP 15 P 18

A bright new modern hotel constructed within one of Belfast's more distinguished Victorian buildings. Beside Queen's University, Ulster Museum, Botanic Gardens and less than 1 mile from the city centre. Golf courses only minutes away. 21 luxury en suite bedrooms, all with satellite TV, hairdryers and direct dial telephones. Gymnasium and saunas also available. Elegant restaurant serving local cuisine. Popular bar for the smart set. A friendly welcome and service is guaranteed.

B&B from £35.00 to £55.00

MICHAEL CAFOLLA
General Manager

American Express
Diners
Mastercard
Visa

☺ Weekend specials from £82.00

21 21

Open All Year

DUNADRY HOTEL AND COUNTRY CLUB

2 ISLANDREAGH DRIVE, DUNADRY,
CO. ANTRIM BT41 2HA
TEL: 028-9443 2474   FAX: 028-9443 3389

HOTEL ★★★★   MAP 15 O 18

This 4**** hotel with country club, and winner of Les Routiers Ireland's Hotel of the Year 1999, offers the last word in comfort and charm. Management's personal attention to detail make every guest feel extra special in experiencing the high standards of excellence in imaginative cuisine, efficient service and total comfort. The fine dining restaurant and Mill Race Bistro provide a tantalising choice of menus and styles to tempt all taste buds. Fully equipped country club. Close to Belfast int. airport. Central reservations Tel:028-9038 5050. Fax: 028-9038 5055.

B&B from £37.50 to £78.95

ROBERT MOONEY
General Manager

American Express
Diners
Mastercard
Visa

☺ Weekend specials from £97.50

83 83

Closed 24 - 26 December

JURYS BELFAST INN

FISHERWICK PLACE, GREAT
VICTORIA ST, BELFAST BT2 7AP
TEL: 028-9053 3500   FAX: 028-9053 3511
EMAIL: info@jurys.com

HOTEL ★★★   MAP 15 P 18

Modern attractive rooms capable of accommodating up to 3 adults or 2 adults and 2 children. All rooms are en suite with multi-channel TV, radio, DD phone, modem points and tea/coffee making facilities. Located in the centre of Belfast on Fisherwick Place, near Opera House, City Hall and business district. 2 minutes walk from major shopping areas of Donegal Place and Castlecourt centre. Public car park close by. Jurys Doyle Hotel Group Central Resv: Tel 01-6070000; Fax 01-6609625.

WEB: www.jurys.com

Room Rate from £63.00 to £65.00

MARGARET NAGLE
General Manager

American Express
Diners
Mastercard
Visa

190 190

Closed 24 - 26 December

B&B rates are per person sharing per night incl. Breakfast

Belfast City
.. touch the spirit, feel the welcome

*...Wherever you go,
wherever you stay you
will find it all in the
Belfast Visitors' Guide.*

For a copy please contact:
Telephone: 028 90 239026
email: info@belfastvistor.com
www.gotobelfast.com
(please quote ref. no. GBROII/ADI4)

A Place to Stay...

"Europe's friendliest regional capital" is how the international travel magazine *Hilton Guest* recently described Belfast City.

Belfast is buzzing with excitement and interesting places to see and visit.

There are many varied places to rest your wearied head.

An unprecedented programme of high quality hotel development is ensuring that excellent

accommodation is being provided in and around Belfast City at very competitive rates.

A traditional welcome can also be found among the many conveniently located family run establishments, most offering the hardy 'Ulster Fry' as a robust start to the day!

Belfast Visitor & Convention Bureau **B** **V** **C** **B**

LA MON COUNTRY HOUSE HOTEL

41 GRANSHA ROAD,
CASTLEREAGH, COMBER BT23 5RF
TEL: 028-9044 8631   FAX: 028-9044 8026

HOTEL ★   MAP 15 P 18

La Mon Country House is a family run hotel located 5 miles from Belfast city centre in the idyllic County Down countryside. This warm and friendly hotel has been extensively refurbished and redeveloped to include a state of the art health and fitness suite. Sleep soundly in the heart of the country with the city lights only 10 mins drive away and enjoy the best of both worlds.

B&B from £30.00 to £40.00

FRANCIS BRADY
Managing Director

American Express
Mastercard
Visa

Open All Year

LISDARA TOWN HOUSE

23 DERRYVOLGIE AVENUE,
MALONE ROAD, BELFAST BT9 6FN
TEL: 028-9068 1549   FAX: 028-9066 8097
EMAIL: elisabeth@lisdara.freeserve.co.uk

GUESTHOUSE ★★   MAP 15 P 18

A luxuriously appointed townhouse, situated in a tree-lined avenue in the university area of south Belfast, convenient to the city centre, theatres, the Lagan Valley parklands and motorways. All rooms have private facilities (one with large 4-poster bed), colour TV and hospitality tray. AA ♦♦♦, featured in Charming Small Hotels Great Britain and Ireland, Guide du Routard. Home cooking and personal attention will help to make your stay relaxing and enjoyable.

B&B from £30.00 to £40.00

ELISABETH GILLESPIE

Mastercard
Visa

Closed 20 December - 03 January

MCCAUSLAND HOTEL

34-38 VICTORIA STREET,
BELFAST BT1 3GH
TEL: 028-9022 0200   FAX: 028-9022 0220
EMAIL: info@mccauslandhotel.com

HOTEL ★★★★   MAP 15 P 18

The McCausland Hotel, a magnificent classical Italianate building which exudes a style that follows through to a beautiful contemporary interior. Individually decorated rooms offer luxury, comfort and the most modern facilities. Gourmet dishes can be enjoyed in Merchants Restaurant; drinks and light meals in Café Marco Polo. The hotel is a short stroll from museums, theatres, shopping and the Waterfront Hall. Sister property to the Hibernian Hotel, Dublin and Woodstock Hotel, Ennis.
UK Toll free 00 800 525 48000.

WEB: www.slh.com/causland/

Members Of Small Luxury Hotels of the World

Room Rate from £100.00 to £200.00

JOSEPH V HUGHES
General Manager

American Express
Diners
Mastercard
Visa

😊 Weekend specials from £130.00

Closed 24 - 28 December

B&B rates are per person sharing per night incl. Breakfast

PARK AVENUE HOTEL

**158 HOLYWOOD ROAD,
BELFAST BT4 1PB
TEL: 028-9065 6520 FAX: 028-9047 1417**

HOTEL ★★★ MAP 15 P 18

Park Avenue Hotel has recently undergone a £2M refurbishment. *56 rooms, with en suite facilities, including TV with satellite channels. *Disabled facilities. *Free parking. Our new Griffin Restaurant offers an extensive menu to suit all tastebuds. Alternatively our bistro menu is served daily in Gelstons Corner Bar. *5 minutes from Belfast City Airport. *10 minutes from Belfast City centre. *Excellent links to the outer ring roads and all transport stations and ferry terminals.

B&B from £39.50 to £42.50

**SHAW STEPHENS
General Manager/Director**

American Express
Mastercard
Visa

☺ Weekend specials from £30.00

56 56

Inet

Closed 25 December

WELLINGTON PARK HOTEL

**21 MALONE ROAD,
BELFAST BT9 6RU
TEL: 028-9038 1111 FAX: 028-9066 5410**

HOTEL ★★★★ MAP 15 P 18

This is truly the place to be seen and enjoys the best location in the fashionable area of South Belfast. Designed to international standards, the hotel offers friendly hospitality and modern comfort in luxuriously appointed suites or spacious family rooms. Indulge in the sumptuous selection of dishes available in the new Piper Bistro. Comfortable overstuffed sofas and side tables are in keeping with the contemporary elegance of the Blackshaw Lounge with its display of Irish Art. Central Reservations Tel: 028-9038 5050 Fax: 028-9038 5055.

Member Of Best Western Hotels

B&B from £40.00 to £74.00

**ARTHUR MOONEY
General Manager**

American Express
Diners
Mastercard
Visa

75 75

Inet FAX

Closed 24 - 26 December

BEECH HILL COUNTRY HOUSE HOTEL

**32 ARDMORE ROAD,
DERRY BT47 3QP
TEL: 028-7134 9279 FAX: 028-7134 5366
EMAIL: info@beech-hill.com**

HOTEL ★★★ MAP 14 L 20

Beech Hill is a privately owned country house hotel, 2mls from the centre of Londonderry. It retains the elegance of country living as restoration has taken place creating a hotel of charm, character and style. Its ambience is complemented by the surrounding grounds, planted with a myriad trees, including beech - after which the hotel is named. Winners of British Airways Best Catering - 1994. CMV & Associates 003531 295 8900. Also Best Kept Secrets of Northern Ireland.

WEB: www.beech-hill.com

Members Of Manor House Hotels

B&B from £55.00 to £67.50

**SEAMUS DONNELLY
Proprietor**

American Express
Mastercard
Visa

27 27

Inet

Closed 25 - 26 December

Room rates are per room per night

DA VINCIS

15 CULMORE ROAD,
DERRY BT48 8JB
TEL: 028-7126 4507 FAX: 028-7137 2074
EMAIL: davincis@god-group.com

UNDER CONSTRUCTION OPENING MAY 2000

HOTEL P MAP 14 L 20

Opening in May 2000, Da Vincis will be the sister hotel of the Trinity. The Da Vincis complex will consist of an award winning bar, à la carte restaurant, function room and 70 en suite rooms. Rates will be on a room only basis, irrespective of number of guests and each room will have 2 double beds. Da Vincis will be a perfect base for a city break or for touring the North West.

Room Rate from £49.95 to £49.95

FINTAN KELLY
General Manager

American Express
Diners
Mastercard
Visa

70 70

inet

HOTELS

Open All Year

TRINITY HOTEL

22-24 STRAND ROAD, DERRY CITY
BT48 7AB, CO. LONDONDERRY
TEL: 028-7127 1271 FAX: 028-7127 1277
EMAIL: trinity@god-group.com

HOTEL ★★★ MAP 14 L 20

Derry's premier city centre hotel provides the ideal meeting place for business/pleasure. It offers 40 en suite rooms which include 2 luxury suites and a standard of comfort and accommodation unrivalled in the area. Nolan's bistro and Porter's café bar provide the ideal environment to pass many a pleasurable hour. For the conference organiser there are 3 dedicated meeting rooms with a maximum capacity of 150 theatre style. Rooms offer latest technology and full air-conditioning.

B&B from £45.00 to £55.00

FINTAN KELLY
General Manager

American Express
Diners
Mastercard
Visa

40 40

 inet

HOTELS

Open All Year

WHITE HORSE HOTEL (BEST WESTERN)

DONNYBREWER ROAD, CAMPSIE,
DERRY BT47 3PA
TEL: 028-7186 0606 FAX: 028-7186 0371
EMAIL: info@whitehorse.demon.co.uk

HOTEL ★★★ MAP 14 L 20

40 bedroom hotel, all en suite with colour TV, trouser press, tea/coffee making facilities. Located 5 miles from Derry city and on the main road to the Giant's Causeway. Ideal touring base for Donegal. Superb golf breaks and over 55s special breaks all year. Carvery lunch served every day, very popular tour stop. Large private car/coach park to rear of hotel, free of charge to guests. 5 mins drive to City of Derry Airport. A perfect choice for both business and pleasure travellers.

B&B from £25.00 to £35.00

SHEILA HUNTER
General Manager

American Express
Diners
Mastercard
Visa

40 40

HOTELS

Open All Year

B&B rates are per person sharing per night incl. Breakfast

BROWN TROUT GOLF & COUNTRY INN

209 AGIVEY ROAD, AGHADOWEY,
COLERAINE, CO. DERRY BT51 4AD
TEL: 028-7086 8209   FAX: 028-7086 8878
EMAIL: bill@browntroutinn.com

HOTEL ★★   MAP 14 N 20

The Brown Trout Golf and Country Inn nestles near the River Bann only 12.8k from the picturesque Causeway coast. This old inn with 17 rooms, and four 5 star cottages, is Northern Ireland's first golf hotel. Bill, Gerry, Jane or Joanna will happily organise golf, horseriding and fishing packages with professional tuition if required or you can just enjoy a relaxing break and the crack with the locals. The warm hospitality and 'Taste of Ulster' restaurant will make your stay enjoyable.

WEB: www.browntroutinn.com

Members Of Coast and Country Hotels

B&B from £30.00 to £42.50

BILL O'HARA
Owner

American Express
Diners
Mastercard
Visa

Weekend specials from £60.00

17 17

Open All Year

BOHILL HOTEL & COUNTRY CLUB

69 CLOYFIN ROAD, COLERAINE,
CO. LONDONDERRY
TEL: 028-7034 4406   FAX: 028-7035 2424

HOTEL ★★★   MAP 14 N 21

In the heart of Co. Londonderry, just a few miles from the beautiful north Antrim coast stands the Bohill Hotel & Country Club bringing together the historic elegance of a country house with the best of today's international hotel facilities. Guests enjoy rooms whose furnishings include baby listening, trouser press, iron and tea/coffee facilities. To complement these relaxing surroundings the Bohill boasts the largest private hotel pool and country club in the north west.

B&B from £40.00 to £80.00

DONAL MACAULEY
Managing Director

Diners
Mastercard
Visa

Weekend specials from £45.00

37 37

Open All Year

LODGE HOTEL

LODGE ROAD, COLERAINE,
CO. DERRY BT52 1NF
TEL: 028-7034 4848   FAX: 028-7035 4555
EMAIL: info@thelodgehotel.com

HOTEL ★★★   MAP 14 N 21

Situated on the outskirts of Coleraine, 10 minutes drive from beaches, golf courses and local attractions. Within walking distance of town centre. En suite bedrooms include TV, phone, hairdryer, trouser press and tea/coffee making facilities. Choice of bistro menu, à la carte or table d'hôte. Entertainment Thurs-Sun in Elliot's (high season). Our friendly staff, good food and comfortable surroundings create a few of the reasons why our guests return again and again.

WEB: www.thelodgehotel.com

B&B from £29.50 to £35.00

NORMA WILKINSON
Managing Director

American Express
Mastercard
Visa

16 16

Open All Year

Room rates are per room per night

EDGEWATER HOTEL

88 STRAND ROAD, PORTSTEWART,
CO. DERRY
TEL: 028-7083 3314   FAX: 028-7083 3315

HOTEL ★★   MAP 14 M 21

Adjacent to Portstewart Golf Club, the hotel is magnificently situated overlooking spectacular views of Portstewart strand, hills of Donegal and Atlantic ocean. All 28 en suite rooms (incl 6 suites with sea views) contain colour TV, radio, DD phone and tea/coffee faciles. Indulge in table d'hôte dinner in O'Malleys split level restaurant or relax and enjoy a bar snack in the Inishtrahull lounge, both with picture windows capturing breathtaking views.

B&B from £30.00 to £45.00

KEVIN O'MALLEY
Proprietor

American Express
Diners
Mastercard
Visa

😊 Weekend specials from £70.00

28   28

Open All Year

MARINE COURT HOTEL

THE MARINA, BANGOR,
CO. DOWN BT20 5ED
TEL: 028-9145 1100   FAX: 028-9145 1200
EMAIL: marine.court@dial.pipex.com

HOTEL ★★★   MAP 15 Q 18

Beautifully situated overlooking the marina on Bangor's seafront, this modern hotel is an ideal location for business or pleasure. All 52 spacious rooms are tastefully fitted and have DD phone, satellite TV, radio, tea/coffee making facilities, trouser press and hairdryer plus many extras. The Stevedore Restaurant offers both table d'hôte and à la carte menus. Lord Nelson's Bistro offers an interesting bistro menu. Residents can enjoy use of Oceanis leisure complex.

WEB: www.nova.co.uk/nova/marine/

B&B from £37.50 to £50.00

PHILIP WESTON
General Manager

American Express
Diners
Mastercard
Visa

😊 Weekend specials from £90.00

52   52

Open All Year

ROYAL HOTEL

26/28 QUAY STREET, BANGOR,
CO. DOWN BT20 5ED
TEL: 028-9127 1866   FAX: 028-9146 7810
EMAIL: TheRoyalHotel@compuserve.com

HOTEL ★★   MAP 15 Q 18

Overlooking Bangor marina this family run hotel is probably the best known landmark on Bangor's seafront. All 50 rooms are en suite and include 7 executive suites, satellite TV, DD phone, courtesy tray and hairdryer are all standard throughout. Renowned for superb food served in a variety of atmospheric restaurants and bars. Nightclub, conference and banqueting facilities. 15 mins from Belfast city airport. Direct rail link from Dublin and Derry.

WEB: www.the-royal-hotel.com

B&B from £40.00 to £45.00

PAUL DONEGAN
Proprietor

American Express
Diners
Mastercard
Visa

😊 Weekend specials from £70.00

50   50

Closed 25 - 26 December

B&B rates are per person sharing per night incl. Breakfast

SHELLEVEN HOUSE

**61 PRINCETOWN ROAD, BANGOR
BT20 3TA, CO. DOWN
TEL: 028-9127 1777 FAX: 028-9127 1777**

GUESTHOUSE ★★★ MAP 15 Q 18

An end of terrace Victorian house set back from Princetown Road, with garden and private parking, convenient to the marina, seafront and shops. We have 10 rooms, all en suite. The front rooms have a view of Bangor Bay and the Irish Sea beyond. Train and bus station is 5 minutes away, with direct link to the Dublin train service, and the city airport. Tee off times can be arranged at several local golf courses.

B&B from £22.50 to £27.50

MARY WESTON

Mastercard
Visa

10 10

Open All Year

CHESTNUT INN

**28/34 LOWER SQUARE, CASTLEWELLAN,
CO. DOWN BT31 9DW
TEL: 028-4377 8247 FAX: 028-4377 0372**

GUESTHOUSE ★ MAP 12 P 16

In the old market town of Castlewellan the Chestnut Inn (King's) is ideally situated to take advantage of the Mournes, the seaside town of Newcastle and all the amenities of south Down. Royal County Down is only 5 minutes away as are the Forest Parks and the beaches of Dundrum bay. The Inn is renowned for excellent bar food and also boasts a superb à la carte restaurant.

B&B from £25.00 to £30.00

JOHN & FIONNUALA KING
Proprietors

Mastercard
Visa

7 7

Open All Year

RAYANNE COUNTRY HOUSE & RESTAURANT

**60 DEMESNE ROAD, HOLYWOOD,
CO. DOWN BT18 9EX
TEL: 028-9042 5859 FAX: 028-9042 3364**

GUESTHOUSE ★★★ MAP 15 P 18

National winner of AA (UK) Best Breakfast of the year award (over 3,500 establishments judged). With a 5 diamond rating and 2 Rosette award from the AA, guests are assured of excellent quality throughout this beautiful family run Victorian residence, full of charm and interest. The intimate restaurant (open to non-residents) is renowned for its superb cuisine and award winning breakfasts. Located just minutes from Belfast centre, city airport, sea and rail terminals, Rayanne House is the ideal base for business or holiday. Fully licenced.

B&B from £35.00 to £45.00

ANNE MCCLELLAND

American Express
Mastercard
Visa

9 9

Open All Year

Room rates are per room per night

BURRENDALE HOTEL AND COUNTRY CLUB

51 CASTLEWELLAN ROAD,
NEWCASTLE, CO. DOWN BT33 0JY
TEL: 028-4372 2599 FAX: 028-4372 2328
EMAIL: reservations@burrendale.com

HOTEL ★★★ MAP 12 P 16

At the foot of the Mournes, the Burrendale is the ideal location for your family, golfing holiday or short break. The hotel comprises of a Country club, Beauty Salon, A La Carte Vine restaurant, Bistro style Cottage Kitchen Restaurant, Cottage Bar and excellent Banqueting / Conference facilities. In close proximity are 15 golf courses including Royal County Down, golden beaches, nature walks, forest parks and pony trekking. Superb hospitality awaits you.

WEB: www.burrendale.com

B&B from £45.00 to £55.00

KEM AKKARI / SEAN SMALL
Manager/Proprietor

American Express
Diners
Mastercard
Visa

68 68

Open All Year

SLIEVE DONARD HOTEL

DOWNS ROAD, NEWCASTLE,
CO. DOWN BT33 0AH
TEL: 028-4372 3681 FAX: 028-4372 4830
EMAIL: res@sdh.hastingshotels.com

HOTEL ★★★★ MAP 12 P 16

Situated at the foot of the mountains of Mourne, the Slieve Donard Hotel stands in 6 acres of private grounds leading to the world-famous Royal County Down golf course. Having completed a total refurbishment programme the Slieve Donard offers deluxe accommodation, Elysium Leisure Complex, restaurants and bars, including the Percy French, an informal pub restaurant in the hotel grounds, truly making it Northern Ireland's most popular holiday hotel.

WEB: www.hastingshotels.com

B&B from £55.00 to £70.00

RICHARD ROBINSON
General Manager

American Express
Diners
Mastercard
Visa

 Weekend specials from £110.00

130 130

Open All Year

CANAL COURT HOTEL

MERCHANTS QUAY, NEWRY,
CO. DOWN BT35 8HF
TEL: 028-3025 1234 FAX: 028-3025 1177
EMAIL: manager@canalcourthotel.com

HOTEL ★★★ MAP 12 O 15

British Airways award winning Canal Court Hotel. 50 en suite rooms with satellite TV, hospitality trays, hairdryer, DD phone and ironing facilities. The Old Mill Restaurant is one of the finest in the area, the Granary Bar has carvery and bar snacks served daily. Conference facilities for up to 300 people with superb suites for wedding receptions and private functions. Health and leisure complex incorporating gym, swimming pools, jacuzzi, sauna and steam room.

WEB: www.canalcourthotel.com

B&B from £50.00 to £65.00

MICHELLE BARRETT
General Manager

American Express
Diners
Mastercard
Visa

 Weekend specials from £110.00

50 50

Closed 25 December

B&B rates are per person sharing per night incl. Breakfast

USEFUL TELEPHONE NUMBERS

Emergency (fire, Garda, (Police) & Ambulance)	999	Delta Airlines (enquiries)	(01) 844 4166
Directory Enquiries (national)	1190	Air France	(01) 844 5633
Directory Enquiries (to Great Britain)	1197	Virgin Altantic	(01) 873 3388
Directory Enquiries (international)	1198	Iberia/Viva Air (Dublin Airport)	(01) 844 4939
Operator Assistance (national)	10	Irish Rail (Passenger information)	(01) 836 6222
Operator Assistance (international)	114	Connolly Station	(01) 836 3333
Dublin Airport	(01) 844 4131	Heuston Station	(01) 836 3333
Shannon Airport	(061) 471 444	Dart Information	(01) 836 3333
Cork Airport	(021) 313131	Irish Bus (Bus Eireann)	(01) 836 1111
Aer Lingus (flight enquiries)	(01) 886 6705	Dublin Bus (Bus Atha Cliath)	(01) 873 4222
British Airways (enquiries)	1 800 62 67 47	Irish Ferries (Enquiries)	1890 31 31 31
Ryanair (flight enquiries)	(01) 844 4411	Irish Ferries	(01) 855 2222
		General Post Office (An Post)	(01) 705 7000
		Bord Fáilte	(01) 602 4000

NARROWS

**8 SHORE ROAD, PORTAFERRY,
CO. DOWN BT22 1JY
TEL: 028-4272 8148   FAX: 028-4272 8105
EMAIL: reservations@narrows.co.uk**

GUESTHOUSE ★★★   MAP 15 Q 17

In the three years since it opened, The Narrows has taken the Northern Ireland hospitality industry by storm. With numerous awards and reviews for its architecture, cuisine, accommodation, accessibility and conference facilities, you will see why our guests keep coming back. We have 13 rooms en suite with views of the Strangford Narrows and our restaurant was recently featured in an all-Ireland Top 10 review. Sauna and walled garden for your relaxation.

WEB: www.narrows.co.uk

B&B from £36.00 to £42.00

WILL & JAMES BROWN

American Express
Mastercard
Visa

☺ Midweek specials from £95.00

13 13

Open All Year

PORTAFERRY HOTEL

**10 THE STRAND, PORTAFERRY,
CO. DOWN BT22 1PE
TEL: 028-4272 8231   FAX: 028-4272 8999
EMAIL: info@portaferryhotel.com**

HOTEL ★★★   MAP 15 Q 17

Charming waterside village inn contained in sensitively renovated 18th Century terrace. AA *** plus 2 rosettes. Local places of interest include NT properties at Castleward, Rowallen & Mt Stewart, Exploris, Castle Espie & Greyabbey with numerous antique shops. Ideal for touring mountains of Mourne. 6 golf courses within 30 mins including Royal Co. Down. Member Ireland's Blue Book. From Belfast A20 via Newtownards & Kircubbin. From Newry A25 via Castlewellan, Downpatrick & Strangford.

WEB: www.portaferryhotel.com

Members Of Ireland's Blue Book

B&B from £40.00 to £47.50

JOHN & MARIE HERLIHY
Proprietors

American Express
Diners
Mastercard
Visa

14 14

Open All Year

HOTEL CARLTON

**2 MAIN STREET, BELLEEK,
CO. FERMANAGH
TEL: 028-6865 8282   FAX: 028-6865 9005
EMAIL: hotelcarlton@btinternet.com**

HOTEL ★★   MAP 13 I 17

The Hotel Carlton's setting on the banks of the river Erne in the heart of the Irish lake district is quite simply breathtaking. Also on the steps of one of Ireland's most famous landmarks, Belleek Pottery, Ireland's oldest pottery. Ideally situated for visitors who wish to tour the nearby counties of Donegal, Sligo, Tyrone and Leitrim. The Hotel Carlton has recently been completely rebuilt in a traditional style and boasts 19 luxurious well appointed en suite rooms.

WEB: www.lakelands.net/hotelcarlton

Members Of MinOtel Ireland Hotel Group

B&B from £30.00 to £37.50

THE GALLAGHER & ROONEY FAMILY

Mastercard
Visa

19 19

Closed 24 - 25 December

B&B rates are per person sharing per night incl. Breakfast

FORT LODGE HOTEL

72 FORT HILL STREET, ENNISKILLEN,
CO. FERMANAGH
TEL: 028-6632 3275 FAX: 028-6632 0275
EMAIL: hotel@fortlodge.freeserve.uk

HOTEL ★★ MAP 11 K 16

John & Mary Sheerin welcome you to their family run hotel which enjoys an enviable reputation for its excellent service and in house entertainment both locally and with visitors. 35 bedrooms all en suite, offering coffee/tea making facilities, DD telephone, central heating and TV. The Medieval Crannog Lounge and Baileys Restaurant provide extensive cuisine and comfort to all clientele. Convenient to water sports & theatre. Golf and fishing packages available.

WEB: www.advert.ie/fortlodge/

B&B from £32.50 to £40.00

JOHN AND MARY SHEERIN
Proprietors

American Express
Mastercard
Visa

35 35
alc

HOTELS

Open All Year

KILLYHEVLIN HOTEL

DUBLIN ROAD, ENNISKILLEN,
CO. FERMANAGH BT74 6RW
TEL: 028-6632 3481 FAX: 028-6632 4726
EMAIL: info@killyhevlin.com

HOTEL ★★★ MAP 11 K 16

Killyhevlin Hotel and chalets are situated on the shores of beautiful Lough Erne, making it a terrific location at the gateway to the west and an ideal base for exploring the many sights of Fermanagh. All 43 bedrooms plus the Belmore suite are fitted to a high standard, each has a bathroom / shower en suite, TV, DD phone, radio and tea facilities. Our scenic lounge and restaurant offer a wide variety of menus. Lunchtime buffet, bar snacks all day. Evenings, table d'hôte or à la carte.

WEB: www.killyhevlin.com

B&B from £40.00 to £50.00

RODNEY J. WATSON
Managing Director

American Express
Diners
Mastercard
Visa

43 43
alc

HOTELS

Closed 24 - 26 December

MANOR HOUSE COUNTRY HOTEL

KILLADEAS, ENNISKILLEN,
CO. FERMANAGH, BT94 1NY
TEL: 028-6862 2211 FAX: 028-6862 1545
EMAIL: manorhousehotel@lakelands.net

HOTEL ★★★ MAP 14 K 16

This fine Victorian country mansion is beautifully situated in the Fermanagh countryside on the shores of lower Lough Erne. The hotel has been extensively refurbished to provide extreme comfort in splendid stately surroundings. All rooms are en suite with satellite TV, D.D. phone and tea making facilities. This is the ideal location for a break away where you can enjoy a range of activities in our ultra modern leisure complex including swimming pool.

WEB: www.lakelands.net/manorhousehotel

B&B from £55.00 to £55.00

DAVID BEGLEY
General Manager

American Express
Mastercard
Visa

Weekend specials from £105.00

40 40

HOTELS

Open All Year

Room rates are per room per night

MAHONS HOTEL

ENNISKILLEN ROAD, IRVINESTOWN,
CO. FERMANAGH
TEL: 028-6862 1656   FAX: 028-6862 8344
EMAIL: mahonhotel@aol.com

HOTEL ★★   MAP 13 K 17

Situated in the heart of the Fermanagh Lakeland. Ideal base for visiting all major tourist attractions - Belleek Pottery 20 minutes, Marble Arch caves 30 minutes, Necarne Equestrian Centre 5 minutes, Lough Erne 5 minutes, Donegal 20 minutes. All rooms en suite, TV, tea making facilities. Bushmills Bar of the Year winner, entertainment at weekends, private car park. Family run from 1883. Visit us in our second century. Cycling, horseriding, tennis and golf all available.

WEB: www.lakelands.net/mahonshotel

B&B from £34.00 to £37.00

JOE MAHON
Manager

American Express
Mastercard
Visa

☺ Weekend specials from £65.00

18 18

Open All Year

CORICK HOUSE & LICENSED RESTAURANT

20 CORICK ROAD, CLOGHER,
CO. TYRONE
TEL: 028-8554 8216   FAX: 028-8554 9531

GUESTHOUSE ★★★   MAP 14 L 17

A warm welcome awaits you at Corick House, a charming 17th century 3*** approved country residence, located in the heart of the Clogher Valley, just off the main A4 Belfast to Enniskillen road. Attractively restored family home offers 10 luxury rooms, licensed restaurant, conference and wedding facilities. Set in mature woodland overlooking the Blackwater river it is the ideal location for trout and salmon fishing. Central to the Fermanagh Lakelands and the Ulster Way.

WEB: www.infowing.ie/tyrone/ad/corick.htm

B&B from £25.00 to £35.00

JEAN BEACOM
Proprietor

American Express
Diners
Mastercard
Visa

☺ Weekend specials from £65.00

10 10

Open All Year

SILVERBIRCH HOTEL

5 GORTIN ROAD, OMAGH,
CO. TYRONE BT79 7DH
TEL: 028-8224 2520   FAX: 028-8224 9061
EMAIL: info@silverbirchhotel.com

HOTEL ★★   MAP 14 L 18

The hotel is situated on the outskirts of Omagh on the B48 leading to the Gortin Glens, Ulster History Park, Sperrins and the Ulster American Folk Park. Set in its own spacious and mature grounds, the hotel now has 40 new en suite bedrooms to 3*** standard. Other facilities include Buttery Grill all day, newly refurbished dining room, function suite for 250 guests for weddings, dinners or conferences. Award winning leisure centre 300 metres away.

WEB: www.silverbirchhotel.com

B&B from £35.00 to £41.00

JAMES DUNCAN
Manager

American Express
Diners
Mastercard
Visa

☺ Weekend specials from £72.00

40 40

Closed 25 December

B&B rates are per person sharing per night incl. Breakfast

As one of the oldest cities in Europe, Dublin provides the visitor with a multitude of cultural riches, from the ancient to the avant-garde: from history, architecture, literature, art and archaeology to the performing arts. Monuments in literature and in stone mark the history, writers, poets and people of Dublin. Medieval, Georgian and modern architecture provide a backdrop to a friendly, bustling port which can boast literary giants such as Wilde, Shaw, Joyce, Yeats, Beckett and O'Casey as native sons. Spawned by the need to ford the river Liffey, fortified by the Danes, developed by the Normans, adorned with fine buildings by the Anglo-Irish, the city has grown in stature and elegance over the century.

When it comes to entertainment, Dubliners with their natural friendly and fun-craving attitude, certainly know how to entertain. The quintessential 'Dublin Pub' provides the focal point of Dublin social life, illuminating the vibrant hues of Dubliners and their culture. It is a place where conversations and "craic" flow freely, unleashing the unique atmosphere that is at the heart of Dublin and its friendly people. Just a twenty-minute journey will bring the visitor from the bustling city centre to the charming coastal towns and villages of the county. These towns and villages provide boundless opportunities for craft-shopping, water-sports, seafood dining and picturesque walks against the spectacular background of Dublin Bay.

Whatever your heart desires, Dublin provides a superb location for all the above activities and many more besides.

Email: reservations@dublintourism.ie
http://www.visitdublin.com

Reservations and Information may be obtained by visiting one of our Information Centres:

- Dublin Tourism Centre, Suffolk St.,
- Arrivals Hall, Dublin Airport,
- Ferry Terminal,
  Dun Laoghaire Harbour,
- Baggot St Bridge.

GUINNESS

St. Patrick's Day Festival, Dublin.
March

Guinness Blues Festival, Dublin.
July

Kerrygold Horseshow, R.D.S. Dublin.
August

Guinness All-Ireland Hurling Championship Final, Croke Park, Dublin.
September

All-Ireland Football Championship Final, Croke Park, Dublin.
September

Dublin Theatre Festival, Dublin.
October

Event details correct at time of going to press

AARONMOR GUESTHOUSE

1B/1C SANDYMOUNT AVENUE,
BALLSBRIDGE, DUBLIN 4
TEL: 01-668 7972   FAX: 01-668 2377
EMAIL: aaronmor@goirl.com

GUESTHOUSE ★★★   MAP 8 O 11

Welcome to Aaronmor, we trust your stay will have pleasant memories. Turn of century home in fashionable Ballsbridge. All rooms en suite, centrally heated, D.D. phones, fax, tea/coffee facilities. Private car park. Convenient R.D.S. showgrounds, Lansdowne Rugby club, Point Depot, embassies, museums, car ferries, airport, bus/train service. 10 mins city centre. Enjoy our relaxed atmosphere. Traditional Irish breakfast. Lift to all floors. AA ♦♦♦♦.

WEB: www.goirl.com/aaronmor

B&B from £25.00 to £49.00
€31.74 to €62.22

BETTY & MICHAEL DUNNE

American Express
Mastercard
Visa

17 17

Closed 24 - 26 December

ABBERLEY COURT HOTEL

BELGARD ROAD, TALLAGHT,
DUBLIN 24
TEL: 01-459 6000   FAX: 01-462 1000
EMAIL: abberley@iol.ie

HOTEL ★★★   MAP 8 O 11

The Abberley Court Hotel is a newly built hotel situated at the foothills of the Dublin mountains, beside the Square towncentre in Tallaght. The facilities include 40 en suite bedrooms, Kilcawleys traditional Irish pub, Court restaurant. Conference/meeting/training facilities with private car parking. Activities in the locality include golf, pitch & putt, ten pin bowling, horse riding, pony trekking, fishing, watersports.

B&B from £30.00 to £49.00
€38.09 to €62.22

ENDA CREEGAN
Senior Manager

American Express
Diners
Mastercard
Visa

40 40

Open All Year

ABERDEEN LODGE

53/55 PARK AVENUE, OFF AILESBURY
ROAD, BALLSBRIDGE, DUBLIN 4
TEL: 01-283 8155   FAX: 01-283 7877
EMAIL: aberdeen@iol.ie

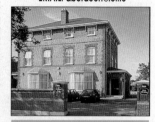

GUESTHOUSE ★★★★   MAP 8 O 11

Award-winning Aberdeen Lodge, 4****, a luxurious combination of Edwardian grace, fine food and modern comforts, all that one expects of a private hotel, aircon suites with jacuzzi, executive facilities, landscaped gardens and guest carpark. Close to city centre, airport and car ferry terminals by DART or bus. Accolades - RAC AAA, Best Loved Hotels, Green Book, Johansens. Sister property of Merrion Hall, Dublin and Halpins Hotel in Co. Clare. USA toll free 800 223 6510. DD 353 1 283 8155.

WEB: www.greenbook.ie/aberdeen

Members Of Charming Hotels

B&B from £35.00 to £70.00
€44.44 to €88.88

PAT HALPIN
Proprietor

American Express
Diners
Mastercard
Visa

☺ Midweek specials from £115.00

20 20

alc Inet FAX

Open All Year

B&B rates are per person sharing per night incl. Breakfast

ABRAE COURT

9 ZION ROAD, RATHGAR,
DUBLIN 6
TEL: 01-492 2242 FAX: 01-492 3944

GUESTHOUSE ★★★ MAP 8 O 11

Built in 1864, family run, 3*** Victorian guesthouse is located in the prestigious residential area of Rathgar, just ten minutes from the heart of Dublin city. Guestrooms are furnished with en suite bathroom, colour TV, direct dial phone and coffee/tea making facilities. Laundry service and a lock up car park are available. Bus routes, a good selection of restaurants, pubs, tourist attractions and various sports.

B&B from £35.00 to £45.00
€44.44 to €57.14

NEVILLE KEEGAN
Owner

Mastercard

Visa

14 14

IRISH HOTELS FEDERATION

Open All Year

ACADEMY HOTEL

FINDLATER PLACE, OFF UPPER
O'CONNELL STREET, DUBLIN 1
TEL: 01-878 0666   FAX: 01-878 0600
EMAIL: stay@academy-hotel.ie

HOTEL N MAP 8 O 11

The natural choice for the discerning visitor to Dublin, the Academy Hotel offers the ultimate in comfort and convenience. Located off the city's main thoroughfare, O'Connell St, we are only a short stroll from the very best of international shopping, galleries, theatres and the cosmopolitan area of Temple Bar. Our beautifully appointed en suite rooms represent the perfect retreat after a demanding meeting or a hectic day of shopping or sightseeing.

WEB: www.academy-hotel.ie

Room Rate from £60.00 to £149.00
€76.18 to €189.19

ROSS MACSWEENEY
Manager

American Express

Diners

Mastercard

Visa

98 98

Inet

IRISH HOTELS FEDERATION

Closed 24 - 26 December

ADAMS TRINITY HOTEL

28 DAME STREET,
DUBLIN 2
TEL: 01-670 7100 FAX: 01-670 7101
EMAIL: adamshtl@indigo.ie

HOTEL ★★★ MAP 8 O 11

What better location in Dublin than the Adams Trinity Hotel? Located mid-way between Dublin Castle, Grafton Street and Trinity College; it faces the vibrant Temple Bar area. Traditional style bedrooms are finished to an exceptionally luxurious standard. The hotel features the 'Black and White' award winning Mercantile bar and restaurant. The Adams Trinity Hotel offers all guests that same personal attention and warmth, it has that little something special.

B&B from £49.50 to £70.00
€62.85 to €88.88

HELEN O'DWYER
Marketing Manager

American Express

Diners

Mastercard

Visa

28 28

Inet

IRISH HOTELS FEDERATION

Closed 25 - 27 December

Room rates are per room per night

AISHLING HOUSE

19/20 ST. LAWRENCE ROAD,
CLONTARF, DUBLIN 3
TEL: 01-833 9097   FAX: 01-833 8400
EMAIL: englishr@gofree.indigo.ie

GUESTHOUSE ★★★   MAP 8 O 11

Elegant Victorian family-run residence situated in Clontarf, north Dublin's most exclusive suburb. Ideally located close to Point Theatre, city centre and Dublin port yet only 15 minutes from airport. Recently extensively refurbished to a high standard. We offer superb luxury accommodation at affordable prices. Tranquil elegant lounge, children's play area, half acre of manicured grounds, fax facilities, private car park. A warm welcome awaits you.

B&B from £25.00 to £30.00
€31.74 to €38.09

ROBERT & FRANCES ENGLISH
Owners

Mastercard
Visa

☺ Midweek specials from £70.00

🛏🌫☎📺🄣Ⓜ️CM❄️♩P▫️
9 9

Closed 24 - 27 December

ALEXANDER HOTEL

AT MERRION SQUARE,
DUBLIN 2
TEL: 01-607 3700   FAX: 01-661 5663
EMAIL: alexanderres@ocallaghanhotels.ie

HOTEL U MAP 8 O 11

Contemporary style deluxe hotel ideally located in Dublin city centre beside Trinity College, 5 mins walk from museums, shops and business districts. 102 air-conditioned guestrooms and suites with satellite TV, phone, tea/coffee facilities, safe, trouser press, iron and board and 24 hour room service. Caravaggio's restaurant specialises in European cuisine. Winners bar pays tribute to world champions. Free private valet car parking and fitness room for residents.
USA Toll Free 1800 5699983.

WEB: www.ocallaghanhotels.ie

Member Of O'Callaghan Hotels

B&B from £90.00 to £139.00
€114.28 to €176.49

JOHN CLESHAM
Operations Manager

American Express
Diners
Mastercard
Visa

☺ Weekend specials from £167.00

🛏🌫☎📺🄣↕️🄣CM📷P🅿️aid▫️
102 102

Inet

IRISH HOTELS FEDERATION

Open All Year

AMBASADOIR HOUSE

36 KENILWORTH SQUARE,
RATHGAR, DUBLIN 6
TEL: 01-497 9332   FAX: 01-497 9332

GUESTHOUSE ★★★   MAP 8 O 11

Ambasadoir House is a 3*** Victorian residence overlooking Kenilworth Park in the prestigious residential area of Rathgar. Just 10 minutes from the heart of Dublin city, with an excellent bus service. All our guest rooms are en suite, with tea/coffee facilities, colour TV and direct dial phone. At Ambasadoir House we provide a very high standard of accommodation with excellent food and very friendly atmosphere. Central reservations: 01-497 9332.

B&B from £25.00 to £35.00
€31.74 to €44.44

RACHEL MCDAID

Mastercard
Visa

🛏🌫☎📺🄣CM
7 7

IRISH HOTELS FEDERATION

Open All Year

B&B rates are per person sharing per night incl. Breakfast

ANCHOR GUEST HOUSE

49 LOWER GARDINER STREET,
DUBLIN 1
TEL: 01-878 6913   FAX: 01-878 8038
EMAIL: gtcoyne@gpo.iol.ie

GUESTHOUSE ★★★   MAP 8 O 11

The Anchor Guesthouse is located in the heart of the city centre. It is a tastefully refurbished Georgian house with a modern purpose built bedroom wing attached. Our location is a perfect base for city exploration. Temple Bar, Trinity College, Grafton Street, theatres, galleries and museums are but a stone's throw. We are 2 minutes walk from the central bus station, which has connections to the airport and ferry terminals.

WEB: www.anchorguesthouse.com

B&B from £22.00 to £35.00
€27.93 to €44.44

JOAN & GERRY COYNE
Proprietors

Mastercard

Visa

😊 Midweek specials from £60.00

🚲🐕📞📺©🍴♿🅿🛗
21 21

IRISH
HOTELS
FEDERATION

Open All Year

ANGLESEA TOWN HOUSE

63 ANGLESEA ROAD, BALLSBRIDGE,
DUBLIN 4
TEL: 01-668 3877   FAX: 01-668 3461

GUESTHOUSE ★★★★   MAP 8 O 11

This is a world-renowned guesthouse of national breakfast award fame. It has been featured on TV in both Ireland and the UK and has won entry in British, Irish, European and American travel guides and journals. It is a fine Edwardian residence of 7 en suite rooms with phone and TV, offering quiet elegance to discerning guests who wish to combine country-style charm with convenience to town. A warm welcome awaits you from your hostess Helen Kirrane and her family.

B&B from £45.00 to £50.00 .
€57.14 to €63.49

HELEN KIRRANE
Owner

American Express

Mastercard

Visa

🚲🐕📞📺TC🍴❄🅿
7   7

Closed 15 December - 08 January

ARDAGH HOUSE

NO.1 HIGHFIELD ROAD, RATHGAR,
DUBLIN 6
TEL: 01-497 7068   FAX: 01-497 3991
EMAIL: enquiries@ardagh-house.ie

GUESTHOUSE ★★★   MAP 8 O 11

Having been recently totally refurbished, Ardagh House is conveniently situated in a premier residential area. This imposing turn of the century premises contains many of the gracious and spacious features of a fine detached residence of that era and yet incorporating modern creature comforts. Within easy distance of the city centre, RDS, etc. This fine property stands on approximately 1/2 acre with ample off street car parking and good gardens.

WEB: www.ardagh-house.ie

B&B from £27.50 to £45.00
€34.92 to €57.14

WILLIE AND MARY DOYLE
Proprietors

Mastercard

Visa

🚲🐕📞📺TC❄🅿🛗
19 19

IRISH
HOTELS
FEDERATION

Open All Year

B&B rates are per person sharing per night incl. Breakfast

ARIEL HOUSE

52 LANSDOWNE ROAD,
BALLSBRIDGE, DUBLIN 4
TEL: 01-668 5512 FAX: 01-668 5845

GUESTHOUSE ★★★★ MAP 8 O 11

Ariel House is a historic listed Victorian mansion that has recently been carefully restored to its former splendour. Classified 4**** by Bord Failte, it offers an air of quiet luxury and elegant decor in a large variety of rooms, all with private bathroom. Situated in the fashionable tree-lined suburb of Ballsbridge only 3 minutes on the DART to the city centre and within easy access of the airport, ferryports and mainline rail stations.

Room Rate from £68.00 to £79.00
€86.34 to €100.31

MICHAEL O'BRIEN
Managing Director

Mastercard

Visa

☺ Midweek specials from £100.00

🛏️📠☎️📋T P ⓟ ▣
40 40

IRISH HOTELS FEDERATION

Closed 23 December - 09 January

ARLINGTON HOTEL

23/25 BACHELORS WALK,
O'CONNELL BRIDGE, DUBLIN 1
TEL: 01-804 9100 FAX: 01-804 9112
EMAIL: arlington@eircom.net

HOTEL U MAP 8 O 11

Overlooking the river Liffey at O'Connell Bridge, the Arlington is Dublin's most central hotel. Nestled between Trinity College, Temple Bar, the Point Theatre and the Abbey Theatre; close to Jervis St and Grafton St shopping districts. 115 modern en suite rooms, private function and meeting room facilities, featuring a restaurant, lively Knightsbridge bars, nightclub and underground car parking. The perfect location for business or pleasure.

B&B from £45.00 to £75.00
€57.14 to €95.23

PAUL KEENAN
General Manager

American Express

Diners

Mastercard

Visa

✒️🍴

☺ Weekend specials from £99.00

🛏️📠☎️📋TCCM♪PS☕ⓐⓒ▣
115 115

IRISH HOTELS FEDERATION

Open All Year

Room rates are per room per night

ASHFIELD HOUSE

**5 CLONSKEAGH ROAD,
DUBLIN 6**
TEL: 01-260 3680   FAX: 01-260 4236

GUESTHOUSE U   MAP 8 O 11

One of Dublin's friendliest family run guesthouses. Providing comfort and service of a very high standard to the tourist and business sector. Rooms are en suite with TV, DD phones, tea/coffee facilities, hairdryer etc. A fax service is available. 10 mins from city centre, RDS, Lansdowne road, Leopardstown racecourse, ferry ports etc. Many top class pubs and restaurants adjacent to Ashfield House. We provide off street parking. There is an excellent bus service directly to city centre.

B&B from £30.00 to £60.00
€38.09 to €76.18

FRANK AND OLIVE TAYLOR

Mastercard
Visa

10 10

Open All Year

ASHLING HOTEL

**PARKGATE STREET,
DUBLIN 8**
TEL: 01-677 2324   FAX: 01-679 3783
EMAIL: info@ashlinghotel.ie

HOTEL ★★★   MAP 8 O 11

Why choose us? Stylish refurbishment. New spacious rooms, secure parking, conference/meeting rooms. Under 8 mins by taxi/bus to city centre / Temple Bar. Lovely quaint pubs, Guinness Brewery, Phoenix Park and other attractions nearby. Easily found location by car/rail/bus. By car take city centre route & briefly follow river Liffey westward. Taxi or airlink bus from airport, Heuston Intercity rail station opposite. For onward journeys we are within easy access of all major roads.

WEB: www.bestwestern.com

Members Of Best Western Hotels

B&B from £36.00 to £68.00
€45.71 to €86.34

ALAN MOODY
General Manager

American Express
Diners
Mastercard
Visa

150 150

Closed 24 - 28 December

ASTON HOTEL

**7/9 ASTON QUAY,
DUBLIN 2**
TEL: 01-677 9300   FAX: 01-677 9007

HOTEL U   MAP 8 O 11

A warm welcome awaits you at the Aston Hotel, located in Temple Bar and overlooking the river Liffey. Friendly staff and pleasant surroundings will make your stay a memorable one. All our 27 rooms are en suite and offer every guest comfort including DD phone, colour TV, hairdryer and tea/coffee making facilities. A leisurely stroll from the Aston brings you to all Dublin's top attractions and amenities and makes it an ideal base for exploring the capital.

B&B from £56.00 to £110.00
€71.11 to €139.67

ANN WALSH
Manager

American Express
Diners
Mastercard
Visa

27 27

Closed 24 - 27 December

B&B rates are per person sharing per night incl. Breakfast

AUBURN GUESTHOUSE

NAVAN ROAD, CASTLEKNOCK, (AT
AUBURN ROUNDABOUT), DUBLIN 15
TEL: 01-822 3535 FAX: 01-822 3550
EMAIL: auburngh@iol.ie

GUESTHOUSE ★★★ MAP 8 O 11

Auburn, family-run, set on its own
grounds, with ample car parking. It
is remarkably secluded, private and
secure. We offer excellent
accommodation with breakfast. It
has an ideal gateway location for
visitors who wish to explore Dublin
city and its environs or for the
traveller who wishes to view
Ireland's countryside. Situated 15
mins from the city centre, it has
immediate accessability to the M50
motorway. 10 mins to Dublin
airport. Close by: fishing,
horseriding, golf courses.

Members Of Premier Guesthouses

B&B from £28.00 to £35.00
€35.55 to €44.44

ELAINE COWLEY
Manageress

Mastercard
Visa

7 7

Closed 24 - 27 December

BEDDINGTON GUESTHOUSE

181 RATHGAR ROAD,
DUBLIN 6
TEL: 01-497 8047   FAX: 01-497 8275

GUESTHOUSE CR MAP 8 O 11

The Beddington guesthouse is
ideally situated on the main Rathgar
road only one mile from Dublin city
centre on the main bus route. Private
parking. All rooms are en suite with
tea/coffee facilities, colour TV, direct
dial telephone, hair dryer. Shoe
shine, trouser press and ironing
facilities are also available.
Restaurants, cinema, library,
swimming pool, tennis, bowling etc,
all within walking distance. The
perfect location for both tourist and
business people.

B&B from £30.00 to £35.00
€38.09 to €44.44

ANGELINA CLERKIN
Manager

American Express
Diners
Mastercard
Visa

14 14

Open All Year

BELGRAVE GUESTHOUSE

8-10 BELGRAVE SQUARE,
RATHMINES, DUBLIN 6
TEL: 01-496 3760 FAX: 01-497 9243

GUESTHOUSE ★★★ MAP 8 O 11

The Belgrave consists of three
interconnecting early Victorian
buildings overlooking a well matured
square. While retaining all the
character and charm of its era, the
Belgrave has all the conveniences of
a modern 3*** guesthouse, each
room is en suite and has colour TV,
direct dial telephone, tea making
facilities. Private car park. Ideally
located. We look forward to hosting
you and according you a warm
welcome for which we are
renowned. AA ◆◆◆.

B&B from £25.00 to £45.00
€31.74 to €57.14

PAUL AND MARY O'REILLY
Owners

Mastercard
Visa

24 24

Closed 22 December - 04 January

Room rates are per room per night

BELVEDERE HOTEL

GREAT DENMARK STREET, DUBLIN 1
TEL: 01-874 1413   FAX: 01-872 8631

HOTEL ★   MAP 8 O 11

Situated only three minutes walking distance from O'Connell Street, it is the ideal base for shopping and taking in the sights of this famous historic city. This area includes the National Wax Museum, major theatres, cinemas, sporting and concert venues, including the Point Theatre where most major acts perform. We are also the most convenient hotel to the new Croke Park, the main venue for all Gaelic Games.

B&B from £40.00 to £45.00
€50.79 to €57.14

MARION HENEGHAN
Manager

Mastercard
Visa

40 40

Closed 24 - 28 December

BERKELEY COURT HOTEL

LANSDOWNE ROAD, BALLSBRIDGE, DUBLIN 4
TEL: 01-660 1711   FAX: 01-661 7238
EMAIL: berkeley@doylehotels.com

HOTEL ★★★★   MAP 8 O 11

Renowned as one of Dublin's premier hotels and host to high-profile international dignitaries and celebrities. This hotel exudes an old-world, club-like aura which is nicely complimented by a broad range of modern-day facilities and exceptional services. Located in Dublin's most prestigous district, overlooking some of Dublin's famous Georgian residences, the hotel is just 5 mins drive from the city centre and within 10 mins drive from the International Financial Services Centre.

WEB: www.doylehotels.com

B&B from £86.00 to £139.00
€109.20 to €176.49

JOE RUSSELL
General Manager

American Express
Diners
Mastercard
Visa

186 186

Weekend specials from £160.00

Inet

Open All Year

BEWLEY'S HOTEL BALLSBRIDGE

MERRION ROAD, BALLSBRIDGE, DUBLIN 4
TEL: 01-668 1111   FAX: 01-668 1999
EMAIL: res@bewleyshotel.com

HOTEL P   MAP 8 O 11

A new stylish concept in a prime location on Merrion Road combining the past with the present and accommodating you in style with over 200 deluxe bedrooms and spacious suites. Enjoy an exciting new dining experience in O'Connell's Restaurant within walking distance of the RDS. Bewley's Hotels... an independent collection.

WEB: www.bewleyshotels.com

Room Rate from £69.00 to £138.00
€87.61 to €175.22

CLIO O'GARA
General Manager

American Express
Diners
Mastercard
Visa

220 220

Inet

Closed 24 - 26 December

B&B rates are per person sharing per night incl. Breakfast

BEWLEY'S HOTEL NEWLANDS CROSS

NEWLANDS CROSS, NAAS ROAD (N7),
DUBLIN 22
TEL: 01-464 0140   FAX: 01-464 0900
EMAIL: res@bewleyshotels.com

HOTEL ★★★   MAP 8 O 11

A unique blend of quality, value and
flexibility for independent discerning
guests. Located just off the N7,
minutes from the M50, Dublin
airport and the city centre. Our large
spacious family size rooms are fully
equipped with all modern amenities.
Our Bewley's restaurant offers you a
range of dining options, from
traditional Irish breakfast to full table
service à la carte. Bewley's Hotels...
an independent collection.

WEB: www.bewleyshotels.com

Room Rate from £49.00 to £99.00
€62.22 to €125.70

DAMIEN MOLLOY
General Manager

American Express
Diners
Mastercard
Visa

☺ Free car parking

265 265

Closed 24 - 26 December

Dublin's Viking Adventure
Malahide Castle
Fry Model Railway
James Joyce Museum
Shaw Birthplace
Dublin Writers Museum

Something to write home about

Dear Sarah
    We're having an amazing time, Dublin is
even more than we expected.
    The history here is something else, it's
certainly the land of scholars (though we're
not sure about the saints yet).
We had planned to come home at the weekend
but we're having such a great time we
might just stay another week.

            Bye for now,
                Lots of love -
                Mum & Dad

P.S. A few must sees when in Dublin
Malahide Castle,
Fry Model Railway,
Dublin's Viking Adventure,
Dublin Writers Museum,
James Joyce Museum
Shaw Birthplace

FOR FURTHER INFORMATION PLEASE CONTACT:
Tel:+353 1 846 2184 Fax:+353 1 846 2537
enterprises@dublintourism.ie www.visitdublin.com

Dublin Tourism Enterprises

Room rates are per room per night

BEWLEY'S PRINCIPAL HOTEL

19/20 FLEET STREET, TEMPLE BAR, DUBLIN 2
TEL: 01-670 8122   FAX: 01-670 8103
EMAIL: bewleyshotel@eircom.net

HOTEL ★★★   MAP 8 O 11

We are not just another hotel in Dublin's exciting and vibrant Temple Bar district; we offer the finest traditions of quality and service from both Bewley's and Principal hotels. Small enough to maintain that feeling of old fashioned intimacy yet we have all the facilities expected from a modern 3*** hotel. Our location makes an ideal base for visiting Dublin's major attractions and its renowned shopping malls. Temple Bar passport available here.

WEB: bewleysprincipalhotel.com

B&B from £40.00 to £65.00
€50.79 to €82.53

CAROL MCNAMARA
General Manager

American Express
Diners
Mastercard
Visa

😊 2 B&B specials from £90.00

70   70

Closed 24 - 27 December

BLOOMS HOTEL

6 ANGLESEA STREET, TEMPLE BAR, DUBLIN 2
TEL: 01-671 5622   FAX: 01-671 5997
EMAIL: blooms@eircom.net

HOTEL N   MAP 8 O 11

Every city has one hotel that mirrors the life and humour of its people. Blooms is now at the centre of Dublin's cultural and artistic heart - Temple Bar. Being a small hotel, only 86 bedrooms, there is a feeling of intimacy and familiarity. The proximity of Blooms to both tourist and business locations makes it the ideal point for capturing the atmosphere and essence of Dublin city.

WEB: www.blooms.ie

B&B from £68.87 to £68.87
€87.45 to €87.45

GERALDINE LEECH
General Manager

American Express
Diners
Mastercard
Visa

😊 Weekend specials from £100.00

86   86

Closed 24 - 27 December

BROOKS HOTEL

DRURY STREET, DUBLIN 2
TEL: 01-670 4000   FAX: 01-670 4455
EMAIL: reservations@brookshotel.ie

HOTEL ★★★★   MAP 8 O 11

Located in the fashionable heart of Dublin city, 3 mins from Grafton St, Temple Bar and Trinity College. Brooks' is a designer/boutique hotel with high standards throughout, appealing in particular to the discerning international traveller. With superb accommodation, the Butter Lane bar, residents drawing room, Francesca's Restaurant and the Markets Room meeting room, Brooks is designed to cater for guests needs well into the next century. Secure parking available opposite the hotel.

WEB: www.iol.ie/bizpark/s/sinnott

B&B from £90.00 to £110.00
€114.28 to €139.67

ANNE MCKIERNAN
Resident Manager

American Express
Diners
Mastercard
Visa

😊 2 B&B weekend special from £135.00

75   75

Open All Year

B&B rates are per person sharing per night incl. Breakfast

BURLINGTON HOTEL

**UPPER LEESON STREET,
DUBLIN 4**
TEL: 01-660 5222 FAX: 01-660 8496
EMAIL: burlington@doylehotels.com

HOTEL ★★★★ MAP 8 O 11

Dublin's largest, best known and liveliest hotel. Its popularity with local Dubliners who frequent its busy bars and restaurants, allows overseas guests experience the 'craic' that is synonymous with Dublin. Centrally located just 10 mins walk from the city centre. The Burlington offers the broadest range of facilities in Dublin.

WEB: www.doylehotels.com

B&B from £82.00 to £134.00
€104.12 to €170.14

SEAMUS MCGOWAN
General Manager

American Express
Diners
Mastercard
Visa

☺ Weekend specials from £120.00

504 504

🛗 ■ Inet FAX

IRISH HOTELS FEDERATION

Open All Year

BUSWELLS HOTEL

**23/27 MOLESWORTH STREET,
DUBLIN 2**
TEL: 01-614 6500   FAX: 01-676 2090

HOTEL U MAP 8 O 11

One of Dublin's best kept secrets, this gracious hotel has been recently refurbished to the highest standards, offering every modern amenity, yet retaining the charm of it's Georgian era. Located in the quiet, elegant Molesworth Street, just minutes walk from St. Stephen's Green, Grafton Street, and easy reach of the city's major attractions.
Toll-free: 1800-473-9527.

B&B from £45.00 to £85.00
€57.14 to €107.93

PAUL GALLAGHER
General Manager

American Express
Diners
Mastercard
Visa

69 69

IRISH HOTELS FEDERATION

Closed 24 - 26 December

Room rates are per room per night

BUTLERS TOWN HOUSE

**44 LANSDOWNE ROAD,
BALLSBRIDGE, DUBLIN 4**
TEL: 01-667 4022   FAX: 01-667 3960
EMAIL: info@butlers-hotel.com

GUESTHOUSE ★★★★   MAP 8 O 11

An oasis of country tranquillity in the heart of Dublin, Butlers Town House is an experience as opposed to a visit. Opened in March 1997, fully restored to reflect it's former glory, but with all modern comforts from air-conditioning to modem points. Enjoy our gourmet breakfast in the conservatory or our light room service menu, available for the remainder of the day, in the comfort of your room. Secure parking is available.

WEB: www.butlers-hotel.com

Members Of Manor House Hotels

B&B from £65.00 to £90.00
€82.53 to €114.28

CHRIS VOS
General Manager

American Express
Diners
Mastercard
Visa

🖐🏨🛏📞⬜TC🅿️♿💻 Inet
19 19

HOTELS

Closed 23 - 26 December

CAMDEN COURT HOTEL

**CAMDEN STREET,
DUBLIN 2**
TEL: 01-475 9666   FAX: 01-475 9677
EMAIL: sales@camdencourthotel.com

HOTEL ★★★   MAP 8 O 11

The Camden Court Hotel is situated in the heart of Dublin within a 10 minute walk of Grafton Street. The hotel comprises of 246 well-appointed bedrooms all en suite with hairdryer, DD phone, colour TV, trouser press and tea/coffee making facilities. We also provide excellent conference facilities, restaurant and themed bar. Our state of the art leisure centre consists of a 16m swimming pool, sauna, steamroom, jacuzzi, solarium and a fully equipped gym. Secure carparking.

B&B from £55.00 to £90.00
€69.84 to €114.28

DERRY BRITTON
General Manager

American Express
Diners
Mastercard
Visa

😊 Weekend specials from £125.00

🖐🏨🛏📞⬜TC🅿️CM♿🍽🛏🅿️♿
246 246
alc 🖥 Inet FAX

HOTELS

Closed 24 December - 02 January

CAMDEN DE LUXE HOTEL

**84/87 CAMDEN STREET LOWER,
DUBLIN 2**
TEL: 01-478 0808   FAX: 01-475 0713
EMAIL: info@camden-deluxe.ie

HOTEL N   MAP 8 O 11

The Camden De Luxe Hotel, situated in the heart of Dublin's city centre, is just a short walk from the bustling shopping area of Grafton Street and the lively nightlife quarter of Temple Bar which boasts dozens of restaurants, bars and live music. The hotel is sited on the old Theatre De Luxe and has recently been tastefully renovated and comprises of 34 en suite rooms, Planet Murphy bar and restaurant and also offers corporate facilities.

WEB: www.camden-deluxe.ie

B&B from £70.00 to £100.00
€88.88 to €126.97

JUSTINE POWER
Manager

American Express
Diners
Mastercard
Visa

🖐🏨🛏📞⬜T♿🅿️alc ▪
34 34

Closed 24 - 27 December

B&B rates are per person sharing per night incl. Breakfast

On 1 January 1999, 00.00 a.m., the Euro became the official currency of 11 Member States of the European Union with a fixed conversion rate against their national currencies.

The Euro notes and coins will not appear until 1 January 2002, the new currency can be used by consumers, retailers, companies of all kinds and public administrations from 1 January 1999 in the form of "written money" - that is, by means of cheques, travellers' cheques, bank transfers, credit cards and electronic purses.

EURO CONVERSION RATES

1 Euro =		
40.3399	BEF	
1.95583	DEM	
166.386	ESP	
6.55957	FRF	
0.787564	IEP	
1936.27	ITL	
40.3399	LUF	
2.20371	NLG	
13.7603	ATS	
200.482	PTE	
5.94573	FIM	

CARMEL HOUSE

16 UPPER GARDINER STREET,
DUBLIN 1
TEL: 01-874 1639   FAX: 01-878 6903

GUESTHOUSE ★★★   MAP 8 O 11

Carmel House is located in the heart of Dublin's historic north inner city. Adjacent to all shopping, theatre and cinema facilities and situated on the main bus route to the airport, this small exclusive guesthouse rivals the best in its comfortable ambience. All bedrooms are en suite, have TV, DD phone and tea and coffee making facilities. Secure on-premises parking is included. For an Irish welcome contact Tom or Anne Smyth. No agents please.

B&B from £22.50 to £30.00
€28.57 to €38.09

TOM & ANNE SMYTH
Proprietors

Mastercard

Visa

⌂♨☎⊡P
9 9

IRISH HOTELS FEDERATION

Closed 15 - 31 December

CASSIDYS HOTEL

CAVENDISH ROW, UPPER
O'CONNELL ST., DUBLIN 1
TEL: 01-878 0555   FAX: 01-878 0687
EMAIL: rese@cassidys.iol.ie

HOTEL ★★★   MAP 8 O 11

A little gem in the heart of the city. Cassidys is located at the top of O'Connell St. opposite the Gate Theatre in three redbrick Georgian terraced houses. The building has been newly refurbished boasting 88 tastefully furnished bedrooms. The warm and welcoming atmosphere of Groomes Bar lends a traditional air to Cassidys. Fine dining is assured in the stylish surroundings of Restaurant 6. Limited parking for guests. Conference facilities available.

WEB: www.bookings.org/ie/hotels/cassidys

B&B from £40.00 to £54.00
€50.79 to €68.57

MARTIN CASSIDY
General Manager

American Express

Diners

Mastercard

Visa

88 88

IRISH HOTELS FEDERATION

Closed 24 - 27 December

CASTLE HOTEL

2-4 GARDINER ROW,
DUBLIN 1
TEL: 01-874 6949   FAX: 01-872 7674
EMAIL: hotels@indigo.ie

HOTEL ★★   MAP 8 O 11

Elegant Georgian hotel close to Dublin's main shopping district, renowned for its friendly service. One of Dublin's oldest hotels. Authentically restored the decor and furnishings offer modern comfort combined with olde world features: crystal chandeliers, antique mirrors, marble fireplaces and period staircases. The individually decorated rooms offer private bathroom, satellite TV, DD phone and beverage making facilities. The hotel has an intimate residents bar and private parking.

Members Of Castle Hotel Group

B&B from £35.00 to £45.00
€44.44 to €57.14

YVONNE EVANS
Manageress

Mastercard

Visa

☺ Midweek specials from £110.00

38 38

IRISH HOTELS FEDERATION

Closed 24 - 27 December

B&B rates are per person sharing per night incl. Breakfast

CEDAR LODGE

**98 MERRION ROAD,
DUBLIN 4**
TEL: 01-668 4410 FAX: 01-668 4533
EMAIL: info@cedarlodge.ie

GUESTHOUSE ★★★★   MAP 8 O 11

Cedar Lodge the luxurious alternative to a hotel. Edwardian style, intimate ambience and modern comforts combine to create a truly unique experience. Our 15 beautifully furnished en suite bedrooms are of international standard. This jewel among guesthouses is ideally located adjacent to the RDS and opposite the British Embassy in leafy Ballsbridge. 10 minutes from city centre, close to airport and car ferry terminals. Private guest car park. AA Premier Selected ◆◆◆◆◆.

WEB: www.cedarlodge.ie

B&B from £30.00 to £60.00
€38.09 to €76.18

GERARD & MARY DOODY
Owners

American Express
Mastercard
Visa

🏠🐾☎️🖥️C🍴❄️P🛗
15 15

IRISH HOTELS FEDERATION

Closed 22 - 28 December

CENTRAL HOTEL

**1-5 EXCHEQUER STREET,
DUBLIN 2**
TEL: 01-679 7302   FAX: 01-679 7303
EMAIL: reservations@centralhotel.ie

HOTEL ★★★   MAP 8 O 11

City centre location. Totally refurbished summer '97. 52 restaurants, numerous bars within walking distance. Temple bar, Dublin's left bank 1 block away. Trinity College, Grafton St and Christchurch 5 mins from hotel. Rooms en suite include DD phones, voicemail, hairdryers, tea/coffee making facilities, multi-channel TV. Residents bar. Private meeting rooms. Parking arranged.

WEB: www.centralhotel.ie

Members Of Best Western Hotels

B&B from £54.00 to £75.00
€68.57 to €95.23

JOHN-PAUL KAVANAGH
General Manager

American Express
Diners
Mastercard
Visa

✈️🍴

😊 Midweek specials from £120.00

😊🐾☎️🖥️🛏️T C🍴CMS🔒a/c
70 70

IRISH HOTELS FEDERATION

Closed 24 December - 04 January

Room rates are per room per night

CHARLEVILLE LODGE

268-272 NORTH CIRCULAR ROAD,
PHIBSBORO, DUBLIN 7
TEL: 01-838 6633   FAX: 01-838 5854
EMAIL: charleville@indigo.ie

GUESTHOUSE ★★★   MAP 8 O 11

Charleville Lodge is an elegant terrace of Victorian houses located minutes from the city centre and Temple Bar, en route to Dublin airport and car ferry. Close to Dublin City University and Botanic Gardens, our luxurious en suite bedrooms have direct dial phones and colour TV. Arrangements exist with a local golf club. With car park, we are RAC Highly Acclaimed. AA Selected ♦♦♦♦. Egon Ronay Guide and Premier Guesthouses. Visit our website.

WEB: www.charlevillelodge.ie

Members Of Logis of Ireland

B&B from £25.00 to £55.00
€31.74 to €69.84

VAL & ANNE STENSON
Owners

American Express
Diners
Mastercard
Visa

☺ Midweek specials from £70.00

30 28

Closed 20 - 26 December

CHIEF O'NEILL'S HOTEL

SMITHFIELD VILLAGE,
DUBLIN 7
TEL: 01-817 3838   FAX: 01-817 3839
EMAIL: reservations@chiefoneills.com

HOTEL P   MAP 8 O 11

Chief O'Neill's Hotel is dedicated to the memory of Francis O'Neill, Chicago Chief of Police and one of the most important individual collectors of Irish traditional music this century. Its theme is Irish traditional music expressed through Ireland's finest contemporary design. Each of the 73 en suite luxury rooms is equipped with a CD/Hi-Fi system, multi-channel TV, DD phone and tea/coffee facility. A state-of-the art gym, vibrant shopping area, restaurants and visitor attractions surround the hotel.

WEB: www.chiefoneills.com

Room Rate from £95.00 to £295.00
€120.63 to €374.57

RORY O'LEARY
General Manager

American Express
Diners
Mastercard
Visa

☺ Weekend specials 2 nights B&B
from £98.00

73 73

Open All Year

CLARA HOUSE

23 LEINSTER ROAD, RATHMINES,
DUBLIN 6
TEL: 01-497 5904   FAX: 01-497 5904

GUESTHOUSE ★★★   MAP 8 O 11

Clara House is a beautifully maintained listed Georgian house with many original features skillfully combined with modern day comforts. Each bedroom has en suite bathroom, remote control colour TV, direct dial telephone, radio/alarm clock, tea/coffee making facilities, hair dryer and trouser press. Clara House is a mile from downtown with bus stops 100 metres away. Bus stop for Ballsbridge/RDS is 200 metres. Secure parking at rear of house.

B&B from £30.00 to £35.00
€38.09 to €44.44

PHIL & PAUL REID
Proprietors

Mastercard
Visa

☺ 10% discount for 7 days

13 13

Open All Year

B&B rates are per person sharing per night incl. Breakfast

CLARENCE HOTEL

6-8 WELLINGTON QUAY,
DUBLIN 2
TEL: 01-670 9000   FAX: 01-670 7800
EMAIL: clarence@indigo.ie

HOTEL U   MAP 8 O 11

Built in 1852 and transformed into a contemporary boutique, design hotel in June 1996. Many of the hotel's original features have been revived. Antique panelling sets the backdrop for innovative furnishings. Located in the fashionable Temple Bar district and approx 30 mins from Dublin Airport. 50 rooms and suites, each one individually designed in contemporary, elegant style. The Tea Room and Octagon Bar provide a social focus for The Clarence and the Temple Bar area.

WEB: www.theclarence.ie

Room Rate from £195.00 to £210.00
€247.60 to €266.64

CLAIRE O'REILLY
General Manager

American Express
Diners
Mastercard
Visa

50 50

Closed 24 - 27 December

CLARION STEPHENS HALL HOTEL AND SUITES

THE EARLSFORT CENTRE,
LOWER LEESON STREET, DUBLIN 2
TEL: 01-638 1111   FAX: 01-638 1122
EMAIL: stephens@premgroup.ie

HOTEL ★★★   MAP 8 O 11

Dublin's first all-suite hotel, beside St. Stephen's Green in the heart of Georgian Dublin. Tastefully furnished suites with separate living rooms and fax machines and CD players. Morel's at Stephens Hall, open all day, is popular locally as a great place to eat. Suites available for nightly or long-term occupancy. Free underground car parking. Toll Free USA for Clarion Hotels: 1800.CLARION (1800 252 7466).

WEB: www.premgroup.com

Members Of Choice Hotels Ireland

B&B from £94.00 to £144.00
€119.36 to €182.84

JIM MURPHY
Managing Director

American Express
Diners
Mastercard
Visa

37 37

inet FAX

Closed 24 - 28 December

CLIFDEN GUESTHOUSE

32 GARDINER PLACE,
DUBLIN 1
TEL: 01-874 6364   FAX: 01-874 6122
EMAIL: bnb@indigo.ie

GUESTHOUSE ★★★   MAP 8 O 11

A refurbished city centre Georgian home. Our private car park provides security for guests cars, even after check-out, free. All rooms have shower, WC, WHB, TV, direct dial phone and tea making facilities. We cater for single, twin, double, triple and family occupancies. Convenient to airport, ferryports, Busarus (bus station) and DART. We are only 5 minutes walk from O'Connell Street. AA and RAC approved.

WEB: www.clifdenhouse.com

Members Of Premier Guesthouses

B&B from £25.00 to £55.00
€31.74 to €69.84

JACK & MARY LALOR
Proprietors

Mastercard
Visa

Midweek specials from £70.00

14 14

Open All Year

Room rates are per room per night

CLIFTON COURT HOTEL

O'CONNELL BRIDGE,
DUBLIN 1
TEL: 01-874 3535   FAX: 01-878 6698
EMAIL: cliftoncourt@eircom.net

HOTEL ★★   MAP 8 O 11

Situated in the city centre overlooking the River Liffey at O'Connell Bridge. Beside Dublin's two premier shopping streets. The Abbey Theatre, Point Depot, Tara and Amien Street, Dart/Train stations and Bus Aras (airport terminal) are within 3 minutes walk. Our modern bedrooms are equipped with TV and tea/coffee making facilities. The hotel also incorporates one of Dublin's oldest and most famous pubs known as Lanigans (est 1822) which hosts Irish traditional music.

Room Rate from £35.20 to £43.45
€44.69 to €55.17

TIANA MCHALE
Manager

American Express
Mastercard
Visa

HOTELS FEDERATION

30 30

Closed 24 - 27 December

CLONTARF CASTLE HOTEL

CLONTARF,
DUBLIN 3
TEL: 01-833 2321   FAX: 01-833 0418
EMAIL: info@clontarfcastle.ie

HOTEL ★★★★   MAP 8 O 11

This historic castle, dating back to 1172, has recently undergone a £13m refurbishment transforming it into a luxurious 4**** deluxe, 111 room hotel. Ideally situated only 2 miles from the city centre and 5 from the airport. With superb facilities incl uniquely designed rooms equipped with all the modern facilities. Templar's Bistro specialising in modern international cuisine, 2 unique bars, state of the art conference and banqueting facilities and stunning lobby. Free carparking.

B&B from £60.00 to £90.00
€76.18 to €114.28

ENDA O'MEARA
Managing Director

American Express
Diners
Mastercard
Visa

111 111

HOTELS FEDERATION

Closed 24 - 25 December

COMFORT INN, TALBOT STREET

95-98 TALBOT STREET,
DUBLIN 1
TEL: 01-874 9202   FAX: 01-874 9672
EMAIL: info@talbot.premgroup.ie

GUESTHOUSE ★★★   MAP 8 O 11

Situated just off O'Connell St, the Comfort Inn provides an ideal base to explore Dublin's vibrant city. Lively restaurants, bars, theatres, shops and famous tourist attractions are located in the immediate vicinity. Connolly train station and the central bus depot are within short walking distance. All rooms are en suite with DD phone, tea/coffee facilities and cable TV. Car parking on request. Meeting rooms available.

WEB: www.premgroup.ie

Members Of Choice Hotels Ireland

Room Rate from £30.00 to £47.50
€38.09 to €60.31

JOANNA DOYLE
Manager

American Express
Diners
Mastercard
Visa

Weekend special 2 B&B from £60.00

48 48

HOTELS FEDERATION

Closed 24 - 27 December

B&B rates are per person sharing per night incl. Breakfast

CONRAD INTERNATIONAL DUBLIN

EARLSFORT TERRACE,
DUBLIN 2
TEL: 01-676 5555 FAX: 01-676 5424
EMAIL: info@conrad-international.ie

HOTEL ★★★★★ MAP 8 O 11

Just off St. Stephen's Green, the Conrad International is a short walk from the business, shopping and cultural centres of the city. 191 luxury rooms incl 9 suites with colour TV, free in-house movies, radio, DD phone, writing desk, trouser press, air conditioning, mini bar, 2 fluffy bathrobes and 24 hour room service. Two restaurants, the Alexandra and Plurabelle Brasserie and one of the most traditional Irish pubs in town, Alfie Byrnes. Fitness centre. Courtesy of Choice Member.

WEB: www.conrad-international.ie

B&B from £115.00 to £150.00
€146.02 to €190.46

MICHAEL GOVERNEY
General Manager

American Express
Diners
Mastercard
Visa

☺ Weekend specials from £210.00

191 191

Open All Year

COPPER BEECH COURT GUEST HOUSE

16 HOLLYBROOK PARK, CLONTARF,
DUBLIN 3
TEL: 01-833 3390 FAX: 01-853 2013

GUESTHOUSE ★★★ MAP 8 O 11

A Victorian building of historic interest, built for a wealthy merchant and carefully restored, offers an air of quiet luxury and elegant decor. All rooms en suite, equipped with multi-channel TV, DD phone and dressed with real Irish linen. Friendly staff ensure a superb standard of service. City centre shopping 15 minutes, airport 20 minutes. Choice of golf courses include Royal Dublin, Portmarnock and St Margarets.

B&B from £30.00 to £60.00
€38.09 to €76.18

FRANCES CAMPBELL
Owner

Mastercard
Visa

9 9

Open All Year

DAVENPORT HOTEL

AT MERRION SQUARE,
DUBLIN 2
TEL: 01-607 3500 FAX: 01-661 5663
EMAIL: davenportres@ocallaghanhotels.ie

HOTEL U MAP 8 O 11

This elegant deluxe hotel is located at Merrion Square in Dublin city centre, beside Trinity College and just a 5 minute walk from the principal business, shopping and cultural districts. Fully air-conditioned with 115 deluxe guestrooms, state of the art conference and banqueting suites, discreet drawing room bar and fine dining restaurant; it offers that rare blend of the elegance of the 1800's combined with the high expectations of today's guests. Free private valet car parking.
USA Toll Free 1800 5699983.

WEB: www.davenporthotel.ie

Member Of O'Callaghan Hotels

B&B from £90.00 to £139.00
€114.28 to €176.49

WELDON MATHER
General Manager

American Express
Diners
Mastercard
Visa

☺ Weekend specials from £167.00

115 115

Inet

Open All Year

Room rates are per room per night

DERGVALE HOTEL

4 GARDINER PLACE,
DUBLIN 1
TEL: 01-874 4753   FAX: 01-874 8276

HOTEL ★★   MAP 8 O 11

The Dergvale hotel is located within walking distance of all principal shopping areas, cinemas, museums, Trinity College, Dublin Castle and airport bus. Luxury bedrooms with showers en suite, colour TV and direct dial telephone. Fully licensed. A courteous and efficient staff are on hand to make your stay an enjoyable one. The hotel is under the personal supervision of Gerard and Nancy Nolan.

B&B from £28.50 to £38.50
€36.19 to €48.88

GERARD NOLAN
Owner

American Express
Mastercard
Visa

☺ 2 nights value weekend from £70.00

20 17

IRISH HOTELS FEDERATION

Closed 24 December - 07 January

DONNYBROOK HALL

6 BELMONT AVENUE,
DONNYBROOK, DUBLIN 4
TEL: 01-269 1633   FAX: 01-269 1633

GUESTHOUSE ★★★   MAP 8 O 11

Situated in the fashionable Donnybrook district of Dublin, this beautifully restored Victorian residence retains many original features. Each of our en suite rooms are of international standard and are individually designed in elegant style. This guesthouse is ideally located just a short walk from the cultural, commercial and entertinament heart of the city. Nearby is the RDS, RTE, UCD, Lansdowne Road, St. Stephens Green and Trinity College.

B&B from £30.00 to £50.00
€38.09 to €63.49

DOROTHY GLENNON
Owner

Mastercard
Visa

☺ Midweek specials from £90.00

6 6

Open All Year

DONNYBROOK LODGE

131 STILLORGAN ROAD,
DONNYBROOK, DUBLIN 4
TEL: 01-283 7333   FAX: 01-260 4770

GUESTHOUSE ★★★   MAP 8 O 11

Relax in comfortable surroundings in the heart of Dublin's most exclusive area. Ideally situated close to city centre, ferryports and adjacent to RDS, Lansdowne, UCD and RTE. A short stroll from a host of restaurants and entertainment. Recently refurbished, our well-appointed rooms feature en suites, DD phone and TV. Private parking available. Enjoy a leisurely breakfast in our elegant dining room, overlooking gardens. A relaxed atmosphere and warm welcome awaits you.

B&B from £25.00 to £40.00
€31.74 to €50.79

AIDAN & AILEEN O'ROURKE

Mastercard
Visa

☺ Midweek specials from £60.00

7 7

IRISH HOTELS FEDERATION

Open All Year

B&B rates are per person sharing per night incl. Breakfast

DRUMCONDRA HOUSE

27 LOWER DRUMCONDRA ROAD,
DUBLIN 9
TEL: 01-855 0918   FAX: 01-836 5549

GUESTHOUSE U   MAP 8 O 11

Drumcondra House is situated on the main thoroughfare between Dublin international airport and the city centre. It boasts exquisitely decorated en suite rooms, each with its own TV, DD phone, tea/coffee making facilities and is furnished in solid pine. This family run guesthouse is 5 mins from city centre and Temple Bar, having theatres, restaurants and shops all within walking distance.

B&B from £25.00 to £35.00
€31.74 to €44.44

CLARE TYNAN

Mastercard
Visa

6 6

Closed 23 - 27 December

DRURY COURT HOTEL

28-30 LOWER STEPHEN STREET,
DUBLIN 2
TEL: 01-475 1988   FAX: 01-478 5730
EMAIL: druryct@indigo.ie

HOTEL ★★★   MAP 8 O 11

Located in the heart of Dublin's theatre and most fashionable shopping area. The Drury Court Hotel comprises of 30 large luxurious en suite bedrooms and two suites, all with DD phone, computer lines, fax lines, multi channel TV/ radio and secure public parking. The Drury Court, incorporating the fashionable Digges Lane Bar, has everything of interest for the discerning visitor and is an ideal location for todays business person. National Museum, Art Gallery, St Stephens Green nearby.

WEB: www.indigo.ie/~druryct/

Members Of MinOtel Ireland Hotel Group

B&B from £60.00 to £85.00
€76.18 to €107.93

RACHEL SEXTON

American Express
Diners
Mastercard
Visa

32 32

Inet

I R I S H
HOTELS
FEDERATION

Closed 23 - 27 December

EARL OF KILDARE HOTEL

KILDARE STREET,
DUBLIN 2
TEL: 01-679 4388   FAX: 01-679 4914

HOTEL ★   MAP 8 O 11

Overlooking Trinity College, close to Dublin Castle, Dail Eireann and the National Gallery and two minutes walk from Dublin's main shopping area, Grafton Street. All rooms are elegantly furnished with colour TV, DD phone, tea/coffee making facilities and hairdryer. Fax service is also available. A public car park is located nearby. An excellent carvery lunch is available daily followed by an evening menu served until late in the Kildare bar.

WEB: www.earlofkildarehotel.com

B&B from £35.00 to £45.00
€44.44 to €57.14

RICHARD CROSS
Manager

American Express
Diners
Mastercard
Visa

32 24

Closed 24 - 26 December

Room rates are per room per night

EGAN'S GUESTHOUSE

7/9 IONA PARK, GLASNEVIN,
DUBLIN 9
TEL: 01-830 3611   FAX: 01-830 3312
EMAIL: eganshouse@eircom.net

GUESTHOUSE ★★★   MAP 8 O 11

Egans house is a charming 3*** family run guesthouse situated away from the bustle of centre city yet convenient to the airport, ferryports, city centre and within walking distance of the Botanical Gardens. There are 23 rooms, all beautifully decorated, each with bathrooms, TV, phone, hair dryer and tea/coffee facilities. Our comfortable drawing rooms invite you to enjoy and relax in their pleasant, warm atmosphere. Car parking. US freephone 1 800 937 9767.

WEB: www.holiday/ireland.com

Members Of Premier Guesthouses

B&B from £28.00 to £31.00
€35.55 to €39.36

SINEAD EGAN
Proprietor

Mastercard

Visa

Midweek specials from £75.00 low season

23 23

Closed 24 - 27 December

EGLINTON MANOR

83 EGLINTON ROAD,
DONNYBROOK, DUBLIN 4
TEL: 01-269 3273   FAX: 01-269 7527

GUESTHOUSE ★★★★   MAP 8 O 11

This gracious red-bricked Victorian Old House which has just been refurbished to the highest standard is situated in the very elegant suburb of Donnybrook. It is very close to the city centre and the RDS. All rooms have a bathroom and tea/coffee makers, TV, radio, and direct dial telephones. Private free car parking. 4**** premises with lovely garden.

B&B from £35.00 to £40.00
€44.44 to €50.79

ROSALEEN CAHILL O'BRIEN

American Express

Mastercard

Visa

7 7

Open All Year

EIGHTY EIGHT

88 PEMBROKE ROAD,
BALLSBRIDGE, DUBLIN 4
TEL: 01-660 0277   FAX: 01-660 0291

GUESTHOUSE ★★★★   MAP 8 O 11

Eighty Eight is conveniently located in Ballsbridge adjacent to St. Stephen's Green, the American Embassy, the Royal Dublin Society, Herbert Park and Lansdowne Road. Each of our 40 en suite rooms is equipped to today's exacting international standards. Eighty Eight offers it's guests a finely tuned blend of the best traditions of Irish hospitality with a combination of comfort, convenience, service and outstanding value.

B&B from £40.00 to £70.00
€50.79 to €88.88

MICHEL COLACI
General Manager

American Express

Diners

Mastercard

Visa

40 40

Closed 22 December - 02 January

B&B rates are per person sharing per night incl. Breakfast

FITZSIMONS HOTEL

**21-22 WELLINGTON QUAY,
TEMPLE BAR, DUBLIN 2**
TEL: 01-677 9315 FAX: 01-677 9387
EMAIL: info@fitzsimons-hotel.com

HOTEL ★★ MAP 8 O 11

The Fitzsimons, situated on the banks of the River Liffey, in the heart of the city's thriving Left Bank - Temple Bar. Its location offers the visitor doorstep access to this vibrant, colourful and exciting locale and all it has to offer - theatres, galleries, studios, bars, restaurants, live music venues and alternative shops. Home to Dublin's top entertainment venues: Fitzsimon's Bar & Restaurant, and Club.

B&B from £50.00 to £80.00
€63.49 to €101.58

KEVIN FITZSIMONS
Proprietor

American Express

Mastercard

Visa

⌂🅿🚲☎🖥♨Ⓣ C CM♪ 🎵🎵 alc
26 26

Closed 24 - 26 December

FITZWILLIAM

**41 UPPER FITZWILLIAM STREET,
DUBLIN 2**
TEL: 01-662 5155 FAX: 01-676 7488

GUESTHOUSE ★★★ MAP 8 O 11

Centrally located in the heart of elegant Georgian Dublin, minutes walk from St. Stephen's Green, National Concert Hall and Galleries. Enjoy the charm of this spacious town house. Rooms with en suite facilities, colour TV, direct dial telephone, clock/radios and hair dryers. Overnight car parking available. Relax at our excellent restaurant. Our friendly staff will ensure your stay is a relaxed and memorable one.

B&B from £35.00 to £42.50
€44.44 to €53.96

DECLAN CARNEY
Manager

American Express

Diners

Mastercard

Visa

⌂🅿🚲☎ Ⓣ C P SY alc
12 12

Closed 21 - 31 December

FITZWILLIAM HOTEL

**ST. STEPHEN'S GREEN,
DUBLIN 2**
TEL: 01-478 7000 FAX: 01-478 7878
EMAIL: enq@fitzwilliamh.com

HOTEL N MAP 8 O 11

A modern classic uniquely positioned on St. Stephen's Green, paces away from Grafton Street, Ireland's premier shopping location. Understated luxury, a fresh approach and impeccable service make the Fitzwilliam the perfect retreat for business and pleasure travelers. Dine in the highly acclaimed Restaurant Peacock Alley or Christopher's all day brasserie. Other facilities include three conference rooms, complimentary car parking for all residents and Ireland's largest roof garden.

WEB: www.fitzwilliamh.com

Members Of Summit Hotels

Room Rate from £105.00 to £105.00
€133.32 to €133.32

JOHN KAVANAGH
General Manager

American Express

Diners

Mastercard

Visa

☺ 2 B&B from £160.00

⌂🅿🚲☎🖥♨Ⓣ C ⬆CMP🅿 alc
130 130

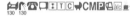

Open All Year

Room rates are per room per night

FITZWILLIAM PARK

5 FITZWILLIAM SQUARE,
DUBLIN 2
TEL: 01-662 8280   FAX: 01-662 8281
EMAIL: info@fitzpark.ie

GUESTHOUSE ★★★★   MAP 8 O 11

Fitzwilliam Park is a luxurious and beautifully restored Georgian town house situated in one of Dublin's most elegant squares, a short stroll from Dublin City centre. Each room with its high ceilings, decorative friezes, tall windows, fine drapes, pastel decor, gold framed mirrors and picture's, is a stylish reminder of Georgian grace. All 20 bedrooms are ensuite with telephone, satellite TV, computer point, tea/coffee tray and hair care facilities. Enjoy breakfast in the Grand Salon. Conference facilities provided.

WEB: www.fitzpark.ie

Member of Manor House Hotels

Room Rate from £75.00 to £150.00
€95.23 to €190.46

CATHERINE O'REILLY
General Manager

American Express
Diners
Mastercard
Visa

20   20

Closed 23 - 27 December

FORTE TRAVELODGE

AUBURN AVENUE ROUNDABOUT,
NAVAN ROAD, DUBLIN 15
TEL: 1800-709709   FAX: 01-820 2808

HOTEL U   MAP 8 O 11

Situated on the N3 route only 5 miles from Dublin city centre, just off the M50 Dublin ring road and mins from the Airport, this superb hotel offers comfortable yet affordable accommodation. Each room is large enough to sleep up to three adults, a child under 12 and a baby in a cot. Price is fixed per room regardless of the number of occupants. Each room has ensuite bathroom, colour satellite TV including Sky Sports and Sky Movies and DD phone. Sited next to Little Chef restaurant.

Room Rate from £44.95 to £59.95
€57.07 to €76.12

BRIDGET AIKEN
General Manager

American Express
Diners
Mastercard
Visa

60   60

Open All Year

GEORGE FREDERIC HANDEL HOTEL

16-18 FISHAMBLE STREET,
CHRISTCHURCH, TEMPLE BAR, DUBLIN 8
TEL: 01-670 9400   FAX: 01-670 9410
EMAIL: info@handelshotel.com

HOTEL U   MAP 8 O 11

A modern hotel, steeped in musical history, situated on the edge of Temple Bar, next to Christchurch Cathedral. Within easy walking distance of main tourist attractions and financial districts, our popular small hotel is built on the site where Handel's Messiah was first performed in 1742. We will offer you a warm welcome and a high standard of accommodation for your stay in Dublin.

WEB: www.handelshotel.com

B&B from £35.00 to £70.00
€44.44 to €88.88

BARBARA BRANGAN
Sales & Marketing Exec.

American Express
Diners
Mastercard
Visa

40   40

Closed 24 - 27 December

B&B rates are per person sharing per night incl. Breakfast

GEORGIAN COURT GUESTHOUSE

77-79 LOWER GARDINER STREET, DUBLIN 1
TEL: 01-855 7872   FAX: 01-855 5715

GUESTHOUSE U   MAP 8 O 11

Situated in the centre of Dublin city, 200m from O'Connell St, Dublin's main shopping street, 50m from the city centre bus station. The 41 bus direct from Dublin airport stops outside our door. 150m to Connolly rail station. 10 mins walk to Temple Bar. Secure car park available. Built in 1805 and located in a fine Georgian terrace. All rooms are en suite, colour TV, tea/coffee facilities, internal phones, hairdryer, electric iron available.

B&B from £25.00 to £35.00
€31.74 to €44.44

EILEEN CONROY
Owner

Mastercard
Visa

43 43

Closed 24 - 27 December

GEORGIAN HOUSE HOTEL

18 BAGGOT STREET LOWER, DUBLIN 2
TEL: 01-661 8832   FAX: 01-661 8834
EMAIL: hotel@georgianhouse.ie

HOTEL ★★★   MAP 8 O 11

This very comfortable 200 year old house with new extension in the heart of Georgian Dublin, next to St. Stephen's Green and a 5 minute walk to the major sites including Trinity College, galleries, museums, cathedrals, theatres and to fashionable shopping streets and pubs. Bathrooms en suite, TV, telephones. Perfect location for business or holiday travellers and offers all the amenities of an exclusive small hotel. Private car park.

B&B from £45.00 to £73.00
€57.14 to €92.69

ANNETTE O'SULLIVAN
Managing Director

American Express
Diners
Mastercard
Visa

😊 Midweek special from £120.00

21 21

IRISH HOTELS FEDERATION

Open All Year

GLASNEVIN MAPLES HOTEL

79-81 IONA ROAD, GLASNEVIN, DUBLIN 9
TEL: 01-830 4227   FAX: 01-830 3874

HOTEL ★★   MAP 8 O 11

Gracious Edwardian house, refurbished hotel is family run and offers a friendly atmosphere and personal attention to your needs. Located 1 mile from city centre and 3 miles from Dublin Airport the hotel is within walking distance of the Botanic Gardens and Croke Park, also close to the Point Depot and Ferryport. Our Lounge Bar offers live weekend entertainment (traditional Irish and Jazz). Exceptional restaurant, banqueting and conference facilities.

B&B from £35.00 to £45.00
€44.44 to €57.14

GRAHAM & LIZ MULLAN

Mastercard
Visa

😊 Weekend specials from £95.00

22 22

IRISH HOTELS FEDERATION

Open All Year

Room rates are per room per night

GLEN GUESTHOUSE

84 LOWER GARDINER STREET,
DUBLIN 1
TEL: 01-855 1374   FAX: 01-456 6901
EMAIL: theglen@eircom.net

GUESTHOUSE ★★★   MAP 8 O 11

The Glen is a beautifully restored
and maintained guesthouse. Located
in the heart of Dublin city, adjacent
to shops, theatres, cinemas,
galleries, museums and Dublin's
famous night spots. Close to bus
and train stations on route to airport.
Rooms en suite, TV, D.D. phones,
tea and coffee available.

WEB: homepage.eircom.net/~theglen

B&B from £20.00 to £35.00
€25.39 to €44.44

THREASA MURRAY
Manageress

Mastercard

Visa

🏠🔥🕿☎TC🥢♪🏃S
15 15

Open All Year

GLENOGRA HOUSE

64 MERRION ROAD, BALLSBRIDGE,
DUBLIN 4
TEL: 01-668 3661   FAX: 01-668 3698
EMAIL: glenogra@indigo.ie

GUESTHOUSE ★★★★   MAP 8 O 11

Located opposite the RDS and Four
Seasons Hotel, close to city centre,
bus, rail, embassies, restaurants,
car ferries. Glenogra provides luxury
and elegance in a personalised,
family run environment. The cosy
drawing room is perfect for a
restoring afternoon tea. En suite
bedrooms are decorated in harmony
with a period residence, are all non-
smoking with phone, TV, coffee
making facilities. Private car parking.
Attractive off season specials.
AA ◆◆◆◆◆.

Members Of Premier Guesthouses

Room Rate from £45.00 to £75.00
€57.14 to €95.23

CHERRY AND SEAMUS MCNAMEE
Proprietors

American Express

Diners

Mastercard

Visa

😊 Midweek specials from £90.00

🏠🔥🕿☎TC✷P🅂🍴🍷
10 10

TRISH
HOTELS
FEDERATION

Closed 20 - 31 December

GLENVEAGH TOWNHOUSE

31 NORTHUMBERLAND ROAD,
BALLSBRIDGE, DUBLIN 4
TEL: 01-668 4612   FAX: 01-668 4559
EMAIL: glenveagh@eircom.net

GUESTHOUSE ★★★   MAP 8 O 11

Charming Victorian residence in the
most exclusive and sought after
neighbourhood in Dublin. Our
proximity to Trinity College,
Lansdowne Road, The R.D.S., Point
Depot, Government buildings, and
fashionable Grafton Street is ideal for
business people and tourists alike. A
family run business where every
care is taken to guarantee a most
pleasant stay whilst away from
home. A haven of outstanding
quality, offering true Irish hospitality
and warmth.

WEB: www.glenveagh.com

B&B from £60.00 to £120.00
€76.18 to €152.37

JOSEPH CUNNINGHAM
Proprietor

Mastercard

Visa

🏠🔥🕿☎TC✷P
10 10

Closed 22 December - 03 January

B&B rates are per person sharing per night incl. Breakfast

GRAFTON HOUSE

26-27 SOUTH GREAT GEORGES
STREET, DUBLIN 2
TEL: 01-679 2041   FAX: 01-677 9715
EMAIL: graftonguesthouse@eircom.net

GUESTHOUSE ★★★   MAP 8 O 11

This charming 3*** guesthouse ideally located in the heart of the city within 2 minutes walking distance of Dublin's premier shopping centre Grafton Street, St. Stephen's Green, Trinity College and Dublin Castle. All bedrooms newly decorated with bathroom/shower, direct dial telephone, TV, hairdryers, tea and coffee making facilities. Car parking close by in enclosed car park. Grafton House is the ideal location for business or holidays.

B&B from £32.00 to £50.00
€40.63 to €63.49

BRIDGET COLLINS

Mastercard
Visa

😊 Midweek specials from £96.00

15 15

Closed 23 - 30 December

GRAFTON PLAZA HOTEL

JOHNSONS PLACE,
DUBLIN 2
TEL: 01-475 0888   FAX: 01-475 0908
EMAIL: info@graftonplaza.ie

HOTEL ★★★   MAP 8 O 11

Nestling in the heart of Dublin's most fashionable and cultural areas, the Grafton Plaza Hotel presents the facade of a traditional Georgian townhouse while affording a wealth of comforts for the most discerning guest. The hotel provides the luxury of its superbly appointed en suite bedrooms, each designed to afford the highest levels of comfort. The hotel is just two minutes walk from Grafton Street.

B&B from £73.00 to £79.00
€92.69 to €100.31

JOSEPHINE PEPPER
General Manager

American Express
Diners
Mastercard
Visa

😊 Midweek specials from £165.00

75 75

Inet

Closed 24 - 26 December

GREEN ISLE HOTEL

NAAS ROAD,
DUBLIN 22
TEL: 01-459 3406   FAX: 01-459 2178
EMAIL: greenisle@doylehotels.com

HOTEL ★★★   MAP 8 O 11

Superior modern 3*** hotel offering high quality international service standards and friendly Irish service. Strategically located in Dublin south west, 12 miles from Dublin international airport and 7 miles from Dublin city centre. The hotel is within 5-10 mins drive from Dublin's most important multi-national business parks and 3 mins drive of major national routes leading to the south and west of Ireland.

WEB: www.doylehotels.com

B&B from £47.00 to £64.00
€59.68 to €81.26

JIM FLYNN
General Manager

American Express
Diners
Mastercard
Visa

😊 Weekend specials from £84.00

90 90

Open All Year

GRESHAM HOTEL

23 UPPER O'CONNELL STREET,
DUBLIN 1
TEL: 01-874 6881 FAX: 01-878 7175
EMAIL: ryan@indigo.ie

HOTEL ★★★★ MAP 8 O 11

The Gresham provides the ultimate in luxury and service. 288 bedrooms incl. 100 new air-conditioned superior rooms in the Lavery Wing and 6 penthouse suites. A conference centre with 10 air-conditioned suites, and a fitness centre complement the spacious ground floor facilities which feature the Aberdeen Restaurant, Toddys Bar, the Gresham lounge and a fully equipped business centre. Multi-storey carpark (£5/day). 15 minutes drive to airport. AA, RAC and Egon Ronay recommended.

B&B from £90.00 to £140.00
€114.28 to €177.76

SHAY LIVINGSTONE
General Manager

American Express
Diners
Mastercard
Visa

☺ Weekend specials from £109.00

288 288

Open All Year

HARCOURT HOTEL

60 HARCOURT STREET,
DUBLIN 2
TEL: 01-478 3677 FAX: 01-475 2013
EMAIL: reservations@harcourthotel.ie

HOTEL ★★★ MAP 8 O 11

Centrally located close to Grafton St and St Stephen's Green, convenient to the city's theatres, museums and tourist attractions. Our elegantly refurbished bedrooms are fully equipped and include tea/coffee making facilities. Once the home of George Bernard Shaw, now the home of traditional Irish music.

Members Of Holiday Ireland Hotels

B&B from £35.00 to £75.00
€44.44 to €95.23

MARY CASHIN
General Manager

American Express
Diners
Mastercard
Visa

46 46

Closed 24 - 25 December

HARDING HOTEL

COPPER ALLEY, FISHAMBLE STREET,
DUBLIN 2
TEL: 01-679 6500 FAX: 01-679 6504
EMAIL: harding@usit.ie

HOTEL ★★ MAP 8 O 11

Harding Hotel is a stylish city centre hotel located within Dublin's thriving left bank, Temple Bar. This historic area with its cobbled streets offers the visitor a variety of shops, restaurants, pubs and theatres. All 53 rooms are equipped to the highest standard with DD phone, TV, hairdryer and tea/coffee making facilities. The lively Darkey Kelly's bar & restaurant is the perfect setting for business or pleasure. Overnight parking is available at special rates in nearby car park.

Members Of USIT Accommodation Centres

Room Rate from £45.00 to £65.00
€57.14 to €82.53

EDEL KINSELLA
Manager

Mastercard
Visa

53 53

Closed 23 - 27 December

B&B rates are per person sharing per night incl. Breakfast

HARRINGTON HALL

70 HARCOURT STREET,
DUBLIN 2
TEL: 01-475 3497 FAX: 01-475 4544
EMAIL: harringtonhall@eircom.net

GUESTHOUSE ★★★★ MAP 8 O 11

Harrington Hall with its secure private parking in the heart of Georgian Dublin, provides the perfect location for holiday and business visitors alike to enjoy the surrounding galleries, museums, cathedrals, theatres, fashionable shopping streets, restaurants and pubs. All rooms are equipped to todays exacting standards with en suite, DD phone, hospitality tray, trouser press and multi channel TV, access to fax facilities, e-mail and internet. All floors are serviced by elevator.

WEB: www.harringtonhall.com

B&B from £45.00 to £70.00
€57.14 to €88.88

HENRY KING
Proprietor

American Express
Mastercard
Visa

😊 Midweek specials from £135.00

🛏🛌☎🖥🚻TC🍴P
28 28

IRISH HOTELS FEDERATION

Open All Year

HARRINGTON HOUSE

21 HARRINGTON STREET, SOUTH
CIRCULAR ROAD, DUBLIN 2
TEL: 01-475 4008   FAX: 01-478 0877
EMAIL: hubandhouse@eircom.net

GUESTHOUSE N MAP 8 O 11

Harrington House is a delightful residence for tourists and business travellers alike. Situated 10-15 mins walk from the heart of the city: vibrant Temple Bar district with it's restaurants pubs & clubs. Trinity College, National Concert Hall, Dublin Castle, Cathedrals, St Patrick's Christ Church. Grafton St, Stephen's Green, Henry St for shopping. All rooms are en suite with cable TV, DD phone, hairdryers, trouserpress and lap-top facilities. Secure free carparking. Bus stops nearby.

WEB: www.hubandhouse.ie

B&B from £25.00 to £50.00
€31.74 to €63.49

RONALD MCCOURT
Owner

Mastercard
Visa

🛏🛌☎🖥TC🍴P🚭S Inet FAX
8 8

IRISH HOTELS FEDERATION

Open All Year

HARVEY'S GUEST HOUSE

11 UPPER GARDINER STREET,
DUBLIN 1
TEL: 01-874 8384   FAX: 01-874 5510

GUESTHOUSE ★★★ MAP 8 O 11

This popular Georgian Guest House, only minutes away from City Centre and conveniently reached by the number 41 airport bus, 1st stop on Upper Gardiner St, by the church. All rooms en suite, TV, hairdryer and telephone. We also have free car parking. Our aim is to make our visitors stay as pleasant and homely as possible.

B&B from £28.00 to £50.00
€35.55 to €63.49

EILISH FLOOD
Proprietor

Mastercard
Visa

😊 Midweek specials from £67.50

🛏🛌☎🖥TCP
14 14

IRISH HOTELS FEDERATION

Open All Year

Room rates are per room per night

HAZELBROOK HOUSE

85 LOWER GARDINER STREET,
DUBLIN 1
TEL: 01-836 5003   FAX: 01-855 0310

GUESTHOUSE N   MAP 8 O 11

Hazelbrook House offers superb accommodation with 19 en suite rooms including family rooms. All have remote control TV, iron, tea/coffee facilities and hairdryer. We provide a good Irish breakfast, cater for vegetarians and childrens special needs. Fax/phone on premises. For tourists there are attractions nearby: Trinity College, St Stephens Green and Dublin's trendy Temple Bar area. Our staff are always friendly and, most important, a warm welcome is assured.

B&B from £30.00 to £35.00
€38.09 to €44.44

DOLORES BURNETT
Manager

Mastercard

Visa

🏨🛏️☎️🅃🄲CMP▪️
19 19

Closed 23 - 28 December

HEDIGAN'S

TULLYALLAN HOUSE, 14 HOLLYBROOK
PARK, CLONTARF, DUBLIN 3
TEL: 01-853 1663   FAX: 01-833 3337

GUESTHOUSE ★★★   MAP 8 O 11

Hedigan's is a late Victorian listed residence in Clontarf located 15 mins from the airport, Dublin port, Point Theatre 5 mins, city centre 10 mins. Local facilities include 3 golf courses, beach and Stann's Rose Gardens. This elegant house offers a choice of single, double and twin luxurious en suite rooms. Also available is a gracious drawing room and gardens. RAC Highly Acclaimed. AA selected ♦♦♦♦.

B&B from £28.00 to £35.00
€35.55 to €44.44

MATT HEDIGAN
Proprietor

Mastercard

Visa

☺️ Midweek specials from £75.00

🏨🛏️☎️🅃🄲🐾❄️PS▪️
9 9

IRISH HOTELS FEDERATION

Open All Year

HERBERT PARK HOTEL

BALLSBRIDGE,
DUBLIN 4
TEL: 01-667 2200   FAX: 01-667 2595
EMAIL: reservations@herbertparkhotel.ie

HOTEL ★★★★   MAP 8 O 11

Ideally located in Ballsbridge, this contemporary hotel is central yet pleasantly secluded next to the Herbert Park. All rooms are fully air-conditioned and individually temperature controlled. Remote control cable television, DD phone, voice mail, trouser press, hair dryer, mini-bar and safe are standard in every room. 24 hour room service. Complimentary secure carpark. The Pavilion Restaurant and Exhibition Bar complete the luxury experience which is the Herbert Park Hotel.

WEB: www.herbertparkhotel.ie

Members Of UTELL International

B&B from £111.00 to £111.00
€140.94 to €140.94

EWAN PLENDERLEITH
General Manager

American Express

Diners

Mastercard

Visa

☺️ 2 nights B&B from £125.00

🏨🛏️☎️🅱️🅃🄲CM🄶UP🄰alc
153 153
♿ Inet FAX

IRISH HOTELS FEDERATION

Open All Year

B&B rates are per person sharing per night incl. Breakfast

HIBERNIAN HOTEL

EASTMORELAND PLACE,
BALLSBRIDGE, DUBLIN 4
TEL: 01-668 7666 FAX: 01-660 2655
EMAIL: info@hibernianhotel.com

HOTEL U MAP 8 O 11

The Hibernian Hotel, a splendid Victorian building offering guests a tranquil haven of true hospitality in bustling downtown Dublin. Each room is elegant and luxurious and equipped with the most modern facilities. The Patrick Kavanagh restaurant prepares gourmet masterpieces for its diners. Close to museums, theatres, concert halls and Grafton St. Winners of the AA Courtesy & Care Award Ireland 2000 and hotel of the year '97 from Small Luxury Hotels. USA Toll free 011 800 525 48000.
GDS Access Code: LX

WEB: www.slh.com/hibernia/

Members Of Small Luxury Hotels of the World

Room Rate from £120.00 to £185.00
€152.37 to €234.90

SIOBHAN MAHER
General Manager

American Express
Diners
Mastercard
Visa

😊 Weekend specials from £130.00

40 40

 Inet

Closed 24 - 27 December

HILTON DUBLIN
(FORMERLY STAKIS DUBLIN)

CHARLEMONT PLACE,
DUBLIN 2
TEL: 01-402 9988 FAX: 01-402 9966

HOTEL U MAP 8 O 11

The Hilton Dublin is a modern, superior hotel which opened in August '97. Overlooking the Grand Canal, the Hilton is centrally located for easy access to all of Dublin's major tourist attractions and road connections network. This excellent hotel has 189 bedrooms. Our Waterfront restaurant serves the best in traditional and international cuisine. Champions bar has a sports theme and beer garden. Private complimentary carpark for residents. Conference and banqueting for up to 300 people.

Room Rate from £135.00 to £220.00
€171.41 to €279.34

PATRICK STAPLETON
General Manager

American Express
Diners
Mastercard
Visa

😊 Weekend specials from £115.00

189 189

 Inet

Closed 24 - 28 December

HOLIDAY INN

99-107 PEARSE STREET,
DUBLIN 2
TEL: 01-670 3666 FAX: 01-670 3636
EMAIL: info@holidayinndublin.ie

HOTEL ★★★ MAP 8 O 11

Ireland's first Holiday Inn, located in the heart of the city centre. 92 superb en suite rooms with satellite TV, fax/modem line, hairdryer, trouser press and tea/coffee facilities. Executive rooms, disabled and designated non-smoking rooms are also available. Each room has either a king bed or two queen beds. Health and fitness centre. Esther Keogh's traditional Irish pub. Function rooms and conference facilities for up to 80 people. Secure private paid carpark.

WEB: www.holidayinndublin.ie

B&B from £52.50 to £84.50
€66.66 to €107.29

PAUL CULLEN
General Manager

American Express
Diners
Mastercard
Visa

92 92

Open All Year

Room rates are per room per night

HOLLYBROOK HOTEL

HOLLYBROOK PARK, CLONTARF,
DUBLIN 3
TEL: 01-833 2979   FAX: 01-833 5458

HOTEL ★★   MAP 8 O 11

Situated in the quiet suburb of Clontarf, 3km from city centre on main bus and DART routes. Local amenities include 6 golf courses in a 5 mile radius, the famous Bull Island, bird sanctuary and Dollymount strand. All rooms en suite with telephone and TV. Convenient to airport, ferry and Point Theatre. Lock-up car park. Excellent banqueting and conference facilities available.

B&B from £40.00 to £50.00
€50.79 to €63.49

JOSEPHINE MCCOOEY
Manager

American Express
Mastercard
Visa

22 20

Closed 24 - 26 December

HOTEL ISAACS

STORE STREET,
DUBLIN 1
TEL: 01-855 0067   FAX: 01-836 5390
EMAIL: hotel@isaacs.ie

HOTEL ★★★   MAP 8 O 11

Situated in the heart of Dublin city, 5 mins by foot from O'Connell St Bridge, Hotel Isaacs, a converted wine-ware house, is the perfect location for the visitor to Dublin, at the perfect price, close to the shopping & financial centre. All rooms are tastefully furnished & are en suite with telephone, TV, tea/coffee making facilities & iron/ironing board. The restaurant, Il Vignardo, serves great tasting Italian food 7 days a week. Nearby overnight parking available at special rates.

WEB: www.isaacs.ie

B&B from £35.00 to £60.00
€44.44 to €76.18

EVELYN HANNIGAN
General Manager

American Express
Mastercard
Visa

58 58

Closed 23 - 27 December

HOTEL ST. GEORGE

7 PARNELL SQUARE,
DUBLIN 1
TEL: 01-874 5611   FAX: 01-874 5582
EMAIL: hotels@indigo.ie

HOTEL U   MAP 8 O 11

The historical Hotel St. George is located on Parnell Square at the top of O'Connell street, Dublin's principal thoroughfare. Within walking distance of the Abbey and the Gate theatre, Municipal Art Gallery, Dublin's writers Museum, Principal shopping district and other major tourist attractions. Each bedroom is en suite, individually decorated, every modern comfort, including D.D. phone, colour TV and tea/coffee making facilities. Private car park.

WEB. www.indigo.io/hotels

B&B from £40.00 to £45.00
€50.79 to €57.14

JIM STAUNTON
Proprietor

Mastercard
Visa

Midweek specials from £99.00

36 36

Closed 24 - 27 December

B&B rates are per person sharing per night incl. Breakfast

IONA HOUSE

5 IONA PARK, GLASNEVIN,
DUBLIN 9
TEL: 01-830 6217   FAX: 01-830 6732

GUESTHOUSE ★★★   MAP 8 O 11

Iona House is a popular 3*** guesthouse, near the city centre, in one of Dublin's unique Victorian quarters, full of charming red brick houses built around the turn of the century. Rooms with private shower and wc en suite, colour TV, self dial phone and central heating. A comfortable lounge and private patio round off the friendly atmosphere of Iona House. Listed with ADAC, AVD, ANWB, International Hotels-Restaurants-Tourisme, Beth Byrant and Fodors Guide.

B&B from £34.00 to £34.00
€43.17 to €43.17

JACK SHOULDICE
Owner

American Express
Mastercard
Visa

🛏🅿☎️🔲⊺©❄️7🍴▪️
10 10

IRISH HOTELS FEDERATION

Closed 01 December - 31 January

JACKSON COURT HOTEL

29/30 HARCOURT STREET,
DUBLIN 2
TEL: 01-475 8777   FAX: 01-475 8793
EMAIL: jackson@destination-ireland.com

HOTEL ★★   MAP 8 O 11

Minutes walk from Grafton Street, Stephens Green and most of Dublin's historic landmarks. Enjoy the combination of local Dubliners and visitors from abroad in our hotel, busy bar and Dublin's hottest night spot, Copper Face Jacks. Rates include full Irish breakfast, night club admission, service and taxes. We look forward to welcoming you!

B&B from £45.00 to £45.00
€57.14 to €57.14

GRACE-ANN FALLON
Manager

American Express
Diners
Mastercard
Visa

😊 Sunday 50% reduction

🛏🅿☎️🔲▪️⊺©↩CMS🔲aⒹc▪️
25 25

IRISH HOTELS FEDERATION

Closed 24 - 27 December

JURYS CHRISTCHURCH INN

CHRISTCHURCH PLACE,
DUBLIN 8
TEL: 01-454 0000   FAX: 01-454 0012
EMAIL: info@jurys.com

HOTEL ★★★   MAP 8 O 11

Modern attractive rooms capable of accommodating up to 3 adults or 2 adults and 2 children. All rooms are en suite with multi-channel TV, tea/coffee making facilities, radio and DD phone. Located in the heart of Dublin city, opposite Christ Church, the Inn has an informal restaurant and a lively pub. It also has the added convenience of an adjoining public multi-storey car park (fee payable). Jurys Doyle Hotel Group central reservations Tel. 01-607 0000 Fax. 01-631 6999.

WEB: www.jurys.com

Room Rate from £62.00 to £65.00
€78.72 to €82.53

EDWARD STEPHENSON
General Manager

American Express
Diners
Mastercard
Visa

🛏🅿☎️🔲▪️⊺↩CM🔲aⒹc♿▪️
182 182

IRISH HOTELS FEDERATION

Closed 24 - 26 December

Room rates are per room per night

JURYS CUSTOM HOUSE INN

CUSTOM HOUSE QUAY,
DUBLIN 1
TEL: 01-607 5000   FAX: 01-829 0400
EMAIL: info@jurys.com

HOTEL ★★★   MAP 8 O 11

Modern attractive rooms capable of accommodating up to 3 adults or 2 adults and 2 children. All rooms are en suite with multi-channel TV, radio, DD phone, tea/coffee making facilities. Located in the heart of Dublin city at the I.F.S. Centre, the Inn has an informal restaurant and lively pub, a business centre, conference rooms and a public multi-storey car park (fee payable). Jurys Doyle Hotel Group central reservations Tel. 01-607 0000 Fax. 01-631 6999.

WEB: www.jurys.com

Room Rate from £62.00 to £65.00
€78.72 to €82.53

MONICA FRIEL
General Manager

American Express
Diners
Mastercard
Visa

 239 239

Closed 24 - 26 December

JURYS HOTEL DUBLIN

PEMBROKE ROAD, BALLSBRIDGE,
DUBLIN 4
TEL: 01-660 5000   FAX: 01-660 5540
EMAIL: info@jurys.com

HOTEL ★★★★★   MAP 8 O 11

This 5***** hotel, with 300 large de luxe bedrooms, is situated in the city's prime residential and business district. Recently refurbished ground floor features 2 restaurants, traditional Dubliner bar and Library lounge, an indoor/outdoor pool, gym and ample car parking. Jurys Doyle Hotel Group central reservations Tel. 01-607 0000.

THE TOWERS

LANSDOWNE ROAD, DUBLIN 4
TEL: 01-667 0033   FAX: 01-660 5540

5 Star Superior hotel adjacent to Jury's Hotel Dublin. Jurys Doyle Hotel Group Central Reservations:
Tel: 01-607 0000 Fax: 01 631 6999.

WEB: www.jurys.com

B&B from £97.00 to £142.00
€123.16 to €180.30

RICHARD BOURKE
General Manager

American Express
Diners
Mastercard
Visa

☺ Weekend specials from £125.00

 394 394

Open All Year

KELLYS HOTEL

SOUTH GREAT GEORGES STREET,
DUBLIN 2
TEL: 01-677 9277   FAX: 01-671 3216
EMAIL: kellyhtl@iol.ie

HOTEL ★   MAP 8 O 11

Situated in the heart of Dublin beside fashionable Grafton St. A few minutes walk to Trinity College. Temple Bar and many of Dublin's famous pubs and restaurants are on our doorstep. Places of historical, cultural and literary interest are close by. Kelly's is a budget hotel of unbeatable value for a city centre location. There is no service charge and our prices include breakfast. Frommers recommended. Parking available in adjacent public multi-storey carpark (for fee).

B&B from £28.00 to £38.00
€35.55 to €48.25

TERRY MOSER
General Manager

American Express
Mastercard
Visa

 24 21

Closed 20 - 26 December

B&B rates are per person sharing per night incl. Breakfast

KILRONAN GUESTHOUSE

70 ADELAIDE ROAD,
DUBLIN 2
TEL: 01-475 5266   FAX: 01-478 2841
EMAIL: info@dublinn.com

GUESTHOUSE ★★★   MAP 8 O 11

This exclusive 3*** guesthouse is in a secluded setting, walking distance from St. Stephen's Green, Trinity College and most of Dublin's historic landmarks. Well appointed bedrooms with private shower, DD phone, TV, hairdryers, tea/coffee tray. Private secure car-parking. Commended by New York Times, Beth Byrant, Michelin Guide, Country Inns and Backroads. Under the personal supervision of owners Terry and Rosemary Masterson.

WEB: dublinn.com

B&B from £35.00 to £45.00
€44.44 to €57.14

ROSE & TERRY MASTERSON
Owners

Mastercard
Visa

15 13

Open All Year

KINGSWOOD COUNTRY HOUSE

NAAS ROAD, CLONDALKIN,
DUBLIN 22
TEL: 01-459 2428   FAX: 01-459 2428
EMAIL: kingswoodcountryhse@eircom.net

GUESTHOUSE ★★★   MAP 8 O 11

A warm and welcoming Country House nestling within beautiful walled gardens. Strategically located 3Km from the M50 at the beginning of the N7(Naas road) the gateway to the west and south west. Enjoy the intimate atmosphere of the restaurant which features open fires and sophisticated Irish dishes with a French influence. The seven tastefully decorated bedrooms are all en suite with TV, direct dial phone. Recommended - Egon Ronay, Good Hotel Guide, RAC, AA ♦♦♦♦.

B&B from £47.50 to £52.00
€60.31 to €66.03

SHEILA O'BRYNE
Manageress

American Express
Diners
Mastercard
Visa

7 7

😊 Weekend specials from £65.00

Closed 24 - 27 December

LANSDOWNE HOTEL

27-29 PEMBROKE ROAD,
BALLSBRIDGE, DUBLIN 4
TEL: 01-668 2522   FAX: 01-668 5585
EMAIL: lanhotel@iol.ie

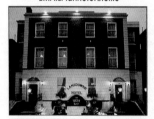

HOTEL ★★★   MAP 8 O 11

The Lansdowne Hotel is a 3*** Georgian hotel just minutes walk from city centre. We combine olde world charm with modern facilities. Ideally located, with Lansdowne Stadium, RDS, Point Theatre and Dublin's business district just a short stroll. You can relax and enjoy fine Irish cuisine in our Celtic restaurant or savour the local atmosphere in our Den bar while enjoying mouth-watering food from our bar menu. We have a fully equipped conference and banqueting hall. Private car park.

WEB: www.lansdownehotel.com

Members Of MinOtel Ireland Hotel Group

B&B from £35.00 to £75.00
€44.44 to €95.23

MARGARET ENGLISH
Assistant Manager

American Express
Diners
Mastercard
Visa

40 40

Closed 23 - 27 December

Room rates are per room per night

LANSDOWNE LODGE

6 LANSDOWNE TERRACE, SHELBOURNE
ROAD, BALLSBRIDGE, DUBLIN 4
TEL: 01-660 5755   FAX: 01-660 5662
EMAIL: info@dublinhotels.com

GUESTHOUSE ★★★   MAP 8 O 11

We offer superior 3*** executive
accommodation in the prestigious
embassy belt area of Dublin 4. A 15
minute stroll from the city centre, we
are adjacent to Lansdowne DART
station, which provides regular
services to both the city and our
neighbouring Co. Wicklow. We offer
superb bed and breakfast
accommodation in an ambience of
traditional elegance. A delightful
residence for tourists and business
travellers alike. You will find a warm
welcome at Lansdowne Lodge.
Private parking.

WEB: www.dublinhotels.com

B&B from £25.00 to £70.00
€31.74 to €88.88

ELAINE SUTTON
Manager

Mastercard

Visa

😊 Midweek specials from £75.00

12 12

IRISH HOTELS FEDERATION

Closed 23 - 28 December

LANSDOWNE MANOR

46-48 LANSDOWNE ROAD,
BALLSBRIDGE, DUBLIN 4
TEL: 01-668 8848   FAX: 01-668 8873
EMAIL: lansdownemanor@eircom.net

GUESTHOUSE ★★★★   MAP 8 O 11

Lansdowne Manor, situated in
Ballsbridge, comprises of two early
Victorian mansions which maintain
the elegance of their original era. The
furnishings were specially
commissioned in the style of 18th
century France. Bedrooms range
from single to executive, each with
en suite, DD phone, multi channel
TV, trouser press and tea/coffee
making facilities. Laundry service,
private meeting room and secretarial
services are available. AA Selected
premises ◆◆◆◆.

WEB: www.booking.org/io/hotels/lansdowne

B&B from £42.50 to £50.00
€53.96 to €63.49

BRENDA O'FLYNN
Manager

American Express

Mastercard

Visa

😊 Midweek specials from £112.00

22 22

IRISH HOTELS FEDERATION

Closed 23 - 27 December

LEESON COURT HOTEL

26/27 LOWER LEESON STREET,
DUBLIN 2
TEL: 01-676 3380   FAX: 01-661 8273

HOTEL ★★   MAP 8 O 11

Beautifully restored Georgian
building to encompass all modern
facilities including air conditioning,
TV, iron/trouser press, tea/coffee
facilities, DD phone, hairdryer,
double/triple glazing. Five minutes
walk from Stephens Green and set in
the southside, this small hotel offers
the discerning client everything they
could wish for whilst on holiday or
business trip at very reasonable
rates.

B&B from £40.00 to £53.00
€50.79 to €67.30

LAURA PRINCE
General Manager

Mastercard

Visa

20 20

Closed 24 December - 01 January

B&B rates are per person sharing per night incl. Breakfast

LONGFIELDS

9/10 FITZWILLIAM STREET LOWER,
DUBLIN 2
TEL: 01-676 1367 FAX: 01-676 1542
EMAIL: lfields@indigo.ie

HOTEL ★★★ MAP 8 O 11

Longfield's, a charming and intimate
hotel in the heart of Ireland's capital
where, with its award winning No.
10 Restaurant, one can relax in
oppulence reminiscent of times past.
Avid followers of good food guides
and well known accommodation
publications will have noted
numerous accolades bestowed upon
this renowned residence. Its central
location and its impeccable service
make it a must for discerning
travellers.

Members Of Manor House Hotels

B&B from £55.00 to £75.00
€69.84 to €95.23

UNA YOUNG
Manager

American Express
Diners
Mastercard
Visa

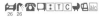

26 26

Closed 24 - 27 December

LYNDON GUESTHOUSE

26 GARDINER PLACE,
DUBLIN 1
TEL: 01-878 6950 FAX: 01-878 7420

GUESTHOUSE ★★ MAP 8 O 11

Lyndon House is an extremely
popular, beautifully restored,
modernly designed, Georgian
guesthouse. It is excellently located
in the heart of Dublin's city centre off
Parnell Square at the top of
O'Connell Street & is on 41/41c
airport bus route. It is family run, so
emphasis is on good value, warm
atmosphere and friendly service.
Rooms are bathroom en suite, with
TV, internal telephone and hospitality
tray. Secure lock up car park. R.A.C.
Highly Acclaimed AA ♦♦♦.

B&B from £25.00 to £35.00
€31.74 to €44.44

FRANK & NEASA MARTINEZ

American Express
Mastercard
Visa

9 9

Closed 24 - 27 December

MAPLE HOTEL

LOWER GARDINER STREET,
DUBLIN 1
TEL: 01-874 0225 FAX: 01-874 5239

HOTEL ★★ MAP 8 O 11

The Maple Hotel is situated in the
heart of the city, just off O'Connell
street, beside all theatres, cinemas,
main railway, bus and DART stations
with a direct bus link to Dublin
airport. The hotel is owned and run
by the Sharkey family who have
been welcoming guests here for over
35 years. All luxurious bedrooms en
suite, colour TV, direct dial
telephones, hair dryer, coffee/tea
facilities. Private car parking.

B&B from £25.00 to £40.00
€31.74 to €50.79

THE SHARKEY FAMILY

Mastercard
Visa

12 12

Closed 20 December - 09 January

Room rates are per room per night

MARIAN GUEST HOUSE

**21 UPPER GARDINER STREET,
DUBLIN 1
TEL: 01-874 4129**

GUESTHOUSE ★ MAP 8 O 11

Situated in Georgian Dublin, just off Mountjoy Square and five minutes walk from city centre and all principal shopping areas, cinemas, theatres, museums. All our rooms are tastefully decorated, with central heating and all usual amenities are available. There is tea/coffee making facilities. The Marian is family run and you are sure to get a warm welcome. On the 41 bus route from Dublin airport. Open all year.

B&B from £19.00 to £19.00
€24.13 to €24.13

CATHRINE MCELROY
Owner

Mastercard
Visa

6

HOTELS
FEDERATION

Open All Year

MERCER HOTEL

**MERCER STREET LOWER,
DUBLIN 2
TEL: 01-478 2179 FAX: 01-478 0328
EMAIL: stay@mercerhotel.ie**

HOTEL ★★★ MAP 8 O 11

The Mercer Hotel is ideally located in the heart of Dublin's most fashionable and cultural areas adjacent to the superb landscape gardens of St. Stephens Green. The Mercer is a boutique style hotel with 21 superbly appointed en suite rooms. Discreetly blended into the decor is a full complement of modern amenities including individually controlled air conditioning, TV/video, CD player, trouser press, fax modem points, DD phone, hairdryer. Conference and restaurant facilities.

WEB: www.mercerhotel.ie

B&B from £48.00 to £73.50
€60.95 to €93.33

MAURICE SUPPLE
General Manager

American Express
Diners
Mastercard
Visa

21 21

Inet FAX

HOTELS
FEDERATION

Open All Year

MERRION HALL

**54/56 MERRION ROAD,
BALLSBRIDGE, DUBLIN 4
TEL: 01-668 1426 FAX: 01-668 4280
EMAIL: merrionhall@iol.ie**

GUESTHOUSE ★★★★ MAP 8 O 11

Award-winning Merrion Hall 4****, an elegant combination of Edwardian grace, fine food and modern comforts, all one expects of a private hotel, aircon suites, executive facilities, jacuzzis, 4-poster beds, private carpark and gardens. Adjacent to RDS, close to city centre, airport and car ferry terminals by DART or bus. Accolades, AAA 5 Diamond, RAC Property of Year, Times, Bestloved Hotels, Johansens. Sister hotel of nearby Aberdeen Lodge & Halpins Hotel in Clare.
US Toll Free 1800 2236510.

WEB: www.greenbook.ie/merrionhall

Members of Green Book Of Ireland.

B&B from £35.00 to £70.00
€44.44 to €88.88

PAT HALPIN
Proprietor

American Express
Diners
Mastercard
Visa

☺ Midweek specials from £115.00

25 25

HOTELS
FEDERATION

Open All Year

B&B rates are per person sharing per night incl. Breakfast

MERRION HOTEL

**UPPER MERRION STREET,
DUBLIN 2**
TEL: 01-603 0600   FAX: 01-603 0700
EMAIL: info@merrionhotel.com

HOTEL ★★★★★   MAP 8 O 11

The Merrion Hotel, Dublin's most luxurious 5★★★★★ hotel is situated in the city centre opposite the Irish Parliament on Upper Merrion Street. This hotel brings new standards of excellence to Ireland's capital by the nature of the discreet but friendly service offered to guests. With the meticulous restoration of four grade 1 listed Georgian town houses, the Merrion provides 145 beautifully appointed guest rooms and suites, many overlooking magnificent 18th century gardens.

WEB: www.merrionhotel.com

Members Of Leading Hotels of the World

Room Rate from £210.00 to £275.00
€266.64 to €349.18

PETER MACCANN
General Manager

American Express
Diners
Mastercard
Visa

145 145

alc Inet FAX

Open All Year

MERRION SQUARE MANOR

**NO 31 MERRION SQUARE NORTH,
DUBLIN 2**
TEL: 01-662 8551   FAX: 01-662 8556
EMAIL: merrionmanor@eircom.net

GUESTHOUSE ★★★   MAP 8 O 11

Merrion Square Manor is situated overlooking Dublin's most gracious Georgian square. Located a 5 minute stroll from the city centre this beautiful house has been tastefully restored and extends the welcome of Georgian days gone by. Bedrooms are individually designed and decorated, all are en suite and have been appointed to the highest standards. Private parking available. AA selected premises ◆◆◆◆.

WEB: www.merrionsquare.com

B&B from £42.50 to £50.00
€53.96 to €63.49

VALERIE GANNON
Manager

American Express
Mastercard
Visa

☺ Midweek specials from £112.50

18 18

Closed 24 - 26 December

MESPIL HOTEL

**MESPIL ROAD,
DUBLIN 4**
TEL: 01-667 1222   FAX: 01-667 1244
EMAIL: mespil@leehotels.ie

HOTEL ★★★   MAP 8 O 11

Located on the banks of the Grand Canal at Baggot Street Bridge, the Mespil is one of Dublin's most popular places to stay. The hotel has 153 bedrooms with 100 new bedrooms and 7 two-bedroom apartments due to open in March 2000. Modern design and decor is reflected in The Kenmare Room restaurant and in the Terrace bar. Free secure parking is available to our guests. Close to all cultural and shopping amenities the Mespil offers excellent value for money in a great location.

WEB: www.iol.ie/lee

Members Of Lee Hotels

Room Rate from £85.00 to £90.00
€107.93 to €114.28

MARTIN HOLOHAN
General Manager

American Express
Diners
Mastercard
Visa

☺ Midweek specials from £129.00

153 153

Inet

Closed 24 - 26 December

Room rates are per room per night

MONT CLARE HOTEL

**MERRION SQUARE,
DUBLIN 2**
TEL: 01-607 3800   FAX: 01-661 5663
EMAIL: montclareres@ocallaghanhotels.ie

HOTEL ★★★   MAP 8 O 11

Welcome to a special corner of
Dublin! The Mont Clare features 74
luxurious fully air conditioned
bedrooms, traditional lounge bar,
Goldsmith's Restaurant, convention
facilities and free private valet
parking. Overlooking Merrion Square
the Mont Clare Hotel is the ideal city
centre location, just a few minutes
walk to all major attractions
including Trinity College, museums,
theatres, exhibition centres and
shopping areas. Reservations via
UTELL International Worldwide.
USA Toll Free 1800 5699983.

WEB: www.ocallaghanhotels.ie

Member Of O'Callaghan Hotels

B&B from £82.00 to £98.00
€104.12 to €124.43

KILLIAN O'GRADY
General Manager

American Express
Diners
Mastercard
Visa

74 74

Open All Year

MONTROSE HOTEL

**STILLORGAN ROAD,
DUBLIN 4**
TEL: 01-269 3311   FAX: 01-269 1164

HOTEL ★★★   MAP 8 O 11

Quality, modern 3★★★ hotel, located
just 2 miles from Dublin city centre,
8 miles from Dublin international
airport and within 10-15 mins drive
of all major southside business and
entertainment districts. Overlooking
the impressive grounds of University
College Dublin and attractive
residences, the hotel offers a warm,
friendly atmosphere coupled with
quality international standards.

WEB: www.doylehotels.com

B&B from £47.00 to £64.00
€59.68 to €81.26

PADRAIG BLIGHE
General Manager

American Express
Diners
Mastercard
Visa

☺ Weekend specials from £84.00

179 179

Open All Year

MORGAN HOTEL

**10 FLEET STREET, TEMPLE BAR,
DUBLIN 2**
TEL: 01-679 3939   FAX: 01-679 3946
EMAIL: sales@themorgan.com

HOTEL U   MAP 8 O 11

The Morgan is a boutique
contemporary style hotel with great
emphasis on aesthetic detail. The
rooms provide the ultimate in
comfort and luxury with spacious 6ft
beds in light beechwood covered in
crisp pure white Egyptian cotton and
oversized pillows. All rooms are
equipped with TV/video, mini hi-fi,
voicemail and ISDN lines. The cool
foyer is refreshingly simple and
elegant. Situated in Temple Bar, the
most vibrant and cosmopolitan area
of Dublin.

WEB: www.themorgan.com

Room Rate from £120.00 to £140.00
€152.37 to €177.76

MARIE O'HALLORAN
Sales & Marketing Manager

American Express
Diners
Mastercard
Visa

☺ Midweek specials from £150.00

61 61

Closed 24 - 27 December

B&B rates are per person sharing per night incl. Breakfast

MORRISON

LOWER ORMOND QUAY,
DUBLIN 1
TEL: 01-887 2400   FAX: 01-878 3185
EMAIL: info@morrisonhotel.ie

HOTEL P   MAP 8 O 11

A contemporary Irish hotel. Located between the Ha'penny Bridge and Capel Street Bridge overlooking the river Liffey. Designed by John Rocha the hotel has 95 bedrooms that include 6 suites and a penthouse, all equipped with high-tech efficiency to suit the modern traveller. Features include the Morrison Bar, a triumph of design and comfort, Halo Restaurant offering fusion cooking, and Lobo Bar and Restaurant with an oriental theme.

WEB: www.morrisonhotel.ie

Members Of Sterling & Resort Hotels

Room Rate from £175.00 to £250.00
€222.20 to €317.43

ANTHONY KENNA
General Manager

American Express
Diners
Mastercard
Visa

☺ Midweek specials from £195.00

🛏🚗☎🖥🛁T C🍴CM♫🅿🔲aic
95 95
Inet FAX

MOUNT HERBERT HOTEL

HERBERT ROAD, LANSDOWNE
ROAD, DUBLIN 4
TEL: 01-668 4321   FAX: 01-660 7077
EMAIL: info@mountherberthotel.ie

HOTEL U   MAP 8 O 11

This gracious Victorian residence is 5 mins south of the city centre in Ballsbridge, Dublin's most exclusive area, where most diplomatic embassies are based. Facilities include 185 modern bedrooms, licensed restaurant, private car park, sauna/sunbed, conference centre, gift shop, picturesque gardens. The Loughran family have been welcoming guests for over 40 years, and it is renowned for its superb value, and its warm and friendly atmosphere.

WEB: www.mountherberthotel.ie

B&B from £34.50 to £49.50
€43.81 to €62.85

MICHELLE SWEENEY
Manager

American Express
Diners
Mastercard
Visa

🏌

🛏🚗☎🖥🛁T/🅰C🍴CM❄🅂🅿🅈
185 185
🔲aic🖥

🎩HOTELS FEDERATION

NORTH STAR HOTEL

AMIENS STREET,
DUBLIN 1
TEL: 01-836 3136   FAX: 01-836 3561
EMAIL: norths@regencyhotels.com

HOTEL U   MAP 8 O 11

Centrally located within walking distance of all theatres, principal shopping areas, cinemas, museums, Trinity College and Dublin's Financial Centre. This elegant hotel now features 90 new executive rooms and penthouse suites each with every modern convenience. The hotel has been further enhanced by a new reception, lobby and restaurant together with a newly appointed lounge. Convenient to DART service, Bus Aras and opposite Connolly Station. Close to main shopping precinct. Carpark.

WEB: www.regencyhotels.com

Members Of Holiday Ireland Ltd

B&B from £50.00 to £80.00
€63.49 to €101.58

FRANK RUANE
Manager

American Express
Diners
Mastercard
Visa

🍸

☺ Weekend specials from £79.00

🛏🚗☎🖥🛁T C🍴CMP🔲aic Inet
129 123
FAX

🎩HOTELS FEDERATION

Room rates are per room per night

NORTHUMBERLAND LODGE

**68 NORTHUMBERLAND ROAD,
BALLSBRIDGE, DUBLIN 4
TEL: 01-660 5270   FAX: 01-668 8679**

GUESTHOUSE ★★★   MAP 8 O 11

Luxurious Victorian house, built in the 1850s, situated in the prestigious Embassy belt of Ballsbridge, Dublin 4. Close to the RDS, Shelbourne Park, bus and Dart station city centre. We offer executive accommodation - fully equipped rooms with multi channel TV, DD phone, hairdryer, etc. Secure car parking. A friendly welcome and service is guaranteed.

B&B from £37.50 to £80.00
€47.62 to €101.58

AVRIL MORDAUNT
Manager

Mastercard

Visa

8 8

HOTELS

Open All Year

NUMBER 31

**31 LEESON CLOSE,
DUBLIN 2
TEL: 01-676 5011   FAX: 01-676 2929
EMAIL: number31@iol.ie**

GUESTHOUSE ★★★★   MAP 8 O 11

An award winning guest house right in the heart of Georgian Dublin. The former home of Ireland's leading architect Sam Stephenson just a few minutes walk from St. Stephen's Green and galleries. An oasis of tranquility and greenery, where guests are encouraged to come back and relax and feel at home at any time of the day. Vast breakfasts in the dining room or in a sunny plant filled conservatory. Recommended by the Good Hotel Guide, Egon Ronay, Bridgestone 100 Best Places, Fodors.

WEB: www.number31.ie

B&B from £42.00 to £65.00
€53.33 to €82.53

NOEL & DEIRDRE COMER

American Express
Mastercard
Visa

18 18

Open All Year

ORMOND QUAY HOTEL

**7-11 UPPER ORMOND QUAY,
DUBLIN 7
TEL: 01-872 1811   FAX: 01-872 1362
EMAIL: ormondqh@indigo.ie**

HOTEL U   MAP 8 O 11

Overlooking the river Liffey and just minutes from Dublin's vibrant Temple Bar and bustling O'Connell St. The Ormond Quay Hotel is one of the city's best known. Alongside our 60 fully equipped en suite rooms, excellent conference and meeting facilities, food and entertainment in our acclaimed Sirens Bar and the unique Grosvenor Room art gallery. The Ormond Quay Hotel can proudly boast a friendly and welcoming atmosphere right at the heart of it.

WEB: www.ormondquayhotel.com

B&B from £30.00 to £75.00
€38.09 to €95.23

DEIRDRE MCDONALD
General Manager

American Express
Mastercard
Visa

60 60

HOTELS

Open All Year

B&B rates are per person sharing per night incl. Breakfast

ORWELL LODGE HOTEL

77A ORWELL ROAD, RATHGAR, DUBLIN 6
TEL: 01-497 7258 FAX: 01-497 9913

HOTEL ★ MAP 8 O 11

The Orwell is a comfortable hotel situated in the leafy garden suburb of Rathgar dating back to the elegant Victorian era. It enjoys a fine reputation for convivial atmosphere and good quality food of an international flavour. Under the personal management of Michael Lynch with friendly qualified staff who insure that your visit is enjoyable. We serve breakfast, lunch, dinner and bar food. Family and corporate functions are catered for. Off street parking available.

B&B from £47.30 to £69.30
€60.06 to €87.99

MICHAEL LYNCH
Owner

American Express
Diners
Mastercard
Visa

♿🛏️☎️🅒⟲CMP♨️aic
10 10

Closed 24 - 26 December

OTHELLO HOUSE

74 LOWER GARDINER STREET, DUBLIN 1
TEL: 01-855 4271 FAX: 01-855 7460

GUESTHOUSE ★★ MAP 8 O 11

Othello is 150m from Abbey Theatre, 200m from Dublin's main O'Connell Street, 50m from centre bus station. 41 bus direct from Dublin Airport stops outside door. 150m to Connelly railway station, 1 mile to ferry terminal, 800m to Point Theatre. Lock up secure car park. All rooms en suite with TV, telephone, tea/coffee making facilities. Trinity College, National Museum, National Library all within walking distance.

B&B from £33.00 to £35.00
€41.90 to €44.44

ROBERT LIPSETT
Proprietor

American Express
Diners
Mastercard
Visa

♿🛏️☎️TCPS⏻
22 22

Open All Year

PARAMOUNT HOTEL

PARLIAMENT STREET & ESSEX GATE, TEMPLE BAR, DUBLIN 2
TEL: 01-677 9062 FAX:01-677 9087
EMAIL: paramount@iol.ie

HOTEL P MAP 8 O 11

Paramount Hotel is one of Dublin's most cosmopolitan of hotels, tastefully designed to the very elegant 1930's style of architecture. It is situated on Parliament Street and Essex Gate in the heart of Temple Bar, Dublin's cultural quarter, adjacent to some of the city's finest restaurants, bars, theatres, galleries and design studios.
The Hotel offers 70 luxurious en-suite bedrooms, each appointed to the highest of international standards with data point connection. The hotel bar and bistro offer first class cuisine in a warm and vibrant ambience.

WEB: www.paramounthotel.ie

B&B from £50.00 to £70.00
€63.49 to €88.88

RITA BARCOE
General Manager

American Express
Diners
Mastercard
Visa

:/1

☺ Special Offer 2 nights B&B from £90.00

♿🛏️☎️🚻TCU⏻▪Inet FAX
70 70

Closed 24 December - 28 December

Room rates are per room per night

PARK LODGE HOTEL

7 NORTH CIRCULAR ROAD, DUBLIN 7
TEL: 01-838 6428   FAX: 01-838 0931

HOTEL ★   MAP 8 O 11

A hotel with the unique situation of being right next to the Phoenix Park, with all its leisure facilities (including Dublin zoo and horse riding) and at the same time being just a few minutes from Dublin city centre. All rooms with multi channel TV & direct dial phone. Ideal venue for people coming to Dublin for shopping. Lock up car park. Hotel German/Irish owned.

B&B from £22.50 to £40.00
€28.57 to €50.79

HORST FLIERENBAUM
Owner

Mastercard

Visa

🛏🚗☎️TP🅿️
20 20

HOTELS

Closed 23 - 28 December

PARNELL WEST HOTEL

38/39 PARNELL SQUARE WEST, DUBLIN 1
TEL: 01-878 2694   FAX: 01-872 5150
EMAIL: par.west@indigo.ie

HOTEL ★★   MAP 8 O 11

Located on Parnell Square at the top of O'Connell Street this newly refurbished and decorated building preserves its charming Georgian character and supplements it with facilities necessary for comfort, relaxation and convenience. It is within walking distance of all theatres, galleries, museums and Dublin's historic and commercial areas. All bedrooms en suite with DD phone, TV and tea/coffee facilities. Conference rooms and secretarial services supplied. On-Street car parking.

B&B from £45.00 to £65.00
€57.14 to €82.53

PETER J O'BRIEN
Proprietor

American Express

Diners

Mastercard

Visa

🍽🍸

🛏🚗☎️🛁TC☕CMPS🅿️ac▪
34 34

Inet

Closed 24 - 26 December

PHOENIX PARK HOUSE

38-39 PARKGATE STREET, DUBLIN 8
TEL: 01-677 2870   FAX: 01-679 9769
EMAIL: phoenixparkhouse@eircom.net

GUESTHOUSE ★★   MAP 8 O 11

This friendly AA listed family run guesthouse directly beside the Phoenix Park with its many facilities is ideally located 2 minutes walk from Heuston Station with direct bus service to ferry ports, Dublin airport, Connolly bus station and central bus station. Close to the Guinness Brewery, Whiskey corner, the re-located National Museum and Kilmainham Museum of Modern Art, the popular Temple Bar and numerous pubs and restaurants. Secure car parking available nearby.

B&B from £19.50 to £35.00
€24.76 to €44.44

MARY SMITH & EMER SMITH
Proprietors

American Express

Mastercard

Visa

🛏🚗☎️TC⋃
24 19

HOTELS

Closed 23 - 28 December

B&B rates are per person sharing per night incl. Breakfast

PLAZA HOTEL

BELGARD ROAD, TALLAGHT, DUBLIN 24
TEL: 01-462 4200   FAX: 01-462 4600
EMAIL: reservations@plazahotel.ie

HOTEL N   MAP 8 O 11

AA 4**** hotel, 120 bedrooms, 2 suites. Convenient location on Belgard Rd, short drive from Dublin airport, 6 miles city centre. Secure car parking. Extensive conference & banqueting facilities. The Olive Tree Restaurant (AA 2 rosettes) serves fine mediterranean cuisine. The Vista Cafe is the ideal venue for informal snacks. Di Maggios, a sports & movie themed restaurant and bar is an informal venue. Grumpy McClafferty's traditional pub offers a warm welcome.

WEB: www.plazahotel.ie

Room Rate from £50.00 to £120.00
€63.49 to €152.37

CHARLES COSTELLOE
General Manager

American Express
Diners
Mastercard
Visa

Weekend specials from £70.00

122 122

Inet

Closed 24 - 27 December

PORTOBELLO HOTEL

33 SOUTH RICHMOND STREET, DUBLIN 2
TEL: 01-475 2715   FAX: 01-478 5010
EMAIL: portobellohotel@indigo.ie

HOTEL N   MAP 8 O 11

This landmark building is located in the heart of Dublin city along the Grand Canal. First opened in 1793, the Portobello Hotel boasts a long tradition in hospitality and this new revival combines to provide all guests with comfortable accommodation, good food and a traditional Irish pub.

B&B from £39.50 to £44.50
€50.15 to €56.50

PAT GROGAN

American Express
Diners
Mastercard
Visa

22 22

FAX

Open All Year

QUALITY CHARLEVILLE HOTEL AND SUITES

LOWER RATHMINES ROAD, DUBLIN 6
TEL: 01-406 6100   FAX: 01-406 6200
EMAIL: charleville@charleville.premgroup.ie

HOTEL ★★★   MAP 8 O 11

Ideally located for business or leisure, situated in the popular suburb of Rathmines village, only a 15 min walk to Dublin's famous Grafton St, museums, galleries and theatres. Most rooms are suites offering sittingroom, kitchenette, separate bedrooms and bathroom. All equipped with fax machine, voice mail, CD player and modem point. Carmines restaurant has an extensive European menu, also there is a multi-level themed bar. Free underground parking for residents.

WEB: www.premgroup.ie

Members Of Choice Hotels Ireland

B&B from £75.00 to £100.00
€95.23 to €126.97

EVELYN HARAN
Hotel Manager

American Express
Diners
Mastercard
Visa

2 B&B weekend special from £95.00

51 51

 Inet FAX

Closed 24 - 27 December

Room rates are per room per night

RAGLAN LODGE

10 RAGLAN ROAD, BALLSBRIDGE, DUBLIN 4
TEL: 01-660 6697 FAX: 01-660 6781

GUESTHOUSE ★★★★ MAP 8 O 11

Raglan Lodge is a magnificent Victorian residence dating from 1861. It is just ten minutes from the heart of Dublin in a most peaceful location. There are seven guest rooms, all of which have bathrooms en suite, colour TV, radio/alarm, telephone and tea/coffee facilities. Several of the rooms are noteworthy for their fine proportions and high ceilings. National winner of the Galtee Irish Breakfast Award. Secure car parking facilities. Recommended by RAC, AA and Egon Ronay.

B&B from £40.00 to £55.00
€50.79 to €69.84

HELEN MORAN
Proprietress

American Express
Diners
Mastercard
Visa

🖐🏨☎📺TC❄♨∪⏴PS🕭▪
7 7

IRISH HOTELS FEDERATION

Closed 20 December - 06 January

RATHGAR HOTEL

33-34 KENILWORTH SQUARE, RATHGAR, DUBLIN 6
TEL: 01-497 6392 FAX: 01-496 9110

HOTEL CR MAP 8 O 11

We are a small hotel situated in a leafy suburb, 10 minutes from Dublin city centre. We have 20 bedrooms, all of which are en suite and have remote control TV, DD phone and tea/coffee making facilities. We have a pub/lounge bar with live music on weekends.

B&B from £25.00 to £40.00
€31.74 to €50.79

NOEL HERBERT
Manager

Mastercard
Visa

🖐🏨☎📺T♫PS🕭▪
20 20

Closed 24 - 27 December

RATHMINES PLAZA HOTEL

LOWER RATHMINES ROAD, DUBLIN 6
TEL: 01-496 6966 FAX: 01-491 0603

HOTEL ★★★ MAP 8 O 11

The Rathmines Plaza Hotel, located in a vibrant district of great character, abundant shopping and lively nightlife. Just ten minutes from the city centre. We offer a wealth of comforts for the most discerning guest including en suite facilities, remote control TV, DD phone and many other amenities. The hotel also features a first class themed bar and restaurant with complimentary car parking.

B&B from £40.00 to £50.00
€50.79 to €63.49

FRANCES DEMPSEY
Hotel Manager

American Express
Diners
Mastercard
Visa

☺ Midweek specials from £105.00

🖐🏨☎📺🛏TC🍴CM♫P🅿alc▪
54 54

IRISH HOTELS FEDERATION

Closed 24 - 26 December

B&B rates are per person sharing per night incl. Breakfast

RED COW MORAN'S HOTEL

RED COW COMPLEX, NAAS ROAD,
DUBLIN 22
TEL: 01-459 3650   FAX: 01-459 1588
EMAIL: reservations@morangroup.ie

HOTEL ★★★★ MAP 8 O 11

4**** Red Cow Moran's Hotel combines classic elegance with modern design, situated at the Gateway to the Provinces, convenient to city centre, 15mins from Dublin airport. Bedrooms are fully air-conditioned with colour teletext TV, DD phones/fax, hairdryer, trouser press & tea/coffee facilities. The complex boasts a choice of lively bars and features two superb restaurants and a carvery restaurant, conference facilities, baby sitting service on request. Night Club. Free carparking, AA 4 Star.

WEB: www.morangroup.ie

B&B from £44.00 to £95.00
€55.87 to €120.63

TOM & SHEILA MORAN
Proprietors

American Express
Diners
Mastercard
Visa

😊 Weekend specials from £104.00

Inet FAX

IRISH HOTELS FEDERATION

Closed 24 - 26 December

REGENCY HOTEL

SWORDS ROAD, WHITEHALL,
DUBLIN 9
TEL: 01-837 3544   FAX: 01-836 7121
EMAIL: regency@regencyhotels.com

HOTEL ★★★ MAP 8 O 11

The Regency Hotel is located 3km north of Dublin's city centre on main route to Dublin's International airport and Northern Ireland. All rooms en suite with colour TV, DD phones and tea/coffee making facilities. The hotel incorporates 70 executive bedrooms with hair dryers and trouser press as standard. The hotel features the Shanard Restaurant, the Appian Lounge and its own theatre. With ample secure car parking.

WEB: www.regencyhotels.com

Members Of Holiday Ireland Ltd

B&B from £50.00 to £80.00
€63.49 to €101.58

BRIAN MCGETTIGAN
General Manager

American Express
Diners
Mastercard
Visa

😊 Weekend specials from £79.00

IRISH HOTELS FEDERATION

Open All Year

RIVER HOUSE HOTEL

23/24 EUSTACE STREET, TEMPLE BAR,
DUBLIN 2
TEL: 01-670 7655   FAX: 01-670 7650
EMAIL: 101473.1007@compuserve.com

HOTEL U MAP 8 O 11

A downtown Dublin hotel located in Dublin's colourful and exciting Temple Bar area. With its cobbled streets, shops, art galleries, bars, restaurants and lively night life, Temple Bar has become a tourist attraction itself. All our 29 bedrooms are en suite and have tea/coffee making facilities, remote control TV, radio, hairdryer and direct dial telephone. Hotel facilities include Danger Doyles bar and the sound proofed The Zazu nightclub.

B&B from £35.00 to £80.00
€44.44 to €101.58

SHEELAGH CONWAY
Proprietor

American Express
Diners
Mastercard
Visa

😊 Midweek specials from £93.00

IRISH HOTELS FEDERATION

Closed 24 - 27 December

Room rates are per room per night

ROYAL DUBLIN HOTEL

O'CONNELL STREET,
DUBLIN 1
TEL: 01-873 3666   FAX: 01-873 3120
EMAIL: enq@royaldublin.com

HOTEL ★★★   MAP 8 O 11

Located in the heart of the city on
Dublin's most famous street,
O'Connell Street. Perfect base from
which to explore shops, theatres,
museums and galleries. Guest
rooms include hairdryer, tea/coffee
making facilities, direct dial
telephone and all are en suite. Relax
in the elegant Georgian Room or
enjoy the lively Raffles Bar. Excellent
food available all day in the Cafe
Royale Brasserie. Secure car park
available.

WEB: www.royaldublin.com

Members Of Best Western Hotels

B&B from £52.50 to £77.00
€66.66 to €97.77

MAGGIE NEWMAN
General Manager

American Express
Diners
Mastercard
Visa

117 117
Inet

Closed 24 - 26 December

SACHS HOTEL

19-29 MOREHAMPTON ROAD,
DONNYBROOK, DUBLIN 4
TEL: 01-668 0995   FAX: 01-668 6147

HOTEL ★★   MAP 8 O 11

Set in a quiet exclusive south city
location, yet only a short stroll from
the heart of Dublin. A unique blend
of Georgian excellence and modern
amenities. You will feel the warmth
of our welcome and the charm of the
traditional decor. Spacious
bedrooms individually designed and
with en suite, colour TV and direct
dial telephone. Extensive conference
and banqueting facilities. Leisure
centre nearby and night club
complimentary to guests. We invite
you to be our guest.

B&B from £40.00 to £47.00
€50.79 to €59.68

BRENDA FLOOD
Manager

American Express
Diners
Mastercard
Visa

20 20

Open All Year

SCHOOL HOUSE HOTEL

2-8 NORTHUMBERLAND ROAD,
BALLSBRIDGE, DUBLIN 4
TEL: 01-667 5014   FAX: 01-667 5015

HOTEL ★★★★   MAP 8 O 11

Situated in the heart of one of
Dublin's most fashionable districts
the hotel offers superb
accommodation, good food and
lively pub. All 31 bedrooms are
furnished to the highest international
standard, catering for both business
and leisure visitors to the capital.
Located just a short walk from the
commercial, cultural and
entertainment heart of the city, the
School House Hotel is poised to
become one of the city's leading
new hotels.

Members Of Signature Hotels

B&B from £55.00 to £95.00
€69.84 to €120.63

BERTIE KELLY
General Manager

American Express
Diners
Mastercard
Visa

☺ Weekend specials from £125.00

31 31

Closed 24 - 27 December

B&B rates are per person sharing per night incl. Breakfast

SHELBOURNE DUBLIN

27 ST. STEPHEN'S GREEN,
DUBLIN 2
TEL: 01-676 6471   FAX: 01-661 6006
EMAIL: shelbourneinfo@forte-hotels.com

HOTEL ★★★★★   MAP 8 O 11

Ireland's most distinguished address, provides the ultimate in luxury and service. In the heart of Dublin, overlooking St. Stephen's Green, within walking distance of shopping areas and Dublin's social and cultural life. The hotel has 190 rooms, 2 bars and 2 restaurants. The Lord Mayor's Lounge is a must for afternoon tea. The Shelbourne Club offers exclusive surroundings with fantastic choice of equipment, 18m pool, sauna, steam room, jacuzzi and top class cardiovascular equipment. Strictly over 18's only.

WEB: www.shelbourne.ie

B&B from £120.00 to £161.00
€152.37 to €204.43

JEAN RICOUX
General Manager

American Express
Diners
Mastercard
Visa

☺ Weekend specials from £220.00

190 190

Open All Year

SHELDON PARK HOTEL & LEISURE CENTRE

KYLEMORE ROAD,
DUBLIN 12
TEL: 01-460 1055   FAX: 01-460 1880

HOTEL ★★★   MAP 8 O 11

Warm and friendly, the Sheldon Park Hotel is ideally situated just 15 mins from Dublin airport and 15 mins from the city centre. Just off the M50, we offer easy access to Ireland's most scenic country routes. Spend a relaxing day in our leisure centre, complete with swimming pool, sauna and jacuzzi and finish with a meal in our bistro style restaurant followed by live entertainment.

B&B from £30.00 to £50.00
€38.09 to €63.49

MAURA BISSETT
General Manager

American Express
Diners
Mastercard
Visa

☺ Weekend specials from £85.00

72 72

Closed 24 - 26 December

SKYLON HOTEL

UPPER DRUMCONDRA ROAD,
DUBLIN 9
TEL: 01-837 9121   FAX: 01-837 2778
EMAIL: skylon@doyldhotels.com

HOTEL ★★★   MAP 8 O 11

Modern 3*** hotel offering a warm Irish ambience and high international service standards, located in a residential setting on the main link route between Dublin International Airport (3 miles) and Dublin city centre (2 miles). Facilities include 88 de luxe rooms, bar, meeting room(max 15 persons), complimentary parking and full business services available.

WEB: www.doylehotels.com

B&B from £47.00 to £64.00
€59.68 to €81.26

LOUIS LANGAN
General Manager

American Express
Diners
Mastercard
Visa

☺ Weekend specials from £84.00

88 88

Open All Year

Room rates are per room per night

ST. AIDEN'S GUESTHOUSE

32 BRIGHTON ROAD, RATHGAR,
DUBLIN 6
TEL: 01-490 2011   FAX: 01-492 0234
EMAIL: staidens@eircom.net

GUESTHOUSE ★★★   MAP 8 O 11

St. Aiden's charming family-run guesthouse is modernised to the highest standard of comfort and elegance while preserving its early Victorian character. Located in one of Dublin's most prestigious areas 15 mins from city centre on excellent bus service, 10 mins from the M50 with its links to the airport and national routes, private parking at rear. Hospitality tray and books are provided in lovely drawing room. Under the personal care of Maura O'Carroll and recommended by AA ◆◆◆.

B&B from £27.50 to £45.00
€34.92 to €57.14

MAURA O'CARROLL
Proprietress

Mastercard

Visa

🛏🏠☎💻 T C P
8 8

HOTELS FEDERATION

Open All Year

ST. ANDREWS

1 LAMBAY ROAD, DRUMCONDRA,
DUBLIN 9
TEL: 01-837 4684   FAX: 01-857 0446
EMAIL: andrew@iol.ie

GUESTHOUSE ★★★   MAP 8 O 11

Welcome to St Andrews. Ideally situated just 10 mins from city centre, airport and car ferry. Newly refurbished to a Bord Failte Grade A standard we offer a variety of en suite rooms with DD phone, multi-channel TV, hairdryer and a hospitality trolley is provided in guests' lounge. An excellent base for exploring the famed attractions of Dublin including Temple Bar, Grafton St, Trinity College, museums, theatres, galleries, etc. Recommended by AA and RAC. Visit our website.

WEB: www.travel ireland.com/irl/standrew.htm

Members Of Premier Guesthouses

B&B from £25.00 to £32.00
€31.74 to €40.63

ROSE AND TERRY MASTERSON
Owners

American Express

Mastercard

Visa

🛏🏠☎💻 T P
17 17

HOTELS FEDERATION

Open All Year

ST. JUDE'S GUEST HOUSE

17 PEMBROKE PARK, BALLSBRIDGE,
DUBLIN 4
TEL: 01-668 0928   FAX: 01-668 0483

GUESTHOUSE ★★   MAP 8 O 11

Comfortable newly-refurbished rooms in fashionable Ballsbridge, Dublin 4. Close to American Embassy and 20 mins walk to city centre. All rooms en suite with tea and coffee making facilities and TV.

B&B from £25.00 to £32.50
€31.74 to €41.27

FRANCES & JIM BROOKS

Mastercard

Visa

🛏🏠💻⚠🛏 S
7 7

Open All Year

B&B rates are per person sharing per night incl. Breakfast

STAUNTONS ON THE GREEN

83 ST. STEPHEN'S GREEN,
DUBLIN 2
TEL: 01-478 2300 FAX: 01-478 2263
EMAIL: hotels@indigo.ie

GUESTHOUSE ★★★ MAP 8 O 11

Large Georgian house overlooking St. Stephen's Green, own private gardens. All rooms are en suite and fully equipped with direct dial telephone, TV and tea/coffee welcoming trays, trouser press and hairdryer. It is close to museums, galleries, Grafton Street shopping area and many other major tourist attractions. Stauntons On the Green occupies one of Dublin's most prestigious locations, close to many corporate headquarters and government buildings.

WEB: indigo.ie/~hotels

B&B from £49.50 to £60.00
€62.85 to €76.18

JOANNE NORMAN

American Express
Diners
Mastercard
Visa

36 36

STEPHEN'S GREEN HOTEL

ST. STEPHEN'S GREEN,
DUBLIN 2
TEL: 01-607 3600 FAX: 01-661 5663
EMAIL: stephensgreenres@ocallaghanhotels.ie

HOTEL P MAP 8 O 11

This deluxe boutique hotel enjoys a superb location on St. Stephen's Green, Dublin city centre - in the heart of the business, cultural and shopping districts. Incorporating 2 historically listed Georgian houses, once home to famous Irish political leaders and writers, the hotel is a splendid craft of Georgian elegance and contemporary style with a 4 storey glass atrium overlooking St. Stephen's Green. 64 luxurious airconditioned guestrooms and 11 suites, restaurant, traditional bar, gym. Car parking.
USA Toll Free 1800 5699983.

WEB: www.ocallaghanhotels.ie

Member Of O'Callaghan Hotels

B&B from £96.00 to £150.00
€121.89 to €190.46

SALLY HUGHES
General Manager

American Express
Diners
Mastercard
Visa

Weekend specials from £167.00

75 75

Inet

TARA HOTEL

MERRION ROAD,
DUBLIN 4
TEL: 01-269 4666 FAX: 01-269 1027
EMAIL: tara@doylehotels.com

HOTEL ★★★ MAP 8 O 11

Modern 3*** hotel located just 2 miles from Dublin city centre, 7 miles from Dublin international airport and within 10-15 mins drive of all major southside business and entertainment districts. Commanding breathtaking view of Dublin bay, this intimate hotel offers a warm, friendly Irish atmosphere combined with quality international service standards.

WEB: www.doylehotels.com

B&B from £47.00 to £64.00
€59.68 to €81.26

PAUL O'MEARA
General Manager

American Express
Diners
Mastercard
Visa

Weekend specials from £84.00

113 113

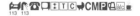

Room rates are per room per night

TAVISTOCK HOUSE

**64 RANELAGH ROAD,
DUBLIN 6
TEL: 01-496 7377   FAX: 01-496 7377
EMAIL: info@tavistockhouse.com**

GUESTHOUSE ★★★   MAP 8 O 11

Magnificent Victorian house, tastefully converted retaining all its original plasterwork - very homely. Situated on the city side of Ranelagh village, on the corner of Ranelagh / Northbrook roads. We are only 7 mins walk from Stephen's Green in the heart of Dublin, near Helen Dillon's world famous garden. All rooms have colour TV, DD phone, hair dryer and tea/coffee making facilities. Private parking. There are a wide variety of restaurants locally. AA ◆◆◆. Internet facilities.

WEB: www.tavistockhouse.com

B&B from £22.50 to £55.00
€28.57 to €69.84

MAUREEN & BRIAN CUSACK
Co-Owners

American Express
Mastercard
Visa

7   7

IRISH HOTELS FEDERATION

Open All Year

TEMPLE BAR HOTEL

**FLEET STREET, TEMPLE BAR,
DUBLIN 2
TEL: 01-677 3333 FAX: 01-677 3088
EMAIL: templeb@iol.ie**

HOTEL ★★★   MAP 8 O 11

A Tower Group Hotel, located in the centre of Dublin in the exciting & vibrant Temple Bar district, the Temple Bar Hotel is the ideal base from which to explore Dublin's cultural centres, bars, restaurants, shops & theatres. Trinity College, Dublin Castle, Christchurch Cathedral and many other places of interest are just a short walk from our door. Avail of the Temple Bar passport offering discounts in a wide selection of shops in the area. All rooms have trouser press and hairdryer.

WEB: www.towerhotelgroup.ie

Members Of Tower Hotel Group

B&B from £55.00 to £95.00
€69.84 to €120.63

DEIRDRE POWER
General Manager

American Express
Diners
Mastercard
Visa

☺ Weekend specials from £89.00

130   130

IRISH HOTELS FEDERATION

Closed 24 - 29 December

TRINITY LODGE

**12 SOUTH FREDERICK STREET,
DUBLIN 2
TEL: 01-679 5044   FAX: 01-679 5223
EMAIL: trinitylodge@eircom.net**

GUESTHOUSE ★★★   MAP 8 O 11

Situated in the heart of Dublin, Trinity Lodge offers superb en suite accommodation in a traditional Georgian townhouse. You will find all of Dublin's business, shopping and historic centres right on our doorstep and you are just steps away from Grafton Street, Trinity College and vibrant Temple Bar. Each room, from our singles to our 650sq' suites is equipped with air conditioning, personal safe, satellite TV, radio alarm, tea/coffee facilities and trouser press.

B&B from £47.50 to £80.00
€60.31 to €101.58

PETER MURPHY
Managing Director

American Express
Diners
Mastercard
Visa

10   10

IRISH HOTELS FEDERATION

Open All Year

B&B rates are per person sharing per night incl. Breakfast

UPPERCROSS HOUSE

26-30 UPPER RATHMINES ROAD,
DUBLIN 6
TEL: 01-497 5486 FAX: 01-497 5361

HOTEL ★★★ MAP 8 O 11

Uppercross House is a hotel providing 25 bedrooms of the highest standard of comfort. All with D.D. phone, TV, tea/coffee maker, central heating and all en suite. Uppercross House has its own secure parking and is ideally situated in Dublin's south-side 2km from St. Stephen's Green and R.D.S., with excellent public transport from directly outside the door. A fully licensed restaurant and bar opens nightly with a warm and friendly atmosphere.

B&B from £35.00 to £45.00
€44.44 to €57.14

DAVID MAHON
Proprietor

American Express
Diners
Mastercard
Visa

🛏️🅿️☎️🍴🇹🇨🍴CM❄️🎵🄿🄰alc🔌
25 25

IRISH
HOTELS
FEDERATION

Open All Year

VIKING LODGE HOTEL

34/36 FRANCIS STREET,
DUBLIN 8
TEL: 01-473 2111   FAX: 01-473 2223
EMAIL: jamesg@esatclear.ie

HOTEL ★★ MAP 8 O 11

A new hotel in the heart of the Liberties. 30 en suite rooms with full facilities. La Venezia restaurant and bar. Close to Christchurch and St Patrick's cathedrals, Guinness Brewery and Dublinia. Within walking distance of main shopping streets and close to Heuston Station. Francis Street is the centre of Dublin's antique trade. Secure car park close by. We offer you convenience, comfort, personal service with the warmest of welcomes.

Members Of Holiday Ireland Hotels

B&B from £40.00 to £80.00
€50.79 to €101.58

JIM GOUGH
General Manager

American Express
Mastercard
Visa

🛏️🅿️☎️🍴🇹🇨🍴CM🎵🅂🄰alc🔌
30 30

IRISH
HOTELS
FEDERATION

Closed 24 - 26 December

WATERLOO LODGE

23 WATERLOO ROAD,
BALLSBRIDGE, DUBLIN 4
TEL: 01-668 5380   FAX: 01-668 5786
EMAIL: info@waterloolodge.com

GUESTHOUSE ★★★ MAP 8 O 11

Waterloo Lodge is centrally located in Ballsbridge on the south side of Dublin city. Just minutes walk from the city centre, Stephen's Green, Temple Bar, museums, theatres, restaurants and pubs with a bus route outside our door. Our rooms are en suite, tastefully decorated, have DD phone, cable TV and hairdryer. Most are non-smoking. Fax and e-mail facilities are available. We assure you of a warm welcome and a pleasant stay.

WEB: www.waterloolodge.com

B&B from £27.50 to £45.00
€34.92 to €57.14

CATHAL DALY
Owner

Mastercard
Visa

🛏️🅿️☎️🍴🇹🇨🍴CM❄️🄿🅂🔌 inet
10 10

IRISH
HOTELS
FEDERATION

Closed 24 - 26 December

Room rates are per room per night

WEST COUNTY HOTEL

**CHAPELIZOD,
DUBLIN 20
TEL: 01-626 4011   FAX: 01-623 1378**

HOTEL ★★   MAP 8 O 11

The West County Hotel, an established hotel, situated on the main West Rd and M50 motorway, convenient to city centre, airport and all main routes. Each of our en suite bedrooms is equipped with TV, DD phone, tea/coffee making facilities, ironing board and hairdryer. Our restaurant offers table d'hôte and à la carte menus and superb wines. 5 excellent golf courses within easy reach. Golf packages available. A warm and friendly welcome awaits you at the West County Hotel.

**B&B from £45.00 to £55.00
€57.14 to €69.84**

GERALD COLGAN
Proprietor

American Express
Diners
Mastercard
Visa

☺ Weekend specials from £95.00

50 50

Closed 24 - 26 December

WESTBURY HOTEL

**GRAFTON STREET,
DUBLIN 2
TEL: 01-679 1122   FAX: 01-679 7078
EMAIL: westbury@doylehotels.com**

HOTEL ★★★★★   MAP 8 O 11

Nestled in the heart of cosmopolitan Grafton Street, in the heart of Dublin's city centre. The Westbury can best be described as a truly international hotel which embraces the warmth and vitality of contemporary Dublin. Chic, modern and as popular with famous personalities from the arts and entertainment world, as with local Dubliners, the hotel is within 2 mins walk to central business districts, theatres, entertainment and cultural attractions.

WEB. www.doylehotels.com

**B&B from £106.00 to £161.00
€134.59 to €204.43**

PADRAIC DOYLE
General Manager

American Express
Diners
Mastercard
Visa

☺ Weekend specials from £185.00

204 204

Inet FAX

Open All Year

WESTLINK LODGE

**PALMERSTOWN VILLAGE,
DUBLIN 20
TEL: 01-623 5494   FAX: 01-623 6214
EMAIL: westlink.lodge@indigo.ie**

GUESTHOUSE ★★★   MAP 8 O 11

Prime location adjacent to all amenities and facilities this superb purpose-built guesthouse adjoins the N4/M50 motorway. Minutes from the city centre and a mere 12 minutes drive to the airport we offer all the features and standards of a luxury hotel. Each elegant en suite bedroom has individual temperature control, ambient lighting, automated door locking system, phone, TV, etc. Separate tea/coffee and iron/trouser press facilities. Private car park. Golf Packages available.

**B&B from £25.00 to £35.00
€31.74 to €44.44**

GERRY O'CONNOR
Owner

Mastercard
Visa

19 19

Open All Year

B&B rates are per person sharing per night incl. Breakfast

RADISSON SAS ST HELEN'S HOTEL

STILLORGAN ROAD, BLACKROCK, CO. DUBLIN
TEL: 01-218 6000 FAX: 01-218 6010
EMAIL: info@dubzh.rdsas.com

HOTEL U MAP 8 O 11

Conveniently located just 3 mls to the city centre, near to golf courses and Wicklow Gardens, we offer luxury accommodation and the highest international service standards. All spacious and air-conditioned rooms are equipped with safe, cable TV with in-house movie channels, minibar, trouser press, hairdryer, bathrobes, fax and modem as well as ice bucket and tea/coffee facilities. Italian and fine dining restaurants, bars, fitness room, beauty salon, snooker and free parking.

WEB: www.radisson.com

Members Of Radisson SAS Hotels

Room Rate from £99.00 to £295.00
€125.70 to €374.57

AILEESH CAREW
General Manager

American Express
Diners
Mastercard
Visa

☺ Weekend specials from £130.00

151 151

Open All Year

STILLORGAN PARK HOTEL

STILLORGAN ROAD, BLACKROCK, CO. DUBLIN
TEL: 01-288 1621 FAX: 01-283 1610
EMAIL: sales@stillorganpark.com

HOTEL ★★★ MAP 8 O 11

The Stillorgan Park Hotel has just invested over £9M in creating a new hotel for Dublin's southside. The result is 100 fully air-conditioned bedrooms, spacious, versatile and fully equipped conference and banqueting suites, a superb restaurant and a comfortable bar. Located just a few minutes from Dublin's city centre on the main N11, parking for 350 cars, 20 mins from Druids Glen golf club and 10 mins from Dun Laoghaire harbour.

WEB: www.stillorganpark.com

B&B from £55.00 to £70.00
€69.84 to €88.88

RONAN DORAN
General Manager

American Express
Diners
Mastercard
Visa

☺ Weekend specials from £115.00

100 100

Open All Year

AIRPORT VIEW

COLD WINTERS, BLAKES CROSS, CO. DUBLIN
TEL: 01-843 8756 FAX: 01-843 8756

GUESTHOUSE P MAP 8 O 11

A luxury 10 roomed en suite guesthouse, built on 2 acres of fine gardens. Located 10 minutes from Dublin airport and 20 minutes from city centre, we are ideally located 50 yards off the main Dublin/Belfast road. Snooker room, hairdryers, remote control TV and conference room. Tennis court, fax / computer outlets, tea/coffee facilities. Full Irish or continental breakfast.

B&B from £25.00 to £38.00
€31.74 to €48.25

ANNE MARIE BEGGS
Proprietor

Mastercard
Visa

☺ Midweek specials from £70.00

10 10

Open All Year

Room rates are per room per night

TUDOR HOUSE

**DALKEY,
CO. DUBLIN**
TEL: 01-285 1528   FAX: 01-284 8133
EMAIL: tudor@iol.ie

GUESTHOUSE ★★★★   MAP O8 P 11

An elegant listed manor house with secluded grounds in the heart of Dalkey. Period ambience and personal friendly service are the hallmarks of Tudor House. Bedrooms are individually decorated and enjoy views of Dublin Bay. Dalkey is a charming heritage town with Norman castles and quaint harbours. It has many excellent restaurants and pubs. It is 3km from Dun Laoghaire ferry port and offers rapid access to Dublin city.

WEB: www.iol.ie/tudor

B&B from £35.00 to £45.00
€44.44 to €57.14

KATIE HAYDON
Owner

Mastercard
Visa

6 6

Open All Year

DUNES HOTEL ON THE BEACH

**DONABATE,
CO. DUBLIN**
TEL: 01-843 6153   FAX: 01-843 6111

HOTEL R   MAP 12 O 12

Occupying one of the best locations on the east coast on the beach at Donabate, our hotel is only 10 minutes north of Dublin airport and 30 minutes from the city centre. Surrounded by 6 golf courses made up of links and parkland courses. Our en suite rooms have spectacular views of Lambay Island and Howth Head. Our bar and carvery offer the ideal ambience for a relaxing meal or drink. Breakfast served till noon.

B&B from £30.00 to £48.00
€38.09 to €60.95

PAULA BALDWIN
Managing Director

Mastercard
Visa

☺ Weekend specials from £75.00

18 18

Closed 24 - 26 December

GREAT SOUTHERN HOTEL DUBLIN AIRPORT

**DUBLIN AIRPORT,
CO. DUBLIN**
TEL: 01-844 6000   FAX: 01-844 6001
EMAIL: res@dubairport.gsh.ie

HOTEL U   MAP 12 O 11

Situated within the airport complex, just 2 mins from the terminal building the Great Southern Hotel, Dublin Airport provides a tranquil haven for the busy traveller. Designed with the international traveller in mind, the guestrooms have every convenience one would expect in an international hotel. Potter's Bistro and Clancy's Bar provide a relaxed setting to unwind before or after a journey. Bookable worldwide through Utell International or central reservations on 01-214 4800.

WEB: www.gsh.ie

Room Rate from £130.00 to £130.00
€165.07 to €165.07

EAMON DALY
General Manager

American Express
Diners
Mastercard
Visa

147 147

Closed 24 - 26 December

B&B rates are per person sharing per night incl. Breakfast

POSTHOUSE DUBLIN AIRPORT

DUBLIN AIRPORT, CO. DUBLIN
TEL: 01-808 0500 FAX: 01-844 6002

HOTEL ★★★★ MAP 12 O 11

A modern hotel located on the Airport complex, offering a choice of standard and Millennium accommodation, and just 11.27km from the city centre. All 249 bedrooms are ensuite with tv and pay movies, mini-bar, trouser press and hair dryer. 24 hour courtesy coach to and from the airport, 24 hour room service, superb choice of Sampans Oriental Restaurant and the Bistro Restaurant, traditional Irish Pub "Bodhran Bar", with live music at weekends. Residents may use the ALSAA Leisure Centre (3 minutes walk) on a complementary basis.

B&B from £45.00 to £90.00
€57.14 to €114.28

BRIAN THORNTON
General Manager

American Express
Diners
Mastercard
Visa

249 249

Closed 24 - 25 December

GLANDORE HOUSE

GLANDORE PARK, LWR MOUNTTOWN ROAD, DUN LAOGHAIRE, CO. DUBLIN
TEL: 01-280 3143 FAX: 01-280 2675

GUESTHOUSE N MAP 8 P 11

Staying at Glandore House allows visitors to take a step back into a more gracious era while at the same time offering the most modern guesthouse facilities. All rooms are en suite with TV, DD phone, tea/coffee facilities. Trouser press/ironing centre. A 6 person lift and off street car parking is also available. Situated 5 min drive from Dun Laoghaire ferry terminal, DART station and bus terminals therefore offering easy accessability to the city centre and surrounding areas.

B&B from £30.00 to £40.00
€38.09 to €50.79

GRAINNE JACKMAN
Manager

Mastercard
Visa

☺ Midweek specials from £105.00

14 14

Closed 22 December - 03 January

MOTORING IN IRELAND

STOP

AND THINK

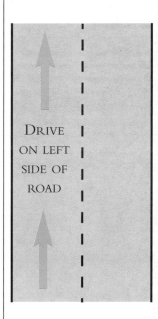

DRIVE ON LEFT SIDE OF ROAD

ENJOY YOUR HOLIDAY

Room rates are per room per night

KINGSTON HOTEL

ADELAIDE ST., (OFF GEORGES ST.),
DUN LAOGHAIRE, CO. DUBLIN
TEL: 01-280 1810   FAX: 01-280 1237

HOTEL ★★   MAP 8 O 11

A delightful 38 bedroomed hotel with panoramic views of Dublin Bay, approximately 15 minutes from city centre. Beside ferryport and DART line. Situated convenient to R.D.S., Point Depot, Lansdowne Road and Leopardstown Racecourse. All rooms are en suite with D.D. phone, TV, tea/coffee making facilities. A family run hotel serving food all day in our lounge/bar and our Cascades restaurant opened nightly.

Members Of MinOtel Ireland Hotel Group

B&B from £37.50 to £42.50
€47.62 to €53.96

JAMES J WALSH

American Express
Diners
Mastercard
Visa

☺ Weekend specials from £89.00

38 38

Closed 25 December

PORT VIEW HOTEL

6/7 MARINE ROAD,
DUN LAOGHAIRE, CO. DUBLIN
TEL: 01-280 1663   FAX: 01-280 0447
EMAIL: portview@clubi.ie

HOTEL U   MAP 8 P 11

The Port View Hotel, Dun Laoghaire, is ideally situated as a base for the social or serious golfer, within easy striking distance of several golf courses. Situated just 200 metres from Dun Laoghaire's high speed ferry port and 15 minutes by train to Dublin city. Why not relax after your long day by the open fire in our bar or sample some home produced food in a variety of surroundings.

B&B from £35.00 to £45.00
€44.44 to €57.14

DONOUGH DUIGNAN
Director

American Express
Diners
Mastercard
Visa

20 8

Closed 25 - 26 December

ROCHESTOWN LODGE HOTEL

ROCHESTOWN AVENUE,
DUN LAOGHAIRE, CO. DUBLIN
TEL: 01-285 3555   FAX: 01-285 3914

HOTEL ★★★   MAP 12 P 11

Located 2 miles from Dun Laoghaire harbour and 5 miles from Dublin city centre. An excellent roads network leads to all areas of interest in Dublin and is a gateway to the sunny south east. The hotel boasts landscaped gardens and has 8 conference rooms, 80 en suite bedrooms, 3 bars and its own famous steak house restaurant. There are several championship golf courses in the area. During 2000 we will be adding a 5* leisure centre including 2 pools, jacuzzis, steam rooms and gym.

B&B from £40.00 to £60.00
€50.79 to €76.18

KEN FETHERSTON
Proprietor

American Express
Diners
Mastercard
Visa

68 68

Open All Year

B&B rates are per person sharing per night incl. Breakfast

ROYAL MARINE HOTEL

MARINE ROAD, DUN LAOGHAIRE,
CO. DUBLIN
TEL: 01-280 1911   FAX: 01-280 1089
EMAIL: ryan@indigo.ie

HOTEL ★★★   MAP 8 O 11

This elegant 1870 hotel with panoramic views of Dublin Bay and the picturesque port of Dun Laoghaire is set in its own landscaped gardens and features 103 en suite bedrooms including 8 Victorian 4 poster suites. The elegant Bay Lounge, the new Toddys Bar and the Powerscourt Room Restaurant provide the ideal location to unwind. Only 20 mins to city centre by light rail, DART. Excellent conference facilities. Complimentary car parking. AA, RAC and Egon Ronay recommended.

WEB: www.ryan-hotels.com

B&B from £45.00 to £110.00
€57.14 to €139.67

PAUL MC CRACKEN
Operations Director

American Express
Diners
Mastercard
Visa

Weekend specials from £99.00

103   103

Open All Year

SANDYCOVE GUESTHOUSE

NEWTOWNSMITH, SANDYCOVE
SEAFRONT, DUN LAOGHAIRE, CO. DUBLIN
TEL: 01-284 1600   FAX: 01-284 1600

GUESTHOUSE ★★★   MAP 8 P 11

Old world refurbished house. Fabulous location on seafront overlooking Dublin/Scotsmans' Bay. All rooms en suite with showers. Tea/coffee making facilities in residents lounge. Convenient to local DART station (fast train). Only 15 mins to Dublin city centre, 5 mins walk to Dun Laoghaire with all its amenities and the triving port of Dun Laoghaire. Local beach, sailing, water skiing, jet skiing, scuba diving etc. Family run guesthouse. Excellent local walks and restaurants etc.

B&B from £21.50 to £29.50
€27.30 to €37.46

CATHERINE DOYLE
Proprietor

Mastercard
Visa

12   12

Closed 22 December - 02 January

BAILY COURT HOTEL

MAIN STREET, HOWTH,
CO. DUBLIN
TEL: 01-832 2691   FAX: 01-832 3730

HOTEL ★★   MAP 12 P 11

Located in the heart of the beautiful fishing village of Howth. Recently refurbished with 20 en suite rooms with TV, DD phone and tea/coffee making facilities. The city centre is 15 minutes away by DART and Dublin airport 12km. A carvery lunch is served daily and Chervil's Bistro offers superb cuisine at affordable prices. Local amenities include golf, fishing and hill walking.

Members Of Logis of Ireland

B&B from £34.00 to £46.00
€43.17 to €58.41

TOM MURPHY
Manager

American Express
Mastercard
Visa

20   20

Closed 24 - 26 December

Room rates are per room per night

DEER PARK HOTEL AND GOLF COURSES

**HOWTH,
CO. DUBLIN**
TEL: 01-832 2624 FAX: 01-839 2405
EMAIL: sales@deerpark.iol.ie

HOTEL ★★★ MAP 12 P 11

14k from Dublin city/airport on a quiet hillside overlooking the bay, Deer Park enjoys spectacular elevated sea views. Featuring Ireland's largest golf complex (5 courses), 18m swimming pool, sauna and steam room and two all-weather tennis courts. Whether on a golfing holiday or a visit to Dublin you will find Deer Park the ideal choice.

WEB: www.deerpark-hotel.ie

Members Of Coast and Country Hotels

B&B from £47.00 to £52.00
€59.68 to €66.03

DAVID & ANTOINETTE TIGHE
Managers

American Express
Diners
Mastercard
Visa

58 58

Closed 23 - 27 December

FITZPATRICK CASTLE DUBLIN

**KILLINEY,
CO. DUBLIN**
TEL: 01-284 0700 FAX: 01-285 0207
EMAIL: dublin@fitzpatricks.com

HOTEL ★★★★ MAP 8 P 10

A warm welcome awaits you at Fitzpatrick Castle, Dublin, set on scenic Killiney Hill with panoramic views of Dublin Bay. The Castle is located 3km from Dun Laoghaire and 14k from Dublin city. The hotel boasts 113 rooms, P.J's restaurant, our cosy Library bar and state of the art fitness centre with a 20m pool. Conference and banqueting facilities for up to 400 with business centre facilities. Nearby to Leopardstown racecourse and ch'ship golf courses such as Druids Glen and Woodbrook.

WEB: www.fitzpatrickhotels.com

B&B from £74.50 to £89.00
€94.60 to €113.01

SANDRA JACKSON
Rooms Division Manager

American Express
Diners
Mastercard
Visa

113 113

Closed 24 - 26 December

QUALITY COURT HOTEL

**KILLINEY BAY,
CO. DUBLIN**
TEL: 01-285 1622 FAX: 01-285 2085
EMAIL: book@killineycourt.ie

HOTEL ★★★ MAP 8 P 10

Elegant Victorian mansion in spectacular setting overlooking breathtaking Killiney Bay. Rapid access to city centre, main train stations, and Dun Laoghaire port from our own DART commuter station. Restaurants popular with locals. International state of art conference centre with simultaneous interpreting equipment. Close to Leopardstown Racecourse and several golf courses: Woodbrook Ch'ship, Druids Glen, The European, Roundwood & Powerscourt. New Year/Christmas packages available.

WEB: www.killineycourt.ie

Members Of Choice Hotels International

B&B from £44.50 to £67.00
€56.50 to €85.07

JOHN O'DOWD
Managing Director

American Express
Diners
Mastercard
Visa

☺ Weekend specials from £109.00

86 86

Open All Year

B&B rates are per person sharing per night incl. Breakfast

BECKETTS COUNTRY HOUSE HOTEL

COOLDRINAGH HOUSE, LEIXLIP,
CO. KILDARE/DUBLIN
TEL: 01-624 7040   FAX: 01-624 7072
EMAIL: becketts@eircom.net

HOTEL ★★★   MAP 8 N 11

Becketts is situated in a quiet scenic area just off the N4 motorway at the Leixlip roundabout close to Dublin's new outer ring with easy access to Dublin airport and all major road networks. Once home to the mother of Samuel Beckett the completely refurbished Cooldrinagh House is now home to Becketts. There are 4 suites and 6 luxury bedrooms and an elegant restaurant with a reputation for superb cuisine and full bar facilities.

B&B from £48.00 to £70.00
€60.95 to €88.88

BRIAN CROKE
General Manager

American Express
Diners
Mastercard
Visa

10 10   Inet FAX

Open All Year

FINNSTOWN COUNTRY HOUSE HOTEL

NEWCASTLE ROAD, LUCAN,
CO. DUBLIN
TEL: 01-628 0644   FAX: 01-628 1088
EMAIL: manager@finnstown-hotel.ie

HOTEL ★★★   MAP 8 N 11

Here is a country house in the grand manner and while it is only 10 minutes drive by dual carriageway (N4) from the centre of Dublin city, it appears to lie in the very depths of the countryside. Being surrounded as it is by imposing grounds and an immaculately maintained 9-hole golf course. A host of facilities include an indoor heated pool, tennis, gymnasium, turkish bath and golf, of course.

WEB: www.finnstown-hotel.ie/finnstown

Members Of Ashley Courtenay Hotels

B&B from £55.00 to £80.00
€69.84 to €101.58

PAULA SMITH
General Manager

American Express
Diners
Mastercard
Visa

☺ Weekend specials from £147.00

45 45

Open All Year

SPA HOTEL

LUCAN,
CO. DUBLIN
TEL: 01-628 0494   FAX: 01-628 0841

HOTEL ★★   MAP 8 N 11

Situated on the N4, the gateway to the west, and 6km from M50, this elegant hotel is ideally located for convenience, comfort and an exceptionally well appointed with central heating, DD phone, colour TV, tea/coffee facilities and ironing board. Our restaurant offers a choice of 3 menus and superb wines. Ideal for conference and weddings alike. Special golf package available.

Members Of Irish Family Hotels

B&B from £45.00 to £50.00
€57.14 to €63.49

FRANK COLGAN
Director

American Express
Diners
Mastercard
Visa

☺ Weekend specials from £99.00

70 70

Closed 25 December

Room rates are per room per night

WESTON WAY GUESTHOUSE

**2 WESTON PARK, LUCAN,
CO. DUBLIN WEST**
TEL: 01-628 2855 FAX: 01-628 2857

GUESTHOUSE ★★★ MAP 8 N 11

Near Castletown House, Japanese Gardens, National Stud, Kilmainham Gaol, Guinness brewery, Christchurch, Trinity College. 20 mins city. 5 mins Ireland's biggest shopping centre, 15 mins direct route to airport.

B&B from £25.00 to £30.00
€31.74 to €38.09

ANGELA MCPARLAND &
BILL DORTON
Proprietors

6 6

Open All Year

CARRIAGE HOUSE

**LUSK (NEAR AIRPORT),
CO. DUBLIN**
TEL: 01-843 8857 FAX: 01-843 8933
EMAIL: carrhous@iol.ie

GUESTHOUSE U MAP 12 O 12

Carriage House is a family run, warm and friendly guesthouse conveniently situated 10 mins from Dublin airport, 20 mins from city. On main Dublin bus route (33). Relax in our indoor heated swimming pool and sauna. Charming award winning gardens and putting green. All rooms en suite with DD phone and colour TV. Tea/coffee making facilities and secure car parking. Semi finalist in Leverclean accommodation awards. Breakfast menu.

WEB: www.iol.ie/~carrhous

B&B from £25.00 to £30.00
€31.74 to €38.09

ROBERT & GEMMA MCAULEY
Proprietors

Mastercard

Visa

14 14

Closed 15 December - 15 January

GRAND HOTEL

**MALAHIDE,
CO. DUBLIN**
TEL: 01-845 0000 FAX: 01-845 0987
EMAIL: booking@thegrand.ie

HOTEL ★★★★ MAP 12 O 12

The Grand Hotel is situated by the sea in six acres of grounds. 8 mins drive from Dublin airport and 20 mins drive from Dublin city centre. The conference and business centre is one of Ireland's largest and most successful. Many bedrooms have spectacular sea views. Nearby are an abundance of golf courses. Leisure centre includes 21 metre swimming pool, jacuzzi, bubble pool, sauna, steam room, state of the art gymnasium and aerobics room.

B&B from £95.00 to £145.00
€120.63 to €184.11

MATTHEW RYAN
Operations Director

American Express

Diners

Mastercard

Visa

Weekend specials from £125.00

100 100

Closed 25 - 26 December

B&B rates are per person sharing per night incl. Breakfast

ISLAND VIEW HOTEL

COAST ROAD, MALAHIDE,
CO. DUBLIN
TEL: 01-845 0099   FAX: 01-845 1498
EMAIL: info@islandviewhotel.ie

HOTEL ★★   MAP 12 O 12

Island View Hotel is ideally located for comfort and convenience and just a 10 minute drive from Dublin airport. Our rooms are all en suite and fully equipped with modern facilities. Oscar Taylors restaurant is an exclusive 150 seater restaurant with a panoramic view of Lambay Island and Malahide coastline. The restaurant is noted for its excellent cuisine. The menu is extensive and moderately priced.

WEB: www.islandviewhotel.ie

B&B from £40.00 to £50.00
€50.79 to €63.49

PHILIP DARBY
Hotel Manager

American Express
Diners
Mastercard
Visa

10 10

Open All Year

MAUD PLUNKETT'S HOTEL

GROVE ROAD, MALAHIDE,
CO. DUBLIN
TEL: 01-845 2208   FAX: 01-845 5837

HOTEL ★   MAP 12 O 12

Situated in the heart of Ireland's tidiest town, Malahide, this 10 bedroom hotel has a friendly welcome for all travellers. The restaurant is popular with locals and tourists alike. It has an extensive menu and offers value for money. Local attractions include Malahide Castle which dates from the 12th Century. Malahide is a golfers paradise with seven excellent courses within a ten-mile radius including Royal Dublin and Portmarnock.

B&B from £40.00 to £50.00
€50.79 to €63.49

ZAC DONOGHUE
Manager

American Express
Diners
Mastercard
Visa

10 10

Open All Year

PORTMARNOCK HOTEL & GOLF LINKS

STRAND ROAD, PORTMARNOCK,
CO. DUBLIN
TEL: 01-846 0611   FAX: 01-846 2442
EMAIL: res@portmarnock.com

HOTEL ★★★★   MAP 12 O 11

Once the home of the Jameson whiskey family, the Portmarnock Hotel and golf links is in a prime location reaching down to the sea, with views over the 18-hole Bernhard Langer designed links golf course. The 19th century character of the ancestral home is retained in the wood panelled walls, marble fireplaces and ornate ceilings of the Jameson Bar. Located just 15 minutes from Dublin airport and 25 minutes from the city centre.

WEB: portmarnock.com

Members Of Summit Hotels

B&B from £60.00 to £102.50
€76.18 to €130.15

SHANE COOKMAN
General Manager

American Express
Diners
Mastercard
Visa

2 B&B, 1 Dinner and 1 golf from £150.00

103 103

Open All Year

WHITE SANDS HOTEL

COAST ROAD, PORTMARNOCK,
CO. DUBLIN
TEL: 01-846 0003   FAX: 01-846 0420
EMAIL: sandshotel@eircom.net

HOTEL ★★★   MAP 12 O 11

Situated in idyllic Portmarnock, facing the velvet strand, the newly renovated 32 en suite rooms, some with spectacular sea views are spacious and tastefully furnished. 15 mins from Dublin airport, 30 mins from the city centre and close to major golf courses. The hotel's facilities comprise of function and meeting rooms, the Oasis bar, the Kingford Smith restaurant serving contemporary food with Irish flair and the renowned Tamango's night club.

B&B from £45.00 to £75.00
€57.14 to €95.23

GEORGINA HIGGINS
General Manager

American Express
Diners
Mastercard
Visa

🛏️🚗📞▯📺Ⓣ©CM♿🎵🅿️🔧
32 32

alc 🔌 Inet

HOTELS
FEDERATION

Open All Year

CITY WEST HOTEL, CONFERENCE, LEISURE & GOLF RESORT

SAGGART,
CO. DUBLIN
TEL: 01-401 0500   FAX: 01-458 8565
EMAIL: info@citywest-hotel.iol.ie

HOTEL ★★★★   MAP 8 N 11

Elegant 4**** hotel with 200 deluxe rooms set in 180 acres of majestic woodland. Facilities include our own championship golf course, Driving Range, MacGregor Golf Academy and 5 star Health and Leisure club. Ideally situated 15 mins from Dublin city centre and 20 mins from Dublin Airport. Our traditional lounges and bars are popular meeting places for locals and visitors alike. The Terrace restaurant offers a gourmet dining experience. Ideal venue for conferences up to 1,800 delegates.

WEB: www.citywesthotel-ireland.com

B&B from £47.50 to £65.00
€60.31 to €82.53

WENDY GREGAN
Sales Director

American Express
Diners
Mastercard
Visa

:/🍴

🙂 Weekend specials from £110.00

🛏️🚗📞▯📺Ⓣ©CM❄️🔧🎱⚲U
🏃18🎵🅿️🔧🔌 Inet

HOTELS
FEDERATION

Open All Year

ABIGAIL HOUSE

COMMONS ROAD, LOUGHLINSTOWN,
SHANKILL, CO. DUBLIN
TEL: 01-282 4747   FAX: 01-272 1068
EMAIL: abigailsguesthouse@irl.com

GUESTHOUSE ★★★   MAP 8 O 11

Nestled in woodlands on the banks of the Shanganagh river just off N11 is Abigails Guesthouse. ITB approved. Large carpark. Beautiful gardens. TV lounge with tea/coffee facilities. 10 ground floor en suite rooms with DD phone, hairdryer, iron, etc. on request. City centre 30 minutes. Dun Laoire ferryport 15 minutes. Convenient Shankill DART and city bus routes. Local amenities: golf, Druid's Glen, Woodbrook, Powerscourt, Leopardstown Races, bars and restaurants.

B&B from £20.00 to £30.00
€25.39 to €38.09

IMELDA REYNOLDS
Proprietor

Mastercard
Visa

:/

🛏️🚗📞📺Ⓣ©❄️⚲U🎵🅿️📶🆂
11 10

HOTELS
FEDERATION

Closed 19 December - 03 January

B&B rates are per person sharing per night incl. Breakfast

REDBANK HOUSE

**6/7 CHURCH STREET, SKERRIES,
FINGAL, CO. DUBLIN
TEL: 01-849 1005 FAX: 01-849 1598
EMAIL: redbank@eircom.net**

GUESTHOUSE ★★★   MAP 12 P 12

Enjoy the extended hospitality of the McCoy's in Redbank House. The world famous seafood restaurant is the dining room of Redbank House. The seven en suite rooms have the McCoys sense of style and elegance. The area is particularly rich in golf courses and a wide variety of leisure activities include sea fishing, boat trips, sailing and horse riding. The Chef Proprietor Terry McCoy cooks the catch of the day landed at Skerries pier specialising in the world famous Dublin Bay prawns.

WEB: www.redbank.ie

B&B from £35.00 to £45.00
€44.44 to €57.14

TERRY MCCOY
Proprietor

American Express
Diners
Mastercard
Visa

Weekend specials from £85.00

7 7

REDBANK LODGE & RESTAURANT

**12 CONVENT LANE, SKERRIES,
CO. DUBLIN
TEL: 01-849 1005   FAX: 01-849 1598
EMAIL: redbank@eircom.net**

GUESTHOUSE ★★★   MAP 12 P 12

Situated in the picturesque fishing port of Skerries, north county Dublin. Each of the five ensuite double bedrooms are elegantly decorated with DD telephone and TV. Adjacent to the award winning Redbank Restaurant, with it's infamous reputation for superb cuisine (fish dishes our speciality) and a well stocked wine cellar. With easy access to Dublin City & Dublin Airport as well as enjoying local attractions such as Ardgillan Demesne, the nearby Boyne Valley & Newgrange.

WEB: www.guesthousesireland.com

B&B from £30.00 to £40.00
€38.09 to €50.79

TERRY MCCOY
Owner

American Express
Diners
Mastercard
Visa

Weekend specials from £85.00

5 5

Room rates are per room per night

MARINE HOTEL

SUTTON CROSS,
DUBLIN 13
TEL: 01-839 0000   FAX: 01-839 0442
EMAIL: info@marinehotel.ie

HOTEL ★★★   MAP 12 P 11

The Marine Hotel 3*** (AA***) overlooks the north shore of Dublin Bay. The two acres of lawn sweep down to the sea shore. All bedrooms are en suite and have trouser press, TV, Direct Dial phone and tea/coffee facilities. The city centre is 6km away and the airport 25 minutes drive. Close by is the DART rapid rail system. The hotel has a heated indoor swimming pool and sauna. Nearby are the Royal Dublin and Portmarnock championship golf courses.

WEB: www.marinehotel.ie

B&B from £80.00 to £85.00
€101.58 to €107.93

SHEILA BAIRD
General Manager

American Express
Diners
Mastercard
Visa

Weekend specials from £99.00

50   50

Closed 25 - 27 December

SUTTON CASTLE HOTEL

REDROCK, SUTTON,
DUBLIN 13
TEL: 01-832 2688   FAX: 01-832 4476
EMAIL: suttoncs@indigo.ie

HOTEL ★★★   MAP 12 O 11

Cloistered in a panoramic setting on the Howth peninsula and set in six acres of landscaped gardens overlooking Dublin Bay. Sutton Castle is 13km from Dublin airport and 16km from Dublin city. All bedrooms are en suite with direct dial phone and multi channel TV. Championship Golf courses including Portmarnock and Royal Dublin, fishing, sailing and horse riding are nearby. Superb cuisine is served in our bistro and carvery. Member of Manor House Hotels (Tel: 01-2958900).

Members Of Manor House Hotels

B&B from £60.00 to £75.00
€76.18 to €95.23

RAY MOONEY
General Manager

American Express
Diners
Mastercard
Visa

3 B&B and 2 Dinners from £139.00

17   17

inet FAX

Closed 25 - 26 December

FORTE TRAVELODGE

PINNOCK HILL, SWORDS ROUNDABOUT,
BELFAST ROAD, CO. DUBLIN
TEL: 1800-709709   FAX: 01-840 9235

HOTEL U   MAP 8 O 11

Situated only 12.8km from Dublin city centre on the Dublin to Belfast road and minutes from the airport, this superb modern hotel offers comfortable yet affordable, accommodation. Each room is large enough to sleep up to three adults, a child under 12 and a baby in a cot. Excellent range of facilities, from en suite bathroom to colour TV including Sky Sports and Sky Movies. Unbeatable value for business or leisure. Sited next to Little Chef restaurant.

Room Rate from £49.95 to £59.95
€63.42 to €76.12

DAVID HURLEY
Manager

American Express
Diners
Mastercard
Visa

100   100

Open All Year

B&B rates are per person sharing per night incl. Breakfast

GLENMORE HOUSE

AIRPORT ROAD, NEVINSTOWN,
SWORDS, CO. DUBLIN
TEL: 01-840 3610   FAX: 01-840 4148

GUESTHOUSE N   MAP 12 O 12

Ideally situated just 1k from Dublin airport and 20 minutes from the city centre, on the main airport/city bus routes, Glenmore House is a spacious family-run guesthouse set in 2 acres of gardens, lawns and private secure carparks. All rooms are beautifully decorated with bathroom, phone, TV, tea/coffee facilities and hairdryer. The warmest of welcomes at a very reasonable cost for business and leisure alike.

B&B from £24.00 to £35.00
€30.47 to €44.44

REBECCA GIBNEY
Proprietor

Mastercard

Visa

Midweek specials from £70.00

20   20

Closed 23 - 27 December

ASHVIEW HOUSE

THE WARD, ASHBOURNE ROAD,
CO. DUBLIN
TEL: 01-835 0499

GUESTHOUSE ★★   MAP 12 O 11

A family run warm and friendly 2* guesthouse with guest sitting room, snooker room, private car park and landscaped gardens, golf, horse riding and swimming nearby. Situated on the main Dublin/Derry road, N2, 11km from Dublin city, 9km from Dublin Airport. Close to Fairyhouse racecourse and Tattersalls sales. Located 5km from Ashbourne it's an ideal touring centre for Newgrange, Slane Castle and the Boyne in Co. Meath.

B&B from £17.00 to £20.00
€21.59 to €25.39

JOSEPHINE FAY
Proprietor

8   3

IRISH
HOTELS
FEDERATION

Closed 24 - 28 December

BEAUFORT HOUSE

GHAN ROAD, CARLINGFORD,
CO. LOUTH
TEL: 042-937 3879   FAX: 042-937 3878

GUESTHOUSE ★★★   MAP 12 O 5

Beaufort House, AA ◆◆◆◆◆, a magnificent shoreside residence with glorious sea and mountain views in medieval Carlingford village. Your hosts, Michael & Glynnis Caine, Bord Fáilte award winners of excellence, will ensure the highest standards. In house activities include sailing school and yacht charter. Tennis court. Golfing arranged in any of five golf courses within 20 mins of Beaufort House. Helipad and private car parking. Dinner by prior arrangement.

B&B from £25.00 to £30.00
€31.74 to €38.09

MICHAEL & GLYNNIS CAINE

Mastercard

Visa

5   5

Open All Year

Room rates are per room per night

MCKEVITT'S VILLAGE HOTEL

MARKET SQUARE, CARLINGFORD, CO. LOUTH
TEL: 042-937 3116 FAX: 042-937 3144

HOTEL ★★ MAP 12 O 15

McKevitts Village Hotel is family owned and personally supervised by Kay & Terry McKevitt. At the Hotel, pride of place is taken in the personal attention given to guests by owners and staff. Carlingford is one of Irelands oldest and most interesting medieval villages. Beautifully situated on the shores of Carlingford Lough and half way between Dublin and Belfast.

Members Of Irish Family Hotels

B&B from £28.00 to £45.00
€35.55 to €57.14

TERRY & KAY MCKEVITT
Owners

Mastercard
Visa

15 15

HOTELS

Open All Year

BELLINGHAM CASTLE HOTEL

CASTLEBELLINGHAM, CO. LOUTH
TEL: 042-937 2176 FAX: 042-937 2766

HOTEL ★★ MAP 12 O 14

Bellingham Castle Hotel is situated close by the pleasant little village of Castlebellingham, Co. Louth, resting in countryside enveloped in history, legend and engaged in beautiful scenery. In the hotel itself, which is an elegant refurbished 17th century castle, you will find all the facilities of a modern hotel, harmonising beautifully with the antique decor and atmosphere of old world splendour.

B&B from £40.00 to £45.00
€50.79 to €57.14

PASCHAL KEENAN
Manager

American Express
Mastercard
Visa

20 20

Closed 24 - 26 December

BOYNE VALLEY HOTEL & COUNTRY CLUB

DROGHEDA, CO. LOUTH
TEL: 041-983 7737 FAX: 041-983 9188
EMAIL: reservations@boyne-valley-hotel.ie

HOTEL ★★★ MAP 12 O 13

Gracious country house on 16 acres of gardens and woodlands, beside historic town of Drogheda, south on the N1. 40k from Dublin and 32k airport. Boyne restaurant with daily supply of fresh fish. Nearby, historic sites of Newgrange, Dowth, Knowth and medieval abbeys Mellifont and Monasterboice. Leisure club, 18 hole pitch & putt on site. 2 tennis courts. 34 new bedrooms opening May 1st 2000.

WEB: www.boyne-valley-hotel.ie

B&B from £54.00 to £54.00
€68.57 to €68.57

MICHAEL MCNAMARA
Proprietor/Manager

American Express
Diners
Mastercard
Visa

Weekend specials from £120.00

37 37

HOTELS

Open All Year

B&B rates are per person sharing per night incl. Breakfast

WESTCOURT HOTEL

WEST STREET, DROGHEDA,
CO. LOUTH
TEL: 041-983 0965 FAX: 041-983 0970

HOTEL ★★★ MAP 12 O 13

At the Westcourt Hotel, our visitors will find the highest standard of courtesy and efficiency coupled with luxurious surroundings in the heart of the historical town of Drogheda. Our bedrooms are all en suite and decorated with television, direct dial phone, tea/coffee making facilities. Our Courtyard restaurant and traditional Irish bar have the finest food, drink and atmosphere for you to enjoy. We pride ourselves on a highly personalised service and look forward to welcoming you.

B&B from £35.00 to £45.00
€44.44 to €57.14

BARRY TIERNEY
Manager

American Express
Diners
Mastercard
Visa

27 27

IRISH HOTELS FEDERATION

Closed 25 December

BALLYMASCANLON HOUSE HOTEL

DUNDALK,
CO. LOUTH
TEL: 042-937 1124 FAX: 042-937 1598
EMAIL: info@ballymascanlon.com

HOTEL ★★★ MAP 12 O 14

Ballymascanlon Hotel is a Victorian mansion set in 130 acre demesne on the scenic Cooley Peninsula. The hotel while retaining its old world ambience has recently had its facilities modernised. Our new leisure centre incorporates a 20m deck level pool, leisure pool, sauna, jacuzzi, steam room, gymnasium and tennis courts. Our 18 hole Parkland golf course surrounding the hotel is both a pleasurable challenge to play and exhilarating to view. Supplement for superior rooms.

WEB: www.globalgolf.com/ballymascanlon

B&B from £45.00 to £48.00
€57.14 to €60.95

OLIVER QUINN

American Express
Diners
Mastercard
Visa

☺ Weekend specials from £105.00

74 74

IRISH HOTELS FEDERATION

Closed 24 - 27 December

CARRICKDALE HOTEL & LEISURE COMPLEX

CARRICKCARNON, RAVENSDALE,
DUNDALK, CO. LOUTH
TEL: 042-937 1397 FAX: 042-937 1740

HOTEL ★★★ MAP 12 O 14

This Hotel, Conference & swimming leisure complex is situated halfway between Dublin and Belfast on the main N1 route just 10km north of Dundalk, 8km south of Newry. All en suite bedrooms are tastefully decorated, the restaurant is the most popular in the area and carvery lunches are served daily. Entertainment each weekend. Ideal touring destination to the mountains of Mourne, Cooley or Carlingford and Northern Ireland tourist areas.

B&B from £40.00 to £40.00
€50.79 to €50.79

JOHN McPARLAND
Proprietor

American Express
Diners
Mastercard
Visa

☺ Weekend specials from £120.00

50 50

IRISH HOTELS FEDERATION

Closed 25 - 26 December

Room rates are per room per night

CLANBRASSIL HOTEL

CLANBRASSIL STREET, DUNDALK,
CO. LOUTH
TEL: 042-34141   FAX: 042-28779

HOTEL ★★   MAP 12 O 14

Ideally situated between the two capitals, Belfast and Dublin, in the heart of Dundalk town, a heavenly location for shopaholics, with an abundance of superb shops. 18 hole golf course within 10km drive, Carlingford Lough, Mourne Mountains, Boyne Valley all a short drive away.

B&B from £35.00 to £35.00
€44.44 to €44.44

ANITA MCCANN

American Express
Diners
Mastercard
Visa

16 16

Closed 25 - 26 December

DERRYHALE HOTEL

CARRICK ROAD, DUNDALK,
CO. LOUTH
TEL: 042-933 5471 FAX: 042-933 5471
EMAIL: info@minotel.iol.ie

HOTEL ★★   MAP 12 O 14

Midway between Dublin and Belfast, Derryhale Hotel is an ideal base for touring the north east of Ireland, mountains of Mourne, Carlingford, Cooley peninsula. Bedrooms contain TV and direct dial telephone. Good quality food is a tradition at the hotel. Derryhale Hotel has wedding and conference facilities. Activities close by include fishing, water skiing, sailing, beaches, horse riding and golf.

Members Of MinOtel Ireland Hotel Group

Room Rate from £35.00 to £45.00
€44.44 to €57.14

LIAM SEXTON
Managing Director

American Express
Diners
Mastercard
Visa

☺ Weekend specials from £85.00

19 19

alc

Open All Year

FAIRWAYS HOTEL

DUBLIN ROAD, DUNDALK,
CO. LOUTH
TEL: 042-932 1500   FAX: 042-932 1511
EMAIL: info@fairways.ie

HOTEL ★★★   MAP 12 O 14

The Fairways Hotel and Leisure Centre, is a busy family-run hotel situated south of Dundalk on the main Dublin/Belfast route N1. The leisure centre contains indoor heated swimming pool, sauna, jacuzzi, steamroom, badminton, squash and tennis courts plus snooker tables. A wide range of food is available throughout the day in the carvery/grill and Modi's bistro. Golf can be organised by the hotel on a choice of local golf courses. Conference facilities available.

WEB. www.fairways.ie

Members Of Business & Leisure Ltd.

B&B from £45.00 to £50.00
€57.14 to €63.49

BRIAN P. QUINN
Managing Director

American Express
Diners
Mastercard
Visa

☺ Weekend specials from £87.00

48 48

Closed 24 - 25 December

B&B rates are per person sharing per night incl. Breakfast

HOTEL IMPERIAL

PARK STREET, DUNDALK,
CO. LOUTH
TEL: 042-933 2241 FAX: 042-933 7909

HOTEL ★★ MAP 12 O 14

Built in the 70's this is a modern hotel of high standard. There is an excellent bar, also a coffee shop which is open from 8am - 10pm. Dining room open all day serving à la carte menu and dinner from 6pm - 10pm. Secure parking can be arranged nearby at no extra charge. Rooms being refurbished at the moment to a 2000 standard.

B&B from £40.00 to £45.00
€50.79 to €57.14

PETER QUINN
Managing Director

American Express
Diners
Mastercard
Visa

:/T

☺ Weekend specials from £85.00

47 47
alc

Closed 25 December

GRANVUE HOUSE

OMEATH,
CO. LOUTH
TEL: 042-937 5109 FAX: 042-937 5415

GUESTHOUSE ★★★ MAP 12 O 15

This large luxuriously appointed family run. Guesthouse is fully licensed - located on the shore of Carlingford Lough with panoramic view of Mourne and Cooley Mountains. Ideal base from which to tour the North. Activities close by include fishing, waterskiing, golf, sailing and hill walking. We pride ourselves on a highly personalised service and look forward to welcoming you.

B&B from £24.00 to £24.00
€30.47 to €30.47

LAURENCE & JOSEPHINE BRENNAN
Owners

Mastercard
Visa

☺ Weekend specials from £63.00

9 9

Closed 23 December - 01 January

AISLING HOUSE

DUBLIN ROAD, ASHBOURNE,
CO. MEATH
TEL: 01-835 0359 FAX: 01-835 1135
EMAIL: duke2@iol.ie

GUESTHOUSE ★★ MAP 12 O 12

Situated on one acre of landscaped gardens on the Dublin/Derry road N2 a mile from Ashbourne village, only 20 minutes from Dublin city centre and airport, convenient to Fairyhouse racecourse and Tattersalls sales. Rooms en suite with guest lounge, games room and private car park. Aisling House is an ideal base for business or holiday. Local amenities include golf, horse riding, clay pidgeon shooting and fishing in the Boyne river.

B&B from £23.00 to £25.00
€29.20 to €31.74

KATHLEEN DAVITT
Proprietor

Mastercard
Visa

10 10

Closed 24 - 28 December

Room rates are per room per night

BROADMEADOW COUNTRY HOUSE & EQUESTRIAN CENTRE

BULLSTOWN, ASHBOURNE,
CO. MEATH
TEL: 01-835 2823 FAX: 01-835 2819
EMAIL: broadmeadow@eircom.net

GUESTHOUSE N   MAP 12 O 12

This exceptional family-run country house is located near Ashbourne village, only 12k from Dublin airport and 20k from the city centre. It is set in 100 acres of farmland with a modern purpose-built equestrian centre. All rooms en suite and designed for maximum guest comfort. Private car parking, tennis court and landscaped gardens. Surrounded by numerous golf courses and restaurants. Ideal location for both tourist and business people. Specialists in equestrian packages.

WEB: www.equine-net.com/broadmeadow

Members Of Equestrian Holidays Ireland

B&B from £28.00 to £36.00
€35.55 to €45.71

ELAINE DUFF
Manager

Mastercard

Visa

8 8

Closed 24 - 26 December

OLD DARNLEY LODGE HOTEL

MAIN STREET, ATHBOY,
CO. MEATH
TEL: 046-32283 FAX: 046-32255

HOTEL ★★★   MAP 11M 12

This 19th century hotel has just recently been refurbished to the very highest standards. The hotel is a haven of tranquility and is ideally located. Dublin and Athlone are only one hours drive away. All bedrooms are en suite and offer a variety of services including, DD phone, multi channel TV, trouser press, hair dryers and tea/coffee making facilities. There are plenty of historic landmarks to see and plenty of activities to enjoy, including golf, fishing, boating, horse riding.

B&B from £25.00 to £30.00
€31.74 to €38.09

TIM O'BRIEN
General Manager

American Express

Diners

Mastercard

Visa

15 15

Open All Year

NEPTUNE BEACH

BETTYSTOWN,
CO. MEATH
TEL: 041-982 7107 FAX: 041-982 7412
EMAIL: info@neptunebeach.ie

HOTEL R   MAP 12 O 13

Located 25 mins north of Dublin Airport with a spectacular setting overlooking Bettystown beach. All 38 rooms are elegantly furnished to provide the comfort and facilities expected of a leading hotel. Enjoy fine dining in the restaurant, afternoon tea in the cosy Winter Garden or a relaxing drink in the Neptune Bar. The leisure club facilities include 20m swimming pool, jacuzzi, sauna and fitness suite. Local golf courses: Laytown & Bettystown, Seapoint and Co. Louth.

WEB: www.neptunebeach.ie

B&B from £50.00 to £100.00
€63.49 to €126.97

DERMOT WALDRON
General Manager

American Express

Mastercard

Visa

Weekend specials from £115.00

38 38

Open All Year

B&B rates are per person sharing per night incl. Breakfast

HEADFORT ARMS HOTEL

**KELLS,
CO. MEATH
TEL: 046-40063 FAX: 046-40587**

HOTEL ★★   MAP 11M 13

Situated in the historical town of Kells, it is 40km from Dublin on the main Derry/Donegal route. This traditional family hotel has 18 bedrooms, all have bath/shower, TV, video, etc. We at the Headfort offer a blend of homeliness, good taste and first class management. Conference facilities provided. Available locally: golf, fishing, tennis. Coffee shop / carvery open 7 days until 10pm.

B&B from £35.00 to £70.00
€44.44 to €88.88

VINCENT DUFF
General Manager

American Express
Mastercard
Visa

Open All Year

Room rates are per room per night

Meath

Where Heritage Lives

Just stand for a few minutes on the Hill of Tara and you'll know what we mean. The sight of Trim Castle's monumental ramparts will do it to you as well. Or the mysterious neolithic wonders of Loughcrew and Newgrange at *Brú na Boinne*. Meath's heritage springs to life, grabbing the imagination with vivid images of the past. Discover Meath's living heritage.

For all your tourism needs and services contact Meath Tourism at:

Callsave 1850 300 789

www.meathtourism.ie   info@meathtourism.ie

Meath
Always a visit to treasure

ARDBOYNE HOTEL

DUBLIN ROAD, NAVAN,
CO. MEATH
TEL: 046-23119 FAX: 046-22355

HOTEL ★★★   MAP 12 N 13

Having been recently refurbished, the Ardboyne Hotel is the newest member of the Quinn Hotel Group and is enjoying its attractive facelift. Situated in its own pleasant grounds, the hotel is conveniently located on the outskirts of Navan and is the perfect base for visiting the many places of interest. Our restaurant offers delicious food in cosy surroundings and our function rooms will cater for every occasion from the grand and gracious to the private and intimate.

—

B&B from £40.00 to £44.00
€50.79 to €55.87

RITA GLEESON
General Manager

American Express
Diners
Mastercard
Visa

😊   Midweek special 2B&B & 1
Dinner from £86.00

29 29

Closed 24 - 26 December

MA DWYERS GUESTHOUSE

DUBLIN ROAD, NAVAN,
CO. MEATH
TEL: 046-77992 FAX: 046-77995

GUESTHOUSE ★★★   MAP 12 N 13

Ma Dwyers newly opened guesthouse possesses many of the qualities of a high class hotel, along with a cosy homely feel which is so vitally important. 9 beautiful ensuite rooms with a D.D. Telephone, TV, Hairdryer and Tea/Coffee facilities with Fax and photocopying services available. Ideally located just minutes walk from the town centre and plenty of historic landmarks to see and activities to enjoy including Golf, Fishing, Boating and Horseriding.

B&B from £25.00 to £28.00
€31.74 to €35.55

DOREEN MULVANEY
Manageress

9 9

Closed 24 - 27 December

NEWGRANGE HOTEL

BRIDGE STREET, NAVAN,
CO. MEATH
TEL: 046-74100 FAX: 046-73977
EMAIL: info@newgrangehotel.ie

HOTEL N   MAP 12 N 13

Centrally located in the heart of a typical Irish market town yet just 30 mins from Dublin airport, the Newgrange Hotel offers a perfect alliance of modern comforts, high standards of food and service. Set within a stylish Gothic design theme, 2 restaurants, 2 bars and a relaxing library lounge await you. (Conference & banqueting facilities to 550). Castles, gardens, craft shops, golfing, shopping, racing all nearby. Heritage and culture abound with the famous Newgrange burial tomb 20mins drive.

WEB: www.newgrangohotol.io

B&B from £35.00 to £44.00
€44.44 to €55.87

MATT O'CONNOR
Managing Director

American Express
Diners
Mastercard
Visa

😊   Weekend specials from £89.50

36 36

alc inet

HOTELS
FEDERATION

Closed 24 - 25 December

B&B rates are per person sharing per night incl. Breakfast

CONYNGHAM ARMS HOTEL

SLANE,
CO. MEATH
TEL: 041-988 4444 FAX: 041-982 4205
EMAIL: conynghamarms@eircom.net

HOTEL ★★ MAP 12 N 13

Located in a lovely manor village
built c. 1850, this traditional family
hotel with 4 poster beds, where you
can enjoy good food and friendly
service, is an ideal base from which
to tour the Boyne Valley - particularly
the tomb of Knowth and Newgrange,
various abbeys, and the birth place
of Francis Ledwidge, all within 15
minutes drive. Available locally: 5
golf courses within 25km. Village
Inn Hotels reservations: 353
419884444; UK 0990 300200 and
USA 1800 44 UTELL.

Members Of Village Inn Hotels

B&B from £27.50 to £50.00
€34.92 to €63.49

KEVIN J. MACKEN
Inn Keeper

American Express
Diners
Mastercard
Visa

14 14
a/c

HOTELS
FEDERATION

Closed 23 - 27 December

HIGHFIELD HOUSE

MAUDLINS ROAD, TRIM,
CO. MEATH
TEL: 046-36386   FAX: 046-38182

GUESTHOUSE N MAP 11M 12

Highfield House guest
accommodation is a beautiful period
residence. Historical building dates
back to the early 18th century. It is
situated overlooking Trim Castle and
the river Boyne just off the main
Dublin road. Inside there are seven
spacious en suite guest rooms with
colour TV, DD phone, coffee/tea
facilities. Beautiful view from all
rooms. 2 mins walking distance to
town.

B&B from £18.00 to £40.00
€22.86 to €50.79

EDWARD & GERALDINE DUIGNAN
Proprietors

Mastercard
Visa

7 7
S

HOTELS
FEDERATION

Closed 23 December - 03 January

WELLINGTON COURT HOTEL

SUMMERHILL ROAD, TRIM,
CO. MEATH
TEL: 046-31516   FAX: 046-36002

HOTEL ★★ MAP 11M 12

The Wellington Court Hotel is family
owned and offers visitors a warm
welcome and old fashioned courtesy
along with excellent facilities. Our 18
rooms are all en suite with DD
phone, colour TV, central heating.
Also tea/coffee facilities. Superb
accommodation, excellent food, set
in Ireland's most historic
surroundings with the magnificent
medieval ruins of King John's
Castle, one of the most enduring
attractions in the area.

B&B from £30.00 to £39.00
€38.09 to €49.52

M & C NALLY
Proprietors

American Express
Mastercard
Visa

18 18
a/c

HOTELS
FEDERATION

Closed 25 - 26 December

Room rates are per room per night

GORMANSTOWN MANOR

FARM GUEST HOUSE, NEAR WICKLOW
TOWN (OFF N11), CO. WICKLOW
TEL: 0404-69432 FAX: 0404-61832
EMAIL: gormanstownmanor@eircom.net

GUESTHOUSE ★★ MAP 8 P 9

A warm welcome awaits you at this charming family guest house. Bright spacious en-suite bedrooms. Peaceful relaxed atmosphere, spectacular surroundings. Golf driving range on farm, landscaped gardens, nature walks and superb personal services. Ideally located for playing golf and touring The Garden of Ireland. Breathtaking scenery, mountains, valleys, rivers, lakes and woodlands. Enjoy stunning sandy beaches of Brittas Bay. Sailing, fishing, gardens, heritage, horseriding and polo.

B&B from £25.00 to £35.00
€31.74 to €44.44

MARGARET MURPHY
Proprietor

Mastercard

Visa

Midweek specials from £75.00

9 9

Open All Year

GRAND HOTEL

WICKLOW,
CO. WICKLOW
TEL: 0404-67337 FAX: 0404-69607
EMAIL: grandhotel@eircom.net

HOTEL ★★★ MAP 8 P 9

This charming hotel is the perfect base for touring the beautiful Garden of Ireland. Situated in Wicklow town, it is only a 40 minute drive from Dublin on the N11. Enjoy golf, fishing, hill walking, sandy beaches and sight seeing locally. 33 large, bright, comfortable bedrooms all en suite with direct dial telephone, multi channel TV and tea/coffee making facilities. Fine food served in the restaurant and grill room all day. Lively lounge bar. Conference facilities.

WEB: www.grandhotel@tinet.ie

B&B from £33.00 to £50.00
€41.90 to €63.49

BARRY MAHER
Managing Director

Mastercard

Visa

33 33

Open All Year

OLD RECTORY COUNTRY HOUSE & RESTAURANT

WICKLOW,
CO. WICKLOW
TEL: 0404-67048 FAX: 0404-69181
EMAIL: mail@oldrectory.ie

GUESTHOUSE ★★★★ MAP 8 P 9

Award-winning, elegant Victorian house where keynotes are charm, tranquility, service and superb cuisine. Enjoy delightful rooms furnished in country house style and gourmet dining, exquisitely presented with herbs and edible flowers. Featured on TV's Gourmet Ireland and Europe's Classic Inns. Winner of National Breakfast, AA Inspectors Award and Egon Ronay Healthy Eating award. Nearby: Powerscourt, Mt Usher, Druids Glen, Glendalough and Wicklow's Historic Gaol.

WEB: indigo.ie/~oldrec

Members Of Ireland's Blue Book

B&B from £54.00 to £54.00
€68.57 to €68.57

PAUL & LINDA SAUNDERS
Proprietors

American Express

Mastercard

Visa

Weekend specials from £119.00

8 8

Closed 01 January - 04 March

B&B rates are per person sharing per night incl. Breakfast

ARKLOW BAY HOTEL

ARKLOW,
CO. WICKLOW
TEL: 0402-32309 FAX: 0402-32300
EMAIL: arklowbay@eircom.net

HOTEL ★★★ MAP 8 O 8

The Arklow Bay Hotel is situated in the heart of Wicklow and is an ideal base for touring this beautiful countryside. New leisure centre due to open in May 2000. Lively bar. Excellent cuisine in our Windermere Restaurant. Extensive conference facilities in a range of suites. Carpark. Enjoy golf, fishing, hillwalking, all available locally. Sister to Springhill Court Hotel, Kilkenny. Member of Business & Leisure Ireland.

WEB: www.arklowbay.com

Members Of Chara Hotel Group

B&B from £40.00 to £59.50
€50.79 to €75.55

ROBERT MCCARTHY
General Manager

American Express
Diners
Mastercard
Visa

🛏️🐾☎️TC❄️CM✳️🫖🛶🎵P
55 55

Open All Year

BRIDGE HOTEL

BRIDGE STREET, ARKLOW,
CO. WICKLOW
TEL: 0402-31666   FAX: 0402-31666

HOTEL ★★ MAP 8 O 8

The Bridge Hotel is a family-run 18 bedroomed hotel situated at the bridge in Arklow beside the Avoca river and only 10 mins walk to the sea. Arklow has a strong seafaring heritage and is famous for its pottery. The town offers a great variety of holiday activities whether you swim, play golf, tennis, fish or walk. Arklow is an ideal base from which to see the beautiful scenery of Wicklow. Only 6.5km to Ballykissangel.

B&B from £25.00 to £29.00
€31.74 to €36.82

JIM HOEY
Proprietor

🛏️🐾☎️TCCM🛶JPS
18 14

Closed 25 December

CLOGGA BAY HOTEL

CLOGGA, ARKLOW,
CO. WICKLOW
TEL: 0402-39299 FAX: 0402-91538

HOTEL ★★ MAP 8 O 8

Situated in the garden of Ireland by the sea. Family owned and managed, set on a 2 acre garden. Only 60km from Dublin, located 3km south of Arklow town in secluded countryside with direct access to the beach from the hotel. All rooms en suite, direct dial telephone with colour TV. Local amenities include pony trekking, golf, fishing, swimming etc. Our restaurant offers superb food, extensive à la carte and table d'hôte menus.

B&B from £25.00 to £27.50
€31.74 to €34.92

FIOUNNUALA JAMESON
Manageress

American Express
Mastercard
Visa

🛏️🐾☎️TCCM✳️JP🛟S
10 10

Open All Year

OSTAN BEAG HOTEL

62/63 MAIN STREET, ARKLOW,
CO. WICKLOW
TEL: 0402-33044 FAX: 0402-33060

HOTEL ★★ MAP 8 O 8

Ostan Beag is situated in the centre of Arklow, walking distance from stretches of sandy beaches and some of the finest Golf clubs. All rooms en suite, D.D. phone and TV. Old style restaurant has a reputation for good food, value for money with bar menu available all day. Whether you're away for romance or a night in the town you will enjoy the craic and porter in the Tunnel Night Club where entertainment is at its best.

B&B from £30.00 to £50.00
€38.09 to €63.49

MICHEAL HENNEBRY
Proprietor

Mastercard

Visa

20 20

alc

HOTELS
FEDERATION

Closed 25 - 26 December

BEL-AIR HOTEL

ASHFORD,
CO. WICKLOW
TEL: 0404-40109 FAX: 0404-40188

HOTEL U MAP 8 P 9

Bel-Air Hotel is a family run hotel and riding school situated in the centre of 81 hectares of farm and parkland. Managed by the Murphy-Freeman family since 1937. The lovely gardens have a breathtaking view to the sea. The homely atmosphere, big log fires and rich history make the hotel a popular venue. Good home cooking and delicious afternoon teas. Rooms en suite with tea making facilities, TVs and hairdryers. EHI Equestrian Wicklow.

B&B from £30.00 to £32.00
€38.09 to €40.63

FIDELMA FREEMAN
Owner

American Express

Diners

Mastercard

Visa

☺ Weekend specials from £78.00

10 10

alc

HOTELS
FEDERATION

Closed 01 - 07 January

CHESTER BEATTY INN

ASHFORD VILLAGE,
CO. WICKLOW
TEL: 0404-40206 FAX: 0404-49003
EMAIL: hotelchesterbeatty@eircom.net

HOTEL N MAP 8 P 9

The Chester Beatty Inn situated in the village of Ashford on the main N11 road, 35 mins south of Dublin. Ideally situated for touring, golfing (adjacent to Druids Glen home of the Murphy's Irish Open), fishing, hill walking and gardens (opposite Mount Usher Gardens, 15 mins from Powerscourt Gardens). Charming country inn style family run hotel comprising 12 luxury en suite bedrooms, award-winning restaurant, lounge and traditional Irish bar all with open log fires. Secure private car parking.

B&B from £30.00 to £55.00
€38.09 to €69.84

KITTY & PAUL CAPRANI

American Express

Diners

Mastercard

Visa

☺ Weekend specials from £79.00

12 12

alc

HOTELS
FEDERATION

Closed 24 - 26 December

B&B rates are per person sharing per night incl. Breakfast

CULLENMORE HOTEL

ASHFORD,
CO. WICKLOW
TEL: 0404-40187   FAX: 0404-40471
EMAIL: cullenmore@eircom.net

HOTEL ★★   MAP 8 P 9

The Cullenmore hotel is a pleasant, friendly, family run hotel, located near Ashford in the garden of Ireland. All bedrooms are modern, en suite, with two designed for wheelchair users. TV (satellite) and DD phone are standard throughout. Extensive bar food menu served all day. Ideal venue for a relaxing break. Very reasonable rates.

B&B from £28.00 to £35.00
€35.55 to €44.44

OLIVE & DIRK VAN DER FLIER

American Express
Diners
Mastercard
Visa

17 17

Closed 24 - 27 December

BROOKLODGE AT MACREDDIN

MACREDDIN VILLAGE,
CO. WICKLOW
TEL: 0402-36444   FAX: 0402-36580
EMAIL: brooklodge@macreddin.ie

UNDER CONSTRUCTION OPENING DEC 1999

HOTEL P   MAP 8 O 8

A welcome as warm as our real fires...a 4 star standard countryhouse hotel in spectacular Wicklow countryside, yet less than an hour from south Dublin...a relaxed drink in the charming Waterside lounge or the perfect pint in Actons country pub...sumptuous, real cuisine using wild, free range and organic foods... deep baths and crisp linen on luxurious beds...golf, horseriding, country walks, field and clay shooting...food, wine and tabletop shops...live the dream...

WEB: www.brooklodge.com

Members Of Manor House Hotels

B&B from £65.00 to £75.00
€82.53 to €95.23

EVAN DOYLE & FREDA DOYLE
Directors

American Express
Diners
Mastercard
Visa

40 40

Inet

Open All Year

LAWLESS HOTEL

AUGHRIM,
CO. WICKLOW
TEL: 0402-36146   FAX: 0402-36384
EMAIL: lawhotel@iol.ie

HOTEL ★★★   MAP 8 O 8

Lawless Hotel, established in 1787, is a charming family run hotel which has been tastefully renovated. The award-winning restaurant enjoys a well established reputation for fine cuisine. Approximately one hour from Dublin, nestling in the Wicklow hills, there is a wide choice of excellent golf courses nearby as well as scenic hill-walking, pony treking and trout fishing in the adjacent river. Other accommodation available in hotel grounds.

WEB: www.lawhotel.com

Members Of Village Inn Hotels

B&B from £39.00 to £47.00
€49.52 to €59.68

SEOIRSE & MAEVE O'TOOLE
Proprietors

American Express
Diners
Mastercard
Visa

😊 Weekend specials from £85.00

14 14

Closed 24 - 27 December

Room rates are per room per night

VALE VIEW HOTEL

AVOCA,
CO. WICKLOW
TEL: 0402-35236 FAX: 0402-35144
EMAIL: valeview@indigo.ie

HOTEL ★★ MAP 8 O 8

Situated in the beautiful Vale of Avoca. All bedrooms en suite with tea/coffee making facilities, DD phone, TV. Function room to cater for different types of functions. Bar food, extensive à la carte and dinner menus.

WEB: indigo.ie/-valeview/

B&B from £30.00 to £45.00
€38.09 to €57.14

PETER AND MARY KING
Proprietors

American Express
Diners
Mastercard
Visa

10 10

DOWNSHIRE HOUSE HOTEL

BLESSINGTON,
CO. WICKLOW
TEL: 045-865199 FAX: 045-865335

HOTEL ★★★ MAP 8 N 10

Downshire is a family run country hotel on Blessington's main street on route N81. Dublin 25km. Twenty five bedrooms all en suite, large garden, close to horse riding, fishing, hill walking, leisure centre on Blessington lakes. Shopping at The Square in Tallaght and twelve screen cinema. Fresh food is supplied daily and cooked under highly qualified supervision. Ideal location for touring the Wicklow mountains or midlands.

Members Of Irish Family Hotels

B&B from £44.00 to £44.00
€55.87 to €55.87

JOAN FLYNN
Manager

Mastercard
Visa

25 25

TULFARRIS HOUSE HOTEL

BLESSINGTON LAKES,
CO. WICKLOW
TEL: 045-867555 FAX: 045-867561

HOTEL ★★★★ MAP 8 N 10

Tulfarris House Hotel is located on the Wicklow/Kildare border, near Blessington, & within 50 minutes drive of Dublin city centre & airport. Built in 1760 Tulfarris nestles between the spectacular Wicklow mountains & Blessington lakes. It has 20 tastefully furnished en suite bedrooms, a courtyard bar, & an excellent restaurant. Facilities include an indoor heated swimming pool, gym, sauna, steam room, sunbed, massage, tennis courts, & a spectacular 18 hole Championship golf course.

B&B from £50.00 to £78.00
€63.49 to €99.04

JIM & MAEVE HAYES
Managing Director & Prop

American Express
Diners
Mastercard
Visa

☺ Weekend specials from £110.00

20 20

B&B rates are per person sharing per night incl. Breakfast

CROFTON BRAY HEAD INN

STRAND ROAD, BRAY,
CO. WICKLOW
TEL: 01-286 7182 FAX: 01-286 7182

GUESTHOUSE ★★ MAP 8 P 10

This 130 year old building is situated on the seafront, under the Bray Head Mountain. A 10 minute walk away from an excellent commuter train to Dublin, but also ideally located for touring Wicklow - The Garden of Ireland. The Bray Head Inn has ample car-parking and is fully licensed. It has a lift, mostly en suite bedrooms with TV and Telephone. Our very reasonable prices include full Irish Breakfast.

B&B from £22.00 to £23.00
€27.93 to €29.20

NANCY REGAN

Mastercard
Visa

40 40

IRISH HOTELS FEDERATION

Closed 01 October - 31 May

ROYAL HOTEL AND LEISURE CENTRE

MAIN STREET, BRAY,
CO. WICKLOW
TEL: 01-286 2935 FAX: 01-286 7373
EMAIL: royal@regencyhotels.com

HOTEL ★★★ MAP 8 P 10

Located in the coastal resort of Bray, ideally positioned at the gateway to the garden county of Ireland and yet only a 30 min DART journey from downtown Dublin. The leisure facilities include pool, sauna, steamroom, whirlpool spa and jacuzzi. Facilities include a beauty salon and creche. The hotel is established for conferences, weddings and corporate banquets. The Dargle Room offers fine dining in luxurious surroundings. 24 hour supervised carpark.

WEB: www.regencyhotels.com

Members Of Best Western Hotels

B&B from £50.00 to £75.00
€63.49 to €95.23

MAUREEN MCGETTIGAN-O'CONNOR
General Manager

Mastercard
Visa

Weekend specials from £79.00

91 91

IRISH HOTELS FEDERATION

Open All Year

ULYSSES GUEST HOUSE

CENTRE ESPLANADE, BRAY,
CO. WICKLOW
TEL: 01-286 3860 FAX: 01-286 3860
EMAIL: cojo@indigo.ie

GUESTHOUSE ★★ MAP 8 P 10

Situated on the promenade in Bray overlooking the sea, Ulysses is a 2** guest house and is ideal for both business or pleasure. It is 35 minutes from Dublin city via DART and minutes drive from the foot of the Wicklow hills. It has been run by the Jones family since 1966 and we offer a high standard of service.

B&B from £25.00 to £25.00
€31.74 to €31.74

COLM & DEIRDRE JONES

Mastercard
Visa

10 8

IRISH HOTELS FEDERATION

Open All Year

Room rates are per room per night

WESTBOURNE HOTEL

QUINSBORO ROAD, BRAY,
CO. WICKLOW
TEL: 01-286 2362 FAX: 01-286 8530

HOTEL ★★   MAP 8 P 10

The Westbourne Hotel is ideally located on the north east coast of the 'Garden of Ireland' in the charming town of Bray. Only minutes from exceptional scenery, beaches and has fast access to Dublin via the DART. Newly refurbished bedrooms en suite, direct dial phone, TV and tea/coffee making facilities. Dusty Millers bar is a live music venue with music Wed-Sun. Clancy's Traditional Irish bar, craic agus ceol. The Tube nite club open Thur-Sun. Food served all day.

B&B from £35.00 to £37.50
€44.44 to €47.62

SUSAN MC CARTHY
General Manager

Mastercard
Visa

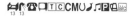
13 13

Closed 25 - 26 December

WOODLANDS COURT HOTEL

SOUTHERN CROSS, BRAY,
CO. WICKLOW
TEL: 01-276 0258 FAX: 01-276 0298

HOTEL N   MAP 8 P 10

Located just minutes from the M11 motorway and 12 miles from Dublin city centre the Woodlands Court Hotel has much to offer the tourist and business traveller. 50 well-appointed en suite rooms, state of the art conference/business centre and excellent value meals in our restaurant. An ideal venue for touring Dublin city and county Wicklow. Special group and business rates available on request.

Room Rate from £50.00 to £90.00
€63.49 to €114.28

EILEEN MURPHY
General Manager

American Express
Diners
Mastercard
Visa

50 50

Open All Year

RATHSALLAGH HOUSE

DUNLAVIN,
CO. WICKLOW
TEL: 045-403112 FAX: 045-403343
EMAIL: info@rathsallagh.com

GUESTHOUSE ★★★★   MAP 8 N 9

Converted from Queen Anne stables in 1798, Rathsallagh nestles in 500 acres of gardens, parkland and an 18-hole championship golf course. There are 17 guest rooms en suite. The O'Flynn Family offer a warm welcome, superb food and fine wines. Set in beautiful countryside near the Wicklow mountains, Glendalough and Russborough, close to Punchestown, Curragh and Goffs, yet only 35 mls. from Dublin. Member of the Blue Book and recommended by international hotel and food guides.

WEB: rathsallagh.com

Members Of Ireland's Blue Book

B&B from £55.00 to £105.00
€69.84 to €133.32

O'FLYNN FAMILY
Owners

American Express
Diners
Mastercard
Visa

☺ Midweek specials from £165.00

17 17

Closed 23 - 27 December

B&B rates are per person sharing per night incl. Breakfast

ENNISCREE LODGE HOTEL

GLENCREE VALLEY, ENNISKERRY,
CO. WICKLOW
TEL: 01-286 3542 FAX: 01-286 6037
EMAIL: enniscre@iol.ie

HOTEL ★★ MAP 8 O 10

A spectacular location is enjoyed by this family operated hotel. Ten en suite bedrooms are comfortably furnished, country style. Our garden terrace restaurant offers superb cuisine and excellent wines, with walls of windows framing skywide views of moors and mountains. Arrive early in the afternoon to enjoy tea of homemade scones in our cosy sitting room. 25kms from Dublin, we are ideally situated for touring our capital, together with exploration of historic Wicklow.

B&B from £40.00 to £50.00
€50.79 to €63.49

JOSEPHINE & RAYMOND POWER
Owners

American Express
Diners
Mastercard
Visa

10 10

Closed 01 - 31 January

POWERSCOURT ARMS HOTEL

ENNISKERRY,
CO. WICKLOW
TEL: 01-282 8903 FAX: 01-286 4909

HOTEL ★ MAP 8 O 10

Powerscourt Arms Hotel owned by the Mc Ternan family. Snuggling in the foothills of the Wicklow mountains the Powerscourt Arms is an ideal base for touring expeditions, it is an intimate family run hotel with 12 bedrooms furnished to include direct dial telephone ensuite bathrooms and multi channel TV, ample car parking facilities. The restaurant seats up to 45 people, our lounge with strong features of american white ash, serves bar food daily. The public bar also has its own atmosphere complete with an open fire.

B&B from £30.00 to £30.00
€38.09 to €38.09

CHARLES MCTERNAN
General Manager

Mastercard
Visa

☺ Weekend specials from £80.00

12 12

Closed 24 - 25 December

SUMMERHILL HOUSE HOTEL

ENNISKERRY,
CO. WICKLOW
TEL: 01-286 7928 FAX: 01-286 7929

HOTEL ★★★ MAP 8 O 10

This charming hotel is just a short walk to the quaint village of Enniskerry, and the famous Powerscourt Gardens. Located on the N11, 19km south of Dublin city & 15km to Dunlaoire ferryport. 57 spacious bedrooms, private free car parking, traditional Irish breakfast, hill walking & nature trails, local golf courses, family rooms (2ad+3ch). Enjoy a rare blend of the Wicklow countryside close to Dublin city.

Members Of Logis of Ireland

B&B from £40.00 to £60.00
€50.79 to €76.18

DENIS KENNEDY
General Manager

American Express
Mastercard
Visa

57 57

Open All Year

Room rates are per room per night

GLENVIEW HOTEL

GLEN-O-THE-DOWNS, DELGANY,
CO. WICKLOW
TEL: 01-287 3399 FAX: 01-287 7511
EMAIL: glenview@iol.ie

HOTEL ★★★ MAP 8 O 10

Tastefully refurbished (1998) to satisfy the most discerning guest. The Glenview Hotel offers a relaxing atmosphere and discreet, friendly service. The Woodlands Restaurant provides unrivalled views over the glen in which to sample its widely acclaimed cuisine and service. Horse riding, golf, shooting, hill walking are all within a 5 minute radius of the hotel. 25 minutes from Dublin on the N11. 5 star fitness & leisure centre. Ideal for conferences.

Members Of Stafford Hotels

B&B from £68.00 to £85.00
€86.34 to €107.93

STEPHEN BYRNE
General Manager

American Express
Diners
Mastercard
Visa

74 74

Open All Year

DERRYBAWN MOUNTAIN LODGE

DERRYBAWN, LARAGH,
GLENDALOUGH, CO. WICKLOW
TEL: 0404-45644 FAX: 0404-45645
EMAIL: derrybawnlodge@eircom.net

GUESTHOUSE ★★★ MAP 8 O 9

Derrybawn Mountain Lodge is a family-run guesthouse, situated on the slopes of Derrybawn mountain. A walkers paradise close by famous Wicklow Way. Tranquil setting, mountain views, all rooms have bath & shower en suite, DD phone, coffee/tea making facilities, hairdryer. Spacious dining and lounge area to relax. Enjoy National Park, Glenmalure, historic Glendalough and Clara Vale. Members of local mountain rescue team. Excellent fresh food & wine. A warm welcome awaits you.

B&B from £25.00 to £30.00
€31.74 to €38.09

TERESA KAVANAGH
Proprietor

American Express
Mastercard
Visa

☺ Weekend specials from £65.00

8 8

Closed 24 - 27 December

GLENDALOUGH HOTEL

GLENDALOUGH,
CO. WICKLOW
TEL: 0404-45135 FAX: 0404-45142
EMAIL: info@glendaloughhotel.ie

HOTEL ★★★ MAP 8 O 9

The Glendalough Hotel, built in the early 1800s, is a family run hotel situated in the heart of Wicklow's most scenic valley and within the Glendalough National Park. The hotel has recently been extended offering 44 beautifully decorated en suite bedrooms with satellite TV and D.D. phone. The hotel's restaurant offers superb cuisine and wines in a tranquil environment overlooking the Glendasan river. The Tavern bar serves good pub food and offers entertainment at weekends.

B&B from £38.50 to £55.00
€48.88 to €69.84

PATRICK CASEY

American Express
Diners
Mastercard
Visa

☺ Weekend specials from £85.00

44 44

Closed 01 - 31 January

B&B rates are per person sharing per night incl. Breakfast

LA TOUCHE HOTEL

TRAFALGAR ROAD, GREYSTONES,
CO. WICKLOW
TEL: 01-287 4401   FAX: 01-287 4504
EMAIL: latouchehotel@hotmail.com

HOTEL ★★   MAP 8 P 10

Our hotel has a superb location overlooking the sea in the garden of Ireland. At our doorstep are Glendalough, Powerscourt and Mount Usher Gardens. All rooms are en suite with remote satellite TV, radio, tea/coffee facilities and DD phone. Our Captains lounge is the main meeting place for locals and visitors alike with a carvery 7 days a week. The Waterfront conference centre caters for parties up to 500. Also available are Bennigans Fun Bar and Club Life night club.

WEB: latouche.jumptravel.com

B&B from £35.00 to £45.00
€44.44 to €57.14

PAT TUFFY
General Manager

American Express
Diners
Mastercard
Visa

Weekend specials from £65.00

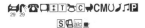

Closed 24 - 25 December

AVONBRAE GUESTHOUSE

RATHDRUM,
CO. WICKLOW
TEL: 0404-46198   FAX: 0404-46198

GUESTHOUSE ★★★   MAP 8 O 9

A small, long established, family run guesthouse, nestling in the Wicklow Hills. We pride ourselves in our good food and personal attention and extend a warm welcome to first time guests and to the many who return again and again. Horse riding, trekking, fishing and excellent golf available locally. We specialise in hill walking holidays and to relax - our own indoor heated pool and games room.

B&B from £24.00 to £24.00
€30.47 to €30.47

PADDY GEOGHEGAN
Proprietor

Mastercard
Visa

Week partial board from £255.00

Closed 30 November - 28 February

MOTORING IN IRELAND

AND THINK

DRIVE ON LEFT SIDE OF ROAD

ENJOY YOUR HOLIDAY

Room rates are per room per night

MOUNT BRACKEN HOUSE

CUNNIAMSTOWN, RATHDRUM,
CO. WICKLOW
TEL: 0404-46311 FAX: 0404-46922

GUESTHOUSE N MAP 8 O 9

Mount Bracken House is situated in beautiful countryside on a private estate on the road to Avoca. Wicklow town is within easy driving distance. All rooms are modern and en suite with magnificent views of the countryside. Fishing, golf and equestrian facilities are nearby. Ideal for touring and walking and only a half hour from beautiful sandy beaches. Via the newly-built N11 Dublin city is less than an hour away.

B&B from £20.00 to £25.00
€25.39 to €31.74

CATHERINE & PETER VAN DIJK
Managers

Mastercard
Visa

🖐🏠🆃🇨❄️🔆🅿️
6 6

Open All Year

HUNTER'S HOTEL

NEWRATH BRIDGE, RATHNEW,
CO. WICKLOW
TEL: 0404-40106 FAX: 0404-40338
EMAIL: hunters@indigo.ie

HOTEL ★★★ MAP 8 P 9

One of Ireland's oldest coaching inns, its award winning gardens along river Vartry provide a haven from the world at large. Restaurant provides the very best of Irish food, fresh fish. Local amenities include golf, tennis, horseriding and fishing. Beautiful sandy beaches and sightseeing in the Garden of Ireland. Dublin 44.8km. Rosslare 115.2km. Off N11 at Rathnew or Ashford. Irish Country Houses and Restaurant Association. Refurbished 95-96. 1996 new Conference Room added.

WEB: indigo.ie/~hunters

Members Of Ireland's Blue Book

B&B from £55.00 to £65.00
€69.84 to €82.53

GELLETLIE FAMILY
Proprietors

American Express
Diners
Mastercard
Visa

🖐🏠☎️🆃🇭CM❄️🔆🅿️🅰️♿

16 16

Closed 24 - 26 December

TINAKILLY COUNTRY HOUSE AND RESTAURANT

WICKLOW, (RATHNEW),
CO. WICKLOW
TEL: 0404-69274 FAX: 0404-67806
EMAIL: wpower@tinakilly.ie

HOTEL ★★★★ MAP 8 P 9

This Victorian mansion was built for Captain Halpin, who laid the world's telegraph cables. The bedrooms, some with 4 posters, are furnished in period style and most overlook the Irish Sea. Award winning cuisine is prepared from garden vegetables, local fish and Wicklow lamb. The family welcome ensures a relaxing, memorable stay. Available locally - golf, horse riding, Powerscourt, Mt. Usher Gardens and Wicklow mountains. Dublin 46km. Awarded RAC Blue Ribbon for Excellence. Blue Book member.

WEB: www.tinakilly.ie

Members Of Small Luxury Hotels

B&B from £68.00 to £96.00
€86.34 to €121.89

WILLIAM AND BEE POWER
Proprietors

American Express
Diners
Mastercard
Visa

☺ Midweek off peak 2 B&Bs &
1 Dinner from £98.00

🖐🏠☎️🇧🆃🇨❄️🔆☀️🔍🅿️🅰️♿
52 52

Open All Year

B&B rates are per person sharing per night incl. Breakfast

VALLEY HOTEL AND RESTAURANT

WOODENBRIDGE, VALE OF AVOCA, ARKLOW, CO. WICKLOW
TEL: 0402-35200 FAX: 0402-35542

HOTEL ★ MAP 8 O 8

Nestled in a scenic valley stands the olde worlde Valley Hotel. A family-run hotel offers a relaxing atmosphere for that break away. Tastefully decorated en suite bedrooms complete with TV and tea/coffee making facilities. Enjoy excellent cuisine in the restaurant and great atmosphere in the bar with music at weekends. Ideal base for touring Wicklow. Visit Avoca village 1.5km away, location for Ballykissangel. Within walking distance of Woodenbridge golf club and 5 others.

B&B from £29.00 to £33.00
€36.82 to €41.90

DOREEN O'DONNELL
Proprietor

American Express
Diners
Mastercard
Visa

Weekend specials from £82.00

10 10

Open All Year

WOODENBRIDGE HOTEL

VALE OF AVOCA, ARKLOW, CO. WICKLOW
TEL: 0402-35146 FAX: 0402-35573
EMAIL: wbhotel@iol.ie

HOTEL ★★★ MAP 8 O 8

Family owned and run with 23 en suite bedrooms, rooms with balconies overlooking scenic 18 hole Woodenbridge golf course. Dating from 1608, the hotel is the oldest in Ireland. Our restaurant and bar serve the very best of food. Winner of tourism menu awards for 1998/'99. Bar food served all day. Horse riding, fishing, golfing, fine beaches and walking are all available locally. Near Avoca, film location for Ballykissangel. Adequate car parking.

B&B from £35.00 to £50.00
€44.44 to €63.49

ESTHER O'BRIEN & BILL O'BRIEN
Proprietors

American Express
Mastercard
Visa

Weekend specials from £85.00

23 23

Closed 25 December

INTERNATIONAL DIAL CODES

Emergency Services: 999 (freephone)

HOW TO DIAL INTERNATIONAL
ACCESS CODE +
COUNTRY CODE +
AREA CODE +
LOCAL NUMBER

SAMPLE CODES:
E.G. UNITED KINGDOM
00 44 + Area Code + Local No.

U.S.A.	00	1	+
Italy	00	39	+
Spain	00	34	+
France	00	33	+
Germany	00	49	+
Iceland	00	354	+
Japan	00	81	+
Luxembourg	00	352	+
Netherlands	00	31	+
Operator (national)			1190
(G. Britain)			1197
(International)			1198

Room rates are per room per night

MIDLANDS/LAKELANDS
East Coast and Lakelands

The East Coast & Lakelands of the Midlands-East Region of Ireland offers a great diversity in scenery and a wealth of attractions to the visitor. Whether you are walking in the Wicklow Mountains or the Slieve Blooms, exploring the Shannon or the Cooley Peninsula or just relaxing on the sandy beaches, this ancient Region has something for everybody. Catch the excitement of the Stradbally Steam Festival, the Wicklow Gardens Festival, Mullingar Bachelor's Festival and the Longford Summer Festival. In addition, there are many Summer Schools and other events, that take place throughout the Region.

MAJOR ATTRACTIONS

The Region is rich in archeological and historical sites of great interest, from the passage graves in the Boyne Valley, and the new Bru Na Boinne Visitor Centre, the early Christian settlements of Clonmacnoise and Glendalough to more recent wonders such as the Japanese Gardens at Tully; Wicklow Gaol, Wicklow Town; Avondale House in Rathdrum; Kilruddery House and Gardens, Bray; Russborough House in Blessington and Powerscourt Gardens and Waterfall, Enniskerry.

Other popular attractions include Newgrange Farm, Slane; Mosney; Crookstown Mill in Ballitore; Charleville Castle, Tullamore; Locke's Distillery, Kilbeggan; Athlone Castle Visitor Centre, Newtowncashel Heritage Centre and the designated Heritage towns of Athy, Kildare Town, Ardagh, Carlingford, Trim, Kells, Baltinglass, Abbeyleix and Tullamore; Heywood Gardens, Gash Gardens and Donaghmore Farm Museum in Co. Laois; Wineport Sailing Centre, Athlone; Holy Trinity Visitor Centre, Carlingford and the National Gardens Exhibition Centre, Kilquade. In addition, Corlea Trackway Exhibition Centre, Kenagh; Ardagh Heritage Centre and the County Museum, Dundalk are also worth a visit as is the new Tullamore Dew Heritage Centre. Indeed there are many other interesting places to visit throughout the Region.

High quality golfing and equestrian facilities are widely available in the Region. Coarse, Game and Sea fishing is also available as is Cruising, Walking and other activities. There is a great variety of accommodation from the most luxurious of Hotels to the more modest family run unit and other types of accommodation, each in their own way offering superb service to the visitor.

Full details on all festivals and events, heritage and special interest activities from angling to walking in the East Coast and Midlands Region are available from the local Tourist Information Office or from East Coast and Midlands Tourism, Market House, Mullingar, Co. Westmeath.

Tel: (00 353) 044-48650
Fax: (00 353) 044-40413
E-mail: midlandseasttourism@eircom.net
Web site: www.midlandseastireland.travel.ie

Budweiser Irish Derby Weekend, The Curragh, Co. Kildare.
June

Guinness Mullingar Batchelor Festival, Mullingar, Co. Westmeath
July

Event details correct at time of going to press

HOTEL KILMORE

DUBLIN ROAD,
CAVAN
TEL: 049-433 2288 FAX: 049-433 2458

HOTEL ★★★   MAP 11 L 14

The Hotel Kilmore is ideally located in the heart of Ireland's Lakeland district. Recently refurbished, the hotel offers 39 luxuriously appointed rooms. Renowned for fine cuisine our AA Rosette Annalee Restaurant boasts a wide selection of dishes including local fish and game, complemented by an extensive wine list. Ideal venue for conferences and private functions the Hotel Kilmore is the perfect base for a business visit or to enjoy the varied leisure pursuits in the area.

B&B from £39.00 to £44.00
€49.52 to €55.87

CYRIL BOYLAN
General Manager

American Express
Diners
Mastercard
Visa

☺ Weekend specials from £90.00

39 39

Open All Year

BAILIE HOTEL

BAILIEBOROUGH,
CO. CAVAN
TEL: 042-966 5334   FAX: 042-966 6506

HOTEL ★★   MAP 11 M 14

Friendly family run hotel. Rooms en suite. TV, DD phone. Excellent reputation for good food. Carvery lunches served daily. Also à la carte and evening dinner. Food served all day in lounge. Coarse fishing close by, golf course and mountain climbing also close by. Newly opened swimming pool and leisure centre in town. Ideal for a relaxing break.

B&B from £23.00 to £25.00
€29.20 to €31.74

KEVIN MURPHY
Manager

American Express
Mastercard
Visa

☺ Weekend specials from £60.00

18 17

Open All Year

ANGLER'S REST

MAIN STREET, BALLYCONNELL,
CO. CAVAN
TEL: 049-952 6391   FAX: 049-952 6777
EMAIL: bycl@iol.ie

GUESTHOUSE ★★   MAP 11 K 15

The Angler's Rest, is a family run guesthouse. All rooms are en suite with TV, D.D. phone and tea making facilities. Private car parking at rear of premises. Golf is available on local championship course or angling on one of the many local lakes. Trips on the Shannon Erne waterway can be arranged.

B&B from £21.28 to £
€27.02 to €0.00

PAULINE & FRANCIS MCGOLDRICK
Proprietors

Mastercard
Visa

9 9

Open All Year

KEEPERS ARMS

BRIDGE STREET, BAWNBOY,
BALLYCONNELL, CO. CAVAN
TEL: 049-952 3318   FAX: 049-952 3008

GUESTHOUSE N   MAP 11 K 15

Enjoy the delights of an Irish pub. The Keepers Arms is situated in Bawnboy, a small peaceful village at the foot of Slieve Rushen. Fully modernised with 11 en suite rooms, home produced/cooked food, pleasant and relaxed atmosphere, the owners and staff will tend to your needs. Specialise in group bookings, angling and golf parties. For a break away from it all, give us a call...

Members Of Unspoilt Ireland

B&B from £18.00 to £22.00
€22.86 to €27.93

SHEILA MCKIERNAN

Closed 24 - 26 December

SLIEVE RUSSELL HOTEL, GOLF & COUNTRY CLUB

BALLYCONNELL,
CO. CAVAN
TEL: 049-952 6444   FAX: 049-952 6474
EMAIL: slieve-russell@quinn-hotels.com

HOTEL ★★★★   MAP 11 K 15

The Slieve Russell Hotel, Golf and Country Club offers a unique experience in relaxation and leisure to our guests. Enjoy excellent cuisine, professional and friendly service and a range of leisure facilities. The 18 hole PGA ch'ship golf course ensures a challenging game, whilst beginners will enjoy the 9 hole par 3 course. Country Club facilities include: a 20m leisure pool, saunas, steamroom, jacuzzi, fitness suite, tennis, squash, snooker, hair/beauty salon, crèche and games room.

WEB: www.quinn-group.com

B&B from £75.00 to £135.00
€95.23 to €171.41

SHEILA GRAY
General Manager

American Express
Diners
Mastercard
Visa

Open All Year

OLDE POST INN

CLOVERHILL,
CO. CAVAN
TEL: 047-55555   FAX: 047-55111
EMAIL: oldepostinn@eircom.net

GUESTHOUSE ★★★   MAP 11 K 15

Nestling in a sylvan setting in Ireland's tranquil lakelands, this 200 year old country inn was the original Cloverhill post office. Stone walls supporting ancient pine beams and rafters create an ambience that complements our award-winning modern Irish cuisine. 6 beautiful en suite rooms offer luxurious accommodation in this olde world atmosphere where service has the 'stamp of quality'. You may come for the fishing, the horse-riding or the golf, but you'll stay for our hospitality.

B&B from £30.00 to £35.00
€38.09 to €44.44

FRANK CASSIDY
Proprietor

Mastercard
Visa

Weekend specials from £60.00

Closed 15 February - 01 March

CABRA CASTLE HOTEL

KINGSCOURT,
CO. CAVAN
TEL: 042-966 7030 FAX: 042-966 7039
EMAIL: cabrach@iol.ie

HOTEL ★★★   MAP 11 M 14

Follow in the footsteps of Oliver Cromwell and James II, and treat yourself to a stay in a Castle. Cabra Castle stands on 88 acres of gardens and parkland, with its own nine hole golf course. The bar and restaurant offer views over countryside famous for its lakes and fishing, as well as Dun a Ri forest park. An ideal venue for that holiday, specialising in golfing and equestrian holidays. Member of: Manor House Hotels Tel: 01-295 8900, GDS Access Code: UI Toll Free 1-800-44-UTEII.

Members Of Manor House Hotels

B&B from £36.00 to £75.00
€45.71 to €95.23

HOWARD CORSCADDEN
Manager

American Express
Mastercard
Visa

☺ Weekend specials from £85.00

70 70

Closed 23 - 27 December

PARK HOTEL

VIRGINIA,
CO. CAVAN
TEL: 049-854 7235 FAX: 049-854 7203

HOTEL ★★★   MAP 11 L 13

Situated 80km northwest of Dublin at the Gateway to the Lake County, this beautifully restored 37 room hotel was built in 1750 as the residence for the Marquis De Headford. Enjoy dinner in the historical Marquis dining room overlooking Lough Ramor, the cavery and a pub atmosphere of the Huntsman Lodge. Golf on property as well as 15 miles of nature trails adjacent to Lough Ramor.

B&B from £25.00 to £80.00
€31.74 to €101.58

KELLY MASSETT
General Manager

American Express
Diners
Mastercard
Visa

37 37

alc

Open All Year

SHARKEYS HOTEL

MAIN STREET, VIRGINIA,
CO. CAVAN
TEL: 049-854 7561 FAX: 049-854 7761
EMAIL: sharkeys@destination-ireland.com

HOTEL ★★   MAP 11 L 13

Egon Ronay awardwinning family run hotel, situated in the heart of Virginia, 80km from Dublin, on the main route to Donegal. It is furnished to the highest standards, DD phone, TV in all rooms. Enjoy a day's fishing or travelling around the lake region and return to relax in the comfort of our restaurant and sample some of the delights of our awardwinning chef. It has both à la carte and dinner menu, carvery and extensive bar menu. Food served all day. 9 hole golf course 5 mins walk.

WEB: www.destination-ireland.com/sharkeys

B&B from £32.50 to £40.00
€41.27 to €50.79

PAT AND GORETTI SHARKEY
Proprietors

Mastercard
Visa

☺ Weekend specials from £69.00

10 10

alc

Open All Year

Room rates are per room per night

CURRAGH LODGE HOTEL

DUBLIN ROAD, KILDARE TOWN,
CO. KILDARE
TEL: 045-522144 FAX: 045-521247

HOTEL ★★   MAP 7 M 10

The Curragh Lodge Hotel is situated in Kildare town on the N7 from Dublin going south. Steaped in history, Kildare is a must for tourists not only for its heritage but for its other attractions such as the Japanese Gardens and the Irish national stud and horse museum. The Curragh Lodge Hotel offers excellent accommodation, food, drink, service and entertainment. Minutes away from the classic Curragh racecourse and midway between Belfast and Cork. It is an ideal stop over.

B&B from £45.00 to £50.00
€57.14 to €63.49

LIAM MCLOUGHLIN
Manager

American Express
Diners
Mastercard
Visa

☺ Weekend special 2 nights B&B +
1 Dinner £100.00

21 21

Open All Year

TONLEGEE HOUSE AND RESTAURANT

ATHY,
CO. KILDARE
TEL: 0507-31473 FAX: 0507-31473
EMAIL: tonlegeehouse@eircom.net

GUESTHOUSE ★★★★   MAP 7 M 9

Tonlegee House has been restored by Mark and Marjorie Molloy as a country house and restaurant of warmth and character, with antique furnishings and open fires. 5 mins from Athy, which is only an hour from Dublin. Tonlegee House is an ideal place to stay for either an activity filled or leisurely break. Egon Ronay recommended and Bridgestone Guide Best 100.

B&B from £37.50 to £37.50
€47.62 to €47.62

MARJORIE AND MARK MOLLOY
Proprietors

American Express
Mastercard
Visa

9 9

Closed 01 - 14 November

ARDENODE HOTEL

BALLYMORE EUSTACE,
CO. KILDARE
TEL: 045-864198 FAX: 045-864139
EMAIL: ardenode@iol.ie

HOTEL ★★   MAP 8 N 10

Situated on the borders of Counties Wicklow and Kildare and just 20k from Dublin City, this hotel is a perfect base for touring. The Ardenode is a family run country house hotel, set in 7 acres of scenic gardens where personal attention, a warm welcome and friendly service awaits you. The Ardenode makes every occasion special, whether it's Sunday lunch, an intimate meal or a business conference. Also the ideal location for any golfer - surrounded by championship courses.

WEB: www.ardenode-hotel.ie

B&B from £50.00 to £100.00
€63.49 to €126.97

MICHELLE BROWNE
Manager

American Express
Mastercard
Visa

17 17

Open All Year

KILKEA CASTLE

CASTLEDERMOT,
CO. KILDARE
TEL: 0503-45156 FAX: 0503-45187
EMAIL: kilkea@iol.ie

HOTEL ★★★★ MAP 7 M 8

Kilkea Castle is the oldest inhabited Castle in Ireland. Built in 1180, offering the best in modern comfort while the charm and elegance of the past has been retained. The facilities include deluxe accommodation, a fine dining room, d'Lacy's Restaurant, restful bar/lounge area, full banqueting and conference facilities and full on site Leisure Centre with an indoor heated swimming pool, sauna, jacuzzi, steamroom and fully equipped gym. 18 hole golf course encircles the Castle.

B&B from £70.00 to £120.00
€88.88 to €152.37

PAUL CORRIDAN
General Manager

American Express
Diners
Mastercard
Visa

36 36

IRISH HOTELS FEDERATION

Closed 23 - 27 December

STANDHOUSE HOTEL LEISURE & CONFERENCE CENTRE

CURRAGH RACECOURSE,
THE CURRAGH, CO. KILDARE
TEL: 045-436177 FAX: 045-436180
EMAIL: standhse@indigo.ie

HOTEL U MAP 7 M 10

Standhouse Hotel has a tradition which dates back to 1700. Situated beside the Curragh Racecourse it has become synonymous with the classics. The premises has been restored to its former elegance and offers the discerning guest a fine selection of quality restaurants, bars, leisure facilities, including 20 metre pool, state of art gym, jacuzzi, steam room, sauna and plunge pool. Conference facilities cater for 2 to 500 delegates.

B&B from £40.00 to £90.00
€50.79 to €114.28

ODHRAN LAWLOR
Manager

American Express
Diners
Mastercard
Visa

☺ Weekend specials from £89.00

63 63

IRISH HOTELS FEDERATION

Closed 25 - 26 December

Visit the...

IRISH NATIONAL STUD
JAPANESE GARDENS
SAINT FIACHRA'S GARDEN

'One visit...
three different worlds'

Opening Hours
12th Feb - 12th Nov.
9.30am to 6.00pm   7 Days
(last admission one hour before closing).

Tully, Kildare Town,
Co. Kildare, Ireland.
Tel. +353-(0)45-521617 / 522963
Fax. +353-(0)45-522964

Email: stud@irish-national-stud.ie
Website: www.irish-national-stud.ie

Room rates are per room per night

AMBASSADOR HOTEL

KILL,
CO. KILDARE
TEL: 045-877064 FAX: 045-877515

HOTEL ★★★ MAP 8 N 10

Situated just 20km from Dublin city, this 36 bedroomed hotel is ideally located for those travelling from the south or west. Our restaurants boast excellent cuisine and our bar provides music 5 nights per week. Local amenities include 3 race courses, Curragh, Naas and Punchestown, four golf courses, Goffs Horse Sales, (just across the road) and plenty of horse riding. The Ambassador has something for everybody.

B&B from £42.00 to £95.00
€53.33 to €120.63

NIALL DUFF
General Manager

American Express
Diners
Mastercard
Visa

☺ Weekend specials from £92.00

36 36

alc

Open All Year

LEIXLIP HOUSE HOTEL

CAPTAIN'S HILL, LEIXLIP,
CO. KILDARE
TEL: 01-624 2268 FAX: 01-624 4177
EMAIL: manager@lvhh.iol.ie

HOTEL U MAP 8 N 11

A most elegant Georgian house built in 1772, overlooking the village of Leixlip, is a mere 20 mins from Dublin City. Lovingly restored and luxurious, the hotel offers the highest standards of service and amenities. Our convenient location allows easy access from the city and Dublin Airport. The state of the art conference centre can cater for groups of up to 120 persons. Our award winning Signature Restaurant is a culinary delight offering a wide range of modern Irish dishes.

WEB: www.leixliphousehotel.com

Members Of The Small Hotel Company

B&B from £60.00 to £75.00
€76.18 to €95.23

CHRISTIAN SCHMELTER

American Express
Diners
Mastercard
Visa

15 15

Open All Year

LIFFEY VALLEY HOUSE HOTEL

ST. CATHERINES PARK, LEIXLIP,
CO. KILDARE
TEL: 01-624 7415 FAX: 01-624 7413
EMAIL: manager@lvhh.iol.ie

HOTEL U MAP 8 N 11

Liffey Valley House Hotel, set in 29 acres of private parkland, is a most splendid Georgian house. Just 20 mins from Dublin City the hotel is perfectly located off Dublin's motorway network. Be it for business or pleasure our elegant surroundings will delight you. Our newly refurbished conference rooms meet the highest standards required in today's business environment. Relax in our conservatory bar, dine in our elegant restaurant or stroll through our magnificent grounds.

WEB: www.globalgolf.com/ireland/east

B&B from £50.00 to £70.00
€63.49 to €88.88

CHRISTIAN SCHMELTER

American Express
Diners
Mastercard
Visa

27 27

Open All Year

GLENROYAL HOTEL, LEISURE CLUB & CONFERENCE CENTRE

STRAFFAN ROAD, MAYNOOTH, CO. KILDARE
TEL: 01-629 0909 FAX: 01-629 0919
EMAIL: glenroyal-hotel@clubi.ie

HOTEL ★★★ MAP 8 N 11

Premier 3*** hotel with the finest of accommodation and leisure facilities 20 mins from Dublin. Leisure facilities include 20m pool, aerobics studio, gym, sauna, jacuzzi and steamroom. Nancy Spain's bar is always buzzing with conversation and laughter. Food is served here throughout the day, including carvery lunches and an extensive barfood menu. The restaurant has a fine reputation for its Irish and international cuisine. Entertainment a feature.

WEB: www.clubi.ie/glenroyal-hotel

B&B from £37.50 to £47.50
€47.62 to €60.31

HELEN COURTNEY
General Manager

American Express
Diners
Mastercard
Visa

57 57

Closed 25 December

HAZEL HOTEL

DUBLIN ROAD, MONASTEREVIN, CO. KILDARE
TEL: 045-525373 FAX: 045-525810
EMAIL: sales@hazelhotel.com

HOTEL ★★ MAP 7 N 10

The Hazel Hotel is a family run country hotel on the main Dublin/Cork/Limerick road (N7). All bedrooms have bath/shower, colour TV and international direct dial telephone. The hotel's restaurant has extensive à la carte and table d'hôte menus. Ample car parking. Entertainment is provided. Ideal base for going to the Curragh, Naas or Punchestown racecourses. Several golf courses close by. National Stud and Japanese Gardens only 7 miles from hotel. No service charge.

WEB: hazelhotel.com

Members Of Logis of Ireland

B&B from £27.50 to £27.50
€34.92 to €34.92

MARGARET KELLY
Proprietor

American Express
Diners
Mastercard
Visa

☺ Weekend specials from £65.00

15 15

Closed 25 - 26 December

HARBOUR VIEW HOTEL

LIMERICK ROAD, NAAS, CO. KILDARE
TEL: 045-879145 FAX: 045-874002

HOTEL ★★ MAP 8 N 10

Looking after the needs of our guests and providing quality service is a priority in this family run hotel. All rooms have colour TV, direct dial telephone, hair dryer and teas made. We offer superb home cooked food, extensive à la carte and table d'hôte menus and excellent wine list. Relax and enjoy a drink in our comfortable lounge. Conveniently situated to Dublin City, ferry, airport, Punchestown, The Curragh and Mondello.

B&B from £30.00 to £40.00
€38.09 to €50.79

MARY MONAGHAN
Proprietor

American Express
Diners
Mastercard
Visa

10 10

Closed 25 - 28 December

Room rates are per room per night

HILLVIEW HOUSE

PROSPEROUS, NAAS,
CO. KILDARE
TEL: 045-868252 FAX: 045-892305
EMAIL: hillview@eircom.net

GUESTHOUSE N   MAP 8 N 11

Hillview House near Naas, is situated in golfers' paradise. 6 golf courses within 15 minutes, another 6 within 1/2 hour. 45 mins airport and city centre. Between N4/N7 main routes south and west. Easy reach of Curragh, Punchestown, K-Club, Mondello. All rooms en suite, multi-channel TV, DD phone, tea/coffee facilities. Holistic centre on site, courses / workshops available. Whether touring, a golfer, race-goer, or just in need of a rest, we are here to welcome you.

B&B from £25.00 to £35.00
€31.74 to €44.44

BRENDAN & MOIRA ALLEN
Proprietors

Mastercard

Visa

Closed 15 December - 05 January

ANNAGH LODGE GUESTHOUSE

NAAS ROAD, NEWBRIDGE,
CO. KILDARE
TEL: 045-433518 FAX: 045-433538
EMAIL: annaghlodge@eircom.net

GUESTHOUSE N   MAP 7 M 10

New purpose-built guesthouse in peaceful setting, ideally located beside all town amenities, including hotels, restaurants and leisure centres. Facilities include private parking and sauna. Annagh Lodge provides the highest standard of comfort in superior rooms with all modern conveniences combined with excellent service. Dublin and the airport are 30 mins drive. Curragh, Naas and Punchestown racecourses, 8 golf courses and fishing are a short drive. Access for wheelchairs.

WEB: www.homepage.eircom.net/~annaghlodge

B&B from £30.00 to £45.00
€38.09 to €57.14

DERNA WALLACE
Proprietor

Mastercard

Visa

Closed 23 December - 02 January

GABLES GUESTHOUSE & LEISURE CENTRE

RYSTON, NEWBRIDGE,
CO. KILDARE
TEL: 045-435330 FAX: 045-435355

GUESTHOUSE ★★★   MAP 7 M 10

Set on the banks of the Liffey, our family run guesthouse has 10 bedrooms with bath/shower, multi channel TV, direct dial telephone, hairdryer and teas made. Our leisure centre includes a 14 metre indoor swimming pool, jacuzzi, steam room, sauna and fully equipped gymnasium. Horse racing, golfing and fishing are well catered for locally. A warm and friendly welcome awaits you at the Gables. Brochures available on request.

B&B from £25.00 to £45.00
€31.74 to €57.14

RAY CRIBBIN
Proprietor

Mastercard

Visa

Closed 23 - 28 December

B&B rates are per person sharing per night incl. Breakfast

KEADEEN HOTEL

NEWBRIDGE,
CO. KILDARE
TEL: 045-431666 FAX: 045-434402
EMAIL: keadeen@iol.ie

HOTEL ★★★ MAP 7 M 10

On 8 acres of award winning landscaped gardens, adjacent to the primary Dublin/Cork/Limerick road. This newly refurbished grade A hotel containing The Keadeen Health and Fitness Club is only 40Km from Dublin, 2Km from The Curragh Racecourse and is easily accessible off the M7. All our luxurious en suite bedrooms are equipped to international standards. Our restaurant serves an extensive range of cuisine and has been awarded 2 red rosettes by The Automobile Association.

WEB: www.keadeenhotel.kildare.ie

B&B from £47.50 to £100.00
€60.31 to €126.97

ROSE O'LOUGHLIN
Proprietor

American Express
Diners
Mastercard
Visa

😊 Weekend specials from £99.00

55 55
PSⓋ

Closed 24 December - 04 January

KILDARE HOTEL & COUNTRY CLUB

AT STRAFFAN,
CO. KILDARE
TEL: 01-601 7200 FAX: 01-601 7299
EMAIL: hotel@kclub.ie

HOTEL ★★★★★ MAP 8 N 11

Ireland's only AA 5 Red Star hotel, located 30 minutes from Dublin Airport, invites you to sample its pleasures. Leisure facilities include an 18 hole championship golf course designed by Arnold Palmer, home to the Smurfit European Open and venue for the Ryder Cup in 2005. In addition, both river and coarse fishing are available with full health & leisure club and sporting activities. Meeting and private dining facilities also available.

WEB: www.kclub.ie

Members Of Preferred Hotels & Resorts WW

Room Rate from £310.00 to £360.00
€393.62 to €457.11

RAY CARROLL
Chief Executive

American Express
Diners
Mastercard
Visa

45 45

Open All Year

ABBEYLEIX MANOR HOTEL

ABBEYLEIX,
CO. LAOIS
TEL: 0502-30111 FAX: 0502-30220
EMAIL: info@abbeyleixmanorhotel.com

UNDER CONSTRUCTION OPENING JAN 2000

HOTEL P MAP 7 L 8

Situated in the delightful setting of Abbeyleix heritage town, the brand new Abbeyleix Manor Hotel, with its fabulous bar and restaurant, is the perfect stop-off point halfway between Dublin and Cork on the N8. All the luxury bedrooms are en suite and food is available all day. Abbeyleix's friendly, rural atmosphere will revive the most jaded traveller and with golf, fishing and walking available locally, there's plenty to see and do.

WEB: www.abbeyleixmanorhotel.com

B&B from £35.00 to £40.00
€44.44 to €50.79

JENNY KENT
Owner/Manager

American Express
Mastercard
Visa

23 23

 Inet FAX

Closed 25 - 27 December

Room rates are per room per night

HIBERNIAN HOTEL

ABBEYLEIX,
CO. LAOIS
TEL: 0502-31252 FAX: 0502-31888

HOTEL ★★ MAP 7 L 8

Our family run hotel in Abbeyleix is the ideal place for a short break or holiday. We are situated on the main Dublin/Cork road (N8). Set in the finest Tudor style on the main street. Our excellent restaurant offers extensive à la carte and table d'hôte menus. All bedrooms are en suite with direct dial telephone. Scenic walks, 9 hole golf course, fishing and tennis also available.

B&B from £25.00 to £35.00
€31.74 to €44.44

MARY AND FRANK HARDING
Owners

Mastercard
Visa

🖐🚗🐾📺 T C M U 🖊 S 🏧 alc
10 10

IRISH
HOTELS
FEDERATION

Closed 25 - 27 December

CASTLE ARMS HOTEL

THE SQUARE, DURROW,
CO. LAOIS
TEL: 0502-36117 FAX: 0502-36566

HOTEL R MAP 7 L 8

The Castle Arms Hotel is a family run hotel situated in the award winning picturesque village of Durrow. We are situated one and a half hours from Dublin, two hours from Cork and three hours from Belfast. Our reputation is for good food, service and friendliness. Local amenities include fishing, Granstown Lake is described as being the best Coarse fishing lake in Europe. Trout can be fished from the local rivers Erkina and Nore, horse trekking and many golf courses within easy reach.

B&B from £25.00 to £30.00
€31.74 to €38.09

SEOSAMH MURPHY
General Manager

🖐🚗🐾📺 C M 🖊 🏧 alc
10 10

IRISH
HOTELS
FEDERATION

Open All Year

MONTAGUE HOTEL

EMO, PORTLAOISE,
CO. LAOIS
TEL: 0502-26154 FAX: 0502-26229

HOTEL U MAP 7 L 9

This attractive hotel is the perfect touring base to explore many parts of Ireland and our 70 comfortable bedrooms are en suite. Enjoy our de luxe carvery open daily for snacks, lunches and our Maple Room for evening meals. The Oak Room bar with its relaxing atmosphere is ideal for the quiet drink. We have an excellent reputation for weddings, seminars and conferences. A warm friendly welcome awaits you at the Montague Hotel.

B&B from £38.50 to £66.00
€48.88 to €83.80

P J MCCANN
General Manager

American Express
Diners
Mastercard
Visa

🖐🚗🐾📺 T C M ✲ U J P S 🏧
70 70
alc ♿

IRISH
HOTELS
FEDERATION

Open All Year

ARLINGTON TOWER HOTEL

MAIN STREET, PORTARLINGTON,
CO. LAOIS
TEL: 0502-23225 FAX: 0502-23901
EMAIL: arlingtontower@oceanfree.net

HOTEL U MAP 7 L 10

This well established hotel, situated in the town of Portarlington, only 5 mins from railway station, is well known for good food, excellent service and friendly efficient staff. The hotel is close to all amenities, golf, fishing, pony trekking, etc. In-house entertainment three nights weekly. All bedrooms are tastefully decorated with tea/coffee facilities, direct dial telephone, multi-channel TV. If in the area, or in need of a break, it has to be the Arlington Tower Hotel.

B&B from £30.00 to £45.00
€38.09 to €57.14

JIMMY KELLY
Owner Manager

American Express
Diners
Mastercard
Visa

😊 Weekend specials from £65.00

12 12

Closed 25 December

KILLESHIN HOTEL

PORTLAOISE,
CO. LAOIS
TEL: 0502-21663 FAX: 0502-21976

HOTEL ★★★ MAP 7 L 9

Centrally located just off the M7 approximately one and a half hours south of Dublin, you will find the ideal location for your weekend break. The Killeshin Hotel is the ideal stopover for the tourist or traveller. The location, cuisine and ambience together with our friendly relaxed style will ensure a memorable stay. Leisure centre which comprises 20 metre swimming pool, steam room, sauna, jacuzzi and state of the art gymnasium are now open.

B&B from £35.00 to £45.00
€44.44 to €57.14

NIALL CALLALY
General Manager

American Express
Diners
Mastercard
Visa

😊 Weekend specials from £75.00

50 50

Open All Year

O'LOUGHLIN'S HOTEL

30 MAIN STREET, PORTLAOISE,
CO. LAOIS
TEL: 0502-21305 FAX: 0502-60883
EMAIL: oloughlins@eircom.net

HOTEL ★★ MAP 7 L 9

O'Loughlin's Hotel is situated in the heart of Portlaoise town. It has been completely refurbished by new owners Declan & Elizabeth O'Loughlin. There are 14 en suite bedrooms beautifully decorated with charm, character and comfort. The hotel provides entertainment 3 nights in the exclusive Club 23. Food is served all day from 8am to 9pm. There is an excellent lunch and an à la carte menu. Guests are assured of personal attention and a warm welcome from owners, management and staff.

B&B from £30.00 to £30.00
€38.09 to €38.09

DECLAN & ELIZABETH O'LOUGHLIN
Owners

Mastercard
Visa

14 14

Closed 25 December

Room rates are per room per night

LONGFORD ARMS HOTEL

MAIN STREET,
LONGFORD
TEL: 043-46296 FAX: 043-46244
EMAIL: longfordarms@eircom.net

HOTEL ★★★ MAP 11 J 13

Ideally located in the heart of the midlands, this comfortable hotel, newly renovated to exacting standards has a vibrant and relaxing atmosphere. The hotel boasts a state of the art conference centre, excellent restaurant and award winning coffee shop where you can be assured of fine food, service and a warm welcome in relaxing convivial surroundings. Available locally: 18 hole golf course, angling, equestrian centre and watersports on the Shannon.

B&B from £45.00 to £80.00
€57.14 to €101.58

JAMES REYNOLDS
Manager

American Express
Diners
Mastercard
Visa

☺ Weekend specials from £95.00

62 62

Closed 25 - 26 December

FOUR SEASONS HOTEL & LEISURE CLUB

COOLSHANNAGH,
MONAGHAN
TEL: 047-81888 FAX: 047-83131
EMAIL: info@4seasonshotel.ie

HOTEL ★★★ MAP 11 M 16

Elegance without extravagence! Enjoy the excellent service, warmth and luxury of this family run hotel. Relax by the turf fire in the Poitin Still bar or savour the superb food and wine in the Range restaurant. The bedrooms have all modern facilities and residents have unlimited use of the leisure club :- 18m pool, steamroom, jacuzzi, gymnasium and sunbed. Available locally :- 18 hole golf course, angling, equestrian centre and watersports. AA *** member.

B&B from £38.00 to £55.00
€48.25 to €69.84

FRANK McKENNA
Managing Director

American Express
Diners
Mastercard
Visa

40 40

Closed 25 - 26 December

HILLGROVE HOTEL

OLD ARMAGH ROAD,
MONAGHAN
TEL: 047-81288 FAX: 047-84951

HOTEL ★★★★ MAP 11 M 16

This 4**** hotel combines comfort and genuine Irish hospitality, only 2hrs from Dublin, it offers 44 superbly appointed rooms, comfortable surroundings and a delightful restaurant. On the boundaries of the ecclesiastical capital of Ireland, the ancient seat of the Kings, the Hillgrove is perfectly situated for those who enjoy the rich tapestry of local history. There is a variety of activities offered by Monaghan, the most northerly town in the Lakeland region.

B&B from £39.00 to £49.00
€49.52 to €62.22

ROSS MEALIFF
General Manager

American Express
Diners
Mastercard
Visa

☺ Weekend specials from £95.00

44 44

Open All Year

RIVERDALE HOTEL

**LOWER MAIN STREET, BALLYBAY,
CO. MONAGHAN**
TEL: 042-974 1188 FAX: 042-974 8121
EMAIL: riverdalehotel@eircom.net

HOTEL ★★ MAP 11 M 15

A small family run hotel in a nice country town offering good accommodation, excellent food, nice homely atmosphere. Overlooking Lough Major the headwaters of the Dromore system, offering 1st class pike and coarse fishing - boats provided, 6 golf courses nearby, horse riding, scenic walks. Good shopping areas within easy reach. Entertainment weekly includes Bingo, live bands, cabaret, discos, traditional music. Catering for functions, parties, meetings (up to 400), conferences etc.

B&B from £30.00 to £37.50
€38.09 to €47.62

PADDY AND PAULINE CONNOLLY
Owners

Mastercard

Visa

☺ Midweek specials from £85.00

19 19

Inet

HOTELS

Closed 24 - 26 December

BREFFNI GUEST HOUSE

**O'NEILL STREET, CARRICKMACROSS,
CO. MONAGHAN**
TEL: 042-966 1361 FAX: 042-966 1361
EMAIL: farneywines@eircom.net

GUESTHOUSE ★★ MAP 12 N 14

A fine Georgian residence 2 mins walk from town centre. Within easy reach of lakes for fishing. Pony trekking, golf and nature walks all close by. Carrickmacross is famous for its lace which you can view at the Lace Co Op at Market Square. All rooms tastefully decorated en suite with TV, phone, tea/coffee making facilities. A home from home cosy house. Car parking at rear.

B&B from £20.00 to £35.00
€25.39 to €44.44

SHEILA MCARDLE
Owner

American Express

Mastercard

Visa

14 11

Open All Year

NUREMORE HOTEL & COUNTRY CLUB

**CARRICKMACROSS,
CO. MONAGHAN**
TEL: 042-966 1438 FAX: 042-966 1853
EMAIL: nuremore@eircom.net

HOTEL ★★★★ MAP 12 N 14

A fine country hotel, Nuremore offers an unrivalled range of sporting and leisure facilities. Our parkland estate boasts a splendid 18 hole championship golf course. The superb country club has a swimming pool, whirlpool, sauna, steam room, gym, squash, tennis courts and snooker. Situated 1.5hrs from Dublin and Belfast. Extensive conference and banqueting facilities on site.

WEB: www.nuremore-hotel.ie

B&B from £65.00 to £95.00
€82.53 to €120.63

JULIE GILHOOLY
Proprietor

American Express

Diners

Mastercard

Visa

☺ Weekend specials from £160.00

69 69

HOTELS

Open All Year

Room rates are per room per night

GLENCARN HOTEL AND LEISURE CENTRE

MONAGHAN ROAD,
CASTLEBLAYNEY, CO. MONAGHAN
TEL: 042-974 6666 FAX: 042-974 6521

HOTEL ★★★ MAP 11 M 15

Situated on the main Dublin route to the north west. This luxury hotel has 27 bedrooms all en suite, with D.D. telephone, TV (family rooms available). Beside Lough Muckno forest park, great for fishing, water skiing, boating or a leisurely stroll. The Glencarn has established its name for quality food and efficient service. Music in the Temple Bar and night club. Our leisure centre boasts a jacuzzi, steam rooms, changing rooms, plunge pool, childrens pool, 21 metre swimming pool.

B&B from £35.00 to £38.00
€44.44 to €48.25

PATRICK MCFADDEN
General Manager

American Express
Diners
Mastercard
Visa

☺ Weekend specials from £85.00

27 27

Closed 24 - 25 December

BROSNA LODGE HOTEL

BANAGHER-ON-THE-SHANNON,
CO. OFFALY
TEL: 0509-51350 FAX: 0509-51521

HOTEL ★★ MAP 7 J 10

Our country hotel, close to the river Shannon, welcomes guests with superb hospitality and relaxed elegance. Mature gardens surround the hotel. With unique peat bogs, mountains, the Shannon and Clonmacnois, you will delight in this gentle little known part of Ireland. Fishing, golf, pony trekking, nature and historical tours arranged locally. Enjoy beautiful food in our famous Snipes Restaurant and drinks in McGabhann's bar. Courtesy of Choice Programme.

B&B from £26.00 to £26.00
€33.01 to €33.01

DAVID & TERESA SMYTH
Proprietors

American Express
Diners
Mastercard
Visa

☺ Weekend specials from £69.00

14 14

Open All Year

COUNTY ARMS HOTEL

RAILWAY ROAD, BIRR,
CO. OFFALY
TEL: 0509-20791 FAX: 0509-21234
EMAIL: countyarmshotel@eircom.net

HOTEL ★★★ MAP 7 J 9

One of the finest examples of late Georgian Architecture (C.1810), its well preserved interior features are outstanding. The atmosphere is warm, cosy & peaceful. Our hotel gardens and glasshouses provide fresh herbs, fruit and vegetables for our various menus. All our recently renovated bedrooms have private bathroom, telephone, colour TV & tea maker. 2 rooms adapted with facilities for disabled. Locally available golf, horseriding, fishing, tennis & heated indoor pool.

Members Of MinOtel Ireland Hotel Group

B&B from £33.00 to £48.00
€41.90 to €60.95

WILLIE & GENE LOUGHNANE
Owners

American Express
Diners
Mastercard
Visa

24 24

Open All Year

DOOLYS HOTEL

EMMET SQUARE, BIRR,
CO. OFFALY
TEL: 0509-20032 FAX: 0509-21332
EMAIL: doolyshotel@esatclear.ie

HOTEL ★★★ MAP 7 J 9

An historic 250 year old coaching inn, this 3*** Bord Failte and AA hotel has been modernised to a very high standard of comfort and elegance. All bedrooms en suite, tastefully decorated with colour TV, video, radio, DD phone, tea/coffee making facilities. The Emmet restaurant offers superbly cooked international dishes and is complemented by our modern Coachouse Grill and Bistro where you can obtain hot meals all day.

WEB: www.doolyshotel.com

Members Of Holiday Ireland Hotels

B&B from £33.00 to £37.50
€41.90 to €47.62

NOEL KEIGHER
General Manager

American Express
Diners
Mastercard
Visa

☺ Weekend specials from £85.00

18 18

Closed 25 December

KINNITTY CASTLE

KINNITTY, BIRR,
CO. OFFALY
TEL: 0509-37318 FAX: 0509-37284
EMAIL: kinnittycastle@eircom.net

HOTEL U MAP 7 J 9

This magnificent country residence, situated 1 hour and 30 mins from Dublin, Galway and Limerick. Kinnitty Castle boasts stately reception rooms filled with antique furnishings, 37 luxurious en suite bedrooms and an elegant restaurant offering gourmet cuisine and fine wines. Extensive conference and banqueting facilities available. Equestrian holidays are a speciality and other activities on the estate include clay pigeon shooting, tennis and walking. Golf and fishing can be arranged.

WEB: www.kinnittycastle.com

B&B from £80.00 to £105.00
€101.58 to €133.32

FEARGHAL O'SULLIVAN
General Manager

American Express
Diners
Mastercard
Visa

☺ Weekend specials from £155.00

37 37

Open All Year

Room rates are per room per night

MALTINGS GUESTHOUSE

CASTLE STREET, BIRR,
CO. OFFALY
TEL: 0509-21345   FAX: 0509-22073

GUESTHOUSE ★★★   MAP 7 J 9

Secluded on a picturesque riverside setting beside Birr Castle, in the centre of Ireland's finest Georgian town. Built circa 1810 to store malt, for Guinness, and converted in 1994 to a ten bedroom guesthouse with full bar and restaurant. All bedrooms are comfortably furnished with bath/shower en suite, colour TV and direct dial phones.

B&B from £22.50 to £25.00
€28.57 to €31.74

MAEVE GARRY
Manageress

Mastercard

Visa

☺ Weekend specials from £59.00

10 10

aic

Open All Year

SPINNERS TOWN HOUSE

CASTLE ST, BIRR,
CO.OFFALY
TEL: 0509-21673 FAX: 0509-21672
EMAIL:spinners@indigo.ie

GUESTHOUSE ★★   MAP 7 J 9

Situated in the heart of 18th Century Georgian Birr in the shadow of the famous Birr Castle gardens and its historic Science Centre and Telescope. Ideally located for touring the beautiful Irish midlands and Ely O'Carroll country. Spinners Townhouse & Bistro is a chic and modern family run establishment with an International reputation. The warm friendly welcome along with stylish comfort and good food creates a perfect haven for your holidays Live-Eat-Sleep.

WEB: www.spinners-townhouse.com

B&B from £17.50 to £22.50
€22.22 to €28.57

JOE & FIONA BREEN
Propreitors

American Express

Diners

Mastercard

Visa

☺ Weekend specials from £60.00

9 9

FAX

Closed 01 November-01 March

BRIDGE HOUSE HOTEL & LEISURE CLUB

TULLAMORE,
CO. OFFALY
TEL: 0506-22000 FAX: 0506-41338

HOTEL P   MAP 7 K 10

The famous Bridge House, is now a luxury 72 room hotel and leisure complex in the heart of Tullamore. With our magnificent award-winning bar, restaurant, and coffee shop we are justifiably proud of our great tradition of hospitality, good food and service. The leisure complex with indoor swimming pool, spa pool, sauna, jacuzzi and gym, two 18 hole golf courses within 5 mins and 12 golf courses within 30 mins. Shopping Centre and numerous attractions and activities available locally.

B&B from £50.00 to £80.00
€63.49 to €101.58

COLM MCCABE
Manager

American Express

Mastercard

Visa

72 72

aic   Inet   FAX

Closed 24 - 26 December

MOORHILL COUNTRY HOUSE HOTEL

MOORHILL, CLARA ROAD,
TULLAMORE, CO. OFFALY
TEL: 0506-21395 FAX: 0506-52424
EMAIL: moorhill@indigo.ie

HOTEL U MAP 7 K 10

Mature chestnut trees and manicured lawns form a tranquil setting for the Victorian elegance of Moorhill. Superbly appointed en suite guestrooms in the old house and garden mews lead from the original stone-cut walls and exposed ceiling beams of the award-winning restaurant and old world bar. Attention to detail and quality in this traditional country inn will ensure your sojourn deep in the heart of Ireland is memorable. Booking through tourist office/travel agent or direct to hotel.

WEB: indigo.ie/~moorhill

B&B from £35.00 to £45.00
€44.44 to €57.14

JEAN & OLIVER TONER

American Express
Diners
Mastercard
Visa

☺ Weekend specials from £79.00

🏠🐾📞🖥️T C♨CM❄UJP🍴S
10 10
🍷alc

IRISH HOTELS FEDERATION

Closed 24 - 26 December

SEA DEW GUESTHOUSE

CLONMINCH ROAD, TULLAMORE,
CO. OFFALY
TEL: 0506-52054 FAX: 0506-52054

GUESTHOUSE ★★★ MAP 7 K 10

Set in a mature garden of trees, Sea Dew is a purpose built guesthouse, providing guests with a high standard of comfort, located only 5 mins walk from the town centre. The conservatory breakfast room will give you a bright start to the day, where there is an excellent selection of fresh produce. All bedrooms are spacious with en suite facilities, TV and direct dial telephones. Golfing, fishing, horse riding and shooting are available nearby. Access for wheelchairs.

B&B from £26.00 to £26.00
€33.01 to €33.01

OLIVE WILLIAMS
Proprietor

Mastercard
Visa

🏠🐾📞🖥️C♨UJP🍴
10 10

IRISH HOTELS FEDERATION

Closed 23 December - 02 January

TULLAMORE COURT HOTEL

TULLAMORE,
CO. OFFALY
TEL: 0506-46666 FAX: 0506-46677
EMAIL: info@tullamorecourthotel.ie

HOTEL U MAP 7 K 10

Situated in the heart of Ireland, the Tullamore Court Hotel is close to a range of amenities including golf courses, Clonmacnoise monastic settlement, the Slieve Bloom mountains and the heritage town of Birr with its castle and gardens, making it the ideal location for a conference, special event or holiday break. The hotel offers 72 luxurious guest rooms, superb restaurant, lively bar, conference and banqueting facilities for up to 550 people and state of the art leisure facilities.

WEB: www.tullamorecourthotel.ie

B&B from £70.00 to £75.00
€88.88 to €95.23

JOE O'BRIEN
Managing Director

American Express
Diners
Mastercard
Visa

☺ Weekend specials from £140.00

🏠🐾📞🖥️🍴T C♨CMCS🛎️📶
72 72
UJ🎵PS🍷alc🍺 Inet

IRISH HOTELS FEDERATION

Closed 24 - 26 December

Room rates are per room per night

HODSON BAY HOTEL

ATHLONE,
CO. WESTMEATH
TEL: 0902-92444 FAX: 0902-92688
EMAIL: info@hodsonbayhotel.com

HOTEL ★★★ MAP 11 J 11

Located on the lakeshore of Lough Ree, commanding breathtaking views of the neighbouring golf club and surrounding countryside. Offering sandy beaches and a modern marina with cruiser berthing, summer season daily lake cruise. The purpose built conference centre, leisure complex and award-winning bar and two rosette AA fish restaurant combine to make the hotel one of the finest in Ireland. Exit Athlone bypass, take the N61 Roscommon road.

WEB: www.hodsonbayhotel.com

B&B from £40.00 to £60.00
€50.79 to €76.18

MICHAEL DUCIE
Director/General Manager

American Express
Diners
Mastercard
Visa

:/ 𝄡 ⍁

☺ Weekend specials from £69.00

100 100

Open All Year

PRINCE OF WALES HOTEL

CHURCH STREET, ATHLONE,
CO. WESTMEATH
TEL: 0902-72626 FAX: 0902-75658

HOTEL ★★★ MAP 11 J 11

The Prince of Wales offers 69 tastefully refurbished en suite bedrooms. Situated in the heart of Athlone on the banks of the river Shannon, we are the ideal base to discover the unspoilt beauty of the midlands and west coast. Our facilities include superb restaurant, bistro and old world bar. Local amenities: cruise of the river Shannon, bog tour, Clonmacnois, championship golf courses, pony riding and bowling.

B&B from £40.00 to £60.00
€50.79 to €76.18

PAUL J RYAN
Managing Director

American Express
Diners
Mastercard
Visa

:/ 𝄡

☺ Weekend specials from £75.00

69 69
àlc

Closed 24 - 26 December

ROYAL HOEY HOTEL

ATHLONE,
CO. WESTMEATH
TEL: 0902-72924 FAX: 0902-75194

HOTEL ★★ MAP 11 J 11

The Royal Hoey hotel offers comfort and cuisine. Today, the Royal is a modern hotel with all the services and comforts associated with today's travellers' needs. There are 38 luxuriously appointed bedrooms, colour TV, telephone, passenger lift to all floors, secure car parking, fully licensed bar and function room. Excellent restaurant. Fast food coffee dock. Restful lounge space, where you can relax and enjoy a slower pace of life.

B&B from £38.00 to £41.00
€48.25 to €52.06

MARY HOEY
Proprietor

American Express
Diners
Mastercard
Visa

:/ 𝄡

38 38
àlc

Closed 25 - 29 December

SHAMROCK LODGE COUNTRY HOUSE HOTEL

CLONOWN ROAD, ATHLONE,
CO. WESTMEATH
TEL: 0902-92601 FAX: 0902-92737

HOTEL U MAP 11 J 11

The Shamrock Lodge Countryhouse Hotel, where you are guaranteed a warm welcome is set on its own landscaped gardens, just 7 minutes walk from Athlone town centre. We offer 27 bedrooms all tastefully decorated with en suite facilities, DD phone, multi-channel TV, tea/coffee making facilities. The hotel is renowned for its excellent cuisine. Carvery lunch and bar food served daily. Restaurant dinner nightly. Golfing packages and angling holidays are on offer.

B&B from £30.00 to £35.00
€38.09 to €44.44

PADDY MCCAUL
Proprietor

American Express
Diners
Mastercard
Visa

27 27

Closed 24 - 26 December

LAKESIDE HOTEL & MARINA

GLASSON, ATHLONE,
CO. WESTMEATH
TEL: 0902-85163 FAX: 0902-85431

HOTEL P MAP 7 J 11

Welcome to the Lakeside Hotel & Marina complex situated on the majestic shores of Lough Ree. Enjoy most comfortable accommodation with all mod cons, serving excellent food and fine wine. The Lakeside Hotel is surrounded by 3 of the finest golf courses in Ireland, anglers can explore shore fishing or hire small boats (when available). Our marina is also home to Ireland's luxury passenger cruise ships, MV Goldsmith and the Spirit of Athlone.

B&B from £30.00 to £35.00
€38.09 to €44.44

KATHY & MICHAEL BARRETT
Proprietors

Mastercard
Visa

10 10

Open All Year

AUSTIN FRIAR HOTEL

AUSTIN FRIARS STREET, MULLINGAR,
CO. WESTMEATH
TEL: 044-45777 FAX: 044-45880

HOTEL N MAP 11 L 12

Offering warm hospitality in the best of Irish tradition, the Austin Friar Hotel provides a range of modern facilities and a dedicated professional and friendly service. Unique in it's structural design, the hotel was built in an elliptical shape and features a central atrium. All rooms are en suite with interiors of warm natural colour and soft furnishing giving a modern, sophisticated appearance. Austins, the Californian-style restaurant is the ideal place to enjoy good food.

WEB: www.globalgolf.com

B&B from £35.00 to £75.00
€44.44 to €95.23

JOHN VARLEY
General Manager

American Express
Diners
Mastercard
Visa

19 19

Closed 24 - 26 December

Room rates are per room per night

BLOOMFIELD HOUSE HOTEL & LEISURE CLUB

TULLAMORE ROAD, MULLINGAR,
CO. WESTMEATH
TEL: 044-40894 FAX: 044-43767
EMAIL: bloomfieldhouse@eircom.net

HOTEL ★★★   MAP 11 L 12

3km S. of Mullingar town on the N52, Bloomfield overlooks 20 acres of woodland on Lough Ennell's shore. 3*** hotel with 65 en suite rooms, conservatory lounge bar, lake-view restaurant and extensive conference and banqueting facilities. Health & leisure club has 20m pool, fully equipped gymnasium, jacuzzi, sauna and steam room. Adjacent to Mullingar's 18-hole ch. golf course with fishing on site at Lough Ennell and full range of equestrian activities available nearby. Private parking.

WEB: www.bloomfieldhouse.com

Members Of Executive Club

B&B from £40.00 to £75.00
€50.79 to €95.23

JERRY HEALY
General Manager

American Express
Diners
Mastercard
Visa

:/▣

☺ Weekend specials from £99.00

65 65

Closed 24 - 26 December

CROOKEDWOOD HOUSE

MULLINGAR,
CO. WESTMEATH
TEL: 044-72165 FAX: 044-72166
EMAIL: cwoodhse@iol.ie

GUESTHOUSE ★★★★   MAP 11 L 12

A crooked road winds you up the hill to Crookedwood House, a 200 year old rectory overlooking Lake Derravaragh, the home of the Children of Lir. This is a wonderful spot to relax and enjoy superb food cooked by Noel, one of Ireland's noted chefs. Crookedwood House is a member of Ireland's Blue Book and is listed in all major guides.

WEB: www.iol.ie/~cwoodhse

Members Of Ireland's Blue Book

B&B from £40.00 to £55.00
€50.79 to €69.84

NOEL & JULIE KENNY
Owners/Proprietors

American Express
Diners
Mastercard
Visa

8 8

Open All Year

GREVILLE ARMS HOTEL

MULLINGAR,
CO. WESTMEATH
TEL: 044-48563 FAX: 044-48052

HOTEL ★★★   MAP 11 L 12

In the heart of Mullingar town, the Greville Arms is a home from home with none of the packaged commerciality offered by so many modern hotels. Bedrooms all en suite, colour TV and direct dial phone. Most bedrooms look on to the unique garden and conservatory which is one of the finest gardens to be found in a town centre hotel. The new Greville Restaurant is noted for fine cuisine and wines. The Greville is the perfect centre for touring and action packed breaks.

B&B from £40.00 to £50.00
€50.79 to €63.49

JOHN COCHRANE
General Manager

American Express
Diners
Mastercard
Visa

:/♪▣

☺ Weekend specials from £85.00

40 40

Closed 25 December

AN TINTAIN GUESTHOUSE

**MAIN STREET, MULTYFARNHAM,
CO. WESTMEATH
TEL: 044-71411 FAX: 044-71434**

GUESTHOUSE ★★★ MAP 11 K 12

A delightful blend of old and new, sympathetically restored cut stone cottage and listed forge on the banks of the river Gaine. Our 8 en suite rooms are furnished to a high standard, all are with TV, DD phone and hairdryer. Enjoy fine cuisine in our fully licensed restaurant with a relaxed fireside atmosphere, only 1.5 miles from N4, an hour from Dublin in the gently rolling hills of the lake district of Ireland.

Members Of Premier Guesthouses

B&B from £21.00 to £25.00
€26.66 to €31.74

	IAN & LIZ MILBURN Proprietors
	Mastercard
	Visa

8 8

Closed 02 - 26 January

VILLAGE HOTEL

**TYRRELLSPASS,
CO.WESTMEATH
TEL: 044-23171 FAX: 044-23491**

HOTEL U MAP 11 L 11

A Village Hotel of Ireland, overlooking the village green, built as part of a Georgian crescent by Jane, Countess of Belvedere. We have 10 cosy, en suite rooms with tv etc, a popular restaurant for fine fare and an award winning Innkeepers' Buffet serving bar food all day. A national tidy towns winner. Tyrrellspass is 85km from Dublin on the road west, beside championship golf courses and the Midland's trout lakes.

B&B from £27.50 to £40.75
€34.92 to €51.74

	GERARD CLERY Proprietor
	American Express
	Diners
	Mastercard
	Visa

☺ Weekend specials from £66.00

10 10

HOTELS

Open All Year

Room rates are per room per night

SOUTH EAST
The Sunny South East

"River Valleys in an Ancient Land" - that's how best to summarise the very special appeal of Ireland's South East.

This is one of the best loved holiday regions among Irish people themselves. It combines the tranquil elegance of historic old towns and villages with the classic splendour of medieval Kilkenny and Waterford, the crystal city and regional capital.

There's a beautiful coastline too, dotted with sandy beaches and a mild warm climate which inspired the term "Sunny South East"

But it is the rivers which give uniqueness to the South East. The Slaney, Barrow, Nore, Suir and Blackwater carve a patchwork of fertile valleys and plains through Carlow, Kilkenny, South Tipperary, Waterford and Wexford as they wind their majestic way to the Celtic Sea.

They criss-cross the picturesque landscape past remnants of ancient times and older peoples, the Celts, Vikings, Normans and Anglo-Saxons. They were the early invaders, explorers, traders and missionaries. Their castles, abbeys, stone bridges and settlements lie scattered across the countryside as constant reminders of bygone times.

There's as much to do as to see in the South East. Golfers may enjoy the 'South East Sunshine Circuit' - 28 golf courses in all, mostly parkland, almost all uncluttered for free-and-easy golf.

Horse back lovers can choose between 29 registered centres. Anglers may enjoy sea, game or coarse fishing. Walkers and cyclists love the undulating countryside, the spectacular coastal ways.

Close to 60 visitor centres are open for visitors to explain the region's unique heritage more fully, e.g. Irish National Heritage Park.

Resorts like Courtown, Rosslare, Kilmore Quay, the Hook, Dunmore East, Tramore, Ardmore and Clonea lure families to the seaside in great numbers. They provide opportunities for endless fun and entertainment.

If you have not yet visited the South East, there's a special welcome in store.

For further details, contact South East Tourism, The Quay, Waterford.

Telephone: 051-875823.

Fax. 051-077388 or call to any of the South East's other year-round Tourist Offices at Carlow, Clonmel, Dungarvan, Kilkenny, Waterford, Wexford and Rosslare.

GUINNESS

Guinness Enniscorthy Strawberry Fair, Enniscorthy, Co. Wexford.
June

Waterford Spraoi & International Rhythm Festival, Co. Waterford.
July

Kilkenny Arts Week, Kilkenny.
August

Wexford Opera Festival, Wexford.
October

Event details correct at time of going to press

BALLYVERGAL HOUSE

**DUBLIN ROAD,
CARLOW**
TEL: 0503-43634 FAX: 0503-40386
EMAIL: ballyvergal@indigo.ie

GUESTHOUSE ★★ MAP 7M 8

A large family run guesthouse conveniently located just outside Carlow town on the Dublin road (N9), adjacent to Carlow's 18 hole championship golf course. We offer our guests en suite rooms with TV, DD phone and hairdryer, a large residents' lounge and extensive private car parking. Most importantly you are assured of a warm friendly welcome. We are ideally located for golf (Carlow, Mt Wolseley, Kilkea Castle, Mt Juliet), angling, shooting, horseriding, and pitch & putt.

B&B from £20.00 to £25.00
€25.39 to €31.74

CON & ITA MARTIN

Mastercard
Visa

😊 Midweek specials from £68.00

9 3

Open All Year

BARROWVILLE TOWN HOUSE

**KILKENNY ROAD, CARLOW TOWN,
CO. CARLOW**
TEL: 0503-43324 FAX: 0503-41953

GUESTHOUSE ★★★ MAP 7M 8

"A Personal Guesthouse of Quality". Barrowville, a period listed residence in own grounds. 4 mins walk to town centre. Well appointed rooms with most facilities. Antique furnishing. Traditional or buffet breakfast served in conservatory overlooking gardens. Ideal location for excellent golf at Carlow, Kilkea or Mt. Wolseley. Touring south east, midlands, Glendalough, Kilkenny, Waterford and various gardens. German spoken. Recommended AA, RAC, Travellers Guide, Bridgestone 100 Best. B&B Ireland.

WEB: www.premier-guesthouses.ie

Members Of Premier Guesthouses

B&B from £22.50 to £25.00
€28.57 to €31.74

RANDAL & MARIE DEMPSEY
Proprietors

American Express
Mastercard
Visa

7 7

Open All Year

DOLMEN HOTEL AND RIVER COURT LODGES

**KILKENNY ROAD,
CARLOW**
TEL: 0503-42002 FAX: 0503-42375
EMAIL: reservations@dolmenhotel.ie

HOTEL ★★★ MAP 7M 8

Nestled along the scenic banks of the river Barrow and set in 20 acres of landscaped beauty is the Dolmen Hotel, 1.5k from Carlow. Fishing, golf, shooting and horseriding are just some of the sporting facilities surrounding the hotel. With 40 beautifully appointed rooms including 3 luxury suites with en suite, TV, DD phone, trouser press and hairdryer. Our 1 bedroomed lodges are ideal for the sporting enthusiast. Largest conference and banqueting facilities in the south east.

WEB: www.dolmenhotel.ie

B&B from £39.50 to £52.50
€50.15 to €66.66

JOHN VILLIERS-TUTHILL
General Manager

American Express
Diners
Mastercard
Visa

😊 Weekend specials from £89.00

40 40

Closed 25 December

Room rates are per room per night

ROYAL HOTEL

DUBLIN STREET,
CARLOW
TEL: 0503-31621   FAX: 0503-31125
EMAIL: royal@iol.ie

HOTEL ★★   MAP 7M 8

34 en suite rooms in the heart of
Carlow this friendly family run
historic hotel prides itself on its
professional service. Ideally based to
tour Dublin, Kilkenny, Wicklow, etc.
and close to the best in golfing,
shooting, angling and hillwalking.
Conference suites, weekly
entertainment programme and
extensive all day carvery or bar
menu. Try the fine cuisine in our
exciting new bistro. Own car park
and peaceful garden.

B&B from £35.00 to £40.00
€44.44 to €50.79

PATRICK & ANNE FINUCANE
Proprietors

American Express
Diners
Mastercard
Visa

Closed 25 December

SEVEN OAKS HOTEL

ATHY ROAD,
CARLOW
TEL: 0503-31308   FAX: 0503-32155
EMAIL: sevenoak@eircom.net

HOTEL ★★★   MAP 7M 8

A hotel of quality, standing in 2
acres of landscaped gardens offering
you detailed personal service. We
specialise in the best of Irish Foods
in our award-winning Tudor Bar
Carvery and intimate restaurant.
Individually designed bedrooms,
combining a selection of executive
and luxury suites, studios and family
rooms, are accessible by lift and
have tea/coffee facilities, TV/Video,
hairdryers, trousers press and
telephone. 18 hole golf courses,
shooting and fishing available
locally.

WEB: www.beourguest.ie

B&B from £35.00 to £40.00
€44.44 to €50.79

MICHAEL MURPHY
Manager/Director

American Express
Diners
Mastercard
Visa

😊 Special offers apply

Open All Year

BALLYKEALEY COUNTRY HOUSE & RESTAURANT

BALLON,
CO. CARLOW
TEL: 0503-59288   FAX: 0503-59297
EMAIL: bh@iol.ie

HOTEL ★★★   MAP 7M 8

Ballykealey House, the seat of the
Lecky family from the time of
Cromwell in 1649. Rising
majestically from lush green
parklands, the present house has
changed little from the original, built
in the 1830s. On the N80, 1hr drive
from Dublin and Rosslare, 30mins
from Kilkenny, Ballykealey offers en
suite rooms individually designed in
keeping with the period. Dine in
splendour with table d'hôte and à la
carte menus served nightly in the
Lecky Restaurant.

WEB: http://indigo.ie/~webworks/ballykealey

B&B from £49.50 to £49.50
€62.85 to €62.85

ELAYNE AND IAN FARRELL
Hosts

American Express
Mastercard
Visa

😊 Weekend specials from £110.00

Closed 24 December - 31 January

B&B rates are per person sharing per night incl. Breakfast

MOUNT WOLSELEY HOTEL, GOLF AND COUNTRY CLUB

TULLOW,
CO. CARLOW
TEL: 0503-51674 FAX: 0503-52123
EMAIL: wolseley@iol.ie

HOTEL P MAP 8 N 8

Sensitive restoration of existing buildings, some dating back to the first half of the last century, coupled with additional construction work, have combined to provide a hotel with conference facilities, health centre and accommodation of exceptional standards with timeless elegance at Mount Wolseley Golf and Country Club. The hotel, itself an architectural delight, offering panoramic views of the golfcourse, featuring bars, lounges, restaurant and function rooms.

WEB: www.golfclubireland.com/mountwolseley.htm

B&B from £35.00 to £45.00
€44.44 to €57.14

ANN MARIE MORRISSEY
Hotel Manager

Mastercard
Visa

🏨📶☎️🛗C📠CM❄️🍽️📷⛰️♨️🎵📶🅿️a|c

40 40

Open All Year

BERKELEY HOUSE

5 LOWER PATRICK STREET,
KILKENNY
TEL: 056-64848 FAX: 056-64829

GUESTHOUSE ★★★ MAP 7 L 7

A warm welcome awaits you here at Berkeley House, a fine period residence, uniquely situated in the very heart of Kilkenny city. Our 10 spacious and tastefully decorated bedrooms are en suite, multi channel TV, DD phone and tea/coffee facilities. We also provide private parking for our guests. We are the ideal venue for the perfect break.

B&B from £27.50 to £37.50
€34.92 to €47.62

DECLAN CURTIS
Manager

Mastercard
Visa

☺ Midweek specials from £69.00

🏨📶☎️🛗TC♨️⛰️♨️🅿️

10 10

Closed 22 - 26 December

BRANNIGANS GLENDINE INN

CASTLECOMER ROAD,
KILKENNY
TEL: 056-21069 FAX: 056-65897
EMAIL: branigan@iol.ie

GUESTHOUSE R MAP 7 L 7

The Glendine Inn has been a licensed tavern for over 200 years. It consists of 7 bedrooms (all en suite), a residents lounge and dining room on 1st floor. Downstairs there are lounge and public bars serving snack or bar lunches. We are ideally located for golf (course 200m away), the railway station and the historic city of Kilkenny only 0.5km away. We assure you of a friendly welcome.

B&B from £21.00 to £26.00
€26.66 to €33.01

MICHAEL BRANNIGAN
Proprietor

American Express
Diners
Mastercard
Visa

🏨📶🛗TC♨️⛰️♨️🅿️

7 7

Open All Year

Room rates are per room per night

BUTLER HOUSE

PATRICK STREET,
KILKENNY
TEL: 056-65707 FAX: 056-65626
EMAIL: res@butler.ie

GUESTHOUSE ★★★ MAP 7 L 7

Sweeping staircases, magnificent plastered ceilings, marble fireplaces and a walled garden are all features of this notable Georgian townhouse. Although secluded and quiet Butler House is located in the heart of the city, close to the castle. The house was restored by the Irish State Design Agency in the early 1970s. The combination of contemporary design and period elegance provides an interesting and unique experience. Suites and superior rooms available. Conference/ function facilities and private car park available. AA ◆◆◆◆.

WEB: www.butler.ie

B&B from £39.50 to £54.50
€50.15 to €69.20

MARTINA CUDDIHY
Manager

American Express
Diners
Mastercard
Visa

13 13

Closed 24 - 29 December

CLUB HOUSE HOTEL

PATRICK STREET,
KILKENNY
TEL: 056-21994   FAX: 056-71920
EMAIL: clubhse@iol.ie

HOTEL ★★ MAP 7 L 7

Situated uniquely in a cultural and artistic centre and against the background of Kilkenny's beautiful medieval city, the magnificent 18th century Club House Hotel maintains a 200 year old tradition of effortless comfort, hospitality and efficiency. The en suite rooms are decorated in both modern and period style with complimentary beverages, TV, hairdryer and phone. Food is locally sourced, cooked and presented to highest standards. Victors Bar old world charm and luxury.

Members Of MinOtel Ireland Hotel Group

B&B from £31.50 to £65.00
€40.00 to €82.53

JAMES P. BRENNAN
Managing Director

American Express
Diners
Mastercard
Visa

😊 Midweek specials from £82.50

28 28

Closed 24 - 27 December

HIBERNIAN HOTEL

33 PATRICK STREET, KILKENNY,
CO. KILKENNY
TEL: 056-71888 FAX: 056-71877
EMAIL: info@hibernian.iol.ie

UNDER CONSTRUCTION OPENING DEC 1999

HOTEL P MAP 7 L 7

City centre location, designed to a 4 star standard incorporating restored Georgian Hibernian Bank building, creating a property with an abundance of character and old world charm. With 40 rooms, an intimate setting is provided with close attention to detail and personal service. Centrally located, just minutes walk from Kilkenny Castle, facilities include deluxe rooms, junior suites, penthouse suite, restaurant, bar and conference rooms.

WEB: www.thehibernian.com

B&B from £49.00 to £59.00
€62.22 to €74.91

JOE KELLY
General Manager

American Express
Diners
Mastercard
Visa

40 40

Inet FAX

Open All Year

B&B rates are per person sharing per night incl. Breakfast

HOTEL KILKENNY

COLLEGE ROAD,
KILKENNY
TEL: 056-62000 FAX: 056-65984
EMAIL: kilkenny@griffingroup.ie

HOTEL ★★★ MAP 7 L 7

Hotel Kilkenny is surrounded by picturesque landscaped gardens, just 5 minutes walk from medieval Kilkenny. The hotel has completed a major development programme to include 23 new deluxe rooms, the complete refurbishment of all our existing bedrooms, a new 5* health & fitness club with 20m pool, new stone conservatory to the front of the original Rosehill House, new stone entrance to the hotel and refurbishment of the bar and lobby areas. The all new Hotel Kilkenny. Why resort to less?

WEB: www.griffingroup.ie

Members Of Griffin Hotel Group

B&B from £46.00 to £58.00
€58.41 to €73.64

RICHARD BUTLER
General Manager

American Express
Diners
Mastercard
Visa

103 103

Open All Year

KILFORD ARMS

JOHN STREET,
KILKENNY
TEL: 056-61018 FAX: 056-61018
EMAIL: phelanp@indigo.ie

GUESTHOUSE U MAP 7 L 7

The Kilford Arms is 50 yards from Bus/Rail station and still in city centre offers you 3 luxury Bars, luxury accommodation, entertainment nightly, a beautiful traditional Irish restaurant, bar food available all day. Late bar every night, games room. A new purpose built car park and state of the art nite club called Club Life all under one roof at a price hard to beat.

B&B from £25.00 to £40.00
€31.74 to €50.79

PIUS PHELAN
Owner

Mastercard
Visa

30 30

Open All Year

KILKENNY HOUSE

FRESHFORD ROAD,
KILKENNY
TEL: 056-70711 FAX: 056-70698

GUESTHOUSE ★★★ MAP 7 L 7

Located 1k from the city on the northside R693 near St. Lukes General Hospital. Set in 2 acres of gardens with ample private car parking. The conservatory breakfast room will give guests a bright start to the day. A full Irish and buffet breakfast is served. Home baking a speciality. All rooms en suite with pine furniture and oak floors. Guests have privacy and peace with their own entrance, reception, stairs and sitting-room. Owner operated guarantees 'rest for the tired'.

B&B from £20.00 to £25.00
€25.39 to €31.74

MICHELENE DORE
Proprietor/Manager

Mastercard
Visa

10 10

Closed 20 December - 11 February

Room rates are per room per night

KILKENNY ORMONDE HOTEL

ORMONDE STREET, KILKENNY,
CO. KILKENNY
TEL: 056-23900 FAX: 056-23977
EMAIL: info@kilkennyormonde.com

UNDER CONSTRUCTION OPENING MAR 2000

HOTEL P MAP 7 L 7

The new Kilkenny Ormonde Hotel is designed to compliment its famous sister hotel, the Aghadoe Heights in Killarney, bringing the same level of service and excellence to Kilkenny city. The Kilkenny Ormonde is centrally located just off High Street and is adjacent to a secure 24hr car park. With 118 large superior rooms, a conference centre with 12 meeting rooms and extensive leisure centre, the Kilkenny Ormonde is ideal for both the leisure and corporate traveller.

WEB: www.kilkennyormonde.com

B&B from £52.50 to £67.50
€66.66 to €85.71

PATRICK CURRAN
General Manager/Director

American Express
Diners
Mastercard
Visa

Weekend specials from £125.00

Open All Year

KILKENNY RIVER COURT HOTEL

THE BRIDGE, JOHN STREET,
KILKENNY
TEL: 056-23388 FAX: 056-23389
EMAIL: krch@iol.ie

HOTEL N MAP 7 L 7

Located in a private courtyard, this elegant hotel is built on the banks of the river Nore with stunning views of Kilkenny Castle. Crystal chandeliers, elegant Georgian furniture, beautifully designed fabrics and furnishings give you a sense of old world grandeur and style. Exquisite cuisine in our Riverside Restaurant complemented by discreet, friendly service in anticipation of your every need is the hallmark of the dedication and enthusiasm of our team.

WEB: www.kilrivercourt.com

B&B from £60.00 to £105.00
€76.18 to €133.32

PETER WILSON
General Manager

American Express
Mastercard
Visa

Weekend specials from £135.00

Open All Year

LACKEN HOUSE

DUBLIN ROAD,
KILKENNY
TEL: 056-61085 FAX: 056-62435
EMAIL: lackenhs@indigo.ie

GUESTHOUSE ★★★ MAP 7 L 7

Stay at Lacken House and enjoy high quality accommodation, superb food and a friendly welcome. We are a family run guesthouse, situated in Kilkenny city, where you can enjoy exploring the medieval city. All bedrooms are en suite, central heating throughout, private car parking. Our restaurant features the home cooking of award winning chef/patron Eugene McSweeney, where fresh food is cooked to perfection. Restaurant closed Sundays and Mondays.

Members Of Logis of Ireland

B&B from £30.00 to £36.00
€38.09 to €45.71

EUGENE & BREDA MCSWEENEY
Owners

Mastercard
Visa

Closed 22 - 28 December

B&B rates are per person sharing per night incl. Breakfast

LANGTON HOUSE HOTEL

**69 JOHN STREET,
KILKENNY
TEL: 056-65133   FAX: 056-63693**

HOTEL ★★★   MAP 7 L 7

Langton's Kilkenny, award-winning bar and restaurant; it has won National Pub of the Year 4 times. Now open, a wonderful new hotel extension with a 'five star' finish and the same standards of excellence that have made Langton's famous. Complete with executive, penthouse and art deco rooms the new Langton's Hotel completes the award-winning picture.

B&B from £40.00 to £65.00
€50.79 to €82.53

EAMONN LANGTON
Proprietor

American Express
Diners
Mastercard
Visa

Closed 25 - 26 December

METROPOLE HOTEL

**HIGH STREET,
KILKENNY
TEL: 056-63778   FAX: 056-70232**

HOTEL ★   MAP 7 L 7

The Metropole Hotel is situated in the heart of Kilkenny city. Occupies a dominant position in Kilkenny's main shopping area (High Street). Within walking distance of all the city's medieval buildings e.g. Kilkenny Castle, Roth House and St. Canices Cathedral. All bedrooms are en-suite with multi channel TV, Direct Dial Telephone and Tea/Coffee facilities. Live entertainment. Bord Failte approved.

B&B from £20.00 to £40.00
€25.39 to €50.79

ROBERT DELANEY
Proprietor

Mastercard
Visa

Open All Year

NEWPARK HOTEL

**CASTLECOMER ROAD,
KILKENNY
TEL: 056-22122   FAX: 056-61111
EMAIL: info@newparkhotel.com**

HOTEL ★★★   MAP 7 L 7

The recently refurbished Newpark Hotel (3***, AA***), set in 40 acres of parkland in Ireland's medieval city. 111 en suite rooms with TV, hairdryer, phone and tea/coffee making facilities. The executive leisure centre includes a 52 ft. pool, sauna, jacuzzi, steam room and gym. The new Scott Dove Bar and Bistro serves carvery lunch and a superb evening bar menu. Damask restaurant specialises in fine dining. Live entertainment most nights. Excellent professional conference facilities.

WEB: www.newparkhotel.com

Members Of Best Western Hotels

B&B from £49.50 to £59.50
€62.85 to €75.55

DAVID O'SULLIVAN
General Manager

American Express
Diners
Mastercard
Visa

☺ Midweek specials from £99.00

Open All Year

Room rates are per room per night

SPRINGHILL COURT HOTEL

WATERFORD ROAD,
KILKENNY
TEL: 056-21122 FAX: 056-61600
EMAIL: springhillcourt@eircom.net

HOTEL ★★★ MAP 7 L 7

Visit the new look Springhill Court Hotel. We now offer en suite spacious rooms. Situated in this charming medieval city, the hotel offers entertainment every w/end in the lively Paddocks Bar, carvery food served daily and snacks throughout the day. This hotel is an ideal base for touring the south east. Golf and angling. Extensive new conference facilities in a range of suites. Carparking. Member of Business & Leisure Ireland. Sister of Arklow Bay Hotel in Wicklow.

WEB: www.springhillcourt.com

Members Of Chara Hotel Group

B&B from £40.00 to £59.50
€50.79 to €75.55

ANTHONY SMITH
General Manager

American Express
Diners
Mastercard
Visa

86 86

Open All Year

BAMBRICKS TROYSGATE HOUSE

KILKENNY CITY,
CO. KILKENNY
TEL: 056-51000 FAX: 056-51200

GUESTHOUSE U MAP 7 L 7

Troysgate House formerly the Jailhouse of the old walled-in medieval city of Kilkenny. 20 en suite rooms newly constructed in 1994. Angling, swimming, horse riding nearby. Kilkenny golf course 1km away. Troysgate House is an historic and charming old world inn which has retained its character while serving the needs of the modern world. Troysgate House incorporates Bambrick's renowned traditional pub which truly has an atmosphere all of its own.

B&B from £22.00 to £45.00
€27.93 to €57.14

GREG FLANNERY
Manager

Mastercard
Visa

20 20

Open All Year

AVALON INN

THE SQUARE, CASTLECOMER,
CO. KILKENNY
TEL: 056-41302 FAX: 056-41963
EMAIL: avalinn@eircom.net

GUESTHOUSE ★★★ MAP 7 L 7

The Avalon Inn, a Georgian building, set in the quiet town of Castlecomer, 16km from Kilkenny. A rural setting with quiet woodland walks nearby. The area has good trout and salmon fishing. 1km away there is a 9 hole golf course. There are many excellent golf courses nearby. Staying in Castlecomer offers you the best of both worlds with Kilkenny 15 mins away and at your doorstep fishing, golfing, horseriding and leisurely walks.

B&B from £25.00 to £30.00
€31.74 to €38.09

ANNE O'REGAN
Director

Mastercard
Visa

5 5

Closed 24 - 25 December

B&B rates are per person sharing per night incl. Breakfast

WATERSIDE

**THE QUAY, GRAIGUENAMANAGH,
CO. KILKENNY
TEL: 0503-24246 FAX: 0503-24733
EMAIL: info@waterside.iol.ie**

GUESTHOUSE ★★★ MAP 7M 7

A beautifully restored 19th century cornstore with feature wooden beams and imposing granite exterior. Riverside location, all rooms having a view of the river Barrow. Excellent base for boating, fishing and hillwalking. 16k from Mount Juliet for golf. Graiguenamanagh boasts 13th century Duiske Abbey and is only 27k from historical Kilkenny. Superb restaurant features continental cuisine and international flavour wine list. Relaxed and friendly approach; also perfect for small groups.

WEB: www.watersideguesthouse.com

B&B from £25.00 to £35.00
€31.74 to €44.44

BRIAN ROBERTS/BRIGID DALY
Managers

Mastercard

Visa

🦶🔔☎🖭TC⌖♪S🅿alc
10 10

Open All Year

CARROLLS HOTEL

**KNOCKTOPHER,
CO. KILKENNY
TEL: 056-68082 FAX: 056-68290**

HOTEL N MAP 7 L 6

Situated on the N10 between Kilkenny and Waterford. Enjoy the excellent service, warmth and luxury of our newly opened family-run hotel. All rooms en suite with TV, and DD phone. Our Sionnach St Restaurant has an excellent reputation for good food. The hotel provides live music 3 nights a week. Golfing, fishing, horse riding and shooting are available nearby.

B&B from £30.00 to £35.00
€38.09 to €44.44

WILLIAM CARROLL
Proprietor

Mastercard

Visa

😊 Midweek specials from £75.00

🦶🔔☎🖭TC⌖CM❄☾♪🅿🅟
alc ▪

Closed 25 December

RISING SUN

**MULLINAVAT, VIA WATERFORD,
CO. KILKENNY
TEL: 051-898173 FAX: 051-898435**

GUESTHOUSE ★★★ MAP 4 L 6

A family run guesthouse, 12.8km from Waterford city on the main Waterford - Dublin road. It has 10 luxurious bedrooms all en suite with D/D telephone and TV. The Rising Sun guesthouse is an ideal base for sports enthusiasts, surrounded by some beautiful golf courses within 15-30 mins drive. The old world charm of stone and timberwork sets the tone of comfort and relaxation in the bar and lounge. Traditional home cooked lunches and bar food served daily. Full à la carte menu and wine list.

B&B from £25.00 to £30.00
€31.74 to €38.09

PATRICIA PHELAN
Manager

Mastercard

Visa

🦶🔔☎🖭TC⌖CMP S🅐alc ▪
10 10

Closed 24 - 27 December

Room rates are per room per night

MOUNT JULIET ESTATE

THOMASTOWN,
CO. KILKENNY
TEL: 056-73000 FAX: 056-73019
EMAIL: info@mountjuliet.ie

HOTEL ★★★★   MAP 7 L 6

Mount Juliet Estate, Ireland's premier hotel and sporting estate offers several styles of deluxe accommodation. Guests can choose between the elegance of the 18th century Mount Juliet House or the more sporting ambience of the Hunters Yard or Rose Garden lodges. Estate activities include Jack Nicklaus golf course, fishing, shooting, archery, Iris Kellet equestrian centre, tennis, leisure centre, cycling, 18-hole putting course. Chauffeur driven tours available.

WEB: www.mountjuliet.ie

Members Of Small Luxury Hotels

Room Rate from £115.00 to £340.00
€146.02 to €431.71

RICHARD HUDSON
General Manager

American Express
Diners
Mastercard
Visa

59 59

Open All Year

BALLYGLASS COUNTRY HOUSE HOTEL

GLEN OF AHERLOW ROAD,
BALLYGLASS, TIPPERARY TOWN
TEL: 062-52104 FAX: 062-52229

HOTEL ★   MAP 3 I 6

Family run Ballyglass Country House is set in its own peaceful grounds just 2 miles from Tipperary town at the entrance to the beautiful Glen of Aherlow. Recently refurbished to a high standard with all facilities. We have a fine restaurant serving the best of local produce. The Forge bar is adjacent to the hotel for those who would like a pleasant drink in comfortable Olde Worlde surroundings.

B&B from £26.00 to £28.00
€33.01 to €35.55

JOAN AND BILL BYRNE
Proprietors

American Express
Mastercard
Visa

☺ Weekend specials from £59.00

10 10

Closed 24 - 25 December

ROYAL HOTEL

BRIDGE STREET, TIPPERARY TOWN,
CO. TIPPERARY
TEL: 062-33244 FAX: 062-33596
EMAIL: royalhtl@iol.ie

HOTEL ★★   MAP 6 I 6

The Royal Hotel is situated just off the Main Street by the River. The family Hotel owned and run by Andy & Angela Lacey has 16 en suite rooms with TV and telephone (Fax service available). Our Green Room Restaurant specialises in Steaks, Fish & Poultry (All purchased locally). Tourist Value Menu available each evening from 6-9pm. Andy (a golfer himself) can arrange Golf at the three 18 hole courses 10 minutes from the Hotel. Sport & Leisure Centre only 3 minutes from Hotel.

WEB: www.iol.ie/tipp/royalhtl.htm

B&B from £25.00 to £40.00
€31.74 to €50.79

ANDY LACEY
Proprietor

American Express
Diners
Mastercard
Visa

16 16

Closed 25 - 26 December

B&B rates are per person sharing per night incl. Breakfast

CAHIR HOUSE HOTEL

THE SQUARE, CAHIR,
CO. TIPPERARY
TEL: 052-42727 FAX: 052-42727
EMAIL: cahirhousehotel@eircom.net

HOTEL ★★★ MAP 3 J 6

A Georgian building situated in the picturesque heritage town of Cahir nestled among some of Tipperary's most beautiful scenery surrounded by an abundance of leisure pursuits including golfing, horseriding, fishing, hunting etc. Our award winning restaurant The Butler's Pantry, serves only the best of local produce specialising in steaks, fish & poultry. Food served throughout the day in O'Briens Bar. Music sessions.

B&B from £35.00 to £55.00
€44.44 to €69.84

LIAM DUFFY M.I.H.C.I.

American Express
Diners
Mastercard
Visa

41 41

Closed 24 - 26 December

KILCORAN LODGE HOTEL

CAHIR,
CO. TIPPERARY
TEL: 052-41288 FAX: 052-41994

HOTEL ★★★ MAP 3 J 6

Kilcoran, a former hunting lodge set in spacious grounds overlooking beautiful countryside. An ideal holiday base located equal distance (15 min drive) between Tipperary, Cashel, Clonmel and Mitchelstown and 45 mins drive from Cork, Kilkenny and Limerick on the main Cork-Dublin road. The hotel has the charm of bygone days yet all the modern facilities of a 3 star hotel. Guests have free access to Shapes leisure centre with indoor pool etc. Golf, hillwalking, fishing etc locally.

B&B from £39.00 to £85.00
€49.52 to €107.93

JACQUELINE MULLEN
Managing Director

American Express
Diners
Mastercard
Visa

☺ Weekend specials from £89.50

23 23

Open All Year

CARRAIG HOTEL

MAIN STREET, CARRICK-ON-SUIR,
CO. TIPPERARY
TEL: 051-641455 FAX: 051-641604

HOTEL ★★★ MAP 3 K 5

An ideal base from which to explore the south east's many attractions, walk or drive through the Knockmealdown and Comeragh mountain ranges, fish on the world famous river Suir, cycle the route of the Tour de France '98, horse riding or hunting, golf on one of the local courses, visit Tipperary Crystal, Waterford Crystal, the Ormonde castle, the Rock of Cashel or simply enjoy Irish hospitality at its best.

B&B from £30.00 to £40.00
€38.09 to €50.79

WILLIAM HANRAHAN
General Manager

American Express
Diners
Mastercard
Visa

14 14

Closed 24 - 26 December

Room rates are per room per night

BAILEYS OF CASHEL

MAIN STREET, CASHEL,
CO. TIPPERARY
TEL: 062-61937   FAX: 062-62038
EMAIL: baileys@eircom.net

GUESTHOUSE ★★★   MAP 3 J 6

Baileys (Circa 1709) is a listed Georgian Townhouse fondly restored to its original splendor by the Leahy family. Its secure parking incorporates the city wall (1364). The Licenced Cellar Restaurant has the Distinction of Recommendations by most good food guides. Much acclaimed for its friendly welcome and efficient service. A stay in Baileys is often the highlight of a visit to Cashel of the Kings. We invite you to share a memorable visit to Tipperary with us, in the big house renowned for its hospitality.

WEB: www.euroka.com/cashel/baileys

B&B from £18.50 to £25.00
€23.49 to €31.74

KEVIN AND BEATRICE LEAHY
Hosts

American Express
Diners
Mastercard
Visa

☺ Weekend specials from £55.00

8 8

Closed 25 - 26 December

CASHEL PALACE HOTEL

MAIN STREET, CASHEL,
CO. TIPPERARY
TEL: 062-62707   FAX: 062-61521
EMAIL: reception@cashel-palace.ie

HOTEL ★★★   MAP 3 J 6

Built in 1730 as an Archbishop's Palace, the Cashel Palace has been restored as a hotel, complemented by tranquil walled gardens and a private walk to the famous Rock of Cashel. Our 23 rooms are all en suite with TV, phone, trouser press. Our Bishop's Buttery restaurant is open for lunch and dinner, while the Guinness bar is open for light snacks daily, both offering modern Irish cuisine at affordable prices. Sunday lunch served in our Three Sisters Restaurant.

WEB: www.cashel-palace.ie

B&B from £45.00 to £112.50
€57.14 to €142.85

PATRICK & SUSAN MURPHY
Proprietors

American Express
Diners
Mastercard
Visa

23 23

Closed 24 - 26 December

DUNDRUM HOUSE HOTEL

DUNDRUM, CASHEL,
CO. TIPPERARY
TEL: 062-71116   FAX: 062-71366
EMAIL: dundrumh@iol.ie

HOTEL ★★★   MAP 3 J 7

From the moment one swings through the gates of this 3*** hotel, up the long sweeping drive, bounded on each side by the manicured fairways of its own championship 18 hole golf course, one escapes the stress of the modern world and enters the demesne of Dundrum. This gracious Georgian manor house hotel has been tastefully renovated, with the addition of a new leisure complex, inclusive of a 20m pool/sauna/steamroom/gym/fitness centre, pub/restaurant, enabling guests to relax in style.

WEB: www.tipp.ie/dundrumhh.htm

Members Of Manor House Hotels

B&B from £55.00 to £60.50
€69.84 to €76.82

DEIRDRE & WILLIAM CROWE
Managers

American Express
Diners
Mastercard
Visa

☺ Weekend specials from £100.00

60 60

Open All Year

B&B rates are per person sharing per night incl. Breakfast

LEGENDS GUESTHOUSE & THE KILN RESTAURANT

THE KILN, CASHEL,
CO. TIPPERARY
TEL: 062-61292 FAX: 062-62876
EMAIL: legendsguesthouse@indigo.ie

GUESTHOUSE U MAP 3 J 5

Legends Guesthouse & The Kiln restaurant are uniquely located overlooking the Rock of Cashel with most rooms having spectacular panoramic views. Quality and comfort are the hallmarks of your stay. The Kiln Restaurant offers quality cuisine with many recommendations from noted food guides. Sample also the best of Irish breakfast using local produce. All rooms are tastefully decorated. Local amenities include golf, pony trekking, fishing and hill walking.

WEB: www.tipp.ie/legends.htm

B&B from £22.50 to £32.00
€28.57 to €40.63

MICHAEL & ROSEMARY O'NEILL

American Express
Mastercard
Visa

😊 Weekend specials from £59.00

Closed 24 - 30 December

RECTORY HOUSE HOTEL

DUNDRUM, CASHEL,
CO. TIPPERARY
TEL: 062-71266 FAX: 062-71115
EMAIL: rectoryh@iol.ie

HOTEL ★★★ MAP 3 I 7

The Rectory House Hotel is a family run hotel standing amidst its tree lined grounds. It is a gracious country house providing an ideal haven for the country lover. Comfort and tranquility are offered to our guests in tastefully decorated rooms en suite. Our candlelit restaurant and conservatory provides home cooking. Member Best Western International Group. 1k from 18-hole golf course and leisure complex.

Members Of Best Western Hotels

B&B from £35.00 to £45.00
€44.44 to €57.14

UNA DOYLE
Proprietor

Mastercard
Visa

😊 Oct-Mar weekend specials from £75.00

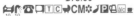

Open All Year

BRIGHTON HOUSE

1 BRIGHTON PLACE, CLONMEL,
CO. TIPPERARY
TEL: 052-23665 FAX: 052-25210
EMAIL: brighton@iol.ie

GUESTHOUSE ★★ MAP 3 K 5

Family run 3 storey Georgian guest house, with a hotel ambience and antique furnishings. Clonmel town centre - the largest inland town in Ireland bridging Rosslare Harbour (132km) with Killarney (160km) and the south west. Host to Fleadh Cheoil na hEireann 1993/94. Visit Rock of Cashel, Mitchelstown Caves, Cahir Castle etc. Golf, fishing and pony trekking arranged locally. All rooms direct dial phones, TV, radio, hairdryer and tea/coffee making facilities.

WEB: www.iol.ie/tipp/brighton.htm

B&B from £25.00 to £35.00
€31.74 to €44.44

BERNIE MORRIS
Proprietor

Mastercard
Visa

😊 Midweek specials from £60.00

Open All Year

Room rates are per room per night

CLONMEL ARMS HOTEL

CLONMEL,
CO. TIPPERARY
TEL: 052-21233 FAX: 052-21526

HOTEL ★★★ MAP 3 K 5

Town centre hotel ideally situated either for business or pleasure. All 31 rooms en suite, direct dial telephone & colour TV. Full conference facilities available. The Paddock restaurant open until 9.30pm each day provides the perfect setting for your personal or business requirements. The Paddock bar is ideal for a quiet drink or alternatively a lively night out with the Paddock music sessions every weekend. Food in the Paddock is served daily.

Members Of Choice Hotels International

B&B from £35.00 to £70.00
€44.44 to €88.88

MARY MALONEY
Assistant Manager

American Express
Diners
Mastercard
Visa

31 31

Closed 25 December

FENNESSY'S HOTEL

GLADSTONE STREET, CLONMEL,
CO. TIPPERARY
TEL: 052-23680 FAX: 052-23783

HOTEL ★★ MAP 3 K 5

Established old hotel. A beautiful Georgian building, it is newly restored and refurbished. Right in the centre of Clonmel, it is easily located by spotting from afar the green steeple of the town's main church, opposite which it stands. All bedrooms have DD phone, TV, en suite, some with jacuzzi. Family run hotel. Elegant and antique decor throughout. After your visit, you will want to return.

B&B from £25.00 to £30.00
€31.74 to €38.09

ESTHER AND RICHARD FENNESSY
Proprietors

American Express
Mastercard
Visa

10 10

Open All Year

HEARNS HOTEL

PARNELL STREET, CLONMEL,
CO. TIPPERARY
TEL: 052-21611 FAX: 052-21135

HOTEL U MAP 3 K 5

Situated in the centre of Clonmel town, the historical Bianconi house, is ideal as a touring base for Cahir Castle, Rock of Cashel, Holycross Abbey, the Vee, Mitchelstown caves and seaside resorts of Tramore and Clonea. All bedrooms are fully en suite with DD phone and TV. Ample parking, relaxing bar, live entertainment at weekends. A la carte restaurant, room service available, attractive conference facilities, good food served all day.

B&B from £37.00 to £42.00
€46.98 to €53.33

VERONICA M BARRY
General Manager

American Express
Diners
Mastercard
Visa

☺ Weekend specials from £80.00

25 25

Closed 25 - 26 December

B&B rates are per person sharing per night incl. Breakfast

HOTEL MINELLA & LEISURE CENTRE

CLONMEL,
CO. TIPPERARY
TEL: 052-22388 FAX: 052-24381
EMAIL: hotel-minella@eircom.net

HOTEL ★★★ MAP 3 K 5

A magnificent country house hotel and 4 star leisure centre situated on the banks of the river Suir. Rooms throughout are elegantly furnished, 5 suites with jacuzzis and 3 suites with 4-poster beds and private steam rooms. Leisure centre: 20m pool, outdoor hot tub, gym, aqua cruises, sauna, steamroom, massage. Outdoor tennis court (all weather), putting green and pleasure boats. AA Rosette. Restaurant. Conference facilities for 500. Family owned and managed by the Nallen family.

WEB: www.tipp.ie/hotel-minella.htm

Members Of Signature Hotels

B&B from £45.00 to £75.00
€57.14 to €95.23

ELIZABETH NALLEN
Proprietor

American Express
Diners
Mastercard
Visa

🙂 Weekend specials from £110.00

70 70

Closed 23 - 29 December

KNOCKLOFTY COUNTRY HOUSE

KNOCKLOFTY, CLONMEL,
CO. TIPPERARY
TEL: 052-38222 FAX: 052-38300
EMAIL: knocklofty@eircom.net

HOTEL U MAP 3 K 5

Knocklofty House is superbly set in 105 acres of sweeping parklands, 6.4km from the lovely town of Clonmel. At Knocklofty you will find a warmth of welcome, intimate tranquil atmosphere and people who care about your needs. Formerly the country residence of the Earls of Donoughmore, the house dates from the 16th Century. The house embodies the best of Georgian decorative architecture and commands magnificent views of the surrounding country and the river Suir - of which we own 1.6km.

WEB: www.iol.ie/tipp/knocklof.htm

B&B from £45.00 to £55.00
€57.14 to €69.84

B. CULLEN/
S. WEIR / G. RUDDY

American Express
Mastercard
Visa

🙂 Oct-Apr weekend specials from £95.00

17 17

Closed 25 - 27 December

AHERLOW HOUSE HOTEL

GLEN OF AHERLOW,
CO. TIPPERARY
TEL: 062-56153 FAX: 062-56212

HOTEL ★★★ MAP 3 I 6

Set in the middle of a coniferous forest just 4 miles from Tipperary town. Originally a hunting lodge now converted into an exquisitely furnished hotel. All bedrooms have en suite facilities. Aherlow House welcomes you to its peaceful atmosphere, enhanced by a fine reputation for hospitality, excellent cuisine and good wines. Overlooks the Glen of Aherlow and has beautiful views of the Galtee mountains. Golf, fishing, hunting, mountain climbing can be arranged.

B&B from £37.00 to £47.00
€46.98 to €59.68

FRANCES FOGARTY
Manager

American Express
Diners
Mastercard
Visa

30 30

Open All Year

Room rates are per room per night

GLEN HOTEL

**GLEN OF AHERLOW
CO. TIPPERARY
TEL: 062-56146 FAX: 062-56152**

HOTEL ★★ MAP 3 I 6

The Glen Hotel set in the shadows of
the majestic Galtee mountains,
amidst the splendour of the Aherlow
Valley is just 5 miles from Tipperary
town. To relax, dream, reminisce or
plan this is the ideal haven. Our
bedrooms are all en suite and have
been recently tastefully redecorated.
This family operated hotel has built
up a fine reputation for excellent
cuisine and offers friendly and
efficient service. Hill walking, horse
riding, fishing and golf.

B&B from £26.00 to £37.00
€33.01 to €46.98

MARGOT AND JAMES COUGHLAN
Proprietors

American Express
Diners
Mastercard
Visa

☺ Weekend specials from £69.00

🛏🔥☎Ⓣ©◻CM☀♂♩🄿🅿🅂
24 24
🄫ᴀʟᴄ

I R I S H
HOTELS
FEDERATION

Open All Year

ARDAGH HOUSE

**KILLENAULE,
CO. TIPPERARY
TEL: 052-56224 FAX: 052-56224
EMAIL: ahouse@iol.ie**

GUESTHOUSE ★ MAP 3 K 7

Fully licensed family guesthouse,
piano lounge bar, residents' lounge,
rooms en suite, home cooking. Set
in the shadow of romantic
Slievenamon, in the area of the
Derrynaflan Chalice, the famous
Coolmore Stud, in the heart of the
Golden Vale. Near Holycross Abbey,
Cashel and Kilkenny. Central for
hunting, fishing, shooting, golf,
horse riding and less strenuous
walks through the hills of Killenaule.
Finally, just one hour from the sea.

B&B from £18.00 to £20.00
€22.86 to €25.39

KATHLEEN & DAVID CORMACK
Proprietors

🛏🔥☎Ⓣ©CM♂🄿🅿7🄫ᴀʟᴄ
6 6

I R I S H
HOTELS
FEDERATION

Closed 25 December

TEMPLEMORE ARMS HOTEL

**MAIN STREET, TEMPLEMORE,
CO. TIPPERARY
TEL: 0504-31423 FAX: 0504-31343
EMAIL: decor@iol.ie**

HOTEL ★★ MAP 7 J 8

The Templemore Arms Hotel, located
in the shadow of one of Ireland's
most prominent landmarks, The
Devil's Bit, in the centre of the town
of Templemore. Recently rebuilt to
match the demands of the most
discerning guests, it boasts lounge
bars, carvery, restaurant, banqueting
suite and conference room,
providing first class service. Visit the
Templemore Arms Hotel and
experience an enjoyable getaway.

WEB: www.tipp.ie/templeah.htm

B&B from £30.00 to £30.00
€38.09 to €38.09

DAN WARD

Mastercard
Visa

🛏🔥☎◻©CM☀♂♩🄫ᴀʟᴄ🍴
10 10

I R I S H
HOTELS
FEDERATION

Closed 25 December

B&B rates are per person sharing per night incl. Breakfast

BRIDGE HOTEL

NO 1 THE QUAY, WATERFORD
TEL: 051-877222 FAX: 051-877229
EMAIL: bridgehotel@treacyhotelsgroup.com

HOTEL ★★★ MAP 4 L 5

One of Waterford's finest hotels enjoying a superb view overlooking the river Suir and just 5 mins walk from the city centre. Family run with an emphasis on traditional hospitality and service for which we are justifiably proud. 100 elegantly furnished en suite rooms equipped with all modern conveniences. Enjoy live entertainment in Timbertoes lounge or our new O'Caseys bar. The cuisine in Crokers restaurant is second to none with traditional and international dishes. Car parking.

WEB: www.treacyhotelsgroup.com

Members Of MinOtel Ireland Hotel Group

B&B from £45.00 to £65.00
€57.14 to €82.53

BRIDGET & JIM TREACY
Proprietors

American Express
Diners
Mastercard
Visa

Weekend specials from £85.00

100 100

Inet

IRISH HOTELS FEDERATION

Closed 24 - 26 December

COACH HOUSE

BUTLERSTOWN CASTLE, BUTLERSTOWN, CORK ROAD, WATERFORD
TEL: 051-384656 FAX: 051-384751
EMAIL: coachhse@iol.ie

GUESTHOUSE ★★★ MAP 4 L 5

Surround yourself with comfort in this elegantly restored 19th century house. Situated 3 miles from Waterford city (Waterford Crystal 5 mins away) in an historic, tranquil, romantic setting (13th century castle in grounds). All rooms en suite. Private sauna available. 5 golf courses within 6 miles radius. Excellent pubs, restaurants nearby. 3*** Irish Tourist Board, AA ♦♦♦♦, Michelin recommended, Best magazine's No.1 in Ireland. 'Crackling log fires and personal attention'.

WEB: homepages.iol.ie/~coachhse

B&B from £26.00 to £33.50
€33.01 to €42.54

DES O'KEEFFE
Proprietor

American Express
Diners
Mastercard
Visa

7 7

IRISH HOTELS FEDERATION

Closed 20 December - 20 January

DIAMOND HILL COUNTRY HOUSE

SLIEVERUE, WATERFORD
TEL: 051-832855 FAX: 051-832254

GUESTHOUSE ★★★ MAP 4 L 5

Situated 1.2km from Waterford City off the Rosslare Waterford road N25, this guesthouse has been refurbished to a Bord Failte grade A standard. Set in its own award winning gardens, all rooms en suite, direct dial phone, multi channel TV, tea/coffee making facilities. Recommended by Frommers, Foders, Michelin, AA, RAC. Member of Premier Guesthouses and Les Routiers. A warm welcome awaits you here at Diamond Hill.

B&B from £22.00 to £27.50
€27.93 to €34.92

MARJORIE SMITH LEHANE
Owner

Mastercard
Visa

12 12

IRISH HOTELS FEDERATION

Closed 25 - 26 December

Room rates are per room per night

DOOLEY'S HOTEL

THE QUAY,
WATERFORD
TEL: 051-873531 FAX: 051-870262
EMAIL: hotel@iol.ie

HOTEL ★★★ MAP 4 L 5

The waters of the river Suir swirl and eddy past the door of this renowned hotel, which is situated on the quay at Waterford. With its high levels of comfort and very personal service Dooley's is our choice for a centrally located hotel in the city. Latest edition conference centre, Rita Nolan suite.

WEB: www.dooleys-hotel.ie

Members Of Holiday Ireland Ltd

B&B from £35.00 to £63.50
€44.44 to €80.63

JUNE DARRER
Proprietor/Manager

American Express
Diners
Mastercard
Visa

☺ Weekend specials from £95.00

113 113 Inet FAX

Closed 25 - 27 December

FORTE TRAVELODGE

CORK ROAD (N25),
WATERFORD
TEL: 1800-709709 FAX: 051-358882

HOTEL U MAP 4 L O5

Situated on the N25 primary route from Rosslare Harbour to Cork, 1 mile from Waterford city and mins from the Waterford Crystal factory, this superb hotel offers comfortable yet affordable accommodation. Each room can sleep up to 3 adults, a child under 12 years and a baby in a cot. Price is fixed per room regardless of the number of occupants. Each room is en suite, has colour TV, Sky Sports and Movies. Sited next to Little Chef restaurant.

Room Rate from £39.95 to £54.95
€50.73 to €69.77

MARY KELLY
General Manager

American Express
Diners
Mastercard
Visa

32 32

Open All Year

GRANVILLE HOTEL

MEAGHER QUAY,
WATERFORD
TEL: 051-305555 FAX: 051-305566
EMAIL: stay@granville-hotel.ie

HOTEL ★★★ MAP 4 L 5

Waterford's most prestigious city centre hotel RAC**** overlooking the river Suir. This family run hotel is one of Ireland's oldest with significant historical connections. Justly proud of the Granville's heritage owners Liam and Ann Cusack today vigorously pursue the Granville's long tradition of hospitality, friendliness and comfort. It has been elegantly refurbished, retaining its old world Georgian character. Award winning Bianconi restaurant, Thomas Francis Meagher Bar.

WEB: www.granville-hotel.ie

Members Of Best Western Hotels

B&B from £50.00 to £70.00
€63.49 to €88.88

LIAM AND ANN CUSACK
Managers/Proprietors

American Express
Diners
Mastercard
Visa

☺ Weekend specials from £90.00

100 100 alc Inet

Closed 25 - 27 December

B&B rates are per person sharing per night incl. Breakfast

IVORY'S HOTEL

TRAMORE ROAD,
WATERFORD
TEL: 051-358888 FAX: 051-358899
EMAIL: ivory@voyager.ie

HOTEL U   MAP 4 L 5

A friendly, family run hotel, Ivory's Hotel is Waterford's best value. Ideally located adjacent to Waterford Crystal factory and city centre. Each en suite combines the convenience of DD phone, multi channel TV with welcoming tea/coffee making facilities, in comfortable surroundings. The hotel boasts an excellent restaurant emphasising the very best fresh local produce. Unwind with a drink and allow us to arrange golf, fishing or choice of activity. Secure carpark. Groups welcome.

WEB: ivoryhotel@voyager.ie

B&B from £27.50 to £47.50
€34.92 to €60.31

DECLAN & NATALIE IVORY
Managing Proprietors

American Express
Diners
Mastercard
Visa

Weekend specials from £89.00

40 40

Open All Year

JURYS HOTEL WATERFORD

FERRYBANK,
WATERFORD
TEL: 051-832111 FAX: 051-832863
EMAIL: info@jurys.com

HOTEL ★★★   MAP 4 L 5

3*** hotel set in 38 acres of parkland with spectacular views of the city and river Suir, just half a mile from the city centre. Each spacious bedroom provides the extra amenity of tea/coffee making facilities. Enjoy a meal in Bardens, a relaxing drink in the Conor Bar, or the many activities available in the superb leisure centre. Ample car parking. Jurys Doyle Hotel Group central reservations Tel. 01-6070000 Fax. 01-6316999.

WEB: www.jurys.com

B&B from £59.00 to £75.00
€74.91 to €95.23

MICHAEL WALSH
General Manager

American Express
Diners
Mastercard
Visa

Weekend specials from £98.00

98 98

Closed 24 - 26 December

MARSUCI COUNTRY HOUSE

OLIVER'S HILL, BUTLERSTOWN,
WATERFORD
TEL: 051-370429 FAX: 051-350983
EMAIL: marsuci@indigo.ie

GUESTHOUSE ★★★   MAP 4 L 5

Marsuci is a refreshingly different 3*** ITB-approved guesthouse. Situated in a semi-rural area just 10 minutes drive from Waterford town, Marsuci is the perfect base for tourists, golfers and business people. All rooms are comfortable with en suite and tea/coffee facilities. A fax/e-mail service is available. Our extensive breakfast menu is second to none. Fluent English, French and Italian spoken.

B&B from £23.00 to £25.00
€29.20 to €31.74

CATHERINE/J-PIERRE OSTINELLI
Proprietors

Mastercard
Visa

6 6

Closed 24 December - 10 January

Room rates are per room per night

O'GRADY'S RESTAURANT & GUESTHOUSE

CORK ROAD,
WATERFORD
TEL: 051-378851   FAX: 051-374062

GUESTHOUSE U   MAP 4 L 5

O'Gradys Restaurant and guesthouse is ideally located on the main Cork road adjacent to the Waterford Crystal factory and city centre. Family-run by Euro Toque chef Cornelius and his wife Sue; they offer the excellent combination of reasonably priced accommodation and a superb licensed Michelin recommended restaurant which specialises in fresh local seafood. Private off street parking. 4 championship golf courses nearby. Tennis, horseriding and fishing. French and Gaelic spoken.

B&B from £25.00 to £35.00
€31.74 to €44.44

SUE AND CORNELIUS
Proprietors

American Express
Diners
Mastercard
Visa

⌂🦽☎️🖨️TC⌴P🅿️🅰️alc
8 8

IRISH HOTELS FEDERATION

Closed 23 - 28 December

RHU GLEN COUNTRY CLUB HOTEL

LUFFANY, SLIEVERUE,
WATERFORD
TEL: 051-832242   FAX: 051-832242

HOTEL N   MAP 4 L 5

Built within its own grounds with parking for cars, coaches etc. the hotel is family run. Situated on the N25 Rosslare to Waterford road, convenient to ferries, it offers a superb location whether your pleasure be golfing, fishing, or simply exploring the south east. All rooms are en suite with DD phone and multi-channel TV. The restaurant is renowned for its service of fine food. Relax and enjoy our lounge bars and ballroom with live entertainment provided by Ireland's top artistes.

B&B from £25.00 to £40.00
€31.74 to €50.79

LIAM MOONEY
Proprietor

American Express
Diners
Mastercard
Visa

☺ Weekend specials from £65.00

⌂🦽☎️🖨️TC⌴CM❄️☽♪♫P🆂
19 19
🅰️alc ☕

IRISH HOTELS FEDERATION

Closed 25 December

RICE GUESTHOUSE BATTERBERRY'S BAR

35 & 36 BARRACK STREET,
WATERFORD
TEL: 051-371606   FAX: 051-357013

GUESTHOUSE U   MAP 4 L 5

We are situated next to Mount Sion Christian Brothers school which Blessed Edmund Ignatius Rice founded in 1802. Tours of the shrine and museum may be arranged, so the name Rice Guesthouse. 20 en suite rooms have cable TV and DD phone. Ideally situated to the main shopping centre, Waterford Crystal and train and bus station. Ideal base for touring the south east or golf breaks. Tee times can be arranged and afterwards enjoy live entertainment most nights in our lounge.

B&B from £26.50 to £32.50
€33.65 to €41.27

JOHN & OLIVE O'DRISCOLL

Mastercard
Visa

⌂🦽☎️🖨️TC⌴CM☽♪♫🅰️
20 20

Open All Year

B&B rates are per person sharing per night incl. Breakfast

ST. ALBANS GUESTHOUSE

CORK ROAD,
WATERFORD
TEL: 051-358171

GUESTHOUSE ★★ MAP 4 L 5

St. Alban's is a well established
family run guesthouse. Ideally
located minutes walk from Waterford
city centre and Waterford Crystal.
Our very spacious superbly
appointed rooms are all en suite
with multi-channel TV, tea/coffee
facilities and hairdryer. Secure
parking at rear of premises. 4
championship golf courses in
vicinity. Horse riding 3km. Tennis
courts, swimming pool 2 mins.
Several local beaches and
breathtaking scenery. Bus and train
station a short distance.

B&B from £20.00 to £27.50
€25.39 to €34.92

TOM & HELEN MULLALLY
Proprietors

Mastercard
Visa

Open All Year

TOWER HOTEL & LEISURE CENTRE

THE MALL,
WATERFORD
TEL: 051-875801 FAX: 051-870129
EMAIL: towerw@iol.ie

HOTEL ★★★ MAP 4 L 5

A Tower Group Hotel, situated in the
heart of Waterford city with 141 en
suite bedrooms, the Tower Hotel &
Leisure Centre is Waterford's leading
hotel and the flagship hotel of the
Tower Group. All rooms have colour
multi-channel TV and direct dial
telephone. Leisure and fitness centre
with 20m pool. Explore the
surrounding coastal resorts and
villages or simply relax and unwind
in the Tower Restaurant and Adelphi
Riverside bar.

WEB: www.towerhotelgroup.ie

Members Of Tower Hotel Group

B&B from £50.00 to £70.00
€63.49 to €88.88

PAUL MCDAID
General Manager

American Express
Diners
Mastercard
Visa

☺ Weekend specials from £79.00

Closed 24 - 29 December

WATERFORD CASTLE

THE ISLAND, BALLINAKILL,
WATERFORD
TEL: 051-878203 FAX: 051-879316
EMAIL: info@waterfordcastle.com

HOTEL U MAP 4 L 5

Waterford Castle hotel, set amidst
310 acres of woodlands
accompanied with an 18 hole
championship golf course located on
a private island, accessible only by
car ferry. The rooms offer panoramic
views of the surrounding river and
estate. For the leisure enthusiast
enjoy a game of golf or perhaps a
refreshing swim in the indoor pool or
a leisurely game of tennis.
Alternatively a scenic walk around
the castle grounds.

WEB: www.waterfordcastle.com

Room Rate from £155.00 to £235.00
€196.81 to €298.39

NIALL EDMONDSON
General Manager

American Express
Diners
Mastercard
Visa

☺ Weekend specials from £180.00

Open All Year

Room rates are per room per night

WATERFORD MARINA HOTEL

CANADA STREET,
WATERFORD
TEL: 051-856600   FAX: 051-856605
EMAIL: stay@irishcourthotels.com

HOTEL ★★★ MAP 4 L 5

The Marina Hotel is located on the waterfront just 2 mins from the city centre. The hotel which has a distinctive art deco, incorporates superbly designed rooms. All rooms are en suite with multi-channel TV, DD phone, hairdryer, trouser press and tea/coffee making facilities. The Waterfront Bar & Bistro restaurant offer an excellent choice of dishes. Guests have complimentary use of a secure indoor carpark, sauna.

WEB: www.irishcourthotels.com

Members Of Irish Court Hotel Group

B&B from £30.00 to £75.00
€38.09 to €95.23

GRAINNE LYNE
Proprietor

American Express
Mastercard
Visa

Weekend specials from £75.00

81 81

alc Inet

IRISH HOTELS FEDERATION

Open All Year

WOODLANDS HOTEL

DUNMORE ROAD,
WATERFORD
TEL: 051-304574   FAX: 051-304575
EMAIL: woodhl@iol.ie

HOTEL P MAP 4 L 5

This new hotel is located 3 miles from Waterford city centre and yet has all the facilities of a countryside hotel with open spaces, a river view and parking for 150 cars. The hotel facilities include 47 en suite rooms with all modern amenities, a split level bar designed to generate a great pub atmosphere. Our restaurant offers the very best cuisine in an intimate setting, state of the art leisure centre plus full conference and banqueting facilities.

B&B from £35.00 to £55.00
€44.44 to €69.84

DERMOT KEENAN
General Manager

American Express
Diners
Mastercard
Visa

Weekend specials from £75.00

47 47

alc Inet FAX

Open All Year

CLIFF HOUSE HOTEL

ARDMORE,
CO. WATERFORD
TEL: 024-94106   FAX: 024-94496
EMAIL: cmv@indigo.ie

HOTEL ★★ MAP 3 K 3

With breathtaking views overlooking Ardmore bay, this owner run family hotel is the ideal location for a peaceful break. All of our comfortable rooms have magnificent sea views and have bathroom/shower en suite. Fresh locally caught fish are a feature of our extensive bars and restaurant menus. This tranquil fishing village was Ireland's 1992 National Tidy Towns winner. The Cliff Hotel is a member of the Village Inns Group Tel: 01-2958900.

Members Of C.M.V.

B&B from £32.50 to £42.00
€41.27 to €53.33

EDDIE IRWIN
Proprietor

American Express
Diners
Mastercard
Visa

13 13

alc

IRISH HOTELS FEDERATION

Closed 01 November - 01 March

B&B rates are per person sharing per night incl. Breakfast

NEWTOWN FARM GUESTHOUSE

GRANGE, ARDMORE, VIA
YOUGHAL, CO. WATERFORD
TEL: 024-94143 FAX: 024-94054
EMAIL: newtownfarm@eircom.net

GUESTHOUSE ★★★ MAP 3 K 3

Family-run farm guesthouse in scenic location, surrounded by its own farmland with dairying as main enterprise. With view of Atlantic ocean, hills and cliff walks, comfortable spacious rooms, all en suite with DD phone, TV and tea/coffee facilities, some with balcony. Seafood award dishes a speciality. Hard tennis court, pony, games room, large garden, sandy beaches 4k. Signposted on N25 Rosslare Road, half way between Dungarvan/Youghal. Turn left at Flemings pub.

WEB: homepage.eircom.net/~newtownfarm

B&B from £21.00 to £28.00
€26.66 to €35.55

TERESA O'CONNOR
Proprietor

☺ Weekend specials from £58.00

Open All Year

ROUND TOWER HOTEL

COLLEGE ROAD, ARDMORE,
CO. WATERFORD
TEL: 024-94494 FAX: 024-94254
EMAIL: rth@eircom.net

HOTEL ★ MAP 3 K 3

Situated within walking distance of Ardmore's award-winning beach, the Round Tower Hotel offers 10 well appointed en suite bedrooms. Fresh local produce feature prominently on both the bar and restaurant menus. The ancient monastic settlement of St. Declan & the Round Tower are situated behind the hotel. Ardmore also boasts some world famous cliff walks, & breathtaking scenery. Ardmore is 21 kms from Dungarvan & a 2hr drive from the port of Rosslare on the Primary N25 route.

WEB: www.waterfordtourism.org

B&B from £25.00 to £30.00
€31.74 to €38.09

AIDAN QUIRKE
Proprietor

Mastercard
Visa

Closed 01 November - 28 February

CLONANAV FARM GUESTHOUSE

NIRE VALLEY, BALLYMACARBRY, VIA
CLONMEL, CO. WATERFORD
TEL: 052-36141 FAX: 052-36294
EMAIL: clonanav@iol.ie

GUESTHOUSE ★★★ MAP 3 K 5

Relax and enjoy the hospitality of the Ryan family at award-winning Clonanav. Situated in the Nire Valley on a farm serving excellent home produced meals. Complimentary tea/coffee bar in conservatory, drying room, hard tennis/basketball court. French and Spanish spoken. Ireland's best dry fly fishing with guidance from Andrew on the Suir, Nire and Tar. Permits, school, tackle hire and shop on premises. Explore the wonderful walking, mountain lakes and valley. Choice of 10 golf courses.

WEB: www.clonanav.com

Members Of Great Fishing Houses of Irl.

B&B from £25.00 to £35.00
€31.74 to €44.44

EILEEN RYAN
Proprietor

American Express
Diners
Mastercard
Visa

☺ Weekend specials from £77.00

Closed 01 November - 01 February

Room rates are per room per night

HANORAS COTTAGE

NIRE VALLEY, BALLYMACARBRY,
CO. WATERFORD
TEL: 052-36134 FAX: 052-36540

GUESTHOUSE ★★★ MAP 3 K 5

Delightfully situated in the Comeragh mountains, Hanoras Cottage has every comfort for discerning guests. Relax in the sheer bliss of an adult only house with spa tub and the soothing sounds of the Nire river running by. Spoil yourselves in our spacious rooms with jacuzzi baths. Superior rooms for that special occasion! Enjoy excellent cuisine from our Ballymaloe School chefs who cater for all diets. We specialise in walking holidays, golf, horse riding and just relaxing.

B&B from £40.00 to £60.00
€50.79 to €76.18

SEAMUS & MARY WALL
Proprietors

Mastercard

Visa

☺ Autumn/Spring specials from £100.00

🛏🚪☎🖥T❄️Ụ💲🅿🍴
10 10

HOTELS

Closed 20 - 28 December

RICHMOND HOUSE

CAPPOQUIN,
CO. WATERFORD
TEL: 058-54278 FAX: 058-54988

GUESTHOUSE ★★★★ MAP 3 J 4

Charming 18th century Georgian countryhouse. AA ◆◆◆◆, RAC highly acclaimed. Of olde world charm & character, yet with all the comforts for the discerning tourist. Relax in total tranquility in front of log fires or treat yourself to a gourmet meal in our fully licensed restaurant. All bedrooms en suite, tea making facilities, TV, & DD phone. Ideal location for walking, golfing, fishing or touring the south east. Recommended in all good travel guides.

WEB: www.amireland.com/richmond

B&B from £45.00 to £70.00
€57.14 to €88.88

PAUL & CLAIRE DEEVY
Proprietors

American Express

Diners

Mastercard

Visa

☺ Weekend specials from £110.00

🛏🚪☎🖥T❄️CM❄️Ụ💲🅿🍴alc
9 9

HOTELS

Closed 23 December - 14 February

THREE RIVERS GUEST HOUSE

CHEEKPOINT,
CO. WATERFORD
TEL: 051-382520 FAX: 051-382542
EMAIL: 3rivers@iol.ie

GUESTHOUSE ★★★ MAP 4 M 5

AA selected ◆◆◆◆. Newly refurbished Guesthouse overlooking Waterford Estuary. Situated on the outskirts of the Historic Village, Cheekpoint, with its award winning Pubs and seafood Restaurants. Sample the delights of breakfast in our Estuary View dining room or relax over coffee in our spacious lounge. Ideal base for touring the sunny south east; close to Waterford, Dunmore East, Tramore and 2km from Faithlegg Golf Course. All rooms en suite, direct dial telephones.

Members Of Premier Guesthouses

B&B from £22.00 to £30.00
€27.93 to €38.09

STAN AND MAILO POWER
Proprietors

American Express

Diners

Mastercard

Visa

☺ Stay 3 nights and 4th night free

🛏🚪☎🖥TC❄️Ụ💲🅿🍴
14 14

Closed 20 December - 10 January

B&B rates are per person sharing per night incl. Breakfast

CLONEA STRAND HOTEL, GOLF & LEISURE

CLONEA, DUNGARVAN,
CO. WATERFORD
TEL: 058-42416 FAX: 058-42880
EMAIL: clonea@indigo.ie

HOTEL ★★★ MAP 3 K 4

Clonea Strand Hotel overlooking Clonea beach. Family run by John and Ann McGrath. All rooms en suite with tea/coffee making facilities, hair-dryer and colour TV. Indoor leisure centre with heated pool, jacuzzi, sauna, Turkish bath, gymnasium and ten pin bowling alley. Situated close by is our 18 hole golf course bordering on the Atlantic ocean with a scenic background of Dungarvan Bay and Comeragh Mountains. Our Bay restaurant specialises in locally caught seafood.

WEB: www.amireland.com/clonea

B&B from £32.00 to £50.00
€40.63 to €63.49

MARK KNOWLES
General Manager

American Express
Diners
Mastercard
Visa

☺ Weekend specials from £79.00

58 58

🔒 HOTELS FEDERATION

Open All Year

GOLD COAST GOLF HOTEL & LEISURE CENTRE

BALLINACOURTY, DUNGARVAN,
CO. WATERFORD
TEL: 058-42249 FAX: 058-43378
EMAIL: clonea@indigo.ie

HOTEL ★★★ MAP 3 K 4

Gold Coast Golf Hotel overlooking Dungarvan Bay, family run by John & Ann McGrath. All rooms en suite with tea/coffee making facilities, colour TV, direct dial telephone, leisure centre with heated pool and children's pool, sauna, gym, jacuzzi, bubble pool. Leisure centre with view of our 18 hole golf course. Our tower and bay restaurants specialises in locally caught seafood. Food available all day in bunker bar, with panoramic view of bay.

WEB: www.amireland.com/clonea

B&B from £32.00 to £50.00
€40.63 to €63.49

MAIRE MCGRATH
Manager

American Express
Diners
Mastercard
Visa

☺ Midweek specials from £95.00

36 36

Open All Year

LAWLORS HOTEL

BRIDGE STREET, DUNGARVAN,
CO. WATERFORD
TEL: 058-41122 FAX: 058-41000
EMAIL: info@lawlors-hotel.ie

HOTEL ★★★ MAP 3 K 4

Lawlors hotel is family run with 89 bedrooms, all en suite with tea/coffee making facilities, TV and DD phone. Lawlors is the ideal choice for your stay in the beautiful West Waterford countryside. Conferences, Weddings, Parties, Seminars are especially catered for. Good food is a speciality at Lawlors and the friendly atmosphere of Dungarvan town is brought to life in the Old Worlde bar surroundings.

B&B from £32.00 to £48.00
€40.63 to €60.95

MICHAEL BURKE
Proprietor

American Express
Diners
Mastercard
Visa

89 89

🔒 HOTELS FEDERATION

Closed 25 December

Room rates are per room per night

PARK HOTEL

**DUNGARVAN,
CO. WATERFORD
TEL: 058-42899   FAX: 058-42969
EMAIL: photel@indigo.ie**

HOTEL ★★★   MAP 3 K 4

Overlooking the Colligan river estuary, owned and run by the Flynn family, whose experience in the hotel business is your best guarantee of an enjoyable and memorable stay. The hotel's spacious and comfortable bedrooms have been furnished with flair and imagination. All have private bathroom, direct dial telephone, 16 channel satellite TV. The hotel's leisure centre has a 20m swimming pool, sauna, steam room & gym.

B&B from £34.00 to £45.00
€43.17 to €57.14

PIERCE FLYNN
Manager

American Express
Diners
Mastercard
Visa

29 29

Open All Year

SEAVIEW

**WINDGAP, DUNGARVAN,
CO. WATERFORD
TEL: 058-41583   FAX: 058-41679
EMAIL: tiodgar@indigo.ie**

GUESTHOUSE N   MAP 3 K 4

Want your vacation to never stop being a vacation? Enjoy breakfast overlooking the sea? Play one of Dungarvans three 18 hole golf courses or take a bus tour of the area and let someone else do the driving. How about dinner, entertained by traditional Irish musicians, at the nearby Marine bar? Make every ounce of your vacation count. Try Seaview on N25 between Waterford and Cork. All rooms en suite with TV and tea/coffee facilities.

WEB: http://amireland.com/seaview

B&B from £25.00 to £30.00
€31.74 to €38.09

NORA & MARTIN & MEALLA FAHEY

Mastercard
Visa

8 8

Open All Year

CANDLELIGHT INN

**DUNMORE EAST,
CO. WATERFORD
TEL: 051-383215   FAX: 051-383289**

HOTEL ★★   MAP 4M 5

The Candlelight Inn is small intimate and family run, with home cooked food and a homely feeling. We welcome you and offer good service, very fresh fish, seasonal meats, fruits and vegetables all bought locally. Golfers are especially welcome. Bridge parties welcome to play local club. Painting weekends and activity weekends. Heated outdoor swimming pool in June, July and August.

B&B from £25.00 to £35.00
€31.74 to €44.44

ANTOINETTE BOLAND
Manager

American Express
Diners
Mastercard
Visa

11 11

Closed 01 November - 01 March

B&B rates are per person sharing per night incl. Breakfast

HAVEN HOTEL

DUNMORE EAST,
CO. WATERFORD
TEL: 051-383150 FAX: 051-383488

HOTEL ★★ MAP 4M 5

The Haven Hotel is family owned and managed. Situated in Dunmore East, one of Ireland's most beautiful seaside resorts. The restaurant is renowned for its first class food and specialises in prime rib beef, steaks and locally caught seafood. The Haven is an ideal location for day trips to the many surrounding golf clubs. Children are also made especially welcome with our motto being - the children of today are the customers of tomorrow.

B&B from £35.00 to £40.00
€44.44 to €50.79

JEAN & JOHN KELLY
Managers/Owners

Mastercard
Visa

24 24

Closed 01 November - 28 February

OCEAN HOTEL

DUNMORE EAST,
CO. WATERFORD
TEL: 051-383136 FAX: 051-383576

HOTEL ★★ MAP 4M 5

The Ocean Hotel, 15 minutes drive from Waterford city, is situated in one of the most picturesque villages in Ireland's sunny south east. We offer you the personal attention and service that only a family run hotel can provide. A la carte, set dinner menu and an extensive bar food menu specialising in steaks and fresh fish dishes and giving good value for money. Golf packages arranged. Alfred D Snow bar is air-conditioned throughout with decor depicting a nautical theme.

B&B from £27.50 to £35.00
€34.92 to €44.44

BRENDAN GALLAGHER
Proprietor

American Express
Diners
Mastercard
Visa

12 12

Closed 25 December

FAITHLEGG HOUSE HOTEL

FAITHLEGG,
CO. WATERFORD
TEL: 051-382000 FAX: 051-382010
EMAIL: faithleg@iol.ie

HOTEL N MAP 4M 5

A Tower Group Hotel, Faithlegg House Hotel opened in May '99, located on the already renowned 18-hole Faithlegg championship golf course, overlooking the estuary of the River Suir. The 18th century manor house has been tastefully refurbished and extended to incorporate 82 rooms, including 14 master rooms in the old house and a unique fitness, health and beauty club which offers a full range of facilities supervised by massage therapists and fitness co-ordinators.

WEB: www.towerhotelgroup.ie

B&B from £65.00 to £100.00
€82.53 to €126.97

MADGE BARRY
General Manager

American Express
Diners
Mastercard
Visa

☺ Weekend specials from £125.00

82 82

Closed 03 January - 07 February

Room rates are per room per night

BALLYRAFTER HOUSE HOTEL

LISMORE,
CO. WATERFORD
TEL: 058-54002   FAX: 058-53050
EMAIL: ballyrafter@esatclear.ie

HOTEL ★★ MAP 3 J 4

With its timeless approach through a tree lined ave. this beautiful Georgian Country Hse Hotel, enjoys award winning standards of cuisine as The Majestic Lismore Castle looms across the Blackwater River from the dining room bay window. Retaining the charm & tranquility of the 1800's the Willoughby's ensure their guests of high standards throughout, as recently awarded by The West Waterford's Good Food Tree. Our 10 bedrooms incorporate modern facilities with unhindered comfort.

WEB: www.ballyrafter

Members Of Best Loved Hotels Of The World

B&B from £35.00 to £45.00
€44.44 to €57.14

JOE AND NOREEN WILLOUGHBY
Proprietors

American Express
Diners
Mastercard
Visa

☺ Weekend specials from £95.00

🛏🚭☎📱T/🄰CCM❄∪J🅿🔒🔌
10 10

Closed 31 October - 01 March

LISMORE HOTEL

MAIN STREET, LISMORE,
CO. WATERFORD
TEL: 058-54555   FAX: 058-53068

HOTEL ★★ MAP 3 J 4

Situated in the heart of historical Lismore, on the Munster Blackwater River, this newly refurbished hotel is the ideal location for a relaxing break. Take a walk back through time and enjoy Lismore with its majestic castle and gardens, historical cathedral and peaceful river walks. Horse riding, fishing and golf are all available locally.

B&B from £30.00 to £40.00
€38.09 to €50.79

JAMES J KELLY
Manager

Mastercard
Visa

🛏🚭☎📱TC⚡CM∪J🎵🅿S🔌
20 20

ⓐⓛⓒ 🔌 FAX

Closed 25 December

BELAIR GUEST HOUSE

RACECOURSE ROAD, TRAMORE,
CO. WATERFORD
TEL: 051-381605   FAX: 051-386688

GUESTHOUSE ★★ MAP 4 L 5

Belair is a beautiful Georgian house built in 1797 featuring delightful enclosed gardens. The house, which overlooks Tramore bay and miles of sandy beach, has been newly refurbished throughout. All rooms en suite, TV, phone, tea/coffee facilities. It is quiet and peaceful for that restful break and safe parking. Fishing, tennis, horseriding, surfing, golfing and Splashworld all at hand. Waterford Crystal and six excellent golf courses within an eight mile radius.

B&B from £22.50 to £30.00
€28.57 to €38.09

MARY CURRAN
Manager

Mastercard
Visa

☺ 7 nights B&B from £150.00

🛏🚭TC⚡∪J🅿S🔌
6   6

Open All Year

B&B rates are per person sharing per night incl. Breakfast

GRAND HOTEL

TRAMORE,
CO. WATERFORD
TEL: 051-381414 FAX: 051-386428
EMAIL: grandhotel@eircom.net

HOTEL ★★★ MAP 4 L 5

The Grand Hotel opened its doors in 1790 and for more than two hundred years its name has been synonymous with the grace and style of the era. It overlooks the golden strands of Tramore which are probably the most enchanting and the most popular of the Atlantic Coast resorts. The 83 newly refurbished bedrooms have bathrooms en suite, DD phones, multi channel, tea/coffee facilities, TV and hair dryers.

WEB: www.tramore.ie

B&B from £30.00 to £38.00
€38.09 to €48.25

TOM AND ANNA TREACY
Proprietors

American Express
Diners
Mastercard
Visa

☺ Weekend specials from £75.00

83 83
Inet

Open All Year

MAJESTIC HOTEL

TRAMORE,
CO. WATERFORD
TEL: 051-381761 FAX: 051-381766
EMAIL: info@majestic-hotel.ie

HOTEL ★★★ MAP 4 L 5

A warm welcome awaits you at the newly refurbished Majestic Hotel overlooking Tramore Bay, and only 10km from Waterford City. Family owned and managed, all 60 bedrooms are en-suite with TV, phone, hairdryer, & tea/coffee facilities. Full leisure facilities (incl. steam room, swimming pool and gym) available to guests at Splashworld Health and Fitness Club adjacent to Hotel. Les Routiers "Gold Key" Award 1999.

WEB: www.majestic-hotel.ie

Members Of Les Routiers Ireland

B&B from £29.50 to £42.50
€37.46 to €53.96

ANNETTE & DANNY DEVINE
Proprietors

American Express
Mastercard
Visa

☺ Weekend specials from £75.00

60 60

Open All Year

O'SHEA'S HOTEL

STRAND STREET, TRAMORE,
CO. WATERFORD
TEL: 051-381246 FAX: 051-390144

HOTEL ★★ MAP 4 L 5

O'Shea's is an intimate family run hotel, newly refurbished and extended, situated beside Tramore's famous 5km safe sandy beach and just a few minutes from Splashworld. Sample our seafood and steak restaurant, full bar food menu available. Entertainment every night during Summer. Golfing holiday packages are our speciality - we will organise your tee times at any of the surrounding golf courses. We look forward to meeting you.

B&B from £27.50 to £37.50
€34.92 to €47.62

NOREEN & JOE O'SHEA
Proprietors

American Express
Diners
Mastercard
Visa

30 30

Closed 22 - 29 December

Room rates are per room per night

FAYTHE GUEST HOUSE

THE FAYTHE, SWAN VIEW,
WEXFORD
TEL: 053-22249   FAX: 053-21680
EMAIL: faythhse@iol.ie

GUESTHOUSE ★★   MAP 4 O 6

Faythe House, located in the quiet part of the town centre, will now have all rooms refurbished by Spring 2000. It is built on the grounds of a former castle of which one wall remains today. Some of our rooms overlook the gardens and Wexford harbour. All rooms have satellite colour TV, DD phone, clock radio and tea/coffee making facilities. Rosslare ferryport is only 15 minutes drive (early breakfast on request) and we also have a large private car park.

WEB: www.iol.ie/~faythhse

B&B from £18.00 to £25.00
€22.86 to €31.74

DAMIAN AND SIOBHAN LYNCH
Proprietors

Mastercard
Visa

🦽🏠☎️🍴T☀️P🔌
10 10

IRISH
HOTELS
FEDERATION

Closed 24 - 28 December

FERRYCARRIG HOTEL

FERRYCARRIG BRIDGE,
WEXFORD
TEL: 053-20999   FAX: 053-20982
EMAIL: ferrycarrig@griffingroup.ie

HOTEL ★★★   MAP 4 N 6

Ferrycarrig Hotel boasts one of the most inspiring locations of any hotel in Ireland with sweeping views across the River Slaney estuary. Facilities include a fabulous health & fitness club with award-winning 20m pool, 2 AA Rosette waterside restaurants, the Dry Dock Bar, one of Ireland's most unusual bars and 90 bedrooms and suites, all with fabulous views. The hotel also boasts an excellent conference centre, a purpose-built executive boardroom and an auditorium for training.

WEB: www.griffingroup.ie

B&B from £45.00 to £75.00
€57.14 to €95.23

MARK BROWNE
General Manager

American Express
Diners
Mastercard
Visa

🦽🏠☎️🍴🛵T C🔌CM☀️🎣🏠⛵
♪🎹P S🅿️alc🍴 Inet

IRISH
HOTELS
FEDERATION

Open All Year

RIVERBANK HOUSE HOTEL

THE BRIDGE,
WEXFORD
TEL: 053-23611   FAX: 053-23342
EMAIL: river@indigo.ie

HOTEL ★★   MAP 4 O 6

The Riverbank House Hotel commands magnificent views of the old Viking town, the river Slaney and the miles of golden beach surrounding Wexford. The hotel boasts an excellent à la carte restaurant, delicious light snacks together with an exciting wine list. Benefiting from its own private car park, the hotel offers easy access to five of the best golf courses in the south east, sea angling sites & shooting - ensuring that whatever your stay, business or leisure will be most enjoyable.

B&B from £45.00 to £70.00
€57.14 to €88.88

COLM CAMPBELL
General Manager

American Express
Diners
Mastercard
Visa

⛳

☺ Weekend specials from £115.00

🦽🏠☎️T C🔌CM☀️⛵J P S🅿️
alc🍴

IRISH
HOTELS
FEDERATION

Closed 25 December

B&B rates are per person sharing per night incl. Breakfast

SAINT GEORGE

GEORGE STREET,
WEXFORD
TEL: 053-43474   FAX: 053-24814
EMAIL: stgeorge@eircom.net

GUESTHOUSE ★★   MAP 4 0 6

You are sure of a warm welcome here at the Saint George, a family-run guesthouse in the centre of Wexford town, the heart of the sunny south east. We are close to all amenities and provide a private lock-up car park. All our bedrooms have bathroom en suite. They are equipped with DD phone, colour TV, tea/coffee making facilities and some are reserved for non-smoking guests. Only 15 minutes drive from Rosslare ferryport. Early breakfast on request.

B&B from £18.00 to £25.00
€22.86 to €31.74

JOHN & OLIVE DOYLE
Proprietors

Mastercard
Visa

Closed 21 - 31 December

TALBOT HOTEL CONFERENCE AND LEISURE CENTRE

TRINITY STREET,
WEXFORD
TEL: 053-22566   FAX: 053-23377
EMAIL: talbotwx@eircom.net

HOTEL ★★★   MAP 4 0 6

Located in the heart of Wexford town is the Talbot Hotel Conference & Leisure Centre. Our Quay Leisure Centre offers extensive leisure facilities for the fitness enthusiast and for those who just want pure pampering. Award winning Slaney Restaurant offers fresh Wexford fayre and an extensive wine list. Evening entertainment in the Trinity Bar at weekends. Bedrooms are fully equipped with DD phone, satellite TV and are tastefully decorated for your comfort and relaxation.

WEB: www.talbothotel.ie

B&B from £45.00 to £51.00
€57.14 to €64.76

URSULA SINNOTT
General Manager

American Express
Diners
Mastercard
Visa

☺ Weekend specials from £105.00

Open All Year

THE IRISH NATIONAL HERITAGE PARK

Where Ireland's Heritage Trail Starts

WEXFORD'S PREMIER VISITOR ATTRACTION

WELL WORTH A VISIT

- Guided Tours
- Multi-language Audio-Visual Presentation
- Restaurant
- Craft & Gift shop
- Open 7 days
- Wheelchair Accessible

**Ferrycarrig, Wexford
Tel: (053) 20733
Fax:(053) 20911
Email: inhp@iol.ie**

Room rates are per room per night

WESTGATE HOUSE

WESTGATE,
WEXFORD
TEL: 053-22167   FAX: 053-22167
EMAIL: westgate@wexmail.com

GUESTHOUSE ★★ MAP 4 0 6

Westgate House stands in a charming, traditional area across the road from the famed Selskar Abbey and Westgate Castle. It is an historic house formerly Westgate Hotel in 1812. It has been refurbished in period style with taste and elegance, with beautifully furnished bedrooms which create a sense of ease and timelessness matching this it offers full modern amenities. Situated in the exciting town centre with superb shops, pubs and restaurants. A secure lock-up car park is provided.

WEB: www.wexford-online.com/westgate

B&B from £20.00 to £25.00
€25.39 to €31.74

M & D ALLEN
Owners

Mastercard
Visa

10 10

Open All Year

WHITES HOTEL

GEORGE STREET,
WEXFORD
TEL: 053-22311   FAX: 053-45000
EMAIL: info@whiteshotel.iol.ie

HOTEL ★★★ MAP 4 0 6

Est. 1779, this charming 3*** hotel is centrally located in the historic and picturesque town of Wexford. The hotel's facilities include a health & fitness club, Harpers superb brasserie restaurant offering the finest local and international dishes for lunch & dinner and the immensely popular Harpers bar where carvery lunches and bar food is served daily and which is open late Thurs-Sun. The hotel is 5 mins walk from the bus and train station and only 20 mins drive from Rosslare Europort.

WEB: www.wexfordirl.com

Members Of Best Western Hotels

B&B from £35.00 to £50.00
€44.44 to €63.49

MICHAEL CONNOLLY
General Manager

American Express
Diners
Mastercard
Visa

Midweek 3 B&B and 3 Dinners
from £99.00

82 82

Open All Year

WHITFORD HOUSE HOTEL

NEW LINE ROAD,
WEXFORD
TEL: 053-43444   FAX: 053-46399
EMAIL: whitford@indigo.ie

HOTEL ★★★ MAP 4 0 6

One of the leading family run tourist establishments in the south east. Our award winning restaurant receives constant accolades for excellence, presentation and value. Seafood a speciality. Well appointed spacious bedrooms, weekly live entertainment. Unwind in our indoor swimming pool (Mar - mid-Nov) or serve an ace on our tennis court. for the younger members of the party we boast a childrens playground. Locally there is golf, fishing, horse riding and Blue Flag beaches.

WEB: indigo.ie/~whitford

B&B from £34.00 to £41.00
€43.17 to €52.06

KAY WHITTY
Proprietor

American Express
Mastercard
Visa

25 25

Closed 23 December - 13 January

B&B rates are per person sharing per night incl. Breakfast

DUNBRODY COUNTRY HOUSE HOTEL & RESTAURANT

ARTHURSTOWN,
CO. WEXFORD
TEL: 051-389600   FAX: 051-389601
EMAIL: info@dunbrodyhouse.com

HOTEL ★★★★   MAP 4 M 5

Set in 200 acres of beautiful parkland, Dunbrody is an enchantingly intimate 1830s Georgian manor. Spacious and elegantly decorated rooms overlook the magnificent gardens and create a distinctive atmosphere of pure relaxation and luxurious comfort. With an award-winning restaurant and a choice of fine wines to complement master chef Kevin Dundon's innovative culinary creations, guests return again and again to relish the unique ambience that is Dunbrody Country House.

WEB: www.dunbrodyhouse.com

Members Of Ireland's Blue Book

B&B from £55.00 to £110.00
€69.84 to €139.67

KEVIN & CATHERINE DUNDON
Owners

American Express
Diners
Mastercard
Visa

☺ Weekend specials from £125.00

🛏🐕☎⏱T C♨CM✲☺♪P♻S
19   19
♿ⓐⓛⓒ🚽

IRISH HOTELS FEDERATION

Closed 24 - 27 December

CRANDONNELL LODGE HOTEL

BARNTOWN,
CO. WEXFORD
TEL: 053-34300

HOTEL CR   MAP 4 N 6

Choice restaurant facilities with widest selection menus and an elegant lounge bar. Located a few miles outside the Viking town of Wexford and just off the national motorway network linking the country with all major centres on the Wexford/New Ross road. 5 mins drive from the international award-winning Irish National Heritage Park and the ideal centre for horse riding, riding lessons, trekking, golf and driving range, watersports and major Wexford attractions.

B&B from £20.00 to £20.00
€25.39 to €25.39

GEORGE CARROLL

🛏🐕☎⏱TCM✲☺♪P♻🍴ⓐⓛⓒ
10   10

Open All Year

ARDAMINE HOUSE

ARDAMINE, COURTOWN HARBOUR,
GOREY, CO. WEXFORD
TEL: 055-25264   FAX: 055-25548

HOTEL U   MAP 8 O 7

Ardamine House is a fully licensed hotel situated 1.5 miles south of Courtown close to Ardamine Beach famed for safe bathing and angling. The hotel is set on it's own grounds and is an ideal location for family holidays. The premises has been run by the O'Loughlin family for many years and a reputation for good food, friendly service and good value for money brings people back year after year.

B&B from £22.00 to £22.00
€27.93 to €27.93

THOMAS O'LOUGHLIN
Proprietor

American Express
Diners
Mastercard
Visa

🛏🐕⏱T▲☺C♨CM♨☜♪P🚽
24   24
ⓐⓛⓒ🚽

Open All Year

Room rates are per room per night

BAYVIEW HOTEL

COURTOWN HARBOUR,
CO. WEXFORD
TEL: 055-25307 FAX: 055-25576
EMAIL: bayview@iol.ie

HOTEL ★★ MAP 8 O 7

The Bayview is owned and run by the McGarry family. The hotel is overlooking the marina at Courtown Harbour. It is renowned for its good food and friendly atmosphere. All rooms are en suite with TV, video channel and direct dial telephone. Self catering apartments in hotel. Enjoy the Squash & Tennis centre free to guests. Courtown's 18 hole golf course 2km. It is an ideal setting for weddings and parties.

WEB: www.courtown.com/page4

B&B from £35.50 to £38.50
€45.08 to €48.88

BRIAN MCGARRY
Manager

American Express
Diners
Mastercard
Visa

13 13

S ♿ a/c ■

Closed 01 November - 01 March

HARBOUR HOUSE GUESTHOUSE

COURTOWN HARBOUR, COURTOWN,
GOREY, CO. WEXFORD
TEL: 055-25117 FAX: 055-25117

GUESTHOUSE ★★ MAP 8 O 7

Harbour House just off the main Rosslare/Dublin N11 route and only 6.4km from Gorey is ideally located in the renowned seaside resort of Courtown Harbour. Harbour House is the ideal base for both business and holiday travellers and is central to all amenities and only three minutes from Courtown's sandy beaches. All rooms are en suite with your own private car park. Your holiday here is under the personal supervision of the O'Gorman family.

B&B from £22.50 to £25.00
€28.57 to €31.74

DONAL & MARGARET O'GORMAN
Proprietors

American Express
Diners
Mastercard
Visa

10 10

Closed 31 October - 17 March

BORRMOUNT LODGE

BORRMOUNT, ENNISCORTHY,
CO. WEXFORD
TEL: 054-47122 FAX: 054-47133
EMAIL: borrmountlodge@eircom.net

GUESTHOUSE ★★★ MAP 4 N 6

Charming country house with the comfort of a hotel and the warmth of a home. At dinner silver and crystal shine in the candlelight. Gourmet evening meals. Extensive wine list hand picked from Burgundy. Breakfast served until noon. Free salmon fishing. Golf and beautiful walks near by. Central location for touring in the south east.

B&B from £25.00 to £34.00
€31.74 to €43.17

NOREEN & GUY KING-URBIN
Owners

Mastercard
Visa

☺ Weekend specials from £79.00

6 6

Open All Year

B&B rates are per person sharing per night incl. Breakfast

LEMONGROVE HOUSE

BLACKSTOOPS, ENNISCORTHY,
CO. WEXFORD
TEL: 054-36115

GUESTHOUSE N   MAP 4 N 6

Spacious luxury home 1km north of Enniscorthy just off roundabout on Dublin/Rosslare road (N11). Lemongrove house is set in mature gardens with private parking. All rooms en suite with DD phone, TV, hairdryer and tea/coffee making facilities. Recommended by Guide du Routard, AA, and other leading guides. Within walking distance of a choice of restaurants, pubs and new pool and leisure centre. Locally we have beaches, golf, horseriding, walking and quad track.

B&B from £18.00 to £25.00
€22.86 to €31.74

COLM & ANN MCGIBNEY
Owners

Mastercard
Visa

9 9

Open All Year

MURPHY - FLOODS HOTEL

MARKET SQUARE, ENNISCORTHY,
CO. WEXFORD
TEL: 054-33413   FAX: 054-33413
EMAIL: mfhotel@indigo.ie

HOTEL ★★   MAP 4 N 6

Overlooks Market Square of historic 6th century Enniscorthy town on Slaney salmon river. Package rates for golf breaks, midweek and weekends. Elegant restaurant, in Georgian style, presents menus of quality and variety. Room service, excellent bar food, packed lunches available, cots provided, night porter service. Central for touring lovely Slaney Valley and sunny south east. Rosslare ferry 43k, Waterford 56k, Dublin 120k, Shannon 240k. 1k from National 1798 Centre.

WEB: indigo.ie/~mfhotel

Members Of Irish Family Hotels

B&B from £30.00 to £40.00
€38.09 to €50.79

MICHAEL J WALL
Proprietor

American Express
Diners
Mastercard
Visa

Weekend specials from £65.00

19 19

Closed 24 - 28 December

RIVERSIDE PARK HOTEL

THE PROMENADE, ENNISCORTHY,
CO. WEXFORD
TEL: 054-37800   FAX: 054-37900
EMAIL: riversideparkhotel@eircom.net

HOTEL ★★★   MAP 4 N 6

Located on the banks of the picturesque River Slaney, the Riverside Park Hotel is a welcome addition to the bustling market town of Enniscorthy. Comprising 60 delightfully furnished rooms offering every modern convenience, facilities also include the Moorings Restaurant and the Promenade and Mill House bars. Only 30 mins drive from Rosslare the hotel is the perfect base for touring historic Vinegar Hill, the 1798 Visitor Centre, the Castle Museum as well as golf courses and beaches.

WEB: www.riverseideparkhotel.com

B&B from £37.00 to £45.00
€46.98 to €57.14

MR JIM MAHER
General Manager

American Express
Diners
Mastercard
Visa

Weekend specials from £99.00

60 60

Closed 24 - 26 December

Room rates are per room per night

TREACYS HOTEL

TEMPLESHANNON, ENNISCORTHY,
CO. WEXFORD
TEL: 054-37798 FAX: 054-37733
EMAIL: treacyshotel@treacyhotelsgroup.com

HOTEL N   MAP 4 N 6

Treacys Hotel is situated in the town centre. Just 30 minutes from Rosslare ferryport and 1 hour 20 minutes from Dublin city. Boasting 48 De-Luxe bedrooms with bath/power shower, satellite TV, DD phone, hairdryer, tea/coffee. Serving à la carte and table d'hôte menus. Our very own Temple Bar is known to be one of the finest in the South East. New adjacent cineplex and leisure centre (25m swimming pool, gym, sauna, steam room) opened July '99.

B&B from £39.00 to £70.00
€49.52 to €88.88

ANTON & YVONNE TREACY

American Express
Diners
Mastercard
Visa

48 48

Closed 24 - 26 December

HORSE AND HOUND INN

BALLINABOOLA, FOULKSMILLS,
CO. WEXFORD
TEL: 051-428323 FAX: 051-428471

GUESTHOUSE ★★★   MAP 4 N 5

The Horse and Hound Inn, Ballinaboola, Co. Wexford is owned and run by the Murphy Family. Situated six miles from New Ross on the N25 from Rosslare. It is a convenient venue for a meal and a rest. Best Irish produce is used in preparing specialities of fish and beef dishes. There are twelve bedrooms should you wish to stay. Catering for all needs - from private parties, weddings to conferences.

B&B from £25.00 to £30.00
€31.74 to €38.09

CHRISTY MURPHY

Mastercard
Visa

12 12

Open All Year

MARLFIELD HOUSE HOTEL

GOREY,
CO. WEXFORD
TEL: 055-21124 FAX: 055-21572
EMAIL: marlf@iol.ie

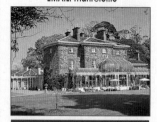

HOTEL ★★★★   MAP 8 O 7

Formerly the residence of the Earls of Courtown, Marlfield has been renovated by your hosts the Bowe family. Enjoy this Regency period house filled with antiques and set amidst 36 acres of woodland walks and flower gardens. The kitchen garden provides fresh produce for its award winning restaurant. Five minutes to an 18 hole golf course and sandy beaches. Very highly rated by Michelin, AA and RAC. Member of Ireland's Blue Book and Relais et Chateaux.

WEB: marlfieldhouse.com

Members Of Relais & Châteaux

B&B from £79.00 to £84.00
€100.31 to €106.66

MARY BOWE
Proprietor

American Express
Diners
Mastercard
Visa

2 B&B and 2 dinners from £198.00

20 20

Closed 15 December - 25 January

B&B rates are per person sharing per night incl. Breakfast

HOTEL SALTEES

KILMORE QUAY,
CO. WEXFORD
TEL: 053-29601 FAX: 053-29602

HOTEL ★★ MAP 4 N 5

Hotel Saltees, is situated in the picturesque fishing village of Kilmore Quay. Renowned for its thatched cottages and maritime flavour, it is located just 22km from Wexford town and 19km from the international port of Rosslare. Offering excellent value accommodation, with all rooms en suite, TV, telephone and all well designed to cater for families. The Coningbeg Seafood Restaurant, specialises in serving the freshest seafood. Shore and deep-sea fishing available locally.

B&B from £25.00 to £32.00
€31.74 to €40.63

TOMMY AND NED BYRNE
Proprietors

Mastercard

Visa

☺ Weekend specials from £68.00

IRISH HOTELS FEDERATION

Closed 25 December

QUAY HOUSE

KILMORE QUAY,
CO. WEXFORD
TEL: 053-29988 FAX: 053-29808
EMAIL: kilmore@esatclear.ie

GUESTHOUSE ★★★ MAP 4 N 5

3*** guesthouse. AA Selected ◆◆◆. Quay House, Kilmore Quay, famous for sea angling and diving with nature trails along the peaceful Ballyteigue Burrow. Enjoy breakfast or entertain friends in our spacious dining room with its high wooden ceiling. All bedrooms and guest lounge have Douglas Fir wooden floors, all bedrooms are en suite with remote control TV, tea/coffee facilities, DD phone service. Private carpark. Coffee shop open during season. Facilities for divers and anglers.

WEB: www.esatclear.ie/~mmaguire/index.htm

B&B from £20.00 to £26.00
€25.39 to €33.01

SIOBHAN MCDONNELL
Proprietor

Mastercard

Visa

☺ Midweek specials from £60.00

IRISH HOTELS FEDERATION

Open All Year

CEDAR LODGE HOTEL & RESTAURANT

CARRIGBYRNE, NEWBAWN, (NEAR NEW ROSS), CO. WEXFORD
TEL: 051-428386 FAX: 051-428222

HOTEL ★★★ MAP 4 N 6

Charming 3*** country hotel located in a picturesque setting, 30 minutes drive from Rosslare port on the N25 New Ross road. All bedrooms en suite with DD phone and TV. The restaurant which concentrates on freshly prepared produce, is noted for its good food. Recommended by Michelin, Good Hotel Guide, RAC. Forest walks nearby. Golf, horse riding, JF Kennedy Park, county museum, heritage park and sandy beaches within easy driving distance.

B&B from £40.00 to £55.00
€50.79 to €69.84

TOM MARTIN
Proprietor

American Express

Diners

Mastercard

Visa

☺ 3 B&B plus 3 Dinners from £185.00

IRISH HOTELS FEDERATION

Closed 20 December - 01 February

Room rates are per room per night

BRANDON HOUSE HOTEL & LEISURE CENTRE

NEW ROSS,
CO. WEXFORD
TEL: 051-421703 FAX: 051-421567
EMAIL: brandonhouse@eircom.net

HOTEL ★★★ MAP 4M 6

A comfortable country manor house hotel set in landscaped grounds with panoramic views overlooking the river Barrow. Dine in the AA award winning Gallery restaurant or relax in the Library bar. All rooms are elegantly furnished. New leisure centre with 20m pool incorporating kiddies pool and fully equipped gym and treatment rooms. Activities nearby- golf, angling, walking and horse riding. An ideal base for touring counties Wexford, Waterford, Kilkenny and Wicklow.

WEB: www.brandonhousehotel.ie

Members Of Choice Hotels Ireland

B&B from £40.00 to £55.00
€50.79 to €69.84

MARIA O'CONNOR
General Manager

American Express
Diners
Mastercard
Visa

😊 Weekend specials from £89.00

60 60

Closed 24 - 25 December

CREACON LODGE HOTEL

CREACON, NEW ROSS,
CO. WEXFORD
TEL: 051-421897 FAX: 051-422560
EMAIL: creacon@indigo.ie

HOTEL U MAP 4M 6

Set amidst the peace and tranquility of the countryside. 45 mins drive from Rosslare, 2 hours from Dublin and only a short scenic drive to the Hook peninsula and JFK park. Relax and enjoy our beautiful gardens, comfy sofas and log fires and sample the delights of our restaurant and bar. All bedrooms are en suite with D.D. phone, colour TV. Local amenities include golf, angling, horse-riding water sports and sandy beaches.

WEB: http://indigo.ie/~creacon

B&B from £30.00 to £40.00
€38.09 to €50.79

JOSEPHINE FLOOD
& NICK CROSBIE

Mastercard
Visa

😊 Weekend specials from £75.00

10 10

Open All Year

OLD RECTORY HOTEL

ROSBERCON, NEW ROSS,
CO. WEXFORD
TEL: 051-421719 FAX: 051-422974
EMAIL: oldrectorynewross@eircom.net

HOTEL ★★ MAP 4M 6

Owner-managed country house hotel combining historic charm and modern comfort. Set in 2.5 acres of beautiful gardens overlooking the river Barrow and New Ross town. All bedrooms en suite with TV, phone and tea/coffee facilities. The intimate restaurant is renowned for it's tempting dishes and fine wines. Centrally located between Wexford, Waterford and Kilkenny. Ideal base for touring the south east. Dublin 85 miles; Rosslare 30 miles. Ample off street car parking. Golf, fishing and horse riding nearby.

WEB: www.amireland.com/oldrectory

Members Of Irish Family Hotels

B&B from £27.50 to £32.50
€34.92 to €41.27

GERALDINE & JAMES O'LEARY
Proprietors

American Express
Diners
Mastercard
Visa

😊 Weekend specials from £79.00

12 12

Open All Year

B&B rates are per person sharing per night incl. Breakfast

CHURCHTOWN HOUSE

TAGOAT, ROSSLARE,
CO. WEXFORD
TEL: 053-32555 FAX: 053-32577
EMAIL: churchtown.rosslare@indigo.ie

GUESTHOUSE ★★★★ MAP 4 O 5

AA Guesthouse of the Year 1998. Premier Selected ◆◆◆◆◆. Churchtown is a period house c.1703 where peace and tranquility, together with country house hospitality combine with modern comforts to make it 'A SPECIAL PLACE TO STAY'. A rural setting in mature gardens, $\frac{1}{2}$ mile off the N25 and 5 mins from Rosslare ferryport/strand. Explore Wexford's 'Land of Living History', gardens, golf, beaches, birdwatching, fishing and riding. Evening meals served Tues-Sat. Please pre-book.

Members Of Best Loved Hotels Of The World

B&B from £25.00 to £35.00
€31.74 to €44.44

AUSTIN AND PATRICIA CODY
Owners

Mastercard

Visa

14 14

Closed 30 November - 01 March

CROSBIE CEDARS HOTEL

ROSSLARE,
CO. WEXFORD
TEL: 053-32124 FAX: 053-32243
EMAIL: info@crosbiecedars.iol.ie

HOTEL ★★★ MAP 4 O 5

The Crosbie Cedars Hotel is a Grade A, AA*** deluxe hotel situated in the heart of Rosslare. The hotel provides elegant and tastefully designed en suite rooms, restaurant and bars, ensuring a comfortable and relaxing stay for all. A haven of outstanding quality, offering true Irish warmth and hospitality. Ideal golf centre within easy reach of 3 excellent courses, Rosslare, St. Helens and Wexford. Golf rates and packages available.

WEB: www.iol.ie/~cch/

B&B from £30.00 to £45.00
€38.09 to €57.14

TOM & ANN CROSBIE
Proprietors

American Express

Diners

Mastercard

Visa

34 34

Open All Year

DANBY LODGE HOTEL

ROSSLARE ROAD, KILLINICK,
ROSSLARE, CO. WEXFORD
TEL: 053-58191 FAX: 053-58191

HOTEL N MAP 4 O 5

Nestling in the heart of south county Wexford, Danby Lodge Hotel has rightfully earned for itself a reputation for excellence in cuisine and accommodation. Once the home of the painter Francis Danby, 1793-1861, this hotel bears all the hallmarks of a charming country residence. Conveniently located on main Rosslare to Wexford road (N25). Danby Lodge Hotel offers the visitor a quiet country getaway yet just minutes drive from the port of Rosslare and the town of Wexford. RAC and AA recommended.

Room Rate from £39.00 to £59.00
€49.52 to €74.91

RAYMOND & MARGARET PARLE
Owners

American Express

Diners

Mastercard

Visa

18 18

Closed 22 - 30 December

Room rates are per room per night

KELLY'S RESORT HOTEL

ROSSLARE,
CO. WEXFORD
TEL: 053-32114   FAX: 053-32222
EMAIL: kellyhot@iol.ie

HOTEL ★★★★   MAP 4 0 5

Since 1895 the Kelly family have created a truly fine resort hotel concentrating on holidays all year round. Good food and wine are very much a part of the tradition. Amenities include indoor/outdoor tennis, squash, snooker, bowls, croquet, crazy golf, bicycles, children's playroom, leisure and beauty centre The Aqua Club, nightly entertainment. 7 day holidays (July and August) 5 day midweek and 2 day weekend (Spring and Autumn). 1995 Egon Ronay Irish Hotel of the Year.

WEB: www.kellys.ie

B&B from £48.00 to £70.00
€60.95 to €88.88

WILLIAM J KELLY
Manager/Director

American Express
Mastercard
Visa

5 Day Midweek Full Board
(B/L/D x 5) From £374.00

99 99

Closed 06 December - 01 March

AILSA LODGE

ROSSLARE HARBOUR,
CO. WEXFORD
TEL: 053-33230   FAX: 053-33581
EMAIL: ailsalodge@eircom.net

GUESTHOUSE ★★   MAP 4 0 5

Ailsa Lodge a family run guesthouse in the town of Rosslare Harbour. Positioned in a quiet location with private grounds and spacious parking, it overlooks the Irish sea, the beach and the Ferryport. 5 minutes walk from the bus/rail/ferry terminal. All rooms en-suite with TV and DD phone. Early breakfasts served. A short walk from all shops, pubs and restaurants. Excellent beaches, fishing, walks and golf courses locally.

WEB: www.ailsalodge.com

Members Of Premier Guesthouses

B&B from £17.00 to £24.00
€21.59 to €30.47

DOMINIC SHEIL
Proprietor

Mastercard
Visa

10 10

Closed 24 December - 07 January

CORAL GABLES

TAGOAT, ROSSLARE HARBOUR,
CO. WEXFORD
TEL: 053-31213   FAX: 053-31414
EMAIL: coralgables@eircom.net

GUESTHOUSE ★★   MAP 4 0 5

Coral Gables is situated on a hilltop in quiet secluded surroundings overlooking the Wexford/Rosslare N25, just 3k from the ferry. Good food and friendly atmosphere provides the perfect stopover for visitors arriving and departing through Rosslare port or for golfing, fishing, horseriding or relaxing on our safe sandy beaches. Our guesthouse has 15 en suite rooms with DD phone, tea/coffee facilities, hairdryer, TV, central heating, private car parking. TV lounge.

B&B from £20.00 to £30.00
€25.39 to €38.09

SARAH & PAUL HASLAM
Proprietors

Mastercard
Visa

15 15

Open All Year

B&B rates are per person sharing per night incl. Breakfast

DEVEREUX HOTEL

HARBOUR LODGE, ROSSLARE
HARBOUR, CO. WEXFORD
TEL: 053-33216 FAX: 053-33301
EMAIL: info@devereuxhotel.com

HOTEL ★★★ MAP 4 O 5

Traditional style hotel, located close to Rosslare ferry port (250m). Ideal for your first or last stay in Ireland. The hotel which is open all year round offers exceptional value - all rooms complete with private bath, colour TV, DD phone, tea/coffee facilities. Our facilities also include a restaurant specialising in prime steak and fresh seafood, also traditional bar. Close by are two 18 hole golf courses, angling and bird watching.

WEB: www.devereuxhotel.com

B&B from £24.20 to £33.00
€30.73 to €41.90

WILLIAM DEVEREUX
General Manager

American Express

Mastercard

Visa

😊 Weekend specials from £70.00

24 24

HOTELS
FEDERATION

Closed 24 - 26 December

EURO LODGE

ROSSLARE HARBOUR,
CO. WEXFORD.
TEL: 053-33118 FAX: 053-33910
EMAIL: eurolodge@eircom.net

GUESTHOUSE N MAP 4 O 5

A new luxury lodge conveniently located beside Rosslare Europort (600m). All 38 rooms have bathroom en suite with colour TV, tea/coffee facilities, phone and private car parking. Twin and family rooms available. An ideal location to stay while touring the south east. Close to all amenities. With two 18-hole golf courses, sandy beaches, fishing, horse riding and leisure centre nearby.

WEB: wexford-online.com/eurolodge

Room Rate from £39.00 to £49.00
€49.52 to €62.22

HELEN SINNOTT
Manager

Mastercard

Visa

38 38

HOTELS
FEDERATION

Open All Year

FERRYPORT HOUSE

ROSSLARE HARBOUR,
CO. WEXFORD
TEL: 053-33933 FAX: 053-33363

GUESTHOUSE ★★★ MAP 4 O 5

A new luxury guesthouse conveniently located close to Rosslare ferryport (400m). The last guesthouse when leaving Ireland and the first on your return. It has 17 en suite bedrooms with DD phone, colour TV, central heating, tea/coffee making facilities, hairdryer and private car parking. Local amenities include golf, fishing, horse riding and safe sandy beaches.

B&B from £19.00 to £29.00
€24.13 to €36.82

BILLY & PATRICA ROCHE
Proprietors

Mastercard

Visa

17 17

HOTELS
FEDERATION

Open All Year

Room rates are per room per night

ROSSLARE GREAT SOUTHERN HOTEL

ROSSLARE HARBOUR,
CO. WEXFORD
TEL: 053-33233 FAX: 053-33543
EMAIL: res@rosslare.gsh.ie

HOTEL ★★★ MAP 4 O 5

In Rosslare, a favourite resort, the Great Southern Hotel provides a warm welcome with traditional hospitality. The hotel is beautifully situated on a clifftop overlooking Rosslare harbour. All rooms are en suite with DD phone, TV, radio, hairdryer, in-house movie channel and tea/coffee facilities. Enjoy the leisure centre with indoor swimming pool, jacuzzi, steam room, the comfortable lounges and excellent food of the Mariner's Restaurant. Ctrl reservations 01-2144800 or UTELL.

WEB: www.gsh.ie

B&B from £48.00 to £57.00
€60.95 to €72.38

PAT CUSSEN
General Manager

American Express
Diners
Mastercard
Visa

☺ Weekend specials from £85.00

100 100

| Closed 06 January - 16 March |

TUSKAR HOUSE HOTEL

ROSSLARE HARBOUR,
CO. WEXFORD
TEL: 053-33363 FAX: 053-33363
EMAIL: thh@iol.ie

HOTEL ★★★ MAP 4 O 5

Family run hotel enjoying panoramic views of Rosslare Bay, just 219m from ferry and train terminals. It has all en suite bedrooms with telephone, TV, central heating and some with balconies. Dinner served nightly until 11pm and Sunday lunch 12.30/2.30, with local seafood a speciality. Regular entertainment in the lively Punters Bar. Local amenities include: golf, fishing, horse riding and safe beaches. Michelin recommended.

B&B from £29.00 to £40.00
€36.82 to €50.79

ORLA ROCHE
General Manager

American Express
Diners
Mastercard
Visa

☺ Week partial board from £279.00

30 30

| Closed 25 December |

GLENGARRIFF ECCLES HOTEL

GLENGARRIFF HARBOUR,
CO. CORK
TEL: 027-63003 FAX: 027-63319
EMAIL: eccleshotel@iol.ie

HOTEL R MAP 1 D 2

Located in beautiful Bantry Bay. The Eccles Hotel is one of the oldest established hotels in Ireland. Recently purchased by the Hanratty family, it contains 71 ensuite bedrooms. The hotel is a wonderful base for the many attractions of the Beara Peninsula and is situated directly opposite Garnish Island. Boating, fishing, golf, pony trekking and hill walking are all catered for nearby.

B&B from £27.00 to £30.00
€34.28 to €38.09

HANRATTY FAMILY
Owners

American Express
Diners
Mastercard
Visa

71 71

| Closed 23 - 28 December |

B&B rates are per person sharing per night incl. Breakfast

SOUTH WEST
The spectacular South West

Located in the south-west corner of Ireland, the Cork and Kerry region offers its visitors a great diversity of scenery, culture and leisure activities. Cork and Kerry claims some of the most varied and spectacular scenery in the country.

The Queenstown Story, Cobh, Co. Cork

Natural attractions abound, from the West Cork coast, the Beara and Dingle peninsulas and the Ring of Kerry to the Lakes of Killarney and the Bandon, Lee and Blackwater valleys.

With its remarkable charm, bumpy bridges, hilly streets and distinctive continental air the city of Cork will not fail, like the rest of the Region, to captivate and welcome all visitors, young and old. Cobh, situated on the southern short of the Great Island, lies in one of the world's largest natural harbours. The Queenstown Story in Cobh tells the story of emigration and the history of sail and steam in Cork Harbour. Cobh was the last port of call for the ill-fated Titanic.

The coast road from Kinsale to Skibbereen passes through many attractive villages and towns giving breath-taking views of the south west coastline. Kinsale, a town which has retained its old world charm and character is firmly established as one of Ireland's leading gourmet centres. Passing onto Clonakilty, Ireland's 1999 national Tidy Towns winners, one of Cork's many picturesque and colourful towns. There are many amenities in the area, with places of interest to visit, sporting and leisure activities and festivals.

The unspoilt coastal and inland waters of Cork and Kerry offer numerous water sports, from fishing to sailing, diving and windsurfing.

The Ring of Kerry is a journey through some of the country's most outstanding scenery. It is not only one of great natural beauty - it is enhanced by the influence of both ancient folklore and local traditions. With its three famous lakes and great mountain ranges Killarney has been

the inspiration of poets and painters over many centuries. A spectacular attraction is the Skellig Experience Centre at Valentia Island which imaginatively tells the story of the history of the Skelligs.

The Dingle Peninsula has some of the most intersting antiquities, historic sites and varied scenery in the whole country. Dingle, the most westerly town in Europe is an excellent centre for the visitor. It still retains much of its old-world atmosphere with its many shops and restaurants.

For further information contact:
Cork Kerry Tourism, Aras Failte,
Grand Parade, Cork.
Tel. (021) 273251. Fax. (021) 273504
email: user@cktourism.ie

Killarney Tourist Office, Beech Road,
Killarney, Co. Kerry.
Tel. (064) 31633. Fax (064) 34506.

The Skellig Experience Visitor
Centre, Valentia Island, Co. Kerry

Event details correct at time of going to press

ACORN HOUSE

14 ST. PATRICK'S HILL,
CORK
TEL: 021-502474 FAX: 021-500225
EMAIL: jackie@acornhouse-cork.com

GUESTHOUSE ★★ MAP 2 H 3

Acorn House is a comfortable refurbished listed Georgian house of architectural merit dating back to 1810. It is a 3 minute walk to St. Patrick Street, Cork city's principal thoroughfare with theatres and excellent choice of restaurants. 5 minutes walk to bus and rail stations; 15 minutes drive to airport and car ferry. Rooms en suite with TV and tea/coffee facilities. Michelin and Stilwell recommended. Children over 12 welcome.

WEB: acornhouse-cork.com

B&B from £22.00 to £30.00
€27.93 to €38.09

JACKIE BOLES
Proprietor

Mastercard

Visa

Closed 22 December - 10 January

AIRPORT LODGE

FARMERS CROSS, KINSALE ROAD,
CORK AIRPORT, CORK
TEL: 021-316920 FAX: 021-316920
EMAIL: airlodge@indigo.ie

GUESTHOUSE U MAP 2 H 3

Located at the gates of Cork airport, 15 minutes drive from Ringaskiddy ferryport and adjacent to all major roads around Cork city, we are ideal as a first/last night stop. Cork city is only 8k away, Kinsale 30k. We have extensive free car parking and provide a welcome break before you continue your journey.

Room Rate from £25.00 to £50.00
€31.74 to €63.49

MARY & MAURICE BERGIN
Proprietors

Mastercard

Visa

Closed 01 - 28 February

AMBASSADOR HOTEL

MILITARY HILL, ST. LUKES,
CORK
TEL: 021-551996 FAX: 021-551997
EMAIL: info@ambassadorhotel.ie

HOTEL U MAP 2 H 3

The Ambassador Hotel has already received excellent reviews since opening in June '97. This historic building of striking architectural design dates back to 1872. Situated on its own private grounds in a quiet central location with breathtaking views over the city, guests can relax in the Cocktail Lounge or Embassy Bar or enjoy gourmet dining in the Seasons Restaurant. 60 spacious bedrooms luxuriously decorated to the highest standards and professional service ensure a memorable stay.

WEB: www.ambassadorhotel.ie

Members Of Distinguished Hotels(Robt F Warner)

B&B from £40.00 to £70.00
€50.79 to €88.88

DUDLEY FITZELL
General Manager

American Express

Diners

Mastercard

Visa

Special Offer 2 B&B + 1 Dinner
from £99.00

Closed 24 - 26 December

B&B rates are per person sharing per night incl. Breakfast

ANTOINE HOUSE

WESTERN ROAD,
CORK
TEL: 021-273494 FAX: 021-273092
EMAIL: antoinehouse@eircom.net

GUESTHOUSE ★★ MAP 2 H 3

Located at gateway to west Cork and
Kerry for business or pleasure. An
ideal base from which to explore,
less than one mile from city centre
and in close proximity to airport,
train, ferry, Blarney and Fota. All
rooms en suite with D.D. phones,
Satellite TV, hairdryer, tea/coffee
facilities. Private lock up car park at
rear, golf, shooting, fishing, horseriding, flying can be arranged.
Children welcome. Frommers
recommended and AA listed.

B&B from £20.00 to £30.00
€25.39 to €38.09

KEVIN CROSS
Proprietor

American Express
Diners
Mastercard
Visa

☺ Midweek specials from £59.00

🛏📞☎🅲❄🕯📶🅿
10 10

IRISH
HOTELS
FEDERATION

Open All Year

ARBUTUS LODGE HOTEL

MONTENOTTE,
CORK
TEL: 021-501237 FAX: 021-502893
EMAIL: info@arbutuslodgehotel.net

HOTEL ★★★ MAP 2 H 3

Elegant townhouse built in the late
18th century, set in its own gardens,
overlooking the River Lee and Cork
city. There are 20 rooms and suites
all individually decorated. An
imaginative fusion of French
influence and Irish produce
combined with an impressive wine
list ensures that Arbutus Lodge has
one of the best restaurants in
Ireland. There is a delightful bar and
patio with a lunchtime bar service.
The hotel is family owned and John
and family look forward to meeting
you.

B&B from £45.00 to £100.00
€57.14 to €126.97

CARMODY FAMILY

American Express
Diners
Mastercard
Visa

✓

☺ Weekend specials from £99.00

🛏📞☎🆃🅲➜CM❄🕯📶🅿🆂🄰alc
20 20

IRISH
HOTELS
FEDERATION

Closed 23 - 27 December

Room rates are per room per night

ASHLEY HOTEL

COBURG STREET,
CORK
TEL: 021-501518 FAX: 021-501178
EMAIL: ashleyhotel@eircom.net

HOTEL U MAP 2 H 3

The Ashley Hotel is family-owned, run by Anita Coughlan and her enthusiastic staff, with all the benefits of the city centre location to shops and other attractions. It is the perfect place to relax and have fun. The Ashley has plenty to offer you with a secure lock-up car park, 27 rooms with bathroom en suite, tea/coffee making facilities and DD phone with a lively bar and restaurant.

WEB: ashleyhotel.com

B&B from £27.50 to £38.50
€34.92 to €48.88

ANITA COUGHLAN

American Express
Diners
Mastercard
Visa

27 27

aic

IRISH
HOTELS
FEDERATION

Open All Year

BRAZIER'S WESTPOINT HOUSE

WESTERN ROAD,
CORK
TEL: 021-275526 FAX: 021-274091
EMAIL: westpoint@eircom.net

GUESTHOUSE N MAP 2 H 3

A warm welcome and friendly service awaits you at the family run Brazier's Westpoint House which is located less than 10 mins walk from Cork city centre and opposite University College Cork. Tastefully decorated, all rooms are en suite with colour TV, DD phone, tea/coffee facilities and we have a private lock-up carpark at the rear. An ideal base to visit Cork and tour the beautiful south west.

B&B from £22.50 to £25.00
€28.57 to €31.74

JOY BRAZIER
Proprietor

Mastercard
Visa

☺ Midweek specials from £60.00

8 8

Closed 23 - 27 December

BROOKFIELD HOTEL

BROOKFIELD HOLIDAY VILLAGE,
COLLEGE ROAD, CORK
TEL: 021-344032 FAX: 021-344327

HOTEL ★★★ MAP 2 H 3

Brookfield Hotel, College road is just 1 mile from Cork city centre. Set on 10 acres of rolling parkland, it is truly a rural setting. *24 bright, modern bedrooms. *Family rooms. *Interconnecting rooms. *Complimentary use of our leisure and fitness centre which incorporates 25m indoor pool. Kiddies pool, water slide, saunas, steam room, spa jacuzzi, outdoor hot tub, massage, gym, sunbeds, outdoor tennis courts.

B&B from £35.00 to £45.00
€44.44 to €57.14

MIRIAM RYAN
Reservations Manager

American Express
Mastercard
Visa

☺ Weekend specials from £83.00

24 24

inet

Closed 23 December - 04 January

B&B rates are per person sharing per night incl. Breakfast

CLARION HOTEL - MORRISONS ISLAND

MORRISON'S QUAY,
CORK
TEL: 021-275858 FAX: 021-275833
EMAIL: morrison@iol.ie

HOTEL ★★★ MAP 2 H 3

Clarion Hotel - Morrison's Island is Cork's first all suite hotel and, as such, has a whole new world in accommodation to offer business people and visitors alike. Our luxury penthouses with our river front suites and Riverbank Bar and Restaurant boast a superb view of Cork. Each suite has a choice of one or two bedrooms. The hotel is centrally located with easy access to shopping, cultural and historic attractions.

Members Of Choice Hotels Ireland

Room Rate from £65.00 to £130.00
€82.53 to €165.07

FRANKIE WHELEHAN
Joint Managing Director

American Express
Diners
Mastercard
Visa

Open All Year

COMMONS INN

COMMONS ROAD,
CORK
TEL: 021-210300 FAX: 021-210333
EMAIL: commons@iol.ie

HOTEL P MAP 3 H 3

Close to Cork city, on the main Cork/Limerick road, this family-run hotel contains the popular Commons Bar, C Restaurant and the Roebuck Room function centre. All rooms contain two queen sized beds and are priced per room. Enjoy carvery lunch in the bar or dinner in our superb restaurant. Whether you're in Cork on business or for pleasure we would be delighted to look after you.

Room Rate from £39.50 to £39.50
€50.15 to €50.15

MYLES O'NEILL
General Manager

American Express
Diners
Mastercard
Visa

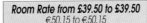

Closed 24 - 27 December

Room rates are per room per night

COUNTRY CLUB HOTEL

MONTENOTTE,
CORK
TEL: 021-502922 FAX: 021-502082

HOTEL ★★★ MAP 3 H 3

A 3*** 58 bedroomed hotel in its own landscaped gardens with breathtaking views of Cork city. All bedrooms have private bath/shower, fifteen channel colour TV, radio, direct dial telephones. Spacious car parks and just minutes walk from city centre, bus and rail terminals. Newly designed restaurant and Pennant Bar with balcony views of the city. Personal service assured at all times. Special group/individual rates available on request.

B&B from £35.00 to £55.00
€44.44 to €69.84

DON MOORE
Director

American Express
Diners
Mastercard
Visa

😊 Weekend specials from £80.00

58 58

alc

IRISH HOTELS FEDERATION

Closed 23 - 27 December

CRAWFORD HOUSE

WESTERN ROAD,
CORK
TEL: 021-279000 FAX: 021-279927
EMAIL: crawford@indigo.ie

GUESTHOUSE N MAP 3 H 3

Luxurious accommodation located close to the city centre. Crawford House is one of Cork's newest guesthouses. This superior guesthouse offers bed & breakfast in a contemporary setting. The rooms provide comfort and luxury with oak-wood furniture and king size beds. Deluxe en suites include jacuzzi baths and/or power showers. Fax/modem points in all rooms. Located directly across from University College Cork and convenient to ferry, airport and bus termini. Car park available.

B&B from £20.00 to £40.00
€25.39 to €50.79

CECILIA O'LEARY
Manager

American Express
Mastercard
Visa

12 12

IRISH HOTELS FEDERATION

Closed 23 - 27 December

D'ARCYS

7 SIDNEY PLACE,
WELLINGTON ROAD, CORK
TEL: 021-504658 FAX: 021-502791

GUESTHOUSE ★ MAP 2 H 3

Not until you enter 7 Sidney Place do you realise what a large building it is. High ceilings and large spacious rooms. The front rooms have views over the city. Rooms are uncluttered, calm, cool places, very peaceful in the centre of the city. Children are welcome. Breakfast is not to be missed. Try freshly squeezed fruit juices, smoked salmon and scrambled eggs and home made preserves.

B&B from £25.00 to £35.00
€31.74 to €44.44

CLARE D'ARCY
Proprietor

American Express
Diners
Mastercard
Visa

6 2

IRISH HOTELS FEDERATION

Closed 23 - 27 December

B&B rates are per person sharing per night incl. Breakfast

DOUGHCLOYNE HOTEL

DOUGHCLOYNE,
CORK
TEL: 021-312535 FAX: 021-316086

HOTEL ★★★ MAP 2 H 3

The Doughcloyne Hotel is situated 2 miles from the city centre, close to the University hospital in Wilton and Cork airport, south link N28 exit Doughcloyne Sarsfields Road roundabout. Our restaurant presents bonne cuisine with friendly service. The lounge bar is noted for its lunch-time barfood and live music at the weekends. Guests have complimentary use of Brookfield leisure centre with a 25m swimming pool located near by.

B&B from £25.00 to £35.00
€31.74 to €44.44

DAVID HARNEY
General Manager

American Express
Diners
Mastercard
Visa

50 50 alc

Closed 24 December - 02 January

EAGLE LODGE GUEST HOUSE

1 WILLOWBROOK, WESTERN ROAD,
CORK
TEL: 021-277380 FAX: 021-276432

GUESTHOUSE ★★★ MAP 2 H 3

Eagle Lodge is a 10 minute walk from city centre and close to bus and train stations. All rooms en suite with TV, tea/coffee making facilities, hair dryer and ironing facilities. An ideal base from which to tour west Cork and Kerry. Situated opposite University College. Eagle Lodge is within a short walk of many traditional Irish pubs and a variety of restaurants to suit all tastes.

B&B from £20.00 to £35.00
€25.39 to €44.44

NORA MURRAY
Proprietor

American Express
Diners
Mastercard
Visa

3 nights B&B from £54.00

7 7

Open All Year

CORK CITY GAOL

CORK CITY GAOL
Sunday's Well, Cork.

A step back in time to see what 19th and early 20th Century life was like in Cork – inside and outside prison walls. Amazingly lifelike figures, furnished cells, sound effects and fascinating exhibitions.

Also at the same location new attraction "Radio Museum Experience" which deals not alone with the early days of Irish & International Radio Broadcasting but with the impact of its invention on all our lives. Open daily throughout the year.

Night Tours July/August.

Tel: (021) 305022.
Admission Charge.

Room rates are per room per night

FAIRY LAWN

WESTERN ROAD,
CORK
TEL: 021-543444 FAX: 021-544337

GUESTHOUSE N MAP 3 H 3

Fairy Lawn, newly refurbished and extended, this luxury guesthouse has 14 en suite rooms, tastefully decorated. Opposite UCC in the heart of Cork with private car parking. This family-run guesthouse with TV, DD phone, hairdryer and tea/coffee making facilities is convenient to all amenities, airport, ferry, bus/train station, pubs, restaurants, etc. Ideal touring base for the south of Ireland. A warm welcome awaits you.

B&B from £20.00 to £35.00
€25.39 to €44.44

TONY & JOAN MCGRATH
Proprietors

Mastercard

Visa

☺ Midweek specials from £60.00

14 14

Open All Year

FITZPATRICK CORK

TIVOLI,
CORK
TEL: 021-507533 FAX: 021-507641
EMAIL: cork@fitzpatricks.com

HOTEL ★★★★ MAP 3 H 3

This 4**** hotel is a 5 min drive from the city centre. 109 rooms with cable TV, hairdryer, trouserpress & tea/coffee maker. PJ's has a relaxed atmosphere and exciting, well-priced menu. The adjoining Gallery lounge is an art-themed modern trendy cafe. Enjoy Sunday jazz brunch in Thady Quill's. Leisure centre and 9 hole golf course in the grounds. Excellent base from which to tour many visitor attractions. Four 18-hole championship courses within a 30 mins drive of Fitzpatrick Cork.

WEB: www.fitzpatrickhotels.com

B&B from £48.00 to £63.00
€60.95 to €79.99

ALAN CRUITE
Deputy General Manager

American Express

Diners

Mastercard

Visa

109 109

Closed 25 - 26 December

FORTE TRAVELODGE

KINSALE ROAD ROUNDABOUT, SOUTH
RING ROAD, BLACKASH, CORK
TEL: 1800-709709 FAX: 021-310707

HOTEL U MAP 3 H 3

Situated a couple of miles from Cork City centre, minutes from the Airport and on the direct routes to/from the car ferry, beautiful Kinsale and West Cork, this superb modern hotel offers comfortable yet affordable accommodation. Each room is large enough to sleep up to three adults, a child under 12 and a baby in a cot. Excellent range of facilities from en suite bathroom to colour TV including Sky Sports and Sky Movies. Sited next to Little Chef restaurant.

Room Rate from £39.95 to £54.95
€50.73 to €69.77

CAROLINE WALSH
Manager

American Express

Diners

40 40

Open All Year

B&B rates are per person sharing per night incl. Breakfast

GABRIEL HOUSE

SUMMER HILL, ST LUKES,
CORK
TEL: 021-500333   FAX: 021-500178

GUESTHOUSE ★★   MAP 3 H 3

Situated in Cork city near bus and rail stations. Supervised private car park. All rooms with bath and shower, DD phone, TV and hair dryer. Most rooms overlook gardens and river Lee. Breakfast served from 5:30am. Wine licence. Refreshments available 24 hours a day. Laundry service. Although situated in Cork city, it is very peaceful and is surrounded by large gardens. Fax and photocopy services available. Pets catered for. Personally supervised by Helen and Vincent Finn. Always open.

B&B from £17.50 to £25.00
€22.22 to €31.74

HELEN & VINCENT FINN
Owners

American Express
Mastercard
Visa

19 16

Open All Year

GARNISH HOUSE

WESTERN ROAD,
CORK
TEL: 021-275111   FAX: 021-273872
EMAIL: garnish@iol.ie

GUESTHOUSE ★★★   MAP 3 H 3

A stay in Garnish House is a memorable one. Our tasteful rooms with optional en suite jacuzzi and our extensive gourmet breakfast is certain to please. 24 hr reception for arrivals, departures and reservations. Situated opposite UCC. Right in the heart of everything. Convenient to ferry, airport and bus terminal. Ideal base for visiting the south. Open all year. Recommended by AA, RAC and Bridgestone Best Places to stay. Car park available. Self catering suites & studios also.

WEB: www.garnish.ie

B&B from £20.00 to £45.00
€25.39 to €57.14

JOHANNA LUCEY
Manageress

American Express
Diners
Mastercard
Visa

14 14

Open All Year

GLENVERA HOTEL

WELLINGTON ROAD,
CORK
TEL: 021-502030   FAX: 021-508180
EMAIL: glenvera@eircom.net

HOTEL U   MAP 3 H 3

Glenvera Hotel is a Victorian mansion in the heart of Cork city. Glenvera Hotel has 34 bedrooms en suite with colour TV, radio, direct dial telephone and personally controlled central heating. Glenvera Hotel is only 3 minutes from bus and rail. Glenvera Hotel is convenient to car ferry and airport. Glenvera Hotel is fully licensed. Glenvera Hotel has a private locked car park. Groups specially catered: rugby, soccer, golf, fishing.

WEB: homepage.eircom.net/~glenvera

B&B from £28.00 to £54.00
€35.55 to €68.56

JOHN O'CONNOR
Proprietor

American Express
Diners
Mastercard
Visa

34 34

Closed 23 December - 03 January

Room rates are per room per night

HAYFIELD MANOR HOTEL

PERROTT AVENUE, COLLEGE ROAD,
CORK
TEL: 021-315600 FAX: 021-316839
EMAIL: enquiries@hayfieldmanor.ie

HOTEL ★★★★★ MAP 2 H 3

Cork's premier 5***** hotel ideally
located 5 mins from the city and 7k
from Cork airport. As a family owned
hotel we endeavour to bring warm
and homely touches to our rooms
whilst retaining the traditional feel of
a country house hotel. Our rooms
are spacious and elegant with direct
access to our private leisure
facilities. Hayfield retains a serene
atmosphere combining the elegance
of an earlier age with every luxury
the modern traveller could wish for.
Conference facilities.

WEB: www.hayfieldmanor.ie

Members Of Small Luxury Hotels of the World

B&B from £90.00 to £120.00
€114.28 to €152.37

MARIE FOLEY

American Express
Diners
Mastercard
Visa

😊 Weekend specials from £155.00

87 87

Open All Year

HOTEL ISAACS

48 MAC CURTAIN STREET,
CORK
TEL: 021-500011 FAX: 021-506355
EMAIL: cork@isaacs.ie

HOTEL ★★★ MAP 3 H 3

A homely city centre hotel set in its
own courtyard garden and Greene's
restaurant even overlooks a waterfall!
Our comfortable en suite rooms with
an Irish literary theme have phone,
TV, tea/coffee making facilities and
hairdryers. We are 5-10 mins from
all amenities (commercial or leisure)
including bus and train stations with
nearby limited free carparking. Hotel
Isaacs Cork is simply an oasis
within Cork city centre.

WEB: www.isaacs.ie

B&B from £30.00 to £60.00
€38.09 to €76.18

PAULA LYNCH
General Manager

American Express
Mastercard
Visa

36 36

Closed 23 - 26 December

IMPERIAL HOTEL

SOUTH MALL,
CORK
TEL: 021-274040 FAX: 021-275375
EMAIL: imperial@iol.ie

HOTEL ★★★ MAP 3 H 3

Located in the heart of the business
and shopping district, this historic
city centre hotel was acquired by
Flynn Hotels in 1998. Since then the
Imperial has undergone extensive
renovations. South's Bar is one of
the most popular in Cork and the
new French style coffee shop is a
must for all visitors. Conference
facilities for up to 450 delegates are
available. Free car parking for
residents.

B&B from £59.50 to £65.00
€75.55 to €82.53

JOHN FLYNN
Proprietor

American Express
Diners
Mastercard
Visa

😊 Weekend specials from £75.00

88 88

Closed 24 - 27 December

B&B rates are per person sharing per night incl. Breakfast

JOHN BARLEYCORN INN HOTEL

RIVERSTOWN, GLANMIRE,
CORK
TEL: 021-821499 FAX: 021-821221

HOTEL ★★ MAP 3 H 3

This fine 18th century residence retains all the atmosphere and charm of a rustic coach stop. Nestling in its own grounds of river and trees, just a short 6km jaunt from Cork city, just off the R639 (alternative Cork/Dublin road). Ideal base for trips to Blarney, Kinsale, Fota and Cobh Heritage Centre. We welcome all guests with enthusiasm and attention. A Village Inn Hotel, Central reservations tel: 01-295 8900, fax: 01-295 8940.

Members Of Village Inn Hotels

B&B from £29.00 to £36.50
€36.82 to €46.35

MICHELLE LANE
Proprietor/Manager

American Express

Diners

Mastercard

Visa

17 17

alc

HOTELS

Closed 25 - 26 December

JURYS CORK INN

ANDERSON'S QUAY,
CORK
TEL: 021-276444 FAX: 021-276144
EMAIL: info@jurys.com

HOTEL ★★★ MAP 2 H 3

Modern attractive rooms capable of accommodating up to 3 adults or 2 adults and 2 children. All rooms are en suite with multi-channel TV, radio, DD phone and tea/coffee making facilities. Located in the centre of Cork city, overlooking the river Lee, it has an informal restaurant and a lively pub, business centre, conference rooms and an adjoining public multi-storey car park (fee payable). Jurys Doyle Hotel Group central reservations Tel. 01-607 0000 Fax. 01-631 6999.

WEB: www.jurys.com

Room Rate from £49.00 to £60.00
€62.22 to €76.18

MELISSA HYNES
General Manager

American Express

Diners

Mastercard

Visa

133 133

HOTELS

Closed 24 - 26 December

JURYS HOTEL CORK

WESTERN ROAD,
CORK
TEL: 021-276622 FAX: 021-274477
EMAIL: info@jurys.com

HOTEL ★★★★ MAP 2 H 3

Centrally located on the banks of the river Lee. Just 5 mins walk from the city centre. Renowned for its distinctly warm welcome, friendly staff and efficient and professional service. The newly refurbished ground floor comprises the Glandore Restaurant with its wide menu selection, a lively atmosphere in Kavanagh's traditional Irish pub and the Library lounge, perfect for a relaxing drink. Jurys Doyle Hotel Group central reservations Tel. 01-607 0000 Fax. 01-631 6999.

WEB: www.jurys.com

B&B from £76.00 to £92.00
€96.50 to €116.82

JOSEPH QUINN
General Manager

American Express

Diners

Mastercard

Visa

☺ Weekend specials from £98.00

185 185

HOTELS

Closed 24 - 26 December

Room rates are per room per night

KILLARNEY GUEST HOUSE

WESTERN ROAD, (OPP. UCC),
CORK
TEL: 021-270290   FAX: 021-271010
EMAIL: killarneyhouse@iol.ie

GUESTHOUSE ★★★ MAP 2 H 3

The Killarney House is a 3*** guest house situated opposite University College Cork - a short drive from Cork airport and ferry. Registered with the AA, RAC and featured in many travel guides it offers exceptional style and comfort within walking distance of Cork city. All the rooms are en suite with direct dial phones, TV and tea/coffee making facilities. Room with jacuzzi bath available. It is ideally situated for touring in the Cork/Kerry region. Large car park at rear of house.

WEB: www.killarneyhouse.com

B&B from £20.00 to £35.00
€25.39 to €44.44

MARGARET O'LEARY
Manageress

American Express
Mastercard
Visa

19 19

Closed 23 - 26 December

KINGSLEY HOTEL

VICTORIA CROSS,
CORK
TEL: 021-800500   FAX: 021-800555
EMAIL: kingsley@eircom.net

HOTEL U MAP 2 H 3

This de luxe Hotel is nestled on the River Lee, located only minutes from Cork's Airport. State of the art facilities, an elegant atmosphere and tranquil surroundings. The Sabrona Lounge and Library with open fires are havens of tranquillity. Otters Brasserie is a creative dining experience. Poachers Bar is a distinctly different hotel bar. For business clients a customised business centre and conference facilities. The Kingsley Club allows guests unwind at leisure. Opened June 1998.

WEB: www.kingsleyhotels.com

B&B from £60.00 to £90.00
€76.18 to €114.28

MICHAEL ROCHE
General Manager

American Express
Diners
Mastercard
Visa

57 57

Closed 24 - 25 December

LANCASTER LODGE

WESTERN ROAD,
CORK
TEL: 021-251125   FAX: 021-251126
EMAIL: lancasterlodge@eircom.net

GUESTHOUSE N MAP 2 H 3

Lancaster Lodge is a purpose-built 39 roomed en suite guesthouse including two luxury suites with jacuzzi baths. Located alongside Jurys Hotel and only five minutes from the city centre, the guesthouse provides private parking, 24-hour reception, an extensive breakfast menu, spacious rooms including wheelchair facilities and lift to each floor. For comfort and convenience Lancaster Lodge awaits you.

B&B from £25.00 to £50.00
€31.74 to €63.49

ROBERT WHITE
Proprietor

American Express
Diners
Mastercard
Visa

39 39

Open All Year

B&B rates are per person sharing per night incl. Breakfast

LOTAMORE HOUSE

TIVOLI,
CORK
TEL: 021-822344 FAX: 021-822219
EMAIL: lotamore@iol.ie

GUESTHOUSE ★★★★ MAP 3 H 3

A beautiful house with 20 en suite rooms, 4****, and all the amenities of a hotel. 9 mins drive from the city centre but having a quiet location surrounded by 4 acres. Cobh Heritage Centre, Fota Island, many golf courses. Blarney, Kinsale within easy reach. Situated 3 mins from the Lee tunnel. Ideally situated for travelling to the airport, ferry terminals, west Cork, Killarney and the Ring of Kerry.

B&B from £29.00 to £32.00
€36.82 to €40.63

MAIREAD HARTY
Proprietor/Manager

American Express
Mastercard
Visa

:/

☺ Midweek specials from £80.00

20 20

Closed 20 December - 07 January

LOUGH MAHON HOUSE

TIVOLI,
CORK
TEL: 021-502142 FAX: 021-501804
EMAIL: loughmahonhse@eircom.net

GUESTHOUSE ★★★ MAP 3 H 3

Family run comfortable Georgian house with private parking. Convenient to city centre, bus and rail station. En suite bedrooms are decorated to a high standard with every comfort for our guests TV, direct dial phone, tea/coffee maker, hair dryer, trouser press and ironing facilities available. Near to Fota Wildlife Park, Cobh Heritage Centre, golf clubs and fishing. Ideal base for trips to Blarney Castle, Kinsale and Killarney. Open all year.

WEB: www.cork-guide.ie/corkcity/
loughmahonhouse/welcome.html
Members Of Premier Guesthouses

B&B from £20.00 to £30.00
€25.39 to €38.09

MARGOT MEAGHER
Proprietor

American Express
Mastercard
Visa

5 5

Closed 24 - 27 December

MARYBOROUGH HOUSE HOTEL

MARYBOROUGH HILL, DOUGLAS,
CORK
TEL: 021-365555 FAX: 021-365662
EMAIL: maryboro@indigo.ie

HOTEL N MAP 3 H 3

Distinctive, delightful and different. Maryborough is set on 24 acres of listed gardens and woodland, located only 10 minutes from Cork city. This charming 18th Century house with its creatively designed extension features exquisite conference, banqueting and leisure facilities. 79 spacious rooms, some with balconies overlooking the magnificent gardens and orchards. Zing's restaurant, contemporary relaxed design is an exciting mix of modern flavours and styles. 4 mins from Lee Tunnel.

WEB: www.maryborough.ie

B&B from £50.00 to £65.00
€63.49 to €82.53

PAT CHAWKE
General Manager

American Express
Diners
Mastercard
Visa

:/ 🍴

☺ Weekend specials from £110.00

79 79

Closed 24 - 27 December

Room rates are per room per night

METROPOLE RYAN HOTEL AND LEISURE CENTRE

MACCURTAIN STREET,
CORK
TEL: 021-508122 FAX: 021-506450
EMAIL: ryan@indigo.ie

HOTEL ★★★ MAP 3 H 3

Newly acquired by the Ryan Hotel Group the recently refurbished Metropole Ryan includes the Riverview Restaurant, the ide Cafe and the Met Bar. Our superb Leisure Centre includes three main pool areas, a whirlpool spa, sauna, steam, sun rooms and a fully equipped gymnasium. Located in the heart of Cork City overlooking the River Lee, close to the train and bus stations and 15 minutes from Cork Airport. Car parking available.

WEB: www.ryan-hotels.com

Members Of Best Western Hotels

B&B from £45.00 to £100.00
€57.14 to €126.97

PAUL MC CRACKEN
Operations Director

American Express
Diners
Mastercard
Visa

Weekend specials from £89.00

123 123

Open All Year

QUALITY SHANDON COURT HOTEL

SHANDON,
CORK
TEL: 021-551793 FAX: 021-551665
EMAIL: choichtl@iol.ie

HOTEL R MAP 2 H 3

Located in the heart of the city centre, close to all amenities and points of interest the Quality Shandon Court Hotel offers the elegance of old world splendour with the facilities of a modern day hotel. Recently refurbished Bells bar and bistro offers an exciting yet reasonably priced menu as well as a regular entertainment schedule.

Members Of Choice Hotels Ireland

B&B from £30.00 to £70.00
€38.09 to €88.88

RICHARD COLLINS
General Manager

American Express
Diners
Mastercard
Visa

Weekend specials from £99.00

24 24

Closed 23 - 30 December

REDCLYFFE GUEST HOUSE

WESTERN ROAD,
CORK
TEL: 021-273220 FAX: 021-278382
EMAIL: chorgan@indigo.ie

GUESTHOUSE ★★ MAP 2 H 3

Redclyffe is a charming Victorian red brick guesthouse, family run and decorated to the highest standard. Opposite University, museum, consultants clinic and Jury's hotel. 13 luxurious bedrooms, all en suite with DD phone, satellite TV, hairdryer & tea/coffee making facilities. 10 mins walk to city centre, No 8 bus at door. Easy drive to airport & car ferry. AA approved. Spacious car park front & rear. Be assured of a warm welcome.

B&B from £20.00 to £25.00
€25.39 to €31.74

MICHAEL SHEEHAN
Proprietor

American Express
Diners
Mastercard
Visa

13 13

Closed 24 - 25 December

B&B rates are per person sharing per night incl. Breakfast

ROCHESTOWN PARK HOTEL

ROCHESTOWN ROAD, DOUGLAS,
CORK
TEL: 021-892233 FAX: 021-892178
EMAIL: info@rochestownpark.com

HOTEL U   MAP 3 H 3

A manor style hotel set in mature gardens on the south side of Cork city. Facilities include an award winning leisure centre and Ireland's premier Thalasso therapy centre. A large proportion of our 115 rooms overlook the gardens, Mahon golf club and bird sanctuary. The hotel caters for weekend breaks, conference, weddings, accommodation for families, individuals and groups. Another 50 rooms will be completed in Sept 2000. Close to the Lee Tunnel linking all main roads into Cork city.

WEB: www.rochestownpark.com

Members Of Conference Connections

B&B from £35.00 to £60.00
€44.44 to €76.18

LIAM LALLY
General Manager

American Express
Diners
Mastercard
Visa

115 115

Open All Year

ROSERIE VILLA GUEST HOUSE

MARDYKE WALK,
OFF WESTERN ROAD, CORK
TEL: 021-272958 FAX: 021-274087
EMAIL: info@roserievilla.com

GUESTHOUSE ★★★   MAP 2 H 3

Roserie Villa is a 10 minute walk from city centre and close to bus and train stations. 16 en suite bedrooms with direct dial telephone, TV, tea/coffee making facilities, hairdryer and ironing facilities. An ideal base for the busy executive or holiday maker to explore the south west. Airport and ferry 15 minutes drive. Golf, tennis, cricket, fishing nearby and just minutes from university college.

WEB: www.roserievilla.com

B&B from £20.00 to £30.00
€25.39 to €38.09

PADDY MURPHY
Proprietor

American Express
Diners
Mastercard
Visa

16 16

Open All Year

SAINT KILDA GUESTHOUSE

WESTERN ROAD,
CORK
TEL: 021-273095 FAX: 021-275015
EMAIL: gerald@stkildas.com

GUESTHOUSE ★★★   MAP 2 H 3

Exclusive overnight accommodation just a 10 min walk to city centre. Directly opposite university with long-established tennis and cricket clubs at rear. Magnificent swimming and leisure centre nearby. Killarney 1 hr, Kinsale 30 mins, airport and Blarney Castle 20 mins. Registered with RAC and recommended by Frommers, Stilwells and Lonely Planet guides. A short pleasant drive to numerous golf courses including Old Head of Kinsale, Fota Island, Lee Valley and Monkstown.

WEB: www.cork-guide.ie/st-kilda/index.htm

B&B from £20.00 to £30.00
€25.39 to €38.09

GERALD COLLINS
Proprietor

Mastercard
Visa

20 20

Closed 18 December - 10 January

Room rates are per room per night

SEVEN NORTH MALL

7 NORTH MALL,
CORK
TEL: 021-397191 FAX: 021-300811
EMAIL: sevennorthmall@eircom.net

GUESTHOUSE ★★★★ MAP 2 H 3

Comfortable 240 year old listed house on tree lined mall, facing south, overlooking River Lee. Adjacent to all sites including theatres, art galleries, Shandon, the university and some of Ireland's best restaurants. Individually decorated en suite bedrooms include direct dial telephone, cable TV, trouser press and hair dryer. Small conference room, private car park and accommodation for disabled guests. Children over 12 welcome. ITB Graded 4****.

B&B from £30.00 to £35.00
€38.09 to €44.44

ANGELA HEGARTY
Proprietor

Mastercard

Visa

🖐🔥☎️⬜T❄P
5 5

HOTELS

Closed 17 December - 08 January

VICTORIA HOTEL

PATRICK STREET,
CORK
TEL: 021-278788 FAX: 021-278790
EMAIL: vicgeneral@eircom.net

HOTEL ★★ MAP 3 H 3

The Victoria Hotel is situated in Cork city centre. All rooms have bath & shower, DD phone, TV and hair dryer. Family suites available. Built in 1810, it was frequented by European Royalty and was home to some of our own great political leaders, including Charles Stewart Parnell who made his major speeches from its upper balcony. James Joyce recounts his stay in one of his novels. Enjoy your stay in this family run hotel.

Members Of MinOtel Ireland Hotel Group

B&B from £20.00 to £50.00
€25.39 to €63.49

EAMON & PAUL KING
Joint Managing Directors

Mastercard

Visa

🖐🔥☎️⬜T C CM🍴S📶alc
29 29

HOTELS

Open All Year

VICTORIA LODGE

VICTORIA CROSS,
CORK
TEL: 021-542233 FAX: 021-542572

GUESTHOUSE ★★★★ MAP 2 H 3

This newly renovated monastery located just minutes from city centre, yet standing in mature gardens, has 28 luxury bedrooms with private bath and shower, colour TV, orthopaedic beds, computerised fire detection, direct dial telephone, central heating, tea making facilities, secure car parking, lift to each floor. Convenient to tennis village, golf clubs, museum and fishing facilities. Light snacks, cold meals and drinks served.

B&B from £26.00 to £30.00
€33.01 to €38.09

BRENDAN & MARION LONG
Proprietors

American Express

Mastercard

Visa

🖐🔥☎️⬜T C❄JP
28 28

Closed 24 - 28 December

B&B rates are per person sharing per night incl. Breakfast

VIENNA WOODS HOTEL

GLANMIRE,
CORK
TEL: 021-821146   FAX: 021-821120
EMAIL: vienna@iol.ie

HOTEL U   MAP 3 H 3

An 18th century mansion set in 20 acres of woodland just 5 minutes from Cork city. Located near the mouth of the Jack Lynch Tunnel, the hotel is within easy reach of all Cork's finest golf courses and leisure destinations. The hotel boasts well appointed en suite rooms and extensive conference and banqueting facilities. In May 2000 a further 38 new luxury rooms open including 6 suites and 4 conference rooms.

WEB: www.viennawoodshotel.com

B&B from £35.00 to £45.00
€44.44 to €57.14

JOHN GATELY/DARINA O'DRISCOLL
Proprietors

American Express
Diners
Mastercard
Visa

☺ Midweek specials from £80.00

19 19
alc

IRISH HOTELS FEDERATION

Closed 24 - 26 December

SEA VIEW GUEST HOUSE

CLUIN VILLAGE, ALLIHIES, BEARA,
CO. CORK
TEL: 027-73004   FAX: 027-73211
EMAIL: seaviewg@iol.ie

GUESTHOUSE ★★★   MAP 1 C 2

Sea View Guest House is a family run concern in the remote and unspoilt Beara Peninsula. All bedrooms are en suite with TV and telephone. Situated in the village of Allihies it is within walking distance of a beach, playground and tennis court. The nearby hills afford excellent opportunities for walking, offering breathtaking views. Traditional Irish music and a friendly welcome can be found in the village pubs.

B&B from £20.00 to £25.00
€25.39 to €31.74

JOHN AND MARY O'SULLIVAN
Proprietors

Mastercard
Visa

10 10
FAX

Closed 31 October - 01 March

WEST PARK HOTEL

BALLINCOLLIG,
CORK
TEL: 021-870700   FAX: 021-876777

HOTEL N   MAP 3 H 3

Elegant suburbian hotel, 3 miles to city centre and gateway to the Ring of Kerry, 6 miles to Blarney. Enjoy warm friendly hospitality and superb restaurant and food. Choice of 2 bars and bar food available all day.

B&B from £37.50 to £40.00
€47.62 to €50.79

JOHN HICKEY
Manager

Mastercard
Visa

☺ Weekend specials from £80.00

9 9
alc   FAX

IRISH HOTELS FEDERATION

Closed 25 - 26 December

Room rates are per room per night

BAYVIEW HOTEL

BALLYCOTTON,
CO. CORK
TEL: 021-646746 FAX: 021-646075
EMAIL: bayhotel@iol.ie

HOTEL ★★★★ MAP 3 J 3

Bayview is a luxury 35 bedroom hotel built in 1992 on the site of the old hotel. Magnificently situated overlooking Ballycotton Bay and fishing harbour. Private gardens with steps leading to the sea and bathing spot. All rooms en suite with direct dial telephone and TV. Luxury suites also available. 4 superb golf courses in the area. 2 rosettes awarded by AA. GDS Access Code: UI Toll Free 1-800-44-UTELL.

Members Of Manor House Hotels

B&B from £55.00 to £67.50
€69.84 to €85.71

STEPHEN BELTON
General Manager

American Express
Diners
Mastercard
Visa

35 35
alc

Closed 31 October - 31 March

SPANISH POINT SEAFOOD RESTAURANT & GUEST HOUSE

BALLYCOTTON,
CO. CORK
TEL: 021-646177 FAX: 021-646179

GUESTHOUSE ★★★ MAP 3 J 3

Spanish Point Seafood Restaurant & Guest accommodation is situated on a cliff face overlooking Ballycotton bay. The conservatory restaurant specialises in seafood which is caught from our own trawler. Mary Tattan, Chef/Owner, trained at Ballymaloe Cookery School.

B&B from £25.00 to £25.00
€31.74 to €31.74

MARY TATTAN
Chef/Owner

Mastercard
Visa

5 5
S alc

Closed 02 January - 13 February

BALLYLICKEY MANOR HOUSE

BALLYLICKEY, BANTRY BAY,
CO. CORK
TEL: 027-50071 FAX: 027-50124
EMAIL: ballymh@eircom.net

GUESTHOUSE ★★★★ MAP 2 E 2

Overlooking beautiful Bantry Bay in 4 hectares of parkland and ornamental gardens, bordered by the Ouvane river, Ballylickey, a 17th century manor house together with cottages around the swimming pool, offers both standard and luxury suite accommodation, an outdoor heated swimming pool, private fishing, 2 golf courses (3 and 8km) and riding nearby. Ballylickey is a member of the Irish Country House and Restaurant Association and of Relais and Châteaux International.

WEB: www.relaischateaux.fr.ballylickey

Members Of Ireland's Blue Book

B&B from £66.00 to £82.50
€83.80 to €104.75

MR AND MRS GRAVES
Owners

American Express
Diners
Mastercard
Visa

11 11

IRISH HOTELS FEDERATION

Closed 05 November - 01 April

B&B rates are per person sharing per night incl. Breakfast

REENDESERT HOTEL

BALLYLICKEY, BANTRY,
CO. CORK
TEL: 027-50153 FAX: 027-50597

HOTEL ★★ MAP 2 E 2

Owner managed hotel overlooking Bantry Bay. Ideal centre for touring West Cork and Kerry. 19 en suite bedrooms with DD phone, colour TV, tea/coffee making facilities, hairdryer. Convenient to 2 golf courses, fishing, walks and horse riding. Extensive bar food menu available all day. Restaurant open in the evenings. Special weekend and short break terms available. A warm and friendly welcome awaits you at Reendesert Hotel. To us you are important.

B&B from £25.00 to £25.00
€31.74 to €31.74

EMILY SMITH
Manageress

American Express
Diners
Mastercard
Visa

🏨🍴☎️🅣🅒➡CM❄️☀️♪🅟🅢🅔
19 19
alc◼

IRISH
HOTELS
FEDERATION

Open All Year

SEA VIEW HOUSE HOTEL

BALLYLICKEY, BANTRY,
CO. CORK
TEL: 027-50073 FAX: 027-51555

HOTEL ★★★★ MAP 2 E 2

Delightful comfortable country house hotel and restaurant, set back in extensive grounds on main Bantry/Glengarriff road. All bedrooms en suite, D.D. telephone and colour TV. Ideal for touring West Cork and Kerry. Two golf courses nearby. Recommended Egon Ronay, Good Hotel Guide etc. For the restaurant, AA Rosettes and Bord Failte Awards of Excellence. Seafood a speciality. Member Manor House Hotels, Tel: 01-295 8900 Fax: 01-295 8940. GDS Access Code: UI Toll Free 1-800-44-UTELL.

Members Of Manor House Hotels

B&B from £45.00 to £60.00
€57.14 to €76.18

KATHLEEN O'SULLIVAN
Proprietor

American Express
Diners
Mastercard
Visa

☺ Midweek specials on request

🏨🍴☎️🅓🅒➡☀️♪🅟
16 16

IRISH
HOTELS
FEDERATION

Closed 15 November - 14 March

ABBEY HOTEL

BALLYVOURNEY,
CO. CORK
TEL: 026-45324 FAX: 026-45449

HOTEL U MAP 2 F 3

Family run hotel nestles in the valley of the Sullane river among the Cork and Kerry mountains on the N22. It combines a friendly atmosphere and excellent catering and is an ideal base for touring Kerry and Cork. A wide range of activities are available to you at the hotel including fishing, mountaineering, nature walks and golfing. 34 bedrooms with private facilities have DD phone and colour TV. Within 20 mins drive are two 18-hole golf courses and trout fishing on the Sullane river.

B&B from £28.00 to £35.00
€35.55 to €44.44

CORNELIUS CREEDON
Proprietor

American Express
Diners
Mastercard
Visa

☺ Weekend specials from £65.00

🏨🍴☎️🅓🅣🅒➡CM❄️☀️♪🅟🅔
34 34
alc◼

IRISH
HOTELS
FEDERATION

Closed 24 - 27 December

Room rates are per room per night

BALTIMORE BAY GUEST HOUSE

THE SQUARE, BALTIMORE,
CO. CORK
TEL: 028-20600   FAX: 028-20495

GUESTHOUSE ★★★   MAP 2 E 1

Baltimore Bay Guest House is a superbly appointed new guesthouse with 8 spacious bedrooms. 5 bedrooms have a magnificent view on the sea. Two restaurants are attached to the guesthouse, La Jolie Brise budget restaurant, Egon Ronay listed, and Chez Youen, Egon Ronay Best Irish fish restaurant of the year in 1994 and listed as one of the best 100 restaurants in the Bridgestone guide. Youen & Mary Jacob and sons, Proprietors. Sailing facilities. In Bridgestone's 100 best places to stay.

B&B from £25.00 to £32.00
€31.74 to €40.63

YOUEN & MARY JACOB
Owner-Managers

| American Express |
| Diners |
| Mastercard |
| Visa |

Weekend specials from £85.00

Open All Year

BALTIMORE HARBOUR HOTEL & LEISURE CENTRE

BALTIMORE,
CO. CORK
TEL: 028-20361   FAX: 028-20466
EMAIL: info@bhrhotel.ie

HOTEL ★★★   MAP 2 E 1

The hotel is situated overlooking the Harbour & Islands in the charming coastal village of Baltimore. It is the ideal haven from which to explore the beauty and wonders of West Cork and the sea and to enjoy the many varied activities available locally, including sailing, golfing, angling, diving, horse-riding, walking, cycling and of course the Islands. We are especially suited for families and offer children's entertainment during peak season. Enjoy our superb indoor leisure centre.

WEB: www.bhrhotel.ie

Members Of Best Western Hotels

B&B from £34.00 to £55.00
€43.17 to €69.84

ANTHONY PALMER
General Manager

| American Express |
| Diners |
| Mastercard |
| Visa |

Weekend specials from £75.00

Closed 03 January - 11 February

CASEY'S OF BALTIMORE

BALTIMORE,
CO. CORK
TEL: 028-20197   FAX: 028-20509
EMAIL: caseys@eircom.net

HOTEL ★★★   MAP 2 E 1

A warm welcome awaits you at Casey's of Baltimore. Situated at the entrance to Baltimore with its lovely views overlooking the bay, this superb family run hotel is the perfect place to spend some time. All rooms feature en suite bathrooms, satellite TV, tea/coffee facility, DD phone, hairdryer and trouser press. The traditional pub and restaurant feature natural stone and wood decor, a spectacular view, extensive menu - seafood is our speciality. Activities can be arranged.

WEB: www.sleeping-giant.ie/baltimore/caseys/

Members Of Coast and Country Hotels

B&B from £39.00 to £55.00
€49.52 to €69.84

ANN & MICHAEL CASEY
Owners

| American Express |
| Diners |
| Mastercard |
| Visa |

Weekend specials from £80.00

Closed 23 - 28 December

B&B rates are per person sharing per night incl. Breakfast

MUNSTER ARMS HOTEL

OLIVER PLUNKETT STREET, BANDON,
CO. CORK
TEL: 023-41562   FAX: 023-41562
EMAIL: kingsley@eircom.net

HOTEL ★★★   MAP 2 G 2

Set at the gateway to west Cork, 30 high quality en suite bedrooms with tea/coffee facilities, direct dial telephone, remote control T.V. radio and hairdryer. Set in beautiful scenic west Cork accessible by the N71 route from Cork city. Renowned for its homely atmosphere and superb quality. Ideal touring base and easily accessible to Kinsale, Cork City, Blarney, Killarney and West Cork. Relax and be pampered!

WEB: www.kingsleyhotels.com

B&B from £30.00 to £35.00
€38.09 to €44.44

ORLA LANNIN
Operations Manager

American Express
Diners
Mastercard
Visa

:-) Weekend specials from £75.00

30 30

Closed 25 - 26 December

ATLANTA HOUSE

MAIN STREET, BANTRY,
CO. CORK
TEL: 027-50237   FAX: 027-50237

GUESTHOUSE ★★★   MAP 2 E 2

Atlanta House is a long established family run guesthouse situated in the centre of Bantry. It is an ideal base from which to tour West Cork and Kerry if you are walking cycling or driving. Golf, fishing and horseriding are all close by. Rooms are en suite with TV, D.D phone & tea/coffee making facilities. We assure you of a warm welcome and we look forward to seeing you in Bantry.

B&B from £18.00 to £20.00
€22.86 to €25.39

RONNIE & ESTHER O'DRISCOLL
Owners

Mastercard
Visa

9 9

Closed 19 - 31 December

BANTRY BAY HOTEL

WOLFE TONE SQUARE, BANTRY,
CO. CORK
TEL: 027-50062   FAX: 027-50261
EMAIL: bantrybay@eircom.net

HOTEL ★★   MAP 2 E 2

The Bantry Bay has been operated by the O'Callaghan family for 53 years in the centre of historic Bantry. Extensively refurbished since 1995, the premises consists of a choice of family, tourist and commercial accommodation. All rooms are en suite with satellite TV, DD phone, teamaker and hairdryer. They are complimented by our beautiful maritime themed bar and restaurant. Carvery in operation daily. Guests assured of a hearty O'Callaghan welcome.

WEB: www.micromagic.ie/bantrybay/

B&B from £33.00 to £36.30
€41.90 to €46.09

VIVIAN O'CALLAGHAN JNR/SNR
Manager/Owner

American Express
Diners
Mastercard
Visa

14 14

Closed 24 - 27 December

Room rates are per room per night

VICKERY'S INN

NEW STREET, BANTRY,
CO. CORK
TEL: 027-50006 FAX: 027-20002
EMAIL: tvickery@iol.ie

GUESTHOUSE ★ MAP 2 E 2

Originally a coaching inn established 1850. Most bedrooms en suite. All with TV, tea/coffee facilities. An extensive bar and grill menu is available all day, reasonably priced lunches and dinner in the restaurant. Guide du Routard recommended. Traditional music in the bar during season. Ideally situated to explore scenic West Cork/Kerry. Golf, river, lake, seafishing and horseriding close by. Groups catered in separate dining room, seating 40. Full internet access available.

WEB: www.westcork.com/vickerys-inn

B&B from £23.00 to £25.00
€29.20 to €31.74

HAZEL VICKERY
Proprietor

American Express
Diners
Mastercard
Visa

Closed 23 - 29 December

WESTLODGE HOTEL

BANTRY,
CO. CORK
TEL: 027-50360   FAX: 027-50438
EMAIL: info@westlodgehotel.ie

HOTEL ★★★ MAP 2 E 2

3*** hotel beautifully situated in the scenic surroundings of Bantry Bay. Super new health and leisure centre including indoor heated swimming pool, children's pool, toddlers pool, sauna, steam room, jacuzzi, gym, aerobics and squash. Outdoor amenities include tennis, pitch & putt and wooden walks. The Westlodge specialise in family holidays with organised activities during July and August. A warm and friendly welcome awaits you at the Westlodge. Self-catering cottages available.

WEB: www.westlodgehotel.ie

B&B from £38.00 to £57.50
€48.25 to €73.01

EILEEN M O'SHEA
General Manager

American Express
Diners
Mastercard
Visa

☺ Weekend specials from £90.00

Closed 23 - 28 December

BLARNEY CASTLE HOTEL

BLARNEY,
CO. CORK
TEL: 021-(4)385116 FAX: 021-(4)385542
EMAIL: castlehb@iol.ie

HOTEL ★★ MAP 2 H 3

Established in 1837, still run by the Forrest family. Picturesque inn on peaceful village green, 5 miles from Cork city. Tastefully appointed bedrooms, unspoilt traditional bar and restaurant specialising in finest local produce. Killarney, Kenmare, West Cork, Kinsale, Cobh, Fota Wildlife Park and numerous golf courses all an easy drive. Immediately to the right Blarney Woollen Mills, to the left the magnificent gardens of Blarney Castle guarding that famous stone. Private carpark for hotel guests. Quality entertainment nightly in village.

WEB: www.blarney-castle-hotel.com

Members Of Irish Family Hotels

B&B from £25.00 to £35.00
€31.74 to €44.44

IAN FORREST
Manager

American Express
Diners
Mastercard
Visa

☺ Weekend specials from £60.00

Closed 25 - 26 December

B&B rates are per person sharing per night incl. Breakfast

BLARNEY PARK HOTEL

BLARNEY,
CO. CORK
TEL: 021-385281   FAX: 021-381506
EMAIL: info@blarneypark.com

HOTEL ★★★   MAP 2 H 3

Situated in the picturesque village of Blarney, with Blarney Castle around the corner and Cork City's attractions at its doorstep, Blarney Park Hotel offers friendly, efficient service and a relaxing atmosphere. Recline by the log fire in our residents lounge, indulge your culinary pleasures in the Clancarty restaurant and enjoy our award-winning leisure centre. Children will love our supervised playroom. Callsave 1850-503010 from within the Republic of Ireland.

WEB: www.blarneypark.com

B&B from £52.00 to £62.00
€66.03 to €78.72

GERRY O'CONNOR
Managing Director

American Express
Diners
Mastercard
Visa

Weekend specials from £95.00

91 91

Open All Year

CHRISTY'S HOTEL

BLARNEY,
CO. CORK
TEL: 021-(4)385011   FAX: 021-(4)385350
EMAIL: christys@blarney.ie

HOTEL ★★★   MAP 2 H 3

Located in Blarney, Christy's Hotel is a 3 star hotel with 49 beautifully appointed bedrooms each en suite with D.D. phone, TV/Radio and tea/coffee making facilities. Blarney is situated 9.6kms from Cork City and just 22.4kms from Cork Airport. In addition to our all day Self Service restaurant the award winning Weaving Room has a reputation for fine foods at reasonable prices. The hotel has a full Health and Sports Centre. Blarney Woollen Mills Shopping Complex adjoins.

WEB: www.blarney.ie

B&B from £36.50 to £49.00
€46.35 to €62.22

THOS O'BRIEN
General Manager

American Express
Diners
Mastercard
Visa

Weekend specials from £79.00

49 49

Closed 24 - 26 December

SUNSET RIDGE HOTEL

KILLEENS, BLARNEY,
CO. CORK
TEL: 021-(4)385271   FAX: 021-(4)385565

HOTEL ★   MAP 2 H 3

Situated on main Cork/Limerick road, Cork City 4.8km/Blarney Village 3.2km. All rooms en suite, TV, DD phone. Fully licensed bar, complimentary entertainment Wed/Sat/Sun, bar food available. Our restaurant offers a selection of lunch, dinner and à la carte menus daily. Local amenities include horse riding, golf and fishing. A scenic nature trail walk links our hotel with Blarney Village. Special rates for group bookings. Bus tours catered for.

B&B from £24.00 to £30.00
€30.47 to €38.09

DENIS CRONIN
Manager

American Express
Diners
Mastercard
Visa

Weekend specials from £60.00

28 28

Closed 25 - 26 December

Room rates are per room per night

WATERLOO INN

WATERLOO, BLARNEY,
CO. CORK
TEL: 021-(4)385113 FAX: 021-(4)382829

GUESTHOUSE ★★ MAP 2 H 3

Enjoy a holiday in an old country inn located just 1.5 miles from Blarney Castle and 6 miles from Cork City. Set in a peaceful location this riverside inn offers comfortable rooms with tea/coffee making facilities. Relax in our conservatory, have a drink in the bar or walk up to the old round tower of Waterloo. All leisure activities nearby (golf, horse riding etc). This is an ideal centre to tour the south of Ireland.

B&B from £18.00 to £18.00
€22.86 to €22.86

PATRICIA DORAN/MARY DUGGAN
Proprietors

Mastercard

Visa

☺ Midweek specials from £50.00

5 3

Closed 31 October - 01 March

CARRIGALINE COURT HOTEL

CARRIGALINE,
CO. CORK
TEL: 021-371300 FAX: 021-371103
EMAIL: carrigcourt@eircom.net

HOTEL N MAP 3 H 3

Cork's newest luxury hotel, situated only minutes from the city centre, airport and ferryport. Our 52 rooms offer the finest in modern comforts including ISDN phone, satellite TV and radio. A distinguished menu of classic and traditional Irish dishes will ensure superb dining in our restaurant. An Carrig leisure centre, luxurious and stress- free facilities include a 20m pool. Local facilities include golf, sailing and a host of other events in this beautiful area.

WEB: www.carrigcourt.com

B&B from £55.00 to £70.00
€69.84 to €88.88

JOHN O'FLYNN
General Manager

American Express

Diners

Mastercard

Visa

☺ Weekend specials from £85.00

52 52

IRISH HOTELS FEDERATION

Closed 25 December

FERNHILL GOLF & COUNTRY CLUB

FERNHILL, CARRIGALINE,
CO. CORK
TEL: 021-372226 FAX: 021-371011
EMAIL: fernhill@iol.ie

GUESTHOUSE ★★★ MAP 3 H 3

Fernhill Golf & Country Club has all the facilities you want for a relaxing holiday. 18 hole golf course, heated indoor pool, sauna, tennis. Fernhill is 10 mins from Cork City, Cork Airport, 5 mins from Cork-Swansea ferry and 15 mins from Kinsale. Horse-riding and fishing. All rooms en suite, DD phone, TV, trouser press and tea/coffee making facilities. Full bar and restaurant facilities all day in the clubhouse. Music Friday and Saturday. Free golf included. Also Holiday Homes.

WEB: www.fernhillgolfhotel.com

B&B from £35.00 to £55.00
€44.44 to €69.84

MICHAEL BOWES
Owner/Manager

American Express

Diners

Mastercard

Visa

☺ Weekend specials from £99.00

18 18

Closed 20 December - 30 January

B&B rates are per person sharing per night incl. Breakfast

LODGE & SPA AT INCHYDONEY ISLAND

CLONAKILTY,
CO. CORK
TEL: 023-33143 FAX: 023-35229
EMAIL: mkj@inchydoneyisland.com

HOTEL ★★★★ MAP 2 G 2

Situated on the idyllic island of Inchydoney, between two EU blue flag beaches, the hotel offers de luxe rooms, a fully equipped thalassotherapy (seawater) spa, restaurant, Dunes pub and function and meeting facilities. Within a short distance guests can enjoy sailing, golf at the Old Head of Kinsale, riding and deep sea fishing. The style of cooking in the Gulfstream Restaurant reflects the wide availability of fresh seafoods and organically grown vegetables.

WEB: www.inchydoneyisland.com

Members Of Concorde Hotels

Room Rate from £140.00 to £180.00
€177.76 to €228.55

MICHAEL KNOX-JOHNSTON

American Express
Diners
Mastercard
Visa

:/ ✈ 🍴

☺ Weekend specials from £165.00

67 67

Open All Year

O'DONOVAN'S HOTEL

PEARSE STREET, CLONAKILTY,
CO. CORK
TEL: 023-33250 FAX: 023-33250
EMAIL: odhotel@iol.ie

HOTEL ★ MAP 2 G 2

Charles Stewart Parnell, Marconi and Gen Michael Collins found time to stop here. This fifth generation, family run hotel is located in the heart of Clonakilty town. Abounding in history, the old world charm has been retained whilst still providing the guest with facilities such as bath/shower en suite, TV etc. Our restaurant provides snacks and full meals and is open to non-residents. Ideal for conferences, private functions, meetings etc., with large lock up car park.

WEB: www.iol.ie/~odhotel

B&B from £30.00 to £40.00
€38.09 to €50.79

O'DONOVAN FAMILY
Proprietors

American Express
Mastercard
Visa

26 26

Closed 24 - 27 December

QUALITY HOTEL AND LEISURE CENTRE

CLONAKILTY,
CO. CORK
TEL: 023-35400 FAX: 023-35404

HOTEL N MAP 2 G 2

Clonakilty is a thriving and busy attractive town with a wealth of musical and artistic cultural activities. Facilities include golf, walking, horseriding, sea angling. Excellent visitor attractions, model village, animal park, ringfort, Lisselan gardens and more, plus access to superb sandy beaches makes Clonakilty the perfect gateway to West Cork. This new hotel with full indoor leisure centre and exciting bar and restaurant is your value for money choice.

Member of Choice Hotels Ireland

B&B from £30.00 to £50.00
€38.09 to €63.49

MAURICE J BERGIN
General Manager

American Express
Diners
Mastercard
Visa

:/ 🍴

☺ Midweek specials from £60.00

58 58

Closed 24 - 27 December

Room rates are per room per night

BELLA VISTA MANOR HOUSE HOTEL

BISHOP'S ROAD, SPY HILL, COBH,
CO. CORK
TEL: 021-812450 FAX: 021-812215
EMAIL: bellavis@indigo.ie

HOTEL N MAP 313

Bella Vista is a beautiful historic Victorian villa which enjoys a perfect location situated in the picturesque town of Cobh with tremendous views of Cork Harbour and Cobh Cathedral. Rooms are individually and luxuriously decorated some historically themed. Enjoy excellent cuisine in Napoleon's restaurant which is located in the stunning conservatory. The peaceful ambience of the house and gardens makes Bella Vista the ideal setting for an intimate weekend or relaxing break.

WEB: indigo.ie/~bellavis

B&B from £40.00 to £55.00
€50.79 to €69.84

ANGELA & STEVEN WARD
Hosts/Proprietors

American Express
Mastercard
Visa

Weekend specials from £99.00

16 16

Inet

Closed 23 - 28 December

COMMODORE HOTEL

COBH,
CO. CORK
TEL: 021-811277 FAX: 021-811672
EMAIL: commodorehotel@eircom.net

HOTEL ★★ MAP 313

The Commodore Hotel newly refurbished, owned by the O'Shea family for 30 years overlooks Cork Harbour. 25 minutes from city centre. Facilities: indoor pool, snooker, entertainment, roof garden. Available locally free golf and pitch & putt. Ideal for visiting Fota, Blarney, The Jameson and Queenstown heritage centres. All 43 rooms have full facilities, 22 overlook Cork Harbour. Ringaskiddy ferryport 15 mins via river car ferry.

Members Of Logis of Ireland

B&B from £25.00 to £65.00
€31.74 to €82.53

PATRICK O'SHEA
General Manager

American Express
Diners
Mastercard
Visa

43 43

Closed 24 - 27 December

RUSHBROOKE HOTEL

RUSHBROOKE, COBH,
CO. CORK
TEL: 021-811407 FAX: 021-812042
EMAIL: info@rushbrooke.com

HOTEL R MAP 313

Nestled on the banks of the River Lee, on the R624 off the N25, this newly renovated hotel has everything to offer the discerning guest. All bedrooms are en suite with state of the art facilities including e-mail and ISDN and many have balconies with spectacular Harbour views. The bar and restaurant overlook the waterfront and offer splendid cuisine with friendly, efficient service. Cork City 15 mins and beside Cobh Heritage town (incorporating Queenstown Story and Titanic Trail).

B&B from £30.00 to £45.00
€38.09 to €57.14

TOM COUGHLAN
Director

Mastercard
Visa

Weekend specials from £74.00

75 75

Open All Year

B&B rates are per person sharing per night incl. Breakfast

WATERSEDGE HOTEL

YACHT CLUB QUAY, COBH,
CO. CORK
TEL: 021-815566   FAX: 021-812011
EMAIL: watersedge@eircom.net

HOTEL P   MAP 313

Situated on the waterfront overlooking Cork Harbour. All rooms en suite with satellite TV, tea making facilities, DD phone, modem, hairdryer and trouser press. Our restaurant, Jacobs Ladder, is renowned for its seafood, steaks, ambience and friendly staff. Open all day. Local activities and sightseeing include Cobh Heritage Centre (next door), Cathedral, Titanic Trail, Fota Wildlife Park, golf, sailing, angling, tennis, horseriding. Ideal touring base for Cork City, Kinsale & Blarney. International airport & ferryport 20 minutes. Rail station 2 minutes walk.

B&B from £30.00 to £60.00
€38.09 to €76.18

MARGARET & MIKE WHELAN
Proprietors

American Express
Diners
Mastercard
Visa

Weekend specials from £69.00

19 19

Inet FAX

Open All Year

COURTMACSHERRY HOTEL

COURTMACSHERRY, NEAR BANDON,
WEST CORK, CO. CORK
TEL: 023-46198   FAX: 023-46137
EMAIL: cmv@indigo.ie

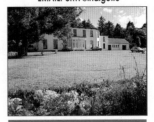

HOTEL ★★   MAP 2 G 2

A friendly, family run hotel, formerly the residence of the Earls of Shannon, offering superb cuisine (AA Rosette) and a connoisseur's wine list, situated in 4 hectares of gardens and woodlands overlooking Courtmacsherry Bay. Self-catering cottages are also available, along with endless local activities, including shore fishing for sea bass and boat angling for deeper water species and our own horse-riding stables and grass tennis court. GDS Access Code UI Toll Free 1-800-44 UTELL

Members Of Coast and Country Hotels

Room Rate from £40.00 to £70.00
€50.79 to €88.88

TERRY & CAROLE ADAMS
Proprietors

Mastercard
Visa

13 13

HOTELS
FEDERATION

Closed 01 October - 10 April

WHISPERING PINES HOTEL

CROSSHAVEN,
CO. CORK
TEL: 021-831448   FAX: 021-831679

HOTEL ★★   MAP 313

Whispering Pines, personally run by the Twomey family is a charming hotel sheltered by surrounding woodland & overlooking the Owenabue River. In this idyllic setting one can enjoy good company, quality homecooked food & a host of amenities to ensure your stay is a restful & memorable experience. All rooms with DD phone, tea/coffee facilities & TV. Our 3 angling boats fish daily from April-Oct. Ideal base for touring Cork/Kerry Region. Cork Airport 12kms & Cork City 19km. AA approved.

B&B from £22.50 to £30.00
€28.57 to €38.09

NORMA TWOMEY
Proprietor

American Express
Diners
Mastercard
Visa

15 15

HOTELS
FEDERATION

Closed 15 December - 01 January

Room rates are per room per night

CO. CORK
DUNMANWAY / FERMOY

DUN-MHUIRE HOUSE

KILBARRY ROAD, DUNMANWAY,
CO. CORK
TEL: 023-45162   FAX: 023-45162

GUESTHOUSE ★★★ MAP 2 F 2

Dun Mhuire is a small exclusive family run guesthouse with award winning restaurant, noted for its excellent cuisine. Situated in the heart of West Cork. It has a lot to offer the holiday maker who will appreciate its relaxed atmosphere and high standards. Ideal base from which to tour Cork and Kerry. Luxury bedrooms, all with bathroom, TV, direct dial telephone. Local amenities include swimming, golf, tennis, fishing, pony riding. Scenic walks nearby.

B&B from £25.00 to £30.00
€31.74 to €38.09

CARMEL & LIAM HAYES
Proprietors

Mastercard
Visa

Week partial board from £280.00

Closed 24 - 26 December

CASTLEHYDE HOTEL

CASTLEHYDE, FERMOY,
CO. CORK
TEL: 025-31865   FAX: 025-31485
EMAIL: cashyde@iol.ie

HOTEL N MAP 3 I 4

Country house hotel accommodation in a fully restored Georgian house and courtyard. Gracious hospitality in gracious surroundings. Only 35 minutes from Cork, a world apart from its bustle! All outdoor pursuits catered for. Heated outdoor pool. Exquisite cuisine served in Mermaids Restaurant, perfect peace in the library. The ideal base in the beautiful north Cork region, be it for leisure or for business.

Members Of Best Loved Hotels Of The World

B&B from £47.50 to £75.00
€60.31 to €95.23

ERIK & HELEN SPEEKENBRINK

American Express
Diners
Mastercard
Visa

Open All Year

GRAND HOTEL

ASHE QUAY, FERMOY,
CO. CORK
TEL: 025-31444   FAX: 025-32630

HOTEL ★ MAP 3 I 4

The Grand Hotel is a family run hotel situated in the heart of Fermoy. Nestling on the banks of the Blackwater river, it offers a superb location whether your pleasure is the local fishing, trekking and horseriding or simply exploring the south. At night, our luxurious lounge, traditional folk bar and Caesars nightclub offer contrasting atmospheres for enjoyable evenings. Friendly staff, quality food and weekend entertainment ensure an enjoyable stay.

B&B from £25.00 to £35.00
€31.74 to €44.44

WINIFRED & SEAN KAVANAGH
Proprietors

American Express
Diners
Mastercard
Visa

Weekend specials from £60.00

Closed 25 December

---

300 SOUTH WEST

B&B rates are per person sharing per night incl. Breakfast

GLANWORTH MILL COUNTRY INN

GLANWORTH, CO. CORK
TEL: 025-38555 FAX: 025-38560
EMAIL: glanworth@iol.ie

GUESTHOUSE ★★★★ MAP 3 I 4

A water mill, a Norman castle, a river, an ancient bridge, gorgeous rooms, a gourmet restaurant, tea rooms, library, courtyard garden and river walk... you'll find it here at Glanworth Mill. Unwind in this 1790 water mill with its sense of history and love of literature. For the more energetic there is a wealth of activities nearby - fishing, horse-riding, golf, hill walking, historic trails and houses and gardens to visit. All in the lush Blackwater Valley of north Cork.

WEB: www.iol.ie/glanworth

B&B from £42.00 to £45.00
€53.33 to €57.14

EMELYN HEAPS & LYNNE GLASSCOE

Mastercard
Visa

CM♦U♪P🔒alc
10 10

IRISH HOTELS FEDERATION

Closed 24 - 27 December

CASEY'S HOTEL

THE VILLAGE, GLENGARRIFF, CO. CORK
TEL: 027-63010 FAX: 027-63072

HOTEL ★★ MAP 1 D 2

Casey's Hotel has been run by the same family since 1884. Recently refurbished to cater for the expectations of the modern traveller. All rooms en suite with DD phones and TV. The hotel offers personal, friendly service with old fashioned courtesy, private car park and gardens. Casey's Hotel is the perfect base for day trips to Barley Cove, Gougane Barra, Killarney and the Ring of Kerry. Come and discover the unspoilt beauty of the Beara peninsula. Hill walking tours arranged.

Members Of Logis of Ireland

B&B from £22.00 to £30.00
€27.93 to €38.09

DONAL & EILEEN DEASY
Owners

American Express
Diners
Mastercard
Visa

♿🐕☎🖥TC🖥CM♦♪P🍽S🔒
19 19
alc

IRISH HOTELS FEDERATION

Closed 15 November - 01 March

GOUGANE BARRA HOTEL

GOUGANE BARRA, BALLINGEARY, CO. CORK
TEL: 026-47069 FAX: 026-47226
EMAIL: gouganebarrahotel@eircom.net

HOTEL ★★ MAP 2 E 3

Situated on its own grounds overlooking Gougane Barra Lake, the source of the River Lee. Most bedrooms enjoy fine views of the lake, glens and hills beyond. Ideally situated for touring the beauty spots of Cork and Kerry, 72km west of Cork city and airport. A walk along the banks of the Lee through the forest park which covers 162 hectares, will take you through varied scenery of mystic beauty. We are members of CMV marketing group. GDS Access Code UI Toll Free: 1-800-44-UTELL

WEB: www.cork-guide.ie

Members Of Coast and Country Hotels

B&B from £34.00 to £40.00
€43.17 to €50.79

BREDA & CHRISTOPHER LUCEY
Owner

American Express
Diners
Mastercard
Visa

♿🐕☎🖥TC🖥CM♦♪P🔒■
28 28

IRISH HOTELS FEDERATION

Closed 15 October - 23 April

Room rates are per room per night

CREEDON'S HOTEL

INCHIGEELA, MACROOM,
CO. CORK
TEL: 026-49012 FAX: 026-49265

HOTEL ★   MAP 2 F 3

One of South West Ireland's best known hotels. In the heart of West Cork's lake district, the hotel is situated en route to Bantry, Glengarriff and Killarney and only 48km from Cork City. Local swimming, golf, tennis & fishing are available - free boat for residents. Great variety of historical / nature walks. Beautiful unspoilt countryside. Creedons have been welcoming guests to their home for 3 generations. It has that special atmosphere of open turf fires, warm welcomes and unexpected conversations.

Members Of Irish Family Hotels

B&B from £20.00 to £35.00
€25.39 to €44.44

JOE & ANNE CREEDON
Proprietors

Mastercard

Visa

🏧🅟🆃CCMU♪🎵S🅰alc
16   8

HOTELS

Open All Year

INNISHANNON HOUSE HOTEL

INNISHANNON,
CO. CORK
TEL: 021-775121 FAX: 021-775609
EMAIL: innishannonhotel@eircom.net

HOTEL ★★★   MAP 2 G 2

The most romantic hotel in Ireland built in 1720 in the Petit Chateau style on the banks of the Bandon river, totally refurbished with Irish country house decor. All rooms en suite with TV, radio, direct dial, etc. Award winning restaurant (AA**, RAC, Egon Ronay) serving daily fresh fish and lobster. Superb wine cellar, stunning art collection, boating and free salmon and trout fishing from the grounds. Horse riding and golf nearby. GDS Code: UI Toll Free 1-800-44 Utell.

WEB: www.iol.ie/hotels

Members Of Manor House Hotels

B&B from £37.50 to £85.00
€47.62 to €107.93

CONAL & VERA O'SULLIVAN
Proprietors

American Express

Diners

Mastercard

Visa

✓♪🍽

😊   Weekend specials from £99.50

🏧🅙☎🅣C🍴CM❄U♪🅟🎶S
13 13
🅟🅰alc

HOTELS

Closed 05 January - 15 March

ACTONS HOTEL

PIER ROAD, KINSALE,
CO. CORK
TEL: 021-772135 FAX: 021-772231
EMAIL: actonsh@indigo.ie

HOTEL ★★★   MAP 2 H 2

Located in private gardens overlooking picturesque Kinsale Harbour and yachting marina. This attractive hotel, renowned for its cuisine and atmosphere, features a modern health and leisure centre including heated pool, sauna, gym, and solarium. Kinsale is famous as the gourmet capital of Ireland and the hotel's Captain's Table Restaurant is a member of Kinsale's Good Food Circle. All bedrooms have multi-channel T.V., hair dryer and tea/coffee making facilities.

B&B from £40.00 to £65.00
€50.79 to €82.53

JACK WALSH
General Manager

American Express

Diners

Mastercard

Visa

✓🍽

😊   Midweek 3 B&B 2 Dinners from £145

🏧🅙☎🅱🅣C🍴CM❄🎿🌐◎♪
76 76
♪🅟S🅰alc🎿🍷

HOTELS

Open All Year

B&B rates are per person sharing per night incl. Breakfast

BLUE HAVEN HOTEL

3/4 PEARSE STREET, KINSALE,
CO. CORK
TEL: 021-772209 FAX: 021-774268
EMAIL: bluhaven@iol.ie

HOTEL ★★★ MAP 2 H 2

The perfect place to stay in Kinsale - Ireland's Gourmet capital and centrally located on the site of the old fish market. Awarded Ireland Hotel of the Year 1996 by Egon Ronay and Jameson Guide. Renowned for its fresh seafood and shellfish cuisine, ambience, atmosphere and friendly staff. Seventeen rooms with an old town house style and all mod cons. The Blue Haven epitomises what a small owner-run hotel should be. Reservations advised.

Members Of Ireland's Blue Book

B&B from £50.00 to £80.00
€63.49 to €101.58

AVRIL & MARCUS

American Express
Diners
Mastercard
Visa

17 17

Closed 04 - 25 January

CAPTAINS QUARTERS

5 DENIS QUAY, KINSALE,
CO. CORK
TEL: 021-774549 FAX: 021-774944
EMAIL: captquarters@eircom.net

GUESTHOUSE ★★★ MAP 2 H 2

This Georgian period townhouse is situated close to the yacht club marina and in easy walking distance of all restaurants and town centre amenities. It offers quality accommodation in a maritime ambience. The spacious and tranquil lounge overlooks the harbour. The wheelchair accessible groundfloor rooms (1 twin/1 single, sharing shower/toilet) are also very convenient for the elderly. TV, DD phone, tea/coffee making facilities, hairdryer in all rooms. German and French spoken.

B&B from £17.00 to £26.00
€21.59 to €33.01

BERNY & CAPT. RUDI TEICHMANN
Co-Owners

Mastercard
Visa

6 4

Closed 30 January - 16 March

COLNETH HOUSE

CAPPAGH, KINSALE,
CO. CORK
TEL: 021-772824 FAX: 021-773357
EMAIL: colnethhouse@eircom.net

GUESTHOUSE ★★★ MAP 3 H 2

We welcome you to relax in the comfort of our home. Colneth House is a newly built guesthouse with very high standards maintained throughout. Ideally situated in a tranquil scenic location, rooms en suite, multi channel TV, DD phone, complimentary tray, hairdryer, canopied beds, breakfast menu, private car parking, landscaped gardens, rooms with beautiful views. Suite available, tastefully decorated to make our guests' stay enjoyable, comfortable and memorable.

WEB: www.euroka.com/cork/colneth

B&B from £25.00 to £35.00
€31.74 to €44.44

LORRAINE O'BRIEN
Proprietress

Mastercard
Visa

Midweek specials from £75.00

8 8

Closed 20 - 29 December

Room rates are per room per night

COTTAGE LOFT

6 MAIN STREET, KINSALE,
CO. CORK
TEL: 021-772803   FAX: 021-772803

GUESTHOUSE ★★   MAP 2 H 2

Located in the heart of Kinsale, the 200 year old town house has an old world charm. Decorated in rich deep tones giving a warm and welcoming ambience. All rooms are en suite with direct dial telephone and TV. Tea & Coffee making facilities in all rooms. Our restaurant, a member of Kinsale's Good Food Circle is noted for its excellent cuisine. All Michael's dishes are created using the finest and freshest ingredients available locally.

B&B from £22.50 to £27.50
€28.57 to €34.92

MICHAEL & CAROLANNE BUCKLEY
Owners

American Express
Mastercard
Visa

☺ Weekend specials from £60.00

🛏🖐☎🖥Ⓒ🔌CM🖥ⓐⓘⓒ▪
6 6

Closed 23 - 27 December

DEASYS LONG QUAY HOUSE

LONG QUAY, KINSALE,
CO. CORK
TEL: 021-774563   FAX: 021-774563

GUESTHOUSE ★★★   MAP 2 H 2

Long Quay House is a Georgian residence which typifies its era with rooms of splendid dimensions, furnished to afford the greatest possible guest comfort. Bedrooms are en suite (majority with bath), TV, DD phone, tea making facilities and hair dryer. Located centrally overlooking inner harbour, yacht marina and within walking distance of all Kinsale's gourmet restaurants and many tourist attractions. Sea angling trips by local skippers arranged. AA recognised establishment ♦♦♦♦.

B&B from £22.50 to £30.00
€28.57 to €38.09

JIM & PETER DEASY
Hosts

Mastercard
Visa

🛏🖐☎🖥Ⓒ🔌CM◡Ⓢ▪ Inet
7 7

Closed 01 - 27 December

KIERANS FOLKHOUSE INN

GUARDWELL, KINSALE,
CO. CORK
TEL: 021-772382   FAX: 021-774085
EMAIL: folkhse@indigo.ie

GUESTHOUSE ★★★   MAP 2 H 2

A charming 250 year old country inn with 27 en suite rooms, including family rooms, finished to the highest standard of comfort. The Cordoba bar features live music nightly in season. Shrimps Bistro, a member of Kinsale's Good Food Circle, offers an imaginative menu featuring steaks and locally caught seafood. Barfood is also available throughout the day. The Bacchus niteclub is the late night meeting place for Kinsale's over 25's. Also a member of Logis of Ireland.

Members Of Premier Guesthouses

B&B from £25.00 to £35.00
€31.74 to €44.44

DENIS & GERALDINE KIERAN
Owners

American Express
Diners
Mastercard
Visa

🛏🖐☎🖥ⓉⒸ🔌CM♫🖥ⓐⓘⓒ▪
27 27

Closed 25 December

B&B rates are per person sharing per night incl. Breakfast

KILCAW HOUSE

KINSALE, SITUATED ON R600,
CO. CORK
TEL: 021-774155 FAX: 021-774755
EMAIL: kilcawhouse@hotmail.com

GUESTHOUSE ★★★ MAP 2 H 2

Kilcaw House is a newly built Guest
House set on 7 acres with
magnificent views. It is built with a
traditional flair, yet is modern and
luxurious. Open fires, wooden floors
and striking colours all add to a
feeling of warmth and character. The
bedrooms are spacious, furnished in
antique pine, en suite with TV, direct
dial phone and tea/coffee making
facilities. Guests comfort is an
absolute priority at this family run
guest house.

WEB: http://homepage.eircom.net/~kilcawhouse

B&B from £20.00 to £25.00
€25.39 to €31.74

HENRY & CHRISTINA MITCHELL
Owners

American Express
Mastercard
Visa

7 7

Closed 01 - 31 January

MOORINGS

SCILLY, KINSALE,
CO. CORK
TEL: 021-772376 FAX: 021-772675
EMAIL: mooring5@indigo.ie

GUESTHOUSE ★★★★ MAP 2 H 2

This superbly appointed guesthouse
has private car parking. The en suite
(power showers) spacious
bedrooms have balconies
overlooking the harbour, TV, DD
phone, tea/coffee making,
hairdryers. The elegantly furnished
resident's lounge and dining room
open onto a large conservatory
which houses exotic cacti and has
panoramic views of the harbour and
yacht marina. The golfing proprietors
can arrange tee times for guests at
preferential green fees.
Recommended by all major guides.

WEB: http://indigo.ie/~mooring5

Room Rate from £90.00 to £120.00
€114.28 to €152.37

PAT & IRENE JONES
Proprietors

American Express
Diners
Mastercard
Visa

8 8

Closed 23 - 29 December

OLD BANK HOUSE

11 PEARSE STREET, NEXT TO P.O.,
KINSALE, CO. CORK
TEL: 021-774075 FAX: 021-774296
EMAIL: oldbank@indigo.ie

GUESTHOUSE ★★★★ MAP 2 H 2

The Old Bank House is a Georgian
residence of great character and
charm. Each room is a perfect blend
of Georgian splendour and modern
comfort with an elevator to all floors
and most rooms enjoying
picturesque views of the ancient
harbour town of Kinsale. Ideally
located for the Old Head Golf Links
and all the great courses in the
south west. Award winning
breakfast. Voted one of the 'Top 100
Places to Stay in Ireland' every year
since 1990 by Bridgestone guides.
The Old Bank House where fine food
is in our nature.

WEB: http://indigo.ie/~oldbank

B&B from £55.00 to £85.00
€69.84 to €107.93

MICHAEL & MARIE RIESE
Proprietors

American Express
Mastercard
Visa

17 17

Closed 23 - 26 December

Room rates are per room per night

QUAYSIDE HOUSE

PIER ROAD, KINSALE,
CO. CORK
TEL: 021-772188   FAX: 021-772664

GUESTHOUSE ★★★   MAP 2 H 2

A family run guesthouse ideally located in a picturesque setting overlooking the Kinsale harbour adjacent to town centre, yachting marina and all amenities. All bedrooms are en suite with direct dial telephone, TV and tea/coffee making facilities. Kinsale's famous gourmet restaurants are all within walking distance and Kinsale's golf club is just a five minute drive. Sea angling trips can be arranged.

B&B from £20.00 to £30.00
€25.39 to €38.09

COTTER FAMILY

Mastercard
Visa

Open All Year

TIERNEYS GUEST HOUSE

MAIN STREET, KINSALE,
CO. CORK
TEL: 021-772205   FAX: 021-774363
EMAIL: mtierney@indigo.ie

GUESTHOUSE ★★   MAP 2 H 2

Tierney's Guest House. A well established guest house perfectly situated in the heart of magnificent award winning Kinsale. Our guest house offers all amenities, TV, en suite, hairdryers, tea/coffee on request. Tastefully decorated and a warm welcome guaranteed. Stay in Tierney's and be in the centre of Kinsale and enjoy the Gourmet Restaurants, various bars & music lounges, breathtaking scenery, water sports, golf & etc.

B&B from £19.50 to £22.00
€24.76 to €27.93

MAUREEN TIERNEY
Owner

American Express
Mastercard
Visa

 Midweek specials from £58.50

Closed 23 - 28 December

TRIDENT HOTEL

WORLD'S END, KINSALE,
CO. CORK
TEL: 021-772301   FAX: 021-774173
EMAIL: info@tridenthotel.com

HOTEL ★★★   MAP 2 H 2

The Trident hotel stands at the water's edge, nestled between the winding streets of historic Kinsale town and one of the prettiest harbours in Europe. Rooms with sea views. The Savannah Waterfront restaurant - a member of Kinsale's Good Food Circle - offers award winning cuisine and service. The Wharf Tavern Bar offers bar food daily. Leisure facilities include: sauna, steamroom, gymnasium and jacuzzi. Excellent golf, sailing, angling etc. available locally.

WEB: tridenthotel.com

B&B from £40.00 to £65.00
€50.79 to €82.53

HAL MCELROY
Managing Director

American Express
Diners
Mastercard
Visa

3 B&B & 2 Dinners from £119.00 midweek

Closed 25 - 26 December

B&B rates are per person sharing per night incl. Breakfast

WHITE HOUSE

PEARSE ST. & THE GLEN, KINSALE,
CO. CORK
TEL: 021-772125 FAX: 021-772045
EMAIL: whitehse@indigo.ie

GUESTHOUSE ★★★ MAP 2 H 2

The White House epitomises Kinsale hospitality with 3*** accommodation, Chelsea's bistro, Le Restaurant D'Antibes and a thoroughly modern bar where all the old values of guest satisfaction, comfort and value for money prevail. We have welcomed both visitors and locals since the 1850s and from its earliest days has enjoyed a reputation for fine food, drinks of good cheer and indulgent service. Today we pride ourselves on enhancing that tradition. A member of Kinsale's Good Food Circle.

WEB: www.whitehouse-kinsale.ie

B&B from £35.00 to £50.00
€44.44 to €63.49

DONNACHA ROCHE
General Manager

American Express
Diners
Mastercard
Visa

Weekend specials from £90.00

10 10

Closed 25 - 26 December

WHITE LADY HOTEL

LOWER O'CONNELL ST, KINSALE,
CO. CORK
TEL: 021-772737 FAX: 021-774641
EMAIL: wlady@indigo.ie

HOTEL ★★ MAP 2 H 2

Looking after your needs and making you feel at home is the priority in this 10 bedroom hotel. All rooms have en suite facilities, TV and DD phone. Our Paddy Garibaldis restaurant provides you with a very varied and reasonably priced menu, while it also offers a selection of fresh seafood. Our on-site nite club ensures a lively atmosphere at weekends. Golf and sea angling trips can be arranged at your request.

B&B from £25.00 to £35.00
€31.74 to €44.44

ANTHONY COLLINS
Owner

American Express
Mastercard
Visa

10 10

Closed 24 - 26 December

CASTLE HOTEL & LEISURE CENTRE

MAIN STREET, MACROOM,
CO. CORK
TEL: 026-41074 FAX: 026-41505
EMAIL: castlehotel@eircom.net

HOTEL ★★★ MAP 2 F 3

Nestled between Blarney and Killarney the Castle Hotel is the ideal centre for your stay in the scenic south west. Guided walks, horse-riding, bicycle hire, coarse and game fishing, free pitch & putt and half-price green fees on one of Ireland's finest parklands 18 hole golf courses are all available locally to our guests. Hotel facilities include our award-winning restaurant (AA Rosette 92/99), new health & leisure club featuring 16m pool, kiddies pool, steam room and gymnasium.

WEB: www.castlehotel.ie

Members Of Village Inn Hotels

B&B from £30.00 to £45.00
€38.09 to €57.14

DON & GERARD BUCKLEY
Proprietors

American Express
Diners
Mastercard
Visa

3 B&B 2 Dinner 2 Golf from £135.00

42 42

Closed 24 - 28 December

Room rates are per room per night

COOLCOWER HOUSE

COOLCOWER, MACROOM,
CO. CORK
TEL: 026-41695   FAX: 026-42119

GUESTHOUSE ★★ MAP 2 F 3

Coolcower House is a large country residence on picturesque grounds. The house is ideally located within easy driving distance of all the tourist attractions in the Cork-Kerry region including Killarney, Kenmare, Kinsale, Blarney and Bantry. Located on the river's edge for coarse fishing and boating. Also outdoor tennis court. Restaurant offers the best of home produce on its à la carte and dinner menus. Fully licensed bar. TV's and Tea/Coffee making facilities in all rooms.

B&B from £21.00 to £23.50
€26.66 to €29.84

EVELYN CASEY
Manager

Mastercard

Visa

⊙⊙ Midweek specials from £58.00

10 10

Closed 14 December - 06 March

LYNCH'S LODGE HOTEL

KILLARNEY ROAD, MACROOM,
CO. CORK
TEL: 026-42122   FAX 026-42988

HOTEL N MAP 2 F 3

A warm welcome awaits you at the Lynch's Lodge Hotel. Located just outside the market town of Macroom on the main Cork to Killarney road (N22) in the beautiful Lee Valley, an ideal base for touring, golfing, sightseeing and fishing. Waders Bar serves bar food all day, using only the best of local products within a lively atmosphere.

Adjacent to Macroom's 18 hole golf course and close to other golf courses, Lee Valley, Bantry, Muskerry and Killarney. On the banks of the River Sullane, an excellent brown trout fishery.

Members of Irish Family Hotels

B&B from £25.00 to £35.00
€31.74 to €44.44

MARTIN O'MAHONY
General Manager

American Express

Diners

Mastercard

Visa

⊙⊙ Weekend specials from £59.00

33 33

Inet FAX

Closed 25 December

MILLS INN

BALLYVOURNEY, MACROOM,
CO. CORK
TEL: 026-45237   FAX: 026-45454

GUESTHOUSE ★★★ MAP 2 F 3

The Mill's Inn is an award-winning country inn, located in the centre of the romantic Gaeltacht village of Ballyvourney with its own landscaped gardens. It provides a warm welcome with traditional Irish hospitality. The Mill's Inn, one of the oldest inns in Ireland, combines the best of old world charm with all the conveniences of modern living.

B&B from £28.00 to £35.00
€35.55 to €44.44

JIM BERMINGHAM
Proprietor

Mastercard

Visa

11 11

Open All Year

B&B rates are per person sharing per night incl. Breakfast

VICTORIA HOTEL

THE SQUARE, MACROOM,
CO. CORK
TEL: 026-41082 FAX: 026-42148

HOTEL ★★ MAP 2 F 3

Situated in the centre of Macroom town, the Victoria is a small friendly hotel, family owned and managed. An ideal base for your visit to the beautiful Lee Valley or the scenic south west. Local amenities include fishing, local 18 hole golf course, hiking, walking and horse riding. All our rooms are en suite with telephone, TV and tea/coffee facilities. A la carte and full dinner menu available. Bar meals served all day.

B&B from £25.00 to £30.00
€31.74 to €38.09

MICHAEL LYONS
Manager

Mastercard

Visa

☺ Weekend specials from £65.00

Closed 24 - 28 December

CORTIGAN HOUSE

GOLF COURSE ROAD, MALLOW,
CO. CORK
TEL: 022-22770 FAX: 022-22732
EMAIL: cortiganhouse@eircom.net

GUESTHOUSE ★★★ MAP 2 G 4

AA selected ◆◆◆◆. Period house in town on 2 acres of landscaped gardens overlooking Mallow Castle, Deerpark and river Blackwater renowned for its game angling. All en suite bedrooms are equipped with orthopaedic beds, power showers, hairdryers, radio, TV and phone. Residents lounges with library and open fires. Adjacent to 18-hole championship golf course. Game angling & horse riding arranged. 5 mins walk to excellent restaurants, pubs and genealogy centre.

WEB: www.cortiganhouse.com

Members Of Premier Guesthouses

B&B from £19.00 to £29.00
€24.13 to €36.82

LIONEL & SHEILA BUCKLEY
Proprietors

Mastercard

Visa

☺ Midweek specials from £55.00

Closed 22 - 30 December

HIBERNIAN HOTEL

MAIN STREET, MALLOW,
CO. CORK
TEL: 022-21588 FAX: 022-22632

HOTEL ★★★ MAP 2 G 4

The Hibernian Hotel blends olde-world surroundings with modern conveniences and comforts in a warm, friendly atmosphere. Situated in the heart of Munster, the Hibernian is an ideal base for touring Cork and Kerry. All rooms are equipped with multi-channel TV, hairdryer, tea/coffee making facilities, trouser press and phone. ISDN lines available. A choice of restaurants and lounge bars are available. Decorated to high standards. A warm welcome awaits you.

B&B from £32.00 to £37.00
€40.63 to €46.98

DÁIRE MANNION
General Manager

American Express

Diners

Mastercard

Visa

Closed 25 - 26 December

Room rates are per room per night

LONGUEVILLE HOUSE & PRESIDENTS' RESTAURANT

MALLOW,
CO. CORK
TEL: 022-47156 FAX: 022-47459
EMAIL: info@longuevillehouse.ie

HOTEL ★★★★ MAP 2 G 4

Longueville stands on a wooded eminence in a 500 acre private estate, overlooking the Blackwater Valley, itself famous for its game fishing and private walks. The aim at Longueville is peace and relaxation and for guests to partake only of its own fresh produce, superbly prepared by William O'Callaghan. Longueville is an ideal base for touring the scenic south-west, to laze by the fire in the drawing room, or to enjoy the peace and serenity of the estate. Member of Relais et Châteaux.

WEB: www.longuevillehouse.ie

Members Of Ireland's Blue Book

B&B from £57.50 to £85.00
€73.01 to €107.93

WILLIAM O'CALLAGHAN
Chef/Proprietor

American Express
Diners
Mastercard
Visa

20 20

S alc

Closed 19 December - 11 February

MALLOW PARK HOTEL

MAIN STREET, MALLOW,
CO. CORK
TEL: 022-21527 FAX: 022-51222
EMAIL: hotel@anu.ie

HOTEL ★★ MAP 2 G 4

The Mallow Park Hotel situated in the centre of Mallow is a handsome structure with an excellent and historical facade. The hotel interior has just recently been completely refurbished and is decorated to the highest standard with a warm and welcoming foyer lounge, coffee dock, An Síbín - traditional bar, Wedgewood Ballroom and carvery rooms plus luxurious rooms. Ideal for touring the south west, Blarney, the Ring of Kerry and West Cork. Excellent angling on the renowned Blackwater, other local facilities include golf and horseriding.

B&B from £30.00 to £40.00
€38.09 to €50.79

SEAN GLEESON
General Manager

American Express
Mastercard
Visa

36 36

alc

☺ Weekend specials from £65.00

Closed 25 December

SPRINGFORT HALL

MALLOW,
CO. CORK
TEL: 022-21278 FAX: 022-21557
EMAIL: stay@springfort-hall.com

HOTEL ★★★ MAP 2 G 4

Springfort Hall 18th century Georgian manor house, owned by the Walsh family. Highly recommended restaurant, fully licensed bar, bedrooms en suite, coloured TV and direct outside dial. 6km from Mallow off the Limerick road, N20. Ideal for touring the southwest, Blarney, Killarney, Ring of Kerry. Local amenities, 18-hole golf course, horse riding, angling on River Blackwater. Gulliver Central Reservations.

WEB: www.springfort-hall.com

Members Of Green Book of Ireland

B&B from £33.00 to £45.00
€41.90 to €57.14

WALSH FAMILY
Proprietors

American Express
Diners
Mastercard
Visa

50 50

alc

☺ Weekend specials from £85.00

Closed 23 December - 02 January

B&B rates are per person sharing per night incl. Breakfast

BARNABROW COUNTRY HOUSE

BARNABROW HOUSE, CLOYNE,
MIDLETON, EAST CORK
TEL: 021-652534
EMAIL: barnabrow@eircom.net

GUESTHOUSE ★★★ MAP 3 1 3

17th century family-run country house set in 35 acres of parkland adjacent to the historic village of Cloyne (580AD). The house has been extensively refurbished to offer a perfect blend of old world charm and new world comfort. Mor Chluana, the restaurant at Barnabrow, is named after Mor, the fairy godess of Cloyne. This is the perfect setting to relax and soak up an atmosphere of peaceful unhurried living with log fires and candlelit dinners. Nearby: Ballymaloe & Stephen Pearse.

WEB: www.indigo.ie/ipress/bch/contact.htm

Members Of Cork Region Marketing

B&B from £35.00 to £45.00
€44.44 to €57.14

GERALDINE O'BRIEN

Mastercard
Visa

Closed 21 - 28 December

MIDLETON PARK HOTEL

OLD CORK ROAD, MIDLETON,
CO. CORK
TEL: 021-631767   FAX: 021-631605
EMAIL: reservations@midletonparkhotel.ie

HOTEL ★★★ MAP 3 1 3

Midleton Park Hotel is situated in scenic east Cork on the N25, only 16k from Cork city. Our friendly professional staff offers attentive service and traditional hospitality which, when combined with its reputation for award-winning cuisine, makes Midleton Park Hotel an ideal choice for business or pleasure. Egon Ronay and AA recommended. Our guest rooms are tastefully furnished. Adjacent to blue flag beaches, championship golf courses, heritage trails and wildlife sanctuary.

WEB: www.kingsleyhotels.com

Members Of Signature Hotels

B&B from £35.00 to £65.00
€44.44 to €82.53

FINBARR MALONE
General Manager

American Express
Diners
Mastercard
Visa

Closed 25 December

FIR GROVE HOTEL

CAHIR HILL, MITCHELSTOWN,
CO. CORK
TEL: 025-24111   FAX: 025-84541

HOTEL ★★ MAP 3 1 5

The Fir Grove Hotel is a modern hotel, set in its own grounds beneath the Galtee Mountains. Situated on the main Cork/Dublin road, we are central to most of Munster's large towns and cities. We have a restaurant that serves good local food with a friendly service. All bedrooms are en suite with central heating and TV. Local facilities include golf, fishing, hill walks and pony trekking.

B&B from £24.00 to £25.00
€30.47 to €31.74

PAT & BRENDA TANGNEY
Proprietors

American Express
Diners
Mastercard
Visa

Closed 24 - 25 December

Room rates are per room per night

CELTIC ROSS HOTEL & LEISURE CENTRE

ROSSCARBERY,
WEST CORK
TEL: 023-48722   FAX: 023-48723
EMAIL: info@celticrosshotel.com

HOTEL ★★★ MAP 2 F 1

The Celtic Ross is a new 3*** luxury hotel, set in Rosscarbery Bay. West Cork is renowned for its beautiful scenery and fresh food. The hotel truly captures this uniqueness. Come and relax in this oasis of peace and allow us to pamper you. Facilities include 67 guest rooms, many overlooking the bay, Druids restaurant, Library & tower, traditional Old Forge pub & eaterie with regular entertainment, leisure centre including pool, gym, steam room and sauna. Reservations: 1800-272737

WEB: www.celticrosshotel.com

B&B from £40.00 to £80.00
€50.79 to €101.58

FRANK NOLAN

American Express
Diners
Mastercard
Visa

:/ ♪⊐♋

67 67

♪PS🌐🅰️ald🍴🍺

Open All Year

COLLA HOUSE HOTEL

COLLA, SCHULL,
CO. CORK
TEL: 028-28105   FAX: 028-28497

HOTEL ★ MAP 2 D 1

An attractive family run hotel situated in a magnificent position overlooking the sea, with panoramic views of the Atlantic Ocean, Cape Clear and Carbery's Hundred Isles. It is surrounded by its own pitch & putt course running direct to the sea. Colla House also has its own horse-riding school on its grounds. All bedrooms en suite with direct dial telephone and TV. Local amenities include 18 hole golf course, deep sea angling and boat trips to islands.

B&B from £25.00 to £35.00
€31.74 to €44.44

MARTIN O'DONOVAN
Proprietor

American Express
Diners
Mastercard
Visa

:/♩

☺ Weekend specials from £65.00

10 10

🅰️ald

Open All Year

EAST END

SCHULL,
CO. CORK
TEL: 028-28101   FAX: 028-28012

HOTEL ★★ MAP 2 D 1

A family run hotel overlooking Schull harbour and within walking distance of the numerous amenities in this cosmopolitan village. The hotel's kitchen uses fresh produce and provides quality food all day. TV and DD phone in all bedrooms. Dine alfresco in our new patio garden. We especially welcome families with young children.

Members Of Irish Family Hotels

B&B from £27.50 to £45.00
€34.92 to €57.14

DERRY & DOROTHY ROCHE
Proprietors

American Express
Diners
Mastercard
Visa

♩

17 15

Closed 23 - 27 December

B&B rates are per person sharing per night incl. Breakfast

BALLYMALOE HOUSE

SHANAGARRY, MIDLETON,
CO. CORK
TEL: 021-652531   FAX: 021-652021
EMAIL: bmaloe@iol.ie

GUESTHOUSE ★★★★   MAP 3 I 3

A large country house on a 400 acre farm. Home and locally grown produce is served in the award winning restaurant. Small golf course, tennis court and outdoor pool. Sea and river fishing and riding can be arranged. The Allen family also run a craft and kitchen shop, the cafe at the Cork Municipal Art Gallery and the Ballymaloe Cookery School. Take the N25 from Cork City for approx 13 miles. Go right at roundabout towards Ballycotton. Ballymaloe House is 2 miles beyond Cloyne.

WEB: www.ballymaloe.ie

Members Of Ireland's Blue Book

B&B from £65.00 to £85.00
€82.53 to €107.93

MYRTLE ALLEN
Proprietor

American Express
Diners
Mastercard
Visa

☺   Reduced winter 2 day rates available

🛏🍴☎️T/A🅲➡CM❄🔍♉UP🅟🔲
32   32

Closed 24 - 26 December

GARRYVOE HOTEL

SHANAGARRY, MIDLETON,
CO. CORK
TEL: 021-646718   FAX: 021-646824

HOTEL ★★   MAP 3 I 3

Situated on Ballycotton Bay, miles of Blue Flag sandy beach, deep sea fishing at Ballycotton (4 miles), own tennis courts. 6 golf courses in the area. All bedrooms en suite with TV and direct dial telephone. The restaurant offers high quality Irish foods, featuring a daily selection of locally caught fish. Midleton 13km, Cork 32km.

B&B from £35.00 to £35.00
€44.44 to €44.44

CARMEL & JOHN O'BRIEN
Proprietors

American Express
Diners
Mastercard
Visa

🛏🍴☎️🔲T🅲➡CM❄🔍♉UP🅟🔲
19   19

alc

Closed 25 December

CASTLE

CASTLETOWNSHEND,
NEAR SKIBBEREEN, CO. CORK
TEL: 028-36100   FAX: 028-36166

GUESTHOUSE ★   MAP 2 F 1

18th century Townshend family home overlooking Castlehaven Harbour. Set in own grounds at water's edge with access to small beach and woods. Most bedrooms en suite on second floor with excellent sea views. Panelled hall/sitting room with TV and open fire. Breakfast in elegant dining room. Mary Ann's restaurant close by. Ideal for touring Cork and Kerry. Also self catering apartments and cottages. For illustrated brochure please apply.

B&B from £25.00 to £50.00
€31.74 to €63.49

MRS COCHRANE-TOWNSHEND

Mastercard
Visa

🛏🍴🅲➡CM❄🔍♉UP🅟▪
7   6

Closed 15 December - 15 January

Room rates are per room per night

ELDON HOTEL

BRIDGE STREET, SKIBBEREEN,
WEST CORK
TEL: 028-22000 FAX: 028-22191
EMAIL: welcome@eldon-hotel.ie

HOTEL ★★ MAP 2 E 1

As a small family hotel our aim is to provide the best of the simple things in life; good food, good drink and good company. Michael Collins found these while visiting the Eldon in the 1920s, our guests tell us they still find them today! Following this tradition, the renowned Restaurant in Blue, Schull, invites you to their new Bistro Blue where the quality and standards of their exclusive kitchens can be enjoyed at the Eldon.

WEB: eldon-hotel.com

Members Of Logis of Ireland

B&B from £25.00 to £45.00
€31.74 to €57.14

ARTHUR LITTLE/LYDIA O'FARRELL
Managers

Mastercard
Visa

☺ Midweek specials from £64.50

19 19

Closed 25 - 26 December

WEST CORK HOTEL

ILEN STREET, SKIBBEREEN,
CO. CORK
TEL: 028-21277 FAX: 028-22333

HOTEL ★★★ MAP 2 E 1

The West Cork Hotel offers one of the warmest welcomes you will find in Ireland, and combines old-fashioned courtesy with the comfort of tastefully decorated and well-equipped accommodation. Guests can enjoy the friendly bar atmosphere or dine in the elegant restaurant. However long your stay the West Cork Hotel is the perfect base from which to discover and explore the glorious surroundings and activities available in West Cork.

B&B from £30.00 to £40.00
€38.09 to €50.79

JOHN MURPHY
General Manager

American Express
Diners
Mastercard
Visa

☺ Weekend specials from £74.00

30 30

Closed 22 - 27 December

AHERNE'S TOWNHOUSE & SEAFOOD RESTAURANT

163 NORTH MAIN STREET,
YOUGHAL, CO. CORK
TEL: 024-92424 FAX: 024-93633
EMAIL: ahernes@eircom.net

GUESTHOUSE ★★★★ MAP 3 J 3

Open turf fires and the warmest of welcomes await you in this family run hotel in the historic walled port of Youghal. Our rooms exude comfort and luxury, stylishly furnished with antiques and paintings. Our restaurant and bar food menus specialise in the freshest of locally landed seafood. Youghal is on the N25, 35 mins from Cork Airport and is a golfers' paradise. There are 18 golf courses within 1 hours drive. Find us in Ireland's Blue Book and other leading guides.

WEB: www.ahernes.com

Members Of Ireland's Blue Book

B&B from £50.00 to £60.00
€63.49 to €76.18

THE FITZGIBBON FAMILY

American Express
Diners
Mastercard
Visa

☺ Weekend specials from £109.00

12 12

Closed 24 December - 03 January

B&B rates are per person sharing per night incl. Breakfast

DEVONSHIRE ARMS HOTEL & RESTAURANT

PEARSE SQUARE, YOUGHAL,
CO. CORK
TEL: 024-92827   FAX: 024-92900

HOTEL ★★ MAP 3 J 3

Luxurious old world family run hotel. Centrally located in the town of Youghal with Blue Flag Beach, 18 hole golf course, riding and historical walking tours. All bedrooms individually decorated, TV, direct dial telephone, hair dryer and valet cleaning unit service. Our restaurant (AA2 Rosettes) offers fresh seafood and a wide range of dishes to suit all tastes, also à la carte bar menu. Half an hour from Cork, two hour drive from Rosslare N25. Member of Logis of Ireland Tel: 01-6689743.

Members Of Logis of Ireland

B&B from £35.00 to £40.00
€44.44 to €50.79

STEPHEN & HELEN O'SULLIVAN
Proprietors

American Express
Diners
Mastercard
Visa

🛏️🐾📞🅿️🆃🆑➡️CM❄️🅾️🎵🎵🄿🆂
10 10

🚪🄰🅖♿

Closed 24 - 31 December

WALTER RALEIGH HOTEL

O'BRIENS PLACE, YOUGHAL,
CO. CORK
TEL: 024-92011   FAX: 024-93560

HOTEL ★★ MAP 3 J 3

A family run and owned hotel where special emphasis is placed on service, comfort and value for money for our guests. We are ideally located on the N25. Youghal is a lovely heritage town steeped in history on the mouth of the river Blackwater. We are within half hour's drive of 10 first class golf courses. We have miles of safe blue flag beaches. There are lots of things for families to do in East Cork/West Waterford which makes our hotel an ideal location.

Members Of MinOtel Ireland Hotel Group

B&B from £30.00 to £40.00
€38.09 to €50.79

EDMUND & MARY MURPHY
Owners

American Express
Mastercard
Visa

😊 Weekend specials from £70.00

🛏️🐾📞🅿️🆃🆑➡️CM🎵🄿🆂🄰🆔▪️
38 38

🏨 HOTELS FEDERATION

Closed 26 - 31 December

CLIFF HOUSE HOTEL

CLIFF ROAD, BALLYBUNION,
CO. KERRY
TEL: 068-27777   FAX: 068-27783

HOTEL ★★★ MAP 5 D 6

The Cliff House Hotel is a natural base from which to explore Ireland's southwest coast. To the north are, the Shannon Estuary, the Burren of Clare, the mighty Cliffs of Moher. To the south are, the Dingle peninsula, the Ring of Kerry, the Lakes of Killarney. Commanding a glorious vantage above Ballybunion beach, this 3*** hotel is a golfers' home from home with the world ranked Ballybunion links nearby. Our Carraig restaurant offers a wholesome menu of fresh local food.

Members Of Holiday Ireland Hotels

B&B from £35.00 to £75.00
€44.44 to €95.23

KEVIN O'CALLAGHAN
Director

American Express
Diners
Mastercard
Visa

🛏️🐾📞🅿️🆃🆑➡️CM🅾️🎵🄿🆂
40 40

🚪🆔▪️

🏨 HOTELS FEDERATION

Closed 24 - 26 December

Room rates are per room per night

EAGLE LODGE

BALLYBUNION,
CO. KERRY
TEL: 068-27224

GUESTHOUSE R MAP 5 D 6

Owner managed, delightful guesthouse situated in town centre. All bedrooms with bathrooms and central heating throughout. A beautiful lounge and private car park for guests. Local amenities include two championship golf courses, sea fishing, tennis, pitch and putt, swimming and boating. Extra value reduced green fees at Ballybunion Golf Club. Cliff walks and surfing also available.

B&B from £20.00 to £30.00
€25.39 to €38.09

MILDRED GLEASURE

88

HOTELS
FEDERATION

Open All Year

HARTY COSTELLO TOWN HOUSE

MAIN STREET, BALLYBUNION,
CO. KERRY
TEL: 068-27129 FAX: 068-27489

GUESTHOUSE ★★★★ MAP 5 D 6

8 luxury bedrooms en suite, in a Townhouse style, all modern conveniences. Elegant dining with traditional high standards of fresh food and wine in our Seafood Restaurant and Bar. Table d'hôte and extensive à la carte menu's available. Local amenities, two championship golf links, cliff walks, hot seaweed baths, fishing, four golden beaches and bird watching. Ideal base for golfers or touring.

B&B from £30.00 to £45.00
€38.09 to €57.14

DAVNET & JACKIE HOURIGAN
Owners

American Express

Mastercard

Visa

88

HOTELS
FEDERATION

Closed 30 October - 01 April

MARINE LINKS HOTEL

SANDHILL ROAD, BALLYBUNION,
CO. KERRY
TEL: 068-27139 FAX: 068-27666
EMAIL: marinelinkshotel@eircom.net

HOTEL ★★ MAP 5 D 6

A small intimate owner-managed hotel with 10 rooms overlooking the mouth of the Shannon which welcomes golfers and holidaymakers from all over the world who enjoy the local amenities of golf, blue flag sandy beaches, hot seaweed baths, cliff walks, fishing, cycling and pony trekking. The restaurant is recognised in the area for fine dining with a table d'hôte and extensive à la carte menu served nightly.

WEB: www.travel-ireland.com/irl/marine.htm

Members Of Irish Family Hotels

B&B from £30.00 to £45.00
€38.09 to €57.14

R. RAFTER & S. WILLIAMSON
Proprietors

American Express

Diners

Mastercard

Visa

Weekend specials from £69.00

10 10

HOTELS
FEDERATION

Closed 01 November - 12 March

B&B rates are per person sharing per night incl. Breakfast

SOUTHERN HOTEL

SANDHILL ROAD, BALLYBUNION,
CO. KERRY
TEL: 068-27022   FAX: 068-27085
EMAIL: southotel@eircom.net

HOTEL U   MAP 5 D 6

The Southern Hotel overlooks
Ballybunion's spacious beaches and
the 9th hole of Ballybunion golf
course. Residents qualify for a
special reduction in green fees from
October to May. All rooms have, in
addition to standard facilities,
elegant designer furniture and many
have stunning sea views. The hotel
is family owned and its size allows
a level of personal attention not often
possible in larger hotels.

WEB: www.iol.ie/kerry-insight/southern

B&B from £25.00 to £50.00
€31.74 to €63.49

THOMAS O'BRIEN

American Express
Mastercard
Visa

Week partial board from
£198.00

15 15

Closed 08 January - 20 April

TEACH DE BROC

LINK ROAD, BALLYBUNION,
CO. KERRY
TEL: 068-27581   FAX: 068-27919
EMAIL: teachdebroc@eircom.net

GUESTHOUSE ★★★★   MAP 5 D 6

This family-run unique property,
noted for its enviable location and
quality accommodation offering
standard and deluxe rooms, is just 2
mins walk to Ballybunion's 1st tee
and 10yds to Ballybunion's practice
ground. Built in 1994 to combine all
modern amenities with the elegance
of an earlier age. Teach de Broc
plays host to the many visitors who
come to golf the great courses of
Kerry. Concession green fees
available from October to June.
Quality 4**** accommodation.

WEB: www.ballybuniongolf.com

B&B from £30.00 to £50.00
€38.09 to €63.49

SEAMUS AND AOIFE BROCK
Owners

Mastercard
Visa

10 10

Open All Year

BRASSILS GUEST HOUSE

MAIN STREET, BALLYHEIGUE,
CO. KERRY
TEL: 066-713 3707   FAX: 066-713 3112

GUESTHOUSE ★★   MAP 1 D 6

Bord Failte registered guesthouse in
the seaside resort located 19.3km
from the county capital, Tralee, and
32km Kerry County airport and
within an hours drive from Killarney
and Ballybunion's 18 hole courses.
Ideal location for touring the Ring of
Kerry. Ballyheigue offers 4.8km of
safe Blue Flag beach with maritime
centre and spectacular 9 hole golf
course and walkway around Kerry
Head overlooking Tralee bay, Mount
Brandon and Shannon estuary. The
village has many other facilities.

B&B from £16.00 to £22.00
€20.32 to €27.93

MARY BRASSIL
Proprietor

Mastercard
Visa

9 9

Closed 01 November - 01 April

Room rates are per room per night

DERRYNANE HOTEL

CAHERDANIEL, RING OF KERRY,
CO. KERRY
TEL: 066-947 5136   FAX: 066-947 5160
EMAIL: info@derrynane.com

HOTEL ★★★   MAP 1 C 2

Amidst the most spectacular scenery in Ireland, halfway round the famous Ring of Kerry (on the N70) lies the Derrynane Hotel offering you all the pleasures of an elegant modern 3*** hotel with 74 en suite bedrooms. Facilities include 15m outdoor heated pool, steamroom, sauna, gym and tennis court. We are surrounded by beautiful beaches and hills, lovely walks and Derrynane House and National Park. Deep sea angling, lake fishing, golf, horseriding, seasports, boat trips to Skellig Rock all within a short distance.

WEB: www.derrynane.com

Members Of Best Western Hotels

B&B from £38.50 to £49.50
€48.88 to €62.85

MARY O'CONNOR
Manager/Director

American Express
Diners
Mastercard
Visa

😊 Weekend specials from £79.00

74 74

Closed 15 October - 15 April

SCARRIFF INN

CAHERDANIEL,
CO. KERRY
TEL: 066-947 5132   FAX: 066-947 5425
EMAIL: scarriff@indigo.ie

GUESTHOUSE R   MAP 1 C 3

This family-run guesthouse overlooks the best view in Ireland, with majestic views of Derrynane, Kenmare and Bantry Bay, situated halfway round the Ring of Kerry. All our rooms have seaview. Dine in our seafood restaurant and enjoy outstanding cuisine as recommended by Sir Andrew Lloyd Webber or relax in our Vista bar and enjoy scenery and ambience. The area is varied in activities, the Kerry Way, several beautiful beaches within walking distance. Day trips to Skellig Rocks.

WEB: www.caherdaniel.net

B&B from £19.95 to £25.95
€25.33 to €32.95

KATIE O'CARROLL
Proprietor

Mastercard
Visa

6 6

Closed 30 October - 05 March

BARNAGH BRIDGE COUNTRY GUEST HOUSE

CAMP, TRALEE,
CO. KERRY
TEL: 066-713 0145   FAX: 066-713 0299
EMAIL: mwarch@iol.ie

GUESTHOUSE ★★★   MAP 1 C 5

Between the mountains and sea on the Dingle peninsula. In landscaped grounds, architect's guesthouse combines modern character with traditional cooking and friendly atmosphere. Family run with delightful breakfasts. Local golfing, fishing, walking & horse riding. AA ◆◆◆◆ Selected and Frommers listed as stunning house offering exceptional value. Peaceful rural retreat with a 'friendly welcome, a good bed & beauty all around'. Leave the N86 at Camp, follow Conor Pass Rd R560 for 1 mile.

Members Of Premier Guesthouses

B&B from £16.00 to £25.00
€20.32 to €31.74

HEATHER WILLIAMS
Host

American Express
Mastercard
Visa

5 5

Closed 31 October - 01 March

B&B rates are per person sharing per night incl. Breakfast

ARD-NA-SIDHE

CARAGH LAKE, KILLORGLIN,
CO. KERRY
TEL: 066-976 9105   FAX: 066-976 9282
EMAIL: khl@iol.ie

HOTEL ★★★★   MAP 1 D 4

20 bedroom 4**** de luxe Victorian mansion delightfully located in its own park on Caragh Lake. Highest standards of comfort. Tastefully furnished with antiques and open fireplaces. Luxurious lounges and restaurant. Cosy spot for a quiet holiday. Free boating, fishing and facilities of sister hotels Europe and Dunloe Castle available to guests. 11 major golf courses nearby. Special green fees. Central Reservations Tel: 064-31900 Fax: 064-32118.

WEB: www.iol.ie/khl

B&B from £62.00 to £83.00
€78.72 to €105.39

KATHLEEN DOWLING
Resident Manager

American Express
Diners
Mastercard
Visa

Closed 01 October - 30 April

CARAGH LODGE

CARAGH LAKE,
CO. KERRY
TEL: 066-976 9115   FAX: 066-976 9316
EMAIL: caraghl@iol.ie

GUESTHOUSE ★★★★   MAP 1 D 4

A Victorian fishing lodge standing in 7.5 acres of parkland containing many rare and subtropical trees and shrubs. Winner of the National Garden Award. The gardens sweep down to Caragh Lake, ideal for trout fishing. The lounges and dining room are very comfortably furnished and overlook the gardens and lake. Excellent cuisine includes local lamb and wild salmon. Golf and beaches within 5 minutes.

Members Of Ireland's Blue Book

B&B from £57.50 to £72.50
€73.01 to €92.06

MARY GAUNT
Owner

American Express
Diners
Mastercard
Visa

Closed 17 October - 21 April

GLENCAR HOUSE HOTEL

GLENCAR,
CO. KERRY
TEL: 066-976 0102   FAX: 066-976 0167
EMAIL: glencarh@iol.ie

HOTEL ★★   MAP 1 C 4

The Glencar House Hotel, built in 1732, lies framed by the McGillycuddy Reeks mountains and is 2k from Caragh Lake. Declared an area of Special Conservation in 1997, it is the perfect base for a relaxing or activity holiday. Local golf courses include Dooks, Beaufort and Killarney. Traditional Irish cuisine is served in our restaurant. Salmon and trout fishing is available on the Caragh fishery and boats are for hire on Caragh Lake. All bedrooms have private bath/shower and TV.

WEB: glencarhouse.com

B&B from £36.00 to £48.00
€45.71 to €60.95

SANDY HEPPEL
Manager

American Express
Diners
Mastercard
Visa

Open All Year

Room rates are per room per night

CRUTCH'S HILLVILLE HOUSE HOTEL

CONOR PASS ROAD, CASTLEGREGORY,
DINGLE PENINSULA, CO. KERRY
TEL: 066-713 8118   FAX: 066-713 8159
EMAIL: macshome@iol.ie

HOTEL ★★   MAP 1 C 5

Delightful country house owned and managed by Ron & Sandra. Situated near Fermoyle Beach on Kerry's scenic Dingle Peninsula. Close to the highest mountain pass in Ireland - The Conor Pass, Slea Head Dingle & Killarney. The Fermoyle Room Restaurant offers traditional home cooking using fresh local produce, vegetarians, special diets catered for on request. A friendly country house atmosphere, generously sized rooms, some with four poster beds & sea views, cosy bar and open fires.

Members Of Coast and Country Hotels

B&B from £35.00 to £47.00
€44.44 to €59.68

RON & SANDRA
Proprietors

American Express
Diners
Mastercard
Visa

Open All Year

O'CONNOR'S GUESTHOUSE

CLOGHANE, DINGLE PENINSULA,
CO. KERRY
TEL: 066-713 8113   FAX: 066-713 8270
EMAIL: o'connorsguesthouse@eircom.net

GUESTHOUSE ★★   MAP 1 B 5

A long established, spacious country home with spectacular views of sea and mountains, overlooking Brandon Bay and within easy reach of Dingle on the Dingle Way. Private car park, guest lounge, open fire, home cooked meals, pub and a warm welcome are just some of the things awaiting our guests.

B&B from £18.00 to £21.00
€22.86 to €26.66

MICHEAL & ELIZABETH O'DOWD
Owners

Closed 01 November - 28 February

ALPINE HOUSE

MAIL ROAD, DINGLE,
CO. KERRY
TEL: 066-915 1250   FAX: 066-915 1966

GUESTHOUSE ★★★   MAP 1 B 4

Superb guesthouse run by the O'Shea family. AA ♦♦♦♦ and RAC highly acclaimed. Elegant en suite bedrooms with TV, DD phone, hairdryers, central heating and tea/coffee facilities. Spacious dining room with choice of breakfast. Delightful guest lounge. 2 minutes walk to town centre, restaurants, harbour and bus stop. Local amenities include Slea Head drive and Blasket Islands, also pony trekking, angling and boat trips to Fungi the dolphin.

B&B from £17.50 to £27.50
€22.22 to €34.92

PAUL O'SHEA
Manager

Mastercard
Visa

IRISH
HOTELS
FEDERATION

Open All Year

B&B rates are per person sharing per night incl. Breakfast

BAMBURY'S GUEST HOUSE

MAIL ROAD, DINGLE,
CO. KERRY
TEL: 066-915 1244   FAX: 066-915 1786
EMAIL: bamburysguesthouse@eircom.net

GUESTHOUSE ★★★   MAP 1 B 4

AA selected ◆◆◆◆, new house, excellent location, 2 minutes walk to town centre. Offering peaceful accommodation in spacious, double, twin or triple rooms all with en suite, direct dial telephone and satellite TV. Attractive guest lounge to relax in. Private car parking, choice of breakfast in spacious dining room. Local attractions, Dingle Peninsula, horse riding, angling and golf on local 18 hole golf links. Reduced green fees can be arranged. Listed in all leading guides.

B&B from £18.00 to £30.00
€22.86 to €38.09

BERNIE BAMBURY
Proprietor

Mastercard

Visa

☺ Midweek specials from £45.00

🛏📻☎🖨🚶♨⛵🅿
12 12

IRISH HOTELS FEDERATION

Open All Year

BENNERS HOTEL

MAIN STREET, DINGLE,
CO. KERRY
TEL: 066-915 1638   FAX: 066-915 1412
EMAIL: benners@eircom.net

HOTEL ★★★   MAP 1 B 4

A 300 year old hotel with young ideas. Benners is a timeless part of Kerry's proud holiday tradition. Its part of the emotional experience that lingers on... long after a visit to the magnificent Dingle peninsula. Benners is synonymous with excellence in comfort and cuisine, specialising in a daily fresh Atlantic catch. Our rooms are all en suite with antique furniture, hairdryer, TV, DD phone and tea/coffee facilities. Open all year. Special weekend and midweek packages available.

Members Of Best Western Hotels

B&B from £30.00 to £65.00
€38.09 to €82.53

PAT GALVIN
General Manager

American Express

Diners

Mastercard

Visa

☺ Weekend specials from £69.00

🛏📻☎🖨🈂T C♨CM❄⛵🅿🆂
52 52

🔒🅰⬛

IRISH HOTELS FEDERATION

Closed 25 - 26 December

BOLAND'S GUESTHOUSE

GOAT STREET, DINGLE,
CO. KERRY
TEL: 066-915 1426

UNDER CONSTRUCTION OPENING JAN 2000

GUESTHOUSE P   MAP 1 B 4

A warm welcome awaits you in our family run guesthouse. Situated in Dingle town with panoramic views of Dingle Bay. All our rooms are en suite with DD phones, TV, hairdryers, tea/coffee making facilities. Full breakfast menu in our conservatory dining room. Relax and enjoy the magnificent views of Dingle Bay from our guest lounge. Boland's is A.A. selected and R.A.C. listed.

B&B from £18.00 to £27.50
€22.86 to €34.92

BREDA BOLAND
Owner

Mastercard

Visa

🛏📻☎🈂T C♨⛵⬛
9 9

Closed 01 December - 01 January

Room rates are per room per night

CAPTAINS HOUSE

**THE MALL, DINGLE,
CO. KERRY**
TEL: 066-915 1531   FAX: 066-915 1079
EMAIL: captigh@eircom.net

GUESTHOUSE ★★★   MAP 1 B 4

A welcome awaits you at the Captains House situated in Dingle town. Approached by foot bridge over the Mall stream and through award winning gardens our three star family run guest house is tastefully furnished with items collected on the Captains voyages. All rooms are en suite with direct dial telephones and TV. A breakfast menu featuring home made bread and preserves is served in the conservatory overlooking the garden.

WEB. homepage.eircom.nct/·-captigh/

B&B from £25.00 to £30.00
€31.74 to €38.09

MARY & JIM MILHENCH
Proprietors
American Express
Diners
Mastercard
Visa

Closed 01 December - 16 March

CLEEVAUN COUNTRY LODGE

**LADYS CROSS, MILLTOWN, DINGLE,
CO. KERRY**
TEL: 066-915 1108   FAX: 066-915 2228
EMAIL: cleevaun@iol.ie

GUESTHOUSE ★★★   MAP 1 B 4

Galtee Regional Breakfast Winner 1994. Cleevaun is set in landscaped gardens overlooking Dingle Bay, 1 mile from Dingle town. Rooms with private bathrooms, TV's, hairdryers, tea/coffee facilities. Relax and enjoy the magnificent views of Dingle Bay from our breakfast room while you choose from our award winning menu. Often described as an oasis of peace and tranquility. Cleevaun is commended by AA, RAC, and Karen Browne. Local amenities golf, walking, pony trekking.

WEB: www.iol.ie~cleevaun index html

B&B from £20.00 to £33.00
€25.39 to €41.90

CHARLOTTE CLUSKEY
Host
Mastercard
Visa

HOTELS

Closed 30 November - 15 March

COASTLINE GUESTHOUSE

**THE WOOD, DINGLE,
CO. KERRY**
TEL: 066-915 2494   FAX: 066-915 2493
EMAIL: coastlinedingle@eircom.net

GUESTHOUSE N   MAP 1 B 4

Beautiful new guesthouse on the water's edge of Dingle Bay. All rooms are en suite with DD phone, TV, hairdryer, tea/coffee making facilities and many have panoramic views of the harbour. Ground floor rooms available. Enjoy our excellent breakfast and relax in our sitting room in the evening and watch the fishing fleet return with their catch. Private car park. 5 minutes walk to town centre. Ideal base to enjoy all Dingle has to offer - excellent restaurants and pubs.

B&B from £17.50 to £26.00
€22.22 to €33.01

VIVIENNE O'SHEA
Proprietor
Mastercard
Visa

HOTELS

Open All Year

B&B rates are per person sharing per night incl. Breakfast

CONNORS

DYKEGATE STREET, DINGLE,
CO. KERRY
TEL: 066-915 1598 FAX: 066-915 2376

GUESTHOUSE ★★ MAP 1 B 4

Welcome to our newly refurbished guesthouse. All rooms en suite with TV, clock radio, hairdryer, DD phone, tea/coffee making facilities, central heating, orthopaedic beds. We are situated in the heart of Dingle town. Within walking distance to all restaurants and pubs.
Recommended Guide Du Routard, Rick Steves Guide to Ireland and Stilwells Guide. Breakfast menu available in our spacious dining room. Packed lunches available on request.

B&B from £18.00 to £27.00
€22.86 to €34.28

CAROL CONNOR
Proprietor

American Express
Mastercard
Visa

15 15

Closed 22 - 26 December

DINGLE SKELLIG HOTEL

DINGLE,
CO. KERRY
TEL: 066-915 1144 FAX: 066-915 1501
EMAIL: dsk@iol.ie

HOTEL ★★★★ MAP 1 B 4

Renowned hotel situated on the beautiful harbour of Dingle Bay. Luxurious leisure club & pool with jacuzzi, geyser pool, children's pool, steamroom and gymnasium. Ki-massage, reflexology and aromatherapy. Fungi kids club and creche available weekends and holidays. Excellent cuisine specialising in locally caught seafood. New conference and banqueting centre with stunning views for up to 250 people. Reduced green fees and guaranteed tee times (including weekends) at Ceann Sibeal.

WEB: www.dingleskellig.com

B&B from £40.00 to £95.00
€50.79 to €120.63

PHILIP GAVIN
General Manager

American Express
Diners
Mastercard
Visa

Weekend specials from £95.00

116 116

IRISH
HOTELS
FEDERATION

Closed 05 January - 11 February

DOYLES SEAFOOD BAR & TOWN HOUSE

JOHN STREET, DINGLE,
CO. KERRY
TEL: 066-915 1174 FAX: 066-915 1816
EMAIL: cdoyles@iol.ie

GUESTHOUSE ★★★★ MAP 1 B 4

Eight bedrooms all generous in size, warm with comfortable furniture, full bathroom attached, direct dial telephone and TV. The restaurant has an old range, sugan chairs, kitchen tables. Natural stone and wood combined give Doyles a cosy country atmosphere. Lobster our speciality, is chosen from a tank in the bar. The menu consists only of fresh food and is chosen on a daily basis from the fish landed by the Dingle boats.

WEB: www.iol.ie/~cdoylesindexhtml

Members Of Ireland's Blue Book

B&B from £25.00 to £40.00
€31.74 to €50.79

SEAN CLUSKEY
Host

Mastercard
Visa

8 8

IRISH
HOTELS
FEDERATION

Closed 15 December - 15 February

Room rates are per room per night

GREENMOUNT HOUSE

UPPER JOHN STREET, DINGLE,
CO. KERRY
TEL: 066-915 1414   FAX: 066-915 1974

GUESTHOUSE ★★★★   MAP 1 B 4

Greenmount House is the proud recipient of the 1997 RAC Guest House of the Year for Ireland. A charming 4★★★★ country house yet centrally located. Spacious lounges to relax in and take advantage of its magnificent scenic location overlooking Dingle town & harbour. Each bedroom has private bathroom TV/radio & DD phone. Award winning buffet breakfasts served in conservatory with commanding views of Dingle. Luxurious, peaceful retreat. Recognised by all leading guides.

WEB: www.greenmounthouse.com

B&B from £20.00 to £40.00
€25.39 to €50.79

JOHN & MARY CURRAN
Owners

Mastercard

Visa

Closed 20 - 26 December

HEATON'S GUESTHOUSE

THE WOOD, DINGLE,
CO. KERRY
TEL: 066-915 2288   FAX: 066-915 2324
EMAIL: heatons@iol.ie

GUESTHOUSE ★★★★   MAP 1 B 4

Superb new family run guesthouse situated on the shore of Dingle bay, 5 minutes walk from the town. All rooms are en suite (pressure shower and bath), with TV, DD phone and tea/coffee welcome tray. Breakfast is our speciality. Local amenities include golf, sailing, fishing, surfing, cycling, walking, horse riding and the renowned gourmet restaurants.

WEB: www.euroka.com/dingle/heatons

B&B from £20.00 to £35.00
€25.39 to €44.44

CAMERON & NUALA HEATON
Proprietors

Mastercard

Visa

Open All Year

HILLGROVE HOTEL

SPA ROAD, DINGLE,
CO. KERRY
TEL: 066-915 1131   FAX: 066-915 1131

HOTEL ★   MAP 1 B 4

Family-owned and managed, the Hillgrove Hotel was upgraded in 1999. All rooms are finished to a high standard and are complete with bathroom, DD phone, TV and hairdryer. Large car park available. The Hillgrove offers a perfect combination of professional service with cheerful and helpful staff. We ensure that your stay is the highlight of your visit to Dingle.

B&B from £25.00 to £40.00
€31.74 to €50.79

SANDRA KENNEDY
Manager

Mastercard

Visa

Midweek specials from £75.00

Closed 01 November - 30 April

B&B rates are per person sharing per night incl. Breakfast

MILLTOWN HOUSE

MILLTOWN, DINGLE,
CO. KERRY
TEL: 066-915 1372 FAX: 066-915 1095
EMAIL: milltown@indigo.ie

GUESTHOUSE ★★★★ MAP 1 B 4

Milltown House is situated on the seashore overlooking Dingle bay. DD phone, satellite TV, tea/coffee making facilities and hairdryer. All rooms en suite. Some rooms offer panoramic views of the bay or have private patios. Some rooms wheelchair friendly. Assistance in planning your day. Milltown is an AA selected ◆◆◆◆, RAC highly acclaimed and is a 4**** award guesthouse by the Irish Tourist Board.

WEB: http://indigo.ie/~milltown/

B&B from £25.00 to £37.50
€31.74 to €47.62

ANNE AND MARK KERRY
Proprietors

Mastercard

Visa

✓

🛏🔌☎🖥C☼∪♩P♀☎
10 10

IRISH HOTELS FEDERATION

Closed 23 - 27 December

PAX HOUSE

UPPER JOHN STREET, DINGLE,
CO. KERRY
TEL: 066-915 1518 FAX: 066-915 2461
EMAIL: paxhouse@iol.ie

GUESTHOUSE ★★★★ MAP 1 B 4

Pax House has undeniably one of the most spectacular views in the whole peninsula. Quotes from our guest book: "a little bit of heaven", "peace, perfect peace". Situated 1km from Dingle town. All rooms luxuriously appointed in keeping with the Celtic theme of the area. A large gourmet breakfast greets guests each morning. Sit on the balcony in the evening and watch the boats return with their catch. AA ◆◆◆◆.

B&B from £25.00 to £35.00
€31.74 to €44.44

RON & JOAN BROSNAN WRIGHT
Owners

Mastercard

Visa

🛏🔌☎🖥TC↩CM☼∪♩P☎
7 7

IRISH HOTELS FEDERATION

Open All Year

SMERWICK HARBOUR HOTEL

BALLYFERRITER, DINGLE,
CO. KERRY
TEL: 066-915 6470 FAX: 066-915 6473

HOTEL ★★ MAP 1 B 5

Smerwick Harbour Hotel, Seafood restaurant with its old world bar, is located on Slea Head drive, 2k from Gallarus Oratory. Our local 18 hole golf course is on your doorstep, 4k away, reduced green fees for guests. All rooms en suite (family rooms also) with TV, DD phone, tea/coffee facilities. Spacious lounge. Enjoy excellent cuisine in our seafood restaurant, specialising in local seafood and char grilled steaks. Quality barfood also available. Old world ambience. The best sandy beaches in Ireland nearby.

B&B from £25.00 to £40.00
€31.74 to €50.79

MARIE HOULIHAN

Mastercard

Visa

✓♫

☺ Weekend specials from £70.00

🛏🔌☎🖥TC↩CM☼∪♩♫PS
16 15
🛏🅐ⓐⓛⓒ🍺

IRISH HOTELS FEDERATION

Closed 01 November - 01 April

Room rates are per room per night

TOWERS HOTEL

**GLENBEIGH,
CO. KERRY**
TEL: 066-976 8212 FAX: 066-976 8260
EMAIL: towershotel@eircom.net

HOTEL ★★★ MAP 1 C 4

The family run Towers Hotel, on the Ring of Kerry, is an ideal place to relax and enjoy the splendours of Kerry. The hotel is a short distance from sandy beaches and dramatic mountains. Paradise for golfers, walkers, fishermen and anyone interested in the Kerry landscape. The Towers internationally known restaurant is renowned for its excellent seafood and distinguished atmosphere. Its traditional pub provides a chance to mingle with the people of Glenbeigh in a real Kerry atmosphere.

Members Of Coast and Country Hotels

B&B from £39.00 to £48.00
€49.52 to €60.95

DOLORES SWEENEY
Proprietor

American Express
Mastercard
Visa

☺ Weekend specials from £70.00

28   28

Closed 30 October - 01 April

VILLAGE HOUSE

**GLENBEIGH,
CO. KERRY**
TEL: 066-976 8128 FAX: 066-976 8486
EMAIL: breensvillagehouse@eircom.net

GUESTHOUSE ★★★ MAP 1 C 4

A family run guesthouse on the Ring of Kerry and Kerry Way route. Rooms tastefully decorated, with all private facilities including TV and direct dial phone. Ideally situated for touring or golfing in Kerry. Dooks golf links is 2.4km. Also available in the area: horseriding, fishing, tennis, paragliding, orienteering, swimming - 13.6km of sandy beach. Year after year guests return to the Village House. Ample proof that you will be make welcome during you stay. R.A.C. Approved.

Members Of Premier Guesthouses

B&B from £20.00 to £25.00
€25.39 to €31.74

JOHN & MARGARET BREEN
Owners

American Express
Mastercard
Visa

9   9

IRISH HOTELS FEDERATION

Closed 23 - 27 December

BRASS LANTERN

**OLD RAILWAY ROAD, KENMARE,
CO. KERRY**
TEL: 064-42601 FAX: 064-42600
EMAIL: thebrasslantern@eircom.net

GUESTHOUSE ★★★ MAP 1 D 3

The Brass Lantern is ideally located just beyond Kenmare town green. Each of the rooms has beautiful custom-made ash furniture, en suite bathroom, TV and phone. The two ground-floor rooms are ideal for anyone who has difficulty with stairs. It's a two minute walk to Kenmare's famous gourmet restaurants and speciality shops. Local amenities include golf courses, fishing, watersports, pony-trekking and cycling. Ideal base from which to explore south Kerry and West Cork.

WEB: www.kenmare-insight.com/brasslantern

B&B from £20.00 to £30.00
€25.39 to €38.09

PADRAIG JONES
Manager

Mastercard
Visa

☺ Midweek specials from £60.00

8   8

IRISH HOTELS FEDERATION

Open All Year

B&B rates are per person sharing per night incl. Breakfast

DROMQUINNA MANOR HOTEL

BLACKWATER BRIDGE P.O.,
KENMARE, CO. KERRY
TEL: 064-41657 FAX: 064-41791
EMAIL: info@dromquinna.com

HOTEL ★★★ MAP 1 D 3

Breathtaking south facing views of sea, islands and mountains. 28 delightful bedrooms, fourposters, suites and Ireland's only tree house. Lace dining room, international cuisine. Informal atmosphere. Coach House annexe with 18 charming rooms including large family rooms. Kitchen gardens, marina, jetty, slipway, small beach, 42ft fishing launch, all watersports, children's playground, Boathouse Restaurant. Golf courses: Ring of Kerry 3mins, Kenmare 5mins. Well placed for sightseeing.

WEB: www.dromquinna.com

Members Of MinOtel Ireland Hotel Group

B&B from £35.00 to £75.00
€44.44 to €95.23

MIKE & SUE ROBERTSON
Proprietors

American Express
Diners
Mastercard
Visa

46 46

Closed 31 October - 01 March

DUNKERRON

SNEEM ROAD, KENMARE,
CO. KERRY
TEL: 064-41102 FAX: 064-41102

GUESTHOUSE ★★★ MAP 1 D 3

Situated on a 70 acre parkland estate with private sea frontage. The 12th century O Sullivan Mor Stronghold adds character to our Victorian home. Standing magnificently on the Ring of Kerry, adjoining the Beara Peninsula, there are wooded walks which add to the tranquil ambience which is an inherent feature of the estate. Log fires, wooden floors and the handcarved hall staircase contribute to the country house atmosphere. 10 en suite bedrooms. Par 2 golf course. Wine licence.

B&B from £25.00 to £45.00
€31.74 to €57.14

MOYA GUBBINS
Proprietor

Mastercard
Visa

10 10

IRISH
HOTELS
FEDERATION

Closed 31 October - 31 March

FOLEYS SHAMROCK

HENRY STREET, KENMARE,
CO. KERRY
TEL: 064-42162 FAX: 064-41799
EMAIL: foleyest@iol.ie

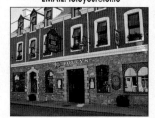

GUESTHOUSE ★★★ MAP 1 D 3

Foleys is situated in Kenmare, Kerry Heritage town, ten very comfortable centrally heated en suite rooms with colour TV, phone & tea making facilities, our chef owned restaurant & pub bistro serves Irish & international cuisine. Traditional session in pub. Foleys is within walking distance of Kenmare 18 hole golf course, horse riding & fishing trips can be arranged. One of Ireland's best Fodors. Also recognised by Routard & Michelin.

B&B from £20.00 to £28.50
€25.39 to €36.19

MARGARET FOLEY
Owner/Manager

Mastercard
Visa

10 10

Open All Year

Room rates are per room per night

KENMARE BAY HOTEL

KENMARE,
CO. KERRY
TEL: 064-41300 FAX: 064-41541
EMAIL: kenmare@leehotels.ie

HOTEL ★★★ MAP 1 D 3

We offer a quiet hospitality with panoramic views of both the Cork and Kerry mountains. By day you can choose from golfing, walking, fishing, touring and cycling; by night we offer quality cuisine followed by traditional Irish music in our lounge. Located in acres of parkland, we are only half a km from Ireland's most colourful heritage town - Kenmare.

Members Of Lee Hotels

B&B from £25.00 to £40.00
€31.74 to €50.79

TERRY O'DOHERTY
General Manager

American Express
Diners
Mastercard
Visa

136 136

Closed 01 November - 01 April

LANSDOWNE ARMS HOTEL

WILLIAM STREET, KENMARE,
CO. KERRY
TEL: 064-41368 FAX: 064-41114
EMAIL: lansdowne@kenmare.com

HOTEL ★★★ MAP 1 D 3

Town centre location established as Kenmare's first hotel by the 1st Marquis of Lansdowne and 2nd Earl of Shelburne when the town was planned, 1761. The basis of Kenmare is a 'heritage town'. The Lansdowne Arms is most ideal for visitors to park up their car and take in all that this town offers, wonderful shops, restaurants, heritage centre, golf links, all a minute's walk from your room. In the heart of the south west it is ideal for touring the gulf stream hinterland.

B&B from £30.00 to £45.00
€38.09 to €57.14

BREDA, BOBBY & PATRICK HANLEY
Owners

Mastercard
Visa

26 26

Closed 01 November - 31 March

LODGE

KILGARVAN ROAD, KENMARE,
CO. KERRY
TEL: 064-41512 FAX: 064-41812

UNDER CONSTRUCTION OPENING MAR 2000

GUESTHOUSE P MAP 1 D 3

Newly-built luxury guesthouse across from Kenmare's 18 hole golf course. Within 3 mins walk of some of the finest restaurants in Ireland. All rooms are elegantly furnished with en suite bathrooms, kingsize beds and central heating. Private parking. Also an ideal location for the activist with walking, cycling and horseriding nearby. 3 of the bedrooms are at ground level with 1 especially equipped for wheelchair use.

B&B from £20.00 to £30.00
€25.39 to €38.09

ROSEMARIE QUILL
Proprietor

American Express
Mastercard
Visa

10 10

Closed 01 November - 01 April

B&B rates are per person sharing per night incl. Breakfast

PARK HOTEL KENMARE

KENMARE,
CO. KERRY
TEL: 064-41200 FAX: 064-41402
EMAIL: phkenmare@iol.ie

HOTEL ★★★★★ MAP 1 D 3

Built in 1897, this Victorian Hotel overlooks the Kenmare estuary. Set in 11 acres of natural gardens it is a 2 minute walk from Kenmare town. Staff lace attentiveness with an attractive friendliness that makes guests feel really welcome. 18 hole golf course, tennis, croquet on property. Renowned for outstanding cuisine featuring the best local seafood. Recognised by all major guides AA Red Star, Michelin, Egon Ronay, Relais et Châteaux, Small Luxury Hotels of the World.

WEB: www.parkkenmare.com

Members Of Ireland's Blue Book

B&B from £122.00 to £175.00
€154.91 to €222.20

FRANCIS BRENNAN
Proprietor

American Express
Diners
Mastercard
Visa

2 B&B plus 1 Dinner from £210.00

49 49

18

Closed 02 January - 14 April

RIVERSDALE HOUSE HOTEL

KENMARE,
CO. KERRY
TEL: 064-41299 FAX: 064-41075
EMAIL: riversdale@eircom.net

HOTEL ★★★ MAP 1 D 3

Located on the scenic shores of Kenmare Bay and backed by the McGillycuddy Reeks and Caha mountains the hotel is the ideal choice to tour the famous Ring of Kerry and beautiful West Cork. Recently refurbished, the hotel boasts 4 luxurious suites, each with panoramic views of the scenery beyond our seven acre garden. Our Waterfront restaurant is renowned for its fine cuisine while local activities include an 18 hole golf course, deep sea angling, hill walking, cycling and water-skiing.

WEB: www.kenmare.com/riversdale

Members Of Best Western Hotels

B&B from £30.00 to £56.00
€38.09 to €71.11

PEGGY O'SULLIVAN
Proprietor

American Express
Diners
Mastercard
Visa

Weekend specials from £75.00

64 64

Closed 06 November - 22 March

ROSEGARDEN GUESTHOUSE

SNEEM RD (N70), KENMARE,
CO. KERRY
TEL: 064-42288 FAX: 064-42305
EMAIL: rosegard@iol.ie

GUESTHOUSE ★★★ MAP 1 D 3

The Rosegarden guesthouse and restaurant is situated within walking distance of Kenmare town, Ring of Kerry (N70). Set in 1 acre of landscaped garden with 350 roses. Private car park. All rooms en suite, power showers, centrally heated. Restaurant open from 6.30 pm. Menu includes lamb, steaks, salmon, stuffed crab, mussels and wine list. Enjoy our peaceful and relaxed ambience. We are looking forward to it. Ask for our 3 and 7 day specials.

WEB: www.euroka.com/rosegarden

B&B from £22.50 to £27.50
€28.57 to €34.92

INGRID & PETER RINGLEVER

American Express
Diners
Mastercard
Visa

Week partial board from £240.00

8 8

Closed 01 November - 31 March

Room rates are per room per night

SEA SHORE FARM

TUBRID, KENMARE,
CO. KERRY
TEL: 064-41270 FAX: 064-41270
EMAIL: seashore@eircom.net

GUESTHOUSE ★★★ MAP 1 D 3

Sea Shore Farm has unique setting on Kenmare Bay, peaceful, private yet only 1 mile from town. Spacious en suite rooms (DD phone, TV, tea facilities etc.), some rooms with king beds and panoramic seascapes. Wheelchair friendly. Our farm is rich in natural habitat and bird life. Unspoilt field walks to shore. Fitness suite and drying room. Private fishing facility on Roughty river. Signposted 300m from Kenmare by Esso station - junction N71/N70 Killarney road/Ring of Kerry Sneem road.

WEB: homepage.eircom.net/~seashore

B&B from £25.00 to £30.00
€31.74 to €38.09

MARY PATRICIA O'SULLIVAN
Proprietor

Mastercard
Visa

Closed 18 November - 14 March

SHEEN FALLS LODGE

KENMARE,
CO. KERRY
TEL: 064-41600 FAX: 064-41386
EMAIL: info@sheenfallslodge.ie

HOTEL ★★★★★ MAP 1 D 3

The lodge presides over a dramatic 300 acre estate above the Sheen Waterfalls and the Kenmare Bay. Superb dining is available in either La Cascade restaurant or Oscars bistro. Facilities on the estate include horseriding, tennis, clay shooting, salmon fishing, heli-pad and two 18 hole golf courses nearby; within the lodge, health and fitness centre, swimming pool, library, billiard room, wine cellar and conference facilities available for up to 120 delegates.

WEB: www.sheenfallslodge.ie

Members Of Relais & Châteaux

Room Rate from £168.00 to £258.00
€213.32 to €327.59

ADRIAAN BARTELS
General Manager

American Express
Diners
Mastercard
Visa

☺ Weekend specials from £205.00

Closed 03 December - 23 December

SHELBURNE LODGE

CORK ROAD, KENMARE,
CO. KERRY
TEL: 064-41013 FAX: 064-42135

GUESTHOUSE ★★★ MAP 1 D 3

Shelburne Lodge is situated on the Cork road just five minutes walk from the town of Kenmare. It is a lovely Georgian farm house set in a large garden with lawns, a herb garden, an orchard and a lawn tennis court. It offers to guests bedrooms which are individually furnished with antiques and polished old wooden floors. Each bedroom has a D.D. phone, a small colour TV and an en suite bathroom.

B&B from £40.00 to £50.00
€50.79 to €63.49

MAURA O'CONNELL-FOLEY
Proprietress

Mastercard
Visa

Closed 31 October - 01 April

B&B rates are per person sharing per night incl. Breakfast

WANDER INN

2 HENRY STREET, KENMARE,
CO. KERRY
TEL: 064-42700 FAX: 064-42569
EMAIL: wanderinn@eircom.net

HOTEL ★★ MAP 1 D 3

A charming family-run hotel, restaurant and bar with entertainment. Ideally located for the Ring of Kerry and the Ring of Beara. Enjoy our golf courses, Kenmare Golf, Ring of Kerry golf and Parknasilla golf. Local activities include deep sea-angling, hill walking, cycling, seawater tours and water sports. Also enjoy local shops and entertainment. All rooms are en-suite, with colour TV and DD. We look forward to your visit.

B&B from £20.00 to £25.00
€25.39 to €31.74

DAN AND JOHN KEANE

Mastercard
Visa

11 11

Open All Year

19TH GREEN

LACKABANE, FOSSA, KILLARNEY,
CO. KERRY
TEL: 064-32868 FAX: 064-32637
EMAIL: 19thgreen@eircom.net

GUESTHOUSE ★★★ MAP 2 E 4

Family run guesthouse 3km from Killarney town. Ring of Kerry road; adjacent to Killarney's 3 x 18 hole championship courses. Ideal for golfers playing Killarney, Beaufort, Dooks, Waterville, Tralee or Ballybunion. All tee times arranged. Putting green for guests' use. Tours arranged: Gap of Dunloe, Ring of Kerry and Dingle Peninsula. All rooms en suite with DD phone and TV. Whether you are sightseeing, fishing, rambling or golfing, the 19th Green will suit you to a tee.

WEB: www.19thgreen-bb.com

B&B from £22.00 to £30.00
€27.93 to €38.09

TIMOTHY AND BRIDGET FOLEY
Proprietors

Mastercard
Visa

🙂 Midweek specials from £60.00

10 10

IRISH
HOTELS
FEDERATION

Closed 01 November - 01 March

ABBEY LODGE

MUCKROSS ROAD, KILLARNEY,
CO. KERRY
TEL: 064-34193 FAX: 064-35877
EMAIL: abbeylodgekly@eircom.net

UNDER CONSTRUCTION OPENING MAR 2000

GUESTHOUSE P MAP 2 E 4

Abbey Lodge, newly refurbished to a very high standard with all rooms en-suite, TV, tea/coffee, DD phone and central heating, is located on the Muckross Road (N71) a three minute walk to town centre. Private car park for guests. The King family invite you to experience the delights of Killarney and Kerry from this ideal location where genuine recommendations for tours and sightseeing is gladly provided. Cead Mile Failte.

B&B from £18.00 to £25.00
€22.86 to €31.74

JOHN G KING
Owner

6 6

Closed 20 - 30 December

Room rates are per room per night

AGHADOE HEIGHTS HOTEL

AGHADOE, KILLARNEY,
CO. KERRY
TEL: 064-31766 FAX: 064-31345
EMAIL: aghadoeheights@eircom.net

HOTEL ★★★★★ MAP 2 E 4

Recently refurbished, this luxury 5***** hotel enjoys panoramic views of Killarney's lakes and mountains. From the luxuriously furnished bedrooms to the highly acclaimed Fredrick's restaurant this hotel is renowned for outstanding comfort and hospitality. Perfect for sports, rest and relaxation with a superb leisure centre including an indoor swimming pool. Within easy reach of the south west championship golf courses and breathtaking scenery.

WEB: www.aghadoeheights.com

B&B from £80.00 to £122.50
€101.58 to €155.54

GILLIAN BUTLER
General Manager

American Express
Diners
Mastercard
Visa

☺ Weekend specials available

77 77

Closed 22 October - 17 April

AISLING HOUSE

COUNTESS ROAD, KILLARNEY,
CO. KERRY
TEL: 064-31112 FAX: 064-30079
EMAIL: aislinghouse@eircom.net

GUESTHOUSE ★★★ MAP 2 E 4

Aisling House located in peaceful surroundings just 800 metres off Muckross Road and 8 minutes walk from the centre of Killarney. All bedrooms are en suite, with tea/coffee facilities, TV and central heating. There is private car park and garden for guests. Aisling House is well within walking distance of Killarney National Park, Ross Castle and Muckross House. Tours of the Ring of Kerry/Dingle may be arranged. Nearby facilities include golf, horse riding, angling.

Members Of Premier Guesthouses

B&B from £18.00 to £25.00
€22.86 to €31.74

PADDY O'DONOGHUE
Owner

Mastercard
Visa

☺ Weekend specials from £65.00

10 10

Closed 20 - 27 December

ARBUTUS HOTEL

COLLEGE STREET, KILLARNEY,
CO. KERRY
TEL: 064-31037 FAX: 064-34033
EMAIL: arbutushotel@eircom.net

HOTEL ★★★ MAP 2 E 4

To get a taste of the real Ireland, stay at a family run hotel with turf fires, good food, personal service with spacious rooms en suite. Oak panelled bar where the best Guinness is filled while traditional music weaves its magic through the air. If you're coming to sightsee, golf, fish or relax, the Arbutus is where you'll find a home away from home.

B&B from £35.00 to £55.00
€44.44 to €69.84

SEAN BUCKLEY
Proprietor

American Express
Diners
Mastercard
Visa

39 39

Closed 17 - 30 December

B&B rates are per person sharing per night incl. Breakfast

ASHVILLE GUESTHOUSE

ROCK ROAD, KILLARNEY,
CO. KERRY
TEL: 064-36405 FAX: 064-36778
EMAIL: ashvillehouse@eircom.net

GUESTHOUSE ★★★ MAP 2 E 4

Ashville is a spacious family run guesthouse, 2 mins walk from town centre, on main Tralee road (N22). Private car park. Comfortably furnished en suite rooms include orthopaedic beds, DD phone, multi channel TV, hairdryer. Sample our varied breakfast menu. Convenient to Killarney National Park, pony trekking, golf and fishing. Ideal touring base for Ring of Kerry, Dingle and Beara. Declan and Elma assure you of a warm welcome at Ashville. Awarded AA ♦♦♦, RAC highly acclaimed.

WEB: www.kerry-insight.com/ashville

B&B from £18.00 to £25.00
€22.86 to €31.74

ELMA & DECLAN WALSH
Proprietors

Mastercard
Visa

10 10

Closed 18 - 30 December

BEAUFIELD HOUSE

PARK ROAD, KILLARNEY,
CO. KERRY
TEL: 064-34440 FAX: 064-34663

GUESTHOUSE ★★★ MAP 2 E 4

Beaufield House is a family run guesthouse, 2km from Killarney town centre on main Cork road (N22). 14 modern centrally heated bedrooms all with bath/shower en suite, direct dial telephone, radio and TV. Spacious visitors' lounge. Relax and enjoy local amenities which include golf, fishing, Killarney's famous lakes, mountains, National Park, tour the Ring of Kerry and Dingle peninsula. You will be made welcome when you stay at Beaufield House.

Members Of Premier Guesthouses

B&B from £20.00 to £22.00
€25.39 to €27.93

MOYA BOWE
Proprietor

American Express
Diners
Mastercard
Visa

14 14

Closed 20 - 28 December

BROOK LODGE HOTEL

HIGH STREET, KILLARNEY,
CO. KERRY
TEL: 064-31800 FAX: 064-35001

UNDER CONSTRUCTION OPENING MAR 2000

HOTEL P MAP 2 E 4

Brook Lodge Hotel is a new hotel, family-run, situated in the heart of Killarney town, set back from the street on over an acre of landscaped garden with private parking. Our spacious and tastefully decorated rooms are all en suite, including tea/coffee facilities, DD phone, hairdryer, multichannel TV, a lift and wheelchair facilities.

B&B from £25.00 to £45.00
€31.74 to €57.14

JOAN COUNIHAN
Owner/Manager

American Express
Diners
Mastercard
Visa

18 18

Closed 01 December - 29 February

Room rates are per room per night

CAHERNANE HOUSE HOTEL

MUCKROSS ROAD, KILLARNEY, CO. KERRY
TEL: 064-31895 FAX: 064-34340
EMAIL: cahernane@eircom.net

HOTEL ★★★★ MAP 2 E 4

Once the private home of the Herbert family, the Earls of Pembroke, 1km from Killarney. 44 bedrooms including 12 master bedrooms and suites. Two award-winning restaurants, a choice of 340 fine wines. RAC - HCR awards. AA 2 rosettes kitchen. An abundance of local activities. Hotel gardens, boutique, tennis. A member of Manor House Hotels of Irl. Tel: 353-1-2958900. Fax: 353-1-2958940. GDS Access Code is: UI and Toll Free: 1-800-44-UTELL.

WEB: www.cahernane.com

Members Of Manor House Hotels

B&B from £55.00 to £67.50
€69.84 to €85.71

CONOR O'CONNELL
Manager

American Express
Diners
Mastercard
Visa

☺ Weekend specials from £140.00

44 44

a|c

Closed 01 November - 31 March

CASTLE OAKS

MUCKROSS ROAD, KILLARNEY, CO. KERRY
TEL: 064-34154 FAX: 064-36980

GUESTHOUSE ★★★ MAP 2 E 4

At the gateway to Killarney National Park and only minutes from the lively town centre, you are always assured of a warm and friendly welcome at this luxury, family-run guesthouse. Enjoy the comfort of the spacious rooms, including large family rooms, all en suite with DD phone, colour TV, hair dryer and power shower; or relax in the guest lounge with our complimentary tea/coffee whilst absorbing breathtaking views of Killarney's lakes and mountains. Private parking.

B&B from £20.00 to £28.00
€25.40 to €35.55

EAMON & VALERIE COURTNEY
Proprietors

Mastercard
Visa

17 17

Closed 10 - 27 December

CASTLELODGE GUESTHOUSE

MUCKROSS ROAD, KILLARNEY, CO. KERRY
TEL: 064-31545 FAX: 064-32325
EMAIL: castlelodge@eircom.net

GUESTHOUSE U MAP 2 E 4

Castlelodge Guesthouse is a newly refurbished guesthouse, situated on the Muckross road, 2 minutes walk from the town centre. 25 rooms en suite including large family rooms, tea/coffee making facilities, satellite TV, direct dial telephone, car park within the grounds. The perfect location for both tourists and business people.

WEB: homepage.eircom.net/~castlelodge/

B&B from £18.00 to £25.00
€22.86 to €31.74

TONY O'SHEA
Proprietor

Mastercard
Visa

25 25

Open All Year

B&B rates are per person sharing per night incl. Breakfast

CASTLEROSSE HOTEL & LEISURE CENTRE

KILLARNEY,
CO. KERRY
TEL: 064-31144   FAX: 064-31031
EMAIL: castler@iol.ie

HOTEL ★★★   MAP 2 E 4

A Tower Group Hotel - situated right on the lakeside, between the golf course and the National Park and a little over a mile from Killarney town centre, the Castlerosse Hotel commands magnificent views of the lakes and mountains, especially from the restaurant and panoramic bar. The impressive range of leisure and fitness facilities, including the 20m swimming pool and 2 floodlit tennis courts, makes the Castlerosse the perfect location for a holiday or leisure break. Opening May 2000, spectacular 9 hole / par 36 golf course.

WEB: www.towerhotelgroup.ie

Members Of Tower Hotel Group

B&B from £35.00 to £50.00
€44.44 to €63.49

DANNY BOWE
General Manager

American Express
Diners
Mastercard
Visa

😊 Weekend specials from £75.00

Closed 01 November - 07 March

COFFEY'S LOCH LEIN GUESTHOUSE

GOLF COURSE ROAD, FOSSA,
KILLARNEY, CO. KERRY
TEL: 064-31260   FAX: 064-36151
EMAIL: ecoffey@indigo.ie

GUESTHOUSE ★★★   MAP 2 E 4

Family run guesthouse, uniquely situated by the shores of Killarney's Lower Lake. Magnificent views of lakes and mountains from lounge and dining room. Ideally situated on Ring of Kerry/Dingle roads, near the famous Gap of Dunloe. Tours arranged. Nearby two 18-hole championship golf courses, horseriding and fishing. Commended by AA, Frommers, Country Inns, Michelin Guide, Penguin and Inside Ireland. A warm welcome awaits you here.

WEB: www.lochlein.com

B&B from £18.00 to £25.00
€22.86 to €31.74

EITHNE COFFEY
Proprietor

Mastercard
Visa

Closed 10 November - 10 March

DARBY O'GILLS COUNTRY HOUSE HOTEL

LISSIVGEEN, MALLOW ROAD,
KILLARNEY, CO. KERRY
TEL: 064-34168   FAX: 064-36794
EMAIL: darbyogill@eircom.net

HOTEL U   MAP 2 E 4

Darby O'Gills Country House Hotel is a charming family run hotel located in an excellent position on the edge of Killarney town in a quiet rural setting only 5 minutes from Killarney town centre. Guest comfort is foremost in our mind and our comfortable rooms reflect this. This is a family friendly hotel where we hope to make your stay a relaxing and memorable occasion.

WEB: www.iol/kerry-insight/darbyogills

Members Of MinOtel Ireland Hotel Group

B&B from £25.00 to £55.00
€31.74 to €69.84

PAT & JOAN GILL & FAMILY

American Express
Diners
Mastercard
Visa

Closed 25 - 26 December

Room rates are per room per night

EARLS COURT HOUSE

WOODLAWN JUNCTION, MUCKROSS ROAD, KILLARNEY, CO. KERRY
TEL: 064-34009 FAX: 064-34366
EMAIL: earls@eircom.net

GUESTHOUSE ★★★★ MAP 2 E 4

RAC Small Hotel of the Year for Ireland 1998. A magical 4**** hideaway, 5 mins walk to town centre. Traditional country house ambience, antique furnishings, log fires, fresh flowers, home baking and fine wines. Here keynotes are charm, tranquillity and unparalleled hospitality afforded to each discerning guest. Breakfast is special - a feast offering tempting choices. Superior rooms with individual themes, full bathroom, TV, ice, phone and individual balconies. Private parking. AA ♦♦♦♦♦.

WEB: www.killarney-earlscourt.ie

B&B from £30.00 to £45.00
€38.09 to €57.14

EMER & RAY MOYNIHAN
Owners

Mastercard
Visa

11 11

Closed 05 November - 28 February

EVISTON HOUSE HOTEL

NEW STREET, KILLARNEY, CO. KERRY
TEL: 064-31640 FAX: 064-33685
EMAIL: evishtl@eircom.net

HOTEL ★★★ MAP 2 E 4

Eviston House Hotel is located in the centre of Killarney yet only a few minutes away from the National Park and championship golf courses. All our luxurious bedrooms are complete with private bathroom, direct dial telephone, tea/coffee facilities, hair dryer and satellite TV. The elegant Colleen Bawn restaurant offers fine food in intimate surroundings. Afterwards visit our famous pub, the Danny Mann, for the best in traditional music and great 'craic'.

Members Of Best Western Hotels

B&B from £29.00 to £60.00
€36.82 to €76.18

EDWARD EVISTON
Proprietor

American Express
Diners
Mastercard
Visa

75 75

Open All Year

FAILTE HOTEL

COLLEGE STREET, KILLARNEY, CO. KERRY
TEL: 064-33404 FAX: 064-36599

HOTEL ★ MAP 2 E 4

The Failte Hotel which was recently refurbished to a very high standard is owned and managed by the O'Callaghan family. Sons Dermot and Donal run the restaurant and kitchen. It is internationally known for its high standard of cuisine. Paudie supervises the award winning bar. It is situated in the town centre, adjacent to railway station, new factory outlet, shopping complex. Also close by are many local cabarets and night clubs. Local amenities include golfing, fishing, walking, etc.

B&B from £25.00 to £40.00
€31.74 to €50.79

DERMOT & EILEEN O'CALLAGHAN
Proprietors

American Express
Mastercard
Visa

12 12

Closed 24 - 26 December

B&B rates are per person sharing per night incl. Breakfast

FOLEY'S TOWNHOUSE

23 HIGH STREET, KILLARNEY,
CO. KERRY
TEL: 064-31217 FAX: 064-34683

GUESTHOUSE ★★★★ MAP 2 E 4

Originally a 19th Century Coaching Inn, this old house has hosted generations of travellers. Newly refurbished, this is a 4**** family-run town centre located guesthouse. Luxury bedrooms are individually designed for comfort complete with every modern amenity. Downstairs is our award-winning seafood and steak restaurant. Chef/owner Carol provides meals from fresh local produce. Choose from approx 200 wines. Personal supervision. Private parking. Awarded AA ♦♦♦♦, RAC highly acclaimed.

B&B from £41.25 to £41.25
€52.38 to €52.38

CAROL HARTNETT
Proprietor

American Express
Mastercard
Visa

28 28

Closed 01 November - 04 April

FRIARS GLEN

MANGERTON ROAD, MUCKROSS,
KILLARNEY, CO. KERRY
TEL: 064-37500 FAX: 064-37388
EMAIL: fullerj@indigo.ie

GUESTHOUSE ★★★★ MAP 2 E 4

Surrounded by Killarney National Park and its attractions, Friars Glen offers you superb accommodation in a tranquil woodland setting, just 3 miles from Killarney town. The guesthouse provides spacious en suite rooms, some family rooms, with all modern requirements. Relax in our comfortable lounge with open turf fire. Sample from our delicious breakfast menu. Wheelchair friendly. Drying room available. Landscaped garden. An ideal base for your holiday in Kerry.

B&B from £22.00 to £30.00
€27.93 to €38.09

MARY & JOHN FULLER
Proprietors

Mastercard
Visa

10 10

Closed 15 December - 15 January

FUCHSIA HOUSE

MUCKROSS ROAD, KILLARNEY,
CO. KERRY
TEL: 064-33743 FAX: 064-36588
EMAIL: fuchsiahouse@eircom.net

GUESTHOUSE ★★★★ MAP 2 E 4

We invite you to enjoy the affordable luxury of Fuchsia House which is set well back from the road in mature, leafy gardens yet is only 7 minutes walk from Killarney towncentre. Purpose built to combine the amenities of a modern 4**** guesthouse with the elegance of an earlier age, Fuchsia House offers orthopaedic beds dressed in crisp cotton & linen, private bath with power shower, DD phone etc. Breakfast room/conservatory overlooks the terrace and gardens, Irish & vegetarian menu.

WEB: www.kerrygems.ie/fuchsiahouse

B&B from £28.00 to £42.00
€35.55 to €53.33

MARY TREACY
Owner

Mastercard
Visa

10 10

Closed 15 December - 28 February

Room rates are per room per night

GLEANN FIA COUNTRY HOUSE

DEERPARK, KILLARNEY,
CO. KERRY
TEL: 064-35035 FAX: 064-35000
EMAIL: gleanfia@iol.ie

GUESTHOUSE ★★★ MAP 2 E 4

Set in a secluded 30 acre wooded river valley, 1 mile from Killarney - Gleann Fia is the perfect holiday setting. Our Victorian style country house offers tasteful en suite rooms, each with phone, TV and orthopaedic beds. Stroll along the river walk admiring the wild flowers and Autumn colours. Relax by the peat fire or enjoy tea/coffee in the conservatory. Wholesome breakfasts include freshly squeezed juice and homemade preserves. Friendly personal attention assured. 300yds from bypass, N22 on Kilcummin Road.

WEB: ireland.iol.ie/kerry-insight/gleannfia

B&B from £22.00 to £30.00
€27.93 to €38.09

JERRY AND NORA GALVIN
Owners

American Express
Mastercard
Visa

Closed 01 December - 01 March

GLENA GUESTHOUSE

MUCKROSS ROAD, KILLARNEY,
CO. KERRY
TEL: 064-32705 FAX: 064-35611
EMAIL: glena@iol.ie

GUESTHOUSE ★★★★ MAP 2 E 4

Glena House, 4**** award-winning guesthouse, AA ◆◆◆◆, RAC acclaimed, Les Routier recommended. It's the simple things that make it right; in a great location, a bed to rest in, a shower/bath to envigorate, tea/coffee when you want. A bowl of ice for a bedroom drink, homebaking and a breakfast as individual as you are. Glena House where memories are made, 5 minutes walk from town centre. Parking.

B&B from £25.00 to £35.00
€31.74 to €44.44

MARINA & TIM BUCKLEY
Owners/Managers

American Express
Diners
Mastercard
Visa

Closed 25 December

GLENCONNOR HOUSE

FOSSA, KILLARNEY,
CO. KERRY
TEL: 064-37534 FAX: 064-36811

GUESTHOUSE P MAP 2 E 4

GlenConnor House offers luxury guesthouse accommodation in superb location overlooking Killarney's lakes and mountains. A short walk to the prestige 5***** Hotel Europe, local pub, Killarney town, the popular Kate Kearney's Cottage and Black Valley. All within 5 mins drive & within easy reach of Killarney golf and fishing club. Enjoy the comfort of large spacious rooms with full bathrooms, DD phone, colour TV, hairdryer or relax in our luxurious guest lounge with a complimentary tea or coffee.

B&B from £25.00 to £36.00
€31.74 to €45.71

ANNE & GER O'CONNOR

Mastercard
Visa

☺ Midweek specials from £50.00

FAX

Closed 01 November - 28 February

B&B rates are per person sharing per night incl. Breakfast

GLENEAGLE HOTEL

**KILLARNEY,
CO. KERRY
TEL: 064-36000 FAX: 064-32646
EMAIL: gleneagl@iol.ie**

HOTEL ★★★ MAP 2 E 4

Ireland's leading leisure hotel, ideally located opposite Killarney's National Park. Many of our beautifully furnished 220 rooms offer a panoramic view. Relaxing lounge rooms with fireplaces and a luxurious spacious lobby area. Our award-winning chefs will delight you in both of our restaurants. We have a great line-up of entertainment all year round. Relax and unwind using our extensive indoor and outdoor leisure facilities.

WEB: www.gleneagle-hotel.com

B&B from £42.00 to £64.00
€53.33 to €81.26

PATRICK O'DONOGHUE G.M.
O'Donoghue Family, Owners

American Express
Diners
Mastercard
Visa

Open All Year

GRAND HOTEL

**MAIN STREET, KILLARNEY,
CO. KERRY
TEL: 064-31159 FAX: 064-35320**

HOTEL ★ MAP 2 E 4

The Grand Hotel is owned by Mr. & Mrs. Patrick Sheehan and is situated in the centre of town within easy reach of shops and restaurants. The 20 bedrooms have recently been refurbished to a very high standard. All are ensuite with T.V., DD Phone, trouser press, iron and tea & coffee making facility. Music in the bar 7 nights, late licence. Discoteque at rear of bar. Local amenities include Golf, Fishing, Horse riding, Boat Trips. Tours can be arranged.

B&B from £25.00 to £45.00
€31.74 to €57.14

JOE MC MAHON
Manager

Mastercard
Visa

Open All Year

HOLIDAY INN KILLARNEY

**MUCKROSS ROAD, KILLARNEY,
CO KERRY
TEL: 064-33000 FAX: 064-33001**

HOTEL N MAP 2 E 4

Holiday Inn Killarney enjoys a quiet but central location close to Killarney town centre. Its 24 suites and spacious en suite rooms are tastefully decorated to the highest standard. Our fully-equipped leisure centre is the perfect place to relax and unwind. Our Library Point Restaurant serves the finest of local cuisine while Saddlers Pub serves food daily and has entertainment nightly. A haven for all seasons!

Members Of Signature Hotels

Room Rate from £39.00 to £109.00
€49.52 to €138.40

JOHN BYRNE
General Manager

American Express
Diners
Mastercard
Visa

Weekend specials from £69.00

Closed 25 - 27 December

Room rates are per room per night

HOTEL DUNLOE CASTLE

KILLARNEY,
CO. KERRY
TEL: 064-44111   FAX: 064-44583
EMAIL: khl@iol.ie

HOTEL ★★★★★   MAP 2 E 4

100 bedroomed resort near
Killarney, facing the famous Gap of
Dunloe. Historical park and botanic
gardens with ruins of castle. Elegant
decor with many valuable antiques.
Luxurious lounges, cocktail bar,
gourmet restaurant. Extensive leisure
facilities: pool, sauna, gym, riding,
putting green, tennis, jogging track.
10 championship courses nearby.
Sister hotels: Ard-na-Sidhe, Europe.
Central Reservations:
Tel 064-31900, Fax 064-32118.

WEB: www.iol.ie/khl

B&B from £62.00 to £86.00
€78.72 to €109.20

CLODAGH DUNWORTH
Resident Manager

American Express
Diners
Mastercard
Visa

☺ Midweek specials from £165.00

100 100

Closed 01 October - 15 April

HOTEL EUROPE

KILLARNEY,
CO. KERRY
TEL: 064-31900   FAX: 064-32118
EMAIL: khl@iol.ie

HOTEL ★★★★★   MAP 2 E 4

De luxe resort known internationally
for its spectacular location on the
Lakes of Killarney. 205 spacious
bedrooms and suites of highest
modern standards, many with lake
view. Elegant lounges, cocktail bar,
panorama restaurant. Boutique.
Health/fitness centre, 25m indoor
pool, sauna, gym. Tennis,
horseriding, fishing, boating,
cycling. 6 championship courses
nearby. Sister hotels: Dunloe Castle,
Ard-na-Sidhe.

WEB: www.iol.ie/khl

B&B from £62.00 to £83.00
€78.72 to €105.39

PHILIP HENNESSY
General Manager

American Express
Diners
Mastercard
Visa

☺ Midweek specials from £165.00

205 205

Closed 01 November - 15 March

HUSSEYS TOWNHOUSE & BAR

43 HIGH STREET, KILLARNEY,
CO. KERRY
TEL: 064-37454   FAX: 064-33144
EMAIL: husseys@iol.ie

GUESTHOUSE ★★★   MAP 2 E 4

Killarney National Park and some of
the best restaurants in town are
within walking distance of this family
owned, centrally located guesthouse
which has been modernised without
losing its old world atmosphere. All
bedrooms are spacious, tastefully
decorated and equipped to a high
standard. This is the discerning
travellers perfect choice with
wonderful breakfasts, home baking,
comfortable guest lounge, a cosy,
friendly pub and private parking too.

B&B from £18.00 to £30.00
€22.86 to €38.09

GERALDINE O'LEARY
Owner

American Express
Mastercard
Visa

5 5

Closed 31 October - 13 March

B&B rates are per person sharing per night incl. Breakfast

INTERNATIONAL BEST WESTERN HOTEL

KENMARE PLACE, KILLARNEY,
CO. KERRY
TEL: 064-31816   FAX: 064-31837
EMAIL: inter@iol.ie

HOTEL ★★★   MAP 2 E 4

A warm welcome awaits you at the International. The hotel has been brought into the 21st century with carefully planned refurbishment. All rooms have TV/radio, tea/coffee, phone & hairdryer. Nearby are Killarney's 18-hole golf courses. Ballybunion, Tralee, Dooks, Waterville within easy reach. Fresh local produce served in our two fully air-conditioned restaurants. Music in our traditional Irish bar nightly in summer. Car hire, foreign exchange on premises. Bus/train 200m. Airport 15k.

WEB: www.killarney-inter.com

Members Of Best Western Hotels

B&B from £25.00 to £60.00
€31.74 to €76.18

PAT TERRY
Manager

American Express
Diners
Mastercard
Visa

☺ Weekend specials from £78.00

🛏♨☎⬇️♨Ⓣ🅲⬅CM☺🕒♫♪🎷
79 79
Ⓢ🅿alc🍴

Closed 22 - 29 December

INVERARAY FARM GUESTHOUSE

BEAUFORT, KILLARNEY,
CO. KERRY
TEL: 064-44224   FAX: 064-44775

GUESTHOUSE ★★   MAP 2 E 4

A luxury farm-guesthouse in a quiet sylvan setting. Views of Killarney lakes, mountains and Gap of Dunloe. 9k west of Killarney, 1k off N72 over bridge at Laune bridge picnic area. Free private trout and salmon fishing available. Anglers, walkers and golfers paradise. Tea-room, games-room, playground and pony for children. Home-baking, seafood and dinner a speciality with good, wholesome home cooking. Tours arranged. Recommended Le Guide du Routard 1999.

B&B from £19.00 to £24.00
€24.13 to €30.47

EILEEN & NOEL SPILLANE
Proprietors

☺ Weekend specials from £53.00

🛏♨☎Ⓣ🅰📷🅲⬅CM☼☺🕒♪🅿
10 10

Closed 01 November - 28 January

KATHLEEN'S COUNTRY HOUSE

TRALEE ROAD, KILLARNEY,
CO. KERRY
TEL: 064-32810   FAX: 064-32340
EMAIL: info@kathleens.net

GUESTHOUSE ★★★★   MAP 2 E 4

Kathleen's is a delightful family run guesthouse. ITB 4★★★★, AA ◆◆◆◆◆ and RAC Small Hotel/Guesthouse of the Year for Ireland are amongst its many awards. Set on 3 acres of mature gardens in peaceful rural surrounds yet only 3k from town centre. Each room furnished in antique pine has bathtub and power shower, tea/coffee facilities, hairdryer, phone, orthopaedic bed. Elegant decor throughout. Art lovers will enjoy the many paintings. Non-smoking house. Easy to get to! Hard to leave!

WEB: www.kathleens.net

B&B from £30.00 to £42.50
€38.09 to €53.96

KATHLEEN O'REGAN SHEPPARD
Proprietor

American Express
Mastercard
Visa

☺ Midweek specials from £85.00

🛏♨☎Ⓣ🅲☼✛🆄🅿Ⓢ🆈🍴
17 17

Closed 07 November - 10 March

Room rates are per room per night

KILLARNEY AVENUE HOTEL

KENMARE PLACE, KILLARNEY,
CO. KERRY
TEL: 064-32522 FAX: 064-33707
EMAIL: towersky@iol.ie

HOTEL R MAP 2 E 4

Killarney Avenue Hotel is a new hotel in the centre of Killarney town. All 66 bedrooms are air-conditioned and also feature TV, radio, DD phone, hairdryer and tea/coffee making facilities. Guests are welcome to use the leisure facilities of our sister hotel (Killarney Towers Hotel), 100m away. Underground garage parking is available to guests. An excellent hotel in an excellent location in downtown Killarney.

B&B from £45.00 to £90.00
€57.14 to €114.28

NOEL O'CONNELL
General Manager

American Express
Diners
Mastercard
Visa

Closed 01 December - 31 January

KILLARNEY COURT HOTEL

TRALEE ROAD, KILLARNEY,
CO. KERRY
TEL: 064-37070 FAX: 064-37060
EMAIL: stay@irishcourthotels.com

HOTEL ★★★ MAP 2 E 4

Opened April '98 the Killarney Court Hotel is a 5 min walk from Killarney town centre, only 15k from Kerry International airport and close to 3 world famous golf courses. Our 100 en suite bedrooms boast a tasteful neo-gothic style decor. Enjoy a meal in our Seasons Restaurant with traditional Irish and international cuisine or a drink in McGillicuddys traditional Irish pub with its wonderful 'ceol, ol agus craic' atmosphere. We assure you your stay will be enjoyable.

WEB: www.Irishcourthotel.com

Members Of Irish Court Hotel Group

B&B from £30.00 to £75.00
€38.09 to €95.23

ROBERT LYNE
Proprietor

American Express
Diners
Mastercard
Visa

Weekend specials from £75.00

Open All Year

KILLARNEY GREAT SOUTHERN HOTEL

KILLARNEY,
CO. KERRY
TEL: 064-31262 FAX: 064-31642
EMAIL: res@killarney.gsh.ie

HOTEL ★★★★ MAP 2 E 4

Experience bygone charm with modern comfort set in scenic gardens in the heart of Killarney. This 4**** hotel offers 180 beautifully appointed bedrooms with DD phone, TV, hairdryer, trouser press. Leisure facilities include swimming pool, sauna, steam room, jacuzzi, plunge pool, gym. Outdoor tennis courts and childrens playground. Creche during July/August. Conference facilities for up to 900 delegates. Bookable worldwide through UTELL International or Central Res: Tel 01-2144800.

WEB: www.gsh.ie

B&B from £49.00 to £94.00
€62.22 to €119.36

CONOR HENNIGAN
General Manager

American Express
Diners
Mastercard
Visa

Weekend specials from £95.00

Open All Year

B&B rates are per person sharing per night incl. Breakfast

KILLARNEY HEIGHTS HOTEL

CORK ROAD, KILLARNEY,
CO. KERRY
TEL: 064-31158 FAX: 064-35198
EMAIL: khh@iol.ie

HOTEL U   MAP 2 E 4

Opened in June 1996, on the site of the Castle Heights, the hotel is strategically located on the approach to Killarney (1km from town centre) overlooking the majestic Torc and Mangerton mountains and Flesk river. Open fires, friendly faces, olde world flag stone floors, pitch pine furnishings create a unique nostalgic atmosphere in the ground floor bars and restaurant - Offering the freshest of local ingredients and the finest of wines to create an unforgetable magical experience.

Members Of Logis of Ireland

B&B from £42.00 to £60.00
€53.33 to €76.18

BERNARD O RIORDAN

Mastercard
Visa

😊 Weekend specials from £85.00

70 70

S🅿aic

IRISH HOTELS FEDERATION

Open All Year

KILLARNEY LODGE

COUNTESS ROAD, KILLARNEY,
CO. KERRY
TEL: 064-36499 FAX: 064-31070
EMAIL: klylodge@iol.ie

GUESTHOUSE ★★★★   MAP 2 E 4

Killarney Lodge, a purpose built guesthouse set in private walled-in gardens, only 2 mins walk from the town centre. The guesthouse provides private parking, spacious en suite air conditioned bedrooms with all modern amenities including wheelchair facilities. Enjoy an extensive breakfast menu in the spacious dining room and relax in comfortable lounges with open fires. The Lodge has already gained an outstanding reputation for quality of service, relaxed atmosphere and friendliness.

B&B from £25.00 to £42.00
€31.74 to €53.33

CATHERINE TREACY
Owner

American Express
Diners
Mastercard
Visa

16 16

IRISH HOTELS FEDERATION

Closed 15 - 28 December

KILLARNEY PARK HOTEL

KENMARE PLACE, KILLARNEY,
CO. KERRY
TEL: 064-35555 FAX: 064-35266
EMAIL: kph@iol.ie

HOTEL ★★★★★   MAP 2 E 4

Superbly located in the heart of Killarney town, this family owned luxury hotel offers the quietness, intimacy and privacy associated with times past. In addition to a country house style lobby, library, drawing room and billiard room, the hotel also offers a magnificent 20m swimming pool, sauna, jacuzzi, outdoor hot tub, fitness suite and treatment room. Dining options include a candlelit dinner in the Park restaurant or an appetising snack in the garden bar.

WEB: www.killarneyparkhotel.ie

B&B from £75.00 to £110.00
€95.23 to €139.67

DONAGH DAVERN
General Manager

American Express
Diners
Mastercard
Visa

😊 Weekend specials from £150.00

76 76

IRISH HOTELS FEDERATION

Closed 24 - 27 December

Room rates are per room per night

KILLARNEY ROYAL

COLLEGE STREET, KILLARNEY,
CO. KERRY
TEL: 064-31853   FAX: 064-34001
EMAIL: royalhot@iol.ie

HOTEL U MAP 2 E 4

The Killarney Royal is not like anywhere else. Family-run and situated in the heart of Killarney, Joe and Margaret Scally have anticipated your needs. Each room has been individually and personally re-designed to meet your comforts with air conditioning throughout, 24 hour personal service, parking facilities available, elegant dining room, local bar atmosphere. Meticulously high standards of service ensure that you can make the most of the charming and graceful surroundings.

WEB: www.killarneyroyal.ie

B&B from £45.00 to £80.00
€57.14 to €101.58

JOE SCALLY
Proprietor

American Express
Diners
Mastercard
Visa

Weekend specials from £110.00

29   29

Closed 22 - 28 December

KILLARNEY RYAN HOTEL & LEISURE CENTRE

CORK ROAD, KILLARNEY,
CO. KERRY
TEL: 064-31555   FAX: 064-32438
EMAIL: ryan@indigo.ie

HOTEL ★★★ MAP 2 E 4

2km from Killarney town centre, this hotel features 168 en suite bedrooms. Savour a meal in the Ross or Herbert rooms, unwind in the Lobby lounge or enjoy nightly entertainment in the bar. Indulge youself in the 18m swimming pool, steam rooms, saunas and jacuzzi. The multi-activity sports hall, tennis courts, the award winning creche, extensive playgrounds and activity programme ensure a fun filled stay. Car park. AA, RAC and Egon Ronay recommended.

WEB: www.ryan-hotels.com

B&B from £45.00 to £85.00
€57.14 to €107.93

PAT GALVIN
General Manager

American Express
Diners
Mastercard
Visa

Weekend specials from £89.00

168   168

Closed 03 January - 04 February

KILLARNEY TOWERS HOTEL & LEISURE CENTRE

COLLEGE SQUARE, KILLARNEY,
CO. KERRY
TEL: 064-31038   FAX: 064-31755
EMAIL: towersky@iol.ie

HOTEL ★★★ MAP 2 E 4

3*** hotel in the centre of Killarney with underground car park, 182 superb en suite bedrooms, satellite TV and video channels, DD phone, hairdryers and tea/coffee facilities. Other guest facilities include a 20m indoor heated pool, sauna, steam room and fully equipped gymnasium. Live music entertainment nightly and green fees reserved at all Kerry courses through our golf department. A great hotel in downtown Killarney.

B&B from £50.00 to £90.00
€63.49 to €114.28

MICHAEL O'DONOGHUE

American Express
Diners
Mastercard
Visa

Weekend specials from £89.00

182   182

Closed 30 November - 01 February

B&B rates are per person sharing per night incl. Breakfast

KILLARNEY TOWN HOUSE

31 NEW STREET, KILLARNEY,
CO. KERRY
TEL: 064-35388 FAX: 064-35259

GUESTHOUSE N MAP 2 E 4

Comfortable family-run 10 roomed guesthouse situated in the heart of Killarney town - within easy walking distance of rail/bus stations. Rooms complete with every modern amenity. Outdoor activities arranged through reception - fishing, golfing and sightseeing.

B&B from £26.00 to £26.00
€33.01 to €33.01

AILISH HALLISSEY

Mastercard
Visa

🖐🏻🔒☎️🖥️T C ✋ U 🎵
10 10

Open All Year

KILLARNEY VIEW HOUSE

MUCKROSS ROAD, KILLARNEY,
CO. KERRY
TEL: 064-33122
EMAIL: killarneyview@ireland.com

GUESTHOUSE U MAP 2 E 4

We are very reasonably priced with a magnificent location overlooking our own river, your ideal base. Six mins walk Killarney town, on main Muckross road at the gateway to Killarney's mountain/lake area. Wonderful river/mountain views from dining and lounge areas. Guest lounge with open fire and tea making facilities. All 12 rooms are en suite with phone. Large private car park. Adjacent to Gleneagle Hotel with new 2000 conference centre. Welcome to our home.

B&B from £16.00 to £22.00
€20.32 to €27.93

MARY GUERIN
Proprietor

Mastercard
Visa

😊 Midweek specials from £45.00

🖐🏻🔒☎️T C C M ✵ 🎵 P S
12 12

IRISH HOTELS FEDERATION

Open All Year

KILLEEN HOUSE HOTEL

AGHADOE, LAKES OF KILLARNEY,
CO. KERRY
TEL: 064-31711 FAX: 064-31811
EMAIL: charming@indigo.ie

HOTEL U MAP 2 E 4

The Killeen House is truly a charming little hotel. With only 23 rooms, 8 of them deluxe, it is the ideal base for touring 'God's own country', the magical Kingdom of Kerry. With our DIY GolfPub and an elegant award-winning dining room you are assured a memorable experience. Go on, do the smart thing and call us now! We look forward to extending the 'hostility of the house' to you!

WEB: www.killeenhousehotel.com

Members Of Logis of Ireland

B&B from £40.00 to £80.00
€50.79 to €101.58

MICHAEL & GEARLDINE ROSNEY
Owners

American Express
Diners
Mastercard
Visa

😊 Weekend specials from £100.00

🖐🏻🔒☎️T ✵ U J P S 🛏️
23 23

IRISH HOTELS FEDERATION

Closed 01 November - 31 March

Room rates are per room per night

LAKE HOTEL

ON LAKE SHORE, MUCKROSS
ROAD, KILLARNEY, CO. KERRY
TEL: 064-31035 FAX: 064-31902
EMAIL: lakehotel@eircom.net

HOTEL ★★★ MAP 2 E 4

Built in 1820 and nestled at the water's edge the Lake Hotel has a unique old world charm with double height ceilings, open log fires, elegant spacious lounges and a friendly and relaxed atmosphere. Sit out in our lakeside garden to enjoy the most breathtaking views in Ireland. 30 new luxury suites with lake view balcony. Jacuzzi bath and some 4 poster beds are on offer at a small supplement. Visitors return year after year for 'a little bit of heaven on earth'.

WEB: lakehotel.com

Members Of Irish Family Hotels

B&B from £33.00 to £50.00
€41.90 to €63.49

TONY HUGGARD
Managing Director

American Express
Diners
Mastercard
Visa

Luxury lake-view suites at a supplement

Closed 04 December - 12 February

LIME COURT

MUCKROSS ROAD, KILLARNEY,
CO. KERRY
TEL: 064-34547 FAX: 064-34121
EMAIL: limecrt@iol.ie

GUESTHOUSE ★★★ MAP 2 E 4

Lime Court has the perfect location, 3*** quality and superb standards. Just 5 mins walk from town, easy off-street parking, on the main entrance route to Killarney National Park (over 26,000 acres) and on the Ring of Kerry road. All room types available, singles, doubles, twins, triples and family rooms. Lime Court is a purpose-built guesthouse and family run to ensure you have a relaxing and pleasurable stay.

WEB: www.iol.io/korry-insight/limecourt

B&B from £18.00 to £30.00
€22.86 to €38.09

ALAN & GERALDINE COURTNEY
Owners/Managers

Mastercard
Visa

10% discount on 3 or more nights

Closed 23 - 27 December

LINDEN HOUSE HOTEL

NEW ROAD, KILLARNEY,
CO. KERRY
TEL: 064-31379 FAX: 064-31196

HOTEL ★★ MAP 2 E 4

Situated in a quiet tree lined avenue 2 minutes walk from the town centre. Linden House is under the personal supervision of Peter and Ann Knoblauch. The Linden restaurant has an enviable reputation for good food prepared by owner chef. Year after year, guests return to Linden House, ample proof that you, too, will be made welcome and comfortable during your stay in beautiful Killarney.

B&B from £22.00 to £30.00
€27.93 to €38.09

PETER KNOBLAUCH
Owner Chef

Mastercard
Visa

3 B&B & 3 Dinners from £111.00 to £125.00

Closed 15 November - 01 February

B&B rates are per person sharing per night incl. Breakfast

MCCARTHY'S TOWN HOUSE

19 HIGH STREET, KILLARNEY,
CO. KERRY
TEL: 064-35655 FAX: 064-35745
EMAIL: mcth@eircom.net

GUESTHOUSE ★★★ MAP 2 E 4

McCarthy's Townhouse is the combination of everything you would expect during a visit to Killarney. Crock O'Gold pub, live traditional music, splendid bedrooms, great restaurant, breakfast room, guests lounge, D.D. telephone, TV and Hairdryer. The twenty five years experience of Con & May McCarthy is reflected in the warm, comfortable and welcoming atmosphere you feel in the McCarthy's Townhouse. Positively enjoy a visit to Killarney. Secure private car park.

WEB: www.iol.ie/kerry-insight/mccarthys

B&B from £22.50 to £30.00
€28.57 to €38.09

CORNELIUS & MAY MCCARTHY
Owners/Managers

American Express
Mastercard
Visa

🖐🅟☎⛁Ⓣ©CM⛛♫₧Ⓢ🅰alc
8 8

IRISH HOTELS FEDERATION

Open All Year

MCSWEENEY ARMS HOTEL

COLLEGE STREET, KILLARNEY,
CO. KERRY
TEL: 064-31211 FAX: 064-34553

HOTEL ★★★ MAP 2 E 4

The McSweeney Arms Hotel is situated in the heart of Killarney town. Small, cosy and run to a very high standard by your hosts Tony and Pauline McSweeney. There are 28 bedrooms with private bathroom, direct dial telephone, colour TV and hairdryer. Our bar and restaurant caters for all tastes with emphasis on traditional Irish food. Local amenities are four 18 hole championship golf courses also two 9 hole courses and the Killarney National Park.

B&B from £35.00 to £55.00
€44.44 to €69.84

TONY MCSWEENEY
Proprietor

American Express
Diners
Mastercard
Visa

🖐🅟☎⛁⬥Ⓣ🅰alc
28 28

IRISH HOTELS FEDERATION

Closed 05 January - 28 February

MOUNTAIN VIEW GUEST HOUSE

MUCKROSS ROAD, KILLARNEY,
CO. KERRY
TEL: 064-33293 FAX: 064-37295
EMAIL: tguerin@indigo.ie

GUESTHOUSE ★★ MAP 2 E 4

Mountain View Guest House offers the highest standard of accommodation by friendly and efficient staff. All rooms are en suite with direct dial phone, tea/coffee making facilities, multi channel televisions and hairdryers. Mountain View Guest House is located only 6 minutes walk from Killarney town centre and 3 minutes from the Gleneagle Country Club on the famous Ring of Kerry scenic route close to Ross Castle, Ross Golf Club, Muckross House, Torc Waterfall.

B&B from £18.00 to £25.00
€22.86 to €31.74

TIMOTHY GUERIN
Owner

Mastercard
Visa

🖐🅟☎⛁Ⓣ❄⛛♫₧Ⓢ▪
6 6

IRISH HOTELS FEDERATION

Closed 03 January - 10 March

Room rates are per room per night

MUCKROSS PARK HOTEL

MUCKROSS VILLAGE, KILLARNEY,
CO. KERRY
TEL: 064-31938 FAX: 064-31965
EMAIL: muckrossparkhotel@eircom.net

HOTEL ★★★★ MAP 2 E 4

Muckross Park Hotel is set in the heart of Killarney's National Park, comprising of 27 superior rooms, including suites. Molly Darcy's, our award winning, traditional Irish pub and restaurant is an experience not to be missed. Situated 4km outside Killarney, and adjacent to Muckross House and Abbey. Local amenities include golf, boating, fishing, horse riding and hillwalking.

WEB: www.muckrosspark.com

B&B from £45.00 to £65.00
€57.14 to €82.53

PATRICIA SHANAHAN
General Manager

American Express
Diners
Mastercard
Visa

Weekend specials from £105.00

27 27

alc

Closed 01 December - 31 February

MURPHYS BAR & GUESTHOUSE

18 COLLEGE STREET, KILLARNEY,
CO. KERRY
TEL: 064-31294 FAX: 064-34507
EMAIL: info@murphysbar.com

GUESTHOUSE N MAP 2 E 4

Killarney's most famous bar and guesthouse situated in the town centre. Experience old world charm and savour the best of Irish home cooking. A family-run business with all guest rooms newly refurbished. Amenities include golf, fishing, horse riding, scenic walks and shopping. Local tours arranged. Enjoy traditional Irish music in our award-winning 'Irish Pub of Distinction'. Sean and Maire assure you a warm welcome at Murphys, Killarney.

WEB: www.murphysbar.com

B&B from £25.00 to £30.00
€31.74 to €38.09

SEAN AND MAIRE MURPHY

American Express
Diners
Mastercard
Visa

11 11

Open All Year

OAKLAND HOUSE

CORK ROAD, KILLARNEY,
CO. KERRY
TEL: 064-37286 FAX: 064-37991
EMAIL: oakland@eircom.net

GUESTHOUSE ★★ MAP 2 E 4

Oakland House is a new family run guesthouse on the main Cork road. 1k from town centre, bus and train stations. All rooms en suite with TV, DD phone. Golf, fishing, pony trekking, leisure centres nearby. All scenic tours arranged. Guest lounge with tea/coffee making facilities. Laundrette, supermarket, post office, bureau de change approx. 100 metres. Visa, MasterCard, vouchers. Personal attention and a warm welcome awaits you at Oakland House.

B&B from £18.00 to £20.00
€22.86 to €25.39

DAVID HEGARTY
Proprietor

Mastercard
Visa

8 8

Closed 24 - 26 December

B&B rates are per person sharing per night incl. Breakfast

OLD WEIR LODGE

MUCKROSS ROAD, KILLARNEY,
CO. KERRY
TEL: 064-35593 FAX: 064-35583

GUESTHOUSE ★★★ MAP 2 E 4

A purpose built, family-run, Tudor designed, magnificent house, conveniently located 500m from the centre of Killarney town, within 1km of Killarney National Park. Set in 3/4 acre of landscaped garden with 15 en suite king size bedrooms with bath and shower, DD phone, orthopaedic beds, multi-channel TV, hairdryer, tea/coffee facilities. 2 spacious lounges, private parking with home baking a speciality. Winner '97 & '98 Best Guesthouse in Killarney Looking Good competition.

B&B from £20.00 to £30.00
€25.39 to €38.09

MAUREEN & DERMOT O'DONOGHUE
Proprietors

American Express
Diners
Mastercard
Visa

15 15

Closed 23 - 26 December

RANDLES COURT CLARION HOTEL

MUCKROSS ROAD, KILLARNEY,
CO. KERRY
TEL: 064-35333 FAX: 064-35206
EMAIL: randles@iol.ie

HOTEL ★★★★ MAP 2 E 4

On main road to Killarney National Park & Lakes 5 mins from town close to championship golf courses fishing etc. Formerly residential rectory, built in 1906, was elegantly developed into superior 50 bedroomed 4**** deluxe hotel in 1992 by the Randles family. Warm, friendly welcome, renowned & exquisite cuisine. Grandly spacious, luxurious bedrooms. Fine art & antique collections and relaxing atmosphere are just a few of the reasons why our guests return again. Own self drive cars.

Members Of Choice Hotels Ireland

B&B from £40.00 to £80.00
€50.79 to €101.58

TOM RANDLES
General Manager

American Express
Diners
Mastercard
Visa

  Weekend specials from £90.00

50 50

Closed 20 - 28 December

RIVERMERE

MUCKROSS ROAD, KILLARNEY,
CO. KERRY
TEL: 064-37933 FAX: 064-37944
EMAIL: rivermereguesthouse@eircom.net

GUESTHOUSE ★★★★ MAP 2 E 4

Rivermere is a custom built, family-run guesthouse within walking distance of Killarney National Park and lakes, 7 mins walk from town centre. All rooms are spacious, equipped with TV, DD phone, private bath/power shower, hairdryer. Private parking. Close to all local amenities. We look forward to welcoming you to Rivermere, where a personal service ensures an enjoyable stay.

B&B from £24.00 to £40.00
€30.47 to €50.79

HANNAH & ANDREW KISSANE
Proprietors

Mastercard
Visa

8 8

Closed 01 November - 28 February

Room rates are per room per night

ROSS HOTEL

KENMARE PLACE, KILLARNEY,
CO. KERRY
TEL: 064-31855   FAX: 064-31139
EMAIL: ross@kph.iol.ie

HOTEL ★★★   MAP 2 E 4

The Ross Hotel is one of the few family-owned and managed hotels in Killarney. Recently refurbished and centrally situated with 32 bedrooms. Renowned locally for its excellent food and comfortable bar, private car parking. Residents of Ross Hotel may use the leisure facilities of our sister hotel, the Killarney Park.

B&B from £36.00 to £48.00
€45.71 to €60.95

JANET & PADRAIG TREACY
Proprietors

American Express
Diners
Mastercard
Visa

😊 Weekend specials from £85.00

🛏🐾☎🖥📺🔌T C🐕CM♨️🎵P🅿️🅰🆑
32 32

IRISH
HOTELS
FEDERATION

Closed 07 December - 28 February

SCOTTS GARDENS HOTEL

KILLARNEY,
CO. KERRY
TEL: 064-31060   FAX: 064-36656

HOTEL N   MAP 2 E 4

Newly refurbished town centre hotel with private carpark facilities. 52 3*** standard bedrooms with DD phone, hairdryer, satellite TV, tea/coffee facilities. Adjacent to shops, restaurants, pubs, churches and Killarney National Park. Tours, cruises, golf, and fishing arranged. Entertainment nightly July/August and on weekends during rest of year.

B&B from £30.00 to £50.00
€38.09 to €63.49

O'DONOGHUE FAMILY
Proprietors

American Express
Mastercard
Visa

🛏🐾☎🖥📺🔌C♨️🎵P🆑
52 52

Closed 24 - 26 December

SLIEVE BLOOM MANOR GUESTHOUSE

MUCKROSS ROAD, KILLARNEY,
CO. KERRY
TEL: 064-34237   FAX: 064-35055

GUESTHOUSE ★★★   MAP 2 E 4

This charming 3*** guesthouse has a premier location on Muckross Rd, only 7 mins walk from Killarney town and gateway to National Park and lakes. Close to restaurants, bars and shops. Rooms are tastefully furnished with all facilities, varied breakfast menu available, private parking and store for bicycles, etc. Local amenities include superb golf at Killarney's two renowned courses, horse riding and fishing. Leisure centre close by. All tours arranged. Be our guest.

B&B from £18.00 to £22.50
€22.86 to €28.57

TERESA CLERY
Proprietor

Mastercard
Visa

🛏🐾☎🔌T C CM♨️🎵P S
11 11

IRISH
HOTELS
FEDERATION

Closed 15 December - 01 February

B&B rates are per person sharing per night incl. Breakfast

TORC GREAT SOUTHERN HOTEL

KILLARNEY,
CO. KERRY
TEL: 064-31611 FAX: 064-31824
EMAIL: res@torc.gsh.ie

HOTEL ★★★ MAP 2 E 4

A 3*** modern hotel situated in beautiful gardens, just 5 minutes from Killarney town. 96 rooms, all en suite, with DD phone, hairdryer, radio, tea/coffee making facilities and colour TV. Leisure facilities include indoor heated swimming pool, steamroom, jacuzzi. Outdoor tennis courts. Superbly located for golfing at Killarney's championship courses. An ideal base from which to tour the Kerry region. Bookable worldwide through Utell International or central reservations 01-2144800.

WEB: www.gsh.ie

B&B from £48.00 to £61.00
€60.95 to €77.45

FREDA DARCY
General Manager

American Express
Diners
Mastercard
Visa

☺ Weekend specials from £85.00

Closed 10 October - 10 April

TUSCAR LODGE

GOLF COURSE ROAD, FOSSA,
KILLARNEY, CO. KERRY
TEL: 064-31978 FAX: 064-31978

GUESTHOUSE ★★ MAP 2 E 4

Tuscar Lodge is a family run guest house. The proprietress Mrs Fitzgerald and her family always ensure that the guests have an enjoyable stay. Situated in scenic surroundings overlooking Loch Lein, with a magnificent view of the Magillycuddy Reeks. With its own car park, it is very central for touring the beauty spots of West Cork and Kerry. Pony trekking, boating, fishing and mountain climbing, all within easy range. Very near Killarney's two golf courses.

B&B from £18.00 to £20.00
€22.86 to €25.39

EILEEN FITZGERALD
Proprietor

Closed 01 November - 28 February

Room rates are per room per night

WOODLAWN HOUSE

WOODLAWN ROAD, KILLARNEY,
CO. KERRY
TEL: 064-37844   FAX: 064-36116
EMAIL: awrenn@eircom.net

GUESTHOUSE ★★★   MAP 2 E 4

Old style charm and hospitality.
Family run. Relaxed atmosphere. All
modern conveniences. Ideally
located 5 mins walk from town
centre. Near leisure centre, lakes and
golf courses. Tours arranged. Private
parking. Decorated with natural pine
wood. Orthopaedic beds dressed in
white cotton and linen. Irish and
vegetarian menus. Our wholesome
breakfasts include freshly squeezed
orange juice, homemade preserves
and bread. Early bird breakfast also
available. A warm welcome assured.

WEB: www.kerry-insight.com/woodlawnhouse

B&B from £22.00 to £29.00
€27.93 to €36.82

ANNE & JAMES WRENN

Mastercard
Visa

9 9

Closed 01 - 29 December

BIANCONI

KILLORGLIN, RING OF KERRY,
CO. KERRY
TEL: 066-976 1146   FAX: 066-976 1950

GUESTHOUSE ★★★   MAP 1 D 4

Family run inn on the Ring of Kerry.
Gateway to Dingle peninsula,
Killarney 18km. On the road to
Glencar - famous for its scenery,
lakes, hill walking and mountain
climbing. Famous for its table. High
standard of food in bar. Table d'hôte
and à la carte available. 1 hour to
Waterville, Tralee & Ballybunion golf
courses. 15 mins to Dooks &
Beaufort courses. 5 mins to
Killorglin course. 15 mins to
Killarney course. Private access to
Caragh Lake. Own boat. Mentioned
by many guides.

B&B from £29.00 to £32.50
€36.82 to €41.27

RAY SHEEHY
Owner

American Express
Diners
Mastercard
Visa

15 15

IRISH HOTELS FEDERATION

Closed 23 - 29 December

GROVE LODGE GUESTHOUSE

KILLARNEY ROAD, KILLORGLIN,
CO. KERRY
TEL: 066-976 1157   FAX: 066-976 2330
EMAIL: gorveldg@iol.ie

GUESTHOUSE ★★★   MAP 1 D 4

Ideally located for all your holiday
activities; golfing, fishing, hill
walking, sightseeing, beaches, Ring
of Kerry/Ring of Dingle, with local
gourmet restaurants & pub
entertainment. (5 min walk from
town centre). We invite you to share
your holiday with us in our newly
refurbished, spacious & luxurious
accommodation, situated on 3 acres
of mature gardens & woodlands,
fronted by the river Laune &
McGillycuddy Reeks mountains &
savour our speciality gourmet
breakfasts. RAC, AA ◆◆◆◆.

B&B from £25.00 to £36.00
€31.74 to €45.71

DELIA & FERGUS FOLEY
Owners & Managers

Mastercard
Visa

10 10

Closed 23 - 29 December

B&B rates are per person sharing per night incl. Breakfast

WESTFIELD HOUSE

KILLORGLIN,
CO. KERRY
TEL: 066-976 1909 FAX: 066-976 1996
EMAIL: westhse@iol.ie

GUESTHOUSE ★★★ MAP 1 D 4

Westfield House is a family run guesthouse. All rooms are bright & spacious en suite, orthopaedic beds, direct dial telephone, TV, tea/coffee maker. Extra large family room available. We are situated on Ring of Kerry in a quite peaceful location only 5 mins walk from town with panoramic views of MacGillycuddy Reeks. There are five 18 hole golf courses within 20 mins drive. Recognised stop for many weary cyclists. Ideal location for the hillwalker and climber.

B&B from £22.50 to £25.00
€28.57 to €31.74

LEONARD CLIFFORD
Proprietor

Mastercard

Visa

🛏🏠☎🖨TCM✳🅿🚲Sa/c
10 10

IRISH
HOTELS
FEDERATION

Open All Year

LISTOWEL ARMS HOTEL

THE SQUARE, LISTOWEL,
CO. KERRY
TEL: 068-21500 FAX: 068-22524

HOTEL ★★★ MAP 2 E 6

In a tranquil corner of Listowel's old square, the Listowel Arms Hotel is a haven of comfort and hospitality, an establishment with a proud tradition of fine food, and discreet service, a quiet retreat, a warm and intimate meeting place. Famous for it's annual race meeting, Listowel is an ideal location to explore the famous Ring of Kerry, Dingle peninsula and lakes of Killarney. Tee times can be reserved at nearby world famous Ballybunion golf club along with Listowel golf club.

B&B from £35.00 to £75.00
€44.44 to €95.23

KEVIN O'CALLAGHAN
Director

American Express

Diners

Mastercard

Visa

🍴🥢🍽

🛏🏠☎🖨⬆TC🍴CM✳♨♪🎵
🚲S♀🅱a/c
37 37

IRISH
HOTELS
FEDERATION

Closed 24 - 26 December

MOORINGS

PORTMAGEE,
CO. KERRY
TEL: 066-947 7108 FAX: 066-947 7220
EMAIL: moorings@iol.ie

GUESTHOUSE ★★★ MAP 1 B 3

The Moorings is a family owned guesthouse and restaurant overlooking the picturesque fishing port in Portmagee. Excellent cuisine, specialising in locally caught seafood. Adjacent to the Moorings is the Bridge Bar, also run by the family, where you can enjoy a wonderful night of music song and dance. The Moorings is central to all local amenities including angling, diving, watersports, 18 hole golf course etc. Trips to Skellig Michael can be arranged.

WEB: www.moorings.ie

B&B from £22.00 to £30.00
€27.93 to €38.09

GERARD & PATRICIA KENNEDY
Proprietors

Mastercard

Visa

🐋

🛏🏠☎🖨TCMU♪🎵🅿a/c🍴
14 14

IRISH
HOTELS
FEDERATION

Closed 01 November - 01 March

Room rates are per room per night

PARKNASILLA GREAT SOUTHERN HOTEL

SNEEM,
CO. KERRY
TEL: 064-45122 FAX: 064-45323
EMAIL: res@parknasilla.gsh.ie

HOTEL ★★★★ MAP 1 C 3

Acknowledged as one of Ireland's finest hotels, Parknasilla is a 19th century house set in 300 acres of grounds. A classically individual hotel with 84 bedrooms equipped with every modern amenity. Leisure facilities include indoor heated swimming pool, sauna, steam room, jacuzzi, hydrotherapy baths, outdoor hot tub, pony trekking, clay pigeon shooting, archery, water skiing, private 9 hole golf course - special green fees for guests. Utell Int. or Central Reservations 01-214 4800

WEB· www.gsh.ie

B&B from £80.00 to £106.00
€101.58 to €134.59

JIM FEENEY
General Manager

American Express
Diners
Mastercard
Visa

😊 Weekend specials from £130.00

Open All Year

TAHILLA COVE COUNTRY HOUSE

TAHILLA, NEAR SNEEM,
CO. KERRY
TEL: 064-45204 FAX: 064-45104
EMAIL: tahillacove@eircom.net

GUESTHOUSE ★★★ MAP 1 D 3

Travel writers have described this family-run, fully licensed seashore guesthouse as the most idyllic spot in Ireland - the haunt of Irish/British dignitaries. Located on the Ring of Kerry seashore, this 14 acre estate boasts mature gardens and private pier. Ideal place for a relaxing holiday or touring centre. Each bedroom has en suite facilities, telephone, television, radio and hair dryer. Log fires, superb views, home cooking. Take Sneem road from Kenmare (N70).

WEB: www.cnoom.com/tahillacove.html

B&B from £35.00 to £40.00
€44.44 to €50.79

JAMES/DOLLY/DEIRDRE WATERHOUSE
Owners/Managers

American Express
Diners
Mastercard
Visa

😊 Special weekly rates on request

Closed 15 October - 01 April

ABBEY GATE HOTEL

MAINE STREET, TRALEE,
CO. KERRY
TEL: 066-712 9888 FAX: 066-712 9821
EMAIL: abbeygat@iol.ie

HOTEL ★★★ MAP 1 D 5

Welcome, the Abbey Gate Hotel is located in the heart of Tralee. All 100 rooms are spacious with full facilities. The Old Market Place pub is Tralee's liveliest venue with great pub grub served all day and casual dining in Bistro Marché at night. Or try our intimate Vineyard Restaurant for the best of Irish and continental dishes. The Abbey Gate Hotel is your gateway to the delights of Kerry!

[handwritten notes: parking-outside, TV., T/k/fee?, ensuite]

B&B from £25.00 to £49.00
€31.74 to €62.22

PATRICK DILLON
General Manager

American Express
Diners
Mastercard
Visa

Closed 24 - 26 December

B&B rates are per person sharing per night incl. Breakfast

BALLYGARRY HOUSE HOTEL

**KILLARNEY ROAD, TRALEE,
CO. KERRY**
TEL: 066-712 1233 FAX: 066-712 7630

HOTEL ★★★ MAP 1 D 5

Ballygarry House Hotel invites you to relax by open fires and experience an air of wellbeing. Ideally situated for Kerry's magnificent golf courses, we can be found less than 1.5k from Tralee en route to Kerry airport and Killarney (N22). This country house hotel boasts 30 luxurious rooms overlooking beautiful landscaped gardens. Our Riverside Restaurant offers modern and traditional cuisine in an intimate atmosphere. A warm welcome awaits you.

Members Of Signature Hotels

B&B from £35.00 to £55.00
€44.44 to €69.84

OWEN MCGILLICUDDY
Proprietor

American Express

Mastercard

Visa

🛏️🅿️☎️📶🇹🇨CM❄️⛵🎵🅿️🅰️alc
30 30

Closed 20 - 28 December

BALLYSEEDE CASTLE HOTEL

**BALLYSEEDY, TRALEE,
CO. KERRY**
TEL: 066-712 5799   FAX: 066-712 5287

HOTEL ★★★ MAP 1 D 5

Ballyseede Castle Hotel is a casual, almost cosy 15th century castle on 35 hectares of parkland. The castle boasts a fine selection of continental cuisine as well as many traditional Irish dishes. Located on the main Tralee/Killarney road within easy reach of Kerry's five magnificent golf courses, Ballybunion, Waterville, Killarney, Dooks and Barrow, the recently designed course for Tralee by Arnold Palmer. Ideally situated for touring the Ring of Kerry and Dingle peninsula.

B&B from £70.00 to £100.00
€88.88 to €126.97

BART W O'CONNOR
Managing Director

Mastercard

Visa

🛏️🅿️☎️🇹❄️⛵🎵🅿️🅰️alc
12 12

**IRISH
HOTELS
FEDERATION**

Open All Year

BARROW HOUSE

**WEST BARROW, TRALEE,
CO. KERRY**
TEL: 066-713 6437 FAX: 066-713 6402

GUESTHOUSE U MAP 1 D 5

Built in 1723, Barrow House is located on Barrow Harbour next to the superb Tralee Golf Club with magnificent views of the Slieve Mish mountains and the Dingle peninsula. This period house has been elegantly refurbished to provide a combination of luxurious suites and deluxe rooms. Each room enjoys the comforts of modern day living in a unique and tranquil setting. Golf, angling, golden beaches, sailing, award-winning restaurants and pubs close by. Former home of Knight of Kerry.

B&B from £30.00 to £50.00
€38.09 to €63.49

NOELLE CROSBIE
Manager

Mastercard

Visa

🛏️🅿️☎️🇹🇨❄️⛵🎵🅿️⚓🇸🇾
15 15

Closed 20 December - 01 April

Room rates are per room per night

BRANDON COURT HOTEL

JAMES STREET, TRALEE,
CO. KERRY
TEL: 066-712 9666   FAX: 066-712 9690

HOTEL U   MAP 1 D 5

The concept - quality at a fixed price. Bright, modern and spacious rooms, each with its own bathroom, colour TV, direct dial telephone and tea/coffee making facilities. The price remains fixed when a room is occupied by 1, 2 or 3 adults or up to 2 adults and 2 children. Bright, spacious public areas, cosy bar facilities and restaurant serving breakfast and light evening meals. Located in Tralee's old quarter, adjacent to Siamsa Tire, Aqua Dome and Kerry County Museum.

Room Rate from £52.00 to £110.00
€66.03 to €139.67

PETER MCDERMOTT
Director/General Manager

American Express
Diners
Mastercard
Visa

49 49

Closed 01 November - 15 March

BRANDON HOTEL

PRINCES STREET, TRALEE,
CO. KERRY
TEL: 066-712 3333   FAX: 066-712 5019

HOTEL ★★★   MAP 1 D 5

This renowned, privately owned premises is located in the heart of Tralee town, close to shopping and cultural interests. The hotel offers a wide range of accommodation - standard, superior and deluxe rooms - and a choice of bars and restaurants. It is also equipped with full leisure centre incorporating swimming pool, sauna and steamroom and has extensive conference facilities. The Brandon Hotel is easily reached by mainline rail or flying to Kerry County Airport just 10 miles away.

B&B from £35.00 to £80.00
€44.44 to €101.58

PETER MCDERMOTT
Director/General Manager

American Express
Diners
Mastercard
Visa

182 182

Closed 24 - 28 December

BROOK MANOR LODGE

FENIT ROAD, TRALEE,
CO. KERRY
TEL: 066-712 0406   FAX: 066-712 7552
EMAIL: brookmanor@eircom.net

GUESTHOUSE ★★★★   MAP 1 D 5

A warm welcome awaits you at our new 4★★★★ luxurious, family-run lodge. Only minutes drive from Tralee, golden beaches and Arnold Palmer designed golf course. 30 minutes from Killarney. 40 minutes from Ballybunion. The Lodge is situated in acres of meadowlands and surrounded by a babbling brook. All our rooms are en suite with full facilities. Brook Manor Lodge is the ideal place for the perfect holiday.

B&B from £28.00 to £40.00
€35.55 to €50.79

MARGARET & VINCENT O'SULLIVAN
Owners

American Express
Mastercard
Visa

6 6

Open All Year

B&B rates are per person sharing per night incl. Breakfast

GLENDUFF HOUSE

KIELDUFF, TRALEE,
CO. KERRY
TEL: 066-713 7105   FAX: 066-713 7099
EMAIL: glenduffhouse@eircom.net

GUESTHOUSE ★★★   MAP 1 D 5

Enter the old world charm of the 19th century in our family run period house set on 6 acres with mature gardens. Refurbished to give the comforts of the modern day, yet keeping its original character with antiques & paintings. Personal attention assured. Evening meals by prearrangement. Relax & enjoy a drink in our friendly bar. Also self catering cottages in courtyard. Ideally situated for golf and sports amenities. From Tralee take route to racecourse off N21 at Clash roundabout.

WEB: glenduffhouse@inkerry.com

B&B from £24.00 to £36.00
€30.47 to €45.71

SHEILA SUGRUE
Owner

Mastercard
Visa

Closed 03 January - 14 March

GRAND HOTEL

DENNY STREET, TRALEE,
CO. KERRY
TEL: 066-712 1499   FAX: 066-712 2877
EMAIL: info@grandhoteltralee.com

HOTEL ★★★   MAP 1 D 5

The Grand Hotel is a 3*** hotel situated in Tralee town centre. Established in 1928, its open fires, ornate ceilings and mahogany furnishings offer guests old world charm in comfortable surroundings. All our rooms are equipped with DD phone, TV and tea/coffee welcoming trays. Residents can avail of green fee reductions at Tralee Golf Club. Also reduced rates to the fabulous Aqua Dome Waterworld complex. Family rooms are available at discounted rates.

B&B from £30.00 to £50.00
€38.09 to €63.49

DICK BOYLE
General Manager

American Express
Mastercard
Visa

Weekend specials from £72.00

Open All Year

IMPERIAL HOTEL

27 DENNY STREET, TRALEE,
CO. KERRY
TEL: 066-712 7755   FAX: 066-712 7800
EMAIL: imptrale@indigo.ie

HOTEL N MAP 1 D 5

The Imperial Hotel is a comfortable and cosy family run hotel situated in Tralee town centre on a beautiful old Georgian street. The hotel offers good food and fine wine all year round in an old world setting. All our rooms are en suite with DD phone and TV. Tralee offers good golfing, greyhound racing, theatre and an excellent selection of restaurants.

B&B from £30.00 to £50.00
€38.09 to €63.49

DAMIEN & MARION SMYTH

Mastercard
Visa

Open All Year

Room rates are per room per night

JOHNSTON MARINA HOTEL

DINGLE ROAD, TRALEE,
CO. KERRY
TEL: 066-718 0177   FAX: 066-718 1881
EMAIL: jjhotel@iol.ie

HOTEL N   MAP 1 D 5

Luxurious new hotel with 35 en suite elegant rooms including multi-channel TV. Overlooking Blennerville windmill and Tralee marina it is ideal for visiting Tralee town (5 mins) and visitor attractions, Dingle or Killarney. Nellies Pub, Loft and beer garden with its thatched roof and traditional style has become a favoured attraction to visitors. Captain Johns Restaurant offers the best in local and international cuisine with a noted selection of fish dishes.

WEB. www.kerry-insight.com/johnston-marina

B&B from £25.00 to £45.00
€31.74 to €57.14

FIONNBAR WALSH
General Manager

American Express
Diners
Mastercard
Visa

☺ Weekend specials from £85.00

35 35

Open All Year

MEADOWLANDS HOTEL

OAKPARK, TRALEE,
CO. KERRY
TEL: 066-718 0444   FAX: 066-718 0964
EMAIL: medlands@iol.ie

HOTEL U   MAP 1 D 5

A charming and intimate hotel, set in a tranquil corner of Tralee, on its own 3 acres with beautiful landscaped gardens. This small luxurious hotel comprises of 27 superbly appointed rooms including suites. Our gourmet restaurant specialises in the freshest of locally-caught seafood and shellfish cuisine. The Meadowlands is an ideal base for golfing enthusiasts and touring the Dingle peninsula, Ring of Kerry, Killarney and west Cork. Experience an experience!

Members Of MinOtel Ireland Hotel Group

B&B from £45.00 to £60.00
€57.14 to €76.18

JOHN PALMER
Manager

Mastercard
Visa

☺ Weekend specials from £100.00

27 27

Closed 24 - 26 December

MOUNTAIN LODGE GUESTHOUSE AND BAR

ANNAGH, BLENNERVILLE, MAIN
DINGLE ROAD, TRALEE, CO. KERRY
TEL: 066-712 2461   FAX: 066-712 0325

GUESTHOUSE ★★   MAP 1 D 5

Family run guesthouse with fully licensed bar serving bar food. Self-catering cottages on grounds. Situated 4.8k from Tralee on the main Tralee/Dingle road (N86). The complex overlooks Tralee Bay with the Kerry mountains at the back. Huge private car park. Convenient to many famous Kerry beaches as well as golf, horse-riding, pony trekking, Aqua Dome, sports complex, Blennerville Windmill, steam train. Owners - Chef, Padraig and Larry. Bar & restaurant in high season only.

B&B from £18.00 to £22.00
€22.86 to €27.93

KATHLEEN & LARRY KERINS
Managers

Mastercard
Visa

8 8

Closed 01 November - 01 March

B&B rates are per person sharing per night incl. Breakfast

OAKLEY HOUSE

BALLYMULLEN, TRALEE,
CO. KERRY
TEL: 066-712 1727 FAX: 066-712 1727

GUESTHOUSE ★★ MAP 1 D 5

Spacious period house with old world charm and character. Situated on main road (N70) to Dingle Peninsula, Killorglin and Ring of Kerry. Overlooking Slieve Mish mountains. Ideal touring base. 8 minutes walk from town centre, National Folk Theatre, Medieval experience. 10 minutes walk from Aqua Dome. Private car park, convenient to beaches, angling, golf, horseriding and pony trekking. Complementary Tea/Coffee available in our spacious TV lounge. A cead mile failte awaits you.

B&B from £20.00 to £22.00
€25.39 to €27.93

MICHAEL & PHILOMENA BENNIS
Proprietors

Mastercard

Visa

☺ Midweek specials from £57.00

7   7

IRISH HOTELS FEDERATION

Open All Year

BAY VIEW HOTEL

WATERVILLE,
CO. KERRY
TEL: 066-947 4122 FAX: 066-947 4504

HOTEL ★★ MAP 1 B 3

The Bay View Hotel has old world charm with beautiful spacious bedrooms with front rooms facing the Atlantic. On the Ring of Kerry in the middle of the village of Waterville the hotel is an ideal location for exploring the peninsula with its breathtaking scenery and archaeological sites. Make sure you visit the Sceilig Rock.

B&B from £25.00 to £40.00
€31.74 to €50.79

MICHAEL O'SHEA
Manager

American Express

Mastercard

Visa

☺ Midweek specials from £75.00

69   69

IRISH HOTELS FEDERATION

Closed 01 November - 01 March

BROOKHAVEN GUESTHOUSE

NEW LINE ROAD, WATERVILLE,
CO. KERRY
TEL: 066-947 4431 FAX: 066-947 4724
EMAIL: brookhaven@esatclear.ie

GUESTHOUSE ★★★ MAP 1 B 3

New, purpose built guesthouse, located on the scenic Ring of Kerry route. Luxury spacious en suite rooms decorated to a high standard with all modern amenities. Rooms overlook the Atlantic ocean and the renowned Waterville golf course. Brookhaven is also within easy reach of other scenic and challenging courses and is central to all local amenities, e.g. golfing, fishing, pony treking, sandy beaches, walking, cycling and gourmet restaurants. AA ♦♦♦. RAC Highly Acclaimed.

WEB: www.euroka.com/waterville/brookhaven

B&B from £20.00 to £28.00
€25.39 to €35.55

MARY CLIFFORD
Proprietor

☺ 10% discount 5 nights stay

5   5

IRISH HOTELS FEDERATION

Closed 31 October - 01 March

Room rates are per room per night

BUTLER ARMS HOTEL

WATERVILLE,
CO. KERRY
TEL: 066-947 4144 FAX: 066-947 4520
EMAIL: butarms@iol.ie

HOTEL ★★★ MAP 1 B 3

Butler Arms Hotel, overlooking the Atlantic, is one of Ireland's best known family run hotels, being the holiday retreat for Charlie Chaplin for many years. Amenities include 30 well appointed bedrooms with sea views, comfortable lounges, seafood restaurant and Fishermens Bar. Green fee reductions on Waterville championship golf links. Salmon/sea trout fishing on Lough Currane and private lakes. Tennis/snooker/horse riding. Manor House Hotels 01-2958900 AA***, RAC***.

WEB. www.kerry-insight.com/butler-arms/

Members Of Manor House Hotels

B&B from £50.00 to £72.50
€63.49 to €92.06

MARY & PETER HUGGARD
Proprietors

American Express
Mastercard
Visa

☺ Weekend specials from £95.00

30 30

Closed 20 October - 01 April

LAKELANDS FARM GUESTHOUSE

LAKE ROAD, WATERVILLE,
CO. KERRY
TEL: 066-947 4303 FAX: 066-947 4678
EMAIL: lakelands@eircom.net

GUESTHOUSE ★★★ MAP 1 B 3

Luxury family run guesthouse in unique location set on 100 acre estate on the south shore of Europe's best free salmon and sea trout lake. Smoking and non smoking lounges. Comfortable spacious bedrooms, all ensuite with D.Dial, TV, Tea/Coffee facilities, hairdryer, some with balcony or jacuzzi. Proprietor professional angler with 10 motor boats. Private pools on River Inny, sea angling arranged. Convenient to Waterville Golf Course. 2,000 acres of forest land for shooting.

WFR· http://www.kerrygems.ie/lakelands

B&B from £20.00 to £26.00
€25.39 to €33.01

ANNE & FRANK DONNELLY
Porprietors

Mastercard
Visa

10 10

Closed 25 December

SMUGGLERS INN

CLIFF ROAD, WATERVILLE,
CO. KERRY
TEL: 066-947 4330 FAX: 066-947 4422

GUESTHOUSE ★★★ MAP 1 B 3

The Smugglers Inn, a family run inn with old world charm and character, quiet location on 2k sandy beach. Adjacent to Waterville golf course, near lake and sea fishing facilities and sporting activities. Very high standard in our gourmet seafood restaurant, meals prepared by chef proprietor Harry Hunt and son Henry. Dining room under supervision of his wife Lucille. Exceptional accommodation. Many good food guides recommend. Breathtaking sea views and spectacular sunsets.

B&B from £23.00 to £40.00
€29.20 to €50.79

LUCILLE & HARRY HUNT
Proprietors

American Express
Diners
Mastercard
Visa

☺ Weekend specials from £73.00

14 14

Closed 30 November - 01 March

B&B rates are per person sharing per night incl. Breakfast

SHANNON
Romantic and Exciting

Your holiday in the Shannon Region can be as active or as placid as you choose. Whichever you choose, you are guaranteed relaxation and enjoyment. All the ingredients are there: the towering cliffs and golden beaches of Clare and North Kerry; the enigmatic rockscapes of the Burren; the gentle beauty of the rolling Slieve Bloom Mountains in South Offaly; Tipperary's fertile pastures and the woodland estates in the heart of County Limerick. And, of course, the mighty Shannon River, which has bestowed its riches on the surrounding countryside and glories in its beauty.

This is one of the few remaining places on earth where clean, unpolluted air is taken for granted.

You have the space to breathe, to refresh your spirit a universe away from frenetic and crowded cities.

There is a sense of timelessness aided by the many physical reminders of Ireland's turbulent past. Castles, forts and ancient churches, spanning centuries of history, abound. many have been lovingly restored.

At the famous Bunratty Castle, visitors can slip back in time and take part in a 15th century Mediaeval Banquet of romance and merriment. The Bunratty Folk Park, in the castle grounds, accurately recreates Irish village life at the turn of the century.

Sporting facilities, in contrast, are very much up to date. Imagine golfing in a magnificent, scenic setting or fishing some of the most productive and versatile fishing waters in Europe. Take to the saddle on horse-back and the countryside is yours.

If boating is your pleasure, the possibilities are, literally, limitless.

There are many elements to a really memorable holiday and the Shannon Region can provide them all. One of the most important is the feeling of being really welcome, of being valued. This intangible but very real feature of a Shannon holiday will be immediately evident in the sense of fun which you will encounter and an eagerness to treat you as an honoured guest.

In Ireland, enjoyment is an art form. Go to one of the many festivals in the Shannon Region and you will experience the art at its best. Entertainment, spontaneous or organised, is everywhere, so too is good food and good company. For further information contact: Tourist Information Office, Arthur's Quay, Limerick. Tel: 061 317522. Fax: 061 317939. Visit our website: www.shannon-dev.ie/tourism

Willie Clancy Summer School, Miltown Malby. Co. Clare **July**

Lisdoonvarna Matchmaking Festival, Lisdoonvarna, Co. Clare. **September / October**

Event details correct at time of going to press

BALLYVAUGHAN LODGE

BALLYVAUGHAN,
CO. CLARE
TEL: 065-707 7292   FAX: 065-707 7287
EMAIL: ballyvau@iol.ie

GUESTHOUSE ★★★   MAP 6 F 10

Located in the heart of
Ballyvaughan, a small fishing village
overlooking Galway bay. A custom
built modern guesthouse, dedicated
to the comfort and relaxation of our
guests. Each room en suite having
TV, DD phone, tea/coffee making
facilities, etc. Allow us to plan your
carefree days in the most unspoilt
natural environment imaginable, the
Burren, including Neolithic caves,
sea fishing, hill walking, cycling,
Cliffs of Moher and the Aran Islands.

B&B from £18.00 to £25.00
€22.86 to €31.74

PAULINE BURKE
Owner

Mastercard

Visa

8 8

Closed 25 - 26 December

CAPPABHAILE HOUSE

BALLYVAUGHAN,
CO. CLARE
TEL: 065-707 7260   FAX: 065-707 7300
EMAIL: cappabhaile@oceanfree.net

GUESTHOUSE ★★★   MAP 6 F 10

Relax, enjoy the peace & quiet,
luxury & comfort and a warm family
welcome at Cappabhaile House. All
rooms are generously sized with
private bathrooms. We have scenic
views of the Burren mountains,
Newtown Castle & Ailwee Cave. We
have a private carpark, pitch & putt
course, games room and the Burren
Gallery, all FREE to our guests.
Nearby: hill walking, nature trails
and beaches. Ideal location for
touring the Burren, Cliffs of Moher,
Aran Islands and Connemara.

B&B from £20.00 to £28.00
€25.39 to €35.55

MARGARET & CONOR FAHY
Proprietors

Mastercard

Visa

:) Midweek specials from £55.00

8 8

S ▪ Inet

Closed 05 November - 01 March

DRUMCREEHY HOUSE

BALLYVAUGHAN,
CO. CLARE
TEL: 065-707 7377   FAX: 065-707 7379
EMAIL: b&b@drumcreehyhouse.com

GUESTHOUSE P   MAP 6 F 10

Delightful country style house
overlooking Galway Bay and the
surrounding Burren landscape. Open
fires, antique furnishings plus a
friendly and personal service by
conscientious hosts Armin and
Bernadette help to make your stay
both enjoyable and memorable.
Tastefully decorated rooms, all en
suite and equipped with TV and DD
phone. Extensive breakfast menu
and simple country style cooking in
a relaxed and homely atmosphere.
Ideally located for touring Clare,
Kerry and Galway.

WEB: www.drumcreehyhouse.com

B&B from £18.00 to £28.00
€22.86 to €35.55

A & B MOLONEY-GREFKES
Proprietors

Mastercard

Visa

:) Weekend specials from £50.00

10 10

Ⓨ

Open All Year

B&B rates are per person sharing per night incl. Breakfast

GREGANS CASTLE HOTEL

BALLYVAUGHAN,
CO. CLARE
TEL: 065-707 7005   FAX: 065-707 7111
EMAIL: res@gregans.ie

HOTEL ★★★★   MAP 6 F 10

4**** luxury hotel amid splendid Burren mountain scenery, overlooking Galway Bay. Country house comforts, turf fires, tranquillity, no TVs in bedrooms. Award winning gardens, food, service, accommodations. Individually designed superior rooms and suites. Nearby ocean swimming, horse riding, hillwalking. Golf at Lahinch. Halfway between Kerry and Connemara using ferry. RAC Blue Ribbon winner. AA Red Stars award. 1 hour from Shannon Airport.

WEB: www.gregans.ie

Members Of Ireland's Blue Book

B&B from £49.00 to £68.00
€62.22 to €86.34

SIMON HADEN
Manager & Director

Mastercard
Visa

☺ Week partial board from £525.00

22 22

Closed 01 November - 01 April

HYLAND'S HOTEL

BALLYVAUGHAN,
CO. CLARE
TEL: 065-707 7037   FAX: 065-707 7131
EMAIL: hylands@eircom.net

HOTEL ★★★   MAP 6 F 10

A charming family run hotel whose present owners are 7th and 8th generation proudly carrying on the tradition for hospitality and good food. Experience bygone charm with modern day facilities, open turf fires, informal bars and restaurants specialising in the finest local seafood. An ideal base for the golfing and walking enthusiasts, exploring the unique Burren landscape, visiting the Aran Islands, touring the unspoilt Clare, Connemara and Kerry countrysides, truly an artists haven.

WEB: www.iol.ie/hotels

Members Of Village Inn Hotels

B&B from £39.00 to £46.50
€49.52 to €59.04

MARIE GREENE
Inn Keeper

American Express
Diners
Mastercard
Visa

☺ Weekend specials from £79.00

30 30

Closed 06 January - 01 March

RUSHEEN LODGE

BALLYVAUGHAN,
CO. CLARE
TEL: 065-707 7092   FAX: 065-707 7152
EMAIL: rusheenl@iol.ie

GUESTHOUSE ★★★★   MAP 6 F 10

Rusheen Lodge is a superb 4**** family run guesthouse, nestling in a valley surrounded by the Burren Limestone mountains noted for their rock formations and unique flora. A previous winner of the Small Hotel & Guesthouse of the Year award. The Lodge provides elegant and tastefully designed en suite bedrooms, dining room and residents lounge ensuring a comfortable and relaxing stay. Excellent location for touring Clare, Kerry and Connemara.

B&B from £25.00 to £30.00
€31.74 to €38.09

JOHN & RITA MC GANN
Proprietors

American Express
Mastercard
Visa

8 8

Closed 30 November - 01 February

Room rates are per room per night

BUNRATTY CASTLE HOTEL

BUNRATTY,
CO. CLARE
TEL: 061-707034 FAX: 061-364891
EMAIL: info@bunrattycastlehotel.iol.ie

HOTEL ★★★ MAP 6 G 7

The new Bunratty Castle Hotel is a 3★★★ Georgian hotel. Situated in the centre of Bunratty village overlooking the historic Bunratty Castle and just across the road from Ireland's oldest pub, Durty Nellies. The rooms have been tastefully decorated in the traditional style. All rooms have air conditioning, satellite TV and have every modern comfort. Relax in Kathleens Irish Pub and restaurant and enjoy great food. We welcome you to experience the warmth and hospitality here.

B&B from £40.00 to £48.00
€50.79 to €60.95

KATHLEEN MCLOUGHLIN
Director

American Express
Diners
Mastercard
Visa

Closed 25 December

BUNRATTY GROVE

CASTLE ROAD, BUNRATTY,
CO. CLARE
TEL: 061-369579 FAX: 061-369561
EMAIL: bunrattygrove@eircom.net

GUESTHOUSE ★★★ MAP 6 G 7

Bunratty Grove is a purpose built luxurious guest house. This guesthouse is located within 3 mins drive from Bunratty Castle and Folk Park and 10 mins from Shannon Airport. Fishing, golfing, historical interests within a short distance. Ideally located for tourists arriving or departing Shannon airport. Bookings for Bunratty and Knappogue Banquets taken on request. All rooms en suite with multi-channel TV, hair dryer, tea/coffee facilities and DD phone.

WEB: http://homepage.eircom.net/~bunrattygrove/

B&B from £20.00 to £27.50
€25.39 to €34.92

PETER & PATSY GOLDEN
Owners

Mastercard
Visa

Closed 30 October - 01 April

BUNRATTY VIEW GUESTHOUSE

CRATLOE, NEAR BUNRATTY,
CO. CLARE
TEL: 061-357352 FAX: 061-357491

GUESTHOUSE ★★★ MAP 6 G 7

Bunratty View is a 3★★★ guesthouse located 10 minutes from Shannon airport, 2 km from Bunratty Castle. Bedrooms have private bathroom, satellite TV, direct dial telephone, hair dryer, tea/coffee facilities, orthopaedic beds. Ideal for tourists arriving or departing Shannon airport. Excellent location for touring Cliffs of Moher, Aillwee Caves, Lakes of Killaloe. Banquets for Bunratty and Knappogue booked on request. Recommended by leading guides for accommodation and hospitality.

B&B from £17.00 to £23.00
€21.59 to €29.20

JOE & MAURA BRODIE
Proprietors

Mastercard
Visa

Closed 20 - 27 December

B&B rates are per person sharing per night incl. Breakfast

BUNRATTY WOODS COUNTRY HOUSE

**LOW ROAD, BUNRATTY,
CO. CLARE
TEL: 061-369689 FAX: 061-369454
EMAIL: bunratty@iol.ie**

GUESTHOUSE ★★★ MAP 6 G 7

Bunratty Woods is a 3*** luxurious guesthouse situated in the old grounds of Bunratty Castle (2 mins drive) to Bunratty Castle and Folk Park and the renowned Durty Nellies pub. All rooms are en suite with DD phone, TV, tea/coffee making facilities and hair dryer. Magnificent mountain views. Bunratty Woods is furnished with style and taste of a bygone era - featuring items such as a settle bed and a famine pot and many, many other items from yesteryear.

WEB: www.iol.ie/~bunratty/

B&B from £22.50 to £25.00
€28.57 to €31.74

MAUREEN & PADDY O'DONOVAN
Owners

Diners
Mastercard
Visa

15 15

Closed 21 - 28 December

CRATLOE LODGE

**SETRIGHTS CROSS, CRATLOE,
NEAR BUNRATTY, CO. CLARE
TEL: 061-357168**

GUESTHOUSE ★★★ MAP 6 G 7

Cratloe Lodge is a 3*** luxury guesthouse purpose built to a high standard. Bedrooms are all en suite with satellite TV, D.D. phone and trouser press. Complimentary tea/coffee available on arrival. This guesthouse is located 10 mins from Shannon airport and 5 mins from Bunratty Castle. Excellent location for those arriving or departing Shannon airport. Ideal as starting point for touring Cliffs of Moher, Ailwee Caves and the Lakes of Killaloe.

B&B from £17.00 to £22.00
€21.59 to €27.93

TOM & MAURA GALVIN

Mastercard
Visa

☺ Midweek specials from £50.00

7 7

Open All Year

FITZPATRICK BUNRATTY

**BUNRATTY,
CO. CLARE
TEL: 061-361177 FAX: 061-471252
EMAIL: bunratty@fitzpatricks.com**

HOTEL U MAP 6 G 7

Situated in wooded grounds in Bunratty village against the backdrop of the medieval castle and folk park. Discover village life with lively pubs, colourful restaurants and shops. 4 miles from Shannon. Hotel facilities include excellent bar and restaurant, fitness centre and rooms with bath, satellite TV and DD phone. Four 18 hole championship golf courses within easy drive. Horse riding available locally. The ideal choice for your stay in the mid-west.

WEB: www.fitzpatrickhotels.com

B&B from £52.50 to £79.50
€66.66 to €100.94

SANDRA DOYLE
General Manager

American Express
Diners
Mastercard
Visa

115 115

alc

Closed 24 - 26 December

Room rates are per room per night

TUBRIDY HOUSE

COORACLARE VILLAGE,
CO. CLARE
TEL: 065-905 9033 FAX: 065-905 9388
EMAIL: tubridyhouse@eircom.net

GUESTHOUSE ★ MAP 5 E 7

Your host Ms. Anne Tubridy extends her welcome to her guests at Cooraclare. Situated 45 minutes from Shannon Airport. With its seas, lakes and rivers, anglers are guaranteed the best of shore and game angling. Tackle shed, cool room, wash room, tennis, pitch and putt, pony trekking, games room and private car park are available. All rooms en suite, direct dial telephones, private TV room. Complete the day with live entertainment nightly in the bar.

B&B from £17.00 to £17.00
€21.59 to €21.59

ANNE TUBRIDY
Owner

Mastercard
Visa

🙂 Week partial board from
£160.00

7   7

Open All Year

ARAN VIEW HOUSE HOTEL & RESTAURANT

COAST ROAD, DOOLIN,
CO. CLARE
TEL: 065-707 4061 FAX: 065-707 4540

HOTEL ★★★ MAP 5 E 9

A Georgian house built in 1736, has a unique position commanding panoramic views of the Aran Islands, the Burren region and the Cliffs of Moher. Situated on 100 acres of farmland, Aran View echoes spaciousness, comfort and atmosphere in its restaurant and bar. Menus are based on the best of local produce, fish being a speciality. All rooms with private bathroom, colour TV and DD phone. Visitors are assured of a warm and embracing welcome at the Aran View House Hotel.

B&B from £35.00 to £50.00
€44.44 to €63.49

THERESA & JOHN LINNANE
Proprietors

American Express
Diners
Mastercard
Visa

🙂 Weekend specials from £90.00

19 19

IRISH HOTELS FEDERATION

Closed 31 October - 01 April

BALLINALACKEN CASTLE COUNTRY HOUSE & RESTAURANT

COAST ROAD, DOOLIN,
CO. CLARE
TEL: 065-707 4025 FAX: 065-707 4025
EMAIL: ballinalackencastle@eircom.net

HOTEL ★★★ MAP 5 E 9

A romantic peaceful oasis steeped in history and ambience offering the most spectacular views of the Cliffs of Moher, Aran Islands, Atlantic Ocean and Connemara hills. Built in 1840 as the home of Lord O'Brien. Family members radiate a warm friendly welcome. Award winning chef Frank Sheedy (son-in-law) makes dining here an experience to remember. Peat and log fires add to the cosy atmosphere. Ideal base for exploring Clare. Recommended by Egon Ronay, Michelin, Fodor, Frommer, RAC.

WEB: homepage.eircom.net/~ballinalackencastle

B&B from £35.00 to £44.00
€44.44 to €55.87

MARY AND DENIS O'CALLAGHAN
Proprietors

American Express
Diners
Mastercard
Visa

🙂 Weekend specials from £90.00

12 12

IRISH HOTELS FEDERATION

Closed 05 October - 31 March

B&B rates are per person sharing per night incl. Breakfast

CULLINAN'S RESTAURANT & GUESTHOUSE

DOOLIN,
CO. CLARE
TEL: 065-707 4183 FAX: 065-707 4239

GUESTHOUSE ★★★ MAP 5 E 9

Cullinan's Restaurant and Guesthouse, centrally located in the heart of Doolin provides spacious and elegant bedrooms, all en suite with tea/coffee making facilities, DD phone, hairdryers and a comfortable TV lounge. Idyllic setting with highly acclaimed restaurant overlooking the Aille river. Imaginative menus are carefully chosen by the chef/owner, specialising in the freshest of locally caught seafood. Natural stone and wood combined gives Cullinan's a cozy, comfortable atmosphere.

B&B from £17.00 to £22.50
€21.59 to €28.57

CAROL & JAMES CULLINAN
Owners

Mastercard
Visa

Closed 24 - 25 December

DOOLIN HOUSE

DOOLIN,
CO. CLARE
TEL: 707 4259 FAX: 065-707 4474

GUESTHOUSE ★★ MAP 5 E 9

Centrally located in the heart of Doolin, Doolin House, A family run Guesthouse offers you a warm Irish welcome. Less than 5 minutes walk to all pubs and local amenities. Each room, en suite , bath or shower , or even cosier why not indulge in our Sauna! We are proud to offer you full usage of your own private sauna. Each room with a telephone at your fingertips. TV Lounge, lock-up bicycle shed, and private car park are just some of the many facilities offered at Doolin House.

B&B from £15.00 to £25.00
€19.05 to €31.74

MICHAEL & ANNE QUEALLY
Owners

Open All Year

DOONMACFELIM HOUSE

DOOLIN,
CO. CLARE
TEL: 065-707 4503 FAX: 065-707 4129

GUESTHOUSE ★★★ MAP 5 E 9

Doonmacfelim House is a 3*** guesthouse, situated on our farm in the village of Doolin, famous for traditional Irish music. Excellent location for visiting Cliffs of Moher, boat to Aran Islands, visiting prehistoric ruins. Its geology, flora, caves, archaeology and history set it apart as a place of mystery and beauty. All rooms en suite, with hairdryers, DD telephone. Shannon airport & Killimer car ferry 70km. Hard tennis court, rackets supplied.

WEB: www.kingsway.ie/doonmacfelim

B&B from £18.00 to £22.00
€22.86 to €27.93

MAJELLA & FRANK MOLONEY
Owners

Mastercard
Visa

Closed 24 - 28 December

Room rates are per room per night

CLARE INN GOLF & LEISURE HOTEL

DROMOLAND,
CO. CLARE
TEL: 065-682 3000 FAX: 065-682 3759
EMAIL: cro@lynchotels.com

HOTEL ★★★ MAP 6 G 8

Located on Dromoland's magnificent 18-hole golf course with stunning views of the Shannon estuary and surrounding Clare. Just 5 mins drive from Ennis, 10 mins from Shannon and 10 mins from Limerick. 183 well furnished en suite rooms, inc. Presidential suite, each with satellite TV & free movies, good food and superb outdoor and indoor leisure facilities including pool, gym, sauna and crazy golf. New Poacher's Pub. Conference facilities for up to 400, parking 300. KidsPlus playcentre.

WEB: www.lynchotels.com

Members Of Lynch Hotels

B&B from £25.00 to £55.00
€31.74 to €69.84

MICHAEL B LYNCH GROUP MD
Noel Mulhaire Gen Mgr

American Express
Diners
Mastercard
Visa

☺ 2 Dinners, B&B from £44.00

Open All Year

ARDILAUN GUESTHOUSE

BALLYCOREE, GALWAY ROAD,
ENNIS, CO. CLARE
TEL: 065-682 2311 FAX: 065-684 3989
EMAIL: purcellsennis@eircom.net

GUESTHOUSE ★★★ MAP 6 F 8

Ardilaun is Gaelic for high island. This is a modern architect-designed 3*** guesthouse overlooking the river Fergus and Ballyallia lake amenity area. Most rooms have panoramic views of the river and all are superbly decorated with en suite, phone, TV, and hairdryer. Our gymnasium sauna facility also overlooks the river and is available to guests only. Ardilaun is just 20 mins drive from Shannon airport on the N18 and is the ideal touring base for Clare, Limerick and Galway.

B&B from £20.00 to £22.50
€25.39 to €28.57

ANNE PURCELL
Proprietress

Mastercard
Visa
-

☺ Midweek specials from £55.00

Closed 24 - 26 December

AUBURN LODGE HOTEL & LEISURE CENTRE

GALWAY ROAD, ENNIS,
CO. CLARE
TEL: 065-682 1247 FAX: 065-682 1232
EMAIL: stay@irishcourthotels.com

HOTEL ★★★ MAP 6 F 8

Located in the historic town of Ennis, the 100 bedroom Auburn Lodge Hotel is the ideal base for the Golf or Fishing Holiday. Convenient to Lahinch, Shannon, Dromoland, Woodstock and Ennis. It offers a wide choice of rolling parkland or link courses - with golf to suit everyone. Within a few miles drive, are the Cliffs of Moher, Scenic Burren, Ailwee Cave and Bunratty Castle and Folkpark. Enjoy nightly traditional music in Tailor Quigleys Pub and re-live the day's golf. Shannon International Airport 15km. Full leisure centre opening summer 2000.

WEB: www.irishcourthotels.com

Members Of Irish Court Hotel Group

B&B from £30.00 to £75.00
€38.09 to €95.23

SEAN LYNE
Proprietor

American Express
Diners
Mastercard
Visa

☺ Weekend specials from £75.00

Open All Year

B&B rates are per person sharing per night incl. Breakfast

CILL EOIN HOUSE

KILDYSERT CROSS, CLARE ROAD,
ENNIS, CO. CLARE
TEL: 065-684 1668   FAX: 065-684 1669

GUESTHOUSE ★★★   MAP 6 F 8

Cill Eoin, named after the nearby 13th Century Abbey, is a 3*** guesthouse on the main tourist route to the west coast of Clare, with its unparalleled beauty in the scenery of the desolate Burren and the majestic vistas, that are the Cliffs of Moher. Golf, with a links and three courses nearby is abundantly available. Horse riding, fishing and many other pastimes are well provided for in the area. Call and see us soon, you will feel at home.

B&B from £22.00 to £24.00
€27.93 to €30.47

PAT & BRIDGET GLYNN LUCEY

American Express
Diners
Mastercard
Visa

14   14

Closed 24 December - 08 January

FOUNTAIN COURT

LAHINCH ROAD, ENNIS,
CO. CLARE
TEL: 065-682 9845   FAX: 065-682 9845
EMAIL: kyran@fountain-court.com

GUESTHOUSE N   MAP 6 F 8

Peaceful rural setting yet only 3 mins drive to Ennis. Rooms and suites furnished to 4 **** standard. Ideally located to tour the Burren National Park, Cliffs of Moher, Bunratty Castle and Folk Park. 6 excellent golf courses within a short distance. Fishing, horseriding and traditional music all within easy reach. Shannon airport 15k.

WEB: www.fountain-court.com

Members Of Premier Guesthouses

B&B from £25.00 to £35.00
€31.74 to €44.44

KYRAN & BREED CARR

American Express
Diners
Mastercard
Visa

☺ Weekend specials from £75.00

12   12

Closed 20 December - 07 January

GLENCAR GUESTHOUSE

GALWAY ROAD, ENNIS,
CO. CLARE
TEL: 065-682 2348   FAX: 065-682 2885
EMAIL: glencar.ennis@eircom.net

GUESTHOUSE ★★★   MAP 6 F 8

Glencar Guesthouse is a newly-refurbished 12 bedroomed 3*** accommodation. Situated on the N18 (Galway R), 1k from Ennis town and 20m from Auburn Lodge Hotel. Shannon Airport 20 mins drive. Glencar is an ideal base for golfing, cycling, fishing or walking holidays. Special attractions: Bunratty Castle, Cliffs of Moher, the Burren and the Ailwee Caves all easily accessible. Ennis is the home of traditional Irish music.

B&B from £20.00 to £25.00
€25.39 to €31.74

PETER & LIZ HOULIHAN

Mastercard
Visa

12   12

Closed 23 - 27 December

Room rates are per room per night

MAGOWNA HOUSE HOTEL

INCH, KILMALEY, ENNIS,
CO. CLARE
TEL: 065-683 9009 FAX: 065-683 9258
EMAIL: magowna@iol.ie

HOTEL ★★★ MAP 6 F 8

Beautifully located, family managed, country house hotel with extensive gardens and lovely views. Ideal for an active or purely relaxing break. Close to excellent golf courses, angling and walks. (Mid-Clare Way 1.5k) Shannon Airport, Cliffs of Moher, the Burren, Doolin, Bunratty Castle, Killimer car ferry to Kerry within easy reach. Conference room (cap. 200). Enjoy hospitality, comfort, good food and a genuine welcome in the heart of county Clare.

Members Of Irish Family Hotels

B&B from £28.00 to £32.00
€35.55 to €40.63

GAY MURPHY
Proprietor

American Express
Diners
Mastercard
Visa

:J🍴

😊 Weekend specials from £72.00

🎣🚭☎🖥🆃CM✳🕽♪P⛽🚬S🅿🔌
10 10

a/c 🛏

IRISH
HOTELS
FEDERATION

Closed 24 - 26 December

OLD GROUND HOTEL

O'CONNELL STREET, ENNIS,
CO. CLARE
TEL: 065-682 8127 FAX: 065-682 8112
EMAIL: oghotel@iol.ie

HOTEL ★★★ MAP 6 F 8

Newly refurbished with 83 deluxe bedrooms completed in April 1997. The ivy clad Old Ground Hotel is situated in Ennis, 30 mins from Shannon Airport. The elegant restaurant offers fine cuisine, lounge & bar snacks available throughout the day. Within a few miles drive are the Cliffs of Moher, the Burren, Ailwee Caves, Bunratty Castle & Folk Park. An ideal base for a golfing holiday with five superb 18 hole courses nearby, Lahinch, Woodstock, Ennis, Dromoland and Shannon.

Members Of Flynn Hotels

B&B from £44.00 to £60.00
€55.87 to €76.18

ALLEN FLYNN-MANAGING DIR
Mary Gleeson-Gen Manager

American Express
Diners
Mastercard
Visa

:J🍴

😊 Weekend specials from £85.00

🎣🚭☎🖥🆃CM✳🕽♪P
83 83

S🅿a/c🛏

IRISH
HOTELS
FEDERATION

Closed 24 - 26 December

QUEENS HOTEL

ABBEY STREET, ENNIS,
CO. CLARE
TEL: 065-682 8963 FAX: 065-682 8628
EMAIL: stay@irishcourthotels.com

HOTEL ★★★ MAP 6 F 8

The Queen's Town Centre Hotel is an ideal base for touring Bunratty Castle and Folk Park, Cliffs of Moher and the Burren. All bedrooms are en suite, with satellite TV, video, radio, phone, hairdryer, tea/coffee. Overlooking the 13th century Franciscan Abbey from which Ennis takes its origin. Adjoins the famous Cruise's Pub and Restaurant built circa 1658. Renowned for its authentic old world charm, superb home cooked Fayre and traditional music nightly. Shannon International Airport 15km.

WEB: www.irishcourthotels.com

Members Of Irish Court Hotel Group

B&B from £30.00 to £75.00
€38.09 to €95.23

MAURICE WALSH
General Manager

American Express
Diners
Mastercard
Visa

:J🎵

😊 Weekend specials from £75.00

🎣🚭☎🖥🆃CM♪S🔌
50 50

a/c🛏

IRISH
HOTELS
FEDERATION

Closed 25 December

B&B rates are per person sharing per night incl. Breakfast

TEMPLE GATE HOTEL

THE SQUARE, ENNIS,
CO. CLARE
TEL: 065-682 3300 FAX: 065-682 3322
EMAIL: templegh@iol.ie

HOTEL ★★★ MAP 6 F 8

Resting on the site of a 19thC Convent, the Gothic style remains throughout this Town House Hotel and combines effortlessly with luxurious charm. A cobblestoned courtyard leads to centre of the historic, yet progressive "Information Age" town of Ennis.
Bedrooms are fitted to exceptional standards. AA Rosettes for food & an acclaimed bar menu in Preachers Pub. Truly unique Great Hall Conference / Banqueting facility. Near Shannon Airport, Bunratty Castle & 5 golf courses including Lahinch.

Members Of Signature Hotels

B&B from £45.00 to £75.00
€57.14 to €95.23

VERA & JOHN MADDEN
Proprietors

American Express
Diners
Mastercard
Visa

☺ Weekend specials from £85.00

70 70

Open All Year

WEST COUNTY CONFERENCE & LEISURE HOTEL

CLARE ROAD, ENNIS,
CO. CLARE
TEL: 065-682 3000 FAX: 065-682 3759
EMAIL: cro@lynchotels.com

HOTEL ★★★ MAP 6 F 8

Centrally located, the West County boasts well furnished en suite rooms, good value food and easy access to all of Clare's famous attractions. 5 mins walk from historic Ennis and all its shopping, 15 mins from Bunratty and Shannon. Conference facilities for up to 1,650 delegates. Health and leisure club with 3 pools, gym, sauna, steamroom, a KidsPlus playcentre, ideal for families, beauty salon. Boru's Porterhouse, award winning traditional Irish pub/carvery.

WEB: www.lynchotels.com

Members Of Lynch Hotels

B&B from £43.00 to £60.00
€54.60 to €76.18

MICHAEL B LYNCH GROUP MD
Brian Harrington Exec Gen Mgr

American Express
Diners
Mastercard
Visa

☺ 2 Dinners, B&B from £44.00

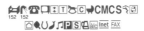
152 152

Open All Year

Room rates are per room per night

WESTBROOK HOUSE

GALWAY ROAD, ENNIS,
CO. CLARE
TEL: 065-684 0173   FAX: 065-684 0173
EMAIL: westbrook.ennis@eircom.net

GUESTHOUSE ★★★   MAP 6 F 8

Westbrook House is the most recently built luxury accommodation in Ennis. All rooms are fitted to exceptionally high standards. Within walking distance of the centre of historic Ennis, with its friendly traditional pubs and fantastic shopping. Ideal base for golfing holidays, special discounts with local golf courses. A short drive to the majestic Cliffs of Moher, the Burren or Bunratty Castle and Folk Park. Only 15 mins from Shannon Airport.

B&B from £20.00 to £25.00
€25.39 to €31.74

SHEELAGH & DOMHNALL LYNCH
Proprietors

Mastercard

Visa

Midweek specials from £50.00

10   10

Closed 23 - 26 December

WOODSTOCK HOTEL & GOLF CLUB

SHANAWAY ROAD, ENNIS,
CO. CLARE
TEL: 065-684 4777   FAX: 065-684 4888
EMAIL: woodstock.ennis@eircom.net

UNDER CONSTRUCTION OPENING MAR 2000

HOTEL P   MAP 6 F 8

Woodstock Hotel & Golf Club is in a setting as scenic as it is historically fascinating. Surrounded by a lake, river, two ancient forts and graceful mature trees, the hotel stands serenely surveying this green and verdant scene. All rooms are equipped with every modern comfort. The restaurant, golf club, leisure and conference rooms provide every facility to cater for company meetings to family holidays. Ideally located to explore the nearby rustic towns and many local attractions. Sister property to the Hibernian Hotel, Dublin and The McCausland Hotel, Bolfast.

B&B from £30.00 to £60.00
€38.09 to €76.18

ANDREW GRIFFITH
Sales & Marketing Manager

American Express

Diners

Mastercard

Visa

Weekend specials from £89.00

65   65

FAX

Open All Year

FALLS HOTEL

ENNISTYMON,
CO. CLARE
TEL: 065-707 1004   FAX: 065-707 1367
EMAIL: falls@iol.ie

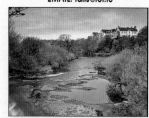

HOTEL ★★★   MAP 5 E 9

3★★★ hotel with 150 en suite spacious bedrooms, set in 50 acres of gardens, woodland and glen overlooking the cascades on the Inagh river. Banqueting and conference facilities for up to 500 guests. Local attractions: the Cliffs of Moher, the Burren National Park and the Ailwee Caves.

B&B from £35.00 to £49.00
€44.44 to €62.22

GERRY O'CONNOR
General Manager

American Express

Mastercard

Visa

150   150

Open All Year

B&B rates are per person sharing per night incl. Breakfast

GROVEMOUNT HOUSE

LAHINCH ROAD, ENNISTYMON,
CO. CLARE
TEL: 065-707 1431 FAX: 065-707 1823

GUESTHOUSE ★★★ MAP 5 E 9

Grovemount House, the Golfers' Paradise. What better than to return to luxurious tranquillity after a refreshing day on Lahinch championship golf course, just 5 minutes drive from here. Or perhaps you would like a rejuvenating sauna in Lahinch's new leisure centre before retiring for the night. We offer easy access to the famous Cliffs of Moher and Burren region. Whatever is your pleasure, be it fishing, golfing or traditional music, this is the place for you.

Members Of Premier Guesthouses

B&B from £18.00 to £22.50
€22.86 to €28.57

SHEILA LINNANE
Owner

Mastercard
Visa

Midweek specials from £51.00

8 8

Closed 31 October - 30 April

SMYTH COUNTRY LODGE HOTEL

FEAKLE,
CO. CLARE
TEL: 061-924000 FAX: 061-924244
EMAIL: smythvil@iol.ie

THE SMYTH COUNTRY LODGE HOTEL

HOTEL ★★★ MAP 6 G 9

Set amidst the breathtaking scenery of east Clare lakelands, the lodge has 35 luxurious rooms and garden suites, gamekeepers restaurant and traditional Irish bar. Log fires, wooden beams, antique furnishings and individually styled rooms symbolise the warmth of the Smyth's hospitality and personal attention. Traditional Irish music nightly in season. Famous for coarse and gamefishing, golf, horseriding, central for touring. Banqueting and conference facility. Cliffs of Moher, Bunratty. Shannon Airport (30 minutes)

WEB: welcome.to/SmythsHotel

Members Of Village Inn Hotels

B&B from £30.00 to £48.00
€38.09 to €60.95

RORY SMYTH
Host

American Express
Diners
Mastercard
Visa

Weekend specials from £69.00

35 35

Open All Year

HALPIN'S HOTEL & VITTLES RESTAURANT

ERIN STREET, KILKEE,
CO. CLARE
TEL: 065-905 6032 FAX: 065-905 6317
EMAIL: halpins@iol.ie

HOTEL ★★★ MAP 5 D 7

The highly acclaimed 3*** Halpin's Hotel and award winning Vittles Restaurant are a combination of old world charm, fine food, vintage wines and modern comforts- overlooking old Victorian Kilkee, close to Shannon Airport- Killimer car ferry- Cliffs of Moher- the Burren and Loop drive. Nearby major golf courses- Lahinch/Ballybunion. Accolades- RAC, AA, Times, Best Loved Hotels, Johansens. Sister property of Aberdeen Lodge & Merrion Hall. USA Toll Free 800 223 6510, DD 353 65 56032.

WEB: www.greenbook.ie/halpins

Members Of Green Book of Ireland

B&B from £27.50 to £45.00
€34.92 to €57.14

PAT HALPIN
Proprietor

American Express
Diners
Mastercard
Visa

Weekend specials from £80.00

12 12

Closed 15 November - 15 March

Room rates are per room per night

MARINE HOTEL & APARTMENT COMPLEX

KILKEE,
CO. CLARE
TEL: 065-905 6722 FAX: 065-905 6550
EMAIL: manager@marinehotel.iol.ie

HOTEL N   MAP 5 D 7

Situated on the seafront in Kilkee, one of the safest resorts on the west coast with breathtaking coastal walks, this newly-refurbished family-owned hotel offers a combination of old world charm and modern comforts. It has 22 well-appointed comfortable rooms. The modern design is reflected in our bar and restaurant where local produce is a speciality. 12 luxury self-catering apartments offer an alternative for a family getaway. Close to Shannon airport, car ferry, Cliffs of Moher etc.

WEB: www.kilmurrylodge.com/marinehotel

B&B from £20.00 to £32.00
€25.39 to €40.63

PAT & SIOBHAN HOARE
Owners

American Express
Diners
Mastercard
Visa

☺ Weekend specials from £45.00

22 22

Open All Year

OCEAN COVE GOLF AND LEISURE HOTEL

KILKEE BAY,
CO. CLARE
TEL: 065-682 3000 FAX: 065-682 3759
EMAIL: cro@lynchotel.com

HOTEL N   MAP 5 D 7

Newly built hotel overlooking Kilkee's sandy bay. 50 en-suite rooms, including seaview and family rooms; PanAsian's à la carte restaurant, Boru's traditional Irish pub/carvery; Sports club gym free to residents; KidsPlus play centre; adjacent to Kilkee waterworld and dive centre; 18 hole golf course also nearby. Ideal for touring Kerry and north Clare. Meeting facilities for 70. Parking 100 cars.

WEB: www.lynchotels.com

Members Of Lynch Hotels

B&B from £25.00 to £45.00
€31.74 to €57.14

MICHAEL B LYNCH GROUP MD
Damian Caldwell Gen Mgr

American Express
Diners
Mastercard
Visa

☺ Dinner, B&B from £39.00

50 50

Open All Year

STELLA MARIS HOTEL

KILKEE,
CO. CLARE
TEL: 065-905 6455 FAX: 065-906 0006
EMAIL: stellamaris@eircom.net

HOTEL ★★   MAP 5 D 7

The Stella Maris is a small family-run hotel in the heart of Kilkee. Its attractions are open peat fires, friendly staff and a veranda overlooking the bay and town of Kilkee. Traditional music in the bar and a variety of home-cooked food all go to make your stay a very memorable and pleasant experience.

Members Of Logis of Ireland

B&B from £20.00 to £28.00
€25.39 to €35.55

ANNE HAUGH

American Express
Mastercard
Visa

☺ Weekend specials from £55.00

10 10

IRISH
HOTELS
FEDERATION

Open All Year

B&B rates are per person sharing per night incl. Breakfast

STRAND GUEST HOUSE

THE STRAND LINE, KILKEE,
CO. CLARE
TEL: 065-905 6177   FAX: 065-905 6177

GUESTHOUSE ★★★★   MAP 5 O 7

Situated on the seafront in Kilkee, one of the most westerly seaside resorts in Europe. Kilkee is built around a 1.5km beach, considered one of the best and safest bathing places in the west with breathtaking coastal walks. The Strand makes an ideal touring base - visit the Burren, Cliffs of Moher, Ailwee Caves. For golf enthusiasts there is a local 18 hole course, Kilrush 13km, Lahinch 42km or Ballybunion 40km (via car ferry). Restaurant fully licenced, specialises in local seafood.

B&B from £22.00 to £35.00
€27.93 to €44.44

JOHNNY & CAROLINE REDMOND

Mastercard
Visa

Open All Year

THOMOND GUESTHOUSE & KILKEE THALASSOTHERAPY CENTRE

GRATTAN STREET, KILKEE,
CO. CLARE
TEL: 065-905 6742   FAX: 065-905 6762
EMAIL: mulcahype@eircom.net

GUESTHOUSE N   MAP 5 D 7

Thomond Guesthouse is a magnificent new premises with 5 en suite rooms coupled with Kilkee Thalassotherapy Centre, offering natural seaweed baths, algae body wraps, beauty salon and other Thalassotherapy treatments. Ideal get-away for those looking for a totally unique and relaxing break. Situated in beautiful Kilkee with golfing (18), scuba diving, deep sea angling, dolphin watching, swimming, pony trekking and spectacular cliff walks, all within walking distance. Specials available.

B&B from £25.00 to £35.00
€31.74 to €44.44

EILEEN MULCAHY
Proprietor

Mastercard
Visa

☺ Midweek specials from £60.00

Closed 31 January - 28 February

KINCORA HALL HOTEL

KILLALOE,
CO. CLARE
TEL: 061-376000   FAX: 061-376665
EMAIL: kincora@iol.ie

HOTEL ★★★   MAP 6 H 8

Kincora Hall in Killaloe (the ancient capital of Ireland) is a comfortable 30 bedroomed hotel on the banks of the river Shannon. This oasis of calm provides a true county Clare welcome combined with friendly service and a wide selection of food and wine in our bistro which overlooks our marina and the river Shannon.

B&B from £60.00 to £60.00
€76.18 to €76.18

JOHN O'CONNOR
General Manager

American Express
Diners
Mastercard
Visa

☺ Midweek 2 B&B + 1 Dinner
from £105.00 to £135.00

Open All Year

Room rates are per room per night

LAKESIDE HOTEL & LEISURE CENTRE

KILLALOE,
CO. CLARE
TEL: 061-376122 FAX: 061-376431
EMAIL: lakesidehotelkilaloe@eircom.net

HOTEL ★★★ MAP 6 H 8

On the banks of the River Shannon, overlooking Lough Derg, the Lakeside is the ideal base for touring Counties Clare, Limerick and Tipperary. Enjoy our fabulous indoor leisure centre with its 40 metre water-slide, swimming pools, sauna and steam rooms, jacuzzi, gym, snooker and creche rooms. Our 3*** hotel has 46 en suite bedrooms, including 10 superior family suites. Fully licensed restaurant and conference facilities available.

Members Of Coast and Country Hotels

B&B from £32.50 to £45.00
€41.27 to €57.14

CHRISTOPHER BYRNES
General Manager

American Express
Diners
Mastercard
Visa

☺ Weekend specials from £75.00

46 46

Closed 23 - 26 December

LANTERN HOUSE

OGONNELLOE, KILLALOE,
CO. CLARE
TEL: 061-923034 FAX: 061-923139

GUESTHOUSE ★★★ MAP 6 H 8

Ideally situated overlooking Lough Derg in a beautiful part of east Clare, 6 miles north of historic Killaloe and 45 minutes drive from Shannon Airport. Our en suite rooms are non-smoking, have semi-orthopaedic beds, DD phone. TV and radio, residents' lounge, homely atmosphere and safe car parking. Enjoy the wonderful views from our fully licenced restaurant. Owner chef. Local activities include golf, watersports, fishing, pony trekking and walking.

B&B from £22.00 to £22.00
€27.93 to €27.93

ELIZABETH COPPEN/PHILIP HOGAN
Owners

American Express
Diners
Mastercard
Visa

6 6

Closed 01 November - 03 March

TINARANA

OGONNELLOE, KILLALOE,
CO. CLARE
TEL: 061-376966 FAX: 061-375369
EMAIL: info@tinarana.com

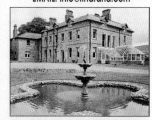

GUESTHOUSE ★★★★ MAP 6 H 8

Tinarana House, a majestic Victorian mansion, on the shores of Lough Derg. A perfect environment for rest and relaxation. What makes a visit to Tinarana really special is its association with the East Clinic in Killaloe, with Hydrotherapy and world - renowned German, Swiss, Austrian and American treatments supervised by medical doctors and trained personnel. At Tinarana we offer Aromatherapy seaweed body wraps, Reflexology, Reiki, massage, facials and skincare treatments.

WEB: www.tinarana.com

B&B from £55.00 to £85.00
€69.84 to €107.93

GARRETT GAVIN
General Manager

American Express
Mastercard
Visa

10 10

Open All Year

B&B rates are per person sharing per night incl. Breakfast

KILLIMER/TARBERT CAR FERRY

M.V. "Shannon Willow" (44 cars) loading at Killimer.

Scenic and Direct Routes via Drive-on/Drive-off Car Ferry Service

From Killimer, Co. Clare
DEPARTURE ON THE HOUR

		FIRST SAILING	LAST SAILING
APRIL/SEPTEMBER.	Weekdays	7.00 a.m.	9.00 p.m.
	Sundays	9.00 a.m.	9.00 p.m.
OCTOBER/MARCH.	Weekdays	7.00 a.m.	7.00 p.m.
	Sundays	10.00 a.m.	7.00 p.m.

From Tarbert, Co. Kerry
DEPARTURE ON THE HALF HOUR

APRIL/SEPTEMBER.	Weekdays	7.30 a.m.	9.30 p.m.
	Sundays	9.30 a.m.	9.30 p.m.
OCTOBER/MARCH.	Weekdays	7.30 a.m.	7.30 p.m.
	Sundays	10.30 a.m.	7.30 p.m.

SAILINGS
Every day of the year except Christmas Day.

TWO FERRY SERVICE
During the peak holiday period both Ferry Boats operate to give half-hourly sailings from each side.

m.v. "Shannon Dolphin" (52 cars)
m.v. "Shannon Willow" (44 cars)

SHANNON FERRY LTD.
KILLIMER, KILRUSH, CO. CLARE
Telephone   Fax
065 9053124   065 9053125

AILLWEE CAVE

In The West. In The Burren.
Ireland's premier showcave.

Add to the holiday experience by taking a stroll underground with one of our expert guides.

Ballyvaughan, Co. Clare. Tel: (065) 7077067

WATERMAN'S LODGE COUNTRY HOUSE HOTEL

BALLINA, KILLALOE,
CO. CLARE
TEL: 061-376333 FAX: 061-375445
EMAIL: info@watermanslodge.ie

HOTEL ★★★ MAP 6 H 8

Waterman's Lodge is perched on a hill overlooking the river Shannon, Clare hills and the lovely un-spoilt village of Killaloe. Old stone steps, high ceilings, timber floors, brass and cast iron beds, together with open fires and books provide all the requirements of the perfect rural hide-away. The philosophy at Waterman's Lodge is very simple - provide a beautiful rural retreat, good food, warm welcome - A home from home. GDS Access Code: UI Toll Free 1-800-44-UTELL

WEB: www.watermanslodge.ie

Members Of Manor House Hotels

B&B from £55.00 to £70.00
€69.84 to €88.88

TOM REILLY
Manager

American Express
Mastercard
Visa

☺ Weekend specials from £99.00

10 10
Inet

Closed 20 December - 10 February

ABERDEEN ARMS HOTEL

LAHINCH,
CO. CLARE
TEL: 065-708 1100 FAX: 065-708 1228
EMAIL: aberdeenarms@eircom.net

HOTEL ★★★ MAP 5 E 9

A haven for the discerning traveller who will appreciate its relaxed and friendly atmosphere. Mackensies Restaurant offers excellent cuisine. The Aberdeen Grill serves imaginative and tempting fair. Lahinch's Golden strand and Golf Course are about 5 minutes from the hotel which is just 51.2km from Shannon Airport on the beautiful Clare coast. Whatever your preference, Golf, Fishing, Horse Riding, Sightseeing all are within easy reach. Conference facilities available.

WEB: www.aberdeenarms.ie

B&B from £25.00 to £49.00
€31.74 to €62.22

BRIAN HEGARTY
General Manager

American Express
Diners
Mastercard
Visa

☺ Weekend specials from £62.00

55 55

Closed 22 - 28 December

ATLANTIC HOTEL

MAIN STREET, LAHINCH,
CO. CLARE
TEL: 065-708 1049 FAX: 065-708 1029

HOTEL ★★★ MAP 5 E 9

The Atlantic Hotel is a family run hotel where comfort and friendliness is our priority. Intimate dining room offering the very best in local seafood. All rooms are en suite and have DD phone, TV, hairdryer and tea/coffee making facilities. 51km from Shannon Airport, 5 minutes from the famous Lahinch championship golf courses, Cliffs of Moher and the Burren. Recently refurbished and upgraded, this charming Little Hotel has much to offer our special guests. A warm welcome awaits you.

B&B from £30.00 to £40.00
€38.09 to €50.79

SEAMUS & ALAN LOGUE
Your Hosts

Mastercard
Visa

14 14

Open All Year

B&B rates are per person sharing per night incl. Breakfast

DOUGH MOR LODGE

STATION ROAD, LAHINCH,
CO. CLARE
TEL: 065-708 2063 FAX: 065-707 1384
EMAIL: dough@gofree.indigo.ie

GUESTHOUSE N MAP 5 E 9

Purpose-built family run guesthouse with residents' lounge and dining room. Private car parking and large garden. You can see Lahinch's famous golflinks from the house. Tee times can be booked and arranged for guests. This is an ideal location for golfing, touring the Burren or visiting the Cliffs of Moher. The beach is within 5 mins walk. Lahinch Sea World has a fine heated indoor swimming pool. The ideal place to unwind and enjoy your holiday.

B&B from £25.00 to £30.00
€31.74 to €38.09

JIM FOLEY
Proprietor

Mastercard

Visa

🏨♿☎🖥C❄☂♨🅿♪
6 6

Closed 31 October - 31 March

GREENBRIER INN GUESTHOUSE

LAHINCH,
CO. CLARE
TEL: 065-708 1242 FAX: 065-708 1247

GUESTHOUSE ★★★ MAP 5 E 9

Luxurious 3*** guesthouse with 14 guest rooms, our diningroom and guest lounge are overlooking Lahinch golf course and the Atlantic Ocean. Totally renovated and extended in '99. Within a short walk of Lahinch village. All rooms are en suite with antique pine furnishings, DD phone, TV, tea/coffee making facilities. An excellent base from which to visit the Cliffs of Moher, the Burren, Aran Islands and Galway or play golf on the nearby Lahinch Championship course. Enjoy our home while away from your own.

B&B from £22.50 to £37.50
€28.57 to €47.62

MARGARET & VICTOR MULCAHY
Proprietors

Mastercard

Visa

☺ Midweek specials from £67.50

🏨♿☎🖥T🅰C❄☂♨🅿S♿
14 14

```
I R I S H
HOTELS
FEDERATION
```

Closed 08 January - 20 February

MOY HOUSE

LAHINCH,
CO. CLARE
TEL: 065-708 2800 FAX: 065-708 2500
EMAIL: moyhouse@eircom.net

GUESTHOUSE N MAP 5 E 9

Moy House prevails over the breathtaking seascape of Lahinch Bay, set on 15 acres of grounds, adorned by mature woodland and a picturesque river. Major restoration has transformed this 18th century country house in keeping with present day expectations of superior standards, yet preserving its unique character style and period ambience. Personal attention and the relaxation of a sanctuary, yet mins away from the many amenities available, are the hallmarks that distinguish us.

B&B from £65.00 to £75.00
€82.53 to €95.23

BERNADETTE KELLEHER
General Manager / Director

American Express

Mastercard

Visa

🏨♿☎🖥T❄☂♨🅿 Inet FAX
7 7

Open All Year

Room rates are per room per night

SANCTA MARIA HOTEL

**LAHINCH,
CO. CLARE
TEL: 065-708 1041   FAX: 065-708 1529**

HOTEL ★★   MAP 5 E 9

The McInerney family have welcomed holiday makers to the Sancta Maria for over 40 years. Many of the attractive bedrooms overlook the famous Lahinch golf links and golden beach, which are within 100 metres of the hotel. Our restaurant specialises in fresh produce and special emphasis is placed on local seafoods and home baking. The Sancta Maria is the ideal base for touring the Burren or visiting the Cliffs of Moher and Aran Islands.

B&B from £24.00 to £28.00
€30.47 to €35.55

THOMAS MCINERNEY
Proprietor

Mastercard

Visa

☺ Weekend specials from £62.00

24 24

HOTELS

Closed 30 October - 03 March

SHAMROCK INN HOTEL

**MAIN STREET, LAHINCH,
CO. CLARE
TEL: 065-708 1700   FAX: 065-708 1029**

HOTEL ★★   MAP 5 E 9

Situated right in the heart of charming Lahinch. All tastefully decorated rooms have DD phone, TV, hairdryer and tea/coffee making facilities. Our restaurant is renowned for its warm and intimate atmosphere offering a choice of excellent cuisine, catering for all tastes. Delicious home cooked bar food is served daily and by night the bar comes to life with the sound of music. Whatever your interest, golf, fishing or horseriding, we can arrange it for you. Also, new self-catering apts.

B&B from £35.00 to £40.00
€44.44 to €50.79

SEAMUS & ALAN LOGUE
Your Hosts

Mastercard

Visa

10 10

Open All Year

CARRIGANN HOTEL

**LISDOONVARNA,
CO. CLARE
TEL: 065-707 4036   FAX: 065-707 4567
EMAIL: carrigannhotel@eircom.net**

HOTEL ★★★   MAP 5 E 9

Small, quiet, friendly and relaxing hotel, set in its own landscaped grounds, just two mins from the village square. Rockeries, rose gardens and lawns can be viewed from our recently refurbished restaurant. Relax and enjoy fresh local produce expertly cooked and served. Ground floor rooms. Laundry/drying facilities. Walking holiday specialists - providing our own maps and notes of the unique Burren region. Logis of Ireland, Tel 01-668 9743.

Members Of Logis of Ireland

B&B from £29.00 to £37.00
€36.82 to €46.98

MARY & GERARD HOWARD
Proprietors

Mastercard

Visa

☺ Weekend specials from £68.00

20 20

HOTELS

Closed 01 November - 28 February

B&B rates are per person sharing per night incl. Breakfast

KINCORA HOUSE

LISDOONVARNA,
CO. CLARE
TEL: 065-707 4300   FAX: 065-707 4490
EMAIL: kincorahotel@eircom.net

GUESTHOUSE ★★★   MAP 5 E 9

A warm welcome awaits you at our award-winning family run inn. Built in 1860 the house exudes charm and character. Individually designed rooms with imaginative decor offer every comfort. Original Irish paintings adorn the walls. Traditional pub/restaurant serving excellent cuisine in an ambient atmosphere. Garden with national award of merit. Ideally situated in the Burren region and nearby are the Cliffs of Moher and Lahinch golf course.

WEB: www.kincora-hotel.com

B&B from £25.00 to £35.00
€31.74 to €44.44

DOREEN & DIARMUID DRENNAN
Proprietors

Mastercard

Visa

⌂⎰☎❑T☀⌖♪🝙alc◼
11 11

Open All Year

LYNCH'S HOTEL

LISDOONVARNA,
CO. CLARE
TEL: 065-707 4010   FAX: 065-707 4611
EMAIL: lynchshotel@eircom.net

HOTEL ★   MAP 5 E 9

Family-owned and run hotel, (currently fifth generation). Comprises 10 bedrooms with all usual facilities. Extensive à la carte menu available till 9.30pm. Located in centre of village with easy access to Burren, Cliffs of Moher and north Clare Atlantic coast. Enjoyable for botanists, bird watchers, anglers, cavers, walkers, swimmers. Most musical tastes catered for nightly in village.

WEB: http://homepage.eircom.net/~joelynch/

B&B from £18.00 to £26.00
€22.86 to €33.01

MAUREEN LYNCH
Owner

Mastercard

Visa

☺ Midweek specials from £59.00

⌂⎰☎❑TCCM♪🝙S🜨alc
10 10

Closed 10 October - 10 May

RATHBAUN HOTEL

LISDOONVARNA,
CO. CLARE
TEL: 065-707 4009   FAX: 065-707 4009

HOTEL ★★   MAP 5 E 9

Rathbaun Hotel on the main street in the centre of Lisdoonvarna is a unique hotel for special guests. Quality accommodation, excellent food served all day, personal service and brilliant value for money are the hallmarks of our hotel. We are also renowned for our bar music and unusual gift shop. We offer maps and helpful information to all our guests on the Burren area. Cead mile failte.

B&B from £18.00 to £25.00
€22.86 to €31.74

JOHN CONNOLLY
Owner

Mastercard

Visa

☺ Midweek specials from £50.00

⌂⎰☎❑TC⟳CMU♪🝙P🝙S🜨
alc◼ Inet
12 12

Closed 05 October - 30 April

Room rates are per room per night

SHEEDY'S RESTAURANT & COUNTRY INN

LISDOONVARNA,
CO. CLARE
TEL: 065-707 4026 FAX: 065-707 4555
EMAIL: cmv@indigo.ie

HOTEL ★★ MAP 5 E 9

Set back from the main street in its own mature gardens, this calm oasis is the ideal retreat after a day trekking the Burren, playing golf at Lahinch or savouring the spectacular views atop the Cliffs of Moher. The restaurant has quietly gained an international reputation for its good value contemporary Irish cuisine. Listed in all major guides, the restaurant has also achieved 2 rosettes for food from AA.

Members Of Village Inn Hotels

B&B from £25.00 to £32.50
€31.74 to €41.27

JOHN & MARTINA
Owners

American Express
Mastercard
Visa

11 11
alc

HOTELS

Closed 01 October - 01 April

ARMADA HOTEL

SPANISH POINT, MILTOWN MALBAY,
CO. CLARE
TEL: 065-708 4110 FAX: 065-708 4632
EMAIL: armada@iol.ie

HOTEL ★★★ MAP 5 E 8

The newly constructed Armada Hotel commands a superb oceanfront setting in the beautiful seaside resort of Spanish Point. All rooms are furnished to a very high standard with TV, tea/coffee facilities, hairdryer etc. The 60 seater Cape restaurant must be the most spectacularly located restaurant in Ireland with a wide selection of local and international cuisine. From the luxurious foyer to the olde world Flagship bar the Armada has something for everyone. Banqueting facilities also.

WEB: www.iol.ie/~armada/index.htm

Members Of MinOtel Ireland Hotel Group

B&B from £30.00 to £40.00
€38.09 to €50.79

JUNE AND CLAIRE BURKE
Hosts

Mastercard
Visa

24 24
  alc

HOTELS

Open All Year

BELLBRIDGE HOUSE HOTEL

SPANISH POINT, MILTOWN MALBAY,
CO. CLARE
TEL: 065-708 4038 FAX: 065-708 4830

HOTEL ★★★ MAP 5 E 8

Situated on the West Clare coastline, this new hotel offers excellent accommodation and cuisine. Adjacent to Spanish Point golf course, sandy beaches, horse riding, fishing, tennis and water sports. Ideal base for touring the Burren, Cliffs of Moher, Aillwee Caves, Bunratty Castle and Folk Park. A family run hotel with friendly and efficient staff whose aim is to make your stay enjoyable and memorable. All rooms have hairdryer, tea/coffee making facilities, direct dial phone and colour TV.

B&B from £25.00 to £40.00
€31.74 to €50.79

PAT O'MALLEY
Proprietor

American Express
Mastercard
Visa

60 60
alc

HOTELS

Closed 04 January - 10 March

B&B rates are per person sharing per night incl. Breakfast

MOUNTSHANNON HOTEL

MOUNTSHANNON,
CO. CLARE
TEL: 061-927162 FAX: 061-927272

HOTEL ★★ MAP 6 H 9

The Mountshannon Hotel, situated in the rural and peaceful village of Mountshannon, offers you first class accommodation in friendly surroundings. All bedrooms are en suite with DD phone, TV, tea/coffee making facilities and hairdryer. Our continental style restaurant, which is known for excellent and reasonably priced cuisine, overlooks our garden and Lough Derg. Private car park. Mountshannon Harbour is four minutes walk away. Fishing, pony trekking and golf are available.

Members Of Irish Family Hotels

B&B from £25.00 to £35.00
€31.74 to €44.44

PAULINE AND MICHAEL MADDEN
Director/Owner

American Express
Mastercard
Visa

14 14

alc

Closed 25 December

DROMOLAND CASTLE

NEWMARKET-ON-FERGUS,
CO. CLARE
TEL: 061-368144 FAX: 061-363355
EMAIL: sales@dromoland.ie

HOTEL ★★★★★ MAP 6 G 8

Located 13km from Shannon airport. Stately halls, elegant public areas & beautifully furnished guest rooms are steeped in a timeless atmosphere that is unique to Dromoland. The international reputation for excellence is reflected in the award-winning cuisine in the castle's Earl of Thomond & The Fig Tree restaurant in the Dromoland Golf & Country Club. A meticulously maintained 18-hole golf course, fishing, horse-riding, clay shooting, health & beauty clinic & much more.

WEB: www.dromoland.ie

Members Of Relais & Châteaux

Room Rate from £140.00 to £336.00
€177.76 to €426.63

MARK NOLAN
General Manager

American Express
Diners
Mastercard
Visa

😊 Weekend specials from £240.00

100 100

Open All Year

HUNTERS LODGE

THE SQUARE, NEWMARKET-ON-
FERGUS, CO. CLARE
TEL: 061-368577 FAX: 061-368057

GUESTHOUSE ★★★ MAP 6 G 8

Ideally situated for visitors arriving or departing from Shannon airport (12km). We offer 6 comfortable bedrooms en suite with telephone and TV. Our olde worlde pub and restaurant specialises in good quality fresh food served in a relaxed atmosphere with a friendly and efficient service. Local tourist attractions include Bunratty Folk Park, Castle banquets and many 18 hole golf courses. Ideal stopover for touring Co. Clare or commencing your trip to the west of Ireland.

B&B from £19.00 to £22.00
€24.13 to €27.93

ROBERT & KATHLEEN HEALY
Proprietors

American Express
Diners
Mastercard
Visa

6 6

Open All Year

Room rates are per room per night

CARRYGERRY COUNTRY HOUSE

SHANNON AIRPORT, NEWMARKET-ON-FERGUS, CO. CLARE
TEL: 061-363739 FAX: 061-363823
EMAIL: carrygerry-hotel@hotmail.com

HOTEL ★★★ MAP 6 G 7

Traditional Irish hospitality is alive and well in our 205 year old Country House, set on 15 acres of woodlands and gardens overlooking the Fergus river. Ideally situated for golf, horseriding and fishing. 10 minutes from Shannon airport. Good Food Circle 3 Toques - outstanding cuisine - seafood specialities in "L'Orangerie". Enchanting courtyard-sylvan setting. Weddings / private parties / banquets / conference facilities. Coach House bar. Ample parking. Languages F/G/E/D.

Members Of Logis of Ireland

B&B from £42.00 to £49.00
€53.33 to €62.22

ANGELA & ELEYNA VAN KOOYK
Proprietors

American Express
Diners
Mastercard
Visa

😊 Weekend specials from £116.00

12 12

Closed 01 January - 01 March

OAK WOOD ARMS HOTEL

SHANNON,
CO. CLARE
TEL: 061-361500 FAX: 061-361414
EMAIL: oakwoarm@iol.ie

HOTEL ★★★ MAP 6 G 7

The Oak Wood Arms Hotel located on the airport road. With its eye-catching tower clock, the hotel retains an unusual charm and character. Sophie's lounge, with its delightful hand carved solid oak panels and old brass, has won national awards for its bar service and food. Also attracting a large following, the Spruce Goose restaurant is cosy and intimate, offering a variety of dishes at a very high standard.

B&B from £39.00 to £49.00
€49.52 to €62.22

STEPHEN KEOGH
General Manager

American Express
Diners
Mastercard
Visa

😊 Weekend specials from £75.00

75 75

Closed 24 - 26 December

SHANNON COURT QUALITY HOTEL

BALLYCASEY, SHANNON,
CO. CLARE
TEL: 061-364588 FAX: 061-364045
EMAIL: sales@qualityshannon.com

HOTEL N MAP 6 G 7

The Quality Shannon Court Hotel, Shannon, located 2 miles from the airport opened in June 1999. This 54 roomed hotel has all rooms en suite with DD phone and multi channel TV. The Old Lodge Bar serves food all day. There is also an all day carvery. Enjoy à la carte meals every evening in the Lodge Restaurant. The hotel has a fine brick finish throughout.

Members Of Choice Hotels Ireland

B&B from £30.00 to £40.00
€38.09 to €50.79

SHANE MCSHORTALL
General Manager

American Express
Diners
Mastercard
Visa

😊 Weekend specials from £60.00

54 54

Closed 25 December

B&B rates are per person sharing per night incl. Breakfast

SHANNON GREAT SOUTHERN HOTEL

SHANNON AIRPORT, SHANNON,
CO. CLARE
TEL: 061-471122 FAX: 061-471982
EMAIL: res@shannon.gsh.ie

HOTEL ★★★ MAP 6 G 7

Shannon Great Southern is a hotel with exceptional style and comfort within walking distance of the terminal building at Shannon airport. All 115 rooms are en suite with DD phone, TV, tea/coffee making facilities, hairdryer and trouser press. Leisure facilities include a gym and steam room. Bookable worldwide through Utell International or central reservations 01-2144800.

WEB: www.gsh.ie

Room Rate from £100.00 to £100.00
€126.97 to €126.97

PAT DOOLEY
General Manager

American Express
Diners
Mastercard
Visa

Weekend specials from £78.00

115 115

Closed 24 - 26 December

ALEXANDRA GUEST HOUSE

5-6 O'CONNELL AVENUE,
LIMERICK
TEL: 061-318472 FAX: 061-400433
EMAIL: info@alexandra.iol.ie

GUESTHOUSE ★★ MAP 6 H 7

Elegant Victorian house situated 5 mins walk to the heart of the city centre and located on the Angela's Ashes trail. Comfortable spacious rooms en suite with TV. Relaxing guest lounge with tea/coffee facilities provided. Conveniently located for bus and rail stations and 20 mins drive to Shannon and Bunratty. Multi guide recommendations with day tours and car hire arranged. Limited off street parking also available. 10% senior citizen discount when booked direct. A very warm welcome.

B&B from £22.00 to £30.00
€27.93 to €38.09

AGNES DONOVAN
General Manager

Mastercard
Visa

10 7

Open All Year

CASTLETROY PARK HOTEL

DUBLIN ROAD,
LIMERICK
TEL: 061-335566 FAX: 061-331117
EMAIL: sales@castletroy-park.ie

HOTEL ★★★★ MAP 6 H 7

Limerick's finest 4**** hotel, the Castletroy Park Hotel, stands on 14 acres of beautifully landscaped gardens overlooking the Clare hills, 3.2km from Limerick city. Our traditionally styled hotel offers McLaughlin's fine dining restaurant, the Merry Pedlar Irish pub and an outstanding health and fitness club. The 101 rooms and 6 suites have been furnished and equipped to the highest international standards, ideally suited to today's discerning traveller.

WEB: www.castletroy-park.ie

B&B from £47.00 to £80.00
€59.68 to €101.58

DARAGH O'NEILL
General Manager

American Express
Diners
Mastercard
Visa

107 107

Open All Year

Room rates are per room per night

CLIFTON HOUSE GUEST HOUSE

ENNIS ROAD,
LIMERICK
TEL: 061-451166   FAX: 061-451224
EMAIL: cliftonhouse@eircom.net

GUESTHOUSE ★★★   MAP 6 H 7

Set in 1 acre of landscape gardens. All sixteen rooms en suite, with multi-channel TV, trouser press, hair dryers, direct dial telephone. Complimentary tea/coffee available in our spacious TV lounge. We are situated on the main Limerick/Shannon road. Within 15 minutes walk of city centre. 22 space car park. AA listed. Friendly welcome awaits you.

B&B from £20.00 to £24.00
€25.39 to €30.47

MICHAEL & MARY POWELL
Proprietor

Mastercard

Visa

🖐📶☎️🔲C✣P
16 16

I R I S H
HOTELS
FEDERATION

Closed 24 December - 06 January

CLONMACKEN HOUSE GUEST HOUSE

CLONMACKEN, OFF ENNIS ROAD,
(AT IVANS), LIMERICK
TEL: 061-327007   FAX: 061-327785
EMAIL: clonmac@indigo.ie

GUESTHOUSE ★★★   MAP 6 H 7

A purpose built, family run guest house, built to the highest standards, with multi-channel TV, DD phone, tea/coffee making facilities and hair dryer in each of its ten en suite superbly decorated bedrooms. Limerick city and King John's Castle are 5 minutes drive, Bunratty and Shannon Airport are situated nearby. Golf outings, coach tours, car hire & Bunratty Banquet can be arranged. Private secure car parking on our own 1 acre site. Home to the Cranberries and Frank McCourt.

WEB: www.euroka.com/limerick/clonmacken

Members Of Premier Guesthouses
B&B from £20.00 to £24.00
€25.39 to €30.47

BRID AND GERRY MCDONALD
Proprietors

American Express

Diners

Mastercard

Visa

🖐📶☎️🔲AC✣U♪P▪
10 10

I R I S H
HOTELS
FEDERATION

Closed 21 December - 07 January

CRUISES HOUSE

DENMARK STREET,
LIMERICK
TEL: 061-315320   FAX: 061-316995
EMAIL: cruiseshouse@eircom.net

GUESTHOUSE ★★★   MAP 6 H 7

Limerick's largest guesthouse, situated in the heart of the city centre. Offering luxurious en suite accommodation with DD phone, satellite TV, tea/coffee making facilities and hairdryer in each room. Convenient to Limerick's finest restaurants, pubs and shops. Additional facilities include a business meeting room, bringing a whole new concept to the guesthouse market.

Members Of Premier Guesthouses
B&B from £20.00 to £35.00
€25.39 to €44.44

CAROLE KELLY
Head Receptionist

American Express

Diners

Mastercard

Visa

🖐📶☎️🔲TC♥U♪♫▪
29 27

I R I S H
HOTELS
FEDERATION

Closed 24 - 28 December

B&B rates are per person sharing per night incl. Breakfast

GLENTWORTH HOTEL

GLENTWORTH STREET,
LIMERICK
TEL: 061-413822 FAX: 061-413073

HOTEL ★★ MAP 6 H 7

The Glentworth Hotel established in 1878 and situated in the city centre is the perfect location for entertainment & shopping. Our hotel features 20 newly refurbished en suite rooms with multi channel TV, hairdryer, tea/coffee facilities and trouser press. Superb restaurant, coffee shop, lounge bar, banqueting & conference facilities. 5 mins walk from bus/train, 25 mins from Shannon and private lock-up carpark. The Glentworth where people matter - Limerick's friendliest hotel.

Members Of UTELL / Robert Reid

B&B from £30.00 to £40.00
€38.09 to €50.79

JEREMIAH FLYNN
Director/General Manager

American Express
Diners
Mastercard
Visa

🙂 Weekend specials from £70.00

50 50

Open All Year

GREENHILLS HOTEL CONFERENCE/LEISURE

ENNIS ROAD,
LIMERICK
TEL: 061-453033 FAX: 061-453307

HOTEL ★★★ MAP 6 H 7

This hotel is set in 3.5 acres of gardens, is 5 minutes from Limerick city, 15 minutes from Shannon international airport. Enjoy our popular theme bar the Jockey club, award winning Bay Leaf Restaurant. Lamb a speciality - hotel's own farm. Also Brasserie Grill and residents' lounge. Super leisure centre, 18m swimming pool. Resident beautician / masseuse. Local amenities include horseriding, bowling and golf.

B&B from £40.00 to £55.00
€50.79 to €69.84

SARAH GREENE
Hospitality Manager

American Express
Diners
Visa

🙂 Weekend specials from £90.00

57 57

Closed 25 - 26 December

HANRATTY'S HOTEL

5 GLENTWORTH STREET,
LIMERICK
TEL: 061-410999 FAX: 061-411077

HOTEL ★★ MAP 6 H 7

Compact, cosy and convenient, our 22 en suite rooms are decorated to a high standard to ensure comfort. Each room has TV, hairdryer and tea/coffee facilities and DD phone. Hanrattys, being Limerick's oldest hotel, retains its character in a modern world. Traditional bar with music most nights. City centre location, near all facilities. Overnight lock-up carpark.

Members Of Irish Family Hotels

B&B from £22.50 to £32.50
€28.57 to €41.27

JOHN LIKELY
Proprietor

American Express
Diners
Mastercard
Visa

22 22

Closed 24 - 26 December

Room rates are per room per night

JURYS HOTEL LIMERICK

ENNIS ROAD,
LIMERICK
TEL: 061-327777   FAX: 061-326400
EMAIL: info@jurys.com

HOTEL ★★★★   MAP 6 H 7

A 4**** hotel set on a quiet 5 acre garden site on the banks of the River Shannon, just a short stroll to the city centre. The multi award-winning Copper Room restaurant offers superb international cuisine while Bridges Restaurant caters for informal dining. Limericks Bar and the extensive leisure facilities provide you with a choice of ways to relax during your stay. Jurys Doyle Hotel Group central reservations Tel. 01-607 0000 Fax. 01-631 6999.

WEB: www.jurys.com

B&B from £64.00 to £84.00
€81.26 to €106.66

AILEEN PHELAN
General Manager

American Express
Diners
Mastercard
Visa

☺ Weekend specials from £95.00

95 95

Closed 24 - 27 December

JURYS INN LIMERICK

LOWER MALLOW STREET,
LIMERICK
TEL: 061-207000   FAX: 061-400966
EMAIL: info@jurys.com

HOTEL ★★★   MAP 6 H 7

Modern attractive rooms capable of accommodating up to 3 adults or 2 adults and 2 children. All rooms are en suite with multi-channel TV, radio, modem points, DD phone and tea/coffee making facilities. Located in the centre of Limerick city, the Inn has an informal restaurant and lively pub and an adjoining public multi-storey car park (fee payable). Jurys Doyle Hotel Group central reservations Tel. 01-607 0000 Fax. 01-631 6999.

WEB: www.jurys.com

Room Rate from £46.00 to £53.00
€58.41 to €67.30

FIONA CLEARY
General Manager

American Express
Diners
Mastercard
Visa

151 151

Closed 24 - 26 December

LIMERICK INN HOTEL

ENNIS ROAD,
LIMERICK
TEL: 061-326666   FAX: 061-326281
EMAIL: limerick-inn@limerick-inn.ie

HOTEL ★★★★   MAP 6 H 7

Just 15 minutes from Shannon and 5 minutes from Limerick city, the Limerick Inn has everything you would expect from a 4**** hotel. All 153 rooms have private bathroom, direct dial telephone, radio and colour TV. The hotel has a full health and leisure centre, well appointed spacious drawing rooms, cocktail bar and lounge, excellent Irish and international cuisine and full conference facilities. USA Toll Free number (800) 223 0888. UTELL Representation.

WEB: limerick-inn.ie

B&B from £50.00 to £70.50
€63.49 to €89.52

JOHN FAHEY
General Manager

American Express
Diners
Mastercard
Visa

☺ Weekend specials from £100.00

153 153

Closed 24 - 26 December

B&B rates are per person sharing per night incl. Breakfast

LIMERICK RYAN HOTEL

ARDHU HOUSE, ENNIS ROAD,
LIMERICK
TEL: 061-453922 FAX: 061-326333
EMAIL: ryan@indigo.ie

HOTEL ★★★ MAP 6 H 7

The original wing of the Limerick Ryan Hotel dates back to 1780. Restored to enhance the original architecture, this hotel combines the spaciousness of an earlier age with the comforts of today - 179 en suite bedrooms, 2 suites, the award winning Ardhu restaurant, gymnasium, superior meeting rooms, a business centre, the new Toddys Bar and a cocktail bar. Located 2km from the city and 15 minutes from Shannon airport. Car parking. AA, RAC and Egon Ronay recommended.

WEB: www.ryan-hotels.com

B&B from £35.00 to £65.00
€44.44 to €82.53

DERMOT FEHILY
General Manager

American Express
Diners
Mastercard
Visa

😊 Weekend specials from £69.00

181 181

Open All Year

RAILWAY HOTEL

PARNELL STREET,
LIMERICK
TEL: 061-413653 FAX: 061-419762

HOTEL ★★ MAP 6 H 7

Family run hotel, owned and managed by the Collins family. Traditional Irish hospitality, good food and personal attention are a way of life in the hotel. Bedrooms are en suite, comfortable and tastefully furnished. An attractive lounge bar is ideal for a quick bar lunch for the tourist and business man. Ideally suited for touring, adjacent to rail and bus station, convenient to city centre. All major credit cards accepted.

B&B from £25.00 to £27.00
€31.74 to €34.28

MICHAEL & UNA COLLINS
Owners/Managers

American Express
Diners
Mastercard
Visa

30 24

Closed 25 December

ROYAL GEORGE HOTEL

O'CONNELL STREET,
LIMERICK
TEL: 061-414566 FAX: 061-317171

HOTEL ★★★ MAP 6 H 7

This family run 3*** hotel is ideally suited for business or pleasure situated in the heart of Limerick city. Enjoy a night in our traditional Irish pub of distinction, The Sibin, with nightly entertainment. 15 mins drive from Shannon International Airport. Local attractions include St. Johns Castle, Bunratty Folk Park, the Hunt Museum, Cliffs of Moher and Adare. Secure lock-up carpark. For special offers Freephone 1800 70 20 70.

Room Rate from £39.00 to £59.00
€49.52 to €74.91

SEAN LALLY

American Express
Diners
Mastercard
Visa

54 54

Closed 25 - 26 December

Room rates are per room per night

SHANNON GROVE GUESTHOUSE

ATHLUNKARD,
LIMERICK
TEL: 061-345756 FAX: 061-343838

GUESTHOUSE ★★★ MAP 6 H 7

Shannon Grove Guesthouse is a charming, family-managed, registered 3*** guesthouse, within 5 mins of Limerick city, yet away from the bustle of city noise and traffic. With 9 beautifully decorated en suite bedrooms, multi channel TV, DD phone and secure car parking, Shannon Grove is the ideal location for your stay in Limerick, being in close proximity to a wide range of leisure activities, university, Shannon Airport, Bunratty and King John's Castle, and Lough Derg. Route R463, from Limerick.

B&B from £25.00 to £30.00
€31.74 to €38.09

NOREEN MARSH
Owner

Mastercard
Visa

🦽🏠T☼🗑P
9 9

IRISH HOTELS FEDERATION

Closed 15 December - 06 January

SOUTH COURT BUSINESS AND LEISURE HOTEL

RAHEEN ROUNDABOUT,
ADARE ROAD, LIMERICK
TEL: 065-682 3000 FAX: 065-682 3759
EMAIL: cro@lynchotels.com

HOTEL R MAP 6 H 7

Few hotels compare to this impressive hotel. 65 large en suite rooms with satellite TV, latest pay per view (movies), fax/modem point; executive rooms have fax, mini bar, trouser press, writing desk etc. Seasons fine dining à la carte restaurant and Boru's Porterhouse traditional Irish pub/bistro. Health suite incl gym, sauna, massage. Business/office support. Parking 200 cars. Limerick 5 mins, Shannon 15 mins. Due 2000, 55 additional rooms, 1250 seater conference centre, leisure club inc. 3 pools.

WEB: www.lynchotels.com

Members Of Lynch Hotels

B&B from £35.00 to £45.00
€44.44 to €57.14

MICHAEL B LYNCH GROUP MD
David Byrne Gen Mgr

American Express
Diners
Mastercard
Visa

😊 2 Dinners, B&B from £44.00

65 65

IRISH HOTELS FEDERATION

Open All Year

TWO MILE INN HOTEL

ENNIS ROAD,
LIMERICK
TEL: 061-326255 FAX: 061-453783

HOTEL ★★★ MAP 6 H 7

123 bedroomed 3*** hotel situated outside Limerick city on the main Limerick/Shannon/Galway road, 15 minutes drive from Shannon International Airport, and 6.44km from Bunratty Castle and Folk Park. All bedrooms have private bathroom, TV, radio & tea/coffee making facilities. À la carte and table d'hôte restaurant and Thady O'Neills old world pub and restaurant with traditional music. Ideal base for scenic tours to the Cliffs of Moher, Galway and Killarney. Toll Free 1800 528 1234.

Members Of Best Western Hotels

B&B from £33.50 to £49.50
€42.54 to €62.85

BRENDAN DUNNE
Proprietor

American Express
Diners
Mastercard
Visa

🦽🏠T☼🗑CM☼♨U♪♫
123 123

PS🅿️🅰️ld♿🛗

IRISH HOTELS FEDERATION

Open All Year

B&B rates are per person sharing per night incl. Breakfast

WOODFIELD HOUSE HOTEL

ENNIS ROAD,
LIMERICK
TEL: 061-453022   FAX: 061-326755

HOTEL U   MAP 6 H 7

Tastefully refurbished in keeping with its old world character and family atmosphere. Personally directed by Austin Gibbons. Renowned locally for its excellent food and conference facilities. Ideally situated on the main Shannon road with Shannon Airport just 16km and conveniently located to Bunratty Castle and Folk Park. All rooms are en suite/modern. Members of MinOtels Ireland Ltd, recommended by RAC and AA. Private Car Park.

Members Of MinOtel Ireland Hotel Group

B&B from £42.50 to £47.50
€53.96 to €60.31

AUSTIN GIBBONS
Proprietor

American Express
Diners
Mastercard
Visa

:✓

🛏🍴☎🖥📺📻🚗CM✳🔆UJPS🏊
alc🔻 Inet FAX

IRISH HOTELS FEDERATION

Closed 25 December

LEENS HOTEL

MAIN STREET, ABBEYFEALE,
CO. LIMERICK
TEL: 068-31121   FAX: 068-32550

HOTEL ★★   MAP 5 E 6

Leens Hotel is located in the square, Abbeyfeale in the heart of West Limerick. It has been recently refurbished to the highest standard and is under the personal supervision of Maurice and Olive Sheehan. It has 20 new bedrooms, tastefully finished to a very high standard. There is a carvery lunch served daily and a wide selection of barfood available throughout the day. There is a very warm atmosphere in the Oak Bar and a very intimate restaurant offering the best in local produce.

B&B from £25.00 to £35.00
€31.74 to €44.44

MAURICE AND OLIVE SHEEHAN

American Express
Diners
Mastercard
Visa

🌶

😊 Weekend specials from £60.00

🛏🍴☎🖥📺📻🚗CMUJ♫🏊🖨alc

IRISH HOTELS FEDERATION

Closed 24 - 26 December

ADARE MANOR HOTEL & GOLF CLUB

ADARE,
CO. LIMERICK
TEL: 061-396566   FAX: 061-396124
EMAIL: reservations@adaremanor.com

HOTEL ★★★★★   MAP 6 G 7

Located 20 miles from Shannon airport. Adare Manor Hotel & Golf Club, set on the banks of the River Maigue, boasts splendour in its luxuriously finished rooms. The Oak Room restaurant provides haute cuisine laced with Irish charm. Indoor facilities include heated pool, fitness centre, sauna and massage therapy. Outdoor pursuits include fishing, horseriding, clay pigeon shooting and the Robert Trent Jones Snr ch'ship golf course. New clubhouse with state of the art conference centre.

WEB: www.adaremanor.ie

Room Rate from £145.00 to £395.00
€184.11 to €501.55

STEPHEN QUINN
Managing Director

American Express
Diners
Mastercard
Visa

:✓🎿🍴

😊 2 nights B&B plus 1 Dinner from £135.00

🛏🍴☎🖥📺📻🚗CM✳🔆🏊🍷🖨🔍
U🎿♫🎵P🏊alc

IRISH HOTELS FEDERATION

Open All Year

Room rates are per room per night

CARRABAWN HOUSE

KILLARNEY ROAD (N21), ADARE,
CO. LIMERICK
TEL: 061-396067 FAX: 061-396925

GUESTHOUSE ★★★ MAP 6 G 7

Beside Adare Manor golf course, multi recommended Carrabawn Guesthouse is a luxury establishment situated in the picturesque village of Adare, renowned for its Tidy Town awards. The Lohan family offer you first class accommodation in friendly surroundings and assure you a most memorable stay. Colour TV, DD phone, tea/coffee making facilities and hairdryer in all rooms. Only 30 mins Shannon Airport / Bunratty Folk Park. Equestrian centre 1k, golf courses too numerous to mention.

B&B from £22.50 to £30.00
€28.57 to €38.09

BRIDGET LOHAN
Proprietor

Mastercard
Visa

Closed 24 - 26 December

DUNRAVEN ARMS HOTEL

ADARE,
CO. LIMERICK
TEL: 061-396633 FAX: 061-396541
EMAIL: dunraven@iol.ie

HOTEL ★★★★ MAP 6 G 7

Established in 1792 Grade A 4**** old world hotel surrounded by ornate thatched cottages, in Ireland's prettiest village. Each bedroom including twelve suites are beautifully appointed with antique furniture, dressing room and bathroom en suite. Award-winning restaurant, AA Three Red Rosettes. Leisure centre comprised of a 17m pool, steam room and gym studio. Equestrian and golf holidays a speciality. 30 mins from Shannon Airport. GDS Access Code UI Toll Free 1-800-44 UTELL

WEB: www.dunravenhotel.com

Members Of Manor House Hotels

B&B from £68.75 to £85.50
€87.29 to €108.56

LOUIS MURPHY
Resident Manager

American Express
Diners
Mastercard
Visa

Open All Year

FITZGERALDS WOODLANDS HOUSE HOTEL & LEISURE CLUB

KNOCKANES, ADARE,
CO. LIMERICK
TEL: 061-605100 FAX: 061-396073
EMAIL: reception@woodlands-hotel.ie

HOTEL ★★★ MAP 6 G 7

Fitzgeralds Woodlands House Hotel, Health & Leisure Club is situated on its own grounds of 44 acres. Luxurious 94 bedroom hotel including deluxe, superior and executive suites with jacuzzi bath. Owned and managed by the Fitzgerald family. Award-winning Brennan Room Restaurant and Timmy Macs Traditional Irish Bar and Bistro serving the best in good food and music - trad sessions. Excellent wedding and conference facilities. An ideal base to explore the mid west. Golf packages a speciality.

WEB: www.woodlands-hotel.ie

Members Of Village Inn Hotels

B&B from £35.00 to £60.00
€44.44 to €76.18

DICK, MARY & DAVID FITZGERALD
Hosts

American Express
Diners
Mastercard
Visa

Closed 24 - 26 December

B&B rates are per person sharing per night incl. Breakfast

CASTLE OAKS HOUSE HOTEL & COUNTRY CLUB

CASTLECONNELL,
CO. LIMERICK
TEL: 061-377666 FAX: 061-377717
EMAIL: info@castle-oaks.com

HOTEL ★★★ MAP 6 H 7

The Castle Oaks Country Hotel and its superb country club leisure centre, including indoor pool, are set on a 26 acre estate on the banks of the river Shannon. All our lavishly furnished bedrooms are en suite. Our luxurious suites contain jacuzzis. The Castle Oaks is renowned for its superb cuisine and ambience. We welcome you to experience the warmth and hospitality of our Georgian mansion. Fishing and golfing available locally. Logis of Ireland member.
Tel: 01-668 9743.

WEB: www.castle-oaks.com

Members Of Logis of Ireland

B&B from £36.30 to £44.00
€46.09 to €55.87

FRANCIS MURPHY/AILEEN KENNEDY
Hosts

American Express
Diners
Mastercard
Visa

Closed 24 - 26 December

KILMURRY LODGE HOTEL

DUBLIN ROAD, CASTLETROY,
LIMERICK
TEL: 061-331133 FAX: 061-330011

HOTEL ★★★ MAP 6 H 7

Kilmurry Lodge Hotel opened in April 1995, set in four acres and boasting 43 beautifully decorated bedrooms. All are fully equipped with TV, hairdryer, tea/coffee making facilities. Bedrooms have either twin or double beds with additional single bed, ideal for families. Situated close to the University and National Technological Park. Excellent Flanagans restaurant, Nelligans Bar and five superb meeting rooms. A friendly hotel providing comfort and value for money.

Members Of Irish Family Hotels

B&B from £32.00 to £32.00
€40.63 to €40.63

ANITA CAREY
General Manager

American Express
Diners
Mastercard
Visa

😊 Weekend specials from £69.00

Closed 25 - 26 December

COURTENAY LODGE HOTEL

NEWCASTLE WEST,
CO. LIMERICK
TEL: 069-62244 FAX: 069-77184
EMAIL: res@courtenaylodge.iol.ie

HOTEL ★★★ MAP 2 F 6

A warm welcome awaits you at the Courtenay Lodge Hotel situated on the main Limerick to Killarney road and only 15 mins from the picturesque village of Adare. The newly-built, tastefully decorated, en suite rooms complete with TV, DD phone, power showers, trouser press, tea/coffee facilities, etc. ensure a level of comfort second to none. The ideal base for touring the Shannon and South West region and the perfect location for golfers to enjoy some of the most renowned courses.

B&B from £25.00 to £40.00
€31.74 to €50.79

DECLAN O'GRADY
General Manager

American Express
Diners
Mastercard
Visa

😊 Weekend specials from £69.00

Closed 25 December

Room rates are per room per night

DEVON INN HOTEL

TEMPLEGLANTINE,
NEWCASTLEWEST, CO. LIMERICK
TEL: 069-84122 FAX: 069-84255

HOTEL ★★★ MAP 6 F 6

The newly refurbished Devon Inn Hotel offers a superb base to explore the wonderful attractions of the South West. Situated midway between Limerick city and Killarney in the heart of West Limerick. The hotel features 40 excellent bedrooms, a superb restaurant featuring the best of local produce, a choice of two bars and conference and banqueting for up to 400 guests. Private car park. Just over an hour's drive from Shannon Airport and under an hour to Killarney.

Members Of Irish Family Hotels

B&B from £25.00 to £40.00
€31.74 to €50.79

WILLIAM SHEEHAN
Manager

American Express
Diners
Mastercard
Visa

☺ Weekend specials from £75.00

40 40

Closed 24 - 26 December

RATHKEALE HOUSE HOTEL

RATHKEALE,
CO. LIMERICK
TEL: 069-63333 FAX: 069-63300
EMAIL: rhh@iol.ie

HOTEL ★★★ MAP 6 G 6

Rathkeale House Hotel a new family-run facility located just 2 minutes off the main N21 Limerick to Killarney road and 4 miles west of Ireland's prettiest village, Adare. A short 20 minute drive from Limerick city, 40 minutes from Shannon Airport and less than 60 minutes from Killarney, the hotel is the ideal base from which to explore the many wonderful amenities of the region. Also a member of Holiday Ireland. Caters for weddings, 21st parties and all family functions.

Members Of Logis of Ireland

B&B from £25.00 to £40.00
€31.74 to €50.79

BRIAN O'CONNOR

American Express
Diners
Mastercard
Visa

26 26

Closed 25 December

DROMINEER BAY HOTEL

DROMINEER, NENAGH,
CO. TIPPERARY
TEL: 067-24114 FAX: 067-24444

HOTEL ★★★ MAP 6 I 8

Family run hotel on the shores of Lough Derg near Nenagh in County Tipperary. Beautiful lake views and a high level of comfort and service. Facilities include Captains Deck Bar serving extensive à la carte menu and Moorings Restaurant. Coarse and game fishing, canoeing, yachting, pony trekking, shooting, walking and golf. Conference facilities available with secretarial back up.

Members Of Coast and Country Hotels

B&B from £45.00 to £65.00
€57.14 to €82.53

MICHELLE DOWLING
Manageress

American Express
Diners
Mastercard
Visa

☺ Weekend specials from £79.00

24 24

Closed 25 - 27 December

B&B rates are per person sharing per night incl. Breakfast

NENAGH ABBEY COURT HOTEL

DUBLIN ROAD, NENAGH,
CO. TIPPERARY
TEL: 067-41111 FAX: 067-41022
EMAIL: abycourt@indigo.ie

HOTEL ★★★ MAP 6 I 8

Located on the main Dublin road (N7) and within easy walking distance of Nenagh Town, the Abbey Court Hotel boasts 46 lavishly appointed rooms decorated to suit the most discerning guests with DD phone, multi-channel TV, tea/coffee making facilities, trouser press/iron centre, etc. Superb conference and banqueting facilities with secretarial back-up. Award winning Rosette Cloister restaurant, Abbots bar and daily carvery lunch. Golf packages available.

WEB: nenagh-abbeycourt.ie

B&B from £45.00 to £130.00
€57.14 to €165.07

TOM WALSH
Managing Director

American Express
Diners
Mastercard
Visa

:/♫👢

🛏🏃☎🖥🇹🇨⬅CM❄☽♪🇵
46 46
🇸🇦álc▪

IRISH
HOTELS
FEDERATION

Open All Year

ST. DAVID'S COUNTRY HOUSE

PUCKANE, NENAGH,
CO. TIPPERARY
TEL: 067-24145 FAX: 067-24388

HOTEL ★★★ MAP 6 I 8

The perfect Irish country house: an elegant Victorian home, nestled on the shores of Lough Derg. The house is restored and refurbished to the highest modern standards and yet retains the cosy relaxed atmosphere of those days gone by. St. David's is set in 17 acres of mature park and woodland. St. David's offers a warm welcome, deliciously good food served with excellent wines and luxurious accommodation at its best.

Members Of Ireland's Blue Book

Room Rate from £120.00 to £180.00
€152.37 to €228.55

BERNHARD KLOTZ
Proprietor

American Express
Mastercard
Visa

:/👢

🛏🏃☎❄☽♪🇺🇵🇸🇦álc
10 10

IRISH
HOTELS
FEDERATION

Closed 15 January - 30 March

GRANT'S HOTEL

CASTLE STREET, ROSCREA,
CO. TIPPERARY
TEL: 0505-23300 FAX: 0505-23209
EMAIL: grantshotel@eircom.net

HOTEL ★★★ MAP 7 J 9

Located on the main link road from Dublin to Kerry, Limerick and Clare (N7). Visit Grant's Hotel, 3***, AA 3*** hotel in the heart of the heritage town of Roscrea. The hotel features 25 en suite bedrooms pleasantly furbished in warm toned colours. Lunch and evening meals served in Kitty's Tavern daily. The award-winning Lemon Tree restaurant is the ideal place to relax after a day's golfing, fishing or exploring Ely O'Carroll country. Special golf packages available.

WEB: www.grantshotel.com

B&B from £30.00 to £40.00
€38.09 to €50.79

EDEL FARRELLY
General Manager

American Express
Diners
Mastercard
Visa

:/

😊 Weekend specials from £80.00

🛏🏃☎🖥🇹🇨⬅CMO☽♪🇵🇸🇦
25 25
álc▪

IRISH
HOTELS
FEDERATION

Closed 24 - 27 December

Room rates are per room per night

RACKET HALL COUNTRY HOUSE HOTEL

DUBLIN ROAD, ROSCREA,
CO. TIPPERARY
TEL: 0505-21748   FAX: 0505-23701
EMAIL: racketh@iol.ie

HOTEL U   MAP 7 J 9

Charming family-run olde world country residence set in the heart of the monastic midlands. Situated on the busy N7 just outside the heritage town of Roscrea, this is the ideal location for the avid golfer, fishing enthusiast or those who wish to explore the abundant historic sites in the area. The Slieve Bloom mountains are also only a stone's throw away. This is a very convenient stopping off point from Dublin to Limerick, Clare or Kerry. Lily Bridges Bar, Willow Tree restaurant.

B&B from £24.50 to £29.50
€31.11 to €37.46

MICHAEL COSTELLO
Proprietor

American Express
Diners
Mastercard
Visa

Weekend specials from £65.00

10 10

Closed 25 December

TOWER

CHURCH STREET, ROSCREA,
CO. TIPPERARY
TEL: 0505-21774   FAX: 0505-22425
EMAIL: thetower@eircom.net

GUESTHOUSE ★★★   MAP 7 J 9

Influenced by its historic environment. The Tower is a unique 3* establishment combining old world style and charm with contemporary service and quality. The 10 guest bedrooms are tastefully decorated and furnished to a very high standard. The Tower has a fully licensed bar & restaurant and special golf week-ends are available. Horse riding & hill walking, forest trail, pitch & putt, angling all available close by to this heritage town.

Members Of Premier Guesthouses

B&B from £20.00 to £25.00
€25.39 to €31.74

GERARD & BRIDIE COUGHLAN
Proprietors

American Express
Diners
Mastercard
Visa

Weekend specials from £58.00

10 10

Closed 25 - 26 December

ANNER HOTEL

DUBLIN ROAD, THURLES,
CO. TIPPERARY
TEL: 0504-21799   FAX: 0504-22111

HOTEL ★★★   MAP 7 J 7

The Anner Hotel is situated on its own private grounds with beautiful landscaped gardens. We offer our guests a warm welcome, excellent food and a friendly service in comfortable surroundings. Each room is spaciously furnished and fully fitted with DD phone, cable TV, tea/coffee making facilities, trouser press and hairdryer. Our luxurious newly-opened health & leisure centre has an 18m pool, kiddies pool, jacuzzi, sauna, steam room, solarium and gym. On the outskirts of Thurles.

WEB: www.iol.ie/annerhtl.htm

B&B from £35.00 to £55.00
€44.44 to €69.84

GERARD MOYLAN

American Express
Diners
Mastercard
Visa

64 64

Open All Year

B&B rates are per person sharing per night incl. Breakfast

HORSE AND JOCKEY INN

HORSE AND JOCKEY, THURLES,
CO. TIPPERARY
TEL: 0504-44192 FAX: 0504-44747
EMAIL: horseandjockeyinn@eircom.net

HOTEL N MAP 7 J 7

The Horse and Jockey Inn, located at the heartland of county Tipperary, midway between Cork and Dublin on the N8 holds great association with people from sporting, cultural and political walks of life. Our new refurbishment includes spacious lounge and bar facilities, a high quality restaurant, deluxe accommodation and a modern conference centre. Experience the atmosphere that's steeped in tradition and share with us the real Ireland, in the comfort of our new inn.

WEB: www.tipp.ie/horse-jockey-inn.htm

B&B from £35.00 to £65.00
€44.44 to €82.53

TOM EGAN
Proprietor

American Express
Diners
Mastercard
Visa

32 32

Inet FAX

FRENCH
HOTELS
FEDERATION

Open All Year

INTERNATIONAL DIAL CODES

Emergency Services:
999 (freephone)

HOW TO DIAL
INTERNATIONAL
ACCESS CODE +
COUNTRY CODE +
AREA CODE +
LOCAL NUMBER

SAMPLE CODES:
E.G. UNITED KINGDOM
00 44 + Area Code + Local No.

U.S.A.	00	1 +
Italy	00	39 +
Spain	00	34 +
France	00	33 +
Germany	00	49 +
Iceland	00	354 +
Japan	00	81 +
Luxembourg	00	352 +
Netherlands	00	31 +

Operator (national)	1190
(G. Britain)	1197
(International)	1198

WATCH FOR THE SYMBOL OF QUALITY

THIS SYMBOL OF QUALITY GUARANTEES YOU, THE VISITOR, A HIGH STANDARD OF ACCOMMODATION AND SERVICE WHICH IS EXPECTED OF IRISH HOTELS & GUESTHOUSES.

QUALITY

Room rates are per room per night

LES ROUTIERS

LES ROUTIERS IRELAND
CONTACT NOEL STEWART
MOBILE: 087 230 9814
FAX: +353 (0) 1 295 1356

Les Routiers offers an unrivalled selection of hotels and restaurants for leisure or business travellers throughout the whole of Ireland. Why not visit one of our award winning establishments and experience excellent accommodation, enjoy innovative cuisine, avail of our conference facilities and varied selection of leisure pursuits or simply relax with a round of golf on one of Ireland's many wonderful courses.

Les Routiers is your guarantee of quality. If you're travelling to Ireland - go Les Routiers.

For brochures please apply to your distribution centre:

Les Routiers 25 Vanston Place
London SW6 1AZ.
Tel: +44 171 385 6644
Fax: +44 171 385 7136
EMAIL: ireland@routiers.co.uk

CHOICE HOTELS IRELAND

32 SOUTH TERRACE,
CORK.
TEL: +353-21-323210 (EUR/INT)
TEL: +353-21-323133 (IRE)
FAX: +353-21-323212
EMAIL: choicehotels@eircom.net

CHOICE HOTELS
IRELAND

Choice Hotels Ireland offer a superb range of Hotels in all principal destinations around Ireland.

All of our properties are independently owned and fulfill the expectations of the discerning Traveller with the atmosphere of genuine hospitality.

Activities within close proximity to Hotels are Golf, Fishing, Cycling and Walking.

Enjoy a Mid-Week or Weekend Break or sample a number of our Hotels with our Go As You Please programme.

Hotels welcome Groups, Conferences and Incentives.

Choice Hotels International represents over 5,000 hotels in 36 countries.

Prompt and personal service guaranteed.

MINOTEL IRELAND HOTEL GROUP

BALLYCANEW, GOREY,
CO. WEXFORD.
TEL: +353-55-27 291
FAX: +353-55-27 398
EMAIL: info@minotel.iol.ie

MinOtel Ireland is a marketing consortium of carefully chosen Owner/Manager style Hotels located throughout Ireland. The Hotels are chiefly 3* standard with their own individual characteristics. The Member Hotels are exposed by MinOtel Ireland to a range of Tour Operator Programmes including:- Car Tours, Fly-Drive, Coach Tours, Activity Holidays, Short Breaks, etc.. MinOtel Ireland has established business links with the Trade in Britain, Europe and North America. Central Reservations/Accounts is an essential service which the Ireland Office provides.

MinOtel International represents over 700 Hotels in 32 countries and the combined initiatives of MinOtel gives Irish Hotels exposure in over a million pieces of MinOtel publications, at the World's major Travel Fairs, in Tour Operator Programmes and on the Internet. The MinOtel Europe Voucher operates on a B+B basis and is accepted at all MinOtel hotels throughout Europe.

Enquiries are invited and will be attended to promptly.

Be Our Guest

2OOO

HOTEL AND GUESTHOUSE
RESERVATIONS
FREEPHONE

To book any of the premises in this Guide
ring toll free on

+800 36 98 74 12 *

Be Our Guest

* + denotes international access code in country where call is made
e.g. from UK   access code 00
        USA   access code 011

Powered by:  **res** ireland

IRELAND FOR

Golf

HOTELS & GUESTHOUSES

Golfing in Ireland is not quite like
golfing any other place else on earth.

Here the game has become part of
the national culture and is for
everyone. That includes you.

Ireland's rugged landscape, perched on the
edge of the Atlantic ocean, has provided
many great golf courses.

And they are relatively uncrowded.
So get in the swing - come golfing in Ireland.

WHERE TO STAY WHEN YOU PLAY!

We invite you to sample the golf, the countryside and the friendship of the Irish people and then to stay in some of Ireland's most charming accommodation. We have listed a range of hotels and guesthouses which are either situated on or close to a golf course. Your host will assist you if necessary in arranging your golfing requirements including tee reservations and green fee charges. A full description of the hotels and guesthouses can be had by looking up the appropriate page number. Premises are listed in alphabetical order in each county.

ACCOMMODATION   COURSES

GALWAY

Accommodation	Courses	Be Our Guest Page Number	Golf On Site	All Inclusive Package	Tuition Available	Cart Available	Arrange Tee Off Times	Advance Reservations	Clubs For Hire	Transport	Preferential Green Fees	Caddy Available
Abbey House	Barna, Galway, Galway Bay, Athenry, Oughterard	24	•					•				
Abbeyglen Castle Hotel	Connemara	45	•	•	•	•	•	•	•	•	•	
Acorn Guesthouse	Galway Bay, Salthill, Oughterard, Athenry, Gort, Loughrea	24	•	•	•	•	•	•	•		•	•
Adare Guest House	Galway Bay, Oughterard	97	•	•	•	•	•	•	•			•
Alcock and Brown Hotel	Connemara	46	•	•	•		•	•		•		
Anno Santo Hotel	Galway, Oughterard, Galway Bay, Athenry, Barna, Glenlo	25						•		•		•
Ardagh Hotel & Restaurant	Connemara	46					•	•		•		
Ardilaun House Hotel, Conference & Leisure Centre	Galway, Oughterard, Galway Bay Golf & Country, Athenry, Lahinch, Connemara	26		•		•	•	•	•	•	•	•
Ballynahinch Castle Hotel	Connemara Championship Golf Course	43	•	•	•	•	•	•		•		•
Ben View House	Connemara	46						•		•		
Boat Inn	Oughterard, Barna, Ballyconneely, Galway Bay, Salthill, Glenlo	55	•	•	•	•	•	•	•		•	•
Connemara Coast Hotel	Barna, Oughterard, Galway Bay	27	•	•		•	•		•		•	•
Connemara Gateway Hotel	Oughterard, Barna Golf and Country Club	55									•	
Corrib House Hotel	Oughterard, Connemara Isles, Galway Bay, Barna, Ballyconneely	55	•	•	•	•	•	•	•		•	•
Corrib Wave Guest House	Oughterard	56						•		•		•
Dun Ri Guesthouse	Connemara	47					•	•		•	•	
Eldons Hotel	Connemara Championship, Oughterard, Westport	37					•	•	•			
Foyles Hotel	Connemara	48					•	•		•		
Galway Bay Golf and Country Club Hotel		29	⚑18	•	•	•	•	•	•	•	•	
Galway Bay Hotel, Conference & Leisure Centre	Galway, Galway Bay, Athenry, Barna, Gort	30	•	•	•	•	•	•	•		•	•

⚑18 = Full 18 Hole   ⚑9 = 9 Hole   ⚑3 = Par 3

Accommodation	Courses	Be Our Guest Page Number	Golf On Site	All Inclusive Package	Tuition Available	Cart Available	Arrange Tee Off Times	Advance Reservations	Clubs For Hire	Transport	Preferential Green Fees	Caddy Available
GALWAY Continued												
Galway Ryan Hotel & Leisure Centre	Galway Bay, Galway, Athenry, Oughterard, Roscam, Rosshill	30							•	•	•	
Guider's Osterley Lodge	Galway, Galway Bay, Barna, Athenry, Oughterard, Glenlo Abbey	31		•	•	•		•	•	•	•	
Hotel Sacre Coeur	Bearna, Galway, Athenry, Tuam, Oughterard, Galway Bay	32		•	•	•		•	•	•	•	•
Inishmore Guesthouse	Barna, Galway Bay, Oughterard, Athenry, Salthill	33		•	•	•		•	•	•	•	
Knockrea Guest House	Galway Bay, Oughterard, Athenry, Barna	34		•	•	•	•	•	•	•	•	•
Lady Gregory Hotel	Gort	51		•	•	•		•	•	•	•	
Lake Hotel	Oughterard Golf Club and other local championship courses	56		•	•	•	•	•	•	•	•	
Lochlurgain Hotel	Barna, Galway, Athenry, Gort, Oughterard and Galway Bay	34		•	•	•	•	•	•	•	•	•
Merriman Inn & Restaurant	Gort, Galway Bay	52							•	•		
Mountain View Guest House	Oughterard, Galway, Connemara, Westport	57		•	•	•		•	•	•	•	•
O'Deas Hotel	Loughrea, Curragh, Gort, Galway Bay	54	•			•		•	•	•	•	
O'Grady's Sunnybank Guesthouse	Connemara, Ballyconneely, Westport, Oughterard	49			•	•		•	•	•	•	
Quality Hotel and Leisure Centre Galway	Athenry, Galway, Galway Bay, Loughrea, Glenlo Abbey, Gort	37		•		•	•	•	•	•	•	•
Renvyle House Hotel	Connemara, Westport, Oughterard	58 [9]		•	•	•	•	•	•	•		
River Run Lodge	Oughterard	57		•	•	•		•	•	•		•
Shannon Oaks Hotel & Country Club	Portumna, Galway Bay, Birr, Glasson, Gort, Lahinch	58	•	•	•	•		•	•	•	•	
Station House Hotel	Ballyconneely (Connemara), Oughterard, Westport	50	•		•		•	•	•	•	•	•
Westwood House Hotel	Barna, Oughterard, Ballyconneely	40				•	•	•	•	•		
MAYO												
Atlantic Coast Hotel	Westport, Enniscrone, Carne, Ballyconneely, Castlebar, Ballinrobe	69		•	•	•		•	•	•		
Augusta Lodge	Westport, Enniscrone, Belmullet (Carne), Mulrany, Clew Bay	69							•	•	•	•

[18] = Full 18 Hole   [9] = 9 Hole   [3] = Par 3

WHERE TO STAY WHEN YOU PLAY!

Accommodation	Courses	Be Our Guest Page Number	Golf On Site	All Inclusive Package	Tuition Available	Cart Available	Arrange Tee Off Times	Advance Reservations	Clubs For Hire	Transport	Preferential Green Fees	Caddy Available
MAYO Continued												
Bartra House Hotel	Enniscrone, Ballina, Cairn, Rosses Point, Strandhill	62		•					•	•	•	•
Belleek Castle	Enniscrone, Sligo, Carne/Belmullet	62							•	•	•	
Castlecourt Hotel Conference and Leisure Centre	Westport, Ballinrobe, Castlebar, Belmullet, Clew Bay, Enniscrone	69	•	•	•	•	•	•	•	•	•	•
Central Hotel	Westport Golf Club	20	•	•	•	•	•	•	•			
Clew Bay Hotel	Westport, Castlebar, Ballinrobe, Carne, Enniscrone	70	•	•	•	•	•	•	•	•	•	•
Daly's Hotel	Castlebar, Westport, Balla, Enniscrone, Belmullet, Three Oaks	64	•	•	•	•	•	•			•	•
Downhill Hotel	Ballina, Enniscrone, Carne (Belmullet), Rosses Point, Strandhill, Westport	62	•	•	•	•	•	•	•	•	•	•
Downhill Inn	Rosses Point	63	•	•	•	•	•	•	•			
Healy's Hotel	Castlebar, Ballina, Westport, Enniscrone, Carne, Swinford, Ballinrobe	68	•	•	•	•	•	•	•	•	•	•
Hotel Westport	Westport, Castlebar, Ballinrobe, Carne	70	•	•	•	•	•	•	•	•	•	•
Jennings Hotel & Travellers Friend	Castlebar, Westport, Three Oaks, Ballinrobe, Belmullet, Enniscrone	65	•	•	•	•	•	•				
Knockranny House Hotel	Westport, Castlebar, Ballinrobe, Clew Bay, Achill, Mulrany	71	•	•	•	•	•	•	•	•	•	•
Knockranny Lodge	Westport Golf Club	71		•	•	•	•	•	•	•		
Lydons Lodge	Ballinrobe, Cross, Ashford	66	•	•	•	•	•	•	•			
Mount Falcon Castle	Enniscrone, Ballina, Carne	63							•	•	•	•
Ryan's Hotel	Westport, Clifden (Ballyconneely), Galway, Ballinrobe	66	•	•	•	•	•	•				
Westport Woods Hotel & Leisure Centre	Westport, Castlebar, Ballinrobe, Clew Bay, Carne (Belmullet)	72	•	•	•	•	•	•	•	•	•	•
ROSCOMMON												
Abbey Hotel	Donegal, Murvagh, Narin	72		•							•	•
Gleesons Guesthouse & Restaurant	Roscommon	72	•	•	•	•	•	•	•			
O'Garas Royal Hotel	Roscommon, Glasson, Longford	73	•									
Regans	Roscommon	73	•		•	•	•	•	•			
White House Hotel	Castlerea	74	•		•	•	•	•	•	•		

 18 = Full 18 Hole   9 = 9 Hole   3 = Par 3

WHERE TO STAY
WHEN YOU PLAY!

NORTH WEST

ACCOMMODATION	COURSES	Be Our Guest Page Number	Golf On Site	All Inclusive Package	Tuition Available	Cart Available	Arrange Tee Off Times	Advance Reservations	Clubs For Hire	Transport	Preferential Green Fees	Caddy Available
DONEGAL												
Abbey Hotel	Roscommon, Glasson, Athlone	76		•	•	•	•	•	•	•	•	•
Arnolds Hotel	Dunfanaghy 18 Hole Links	84		•		•	•	•	•		•	•
Ballyliffin Hotel	Ballyliffin, North West, Buncrana	78		•		•	•	•	•	•		
Bay View Hotel & Leisure Centre	Narin (Portnoo), Donegal Murvagh	85		•		•	•	•	•		•	
Campbell's Pier House	Cruit Island, Narin/Portnoo, Gweedore, Dungloe Pitch & Putt	82	•	•			•	•	•		•	
Castle Grove Country House Hotel	Portsalon, Letterkenny, Rosapenna	86		•			•	•	•		•	
Dorrians Imperial Hotel	Donegal, Bundoran	79										
Fort Royal Hotel	Portsalon, Rosapenna	88	🏴3 •				•	•	•		•	
Great Northern Hotel	Donegal, Strandhill, Rosses Point	82	🏴18				•	•	•		•	
Holyrood Hotel	Bundoran	82		•		•	•	•	•	•	•	
Inishowen Gateway Hotel	North West Lisfannon, Buncrana, Ballyliffin (old and Glashedy links), Derry	81	🏴9 •									
Kee's Hotel	Ballybofey/Stranorlar	78		•		•	•	•	•	•		
Lake of Shadows Hotel	North West, Ballyliffin Old Course, Ballyliffin Glashedy Links, Buncrana	81		•		•	•	•	•	•		
Lake House Hotel	Narin/Portnoo	87		•	•	•	•	•	•	•		
Ostan Na Rosann	Cruit Island	85		•			•	•	•	•		
Ostan Radharc na Mara	Gweedore	80		•								
Redcastle Hotel	Ballyliffen, Greencastle, Foyle, North West	88	🏴9 •				•	•	•	•		
Rosapenna Hotel		83	🏴18 •					•	•			•
Sand House Hotel	Donegal Murvagh, Bundoran, Rosses Point	89		•		•	•	•	•	•	•	
SLIGO												
Ballincar House Hotel	Strandhill, Rosses Point, Enniscrone, Murvagh (Co. Donegal)	90		•	•	•	•	•	•		•	
Castle Arms Hotel	Enniscrone, Ballina	94		•	•	•	•	•	•	•		•

 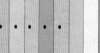

🏴18 = Full 18 Hole   🏴9 = 9 Hole   🏴3 = Par 3

WHERE TO STAY WHEN YOU PLAY!

ACCOMMODATION	COURSES	BE OUR GUEST PAGE NUMBER	GOLF ON SITE	ALL INCLUSIVE PACKAGE	TUITION AVAILABLE	CART AVAILABLE	ARRANGE TEE OFF TIMES	ADVANCE RESERVATIONS	CLUBS FOR HIRE	TRANSPORT	PREFERENTIAL GREEN FEES	CADDY AVAILABLE
SLIGO Continued												
Hotel Silver Swan	Rosses Point, Strandhill, Enniscrone	91		•	•	•	•	•	•	•	•	•
Innisfree Hotel	Strandhill, Rosses Point	91							•		•	
Ocean View Hotel	Strandhill, Enniscrone, Rosses Point, Bundoran, Murvagh	95		•	•	•	•	•	•	•		•
Sligo's Southern Hotel & Leisure Centre	Rosses Point, Strandhill, Bundoran, Enniscrone	92		•	•	•	•	•	•			
Tower Hotel	Co.Sligo (Rosses Point), Strandhill, Enniscrone, Donegal	93		•	•	•	•	•	•			•
Yeats Country Hotel and Leisure Club	Co. Sligo, Strandhill, Enniscrone, Bundoran	95		•	•	•	•	•			•	•

NORTH

ACCOMMODATION	COURSES											
ANTRIM												
Adair Arms Hotel	Galgorm Castle, Moyola Park	97		•	•	•	•	•	•	•	•	•
Alexandra	Royal Portrush, Castlerock, Portstewart, Ballycastle, Bushfoot, Rathmore	99		•	•	•	•	•	•	•	•	•
Beach Hotel	Royal Portrush, Portstewart, Castlerock, Ballycastle, Bushfoot, Galgorm Castle	97		•	•	•	•	•	•	•	•	•
Bushmills Inn	Royal Portrush, Portstewart, Castlerock, Ballycastle, Bushfoot, Gracehill	98		•	•	•	•	•	•	•	•	•
Causeway Coast Hotel & Conference Centre	Royal Portrush, Portstewart, Castlerock, Ballycastle, Bushfort, Gracehill, Galgorm Castle	99		•	•	•	•	•	•	•	•	•
Magherabuoy House Hotel	Royal Portrush, Valley, Portstewart, Castlerock, Bushfoot, Ballycastle	100		•	•	•	•	•	•	•	•	•
Stakis Park		101	18	•		•	•	•	•	•	•	•
Tullyglass House Hotel	Galgorm Castle Golf and Country Club	97		•	•	•	•	•	•	•	•	•
ARMAGH												
Silverwood Golf Hotel and Country Club	Lurgan, Portadown, Banbridge, Tandragee	102	18	•		•		•	•	•	•	

18 = Full 18 Hole   9 = 9 Hole   3 = Par 3   405

WHERE TO STAY WHEN YOU PLAY!

Accommodation	Courses	Be Our Guest Page Number	Golf on Site	All Inclusive Package	Tuition Available	Cart Available	Arrange Tee Off Times	Advance Reservations	Clubs for Hire	Transport	Preferential Green Fees	Caddy Available
DERRY												
Brown Trout Golf & Country Inn	Royal Portrush, Portstewart, Castlerock	109 ►9	•	•	•	•	•	•		•	•	•
Edgewater Hotel	Portstewart, Royal Portrush	110		•	•	•	•	•				
DOWN												
Chestnut Inn	Royal County Down, Ardglass, Spa, Ballynahinch, Bright	111						•				
Marine Court Hotel	Bangor, Clandeboye, Donaghadee, Royal Belfast, Carnalea, Blackwood	110	•	•	•	•	•	•		•	•	•
Royal Hotel	Bangor, Clandeboye, Blackwood	110	•									
Slieve Donard Hotel	Royal Co. Down, Downpatrick, Ardglass, Kilkeel	112		•	•	•	•	•		•		
FERMANAGH												
Mahons Hotel	Castle Hume, Enniskillen	116		•	•	•	•	•		•	•	
TYRONE												
Silverbirch Hotel	Omagh, Newtownstewart, Fintona	116	•							•		

EAST COAST

Accommodation	Courses	Be Our Guest Page Number	Golf on Site	All Inclusive Package	Tuition Available	Cart Available	Arrange Tee Off Times	Advance Reservations	Clubs for Hire	Transport	Preferential Green Fees	Caddy Available
DUBLIN												
Abberley Court Hotel	Citywest	118		•	•	•	•	•	•	•	•	•
Aberdeen Lodge	St. Margarets, Portmarnock, Woodbrook, Dun Laoghaire, Sea Point, Druids Glen	118		•	•	•	•	•	•	•	•	•
Abigail House	Druids Glen, European Club, Woodbrook, Powerscourt, Charlesland, Old Conna	182					•	•	•			
Adams Trinity Hotel	Royal Dublin, Portmarnock, Druids Glen, Citywest, Luttrelstown, Malahide, Clontarf, Hermitage	119						•	•	•		
Airport View	Rush, Skerries, Balbriggan, Swords, Donabate	173	•			•	•	•	•	•		
Alexander Hotel	Royal Dublin, Portmarnock, Druids Glen, St. Margarets	120						•	•	•	•	

►18 = Full 18 Hole   ►9 = 9 Hole   ►3 = Par 3

WHERE TO STAY WHEN YOU PLAY!

DUBLIN Continued

Accommodation	Courses	Be our guest page number	Golf on site	All inclusive package	Tuition package	Cart available	Arrange tee off times	Advance reservations	Clubs for hire	Transport	Preferential green fees	Caddy available
Arlington Hotel	St. Margarets, Portmarnock, Island, Luttrelstown, Citywest, Royal Dublin	123						•	•		•	
Ashview House	St. Margarets, Dublin Country Golf, Hollystown, Ashbourne and Corrstown	185	•	•	•	•	•	•	•	•	•	•
Carriage House	St. Margarets, Portmarnock, Skerries, Balbriggan, Hollywood, Luttrelstown	180	•	•	•	•	•	•	•	•	•	•
Central Hotel	Citywest, St. Margarets Co. Dublin, Edmonstown, Druids Glen, Wicklow	133			•	•	•	•	•	•	•	•
Charleville Lodge	St. Margarets, Luttrelstown, The Links, Portmarnock	134	•	•	•	•	•	•	•	•	•	•
Citywest Hotel, Conference, Leisure & Golf Resort		182 ▶18	•		•	•	•	•	•	•	•	•
Clarion Stephens Hall Hotel and Suites	St. Margarets, Portmarnock Links, Citywest, Luttrelstown Castle	135		•	•	•	•	•	•	•	•	•
Clifton Court Hotel	St. Margarets, Portmarnock, Citywest, Royal Dublin, Luttrelstown	136				•						
Clontarf Castle Hotel	Royal Dublin, Clontarf, St. Anne's, St. Margarets, Portmarnock	136	•				•		•		•	
Davenport Hotel	Druids Glen, Royal Dublin, Portmarnock, St. Margarets	137						•	•		•	
Deer Park Hotel and Golf Courses		178 ▶18	•		•	•	•	•				
Drury Court Hotel	Edmondstown, Luttrelstown Castle, St. Margarets	139						•	•			
Dunes Hotel on the Beach	Donabate, Turvey, Beaverstown, Belcarrick, Island/Corballis	174	•	•	•	•	•	•		•	•	
Fitzpatrick Castle Dublin	Druids Glen, European, Old Conna, Charlesland, Dun Laoghaire	178						•				
Fitzwilliam Hotel	Portmarnock	141		•	•	•	•	•	•	•	•	•
Grand Hotel	Portmarnock, The Island, Royal Dublin, St. Margarets, Malahide	180		•	•	•	•	•	•	•	•	•
Gresham Hotel	St. Margarets, Hollystown, Portmarnock, Grange, Royal Dublin, Howth	146						•	•			
Harrington Hall	St. Margarets, Druids Glen, Powerscourt, Portmarnock Links, Dublin Sport	147			•	•	•	•	•	•	•	•

▶18 = Full 18 Hole   ▶9 = 9 Hole   ▶3 = Par 3

WHERE TO STAY WHEN YOU PLAY!

Accommodation	Courses	Be Our Guest Page Number	Golf On Site	All Inclusive Package	Tuition Available	Cart Available	Arrange Tee Off Times	Advance Reservations	Clubs For Hire	Transport	Preferential Green Fees	Caddy Available
DUBLIN Continued												
Hedigan's	Clontarf, Royal Dublin, St. Anne's, Howth, Portmarnock, Sutton	148				•		•	•	•	•	
Hilton Dublin (formerly Stakis Dublin)	St. Margarets, Druids Glen	149	•					•	•			•
Hollybrook Hotel	Malahide, Sutton, Howth, Clontarf, St. Anne's, Royal Dublin, Portmarnock	150						•		•		•
Island View Hotel	Corballis, Malahide, Portmarnock, Howth, Donabate, Island	181	•	•	•	•	•	•	•	•	•	•
Kingston Hotel	Powerscourt, Charlesland, Old Conna, European, Druids Glen, Portmarnock	176	•	•	•	•	•	•	•	•	•	•
Marine Hotel	Royal Dublin, Portmarnock, St. Margarets, The Island, St. Anne's, The Links Portmarnock	184	•	•	•	•	•	•	•	•	•	•
Merrion Hall	Portmarnock, Royal Dublin, Elm Park, Castle, Milltown and Druids Glen	156	•	•	•	•	•	•	•	•	•	•
Mount Herbert Hotel	Elm Park, Milltown, Royal Dublin, Portmarnock, Druids Glen, European Club	159				•	•					
Paramount Hotel	St. Margarets	161	•	•	•	•	•	•	•		•	•
Parnell West Hotel	Portmarnock, St. Margarets, Hollystown, Elm Green, Citywest, Forest Little	162	•	•	•	•	•	•	•	•	•	•
Plaza Hotel	Ballinascorney, Citywest, Newlands, K Club, Powerscourt	163	•	•	•	•	•	•	•			•
Portmarnock Hotel & Golf Links	Portmarnock, St. Margarets, Royal Dublin, Malahide, The Island	181 ⚑18	•	•	•	•	•	•	•		•	•
Posthouse Dublin Airport	Hollystown, St. Margarets, Portmarnock, Malahide, Forest Little, The Island	175			•	•	•	•	•		•	
Quality Charleville Hotel and Suites	St. Margarets, Portmarnock, Royal Dublin, Citywest, K Club, Luttrelstown	163	•	•	•	•	•	•	•		•	•
Quality Court Hotel	Druids Glen, European, Roundwood, Woodbrook, Charlesland, Powerscourt	178	•	•	•	•	•	•	•		•	•
Redbank House	Skerries, Baltray, St. Margarets, Portmarnock, Balbriggan	183	•	•	•	•	•	•	•	•	•	•
Redbank Lodge & Restaurant	Balbriggan, St. Margarets, Portmarnock, Baltray	183	•	•	•	•	•	•	•	•	•	•
Regency Hotel	Malahide, Clontarf, Hollystown, Howth, St. Anne's, Royal Dublin	165		•	•	•	•	•		•	•	•

⚑18 = Full 18 Hole   ⚑9 = 9 Hole   ⚑3 = Par 3

WHERE TO STAY WHEN YOU PLAY!

ACCOMMODATION	COURSES	BE OUR GUEST PAGE NUMBER	GOLF ON SITE	ALL INCLUSIVE PACKAGE	TUITION AVAILABLE	CART AVAILABLE	ARRANGE TEE OFF TIMES	ADVANCE RESERVATIONS	CLUBS FOR HIRE	TRANSPORT	PREFERENTIAL GREEN FEES	CADDY AVAILABLE
DUBLIN Continued												
Royal Marine Hotel	Dun Laoghaire, Woodbrook, Killiney, Greystones, Seapoint, Druids Glen	177						•		•	•	
Sachs Hotel	Foxrock, Elm Park	166			•				•	•		•
School House Hotel	St. Margarets, Portmarnock	166		•	•		•			•	•	•
Shelbourne Dublin	St. Margarets, Druids Glen	167		•	•			•	•		•	•
Spa Hotel	Hermitage, Citywest, Knockanally, Lucan, Luttrelstown	179	•	•	•	•	•	•	•		•	•
Stephen's Green Hotel	St. Margarets, Druids Glen, Portmarnock, Royal Dublin	169					•	•	•		•	•
Stillorgan Park Hotel	Druids Glen, Portmarnock, Woodbrook, Woodenbridge, Powerscourt, European	173		•	•			•	•		•	•
Sutton Castle Hotel	St. Margarets, St. Anne's, Royal Dublin, Portmarnock	184		•		•	•	•	•		•	
Temple Bar Hotel	St. Margarets, Luttrelstown, Portmarnock Hotel and Golf Links	170			•			•	•		•	•
LOUTH												
Ballymascanlon House Hotel		187 🏌18	•		•		•	•			•	
Boyne Valley Hotel & Country Club	Baltray, Seapoint, Laytown/Bettystown, Dundalk, Headfort (Kells), Ardee	186		•	•		•	•	•		•	•
Fairways Hotel	Ballymascanlon, Dundalk, Killin Park, Greenore, Carnbeg	188		•	•		•	•	•		•	•
Hotel Imperial	Ballymascanlon, Dundalk, Greenore	189		•	•		•	•	•		•	•
McKevitt's Village Hotel	Greenore	186		•			•	•	•		•	•
Westcourt Hotel	Seapoint, Baltray, Balbriggan, Bettystown, Headfort, Dundalk	187		•				•	•		•	
MEATH												
Conyngham Arms Hotel	Sea Point, Ardee, Headford, Royal Tara	193		•				•	•		•	
Headfort Arms Hotel	Headfort, Royal Tara, Trim, Delvin, Moorepark, Racecourse Navan	191			•	•		•	•		•	
Neptune Beach	Laytown & Bettystown, Sea Point, County Louth/Baltray, Royal Tara	190		•	•	•			•		•	•
Old Darnley Lodge Hotel	Royal Tara, Delvin Castle, Headfort, Trim, The Glebe	190		•				•	•	•	•	

🏌18 = Full 18 Hole   🏌9 = 9 Hole   🏌3 = Par 3

WHERE TO STAY WHEN YOU PLAY!

WICKLOW

ACCOMMODATION	COURSES	BE OUR GUEST PAGE NUMBER	GOLF ON SITE	ALL INCLUSIVE PACKAGE	TUITION AVAILABLE	CART AVAILABLE	ARRANGE TEE OFF TIMES	ADVANCE RESERVATIONS	CLUBS FOR HIRE	TRANSPORT	PREFERENTIAL GREEN FEES	CADDY AVAILABLE
Arklow Bay Hotel	European, Arklow, Woodenbridge, Blainroe	195		•	•	•	•	•	•	•	•	•
Chester Beatty Inn	Druids Glen, Woodenbridge, Blainroe, European, Powerscourt, Wicklow	196		•	•	•	•	•	•	•	•	•
Cullenmore Hotel	Druids Glen, Charlesland, Wicklow, Blainroe, European Club, Delgany	197		•			•	•	•	•	•	•
Glendalough Hotel	The European Club, Woodenbridge, Charlesland, Druids Glen, Blainroe	202				•	•	•	•	•	•	•
Glenview Hotel	Charlesland, Druids Glen, Delgany, Powerscourt, Glen-O-The-Downs	202		•		•	•	•	•	•	•	•
Hunter's Hotel	European, Blainroe, Powerscourt, Woodenbridge, Delgany and Druids Glen	204		•		•	•	•	•	•	•	•
La Touche Hotel	Druids Glen, Powerscourt, Greystones, Delgany, Glen-O-The-Downs, Charlesland	203		•		•	•	•		•	•	•
Lawless Hotel	Woodenbridge, Coolatin, European, Blainroe, Arklow, Glenmalure	194		•	•	•	•	•	•	•	•	•
Old Rectory Country House & Restaurant	Druids Glen, Powerscourt, European Club, Blainroe, Wicklow, Woodenbridge	194				•	•	•	•	•	•	•
Ostan Beag Hotel	Blainroe, European, Arklow, Woodenbridge	196		•	•	•	•	•	•	•	•	•
Powerscourt Arms Hotel	Powerscourt, Old Conna, Bray, Druids Glen	201										
Rathsallagh House	Mount Juliet, Carlow, Baltinglass, K Club, Mount Wolseley, Druids Glen	200	⌐18	•	•	•	•	•	•	•	•	•
Royal Hotel and Leisure Centre	Woodbrook, Charlesland, Delgany, The European Club, Greystones, Blainroe	199					•	•	•	•	•	•
Tinakilly Country House and Restaurant	European Club, Druids Glen, Blainroe, Woodenbridge, Wicklow, Delgany	204		•		•	•	•	•	•	•	•
Tulfarris House Hotel	Tulfarris, Rathsallagh, City West	198	⌐18	•	•	•	•	•	•	•	•	•
Vale View Hotel	Woodenbridge	198			•							•
Valley Hotel and Restaurant	Woodenbridge, European, Arklow, Courtown, Blainroe	205								•	•	
Woodenbridge Hotel	Woodenbridge, Blainroe, Arklow, European Club, Mill Brook, Glenmalure	205		•			•	•	•	•	•	•
Woodlands Court Hotel	Powerscourt, Woodbrook, Druids Glen, Charlesland, Old Conna, Kilternan	200		•		•	•	•	•	•	•	•

⌐18 = Full 18 Hole ⌐9 = 9 Hole ⌐3 = Par 3

WHERE TO STAY WHEN YOU PLAY!

Accommodation	Courses	Be Our Guest Page Number	Golf on Site	All Inclusive Package	Tuition Available	Cart Available	Arrange Tee Off Times	Advance Reservations	Clubs for Hire	Transport	Preferential Green Fees	Caddy Available
MIDLANDS / LAKELANDS												
CAVAN												
Angler's Rest	Slieve Russell	207	•	•	•	•	•	•	•		•	
Cabra Castle Hotel		209 ▶9	•	•	•	•	•	•	•		•	
Olde Post Inn	Slieve Russell, Clones, Cavan, Belturbet	208		•	•	•	•	•	•		•	•
Park Hotel		209 ▶9					•	•			•	
Slieve Russell Hotel, Golf & Country Club		208 ▶18	•	•	•	•	•	•	•			•
KILDARE												
Ardenode Hotel	The K Club, Rathsallagh, Curragh, Naas, Slade Valley	210	•			•	•	•		•	•	
Glenroyal Hotel, Leisure Club & Conference Centre	Knockanally, K Club, Killeen, Castlewarden, Bodenstown, City West	213		•	•	•	•	•	•		•	
Hazel Hotel	Cill Dara, Portarlington, Curragh, Heath, Athy	213	•	•		•	•	•			•	
Hillview House	K Club, Citywest, Curragh, Naas, Luttrelstown Castle, Knockanally	214			•	•	•	•	•	•	•	
Keadeen Hotel	Craddockstown, Curragh, Killeen	215	•			•	•	•	•	•	•	
Kildare Hotel & Country Club	Luttrelstown Castle, Druids Glen, Portmarnock Links, Rathsallagh, Hermitage	215 ▶18	•	•	•	•	•	•	•		•	
Standhouse Hotel Leisure & Conference Centre	The Curragh, Athy, Rathsallagh, Cill Dara, K Club, and Naas golf clubs	211	•			•	•	•	•	•	•	
LAOIS												
Arlington Tower Hotel	Portarlington, The Heath, Tullamore, Castlebarnagh, Esker Hills, Curragh	217	•			•	•	•		•	•	•
Hibernian Hotel	Abbeyleix, Mountrath, The Heath, Rathdowney	216							•	•	•	
Killeshin Hotel	Heath, Abbeyleix, Portarlington, Mountrath, Portlaoise	217	•		•	•	•	•		•	•	
Montague Hotel	The Heath - Portlaoise, Garryhinch, Portarlington, Mountrath, Abbeyleix	216	•			•	•	•		•	•	

▶18 = Full 18 Hole   ▶9 = 9 Hole   ▶3 = Par 3

WHERE TO STAY WHEN YOU PLAY!

ACCOMMODATION	COURSES	BE OUR GUEST PAGE NUMBER	GOLF ON SITE	ALL INCLUSIVE PACKAGE	TUITION AVAILABLE	CART AVAILABLE	ARRANGE TEE OFF TIMES	ADVANCE RESERVATIONS	CLUBS FOR HIRE	TRANSPORT	PREFERENTIAL GREEN FEES	CADDY AVAILABLE
LONGFORD												
Longford Arms Hotel	Longford	218		•	•	•	•	•	•		•	
MONAGHAN												
Four Seasons Hotel & Leisure Club	Rossmore, Nuremore, Armagh, Castleblaney	218		•	•					•		•
Glencarn Hotel and Leisure Centre	Castleblayney, Mannon Castle, Rossmore	220		•						•		•
Nuremore Hotel & Country Club	Nuremore, Baltray, Headford, Dundalk, Greenore, Royal Co. Down	219 ⃗18	•	•	•	•	•	•	•	•		
OFFALY												
Bridge House Hotel & Leisure Club	Esker Hills, Tullamore	222		•	•	•	•	•	•	•	•	•
Brosna Lodge Hotel	Birr, Esker Hills, Tullamore, Glasson, Portumna, Ballinasloe	220		•		•	•	•	•	•	•	•
County Arms Hotel	Birr, Tullamore, Nenagh, Roscrea, Mount Temple, Esker Hills	220		•		•	•	•	•	•	•	•
Doolys Hotel	Birr, Esker Hills, Roscrea	221		•	•	•	•	•	•	•	•	•
Kinnitty Castle	Birr, Glasson, Esker Hill, Roscrea, Tullamore	221		•	•	•	•	•	•	•	•	•
Moorhill Country House Hotel	Esker Hills, Tullamore, Daingean, Mount Temple, Birr, Glasson	223	•	•	•	•	•	•	•	•	•	•
Tullamore Court Hotel	Tullamore, Esker Hills, Castlebarna	223		•	•	•	•	•	•	•	•	•
WESTMEATH												
Bloomfield House Hotel & Leisure Club	Mullingar, Glasson, Mount Temple, Esker Hills, Athlone, Tullamore	226		•	•	•	•	•	•	•	•	
Greville Arms Hotel	Mullingar, Glasson, Mount Temple, Tullamore, Longford, Esker Hills	226		•	•	•	•	•	•	•	•	•
Hodson Bay Hotel	Athlone, Glasson, Mountemple, Ballinasloe, Roscommon	224		•	•	•	•	•	•	•	•	•
Prince of Wales Hotel	Glasson, Mount Temple, Athlone, Ballinasloe, Tullamore, Galway Bay, Moate	224		•	•	•	•	•	•	•	•	•
Royal Hoey Hotel	Mount Temple, Glasson, Hodson Bay	224		•	•	•	•	•	•	•	•	•

⃗18 = Full 18 Hole   ⃗9 = 9 Hole   ⃗3 = Par 3

WHERE TO STAY WHEN YOU PLAY!

ACCOMMODATION	COURSES	BE OUR GUEST PAGE NUMBER	GOLF ON SITE	ALL INCLUSIVE PACKAGE	TUITION AVAILABLE	CART AVAILABLE	ARRANGE TEE OFF TIMES	ADVANCE RESERVATIONS	CLUBS FOR HIRE	TRANSPORT	PREFERENTIAL GREEN FEES	CADDY AVAILABLE
WESTMEATH Continued												
Shamrock Lodge Country House Hotel	Glasson, Athlone, Moate, Mount Temple	225		•			•	•		•	•	•
Village Hotel	Mullingar, Tullamore , Athlone	227			•	•	•	•	•	•		•

SOUTH EAST

ACCOMMODATION	COURSES	PAGE										
CARLOW												
Ballyvergal House	Carlow, Mount Wolseley, Kilkea Castle, Mount Juliet	229		•			•	•			•	•
Dolmen Hotel and River Court Lodges	Mount Wolseley, Kilkea Castle	229		•	•		•	•	•	•		•
Mount Wolseley Hotel, Golf and Country Club	Carlow, Rathsallagh, Coolatin	231	🚩18 •	•			•	•	•	•	•	•
Seven Oaks Hotel	Carlow, Mount Wolseley, Kilkea Castle	230		•				•	•			•
KILKENNY												
Brannigans Glendine Inn	Kilkenny, Mount Juliet, Callan, Castlecomer,	231		•		•		•	•			•
Butler House	Kilkenny, Mount Juliet, Carlow, Clonmel, Waterford, Kilkea Castle	232		•			•	•	•	•	•	•
Carrolls Hotel	Mount Juliet, Callan, Mountain View, Kilkenny	237					•	•	•	•		
Club House Hotel	Kilkenny (18), Mount Juliet (18), Callan (18), Castlecomer (9)	232		•	•	•	•	•	•	•		•
Hibernian Hotel	Mount Juliet, Kilkenny, Castlecomer, Kilkea Castle, Mount Wolseley	232		•			•	•	•	•		•
Kilford Arms	Mount Juliet, Kilkenny, Callan, Castlecomer, Borris-in-Ossory, Kilkea Castle	233		•			•	•	•	•		•
Kilkenny River Court Hotel	Callan, Kilkenny, Mount Juliet, Castlecomer, Mount Wolseley	234		•			•	•	•			•
Metropole Hotel	Kilkenny, Callan, Castlecomer and Carrick-on-Suir	235		•				•	•		•	•
Mount Juliet Estate	Kilkenny, Borris-in-Ossory, Callan	238	🚩18 •	•			•	•	•	•		•
Springhill Court Hotel	Kilkenny, Mount Juliet, Castlecomer, Callan, Carlow, Mount Wolseley	236		•	•		•	•	•			•

🚩18 = Full 18 Hole 🚩9 = 9 Hole 🚩3 = Par 3

414

WHERE TO STAY WHEN YOU PLAY!

ACCOMMODATION	COURSES	BE OUR GUEST PAGE NUMBER	GOLF ON SITE	ALL INCLUSIVE PACKAGE	TUITION AVAILABLE	CART AVAILABLE	ARRANGE TEE OFF TIMES	ADVANCE RESERVATIONS	CLUBS FOR HIRE	TRANSPORT	PREFERENTIAL GREEN FEES	CADDY AVAILABLE
TIPPERARY SOUTH												
Cahir House Hotel	Cahir Park, Carrick-on-Suir, Clonmel, Ballykisteen, Fermoy, Dundrum	239		•	•	•	•	•	•	•	•	•
Carraig Hotel	Carrick-on-Suir, Clonmel, Waterford, Waterford Castle, Faithlegg	239		•	•	•	•	•	•	•	•	•
Cashel Palace Hotel	Cahir Park, Thurles, Ballykisteen, Dundrum	240						•	•	•	•	•
Clonmel Arms Hotel	Clonmel, Cahir, Carrick-on-Suir, Ballykisteen	242		•	•	•	•	•	•	•	•	•
Dundrum House Hotel		240	I18	•	•	•	•	•	•	•	•	•
Glen Hotel	Tipperary Golf Club, Ballykisteen, Dundrum, Cahir Park	244		•	•	•	•	•	•	•	•	•
Hearns Hotel	Clonmel, Cahir, Carrick-on-Suir	242		•	•	•	•	•	•	•	•	•
Hotel Minella & Leisure Centre	Clonmel, Dungarvan, Kilkenny, Waterford, Thurles, Faithlegg	243		•			•	•		•		•
Kilcoran Lodge Hotel	Cahir, Clonmel, Mitchelstown	239		•	•	•	•	•	•	•	•	•
Royal Hotel	Tipperary (1.6km), Ballykisteen (3.2km), Dundrum (8km)	238		•	•	•	•	•	•	•	•	•
WATERFORD												
Bridge Hotel	Waterford Castle, Faithlegg, Waterford, Tramore, New Ross	245		•	•	•	•	•	•	•	•	•
Candlelight Inn	Waterford Castle, Waterford, Tramore, Faithlegg and Dunmore East	254	I18									
Clonea Strand Hotel, Golf & Leisure	Gold Coast, West Waterford, Dungarvan, Lismore	253		•	•	•		•	•		•	•
Dooley's Hotel	Waterford, Tramore, Faithlegg, Waterford Castle, New Ross, Gold Coast	246		•	•	•		•	•		•	•
Faithlegg House Hotel	Waterford Castle, Tramore	255	I18	•		•		•	•		•	•
Gold Coast Golf Hotel & Leisure Centre	Gold Coast Golf Course, Dungarvan Golf Course, West Waterford Golf Course	253	I18	•	•	•	•	•	•	•	•	•
Grand Hotel	Tramore, Waterford, Faithlegg, Waterford Castle	257		•	•	•		•	•		•	•
Granville Hotel	Waterford, Faithlegg, Waterford Castle, Tramore, Dunmore East	246		•	•	•		•	•		•	•
Hanoras Cottage	Clonmel, Carrick-on-Suir, Dungarvan, West Waterford, Gold Coast, Cahir Park	252		•	•	•	•	•	•	•	•	•

I18 = Full 18 Hole   I9 = 9 Hole   I3 = Par 3

WHERE TO STAY WHEN YOU PLAY!

ACCOMMODATION	COURSES	Be Our Guest Page Number	Golf on Site	All Inclusive Package	Tuition Available	Cart Available	Arrange Tee Off Times	Advance Reservations	Clubs for Hire	Transport	Preferential Green Fees	Caddy Available
WATERFORD Continued												
Haven Hotel	Faithlegg, Tramore, Waterford, Waterford Castle, Dunmore East	255										
Ivory's Hotel	Dunmore East, Faithlegg, Waterford, Waterford Castle, Tramore, Williamstown	247	●	●	●	●	●	●	●	●	●	●
Jurys Hotel Waterford	Waterford, Waterford Castle & Country Club, Faithlegg, Tramore	247	●	●	●	●	●	●	●	●	●	●
Lawlors Hotel	Dungarvan, West Waterford, Gold Coast	253	●	●	●	●	●	●	●	●	●	●
Majestic Hotel	Tramore, Waterford, Faithlegg, Waterford Castle, Mount Juliet, Dunmore East	257	●	●	●	●	●	●	●	●	●	●
O'Grady's Restaurant & Guesthouse	Waterford Castle, West Waterford, Tramore, Faithlegg, Dungarvan	248							●	●	●	●
O'Shea's Hotel	Tramore, Faithlegg, Waterford Castle, Waterford, Dungarvan, Mount Juliet	257	●	●	●	●	●	●	●	●	●	●
Ocean Hotel	Waterford, Waterford Castle, Faithlegg, Dunmore East, Tramore	255	●	●	●	●	●	●	●	●	●	●
Rice Guesthouse Batterberry's Bar	Dunmore East, Faithlegg, Waterford Castle, Tramore	248							●	●		●
Richmond House	Dungarvan, West Waterford, Ballinacourty, Lismore	252	●	●	●	●	●	●	●	●	●	●
Three Rivers Guest House	Faithlegg, Dunmore East, Tramore, Waterford Castle, Waterford, Mount Juliet	252	●	●	●	●	●	●	●	●	●	●
Tower Hotel & Leisure Centre	Waterford Castle, Waterford, Faithlegg	249		●	●	●	●	●	●		●	●
Waterford Castle	Tramore, Waterford	249	18	●	●	●	●	●	●		●	●
Waterford Marina Hotel	Waterford Castle, Faithlegg, Dunmore East, Tramore, Waterford	250	●	●	●	●	●	●	●	●	●	●
Woodlands Hotel	Waterford Castle, Waterford, Faithlegg, Tramore, Dunmore East	250	●	●	●	●	●	●	●	●	●	●
WEXFORD												
Bayview Hotel	Courtown, Ballymoney, Coolattin, Enniscorthy, European	262	●	●	●	●	●	●	●	●	●	●
Brandon House Hotel & Leisure Centre	New Ross, Mount Juliet, Faithlegg, Rosslare Strand, Waterford, Scarke	266	●	●	●	●	●	●	●	●	●	●

416 ▶18 = Full 18 Hole   ▶9 = 9 Hole   ▶3 = Par 3

WHERE TO STAY WHEN YOU PLAY!

ACCOMMODATION

WEXFORD Continued

COURSES

Accommodation	Courses	Be Our Guest Page Number	Golf On Site	All Inclusive Package	Tuition Available	Cart Available	Arrange Tee Off Times	Advance Reservations	Clubs For Hire	Transport	Preferential Green Fees	Caddy Available
Coral Gables	St. Helen's Bay, Rosslare Strand, Wexford	268					•	•	•	•	•	•
Creacon Lodge Hotel	New Ross, St. Helen's Bay, Faithlegg, Scarke, Mount Juliet	266	•	•	•	•	•	•	•	•		
Devereux Hotel	St. Helen's Bay, Rosslare, Wexford	269	•				•	•			•	
Horse and Hound Inn	New Ross, Wexford, Rosslare, Waterford, Mount Juliet	264	•		•	•	•	•	•			
Kelly's Resort Hotel	Rosslare Championship, Rosslare 9 Hole, St. Helen's Bay, Wexford, Enniscorthy	268	•	•			•	•	•	•	•	
Old Rectory Hotel	New Ross, Scarke, St. Helen's Bay	266	•				•	•	•		•	
Riverbank House Hotel	Wexford, St. Helen's, Rosslare	258	•					•	•			•
Riverside Park Hotel	Enniscorthy	263	•				•	•	•	•		
Talbot Hotel Conference and Leisure Centre	St. Helen's, Wexford, Rosslare, Enniscorthy and Courtown	259	•	•	•		•	•	•	•		
Treacys Hotel	Enniscorthy, Courtown, St. Helen's Bay, Mount Wolsley, Mount Juliet	264	•	•		•	•	•	•	•	•	
Tuskar House Hotel	St. Helen's, Rosslare Strand, Wexford, Mount Juliet, Waterford	270	•				•	•	•	•	•	•
Whites Hotel	Wexford, Rosslare, St. Helen's Bay, Enniscorthy	260	•	•	•	•	•	•	•	•	•	
Whitford House Hotel	St. Helen's Bay, Wexford, Rosslare, Rathaspeck	260	•	•	•	•	•	•	•	•		

SOUTH WEST

CORK

Accommodation	Courses	Be Our Guest Page Number	Golf On Site	All Inclusive Package	Tuition Available	Cart Available	Arrange Tee Off Times	Advance Reservations	Clubs For Hire	Transport	Preferential Green Fees	Caddy Available
Abbey Hotel	Killarney, Kenmare, Macroom, Lee Valley, Dooks	289	•				•	•			•	
Actons Hotel	Kinsale, Old Head of Kinsale	302	•				•	•		•		•
Aherne's Townhouse & Seafood Restaurant	Fota, West Waterford, Youghal, Cork, Faithlegg, Waterford Castle	314		•	•		•	•	•	•	•	•
Ambassador Hotel	Cork, Fota, Douglas, Monkstown, Harbour Point, Water Rock	272	•	•	•		•	•	•			•
Arbutus Lodge Hotel	Fota, Harbour Point, Douglas, Lee Valley, Muskerry	273		•	•	•	•	•	•		•	•

WHERE TO STAY WHEN YOU PLAY!

ACCOMMODATION	COURSES	BE OUR GUEST PAGE NUMBER	GOLF ON SITE	ALL INCLUSIVE PACKAGE	TUITION AVAILABLE	CART AVAILABLE	ARRANGE TEE OFF TIMES	ADVANCE RESERVATIONS	CLUBS FOR HIRE	TRANSPORT	PREFERENTIAL GREEN FEES	CADDY AVAILABLE
CORK Continued												
Ashley Hotel	Fota Island, Little Island, Harbour Point, Muskerry, Kinsale	274			•	•	•	•	•	•	•	•
Ballylickey Manor House	Bantry, Glengarriff	288					•	•	•		•	
Baltimore Bay Guest House	Skibbereen	290					•				•	
Baltimore Harbour Hotel & Leisure Centre	Skibbereen, Bantry	290	•			•	•	•	•		•	•
Barnabrow Country House	Fota Island, East Cork, Water Rock, Youghal, Cork (Little Island)	311			•	•	•	•	•	•	•	•
Blarney Park Hotel	Lee Valley, Harbour Point, Fota, Muskerry, Mallow	293			•	•	•	•	•		•	•
Blue Haven Hotel	Kinsale (Farrangalway, Ringenane), Old Head	303			•		•	•	•		•	•
Carrigaline Court Hotel & Leisure Centre	Old Head of Kinsale, Fernhill, Monkstown, Kinsale, Douglas	294			•	•	•	•	•	•	•	•
Casey's of Baltimore	Skibbereen	290									•	
Celtic Ross Hotel	Skibbereen, Bandon, Lisselan, Old Head, Kinsale	312			•	•	•	•	•		•	•
Christy's Hotel	Muskerry, Lee Valley, Fota Island, Harbour Point, Mallow	293			•	•	•	•	•		•	•
Colla House Hotel	Coosheen, Bantry, Skibbereen	312	•				•	•		•	•	•
Colneth House	Kinsale - Farrangalway, Ringenane, Old Head	303			•	•	•	•	•	•	•	•
Commodore Hotel	Fota, East Cork, Midleton, Cobh	298				•	•	•	•		•	•
Country Club Hotel	Harbour Point, Little Island, Fota, Lee Valley (Ovens), Fernhill	276		•	•	•	•	•	•	•	•	•
Deasys Long Quay House	Kinsale	304		•	•	•	•	•	•		•	
Deerpark Hotel	Charleville	395			•	•	•	•	•		•	•
Dunmore House Hotel	Bandon, Skibbereen, Monkstown, Macroom, The Island	295 🏌9	•			•	•	•		•	•	•
Eldon Hotel	Skibbereen, West Carbery, Bantry, Glengarriff	314			•	•	•	•	•		•	•
Emmet Hotel	Dunmore, Bandon, Skibbereen, Bantry, Lisselan, Macroom	296		•		•	•	•	•		•	•
Fernhill Golf & Country Club	Douglas, Monkstown, Harbour Point, Kinsale - Old Head, Cork, Fota	294 🏌18	•	•	•	•	•	•	•	•	•	•
Fitzpatrick Cork	Cork, Fota, Harbour Point, Lee Valley, Douglas, Monkstown	?? 🏌9	•	•	•	•	•	•	•		•	•

🏌18 = Full 18 Hole   🏌9 = 9 Hole   🏌3 = Par 3

418

WHERE TO STAY WHEN YOU PLAY!

ACCOMMODATION	COURSES	BE OUR GUEST PAGE NUMBER	GOLF ON SITE	ALL INCLUSIVE PACKAGE	TUITION AVAILABLE	CART AVAILABLE	ARRANGE TEE OFF TIMES	ADVANCE RESERVATIONS	CLUBS FOR HIRE	TRANSPORT	PREFERENTIAL GREEN FEES	CADDY AVAILABLE
CORK Continued												
Glanworth Mill Country Inn	Fermoy, Mitchelstown, Lismore, Mallow	301							•	•		
Glenvera Hotel	Fota Island, Harbour Point, Cork, Water Rock, Douglas, Lee Valley	279	•	•	•	•	•	•	•	•	•	•
Hayfield Manor Hotel	Lee Valley, Fota Island, Cork, Harbour Point, Douglas, Old Head of Kinsale	280		•	•	•	•	•	•	•	•	•
Hibernian Hotel	Mallow, Lee Valley, Charleville, Doneraile, Fota Island	309	•							•		
Innishannon House Hotel	Old Head of Kinsale, Bandon, Kinsale, Lee Valley, Lisselan	302	•	•	•	•				•	•	•
Jurys Cork Inn	Little Island, Harbour Point, Lee Valley, Monkstown, Cork	281		•					•			
Jurys Hotel Cork	Lee Valley, Harbour Point, Douglas, Cork, Muskerry	281	•	•	•	•	•	•	•	•	•	•
Kierans Folkhouse Inn	Kinsale, Farrangalway, Fota, Lee Valley, Harbour Point, Old Head of Kinsale	304	•	•	•	•	•	•		•		•
Kingsley Hotel	Fota Island, Cork, Harbour Point, Lee Valley, Muskerry, Old Head	282	•	•	•	•	•	•	•	•	•	•
Lodge & Spa at Inchydoney Island	Old Head of Kinsale, Bandon, Dunmore	297	•	•	•	•	•	•	•		•	
Lotamore House	Cork, Harbour Point, Fota Island, Water Rock, Lee Valley, Kinsale	283	•					•	•	•	•	•
Maryborough House Hotel	Douglas, Fota Island, Cork, Kinsale Old Head, Harbour Point, Monkstown	283	•	•	•	•	•	•	•	•	•	•
Metropole Ryan Hotel and Leisure Centre	Fota Island, Little Island, Harbour Point, Muskerry, Kinsale	284	•	•	•	•	•	•	•	•	•	•
Midleton Park Hotel	Fota Island, Cork - Little Island, Harbour Point, Water Rock, East Cork	311	•	•	•	•	•	•	•	•	•	•
Moorings	Kinsale, Old Head of Kinsale, Bandon, Fota, Cork, Harbour Point	305										
Old Bank House	Old Head of Kinsale, Kinsale, Farrangalway, Little Island, Fota, Lee Valley	305		•	•	•		•	•	•	•	•
Quality Hotel and Leisure Centre	Dunmore, Kinsale, Bandon, Skibbereen, Lisselan	297	•			•	•	•				•
Rochestown Park Hotel	Fota Island, Douglas, Monkstown, Cork (Little Island), Harbour Point, Lee Valley, Old Head of Kinsale	285	•	•	•	•	•	•				

18 = Full 18 Hole   9 = 9 Hole   3 = Par 3

WHERE TO STAY WHEN YOU PLAY!

ACCOMMODATION	COURSES	BE OUR GUEST PAGE NUMBER	GOLF ON SITE	ALL INCLUSIVE PACKAGE	TUITION AVAILABLE	CART AVAILABLE	ARRANGE TEE OFF TIMES	ADVANCE RESERVATIONS	CLUBS FOR HIRE	TRANSPORT	PREFERENTIAL GREEN FEES	CADDY AVAILABLE
CORK Continued												
Rushbrooke Hotel	Cobh, Water Rock, Fota, Harbour Point	298						•	•	•	•	•
Sea View House Hotel	Bantry Park, Glengarriff	289								•		•
Seven North Mall	Cork, Douglas, Fota Island, Harbour Point, Monkstown, Muskerry	286			•	•	•	•	•	•		
Springfort Hall	Mallow, Charleville, Doneraile, Kanturk, Blarney, Adare	310	•					•	•	•		•
Sunset Ridge Hotel	Blarney, Muskerry	293	•			•	•	•	•	•		•
Trident Hotel	Old Head Golf Links, Farrangalway, Ringenane, Harbour Point, Fota	306	•	•		•	•	•	•	•		•
Victoria Hotel, Macroom	Lee Valley, Macroom Golf Club	309						•	•		•	•
Vienna Woods Hotel	Cork, Harbour Point, Fota, Old Head of Kinsale, Water Rock, Silver Springs	287	•		•	•	•	•	•	•		•
Walter Raleigh Hotel	Youghal, Water Rock, West Waterford, Fota Island, Harbour Point	315	•	•		•	•	•	•	•		•
WatersEdge Hotel	Fota Island, Harbour Point, Cobh, Water Rock, East Cork	299	•				•	•	•	•		•
West Cork Hotel	Skibbereen, West Carbery	314				•	•	•				•
Westlodge Hotel	Bantry, Bantry Bay	292	•					•	•			•
White Lady Hotel	Kinsale, Old Head of Kinsale, Farrangalway, Ringenane	307						•	•	•	•	•
KERRY												
Abbey Gate Hotel	Tralee, Ballybunion, Killarney, Dooks, Waterville, Kerries	354	•	•		•	•	•	•			•
Aghadoe Heights Hotel	Waterville, Ballybunion, Kenmare, Killorglin, Beaufort, Ring of Kerry	332						•	•	•		•
Arbutus Hotel	Killarney, Ballybunion, Waterville, Dooks, Tralee, Kenmare	332	•						•	•		•
Ashville Guesthouse	Killarney, Ross, Dunloe, Beaufort, Waterville, Dooks, Ballybunion	333			•	•	•	•	•	•	•	
Ballyseede Castle Hotel	Tralee, Ballybunion, Killarney, Kerries, Dooks, Dingle, Waterville	355			•	•	•	•	•	•		•

▶18 = **Full 18 Hole**   ▶9 = **9 Hole**   ▶3 = **Par 3**

WHERE TO STAY WHEN YOU PLAY!

Accommodation	Courses	Be Our Guest Page Number	Golf on Site	All Inclusive Package	Tuition Available	Cart Available	Arrange Tee Off Times	Advance Reservations	Clubs for Hire	Transport	Preferential Green Fees	Caddy Available
KERRY Continued												
Barrow House	Tralee, Ballybunion, Killarney, Waterville, Dooks, Dingle	355						•	•		•	•
Benners Hotel	Ceann Sibeal (Dingle)	321	•	•	•			•	•	•	•	•
Bianconi	Killarney, Beaufort, Dunloe, Killorglin, Dooks	352	•	•	•		•	•	•		•	•
Brandon Court Hotel	Tralee, Killarney, Ballybunion, Dooks, Kerries	356	•	•	•		•	•	•		•	
Brandon Hotel	Tralee, Ballybunion, Waterville, Dooks, Killarney	356	•	•	•			•	•		•	
Brookhaven Guesthouse	Waterville, Dooks, Parknasilla, Tralee, Killarney, Ballybunion, Ring of Kerry	359						•	•		•	
Butler Arms Hotel	Waterville, Dooks, Killarney, Tralee, Ballybunion, Ring of Kerry	360		•	•		•	•	•		•	•
Cahernane House Hotel	Killarney, Ballybunion, Tralee, Dooks, Kenmare, Waterville, Beaufort	334			•	•	•	•	•		•	•
Caragh Lodge	Dooks, Beaufort, Tralee, Killarney, Waterville, Ballybunion	319			•	•	•	•	•		•	
Castlelodge Guesthouse	Killarney Golf Course, Ross Golf Course	334			•			•	•		•	
Castlerosse Hotel & Leisure Centre	Killarney (3 courses), Beaufort	335 ▶9	•	•	•	•	•	•	•	•	•	•
Cliff House Hotel	Ballybunion Old course and Cashen Course, Tralee, Killarney, Lahinch	315	•	•	•	•	•	•	•		•	•
Dingle Skellig Hotel	Ceann Sibeal Dingle, Castlegregory	323						•			•	
Dromquinna Manor Hotel	Kenmare, Killarney, Waterville, Ring of Kerry, Parknasilla	327		•	•		•	•	•		•	
Earls Court House	Killarney, Waterville, Ballybunion, Tralee, Beaufort, Dooks	336		•	•		•	•	•		•	•
Eviston House Hotel	Killarney, Waterville, Ballybunion, Tralee, Dooks	336	•	•	•		•	•	•		•	•
Foley's Townhouse	Killarney, Barrow, Beaufort, Dooks, Ballybunion, Waterville	337						•	•		•	
Fuchsia House	Killarney, Ballybunion, Waterville, Beaufort, Tralee, Dooks	337	•	•	•			•	•		•	•
Glencar House Hotel	Killarney, Beaufort, Dooks, Waterville, Killorglin	319		•	•		•	•	•	•	•	
Grand Hotel, Tralee	Tralee, Ballybunion, Waterville, Dingle, Dooks, Killarney	357	•	•	•		•	•	•	•	•	•

▶18 = Full 18 Hole   ▶9 = 9 Hole   ▶3 = Par 3

WHERE TO STAY WHEN YOU PLAY!

ACCOMMODATION	COURSES	BE OUR GUEST PAGE NUMBER	GOLF ON SITE	ALL INCLUSIVE PACKAGE	TUITION AVAILABLE	CART AVAILABLE	ARRANGE TEE OFF TIMES	ADVANCE RESERVATIONS	CLUBS FOR HIRE	TRANSPORT	PREFERENTIAL GREEN FEES	CADDY AVAILABLE
KERRY Continued												
Grove Lodge Guesthouse	Killarney, Killorglin, Dooks, Beaufort, Gap of Dunloe, Dingle	352				•	•	•	•		•	•
Harty Costello Town House	Ballybunion, Tralee, Listowel, Ballyheigue	316					•	•	•			•
Holiday Inn Killarney	Killarney Golf & Fishing Club, Ross, Dunloe	339	•			•	•	•	•		•	•
International Best Western Hotel	Killarney, Beaufort, Killorglin, Dooks, Kenmare, Ross	341	•			•	•	•	•	•	•	•
Johnston Marina Hotel	Tralee (Barrow), Ballybunion, Killarney, Dooks, Castlegregory, The Kerries	358					•	•	•		•	•
Kathleen's Country House	Killarney, Beaufort, Dunloe, Ross	341				•	•	•	•		•	•
Kenmare Bay Hotel	Ring of Kerry, Kenmare, Killarney, Tralee, Ballybunion, Waterville	328				•	•	•	•		•	•
Killarney Avenue Hotel	Killarney, Ballybunion, Tralee, Waterville, Beaufort	342	•			•	•	•	•	•	•	•
Killarney Court Hotel	Killarney, Beaufort, Dunloe, Ross	342				•	•	•	•		•	•
Killarney Heights Hotel	Killarney, Beaufort, Waterville, Dooks, Ballybunion, Tralee	343				•	•	•	•		•	•
Killarney Lodge	Killarney, Waterville, Ballybunion, Tralee, Dooks, Beaufort	343				•	•	•	•		•	
Killarney Park Hotel	Killarney, Ballybunion, Tralee, Waterville, Dooks, Beaufort	343				•	•	•	•		•	•
Killarney Royal	Killarney, Tralee, Dooks, Waterville, Beaufort, Ross	344				•	•	•	•		•	•
Killarney Ryan Hotel & Leisure Centre	Killarney, Dooks, Tralee, Ballybunion, Waterville, Beaufort	344				•	•	•	•		•	•
Killarney Towers Hotel & Leisure Centre	Killarney, Ballybunion, Tralee, Waterville, Beaufort	344	•		•	•	•	•	•		•	•
Killeen House Hotel	Killarney, Waterville, Tralee, Dooks, Ballybunion, Beaufort	345				•	•	•	•		•	•
Lake Hotel	Killarney (3 courses), Beaufort, Dooks, Dunloe, Ross, Gleneagle	346	•			•	•	•	•		•	•
Lakelands Farm Guesthouse	Waterville Golf Course	360				•	•	•	•		•	
Listowel Arms Hotel	Ballybunion, Listowel, Tralee, Killarney, Lahinch, Waterville	353			•	•	•	•	•		•	•

422

▶18 = Full 18 Hole ▶9 = 9 Hole ▶3 = Par 3

ACCOMMODATION	COURSES	BE OUR GUEST PAGE NUMBER	GOLF ON SITE	ALL INCLUSIVE PACKAGE	TUITION AVAILABLE	CART AVAILABLE	ARRANGE TEE OFF TIMES	ADVANCE TEE RESERVATIONS	CLUBS FOR HIRE	TRANSPORT	PREFERENTIAL GREEN FEES	CADDY AVAILABLE
KERRY Continued												
Marine Links Hotel	Ballybunion, Old Course & Cashen, Tralee, Killarney, Lahinch, Dooks	316		•	•	•	•	•	•	•	•	•
McSweeney Arms Hotel	Killarney, Ballybunion, Waterville, Dooks, Beaufort, Tralee	347		•	•	•	•	•	•	•	•	•
Meadowlands Hotel	Ballybeggan Park, The Kerries, Tralee, Ballybunion, Castlegregory	358		•				•		•		•
Milltown House	Ceann Sibeal (Dingle), Tralee, Killarney, Ballybunion, Dooks, Castlegregory	325					•	•	•		•	
Muckross Park Hotel	Beaufort, Killeen, O'Mahony's Point, Dunloe, Ross, Lackabane	348		•	•		•	•	•	•	•	•
Oakland House	Killarney, Ross, Beaufort, Waterville, Dunloe, Dooks	348			•		•	•	•		•	
Oakley House	Tralee, Killarney, Dooks, Ballybunion, Waterville	359					•	•	•		•	
Park Hotel Kenmare	Ring of Kerry	329	18	•				•		•		•
Parknasilla Great Southern Hotel		354	3				•	•	•	•	•	•
Riversdale House Hotel	Kenmare, Killarney, Waterville, Parknasilla, Dooks, Ring of Kerry	329					•	•	•		•	
Ross Hotel	Killarney, Ballybunion, Tralee, Waterville, Dooks, Beaufort	350			•		•	•	•		•	
Scarriff Inn	Waterville, Kenmare, Sneem, Killorglin, Tralee, Ballybunion	318			•		•	•	•	•	•	•
Sheen Falls Lodge	Kenmare, Ring of Kerry	330		•	•		•	•	•	•	•	•
Smerwick Harbour Hotel	Ceann Sibeal (Dingle)	325		•	•		•	•	•	•	•	•
Smugglers Inn	Waterville, Killarney, Dooks, Tralee, Ballybunion, Kenmare, Parknasilla	360		•	•		•	•	•	•	•	•
Teach de Broc	Ballybunion Old and Cashen, Tralee, Killarney, Lahinch	317		•	•		•	•	•	•	•	•

SHANNON

CLARE

| Aberdeen Arms Hotel | Lahinch Championship, Lahinch Castle, Woodstock, Dromoland Castle | 378 | | • | • | | • | • | • | • | • | • |

18 = Full 18 Hole   9 = 9 Hole   3 = Par 3   423

WHERE TO STAY WHEN YOU PLAY!

ACCOMMODATION

CLARE Continued

COURSES

Accommodation	Courses	Be Our Guest Page Number	Golf On Site	All Inclusive Package	Tuition Available	Cart Available	Arrange Tee Off Times	Advance Reservations	Clubs For Hire	Transport	Preferential Green Fees	Caddy Available
Aran View House Hotel & Restaurant	Lahinch, Doolin Pitch & Putt	366				•	•	•	•	•	•	•
Armada Hotel	Spanish Point, Lahinch	382		•	•	•	•	•	•	•	•	•
Atlantic Hotel	Lahinch Championship Course and Castle, Woodstock, Ennis, Spanish Point	378		•	•	•	•	•	•	•	•	•
Auburn Lodge Hotel	Ennis, Woodstock, Dromoland, Shannon & Lahinch	368		•	•		•	•	•	•	•	•
Ballinalacken Castle Hotel	Lahinch, Lahinch Castle, Woodstock, Galway Bay, Dromoland Castle, Ennis	366		•	•	•	•	•	•	•	•	•
Bellbridge House Hotel	Spanish Point, Lahinch	382 ⚑9		•		•	•	•	•	•	•	•
Bunratty Castle Hotel	Shannon, Dromoland, Lahinch, Limerick	364		•	•		•	•	•	•	•	•
Carrygerry Country House	Dromoland, Woodstock, Shannon	384		•			•	•	•	•	•	•
Cill Eoin House	Ennis, Woodstock Country Club	369					•	•	•	•	•	•
Dromoland Castle	Lahinch, Ballybunion, Shannon	383 ⚑3		•	•		•	•	•	•	•	•
Falls Hotel	Lahinch, Dromoland, Ennis, Kilkee, Shannon	372		•	•	•	•	•	•	•	•	•
Fitzpatrick Bunratty	Shannon, Dromoland, Woodstock, Ballykisteen, Limerick County	365		•			•	•	•	•	•	•
Fountain Court	Ennis, Woodstock, Dromoland, Lahinch, Shannon, East Clare	369		•			•	•	•	•	•	•
Greenbrier Inn Guesthouse	Lahinch Championship Course, Lahinch Castle Course	379					•	•	•	•	•	•
Grovemount House	Lahinch	373			•		•	•	•	•	•	•
Halpin's Hotel & Vittles Restaurant	Ballybunion, Lahinch, Kilkee, Dromoland, Woodstock, Shannon	373		•	•		•	•	•	•	•	•
Magowna House Hotel	Woodstock, Ennis, Lahinch, Dromoland Castle, Shannon, Kilrush, Kilkee	370		•	•		•	•	•	•	•	•
Oak Wood Arms Hotel	Shannon, Dromoland	384		•	•		•	•	•	•	•	•
Old Ground Hotel	Lahinch, Woodstock, Ennis, Dromoland, Shannon, East Clare	370		•	•		•	•	•	•	•	•
Queens Hotel	Ennis, Woodstock, Shannon, Lahinch	370		•	•	•	•	•	•	•	•	•
Sancta Maria Hotel	Lahinch, Lahinch Castle, Woodstock, Dromoland, Kilkee, Galway Bay	380		•	•		•	•	•	•	•	•

⚑18 = Full 18 Hole   ⚑9 = 9 Hole   ⚑3 = Par 3

WHERE TO STAY WHEN YOU PLAY!

ACCOMMODATION	COURSES	BE OUR GUEST PAGE NUMBER	GOLF ON SITE	ALL INCLUSIVE PACKAGE	TUITION AVAILABLE	CART AVAILABLE	ARRANGE TEE OFF TIMES	ADVANCE RESERVATIONS	CLUBS FOR HIRE	TRANSPORT	PREFERENTIAL GREEN FEES	CADDY AVAILABLE
CLARE Continued												
Shamrock Inn Hotel	Lahinch Championship Course, Spanish Point, Woodstock, Ennis	380		•	•	•	•	•	•	•	•	•
Sheedy's Restaurant & Country Inn	Lahinch Old and Castle Course, Ennis	382						•	•			•
Smyth Country Lodge Hotel	East Clare (5 minutes), Dromoland, Lahinch, Ballyneety, Nenagh, Galway Bay	373		•	•	•	•	•	•		•	•
Strand Guest House	Kilkee, Kilrush	375						•	•			•
Temple Gate Hotel	Woodstock, Ennis, Lahinch, East Clare, Shannon, Dromoland	371		•	•	•	•	•	•	•	•	•
Tinarana	Bodyke	376		•				•	•		•	•
Tubridy House	Kilrush, Kilkee, Lahinch, Woodstock, Spanish Point, Ballybunion, Doughmore	366		•	•	•	•	•	•		•	•
Woodstock Hotel & Golf Club		372 ⛳18	•									
LIMERICK												
Adare Manor Hotel & Golf Club		391 ⛳18	•		•	•	•	•	•	•	•	•
Carrabawn House	Adare Manor, Newcastlewest, Adare, Dromoland, Charleville, Limerick Golf & Country Club	392		•		•	•	•	•	•	•	•
Castle Oaks House Hotel & Country Club	Castletroy, Limerick County, Limerick, Nenagh, Shannon	393 ⛳3		•			•	•	•	•		
Castletroy Park Hotel	Castletroy, Limerick County (Ballyneety), Dromoland, Adare	385		•			•	•	•	•	•	
Clonmacken House Guest House	Dromoland, Shannon, Ballyclough, Castletroy, Ballykisteen, Adare Manor	386		•	•	•	•	•	•		•	•
Devon Inn Hotel	Newcastlewest, Killeline, Ballybunion, Killarney, Tralee	394		•				•	•		•	
Dunraven Arms Hotel	Adare, Adare Manor, Limerick, Ballybunion, Lahinch	392		•				•	•		•	•
Fitzgeralds Woodlands House Hotel	Adare Manor, New Adare, Newcastle West, Ardagh, Charleville, Ballyneety	392		•		•	•	•	•		•	•
Greenhills Hotel Conference/Leisure	Ballyneety, Shannon, Castletroy, Ballykisteen, Dromoland, Limerick	387		•	•	•	•	•	•		•	•

⛳18 = Full 18 Hole   ⛳9 = 9 Hole   ⛳3 = Par 3

WHERE TO STAY WHEN YOU PLAY!

ACCOMMODATION	COURSES	BE OUR GUEST PAGE NUMBER	GOLF ON SITE	ALL INCLUSIVE PACKAGE	TUITION AVAILABLE	CART AVAILABLE	ARRANGE TEE OFF TIMES	ADVANCE RESERVATIONS	CLUBS FOR HIRE	TRANSPORT	PREFERENTIAL GREEN FEES	CADDY AVAILABLE
LIMERICK Continued												
Jurys Hotel Limerick	Castletroy, Limerick (Ballyclough), Co. Limerick (Ballyneety), Shannon	388		•	•	•	•	•	•	•	•	
Kilmurry Lodge Hotel	Castletroy, Ballykisteen, Limerick County, Adare Manor	393		•	•	•	•	•	•	•	•	•
Limerick Inn Hotel	Castletroy, Limerick (Ballyclough), Shannon, Adare, Limerick County	388		•	•	•	•	•	•	•	•	
Limerick Ryan Hotel	Limerick, Castletroy, Adare, Shannon, Ballykisteen, Limerick County	389		•	•	•	•	•	•	•	•	•
Rathkeale House Hotel	Adare, Adare Manor, Killeline, Newcastlewest, Charleville, Ballybunion	394		•	•	•	•	•	•	•	•	•
Shannon Grove Guesthouse	Castletroy, Limerick, Ballyneety, Lahinch, Adare, Clonlard	390						•			•	•
Two Mile Inn Hotel	Castletroy, Limerick, Shannon, Dromoland, Adare	390		•	•	•	•	•	•	•	•	
Woodfield House Hotel	Shannon, Dromoland, Ballykisteen, Limerick Country Club, Woodstock, Bodyke	391		•	•	•	•	•	•	•	•	•
TIPPERARY NORTH												
Anner Hotel	Thurles, Dundrum, Templemore	396		•	•	•	•	•	•	•	•	•
Grant's Hotel	Roscrea, Birr, Nenagh, Mountrath, Esker Hills	395		•	•	•	•	•	•	•	•	•
Nenagh Abbey Court Hotel	Birr, Nenagh, Roscrea	395		•	•		•	•	•	•	•	•
Racket Hall Country House Hotel	Roscrea, Nenagh, Birr, Thurles	396			•	•	•	•	•	•	•	
St. David's Country House	Nenagh, Portumna	395			•			•			•	•
Tower	Roscrea, Birr, Nenagh, Mountrath	396		•			•	•		•	•	

$\blacktriangleright_{18}$ = Full 18 Hole $\blacktriangleright_9$ = 9 Hole $\blacktriangleright_3$ = Par 3

IRELAND FOR

Fishing

HOTELS & GUESTHOUSES

Ireland is accepted as being the outstanding angling holiday resort in Europe. Whether you are a competition angler, a serious specimen hunter, or just fishing while on holiday, you are sure to enjoy yourself here. With over 14,000km of rivers feeding over 4,000 lakes and with no part of Ireland over 112km from sea. Ireland can, in truth, be called an angler's dream.

So come on and get hooked!

ANGLING FOR A PLACE TO STAY!

We invite you to sample the fishing, the countryside and the friendship of the Irish people and then to stay in some of Ireland's most charming accommodation. We have listed a range of hotels and guesthouses which are either situated with or near angling facilities. Your host will assist you in arranging your angling itinerary. A full description of the hotels and guesthouses can be had by looking up the appropriate page number. Premises are listed in alphabetical order in each county.

ACCOMMODATION	TYPES OF FISH	BE OUR GUEST PAGE NUMBER	COARSE FISHING	GAME FISHING	SEA FISHING	BAIT AND TACKLE	BOATS FOR HIRE	DRYING ROOM	PACKED LUNCHES	GILLIE	TACKLE ROOM	FREEZER	PERMITS REQUIRED
WEST													
GALWAY													
Ardilaun House Hotel, Conference & Leisure Centre	Salmon, Brown Trout, Sea Trout, Rainbow Trout	26		•		•	•	•	•	•		•	•
Ballynahinch Castle Hotel	Salmon, Seatrout, Brown Trout	43		•			•	•		•		•	•
Ben View House	Salmon, Trout, Bass, Herring, Whiting, Pollock, Plaice	46		•	•	•		•	•			•	•
Boat Inn	Perch, Pike, Eel, Pike, Salmon, Brown Trout, Sea Trout, Shark, Cod	55	•	•	•	•	•	•	•			•	•
Corrib House Hotel	Salmon, Trout, Perch, Pike, Shark, Cod	55	•	•	•	•	•	•	•			•	•
Corrib Wave Guest House	Pike, Perch, Brown Trout, Salmon	56	•	•		•	•	•	•	•	•	•	•
Day's Hotel	Cod, Plaice, Ling, Pollock, Mackerel	51		•	•		•					•	
Eldons Hotel	Shark, Pollock, Cod, Mackerel, Raywing	59			•		•					•	
Galway Bay Hotel, Conference & Leisure Centre	Bream, Roach, Perch, Rudd, Salmon, Brown Trout, Blue Shark, Cod, Ling, Pollock, Ray, Gurnard, Eel, Plaice	30	•	•	•		•	•	•			•	•
Galway Ryan Hotel & Leisure Centre	Pike, Perch, Bream, Roach, Salmon, Brown Trout	30	•	•			•	•	•			•	•
Lake Hotel	Pike, Perch, Trout, Salmon, All species	56	•	•	•		•	•	•		•	•	•
Lough Inagh Lodge	Salmon, Sea Trout, Brown Trout	58		•			•	•	•	•		•	•
Menlo Park Hotel	Perch, Pike, Trout, Salmon, Mackerel, Pollock, Ray, Tope, Wrasse	35	•	•	•		•		•			•	
Moran's Cloonnabinnia House Hotel	Bream, Roach, Rudd, Hybrids, Pike, Wild Brown Trout, Salmon, Sea Trout, Shark, Bass, Pollock, Cod	54	•	•	•		•	•	•			•	•
Mountain View Guest House	Salmon, Trout, Pike, Perch, Bream	57	•	•			•	•	•			•	•
Pier House Guesthouse	Blue Shark, Cod, Pollock, Ling, Ray, Mackerel	41			•	•	•	•	•			•	

428

ANGLING FOR A PLACE TO STAY!

ACCOMMODATION	TYPES OF FISH	BE OUR GUEST PAGE NUMBER	COARSE FISHING	GAME FISHING	SEA FISHING	BAIT AND TACKLE	BOATS FOR HIRE	DRYING ROOM	PACKED LUNCHES	GILLIE	TACKLE ROOM	FREEZER	PERMITS REQUIRED
GALWAY Continued													
Portfinn Lodge	Bream, Cubb, Pike, Salmon, Trout, Cod, Mackerel, Plaice	53	•	•	•	•	•		•		•		•
Renvyle House Hotel	Brown Trout, Salmon, Sea Trout, Cod, Shark, Eel, Mackerel, Pollock	58		•	•	•	•	•	•		•		•
River Run Lodge	Pike, Perch, Roach, Salmon, Trout	57	•	•	•	•	•	•	•		•	•	•
Station House Hotel	Perch, Roach, Brown Trout, Salmon, Sea Trout, Plaice, Mackerel, Monkfish	50	•	•	•	•	•	•	•	•	•		•
MAYO													
Achill Cliff House & Restaurant	Flat fish, Cod, Ling, Conger, Shark	60			•	•	•		•				
Atlantic Coast Hotel	Eel, Pike, Perch, Salmon, Trout, Sea Trout, Brill, Mackerel, Ling, Pollock, Ray, Shark, Herring	69	•	•	•	•	•	•	•			•	•
Bartra House Hotel	Perch, Pike, Eel, Bream, Salmon, Trout, Wrasse, Cod, Mackerel, Conger, Eel	62	•	•	•	•	•	•	•		•		•
Belleek Castle	Pike, Perch, Trout, Salmon, Cod, Whiting, Red Mullet, Ling	62	•	•	•	•	•	•	•		•	•	•
Clew Bay Hotel	Salmon, Sea Trout, Rainbow Trout, Blue Shark, Skate, Conger Eel, Ling, Wrasse, Gumard, Tope	70		•	•	•	•	•	•		•	•	•
Daly's Hotel	Pike, Perch, Salmon, Sea Trout, Brown Trout, Cod, Whiting, Mackerel, Ling, Pollock, Ray, Shark, Herring	64	•	•	•	•	•	•	•		•	•	•
Downhill Hotel	Pike, Salmon, Trout, Sea Trout, Sole, Bream, Brill, Mackerel, Ling, Cod, Monkfish	62	•	•	•	•	•	•	•	•	•	•	•
Healy's Hotel	Pike, Perch, Salmon, Brown Trout, Sea Trout	68	•	•	•	•	•	•	•		•	•	•
Heneghan's Guest House	Pike, Perch, Salmon, Trout, Sea Trout	64	•	•	•	•	•	•	•	•	•	•	•
Hotel Westport	Pike, Perch, Bream, Salmon, Trout, Pollock, Dog Fish, Cod, Whiting, Blue Shark, Ling, Tope, Skate	70	•	•	•	•	•	•	•		•	•	•
Knockranny House Hotel	Pike, Salmon, Trout, Cod, Sea Trout, Whiting	71	•	•	•	•	•	•	•			•	•

ANGLING FOR A PLACE TO STAY!

ACCOMMODATION	TYPES OF FISH	BE OUR GUEST PAGE NUMBER	COARSE FISHING	GAME FISHING	SEA FISHING	BAIT AND TACKLE	BOATS FOR HIRE	DRYING ROOM	PACKED LUNCHES	GILLIE	TACKLE ROOM	FREEZER	PERMITS REQUIRED
MAYO Continued													
Lydons Lodge	Pike, Trout, Salmon, Cod, Plaice, Mackerel	66	•	•	•	•	•			•		•	•
Mount Falcon Castle	Salmon, Trout, Mackerel, Cod, Skate, Ling	63		•	•	•	•		•	•		•	•
Ryan's Hotel	Brown Trout, Salmon - also Pike, Perch and Roach	66	•	•		•	•		•	•		•	
Westport Woods Hotel & Leisure Centre	Salmon, Trout, Cod	72		•	•				•		•	•	•
ROSCOMMON													
Gleesons Guesthouse & Restaurant	Roach, Rudd, Tench, Bream, Hybrids, Perch, Pike, Brown Trout	72	•	•		•			•		•		•
Regans	Perch, Pike, Rod, Salmon, Trout	73	•	•		•			•				•
White House Hotel	Trout, Salmon	74		•		•			•				

NORTH WEST

ACCOMMODATION	TYPES OF FISH												
DONEGAL													
Abbey Hotel	Pike, Roach, Perch, Bream, Eel, Salmon, Trout, Tope, Cod	76		•		•	•	•			•	•	•
An Chuirt Gweedore Court Hotel	Trout, Salmon, Sea Trout, Mackerel	79		•	•	•			•			•	•
Arnolds Hotel	Brown Trout, Salmon, Sea Trout	84		•	•		•	•	•				•
Bay View Hotel & Leisure Centre	Salmon, Trout, Shark, Pollock, Cod, Conger, Turbot	85		•	•	•	•		•			•	•
Campbell's Pier House	Salmon, Brown Trout, Sea Trout, Cod, Haddock, Whiting, Pollock, Mackerel, Eel	82	•	•	•	•	•		•	•		•	•
Dorrians Imperial Hotel	Pike, Bream, Roach, Perch, Sea Trout, Brown Trout, Salmon, Pollock, Wrasse, Conger, Cod, Shark	79	•	•	•	•	•		•			•	•
Great Northern Hotel	Pike, Perch, Salmon, Trout, Pollock, Cod, Ling, Plaice, Shark, Sole	82	•	•	•	•	•		•			•	•
Inishowen Gateway Hotel	Salmon, Trout, Tope, Spurdog, Cod, Whiting, Ling, Plaice, Pollock, Mackerel	81		•	•	•	•		•				•

ANGLING FOR A PLACE TO STAY!

ACCOMMODATION	TYPES OF FISH	BE OUR GUEST PAGE NUMBER	COARSE FISHING	GAME FISHING	SEA FISHING	BAIT AND TACKLE	BOATS FOR HIRE	DRYING ROOM	PACKED LUNCHES	GILLIE	TACKLE ROOM	FREEZER	PERMITS REQUIRED
DONEGAL Continued													
Lake of Shadows Hotel	Salmon, Sea-Trout, Wild Brown Trout, Tope, Haddock, Cod, Whiting, Pollock, Coalfish, Gurnard, Plaice	81		•	•	•	•		•			•	•
Ostan Na Rosann	Brown Trout, Sea Trout, Salmon, Cod, Mackerel, Shark, Turbot	85		•	•	•	•		•	•		•	•
Ostan Na Tra (Beach Hotel)	Shark, Cod, Haddock, Ling, Conger, Gurnard, Pollock	83			•	•	•	•	•			•	
LEITRIM													
Bush Hotel	Bream, Roach, Rudd, Tench, Pike, Perch, Eel, Trout	90	•	•			•	•		•	•	•	•
SLIGO													
Innisfree Hotel	Bream, Perch, Pike, Trout, Salmon, Mackerel, Cod, Shark	91	•	•		•							•
NORTH													
ANTRIM													
Bushmills Inn	Roach, Bream, Haddock, Salmon, Cod, Plaice, Whiting, Sea Trout	98	•	•	•	•	•	•	•	•		•	•
ARMAGH													
Silverwood Golf Hotel and Country Club	Bream, Pike, Perch, Salmon, Trout	102	•	•			•		•			•	•
DERRY													
Brown Trout Golf & Country Inn	Pike, Bream, Salmon, Trout	109	•	•							•	•	•
DOWN													
Royal Hotel	Cod, Skate, Mackerel, Haddock, Whiting	110			•	•	•		•				•

ANGLING FOR A PLACE TO STAY!

ACCOMMODATION	TYPES OF FISH	BE OUR GUEST PAGE NUMBER	COARSE FISHING	GAME FISHING	SEA FISHING	BAIT AND TACKLE	BOATS FOR HIRE	DRYING ROOM	PACKED LUNCHES	GILLIE	TACKLE ROOM	FREEZER	PERMITS REQUIRED
DOWN Continued													
Slieve Donard Hotel	Pike, Brown and Rainbow Trout, Salmon, Cod, Haddock, Hake, Mackerel	112	•	•	•	•	•	•		•			•
FERMANAGH													
Mahons Hotel	Roach, Bream, Pike, Perch, Trout, Salmon, Pollock, Cod, Conger, Mackerel	116	•	•	•	•	•	•	•	•	•	•	•

EAST COAST

ACCOMMODATION	TYPES OF FISH	BE OUR GUEST PAGE NUMBER	COARSE FISHING	GAME FISHING	SEA FISHING	BAIT AND TACKLE	BOATS FOR HIRE	DRYING ROOM	PACKED LUNCHES	GILLIE	TACKLE ROOM	FREEZER	PERMITS REQUIRED
DUBLIN													
Central Hotel	Bream, Roach, Perch, Salmon, Trout, Plaice, Mackerel	133	•	•	•	•			•				•
Redbank Lodge & Restaurant	Bass, Shark, Skate, Conger Eel	183		•			•		•			•	
Royal Marine Hotel	Cod, Plaice, Pollock, Ling, Dab	177			•	•		•	•		•	•	
Stillorgan Park Hotel	Bass, Sea Trout	173	•		•					•	•	•	•
MEATH													
Headfort Arms Hotel	Pike, Roach, Bream, Perch, Trout, Salmon	191	•	•		•		•		•		•	•
WICKLOW													
Cullenmore Hotel	Trout, Dab, Cod, Ray, Dogfish, Bass	197		•		•			•	•		•	
Rathsallagh House	Pike, Roach, Rudd, Bream, Hybrids, Trout, Salmon	200	•	•		•		•	•	•	•	•	•
Royal Hotel and Leisure Centre	Trout, Salmon, Cod, Plaice, Pollock	199										•	•
Valley Hotel and Restaurant	Brown Trout, Pike, Perch, Roach, Rainbow Trout	205	•	•	•			•	•			•	•

ANGLING FOR A PLACE TO STAY!

		BE OUR GUEST PAGE NUMBER	COARSE FISHING	GAME FISHING	SEA FISHING	BAIT AND TACKLE	BOATS FOR HIRE	DRYING ROOM	PACKED LUNCHES	GILLIE	TACKLE ROOM	FREEZER	PERMITS REQUIRED
ACCOMMODATION	**TYPES OF FISH**												

MIDLANDS / LAKELANDS

CAVAN

Accommodation	Types of Fish	Page	Coarse	Game	Sea	Bait	Boats	Drying	Packed	Gillie	Tackle	Freezer	Permits
Angler's Rest	Pike, Eels, Roach, Bream, Rudd, Trout, Salmon	207	•	•		•	•	•	•	•	•	•	•
Hotel Kilmore	Pike, Perch, Bream, Roach, Trout	207	•	•		•	•	•	•	•		•	•
Keepers Arms	Pike, Bream, Hybrids, Roach, Tench	208	•			•	•	•	•	•	•		
Sharkeys Hotel	Pike, Perch, Bream, Rudd,	209	•			•	•	•	•	•			
Village Hotel	Trout	227		•		•	•	•	•				

KILDARE

Accommodation	Types of Fish	Page	Coarse	Game	Sea	Bait	Boats	Drying	Packed	Gillie	Tackle	Freezer	Permits
Hazel Hotel	Pike, Rudd, Roach, Eel, Tench, Perch, Salmon, Trout	213	•	•		•			•			•	•
Hillview House	Bream, Rudd, Tench, Salmon, Trout	214	•	•		•	•	•	•		•	•	•
Kildare Hotel & Country Club	Salmon, Trout, Carp, Tench, Bream, Rudd	215	•	•		•	•	•	•	•		•	•

LAOIS

Accommodation	Types of Fish	Page	Coarse	Game	Sea	Bait	Boats	Drying	Packed	Gillie	Tackle	Freezer	Permits
Hibernian Hotel	Pike, Roach, Perch, Rudd, Tench, Salmon, Trout	216	•	•		•		•	•			•	•

LONGFORD

Accommodation	Types of Fish	Page	Coarse	Game	Sea	Bait	Boats	Drying	Packed	Gillie	Tackle	Freezer	Permits
Longford Arms Hotel	Perch, Pike, Eel, Bream, Salmon, Trout	218	•	•		•	•	•	•			•	

MONAGHAN

Accommodation	Types of Fish	Page	Coarse	Game	Sea	Bait	Boats	Drying	Packed	Gillie	Tackle	Freezer	Permits
Glencarn Hotel and Leisure Centre	Perch, Bream, Pike, Trout	220	•					•		•			
Riverdale Hotel	Pike, Perch, Bream, Tench, Trout, Salmon	219	•	•		•	•	•	•	•		•	•

ANGLING FOR A PLACE TO STAY!

Accommodation	Types of Fish	Be Our Guest Page Number	Coarse Fishing	Game Fishing	Sea Fishing	Bait and Tackle	Boats for Hire	Drying Room	Packed Lunches	Gillie	Tackle Room	Freezer	Permits Required
OFFALY													
Brosna Lodge Hotel	Bream, Tench, Rudd, Roach, Perch, Brown Trout, Pike, Salmon	220	•	•		•	•	•	•		•	•	•
Doolys Hotel	Trout, Salmon	221		•			•				•		•
Kinnitty Castle	Rudd, Perch, Tench, Pike, Salmon, Brown Trout	221	•	•		•	•	•	•		•		•
WESTMEATH													
Greville Arms Hotel	Pike, Trout	226	•	•		•	•		•	•		•	
Hodson Bay Hotel	Bream, Perch, Pike, Brown Trout	224	•	•		•	•		•			•	
Lakeside Hotel & Marina	Trout, Pike, Roach, Bream, Eel, Hybrids	225	•			•	•	•	•				
Royal Hoey Hotel	Pike, Bream, Perch, Salmon, Trout, Cod, Mackerel	224	•	•		•	•		•		•	•	•
SOUTH EAST													
CARLOW													
Dolmen Hotel and River Court Lodges	Pike, Salmon, Trout	229	•	•		•	•						•
Seven Oaks Hotel	Breem, Perch, Roach, Pike, Eel, Salmon, Trout	230	•	•		•		•	•			•	•
KILKENNY													
Brannigans Glendine Inn		231		•					•				•
Butler House	Brown Trout, Salmon	232		•					•		•	•	•
Kilkenny River Court Hotel	Trout, Salmon	234		•			•		•			•	•
Mount Juliet Estate	Salmon, Trout	238		•				•	•	•			•
Waterside	Dace, Shad, Trout, Salmon	237		•					•		•		•
TIPPERARY SOUTH													
Carraig Hotel	Salmon, Trout	239		•					•			•	•
Cashel Palace Hotel	Perch, Salmon, Brown Trout	240	•	•		•	•	•	•		•	•	•

ANGLING FOR A PLACE TO STAY!

Accommodation	Types of Fish	Be Our Guest Page Number	Coarse Fishing	Game Fishing	Sea Fishing	Bait and Tackle	Boats for Hire	Drying Room	Packed Lunches	Gillie	Tackle Room	Freezer	Permits Required
TIPPERARY SOUTH Continued													
Dundrum House Hotel	Trout, Salmon	240		•				•	•	•		•	•
WATERFORD													
Ballyrafter House Hotel	Salmon, Sea Trout, Brown Trout	256		•		•				•	•	•	•
Bridge Hotel	Salmon, Trout, Sea Bass, Plaice, Cod	245	•	•	•	•	•	•	•	•	•	•	•
Clonanav Farm Guesthouse	Wild Brown Trout, Salmon	250		•					•	•		•	
Lawlors Hotel	Roach, Dace, Salmon, Trout, Shark, Mackerel, Codling, Plaice, Brill, Bass, Turbot, Ray	253	•	•	•	•	•	•	•	•		•	•
Richmond House	Roach, Dace, Tench, Salmon, Trout, Shark, Cod, Mackerel	252	•	•	•	•				•		•	•
WEXFORD													
Hotel Saltees	Cod, Bass, Mackerel, Pollock	265			•	•	•		•	•		•	
Quay House	Bass, Pollock, Coalfish, Codling, Tope, Spurdog, Ballan Wrasse	265			•	•	•		•	•		•	•
Riverside Park Hotel	Salmon, Trout, Bass	263		•	•				•			•	•
Talbot Hotel Conference and Leisure Centre	Salmon, Trout, Roach, Bass, Cod, Pollock, Ling	259	•	•	•	•			•			•	
Whites Hotel	Bream, Roach, Perch, Pike, Salmon, Trout, Cod, Mackerel	260	•	•	•	•			•			•	
SOUTH WEST													
CORK													
Aherne's Townhouse & Seafood Restaurant	Salmon, Trout, Shark, Cod, Ling, Conger Eel	314		•	•				•	•		•	•
Ambassador Hotel	Pike, Bream, Salmon, Sea Trout, Cod, Pollock, Conger, Ling	272	•	•	•	•			•			•	•
Ashley Hotel	Trout, Mackerel, Conger, Pollock, Ling, Cod	274			•	•	•		•	•		•	
Baltimore Bay Guest House	Mackerel, Pollock, Cod, Ling, Turbot, Ray, Blue Shark, Conger Eel	290			•		•			•			•

ANGLING FOR A PLACE TO STAY!

Accommodation	Types of Fish	Be Our Guest Page Number	Coarse Fishing	Game Fishing	Sea Fishing	Bait and Tackle	Boats for Hire	Drying Room	Packed Lunches	Gillie	Tackle Room	Freezer	Permits Required
CORK Continued													
Baltimore Harbour Hotel & Leisure Centre	Bream, Eel, Pike, Trout, Salmon, Pollock, Ling, Cod, Turbot, Skate, Shark	290	•	•	•	•	•	•	•	•		•	•
Barnabrow Country House	Salmon, Trout, Pollock, Ling, Turbot, Blue Shark, Cod, Hake	311	•	•	•		•	•		•		•	•
Blue Haven Hotel	Blue Shark (June-Sept), Pollock, Ling, Conger, Cod	303			•	•	•						•
Carrigaline Court Hotel & Leisure Centre	Blue Shark (June-Sept), Ling, Pollock, Conger, Cod, Sea Trout	294		•	•	•	•		•				•
Casey's of Baltimore	Pike, Ling, Cod, Pollock, Mackerel, Turbot, Skate, Shark	290	•										•
Celtic Ross Hotel	Bream, Roach, Tench, Trout, Salmon, Cod, Shark, Wrasse, Flat Fish	312	•	•	•	•	•	•	•	•		•	•
Colla House Hotel	Shark, Conger Eel, Cod, Mackerel, Ling, Flat Fish	312			•				•				•
Colneth House	Mackerel, Pollock, Ling, Shark, Conger Eel, Cod	303			•	•	•	•	•		•	•	•
Commodore Hotel	Ling, Cod, Pollock, Conger	298			•	•	•						•
Coolcower House	Bream, Rudd, Tench, Eel, Salmon, Trout	308	•	•							•	•	•
Creedon's Hotel	Bream, Pike, Perch	302	•										•
Deasys Long Quay House	Blue Shark, Cod, Ling, Pollock, Conger Eel, Skate, Mackerel, Whiting	304		•	•	•	•						•
Dunmore House Hotel	Bass, Cod, Flat fish, Mackerel, Skate, Whiting, Ling, etc.	295			•								•
East End	Cod, Shark, Ling etc.	312			•		•	•	•				•
Eldon Hotel	Pike, Bream, Tench, Trout, Salmon, Shark, Mackerel, Pollock	314	•	•	•		•				•		•
Emmet Hotel	Bream, Pike, Perch, Shark, Bass, Cod, Conger, Mackerel	296	•		•								•
Glanworth Mill Country Inn	Trout, Salmon	301		•					•	•			•
Hibernian Hotel	Bream, Pike, Perch, Trench, Trout, Salmon	309	•	•				•	•			•	•
Innishannon House Hotel	Salmon, Sea Trout, Brown Trout, Shark, Cod, Ling, Skate, etc.	302		•	•	•	•	•				•	•

ANGLING FOR A PLACE TO STAY!

ACCOMMODATION

CORK Continued

TYPES OF FISH

Accommodation	Types of Fish	Be Our Guest Page Number	Coarse Fishing	Game Fishing	Sea Fishing	Bait and Tackle	Boats for Hire	Drying Room	Packed Lunches	Gillie	Tackle Room	Freezer	Permits Required
Kierans Folkhouse Inn	Ling, Cod, Congor, Blue Shark, Sea Bass, Pollock	304			•	•	•			•			
Kingsley Hotel	Bream, Pike, Perch, Salmon, Trout, Cod, Pollock, Dog Fish	282	•	•	•	•	•	•	•	•	•	•	•
Lodge & Spa at Inchydoney Island	Trout, Salmon, Bass, Cod, Mackerel, Monkfish, Plaice, Skate	297	•	•	•	•			•			•	•
Longueville House & Presidents' Restaurant	Brown Trout, Salmon	310	•	•		•		•	•			•	•
Maryborough House Hotel	Bream, Perch, Pike, Trout, Rudd, Eel, Salmon, Shark, Ling, Conger, Pollock, Cod, Ray, Wrasse	283	•	•	•	•	•		•			•	•
Midleton Park Hotel	Rainbow Trout, Brown Trout, Salmon, Roach, Dace, Shark, Cod	311	•	•	•	•			•			•	
Reendesert Hotel	Salmon, Trout, Mackerel, Ray, Pollock, Shark	289	•	•	•	•	•		•			•	•
Rushbrooke Hotel	Salmon, Trout	298	•	•		•			•	•	•		
Springfort Hall	Trout, Salmon	310	•	•		•			•				
Trident Hotel	Ling, Cod, Conger, Wrasse, Pollock, Mackerel, Blue Shark	306			•	•	•		•				
Victoria Hotel, Macroom	Bream, Pike, Perch	309	•			•			•		•		•
Walter Raleigh Hotel	Salmon, Trout, Blue Shark, Conger Eel, Ling, Cod, Whiting, etc.	315	•	•	•	•			•			•	•
WatersEdge Hotel	Bream, Rudd, Pike, Salmon, Trout, Sea Trout, Blue Shark, Sea Bass, Cod	299	•	•	•	•			•			•	•
White Lady Hotel	Shark fishing our speciality, Cod, Pollock, etc.	307			•	•	•		•			•	

KERRY

Accommodation	Types of Fish	Be Our Guest Page Number	Coarse Fishing	Game Fishing	Sea Fishing	Bait and Tackle	Boats for Hire	Drying Room	Packed Lunches	Gillie	Tackle Room	Freezer	Permits Required
Abbey Gate Hotel	Salmon, Sea Trout, Brown Trout, Mackerel, Pollock, Dog Fish, etc.	354	•	•	•				•			•	•
Aghadoe Heights Hotel	Salmon, Brown Trout, Sea Trout	332		•	•				•	•		•	•
Barrow House	Salmon, Shark, Bass, Wrasse	355		•	•	•			•	•		•	•
Benners Hotel	Pollock, Mackerel, Cod, Sea Trout, Salmon, Ray, Shark	321		•	•	•			•	•		•	•

ANGLING FOR A PLACE TO STAY!

ACCOMMODATION

KERRY Continued

TYPES OF FISH

Accommodation	Types of Fish	Be Our Guest Page Number	Coarse Fishing	Game Fishing	Sea Fishing	Bait and Tackle	Boats for Hire	Drying Room	Packed Lunches	Gillie	Tackle Room	Freezer	Permits Required
Brandon Court Hotel	Cod, Sea Trout	356			•	•	•	•				•	•
Brandon Hotel	Cod, Sea Trout	356			•	•	•	•				•	•
Brookhaven Guesthouse	Bream, Pike, Chub, Rudd, Roach, Tench, Salmon, Trout, Pollock, Mackerel, Whiting, Plaice, Ling	359	•	•	•	•	•	•	•		•	•	•
Butler Arms Hotel	Salmon, Trout, Bass, Pollock, Cod, Shark, Mackerel, Whiting	360		•	•	•	•	•			•	•	•
Cahernane House Hotel	Salmon, Brown Trout	334		•		•	•	•	•	•	•	•	•
Caragh Lodge	Brown Trout, Salmon	319		•		•	•	•	•	•	•	•	•
Castlelodge Guesthouse	Trout, Salmon	334	•	•			•				•	•	•
Castlerosse Hotel & Leisure Centre	Trout, Salmon	335		•		•	•	•	•	•	•		•
Cliff House Hotel	Salmon, Brown Trout, Shark, Monkfish, Bass, Cod, Ray, Pollock, Ling, Tope, Turbot	315	•	•	•	•	•	•	•	•	•	•	•
Derrynane Hotel	Mackerel, Pollock, Shark	318		•	•	•	•	•			•	•	•
Dingle Skellig Hotel	Pollock, Garfish, Blue Shark, Tope, Dogfish, Ling, Whiting, Ray	323			•	•	•	•	•		•	•	•
Dromquinna Manor Hotel	Brown Trout, Rainbow Trout, Sea Trout, Salmon, Ray, Ling, Pollock, Mackerel, Eel, Skate	327		•	•	•	•	•	•	•	•	•	•
Earls Court House	Salmon, Trout	336		•		•	•	•	•	•	•	•	•
Glencar House Hotel	Salmon, Trout, Sea Trout, Tope, Pollock, Cod, Ling, Mackerel, Ray, Shark	319		•	•	•	•	•	•		•	•	•
Grand Hotel, Tralee	Perch, Trout, Pike, Salmon, Dog Fish, Pollock, Ray, Monkfish	357	•	•	•	•	•	•		•		•	•
Inveraray Farm Guesthouse	Salmon, Brown Trout, Perch, Peel	341	•	•			•	•				•	•
Johnston Marina Hotel	Trout, Salmon, Shark, Bass, Pollock, Cod, Mackerel	358		•	•	•	•	•			•	•	•
Killarney Court Hotel	Pike, Trout, Salmon	342	•	•		•	•	•	•	•	•	•	•
Killarney Heights Hotel	Pike, Eel, Trout, Salmon	343	•	•		•	•	•	•	•	•	•	•
Killarney Park Hotel	Tench, Perch, Brown Trout, Salmon	343	•	•		•	•	•	•	•	•	•	•
Killarney Royal	Brown Trout, Salmon	344		•		•	•	•	•	•	•	•	•

ANGLING FOR A PLACE TO STAY!

Accommodation	Types of Fish	Be Our Guest Page Number	Coarse Fishing	Game Fishing	Sea Fishing	Bait and Tackle	Boats for Hire	Drying Room	Packed Lunches	Gillie	Tackle Room	Freezer	Permits Required
KERRY Continued													
Killarney Ryan Hotel & Leisure Centre	Coarse Fish, Salmon, Trout	344	•	•		•		•	•			•	•
Lake Hotel	Salmon, Trout	346		•		•		•	•	•		•	•
Lakelands Farm Guesthouse	Salmon, Sea Trout, Pollock, Bass, Shark, Ling, Mackerel	360	•	•	•	•	•		•		•	•	•
Listowel Arms Hotel	Pike, Perch, Eel, Salmon, Trout, Ling, Ray, Bass, Pollock, Cod, Monkfish, Tope	353	•	•	•	•			•			•	•
Moorings	Salmon, Trout, Cod, Pollock, Mackerel, Shark, Turbot, Sea Trout, Salmon, Plaice	353	•	•	•	•	•		•		•	•	
Muckross Park Hotel	Salmon, Brown Trout, Tench, Rainbow Trout	348	•	•					•			•	•
Park Hotel Kenmare	Trout, Salmon, Skate, Shark, Mackerel	329	•	•	•		•		•			•	•
Scarriff Inn	Mackerel, Pollock, Salmon, Pike, Bass	318	•	•	•		•		•			•	•
Sheen Falls Lodge	Salmon, Trout, Shark, Mackerel, Pollock, Skate, Conger Eel, Dogfish	330		•	•	•	•		•	•		•	•
Smerwick Harbour Hotel	Plaice, Turbot, Sole, Mackerel, Cod, Pollock, Conger, Shark	325			•				•			•	•
Smugglers Inn	Sea Trout, Salmon, Brown Trout, Bass, Cod, Mackerel, Shark, Plaice, Turbot, Sole, Monkfish	360	•	•	•	•	•			•		•	•

SHANNON

Accommodation	Types of Fish	Be Our Guest Page Number	Coarse Fishing	Game Fishing	Sea Fishing	Bait and Tackle	Boats for Hire	Drying Room	Packed Lunches	Gillie	Tackle Room	Freezer	Permits Required
CLARE													
Aberdeen Arms Hotel	Bream, Chub, Tench, Perch, Eel, Dab, Roach, Salmon, Trout, Plaice, Monkfish, Shark, Mackerel, Cod, Ling, etc.	378	•	•	•	•	•	•	•	•	•	•	
Atlantic Hotel	Bream, Eel, Perch, Pike, Tench, Brown Trout, Rainbow Trout, Salmon, Bass, Blue Shark, Cod, Conger Eel, Ling	378	•	•	•	•	•		•		•	•	
Auburn Lodge Hotel	Cod, Trout, Salmon, Bream, Pike, Roach	368	•	•	•	•		•	•		•	•	
Carrygerry Country House	Bream, Pike, Perch, Rainbow and Brown Trout, Mackerel, Bass, Cod	384	•	•	•	•		•	•			•	•

ANGLING FOR A PLACE TO STAY!

Accommodation	Types of Fish	Be Our Guest Page Number	Coarse Fishing	Game Fishing	Sea Fishing	Bait and Tackle	Boats for Hire	Drying Room	Packed Lunches	Gillie	Tackle Room	Freezer	Permits Required
CLARE Continued													
Dromoland Castle	Pike, Trout, Bream	383		•				•		•	•		
Fountain Court	Pike, Bream, Tench, Salmon, Brown Trout, Mackerel, Skate, Pollock, Cod, Hake, Shark	369	•	•	•	•	•	•	•	•	•	•	•
Grovemount House	Roach, Trout	373	•	•		•		•	•		•	•	•
Kincora Hall Hotel	Tench, Bream, Roach, Perch, Pike, Eel, Trout, Salmon	375	•	•		•	•	•	•		•		•
Queens Hotel	Shark, Trout, Salmon, Bream, Roach, Pike, Eel	370	•	•		•	•	•	•	•	•		•
Smyth Country Lodge Hotel	Pike, Rudd, Bream, Tench, Salmon, Trout	373	•	•		•	•	•	•		•		•
Tinarana	Roach, Bream, Tench, Pike, Perch, Trout, Salmon	386	•	•		•	•	•	•	•	•		•
Tubridy House	Brown Trout, Salmon, Bass, Mullet, Mackerel, Pollock, Flatfish, Conger Eel, Tope, Ray	366	•	•	•	•	•	•	•		•		•
Woodstock Hotel & Golf Club	Pike, Bream, Tench, Rudd, Salmon, Rainbow & Brown Trout, Sea Trout, Cod, Conger, Skate, Pollock, Mullet	372	•	•		•	•	•	•	•	•		•
LIMERICK													
Adare Manor Hotel & Golf Club	Salmon, Trout	391		•		•			•	•	•		
Castle Oaks House Hotel & Country Club	Pike, Bream, Tench, Eel, Trout, Salmon	393	•	•		•	•	•	•	•	•	•	•
Fitzgeralds Woodlands House Hotel	Pike, Trout, Salmon	392	•	•		•	•	•	•		•		•
Kilmurry Lodge Hotel	Roach, Pike, Perch, Bream, Hybrids, Salmon, Trout	393	•	•		•	•	•	•	•	•		•
Leens Hotel	Salmon, Trout, Ray, Bass, Pollock, Cod, Monkfish	391	•	•	•	•	•	•	•		•	•	•
Limerick Ryan Hotel	Pike, Perch, Roach, Trout, Salmon	389	•	•		•	•	•	•		•		•
Rathkeale House Hotel	Pike, Perch, Roach, Trout, Salmon	394	•	•		•	•	•	•		•		•
Two Mile Inn Hotel	Pike, Perch, Salmon, Trout	390	•	•		•	•	•	•		•		•
TIPPERARY NORTH													
Nenagh Abbey Court Hotel	Pike, Perch, Bream, Roach, Brown Trout, Salmon	395	•	•		•		•	•	•	•		•

IRELAND FOR

Conferences

HOTELS & GUESTHOUSES

Small meetings or large conferences are part
and parcel of life in Irish hotels and guesthouses.

What makes Ireland special as a venue
is the warmth of the welcome you will receive,
coupled with excellent facilities
which can be tailored to your needs.

If you have an agenda, we can supply
the venue.

SELECT A VENUE FOR YOUR AGENDA

We will be glad to see you and work with you to make your meeting or conference a successful one. Choose from the wide selection of special facilities throughout the country as shown here. A full description of the hotels and guesthouses can be had by looking up the appropriate page number. Premises are listed in alphabetical order in each county.

WEST

GALWAY

Accommodation	Contact Person	Be Our Guest Page Number	500+	400+	300+	200+	100+	50+	50−	Black Out Facilities	Air Conditioning	Interpreting Equipment	Audio Visual Equipment
Abbeyglen Castle Hotel	Paul Hughes	45					1	1	3	•		H	O
Ardilaun House Hotel, Conference & Leisure Centre	Thomas MacCarthy O'Hea	26			1					•	•	H	H
Connemara Coast Hotel	Daniella O'Donnell	27		1	1	2	2	5	8	•		H	O
Corrib House Hotel	Francis Casey	55						1					H
Doonmore Hotel	Aileen Murray	52							3				
Galway Bay Golf and Country Club Hotel	Gerry McKeon	29					2	2	3	•		H	O
Galway Bay Hotel, Conference & Leisure Centre	Terry Brennan	30	1	2	2	2	2	5	5	•	•	H	O
Galway Ryan Hotel & Leisure Centre	Sharon Mulhern Foley	30							2	•	•	H	H
Hotel Spanish Arch	Easter McDonagh Gallagher	32							1	•		H	H
Lady Gregory Hotel	Mary Sheehan	51			1				2	•	•	H	O
Menlo Park Hotel	David Keane	35					1	1	2	•	•	H	O
Oranmore Lodge Hotel, Conference & Leisure Centre	Mary O'Higgins	36			1	1	2	3	5	•	•		H
Park House Hotel & Eyre House Restaurants	Ann Marie Dowd	36							1	•			H
Park Lodge Hotel	Jane Marie Foyle	60					1	1	1	•		H	H
Quality Hotel and Leisure Centre Galway	Rhona Kearney/Dermot Comerford	37						1	6	•			H
Renvyle House Hotel	Vincent Flannery	58					2	1	1	•		H	O
Shannon Oaks Hotel & Country Club	Denis Deery	58	1				1	1	2	•	•	H	O
Station House Hotel	Cian Landers	50				1			2	•	•	H	O
Westwood House Hotel	Rachael Coyle	40			1	1	1	3	4	•	•	H	O

MAYO

Accommodation	Contact Person	Be Our Guest Page Number	500+	400+	300+	200+	100+	50+	50−	Black Out Facilities	Air Conditioning	Interpreting Equipment	Audio Visual Equipment
Atlantic Coast Hotel	Brian Fahy and Jim Mulcahy	69						1	3	•	•	H	O
Belleek Castle	Jacqueline Doran	62						1					
Breaffy House Hotel	Caitriona Gavin	64					1	1	5	•	•	H	O
Castlecourt Hotel Conference and Leisure Centre	Joe Corcoran	69	1	1	1	2	2	3	3	•	•	H	O

H = Can Arrange Hire   O = Available On Premises

442

USEFUL TELEPHONE NUMBERS

Emergency (fire, Garda, (Police) & Ambulance)	999
Directory Enquiries (national)	1190
Directory Enquiries (to Great Britain)	1197
Directory Enquiries (international)	1198
Operator Assistance (national)	10
Operator Assistance (international)	114
Dublin Airport	(01) 844 4131
Shannon Airport	(061) 471 444
Cork Airport	(021) 313131
Aer Lingus (flight enquiries)	(01) 886 6705
British Airways (enquiries)	1 800 62 67 47
Ryanair (flight enquiries)	(01) 844 4411
Delta Airlines (enquiries)	(01) 844 4166
Air France	(01) 844 5633
Virgin Altantic	(01) 873 3388
Iberia/Viva Air (Dublin Airport)	(01) 844 4939
Irish Rail (Passenger information)	(01) 836 6222
Connolly Station	(01) 836 3333
Heuston Station	(01) 836 3333
Dart Information	(01) 836 3333
Irish Bus (Bus Eireann)	(01) 836 1111
Dublin Bus (Bus Atha Cliath)	(01) 873 4222
Irish Ferries (Enquiries)	1890 31 31 31
Irish Ferries	(01) 855 2222
General Post Office (An Post)	(01) 705 7000
Bord Fáilte	(01) 602 4000

SELECT A VENUE FOR YOUR AGENDA

ACCOMMODATION	CONTACT PERSON	BE OUR GUEST PAGE NUMBER	NUMBER OF ROOMS OF VARIOUS SEATING CAPACITIES							AIR CONDITIONING	BLACK OUT FACILITIES	INTERPRETING EQUIPMENT	AUDIO VISUAL EQUIPMENT	
			500+	400+	300+	200+	100+	50+	50-					
MAYO Continued														
Downhill Hotel	Kay Devine & Rachel Moylett	62	1		1	1	1	2	3	•			H	O
Hotel Westport	Gerry Walshe & Ruth Farrell & Rhona Chambers	70		1		1	3	1		•	•		H	O
Jennings Hotel & Travellers Friend	Donal Dunne	65	1	1	2	2	3	3	4	•	•		H	O
Knockranny House Hotel	Derval White	71	1	1	1	2	2	3	3	•	•		H	O
Westport Woods Hotel & Leisure Centre	Michael Lennon	72				1	1	1	2	•	•		H	H
ROSCOMMON														
Abbey Hotel	Adrian Gready	72				1		1	2					O
Gleesons Guesthouse & Restaurant	Eamonn Gleeson	72						1	1	•	•		H	H
O'Garas Royal Hotel	Larry O'Gara	73					1	2	1	•			H	O
Regans	Mary Regan	73						1						O
Shannon Key West Hotel	David O'Connor / Margaret Mitchell	74			1				1	•	•		O	O
White House Hotel	Aidan Kenny	74			1					•	•		H	O

NORTH WEST

ACCOMMODATION	CONTACT PERSON	BE OUR GUEST PAGE NUMBER	500+	400+	300+	200+	100+	50+	50-	AIR CONDITIONING	BLACK OUT FACILITIES	INTERPRETING EQUIPMENT	AUDIO VISUAL EQUIPMENT	
DONEGAL														
Abbey Hotel	Dominic Breslin	76		1	1	1	1	1		•	•		O	O
Bay View Hotel & Leisure Centre	Noel O'Mahony	85			1			1		•	•			O
Dorrians Imperial Hotel	Mary Dorrian	79			1			1	1	•	•			H
Great Northern Hotel	Philip McGlynn	82	1	1	1	1	1	1		•	•		H	O
Holyrood Hotel	Audrey McEniff and Mary Ruane	82	1							•	•		H	O
Hyland Central Hotel	Ann Sharkey	76		1	1	1	1	1		•	•		H	O
Inishowen Gateway Hotel	Patrick Doherty	81			1		1	2	1	•	•			O
Kee's Hotel	Arthur Kee	78			1			1	3	•	•			H
Ostan Na Rosann	Alan Sweeny	85			1	1	1	1		•	•		H	H
Redcastle Hotel	Margaret Patterson	88			1			1			•		H	O
Sand House Hotel	Paul Diver	89						1	3	•			H	H
LEITRIM														
Bush Hotel	Joseph Dolan	90			1	1	3	2	3	•	•		H	H

H = Can Arrange Hire   O = Available On Premises

SELECT A VENUE FOR YOUR AGENDA

NUMBER OF ROOMS OF VARIOUS SEATING CAPACITIES

Key to right‑hand columns: BE OUR GUEST PAGE NUMBER · BLACK OUT FACILITIES · AIR CONDITIONING · INTERPRETING EQUIPMENT · AUDIO VISUAL EQUIPMENT

SLIGO

Accommodation	Contact Person	Page	500+	400+	300+	200+	100+	50+	50–	Black Out	Air Con	Interpreting	Audio Visual
Ballincar House Hotel	The Manager	90						1	3	•			O
Hotel Silver Swan	Helen Burns	91					2		2	•		H	O
Innisfree Hotel	Catherine Gurn	91					1			•		H	O
Sligo's Southern Hotel & Leisure Centre	Kevin McGlynn	92	1	1	1	1	1	2	4	•		H	O
Tower Hotel	Joe Leonard	93					1	1	2	•		H	H

NORTH

ANTRIM

Accommodation	Contact Person	Page	500+	400+	300+	200+	100+	50+	50–	Black Out	Air Con	Interpreting	Audio Visual
Ballymac	Cathy Muldoon	101					1		1	•			O
Beach Hotel	Mary O'Neill	97						2	2	•		H	H
Bushmills Inn	Stella Minogue	98						1	2	•	•	H	O
Causeway Coast Hotel & Conference Centre	Mary O'Neill	99			1	1	2	2	2	•	•	H	H
Magherabuoy House Hotel	Anna Conn	100		1	1	2	2	3		•		H	O
O'Neill Arms Hotel	Kathleen McConville	102	1	1	1	1	1	1	1				
Stakis Park	Wilma Lindsay	101	1			2	5	7	3	•	•	H	O

ARMAGH

Accommodation	Contact Person	Page	500+	400+	300+	200+	100+	50+	50–	Black Out	Air Con	Interpreting	Audio Visual
Silverwood Golf Hotel and Country Club	Miriam Callan	102			1	1	1	2		•			O

BELFAST

Accommodation	Contact Person	Page	500+	400+	300+	200+	100+	50+	50–	Black Out	Air Con	Interpreting	Audio Visual
Dukes Hotel	Yvonne McNally	104					1	2	3	•	•	H	H
Dunadry Hotel and Country Club	Sheree Davis	104			1	2	2	3	8	•		H	O
McCausland Hotel	Adrianne Carr	106						1	1	•	•	H	H
Park Avenue Hotel	Angela Reid	107		1	1	2	3	6	7	•		H	O
Wellington Park Hotel	Malachy Toner	107		1	1	2	3	4	9	•	•	H	O

DERRY

Accommodation	Contact Person	Page	500+	400+	300+	200+	100+	50+	50–	Black Out	Air Con	Interpreting	Audio Visual
Brown Trout Golf & Country Inn	Bill O'Hara	109							2	•	•		

DOWN

Accommodation	Contact Person	Page	500+	400+	300+	200+	100+	50+	50–	Black Out	Air Con	Interpreting	Audio Visual
Marine Court Hotel	Philip Weston	110			2				2	•	•	O	O
Slieve Donard Hotel	Nora Hanna	112	1	1	1	2	2	4	6	•	•		O

H = Can Arrange Hire   O = Available On Premises

SELECT A VENUE FOR YOUR AGENDA

Accommodation	Contact Person	Be Our Guest Page Number	500+	400+	300+	200+	100+	50+	50-	Black Out Facilities	Air Conditioning	Interpreting Equipment	Audio Visual Equipment
FERMANAGH													
Killyhevlin Hotel	David Morrison	115	1			2		2	3	•	•	H	H
Mahons Hotel	Joe Mahon	116		1		1			1	•	•	H	O

EAST COAST

Accommodation	Contact Person	Be Our Guest Page Number	500+	400+	300+	200+	100+	50+	50-	Black Out Facilities	Air Conditioning	Interpreting Equipment	Audio Visual Equipment
DUBLIN													
Abberley Court Hotel	Orla Strumble	118					1		2	•	•	H	O
Aberdeen Lodge	Pat Halpin	118							2		•	H	H
Academy Hotel	Ross MacSweeney	119							4	•	•	H	O
Airport View	Anne Marie Beggs	173							1		•		H
Alexander Hotel	Siobhan O'Hare	120		1	1	2	4	5	1	•	•	H	O
Arlington Hotel	Andrea Inglis	123							2		•	H	O
Ashling Hotel	Dermot Lambe & David Lane	124				1	1	1	5		•	H	H
Becketts Country House Hotel	Emma Mander	179							4			H	H
Belvedere Hotel	Marion Heneghan	126					1					•	
Berkeley Court Hotel	Michelle McDermot	126	1			2	1		3	•	•	H	
Brooks Hotel	Anne McKiornan/Karl Reinhardt	128						1	3	•	•	H	O
Burlington Hotel	John Conmee	129	1	3			3	2	14	•	•	H	H
Buswells Hotel	Michelle McPhillips	129						1	3	•	•	H	O
Camden Court Hotel	Denise Corboy	130							4				O
Cassidys Hotel	Kathryn Tracey	132						1	1		•		H
Central Hotel	John-Paul Kavanagh	133						2	4		•	H	H
Citywest Hotel, Conference, Leisure & Golf Resort	Fiona Killilea	182	1		2			3	10	•	•	H	O
Clarion Stephens Hall Hotel and Suites	Patricia Mulligan	135							3			H	H
Clontarf Castle Hotel	Joanne Rolfe	136		1			3	2	3	•	•	O	O
Comfort Inn, Talbot Street	Joanna Doyle	136							3		•	H	O
Conrad International Dublin	Ann Blake	137				1			4	•	•	H	H
Davenport Hotel	Siobhan O'Hare	137			1	2	2	2	4	•	•	H	O
Eglinton Manor	Rosaleen Cahill O'Brien	140							1		•		
Finnstown Country House Hotel	Oonagh Brien	179						1	4		•		O
Fitzpatrick Castle Dublin	Eoin O'Sullivan	178	1	2	2	2	2	7	5	•	•	H	O
Fitzwilliam Hotel	Lesley Mangan	141						2	1	•	•	H	H

H = Can Arrange Hire   O = Available On Premises

SELECT A VENUE FOR YOUR AGENDA

ACCOMMODATION

DUBLIN Continued

Accommodation	Contact Person	Be Our Guest Page Number	500+	400+	300+	200+	100+	50+	50-	Air Conditioning	Black Out Facilities	Interpreting Equipment	Audio Visual Equipment
Fitzwilliam Park	Catherine O'Reilly	142							1	•		H	H
Georgian House Hotel	Lorraine Loughnane	143						1	3	•	•	H	O
Grand Hotel	Mary O'Reilly	180	2			1	3	6	9	•	•	H	O
Gresham Hotel	Ian Craig	146			1	2	2	4	18	•	•	H	H
Hilton Dublin (formerly Stakis Dublin)	Ann McBride	149				1		4	7	•			O
Holiday Inn	Ciara Hamilton	149						1	1	•	•	H	H
Hollybrook Hotel	Josephine McCooey	150				1				•	•	H	
Hotel St. George	Reception	150						1		•			
Jurys Custom House Inn	Derek McDonagh	152						1	3	•	•	H	H
Jurys Hotel Dublin	Conor O'Kane	152	1				2	2	8	•	•	H	H
Lansdowne Hotel	Margaret English	153					1	1	1	•		H	O
Marine Hotel	Sheila Baird	184						1	6	•	•	H	H
Mercer Hotel	Maurice Supple	156					1	1	3	•	•	H	O
Merrion Hall	Pat Halpin	156							2	•	•	H	H
Merrion Hotel	Ed Kavanagh	157							2	•		H	O
Mespil Hotel	Emma Allen	157							1	•			O
Mont Clare Hotel	Siobhan O'Hare	158					1	3	6	•	•	H	O
North Star Hotel	Dennis McGettigan	159					1	1	1	•	•	H	H
Ormond Quay Hotel	Conor Byrne	160					1	3		•		H	H
Paramount Hotel	Helen Whitty	161						1		•	•	H	O
Parnell West Hotel	B. O'Brien	162						2	1	•		H	H
Plaza Hotel	Deirdre Burns	163			1		2	2	8	•	•	H	H
Portmarnock Hotel & Golf Links	Nicola Meehan	181				1	2	2	2	•	•	H	H
Posthouse Dublin Airport	Valerie Markey	175					1		6	•	•	H	H
Quality Charleville Hotel and Suites	Evelyn Haran	163							3	•		H	H
Quality Court Hotel	Siobhan M. Byrne	178				1	2	2	5	•		O	O
Radisson SAS St Helen's Hotel	John Coleman	173			1	1	3	6	5	•	•	H	O
Rathmines Plaza Hotel	Frances Dempsey	164							2			H	H
Red Cow Moran's Hotel	Karen Moran	165	1	1	1	2	4	4	4	•	•	H	O
Regency Hotel	Catherine McGettigan	165		2				1	3	•	•	H	O
Rochestown Lodge Hotel	John Hickey	176		1	1	2	3	4	5	•			O

H = Can Arrange Hire   O = Available On Premises

SELECT A VENUE FOR YOUR AGENDA

ACCOMMODATION	CONTACT PERSON	BE OUR GUEST PAGE NUMBER	NUMBER OF ROOMS OF VARIOUS SEATING CAPACITIES							BLACK OUT FACILITIES	AIR CONDITIONING	INTERPRETING EQUIPMENT	AUDIO VISUAL EQUIPMENT	
			500+	400+	300+	200+	100+	50+	50-					
DUBLIN Continued														
Royal Dublin Hotel	Elizabeth O'Gorman	166				1	2	3	4	•			H	H
Royal Marine Hotel	Mary Lynch	177	1			1	1	2	4	•	•	•	H	H
Sachs Hotel	Ann Byrne	166					1	1	1				H	H
Shelbourne Dublin	Diarmuid O'Sullivan	167		1			2	2	6	•			H	H
Sheldon Park Hotel & Leisure Centre	Maura Bissett	167	1	1	1	2	2	3	9	•	•		H	O
Spa Hotel	Betty Dolan	179	1	1	1	1	1	1	1					H
Stephen's Green Hotel	Siobhain O'Hare	169							6	•			H	O
Stillorgan Park Hotel	Caroline Daly	173					1	5	9	•	•		H	H
Sutton Castle Hotel	Ray Mooney	184			1			1	1	•	•		H	H
Temple Bar Hotel	Ronda Stockhill	170						1	4	•			H	H
West County Hotel	Gerard Colgan	172					1	1	2	•				H
Westbury Hotel	Jane Howley	172				1	2	1		•			H	H
LOUTH														
Boyne Valley Hotel & Country Club	Michael McNamara	186	1	1	1	2	1	2	3	•			H	O
Carrickdale Hotel & Leisure Complex	Breige Savage/Declan O'Neill/Fiona Clerkin	187	1			1	1	1	1	•	•	•	H	O
Derryhale Hotel	Liam Sexton	188				1			2	•			H	H
Fairways Hotel	Brian Quinn/Chris Brayden	188			1				2	•			H	O
Hotel Imperial	Peter Quinn	189					1	2	2	•				O
McKevitt's Village Hotel	Terry and Kay McKevitt	186						1	1	•				H
Westcourt Hotel	Barry Tierney	187			1	1	2	3	5	•	•			O
MEATH														
Ardboyne Hotel	Bernie McHugh	192					2	2	4	•	•		H	O
Conyngham Arms Hotel	Kevin Macken	193					1	2	1	•	•		H	O
Headfort Arms Hotel	Vincent Duff	191		1						•				O
Neptune Beach	Emma Allen	190				1			2	•	•		H	O
Old Darnley Lodge Hotel	Tim O'Brien	190			1				1	•	•			O
WICKLOW														
Arklow Bay Hotel	Monique Freeman	195	1	1	1	1	1	2	2	•	•		H	H
Brooklodge at Macreddin	Evan Doyle	197			1			1	1	•	•		H	O

H = Can Arrange Hire   O = Available On Premises

SELECT A VENUE FOR YOUR AGENDA

Accommodation	Contact Person	Be Our Guest Page Number	500+	400+	300+	200+	100+	50+	50-	Black Out Facilities	Air Conditioning	Interpreting Equipment	Audio Visual Equipment
WICKLOW Continued													
Cullenmore Hotel	Dirk Van der Flier	197						1	2				H
Glendalough Hotel	Patrick Casey	202			1				2	•	•	H	O
Glenview Hotel	Stephen Byrne	202			1	1	1		2	•	•	H	O
Hunter's Hotel	Nicola Coffey	204							3	•		H	H
La Touche Hotel	Trevor Killeen	203	1	1	1	1	1	1	2	•	•	H	H
Lawless Hotel	Seoirse or Maeve O'Toole	197			1				1	•		H	O
Rathsallagh House	Catherine Lawlor	200						1	2	•		H	O
Royal Hotel and Leisure Centre	Siobhan Ashall	199				1			1	•	•	H	O
Summerhill House Hotel	Denis Kennedy	201			1			1	5	•		H	H
Tinakilly Country House and Restaurant	Louise Barry	204						1	5	•		H	O
Tulfarris House Hotel	Liz Hayes	198				1	1	3	7	•			O
Woodenbridge Hotel	Esther and Bill O'Brien	205			1				1	•			
Woodlands Court Hotel	Eileen Murphy	200							2	•	•	H	O

MIDLANDS / LAKELANDS

Accommodation	Contact Person	Be Our Guest Page Number	500+	400+	300+	200+	100+	50+	50-	Black Out Facilities	Air Conditioning	Interpreting Equipment	Audio Visual Equipment
CAVAN													
Hotel Kilmore	Bernie McHugh	207	1			2	3	3	4	•	•	H	O
Park Hotel	Mary MacMillan	207							1				O
Sharkeys Hotel	Goretti Sharkey	209		1				1	1	•	•	H	O
Slieve Russell Hotel, Golf & Country Club	Vari McGreevy	208	1	1	3	3	3	4	7	•	•	H	O
KILDARE													
Ambassador Hotel	Brian Johnston	212				1	2	2	3	•	•	H	O
Ardenode Hotel	Michelle Browne	210		1	1	1	1	1		•	•		H
Glenroyal Hotel, Leisure Club & Conference Centre	Helen Courtney	213		1	2	2	3	4	7	•	•	H	O
Hazel Hotel	Margaret Kelly	213			1	1	1	1		•	•		O
Hillview House	Brendan Allen	214					1	1		•			
Keadeen Hotel	Michelle Kelly	215	1	1	1	1	3	4	7	•	•	H	O
Kildare Hotel & Country Club	Ann Cronin	215				1	1	3		•		O	O
Standhouse Hotel Leisure & Conference Centre	Tara Tierney	211	1	1	2	3	4	4	7	•	•	H	O

H = Can Arrange Hire   O = Available On Premises

SELECT A VENUE FOR YOUR AGENDA

ACCOMMODATION	CONTACT PERSON	BE OUR GUEST PAGE NUMBER	500+	400+	300+	200+	100+	50+	50-	AIR CONDITIONING	BLACK OUT FACILITIES	INTERPRETING EQUIPMENT	AUDIO VISUAL EQUIPMENT
LAOIS													
Abbeyleix Manor Hotel	Jenny Kent	215				1				•	•	H	H
Arlington Tower Hotel	Jimmy Kelly	217					1				•	O	O
Killeshin Hotel	Marian Keightley	217				2	4	8	5	•	•	H	O
Montague Hotel	Marion Keightley	216		1		2	1	2	4	•	•		O
LONGFORD													
Longford Arms Hotel	James Reynolds	218	1				2	3		•	•	H	H
MONAGHAN													
Four Seasons Hotel & Leisure Club	Orla McKenna	218	1	1	2	2	4	4	5	•	•	H	O
Glencarn Hotel and Leisure Centre	Patrick McFadden/Fiona Dooley/Kathleen Lavelle	220	1	1	1	3	3	3	5	•	•	H	O
Nuremore Hotel & Country Club	Helen Woods	219	1				2	3	4	•	•	H	O
OFFALY													
Bridge House Hotel & Leisure Club	Colm McCabe	222	1	1	2	2	3	4	9	•	•	H	O
County Arms Hotel	William Loughnane	220		1			1	2	2			H	H
Doolys Hotel	Noel Keigher	221			1				2		•		O
Kinnitty Castle	Gerard Lavin	221			1			2	1			H	H
Moorhill Country House Hotel	Oliver Toner	223					1	1	2			H	H
Tullamore Court Hotel	Ann Lynch	223	1	1	2	2	3	4	8	•	•	H	O
WESTMEATH													
Bloomfield House Hotel & Leisure Club	Ita Purcell	226			1	2	3	5	7	•	•	H	O
Greville Arms Hotel	John Cochrane	226				1	2	1	2			H	H
Hodson Bay Hotel	Cathriona Connolly	224	1	1	1	2	3	4	4		•	H	O
Lakeside Hotel & Marina	Jacqueline Mullen	225	1				1	1	1			H	H
Prince of Wales Hotel	Gael C. Allen	224					1		3			H	O
Royal Hoey Hotel	M. Hoey	224					1	2	3		•		O

SOUTH EAST

ACCOMMODATION	CONTACT PERSON	BE OUR GUEST PAGE NUMBER	500+	400+	300+	200+	100+	50+	50-	AIR CONDITIONING	BLACK OUT FACILITIES	INTERPRETING EQUIPMENT	AUDIO VISUAL EQUIPMENT
CARLOW													
Dolmen Hotel and River Court Lodges	Nora Duggan	229	1	2	2	2	2	3	8	•	•	H	O

H = Can Arrange Hire   O = Available On Premises

SELECT A VENUE FOR YOUR AGENDA

Accommodation	Contact Person	Be Our Guest Page Number	500+	400+	300+	200+	100+	50+	50-	Black Out Facilities	Air Conditioning	Interpreting Equipment	Audio Visual Equipment
CARLOW Continued													
Mount Wolseley Hotel, Golf and Country Club	Cathy Walsh	231					1		3	•	•	H	H
Seven Oaks Hotel	Kathleen Dooley	230	1					1	2	•			H
KILKENNY													
Butler House	Martina Cuddihy/Gabrielle Hickey	232					1	2				H	O
Hibernian Hotel	Joe Kelly	232						1	2	•	•		O
Hotel Kilkenny	Brid Crawford	233		1	2	2	3	4	7	•		H	O
Kilkenny Ormonde Hotel	Sheena McCanny	234		2					8	•	•	H	O
Kilkenny River Court Hotel	Patrick Crawford	234			1				4	•	•	H	O
Mount Juliet Estate	Aine O'Hare	238					1	3	2	•		H	O
Newpark Hotel	Orla Gray	235	1	1	1	2	2	7		•		H	O
Springhill Court Hotel	Trish Murphy	236	1	1	1	1	1	2	3	•		H	O
TIPPERARY SOUTH													
Cashel Palace Hotel	Susan Murphy	240					1			•		H	H
Clonmel Arms Hotel	Michael O'Brien	242	1				1		1	•	•	O	H
Dundrum House Hotel	Deirdre Crowe	240	1					1		•		H	O
Glen Hotel	James Coughlan	244			1	1	1	1		•	•	H	
Horse and Jockey Inn	Tom Egan	397					1	2		•			O
Hotel Minella & Leisure Centre	Elizabeth Nallen	243	1		2	2	2	3		•	•	H	H
Kilcoran Lodge Hotel	Linda Coady	239				1		2	3	•	•	H	O
Knocklofty Country House	Stephen/Brona	243						1	2	•			O
WATERFORD													
Bridge Hotel	Rosemary Drinan/Mary Keating	245			1	1	2	3	4	•	•	H	O
Clonea Strand Hotel, Golf & Leisure	Mark Knowles or Ann McGrath	253			2	2	3	4	5	•	•	H	H
Coach House	Des O'Keeffe	345							1	•			
Dooley's Hotel	Margaret Darrer	246			1	2	1	4		•	•	H	O
Faithlegg House Hotel	Tracy McDaid	255				1		1	3	•		H	O
Gold Coast Golf Hotel & Leisure Centre	Ann McGrath	253				1	3	4		•	•	H	H
Grand Hotel	Shane Rossiter	257				1	1	1	1	•		H	O

H = Can Arrange Hire   O = Available On Premises

SELECT A VENUE FOR YOUR AGENDA

Accommodation	Contact Person	Be Our Guest Page Number	500+	400+	300+	200+	100+	50+	50−	Air Conditioning	Black Out Facilities	Interpreting Equipment	Audio Visual Equipment
WATERFORD Continued													
Granville Hotel	Richard Hurley	246					1	2	1	•		H	H
Jurys Hotel Waterford	Aine Aspel	247	1					1	2	•		H	H
Lawlors Hotel	William Buckley & Anne Marie Daffy	253		1		2	3	4	5	•	•	H	O
Majestic Hotel	Annette Devine	257					1	1	1	•	•	H	H
Tower Hotel & Leisure Centre	Michael Skeehan	249	1	1	2	2		5	3	•			H
Waterford Marina Hotel	Grainne Lyne	250							3	•	•		H
Woodlands Hotel	Marguerite Fitzgerald	250	1						2	•	•	H	H
WEXFORD													
Brandon House Hotel & Leisure Centre	Maria O'Connor	266				1			1	•	•	H	O
Danby Lodge Hotel	Margaret Parle	267							1			H	H
Ferrycarrig Hotel	Caroline Roche	258		1	1	1	1	1	2	•	•	H	H
Marlfield House Hotel	Margaret Bowe	264							1			H	O
Riverside Park Hotel	Jim Maher	263	1	1	1	2	1	4	4	•	•	H	O
Talbot Hotel Conference and Leisure Centre	Majella O'Connor	259	1	1	1	1	2	3	4	•	•	H	O
Treacys Hotel	Anton Treacy	264					1	2	4		•	H	O
Whites Hotel	Susan O'Connor	260			1	1	2	3	7	•		H	O
SOUTH WEST													
CORK													
Actons Hotel	Angela Leamy/Anne Marie Cross	302			1				2	•	•	H	H
Ambassador Hotel	Mark Hornibrook	272						1	1	•		H	H
Baltimore Harbour Hotel & Leisure Centre	Fiona O'Sullivan	290				1			1	•		H	H
Barnabrow Country House	Geraldine O'Brien	311							3	•		H	H
Blarney Park Hotel	Eilis Keane	293				1	2	2	3	•	•	H	H
Carrigaline Court Hotel	Bernadette C. Kirby	294			1				2	•	•	H	H
Celtic Ross Hotel	Nollaig Hurley	312				1		1	1	•		H	H
Commodore Hotel	Pat Scannell	298					1		2	•		H	O
Commons Inn	Ashley O'Neill	275			1				3	•	•		H
Country Club Hotel	Don Moore	276				2	2	1	1	•	•		H

H = Can Arrange Hire   O = Available On Premises

SELECT A VENUE FOR YOUR AGENDA

Accommodation	Contact Person	Be Our Guest Page Number	500+	400+	300+	200+	100+	50+	50-	Black Out Facilities	Air Conditioning	Interpreting Equipment	Audio Visual Equipment
CORK Continued													
Doughcloyne Hotel	David Harney	277					1	1	2	•			O
Emmet Hotel	Maria O'Keeffe	296						1	1	•	•	H	H
Fernhill Golf & Country Club	Alan Bowes	294						1		•	•	H	H
Fernhill House Hotel	Teresa O'Neill	296		1						•	•		O
Fitzpatrick Cork	Adeline O'Brien	278	2		4			2	6	•		H	O
Hayfield Manor Hotel	Susan O'Mahony	280					1		3	•	•	H	O
Hibernian Hotel	Catherine Gyves	309				1		2	4	•		O	
Imperial Hotel, Clonakilty	Aideen Murphy	296	1				1	1	4	•		H	O
Innishannon House Hotel	Conal O'Sullivan	302						1				H	H
Jurys Hotel Cork	Niamh Hynes	281	1				1	1	5	•	•	H	H
Kingsley Hotel	Seamus Heaney	282						4		•	•	H	O
Lodge & Spa at Inchydoney Island	Hazel Knox-Johnston	297		1				1	2	•	•	H	O
Longueville House & Presidents' Restaurant	Aisling O'Callaghan	310						2		•	•	H	H
Maryborough House Hotel	Mary Motherway	283		1	1		2	2	2	•	•	H	O
Metropole Ryan Hotel and Leisure Centre	Edel Drinan	284	1	1	1	2	2	4	2	•	•	H	O
Midleton Park Hotel	Daphne Beamish	311			1		2	3	4	•	•	H	H
Quality Hotel and Leisure Centre	Maurice Bergin	297				1	4	4	1	•	•	H	H
Quality Shandon Court Hotel	Tracy Hoary	284					1	3	4	•	•	H	H
Rochestown Park Hotel	Liam Lally/Clair Cullinane	285	2	2	2	2	3	5	9	•	•	H	O
Rushbrooke Hotel	Mary Sydenham	298						1		•		H	H
Springfort Hall	Paul Walsh	310				1	1	2	3	•			O
Trident Hotel	Hal McElroy/Una Wren	306					1		4	•	•	H	O
Walter Raleigh Hotel	Mary Murphy	315	1				1	1	2	•	•	H	H
WatersEdge Hotel	Margaret and Mike Whelan	299						1		•	•	H	H
Westlodge Hotel	Eileen M. O'Shea	292					1			•	•	H	H
KERRY													
Abbey Gate Hotel	Patrick Dillon	354					1		2	•	•	H	O
Aghadoe Heights Hotel	Gillian Butler	332						1	2	•	•		H
Brandon Hotel	Louise Langan/Mark Sullivan	356	1	2	2	3	4	4	4	•	•	H	O
Castlerosse Hotel & Leisure Centre	Michael O'Sullivan	335					1	1	1	•		H	H

H = Can Arrange Hire   O = Available On Premises

SELECT A VENUE FOR YOUR AGENDA

KERRY Continued

Accommodation	Contact Person	Be Our Guest Page Number	500+	400+	300+	200+	100+	50+	50–	Black Out Facilities	Air Conditioning	Interpreting Equipment	Audio Visual Equipment
Dingle Skellig Hotel	Colin Ahern	323			1				2	•	•	H	O
Dromquinna Manor Hotel	Joanna Aydiner	327							1		•		O
Grand Hotel	Dick Boyle	357	1					3	7	•	•	O	O
Holiday Inn Killarney	John Byrne	339							1	•	•	H	O
Johnston Marina Hotel	Fionnbar Walsh	358							1			H	H
Kenmare Bay Hotel	Terry O'Doherty	328	1			1					•	H	O
Killarney Court Hotel	Robert Lyne	342			1					•	•	H	O
Killarney Heights Hotel	Collete Hallinan	343			1				2	•	•		H
Killarney Park Hotel	Niamh O'Shea	343					1	1	1	•	•	H	O
Lake Hotel	Tony Huggard	346						1	2	•	•	H	O
Listowel Arms Hotel	Kevin O'Callaghan	353			1	1	1	1	2	•	•	H	H
Muckross Park Hotel	Patricia Shanahan	348					1		1	•	•	H	H
Park Hotel Kenmare	John Brennan	329						1	2	•	•	H	O
Sheen Falls Lodge	Carmel Flynn	330					1	1	2	•	•	H	O

SHANNON

CLARE

Accommodation	Contact Person	Be Our Guest Page Number	500+	400+	300+	200+	100+	50+	50–	Black Out Facilities	Air Conditioning	Interpreting Equipment	Audio Visual Equipment
Aberdeen Arms Hotel	Brian Hegarty	378			1					•	•		H
Auburn Lodge Hotel	Sean Lyne	368	1		1		1	1		•	•	H	H
Bunratty Castle Hotel	Kathleen McLoughlin	364					1	1	2	•		H	H
Dromoland Castle	Stella Rochford	383		1	1	1	2	3	6	•	•	H	O
Falls Hotel	Gerry O'Connor	372	1					2	2	•	•	O	O
Fitzpatrick Bunratty	Maria O'Gorman Skelly	365	1		2	1	6		1	•	•	H	O
Halpin's Hotel & Vittles Restaurant	Pat Halpin	373							2	•	•	H	H
Kincora Hall Hotel	John O'Connor	375					1					H	H
Magowna House Hotel	Gay Murphy	370					1		2	•	•	H	O
Oak Wood Arms Hotel	Stephen Keogh	384			1			2	3	•	•	H	O
Old Ground Hotel	Marian Kelly	370			1			1	1	•	•	H	O
Smyth Country Lodge Hotel	Rory Smyth/Patricia Coughlan	373			1		1		1	•	•	H	O
Temple Gate Hotel	John Madden	371				1			1	•	•	H	O
Woodstock Hotel & Golf Club	Andrew Griffith	372			1			1	2	•	•	O	O

H = Can Arrange Hire   O = Available On Premises

Accommodation	Contact Person	Be Our Guest Page Number	**Number of Rooms of Various Seating Capacities**							Black Out Facilities	Air Conditioning	Interpreting Equipment	Audio Visual Equipment	
			500+	400+	300+	200+	100+	50+	50-					
LIMERICK														
Adare Manor Hotel & Golf Club	Yvette Kennedy	391				1	1	1	1	•			H	O
Castletroy Park Hotel	Ursula Cullen	385		1	2	4	4	5	9	•	•		H	O
Cruises House	Carol Kelly	388							1		•		H	H
Devon Inn Hotel	William Sheehan	394		1	1	1	1	2	1		•		H	O
Dunraven Arms Hotel	Louis Murphy	392		1	1	1	2	4	5	•	•		H	H
Fitzgeralds Woodlands House Hotel	David Fitzgerald	392			1	1	2	3	3	•	•		H	O
Greenhills Hotel Conference/Leisure	Sarah Greene	387	1	1	1	1	2				•		H	H
Jurys Hotel Limerick	Linda Walsh	388					1		2	•	•		H	H
Kilmurry Lodge Hotel	Ann Devereux	393			1	1	2	2	2				H	O
Limerick Inn Hotel	Patricia Ryan	388	1	1	1	2	2	2	2	•	•		H	H
Limerick Ryan Hotel	Claire Kennedy	389					1	5	5	•			H	H
Rathkeale House Hotel	Brian O'Connor	394			1			1		•	•		H	O
Two Mile Inn Hotel	Shineade Devane	390			1			1			•		H	H
TIPPERARY NORTH														
Anner Hotel	Nollaig Howell	396			1	1	1	3	4		•		H	O
Nenagh Abbey Court Hotel	Lisa Rooney	395	1	1	1	2	3	3	6	•	•		H	O
St. David's Country House	Bernhard Klotz	395							1	•	•	•	O	O

H = Can Arrange Hire O = Available On Premises

Heritage Island

is a group of the most prestigious heritage attractions in all of Ireland...

The centres range from historic houses, castles, monuments, museums, galleries, national parks, interpretative centres, gardens and theme parks.

Visitors can avail of big savings by presenting *Explorer Card* to the following attractions, which will entitle them to reduced admission, many two for one's and special offers...

Armagh • Armagh Planetarium • Palace Stables • St. Patrick's Trian Visitor Complex	**Cavan** • Maudabawn Cultural Centre • Cavan Crystal Visitor Centre	**Clare** • Bunratty Castle & Folk Park • Craggaunowen	**Cork** • Cork City Gaol • Millstreet Country Park • Mizen Vision • Old Midleton Distillery	**Down** • Castle Ward • Exploris • Mount Stewart
Dublin • Ceol - The Irish Traditional Music Centre • Dublin Zoo • Dvblinia • Guinness Hopstore	**Dublin (Continued)** • Icon at the Baileys Centre • Irish Music Hall of Fame • Old Jameson Distillery • St. Patrick's Cathedral • Trinity College	**Fermanagh** • Belleek Pottery Visitor Centre • Castle Coole	**Kerry** • Jeanie Johnston Visitor Shipyard • Kerry the Kingdom	**Kildare** • Irish National Stud & Japanese Gardens • The Steam Museum & Victorian Walled Garden
Galway • Kylemore Abbey • Galway Crystal	**Limerick** • Adare Heritage Centre • Hunt Museum • King John's Castle	**Louth** • County Museum Dundalk • Millmount Museum	**Offaly** • Birr Castle Demesne • Tullamore Dew Heritage Centre	**Roscommon** • Strokestown Park • Lough Key Forest Park
Sligo • Drumcliffe Church **Tipperary** • Brú Ború	**Waterford** • Waterford Crystal • Waterford's Treasures at the Granary & Reginald's Tower	**Westmeath** • Athlone Castle • Belvedere House, Gardens & Park	**Wexford** • Irish National Heritage Park • National 1798 Visitor Centre	**Wicklow** • Avondale • Powerscourt House & Gardens • Russborough • Wicklow's Historic Gaol • The National Sealife Centre

Heritage Island members confirmed as at August 1999. Heritage Island can not accept responsibility for any errors or omissions.

INTRODUCING A 2000

Friends of Heritage Island
EXPLORER CARD

Signed:

Valid to 31 Dec. 2000

To validate please sign this voucher and present to any centre listed above to receive reduced admission. Card is non-transferable.

For full details on centres, opening times, discounts and special offers see Heritage Island Touring Guide 2000 available at Tourist Information Centres, nationwide.

Heritage Island, 37 Main Street, Donnybrook, Dublin 4.
Tel: + 353 1 260 0055
Fax: + 353 1 260 0058
E mail: heritage.island@indigo.ie
Web: www.heritage.island.com

Heritage Island Partners
Houses, Castles and Gardens
Tel: + 353 1 288 9114
Heritage Towns of Ireland
Tel: + 353 62 63175

CUT ALONG DOTTED LINE

KEY TO MAPS

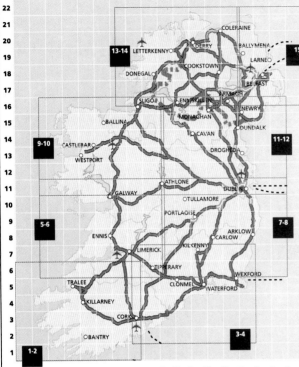

LEGEND

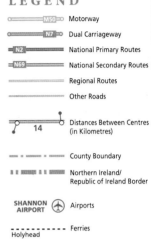

M50	Motorway
N7	Dual Carriageway
N2	National Primary Routes
N69	National Secondary Routes
	Regional Routes
	Other Roads
14	Distances Between Centres (in Kilometres)
	County Boundary
	Northern Ireland/ Republic of Ireland Border
SHANNON AIRPORT ✈	Airports
- - - - - - Holyhead	Ferries
Hill of Tara ◇	Heritage Sites

SHANNON AIRPORT

Variation 10°45' (1990)

DISTANCE CHART
in Kilometres

ARMAGH	ATHLONE	BELFAST	CARLOW	CLIFDEN	CORK	DERRY	DUBLIN	DUNDALK	ENNISKILLEN	GALWAY	KILKENNY	KILLARNEY	LARNE	LIMERICK	PORTLAOISE	ROSSLARE HARBOUR	SHANNON AIRPORT	SLIGO	TRALEE	WATERFORD	WEXFORD	WICKLOW
159																						
66	224																					
211	108	248																				
316	171	370	256																			
380	219	423	187	287																		
114	225	118	309	303	460																	
129	124	167	82	296	256	233																
45	142	82	166	314	340	158	84															
81	127	135	240	237	346	98	175	101														
238	92	303	177	79	206	277	216	233	192													
245	121	282	39	248	148	335	114	200	242	169												
388	229	430	235	295	89	480	303	348	356	214	196											
105	264	40	287	411	462	122	206	121	174	343	320	470										
279	119	320	138	184	101	369	192	238	245	105	114	109	356									
208	71	250	37	229	174	287	82	167	192	150	50	221	285	109								
282	201	320	93	348	206	385	151	237	324	269	100	272	356	204	130							
293	134	345	163	172	126	357	216	261	261	93	138	134	380	24	134	229						
148	116	203	224	167	336	134	213	171	68	142	237	345	240	235	187	319	224					
382	222	423	242	288	121	472	296	341	349	208	216	32	460	103	213	291	127	338				
285	167	324	74	296	126	383	156	240	290	217	48	192	359	124	97	81	148	283	211			
264	184	301	76	330	187	365	132	219	306	250	81	254	338	187	113	19	209	299	272	61		
185	138	222	61	311	256	293	56	140	221	232	100	303	259	193	82	118	216	238	296	135	100	

0   5   10   15   20   25km

0   5   10   15miles

SCALE   1 : 625 000

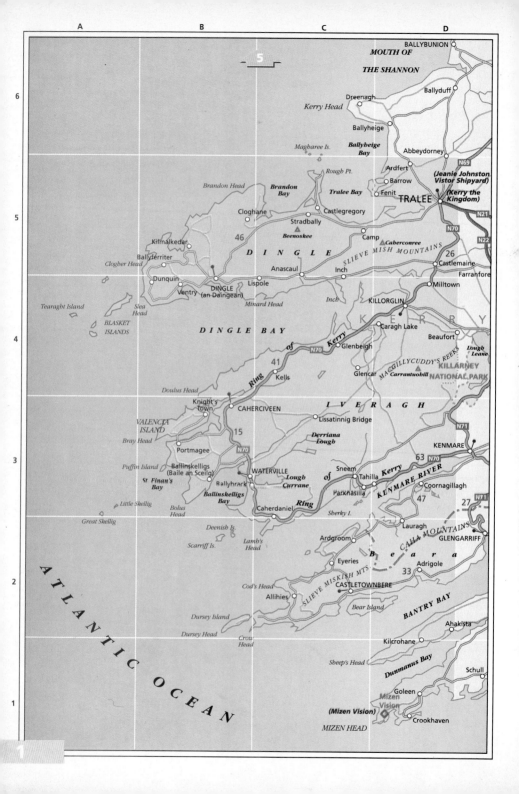

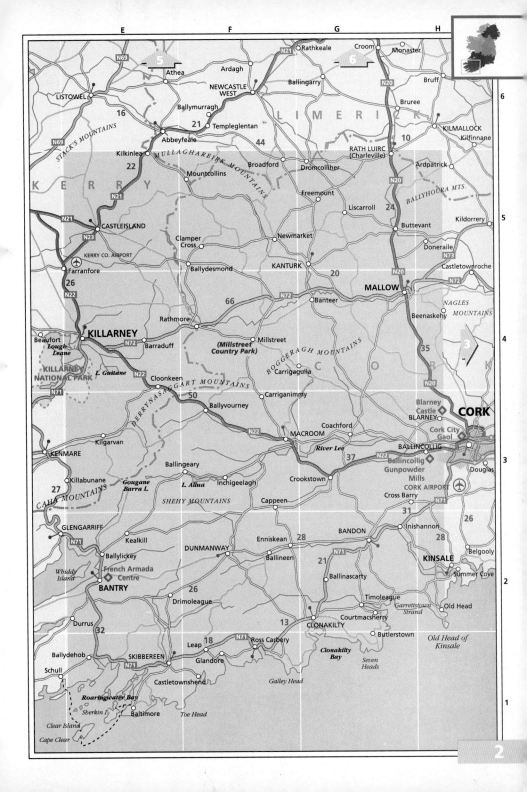

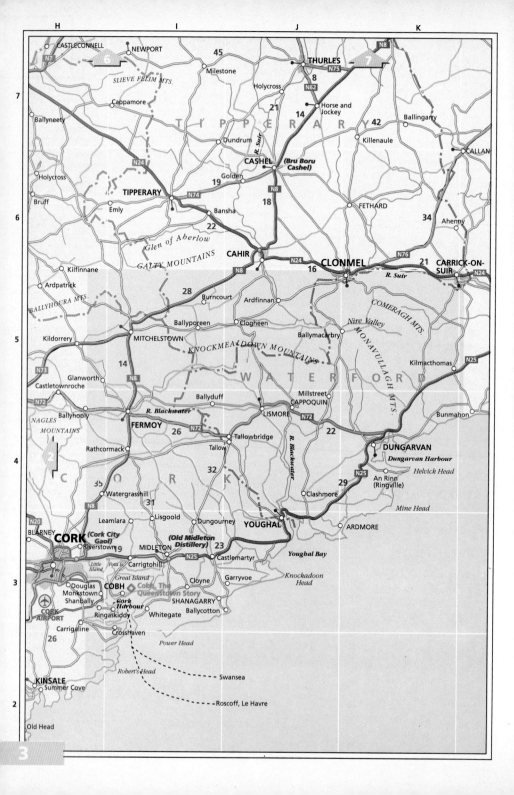

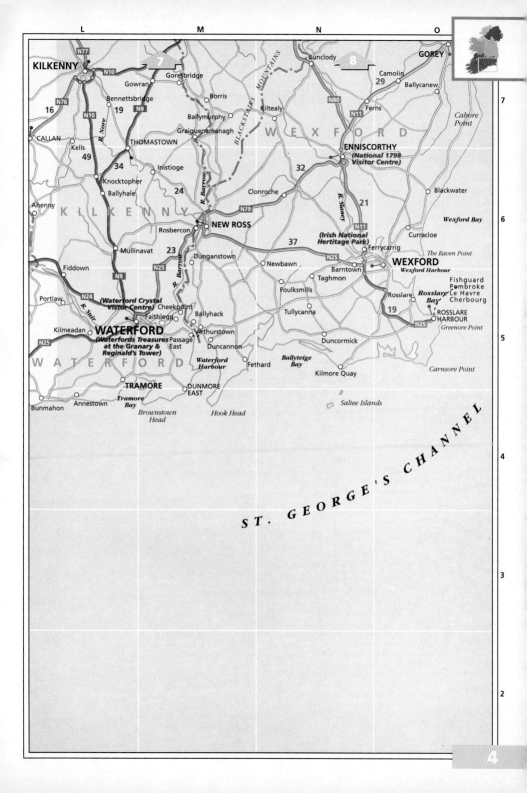

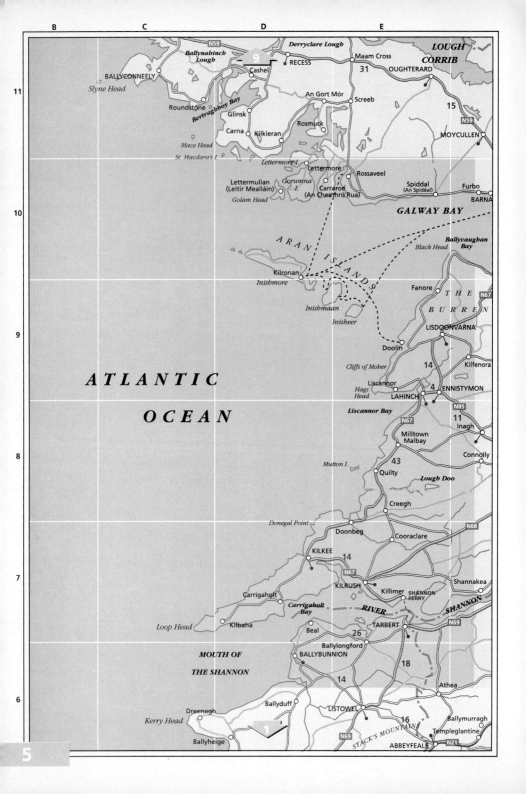

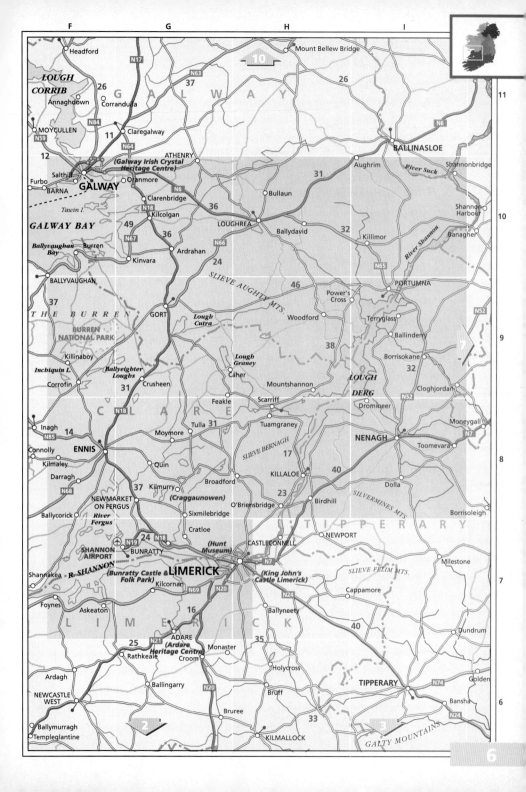

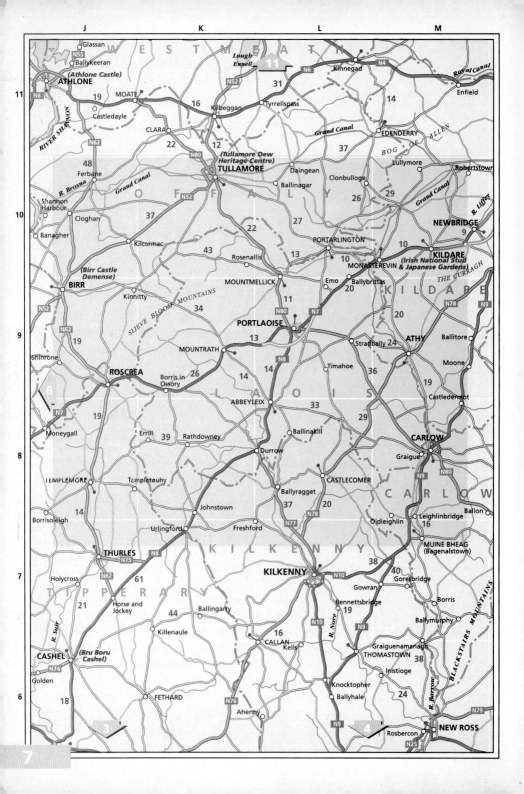

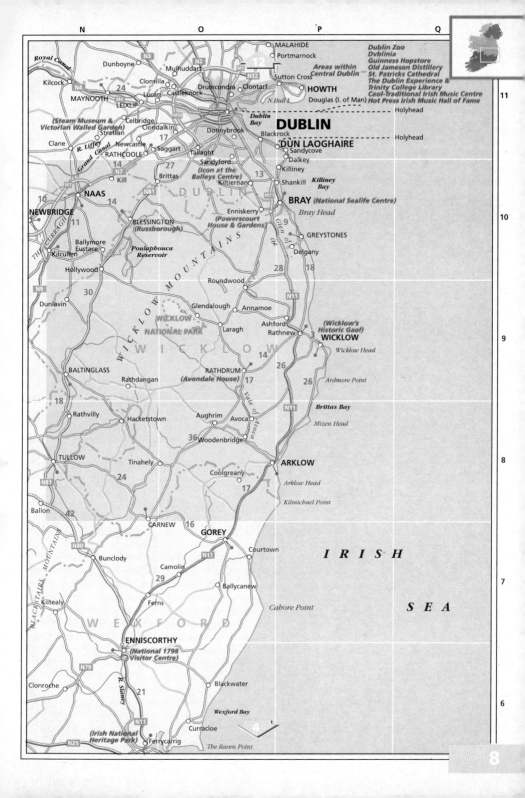

Areas within Central Dublin

Dublin Zoo
Dvblinia
Guinness Hopstore
Old Jameson Distillery
St. Patricks Cathedral
The Dublin Experience &
Trinity College Library
Ceol-Traditional Irish Music Centre
Hot Press Irish Music Hall of Fame

Royal Canal

Dunboyne
Mulhuddart
Clonsilla
MALAHIDE
Portmarnock
Sutton Cross
HOWTH
Douglas (I. of Man)

Kilcock
MAYNOOTH
LEIXLIP
Lucan
Castleknock
Drumcondra
Clontarf
N. Bull I.

Holyhead

(Steam Museum &
Victorian Walled Garden)
Celbridge
Clondalkin
Donnybrook
DUBLIN
Dublin Bay

Straffan
Clane
R. Liffey
Newcastle
RATHCOOLE
Saggart
Tallaght
Sandyford
Blackrock
DÚN LAOGHAIRE
Sandycove
Dalkey
Killiney

Holyhead

Grand Canal

Clondalkin
17
(Icon at the
Balleys Centre)
13
Shankill
Killiney Bay

14
27
Brittas
Kiltiernan
NAAS
N81
DUBLIN
Enniskerry
(Powerscourt
House & Gardens)
BRAY (National Sealife Centre)
Bray Head

NEWBRIDGE
11
BLESSINGTON
(Russborough)
GREYSTONES
Delgany

Ballymore
Eustace
Poulapbouca
Reservoir
28
18

Kilcullen
Hollywood
Roundwood

30
Dunlavin
Glendalough
Annamoe

WICKLOW
NATIONAL PARK
Laragh
Ashford
Rathnew
3
(Wicklow's
Historic Gaol)
WICKLOW
Wicklow Head

WICKLOW MOUNTAINS

BALTINGLASS
Rathdangan
RATHDRUM
(Avondale House)
14
17
26
26
Ardmore Point

WICKLOW

18
Rathvilly
Hacketstown
Aughrim
Avoca
N11
Brittas Bay
Mizen Head

36
Woodenbridge

TULLOW
Tinahely
Coolgreany
ARKLOW
Arklow Head
24
17
Kilmichael Point

Ballon
42
CARNEW
16
GOREY
Courtown
N11

I R I S H

N80
Bunclody
Camolin
29
Ballycanew

Kiltealy
Ferns
Cahore Point
S E A

BLACKSTAIRS MOUNTAINS
W E X F O R D

ENNISCORTHY
(National 1798
Visitor Centre)
N79

Clonroche
R. Slaney
21
Blackwater

Wexford Bay

N11
Curracloe
(Irish National
Heritage Park)
Ferrycarrig
The Raven Point
N25

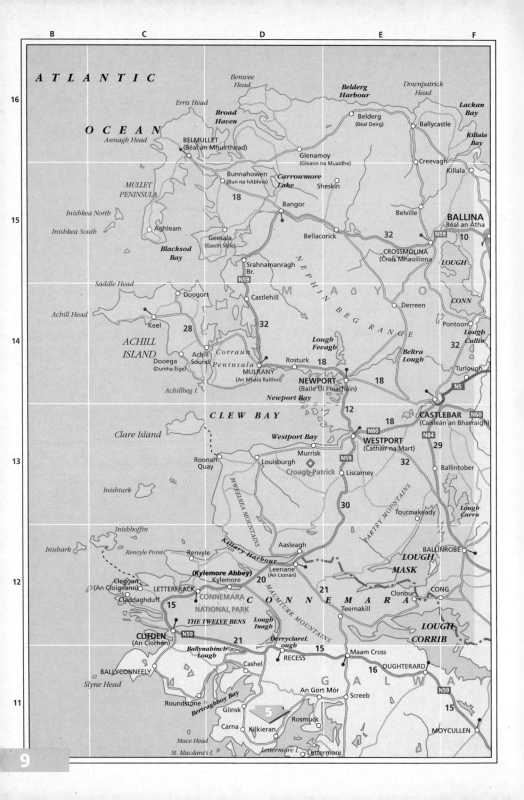

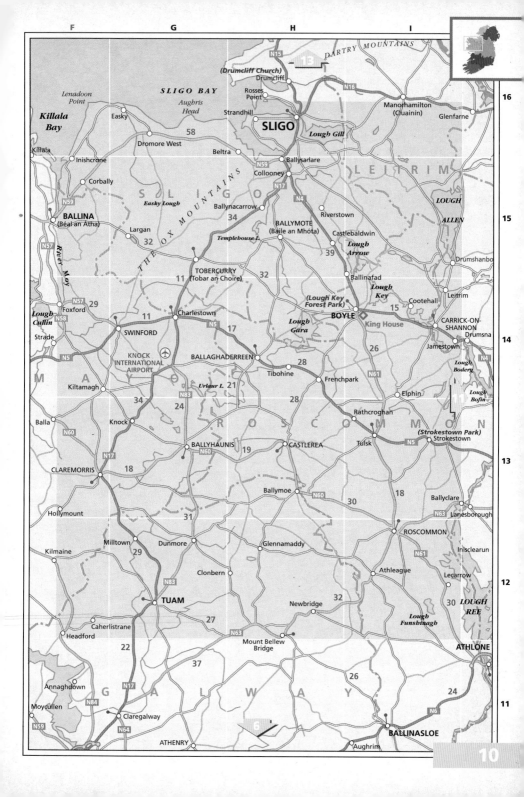

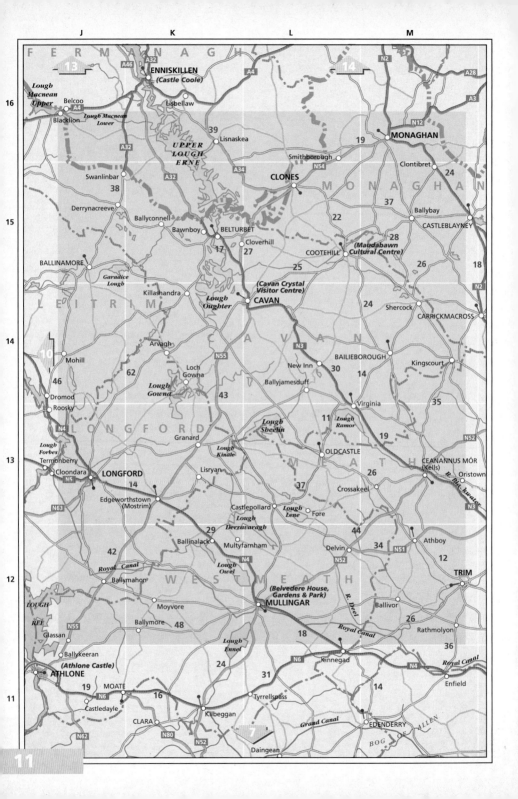

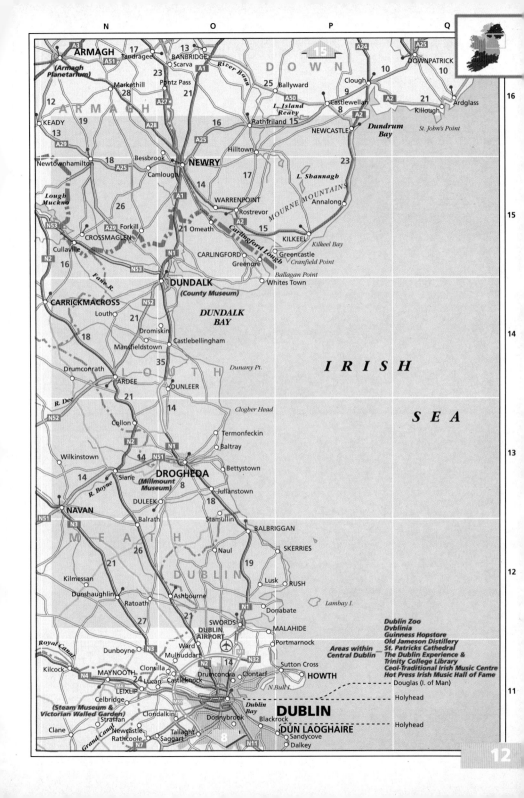

N   O   P   Q

ARMAGH
(Armagh Planetarium)
A3
17 Tandragee
A51
23
Markethill
28
BANBRIDGE
13
Scarva A1
River Bann
Pontz Pass
21
A27

12
A R M A G H
KEADY 19
13
A29
18
A25
Bessbrook
Newtownhamilton

D O W N
15
25 Ballyward
A50
Clough
9
A24
10
A25
DOWNPATRICK
10
Castlewellan
8
Killough
21
Ardglass
A2
NEWCASTLE
Dundrum Bay
St. John's Point
16

16
Rathfriland 15
Hilltown
A28
A25
NEWRY
14
Camlough
17
23
L. Shannagh
26
A29 Forkill
N53
Lough Muckno
CROSSMAGLEN
Cullaville
N2
16
N53
Fane R.
21 Omeath
N1
WARRENPOINT
Rostrevor
A2
15
CARLINGFORD
Greenore
Annalong
M O U R N E   M O U N T A I N S
Carlingford Lough
KILKEEL
Kilkeel Bay
Greencastle
Cranfield Point
15

DUNDALK
(County Museum)
Ballagan Point
Whites Town

CARRICKMACROSS
N52
Louth
21
Dromiskin
18
Mansfieldstown
Castlebellingham
DUNDALK BAY
14

Drumconrath
L O U T H
35
Dunany Pt.
ARDEE
21
DUNLEER

I R I S H

R. Dee
N52
Collon
N2
14
Clogher Head
Wilkinstown
N1
14 N51
Termonfeckin
Baltray
Bettystown
13

S E A

14
Slane
R. Boyne
DROGHEDA
(Millmount Museum) 8
Julianstown
NAVAN
N51
DULEEK
18
Balrath
Stamullin
N3
M E A T H
26
Naul
BALBRIGGAN
19
SKERRIES
12

Kilmessan
21
Dunshaughlin
Ratoath
Ashbourne
D U B L I N
Lusk
RUSH
Lambay I.

27
21
SWORDS
N1
Donabate
DUBLIN AIRPORT
MALAHIDE
Dunboyne
N3
Ward
Mulhuddart
N32
Portmarnock
Sutton Cross

Royal Canal
Kilcock
N4
MAYNOOTH
Clonsilla
14
Clondra
Castleknock
Clontarf
N. Bull I.
HOWTH
Lucan
24
LEIXLIP
M4
M50
Celbridge
(Steam Museum & Victorian Walled Garden)
Straffan
Clondalkin
Donnybrook
Blackrock
Dublin Bay
DUBLIN
Clane
Newcastle
Rathcoole
N7
Tallaght
Saggart
N2
8
N11
DÚN LAOGHAIRE
Sandycove
Dalkey
11

Dublin Zoo
Dvblinia
Guinness Hopstore
Old Jameson Distillery
Areas within Central Dublin
The Dublin Experience &
St. Patricks Cathedral
Trinity College Library
Ceol-Traditional Irish Music Centre
Hot Press Irish Music Hall of Fame
- - - - - Douglas (I. of Man)
- - - - - Holyhead
- - - - - Holyhead

12

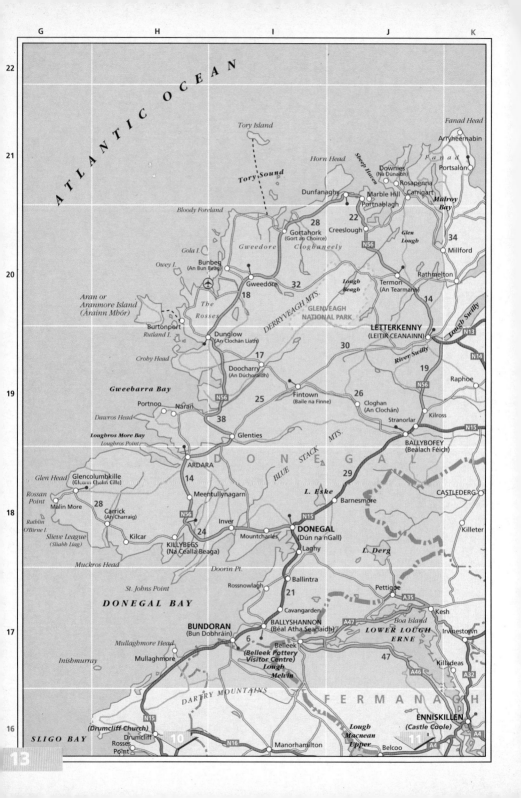

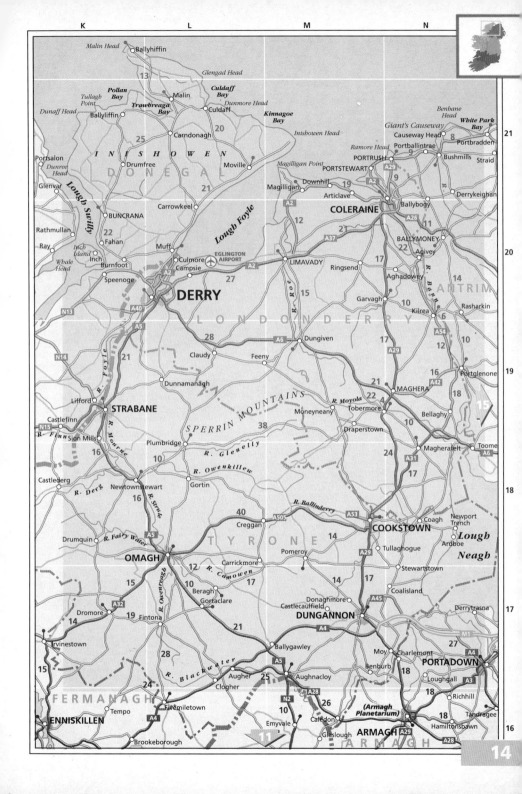

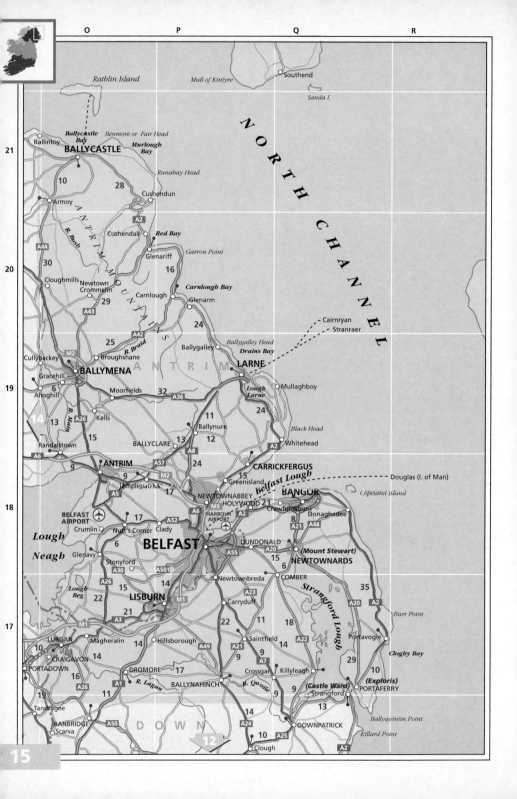

GUINNESS®

Holiday Competition

Guinness invite you to Be Our Guest in any of the hotels or guesthouses featured in Ireland's favourite and most successful accommodation guide. (Value of prize £1,000).

Simply complete the sentence below in 10 words or less:

I would like to win this wonderful prize because

_____

_____

Replies clearly marked Holiday Competition to:

Irish Hotels Federation, 13 Northbrook Road, Dublin 6, Ireland.

Closing Date for Entries 31st August 2000

(Photocopies not accepted)

Name: _____

Address: _____

_____

IRISH HOTELS FEDERATION

Throughout the year, Ireland has a great range of social, cultural and sporting events. The big cities and even the smallest villages have festivals, whether in honour of a goat, as at Puck Fair, or to celebrate the oysters in Galway.

Listed below is a small selection of well known events/festivals which take place. There are, of course, many others, whether music or sport. **Please contact your nearest Irish Tourist Board office for confirmation of dates and a full calendar of events.**

MARCH

Cork City Celtic Flame Festival 2000

Roaring 20's Festival, Killarney, Co. Kerry

St. Patrick's Festival 2000 Dublin

The Benson and Hedges Irish Masters Snooker Tournament Goffs Kill, Co. Kildare

APRIL

Launch of the Jeanie Johnston Ship
Blennerville, Tralee, Co. Kerry

Pan Celtic Festival 2000
Tralee, Co. Kerry

Bord Gais Cork International Choral Festival

World Dancing Championships, Waterford Hall, Belfast

MAY

Murphy's International Mussel Fair,
Bantry, Co. Cork

Galway Early Music Festival "Volta 2000", Galway City

A.I.M.S. Choral Festival
New Ross, Co. Wexford

Irish Amateur Open Golf Championship
Royal Dublin, Co. Dublin

live
life
to
the
power
of

JUNE

Sligo Arts Festival,
Sligo

Writers' Week
Listowel, Co. Kerry (commences late May)

Murphy's Cat Laughs, International Comedy Festival
Co. Kilkenny

Eigse Carlow Arts Festival
Co. Carlow

Enniscorthy Strawberry Fair
Co. Wexford

Tesco/Evening Herald Women's Mini Marathon
Dublin City

Guinness Bloomsday
Dublin

Budweiser Irish Derby Weekend,
The Curragh Racecourse, Co. Kildare

JULY

Willie Clancy Summer School,
Miltown Malby, Co. Clare

Galway Film Festival
Galway City

Galway Arts Festival,
Galway

Ford Cork Week, International Sailing Regatta,
Crosshaven, Co. Cork

Guinness Blues Festival,
Temple Bar, Dublin

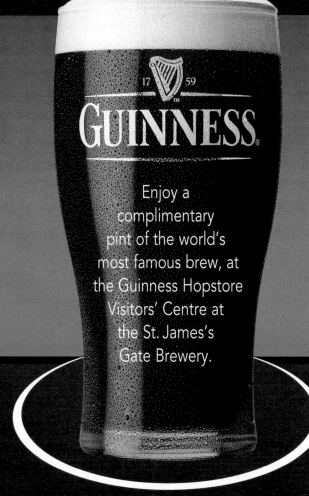

(JULY CONTINUED)

Mitchelstown Music Festival,
Mitchelstown, Co. Cork

AUGUST

Mary from Dungloe International Festival
Dungloe, Co. Donegal (commences late July)

Wicklow Regatta Festival (commences late July)

Guinness Galway Races Meeting
Galway (commences July)

Kerrygold Horse Show
RDS, Dublin 4

Guinness Puck Fair
Killorglin, Co. Kerry

Connemara Pony Show
Clifden, Co. Galway

Kilkenny Arts Week,
Kilkenny

Yeats International Summer School,
Sligo

Rose of Tralee International Festival
Tralee, Co. Kerry

Fleadh Ceoil Na hEireann,
Enniscorthy, Co. Wexford

SEPTEMBER

Matchmaking Festival
Lisdoonvarna, Co. Clare

Clarenbridge Oyster Festival
Co. Galway

(SEPTEMBER CONTINUED)　Guinness All-Ireland Hurling Championship Final
Croke Park, Dublin.

Galway International Oyster Festival
Galway City

National Ploughing Championships
Ballacolla, Co. Laois

Waterford International Festival of Light Opera
Waterford

OCTOBER　Matchmaking Festival, Lisdoonvarna
Co. Clare

Ballinasloe International Horse Fair and Festival
Ballinasloe, Co. Galway (commences late September)

Guinness Cork Jazz Festival
Cork City

Cork Film Festival,
Cork

Dublin Theatre Festival
Dublin

98FM Dublin City Marathon
Dublin City

24th International Gourmet Festival,
Kinsale, Co. Cork

Wexford Festival Opera
Wexford

INDEX OF HOTELS & GUESTHOUSES · GUINNESS.

INDEX OF HOTELS & GUESTHOUSES   GUINNESS

HOTEL

whether you're offering...

bedrooms & ballrooms
saunas & swimming pools
cabaret & craic...

to brighten up your brochure
pick up the phone
and have a word with **'the wood'**.

wood **printcraft** *group*

for the full package in brochure production

contact stanley crawford
sales director
greencastle parade clonshaugh dublin 17
telephone 847 0011 facsimile 847 5570
e-mail s.crawford@wpg.ie

SINCE 1866

Magee

*Handwoven Donegal Tweed Mens & Ladies Garments
Woven & Tailored by Magee in Co. Donegal*

*Hand woven
Donegal Tweed*

Ireland's Tourist Information Network

Tourist Information

WELCOME TO IRELAND and to the services provided by our Tourist Information Network. In addition to tourist information and room reservation, many of our offices provide a wide range of services, all designed to aid you in your holiday planning and help you to enjoy to the full, all that Ireland has to offer.

OUR SERVICES AT A GLANCE

- Accommodation Booking Service
- Bureau de Change Facilities
- Computer speeded Gulliver reservation service
- Guide Books for sale
- Itinerary and route planning
- Local and national Information

- Local Craft Display
- Map Sales
- Multi-lingual facilities
- Souvenirs
- Stamps and postcards
- What's on in the area and nationally

* Some tourist information offices may not provide all of the service or facilities listed here.

Follow the Shamrock

LOOK FOR THE SHAMROCK SIGN on accommodation. It is your guarantee that premises on which it is displayed provide accommodation which is inspected and whose standards are approved and regulated by agencies supervised by Bord Fáilte, the Irish Tourist Board.

Of course all accommodation booked on your behalf through Tourist Information Offices is fully approved and regulated in this manner.

Ask for our free guide to the locations of all 89 Tourist Information Offices throughout the country - your guide to better service and a happier holiday.

For the best introduction to Ireland...

...make Irish Ferries your first connection

When it comes to taking you or your car to Ireland, choose to travel with the experts Irish Ferries.

With the most modern fleet of ships on the Irish Sea, great value fares and inclusive package holidays we have the island covered.

IRISH FERRIES

Ask Irish Ferries first

Call us now on 08705 17 17 17

and quote A392, or see your travel agent.

Bookings: www.irishferries.ie

Lawnhourst
pearse Rd Sligo